Lecture Notes in Computer Science 6418

Commenced Publication in 1973
Founding and Former Series Editors:
Gerhard Goos, Juris Hartmanis, and Jan van Leeuwen

Howard Barringer   Ylies Falcone
Bernd Finkbeiner   Klaus Havelund
Insup Lee   Gordon Pace   Grigore Roşu
Oleg Sokolsky   Nikolai Tillmann (Eds.)

Runtime Verification

First International Conference, RV 2010
St. Julians, Malta, November 1-4, 2010
Proceedings

 Springer

Volume Editors

Howard Barringer
University of Manchester, UK, E-mail: howard.barringer@manchester.ac.uk

Ylies Falcone
IRISA/INRIA Rennes, France, E-mail: ylies.falcone@inria.fr

Bernd Finkbeiner
Saarland University, Saarücken, Germany, E-mail: finkbeiner@cs.uni-sb.de

Klaus Havelund
Jet Propulsion Laboratory, Pasadena, CA, USA,
E-mail: klaus.havelund@jpl.nasa.gov

Insup Lee
University of Pennsylvania, Philadelphia, PA, USA, E-mail: lee@cis.upenn.edu

Gordon Pace
University of Malta, Malta, E-mail: gordon.pace@um.edu.mt

Grigore Roşu
University of Illinois at Urbana-Champaign, Urbana, IL, USA
E-mail: grosu@cs.uiuc.edu

Oleg Sokolsky
University of Pennsylvania, Philadelphia, PA, USA
E-mail: sokolsky@cis.upenn.edu

Nikolai Tillmann
Microsoft Research, Redmond, WA, USA, E-mail: nikolait@microsoft.com

Library of Congress Control Number: 2010966903

CR Subject Classification (1998): D.2, F.2, D.2.4, D.1, F.3, D.3

LNCS Sublibrary: SL 2 – Programming and Software Engineering

ISSN   0302-9743
ISBN-10   3-642-16611-3 Springer Berlin Heidelberg New York
ISBN-13   978-3-642-16611-2 Springer Berlin Heidelberg New York

springer.com

© Springer-Verlag Berlin Heidelberg 2010
Printed in Germany

Typesetting: Camera-ready by author, data conversion by Scientific Publishing Services, Chennai, India
Printed on acid-free paper   06/3180

Preface

This volume contains the proceedings of the 2010 Runtime Verification conference (RV 2010), which was held in St. Julians, Malta on November 1–4, 2010. The conference program included a mix of invited talks and peer reviewed presentations, tutorials, and tool demonstrations.

The 2010 Runtime Verification conference was a forum for researchers and industrial practitioners to present theories and tools for monitoring and analyzing system (software and hardware) executions, as well as a forum for presenting applications of such tools to practical problems. The field of runtime verification is often referred to under different names, including dynamic analysis, runtime analysis, and runtime monitoring, to mention a few. Runtime verification can be applied during the development of a system for the purpose of program understanding, debugging, and testing, or it can be applied as part of a running system, for example for security or safety policy monitoring, and can furthermore be part of a fault protection framework. A number of sub-fields of runtime verification have emerged over time, such as specification languages and logics for execution analysis, dynamic analysis algorithms, program instrumentation, security monitoring, fault protection, specification mining, and dynamic system visualization. Runtime verification has strong connections to other fields of computer science research, such as combinations of static and dynamic analysis, aspect-oriented programming, and model-based testing.

Runtime Verification events started with a workshop in 2001 and continued as an annual workshop series through 2009. The workshops were organized as satellite events to such established forums as CAV (2001–2003, 2005–2006, and 2009), ETAPS (2004 and 2008), and AoSD (2007). In 2006, RV was organized jointly with the FATES workshop (Formal Aspects of Testing). The proceedings for RV from 2001 to 2005 were published in *Electronic Notes in Theoretical Computer Science (ENTCS)*. Since 2006, the RV proceedings have been published in *Lecture Notes in Computer Science (LNCS)*.

This year marks an important transition for RV from workshop to a standalone conference. In the decade that has passed since the inception of the series, the field has matured considerably and a sense of community has emerged. By broadening the event to a conference, we hoped to enlarge the community even further, increasing the visibility of RV events and making submission and participation more attractive to researchers.

As we expected, the change to a conference received a welcome response from the community. RV 2010 received a record number of submissions, exceeding the previous record twofold. Overall, 74 submissions were received, of which 15 were tutorial and tool demonstration proposals. All regular submissions were reviewed by the Program Committee, with each paper receiving at least three reviews. The Program Committee selected 23 papers for presentation at the conference. Tutorial and tool demonstration proposals were evaluated by the respective chairs with the help of external reviewers. Six tutorials and four tool demonstrations were selected.

The organizers would like to thank the Program Committee for their hard work in evaluating the papers. Financial support for the conference was provided by the International Federation for Computational Logic, by the ARTIST Network of Excellence on Embedded Systems Design, by Microsoft Research, and by the University of Illinois. We also would like to thank University of Malta for the extensive and competent help in handling local organization and providing registration services. Submission and evaluation of papers, as well as the preparation of this proceedings volume has been handled by the EasyChair conference management service.

We hope that the strong program of RV 2010 will provide a focal point for the RV community and foster collaborations with researchers in related fields.

August 2010

Howard Barringer
Klaus Havelund
Insup Lee
Grigore Roşu
Oleg Sokolsky
Gordon Pace
Bernd Finkbeiner
Nikolai Tillmann
Ylies Falcone

Conference Organization

General Chairs

Howard Barringer   University of Manchester, UK
Klaus Havelund   NASA/JPL, USA
Insup Lee   University of Pennsylvania, USA

Program Chairs

Grigore Roşu   University of Illinois, Urbana-Champaign, USA
Oleg Sokolsky   University of Pennsylvania, USA

Local Organization Chair

Gordon Pace   University of Malta, Malta

Tutorials Chair

Bernd Finkbeiner   Saarland University, Germany

Tool Demonstrations Chair

Nikolai Tillmann   Microsoft Research, USA

Publicity Chair

Ylies Falcone   INRIA Rennes, France

Program Committee

Jamie Andrews   University of Western Ontario, Canada
Thomas Ball   Microsoft Research Redmond, USA
Saddek Bensalem   Verimag, France
Eric Bodden   Technical University Darmstadt, Germany
Rance Cleaveland   University of Maryland, USA
Mads Dam   KTH, Sweden
Matthew Dwyer   University of Nebraska, USA
Bernd Finkbeiner   Saarland University, Germany
Cormac Flanagan   University of California at Santa Cruz, USA

Patrice Godefroid	Microsoft Research Redmond, USA
Jean Goubault-Larrecq	ENS Cachan, France
Susanne Graf	Verimag, France
Radu Grosu	State University of New York at Stony Brook, USA
Lars Grunske	Swinburne University of Technology, Australia
Rajiv Gupta	University of California at Riverside, USA
John Hatcliff	Kansas State University, USA
Mats Heimdahl	University of Minnesota, USA
Sarfraz Khurshid	University of Texas at Austin, USA
Kim Larsen	Aalborg University, Denmark
Martin Leucker	Technical University Muenchen, Germany
Paul Miner	NASA Langley, USA
Greg Morrisett	Harvard University, USA
Brian Nielsen	Aalborg University, Denmark
Klaus Ostermann	University of Marburg, Germany
Corina Pasareanu	NASA Ames Research Center, USA
Doron Peled	Bar Ilan University, Israel
Martin Rinard	Massachussets Institute of Technology, USA
Wolfram Schulte	Microsoft Research Redmond, USA
Koushik Sen	University of California at Berkeley, USA
Peter Sestoft	University of Copenhagen, Denmark
Scott Smolka	State University of New York at Stony Brook, USA
Serdar Tasiran	Koc University, Turkey
Shmuel Ur	IBM Haifa Research Laboratory, Israel
Willem Visser	University of Stellenbosch, South Africa
Mahesh Viswanathan	University of Illinois at Urbana-Champaign, USA
Brian Williams	MIT, USA

External Reviewers

Ayman Amin	Reinhold Heckmann
Andrea Avancini	Xiaowan Huang
Marina Biberstein	Pallavi Joshi
Benedikt Bollig	Lars Kuhtz
Elie Bursztein	Axel Legay
Christoph Csallner	Gurvan Le Guernic
Rüdiger Ehlers	Jay Ligatti
Tayfun Elmas	Changhui Lin
Peter Faymonville	Nicolas Markey
Min Feng	Brink van der Merwe
Jaco Geldenhuys	Marius Mikučionis
Alexander Gruler	Petur Olsen

Chang-Seo Park
Suzette Person
Pavithra Prabhakar
Kishore Pusukuri
Anders P. Ravn
Christian Schallhart
Justin Seyster
Ali Sezgin
Junaid Siddiqui
Emmanuel Sifakis

Nadia Tawbi
Suresh Thummalapenta
Chen Tian
Margus Veanes
Tomas Vojnar
Yan Wang
Tao Xie
Razieh Zaeem
Pengcheng Zhang

Table of Contents

III. Regular and Short Papers

IV. Tool Demonstrations

Automatic Requirement Extraction from Test Cases

Chris Ackermann[1], Rance Cleaveland[1], Samuel Huang[1], Arnab Ray[2],
Charles Shelton[3], and Elizabeth Latronico[3]

[1] Dept. of Computer Science, University of Maryland, College Park, MD 20742 USA
{chris_ack,rance,srhuang}@cs.umd.edu
[2] Fraunhofer USA Center for Experimental Software Eng., College Park,
MD 20740 USA
arnabray@fc-md.umd.edu
[3] Robert Bosch RTC, P.O. Box 6762, Pittsburgh PA 15212 USA
{charles.shelton,elizabeth.latronico}@us.bosch.com

Abstract. This paper describes a method for extracting functional requirements from tests, where tests take the form of vectors of inputs (supplied to the system) and outputs (produced by the system in response to inputs). The approach uses data-mining techniques to infer invariants from the test data, and an automated-verification technology to determine which of these proposed invariants are indeed invariant and may thus be seen as requirements. Experimental results from a pilot study involving an automotive-electronics application show that using tests that fully cover the structure of the software yield more complete invariants than structurally-agnostic black-box tests.

1 Introduction

Software development, maintenance and evolution activities are frequently complicated by the lack of accurate and up-to-date requirements specifications. In addition to providing developers with guidance on their design and implementation decisions, good requirements documentation can also give an overview of system purpose and functionality. Such an overview gives maintainers and development teams a clear snapshot of expected system behavior and can be used to guide and assess modification decisions necessitated by bug fixes and upgrades.

Implementations can deviate from their requirements specifications for a number of reasons. Miscommunication among the requirements, design and development teams is one; churn in the requirements is another. So-called implicit requirements can also arise during development, especially with experienced programmers familiar with the problem domain; such programmers may rely on their intuitions about what ought to be required rather than what is actually in the requirements documentation. Regardless of the source, such deviations confound development, maintenance and evolution efforts, especially when teams are geographically distributed and possess differing levels of experience with the system domain.

G. Roşu et al. (Eds.): RV 2010, LNCS 6418, pp. 1–15, 2010.

In this paper, we propose and assess a methodology, based on data mining, for automatically extracting requirements from executable software artifacts. The motivation of the work is to make requirements documents more accurate and complete. Our approach is intended for use with software following a read-execute-write behavioral model: input variables are assigned values, computations performed, and values written to output variables. The method first uses an automated test-generator to generate collections of input sequences that cover the model according to several structural-coverage criteria; the resulting outputs for each input vector are also collected. Data-mining tools are then applied to the test data to infer relationships among the input and output variables that remain constant over the entire test set (*invariants*). In a subsequent validation step, an automated tool is used to check which of the proposed invariants are indeed invariant; invariants passing this step are then proposed as requirements.

The rest of the paper is structured as follows. Section 2 gives background on data mining, invariant inference, and the artifacts and verification technique used to conduct the studies in this paper. Section 3 then outlines our approach in more detail, while Sections 4 and 5 present the results of a pilot study involving a production automotive application. Section 6 discusses related work, and the final section contains our conclusions and ideas for future work.

2   Background

Our work is inspired by Raz *et al.* [18, 17], which used data-mining tools to deduce invariants from the execution traces of running systems for the purposes of anomaly detection. Our motivation differs in that our work is aimed at reconstructing requirements from program test data arising in the context of model-based development of automotive systems. In this section we review the results of Raz et al. and also describe the model-based development environment for automotive software in which the results of our work are assessed. An approach for verifying automotive software models, *Instrumentation-Based Verification* [1], is also briefly described.

2.1   Invariant Inference from Executions

Invariants are commonly employed in program verification and express a relation between variables that holds for all executions of a piece of code. For example the invariant $(x > y)$ means that the value of variable x is always greater than the value of variable y. Invariants have a long history in software specification and development, as they define relationships that must hold among program variables even as these variables change values.

The work of Raz *et al.* was motivated by the desire to study the emergent behavior of systems when access to software and other development artifacts for the systems was impossible. The technical approach taken was to observe input / output sequences at the system interface and to use data-mining tools to infer invariants on the input and output variables. Several such tools are capable of discovering so-called *association rules* from time-series data given to them; these rules take the form of implications involving variables in the data that appear to hold throughout the data set. For example, in a data set recording values at different time instants for two variables, `speed` and `active`, which reflect the vehicle speed and the status (active or not) of a vehicle cruise control, one possible association rule that could be inferred is `'speed < 30.0' -> 'active = false'`; in other words, the data set might support the conclusion that whenever the speed is below 30.0, the cruise control is inactive.

In the case of Raz *et al.*, inferred association rules are viewed as invariants that, if true, yield insight into system behavior. Because the invariants deduced by these tools are only based on a subset of system executions, they may in fact not be invariants when considering the entire system. In Raz *et al.* this issue was addressed by presenting inferred invariants in a template form to an expert, who would use his / her understanding of the system to decide whether these candidate invariants were actual invariants on system behavior or had merely been flagged as invariants by the automated tools based on the characteristics of the analyzed traces. If accepted, this invariant would be then used to build up a model of program execution and then when anomalous behavior was observed, it would be flagged either as an error or used to update the set of invariants and consequently the model of proper operation [18].

In this paper, we interpret requirements to be invariants that hold true on all possible runs of the software system. Such requirements can constitute a document of formal properties for the model under inspection (containing properties such as the relationship between inputs, for example), which can serve as the basis for a comparison between the model's observed and intended behavior.

Unlike [18], whose primary goal was anomaly detection, our aim is to efficiently identify a complete set of invariants with minimal and targeted effort for the expert. This includes deducing previously unknown implicit requirements, eliminating candidate invariants that are not valid, and demonstrating that our procedure is robust in that multiple runs will produce converging results.

2.2 Automotive Model-Based Development

The work in this paper grew out of a project devoted to improving the efficiency of software development processes for automotive software. The pilot study in particular involves an external-lighting control feature in a Bosch production application. As automotive software is increasingly developed using model-based development, the software-artifact analyzed in later takes the form of a model in the MATLAB® / Simulink® / Stateflow®[1] modeling notation. This section discusses some of the uses of such models in the automotive industry.

Modern automobiles contain significant amounts of software. One estimate put the average amount of source code in high-end models at 100 million lines of code, with the amount growing by an order of magnitude on average every decade [6]. At the same time, the business importance of software is growing, with new (and profitable) features relying on software for their functionality.

---

[1] MATLAB®, Simulink® and Stateflow® are trademarks of The MathWorks, Inc.

For these reasons, automotive companies, and their suppliers such as Bosch, have strong incentives to improve the efficiency of their software development processes. At the same time, safety, warranty, recall and liability concerns also require that this software be of high quality and dependability.

One approach that is garnering rapidly growing acceptance in the industry is *model-based development* (MBD). In MBD traditional specification and design documents are supplemented with executable models in notations such as MAT-LAB / Simulink / Stateflow or ASCET®2 that precisely define the expected behavior of eventual software and system implementations. These models are often developed upstream of the software-development teams by controls engineers, and the notations are often based on block-diagram notations favored by members of the controls community.

From a programming language perspective, Simulink (and its Statecharts-like sub-language Stateflow) may be seen as a synchronous dataflow language. Blocks in the diagram's design represent functions that compute output values given inputs. Because Simulink and related models are executable, they may be simulated and debugged; they may also be used as test oracles for downstream software development. As the gap between design models and implementation narrows, design models also become increasingly attractive as test oracles.

2.3 Instrumentation-Based Verification

Because of the centrality of models in model-based development processes, it is important that they behave correctly, i.e. in accordance with functional requirements specified for them. Several model-checking tools, including commercial ones such as The MathWorks' DesignVerifier, have been developed for this purpose. Such tools take models to be verified (we call these *design models* in what follows, because they are often the outputs of design processes) and requirements specifications, typically in a temporal logic, and attempt to prove automatically that model behavior conforms to the requirements.

A related approach, called *Instrumentation-Based Verification* (IBV) [1], advocates the formalization of requirements instead as so-called *monitor models* in the same modeling notation used for the other models in the MBD process. Each discrete requirement has its own monitor model, whose purpose is to monitor the data flowing through the design model and determine if the associated requirement is being violated or not via a boolean-valued output. The design model is then instrumented with the monitor models, and structural-coverage testing performed to determine if any monitor models can report an error. The advantages of IBV are that a separate notation for formalizing requirements need not be learned; that monitor models can be executed and debugged; that the monitor models (and the requirements they express) are likely to be updated with the design models, and that testing-based approaches scale better than model checkers. The disadvantage is that IBV cannot produce the iron-clad guarantees of correctness that model checkers can when the latter do indeed terminate.

---

2 ASCET® is a trademark of the ETAS Group.

Commercial tools like Reactis®³ provide support for IBV by supporting the instrumentation process and automating the generation of test suites that maximize coverage of models.

2.4   Reactis

The experimental work described later in this paper makes heavy use of the aforementioned Reactis tool, so this section gives more detail about it.

Reactis is a model-based testing tool. Given an open-loop model (i.e. one with unconnected inputs and outputs) in the MathWorks' Simulink / Stateflow notation, Reactis generates test cases in the form of sequences of input vectors for the model. The goal of the generated tests is to provide full coverage of the model according to different model-based adaptations of structural coverage criteria. In general, for reasons of undecidability, full coverage cannot be guaranteed; Reactis uses different heuristics in to try to maximize the coverage of the test cases it creates. The tool also evaluates the model while it is constructing the test suites and stores the model-generated output vectors in the test cases.

Reactis also supports the Instrumentation-Based Verification (IBV) technique mentioned in the previous subsection. To use this feature, a user first creates a Simulink library containing the monitor models for the requirements of interest. S/he then uses Reactis to instrument the model to be verified with the monitor models, and to generate test cases that cover the instrumented model, including the constructs contained in the monitor models. While the tests are being constructed, Reactis also evaluates the monitor model outputs, and if any reports "false" then the resulting test is evidence that a requirement is violated. The coverage criteria guarantee that the test generator will attempt to generate tests that cause outputs of "false" from the monitor models.

The Reactis test-generation algorithm employs a three-phase approach, including a Monte Carlo simulation step. For space reasons, further details are omitted here; the core of the technique is covered by US Patent #7,644,398. It is important to note that Reactis test suites include randomly generated test cases that are subsequently refined. For this reason, different executions of the tool, even on the same model, will in general yield very different test suites.

3   Extracting Requirements

This section outlines our approach to inferring requirements from executable software artifacts. The steps in our methodology are depicted graphically in Figure 1; they rely on the use of coverage testing and data-mining tools to propose invariants from test data generated from simulated execution runs of the model, and the subsequent validation of these invariants. What follows describes each step in more detail.

---

³ Reactis® is a registered trademark of Reactive Systems, Inc. (RSI). In the interest of full disclosure, one of the authors is a co-founder of this company.

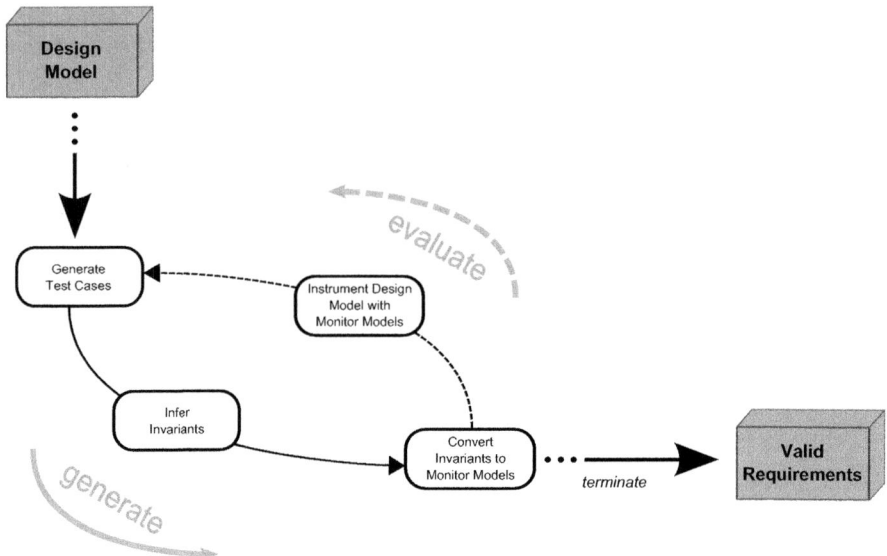

Fig. 1. Overview of requirements-extraction process

Step 1: Generate Test Cases. Test data is generated from design models by running a sequence of generated inputs on the design models using automated, coverage-based test-generation tools.

Step 2: Invariant Inference. Invariants are discovered using an association rule-mining tool on the test data from Step 1. The tool proposes a set of association rules that are ~~believed~~ suspected to be invariants of the model under inspection. We report only invariants having a *strength* value equal to 1.0, the maximum value a strength score can take [22]. This equivalently means that any invariant reported has no counter example in the observed data, namely it is a true invariant for the evidence which the inference is performed over.

Step 3: Invariant Validation. Model-coverage metrics merely assure that critical elements (blocks, conditions, decisions, etc.) have been executed at least once in a test-suite. They of course cannot enforce full coverage of all possible behavior (i.e. path coverage). This is why the inferred invariants cannot be assumed to be true requirements, and must be further validated in order to be reported as such.

In Raz *et al.*'s approach, this validation was carried out manually. We instead automate this validation step by converting each candidate requirement into a monitor model and using IBV to determine if the proposed invariant can be invalidated. While performing this verification, the validation tool will generate a new test-suite that, in its attempt to maximize model coverage, will attempt to violate the monitor model.

If the monitor model is not satisfied, then the putative invariant that it represents does not hold true for all traces and is thus discarded. If the monitor model is satisfied, then we can say, with a high level of confidence, that a valid invariant has been inferred from the design model and can be seen as a requirement.

As indicated in Figure 1, our technique can be iterated. By the nature of IBV, the extra step of validating the invariants involves instrumenting the original design model with monitor model representations of the invariants themselves. The result of this instrumentation is a well-defined design model which has at its core the original design model whose behavior has not been altered due to the manner in which the instrumentation takes place. Thus, we can repeat steps 1-3 on this new, instrumented model and obtain a different, richer set of invariants.

4   Experimental Configuration

We evaluate the requirements extraction process in the previous section using a production automotive pilot study. This section details the experimental set-up used, including the application and tool chain used to implement the steps of the procedure, the specific questions studied, and the analysis framework for assessing the results. The section following then reports the results themselves.

4.1   Test Application

The model used to evaluate our framework is a Simulink diagram encoding the design of an automotive software function taken from existing production C source code developed by Bosch. The model consists of approximately 75 blocks and has two inputs and two outputs. Existing documentation was present that described, among other things, a state machine describing expected behavior. The requirements extraction process corresponds to inferring valid edges between the set of states on this machine. In this state machine there are nine states and 42 transitions, and thus 42 possible invariants that can be discovered. We refer to this automotive model as $\mathcal{D}$ in what follows.

4.2   Tool Chain

The specific tasks that need to be performed in order to implement our requirements-extraction approach include: (1) generation of full-coverage test suites from $\mathcal{D}$; (2) production of proposed invariants from test data; (3) creation of monitor models from invariants; (4) instrumentation of $\mathcal{D}$ with monitor models; (5) generation of coverage test-suites from instrumented $\mathcal{D}$. As indicated in Section 2, the Reactis tool generates high-coverage test suites from Simulink models and also supports the instrumentation of models with monitor models and subsequent validation testing. This tool was used for tasks 1 and 5.

To mine invariants (task 2), we used the Magnum Opus data-mining tool [21], mainly based on its relative ease of use efficiency. For our model, all the variables under consideration are nominal rather than numeric. Thus, we focus on discovering rules of the form

$$\left(\bigwedge a = a_i\right) \longrightarrow \left(\bigwedge b = b_i\right),$$

where the premise and consequent are conjunctions of terms involving equalities of variables to specific values.

Because we have existing ground truth data regarding $\mathcal{D}$ in the form of a state machine, we rewrite all invariants discovered to contain state information on both the premise and the consequent of rule. When considering invariants of this form, there is a one-to-one correspondence with state transitions on the state machine. This allows us to easily check what rules are recovered and what are not. For example, a rule such as `'button=pressed' -> 'new_state=2'` would be expanded to the set of rules (assuming possible values of `state` are 1,2).

```
'state=1' ∧ 'button=pressed' -> 'new_state=2'
'state=2' ∧ 'button=pressed' -> 'new_state=2'
```

To streamline the process, we also wrote scripts that: translate Reactis-generated test data into the Magnum Opus format; convert Magnum Opus association rules into monitor models; and create the file Reactis uses to instrument models with monitors (tasks 3 and 4). The result is a fully automated system that requires no manual involvement.

To use the resulting tool-chain, a user first runs Reactis on $\mathcal{D}$ to create a test suite (set of sequences of input/output vectors). The suite is then automatically translated into Magnum Opus format, and that tool then run infer invariants. Another conversion transforms these invariants into monitor models, along with the proper information for wiring monitor-model inputs into $\mathcal{D}$. Finally, the user runs Reactis a second time on the instrumented $\mathcal{D}$ ($\mathcal{D}$ + monitor models); Reactis creates a second test suite that attempts to cover the instrumented model (and also tries to invalidate the monitor models), reporting when it terminates which monitor models were found to be violated in the second round of testing. Violated monitor models correspond to invariants that are in fact not valid invariants and thus should not be considered requirements.

Note that, as discussed in Section 3, this process can be iterated. Furthermore, because the test suite created during the validation phase of the monitor models is constructed using the same heuristics as that of the standard test suites, it can be used as the basis for a second round of invariant inference and by being combined with the first round's data. Because the second batch of tests includes any counterexamples that where constructed to invalidate some of the invariants generated from the first batch of tests, the already-violated invariants will not reappear in subsequent iterations of this procedure due to our criterion that proposed invariants must satisfy all test data known at the time.

4.3   Structural vs. Random Testing

One hypothesis we wish to test in our experiments is that using full-coverage tests as a basis for invariant inference yields better invariants than tests that do not have coverage guarantees. We quantify the notion of "better" in two dimensions: how *accurate* are the invariants (i.e. what proportion of a set of proposed invariants are found to be valid in the validation-testing phase), and how *complete* are they (what proportion of the total set of invariants from the requirements documentation are generated).

To conduct this assessment empirically, we first produce a test suite having maximal coverage. This suite is then mined for invariants. Finally, we validate these proposed invariants by encoding them as monitor models and generating new test cases with these monitor models instrumenting the original design model. This experiment, which we call E_{full}, is repeated five times to increase statistical confidence in the results.

As a baseline comparison, we then generate a suite of test cases randomly with no structural constraints imposed (a limit on test length was instead imposed). In the exact same way as E_{full}, this test suite is then mined for invariants which are then converted into monitor models and validated using Reactis. We refer to this configuration as $E_{partial}$, indicating that full coverage is not guaranteed for the design model. As before for E_{full}, five separate experiments of configuration $E_{partial}$ are performed.

We hypothesize that because coverage is complete for E_{full} runs and incomplete for those generated by $E_{partial}$ runs, less of the state space of the design model is covered, and thus E_{full} runs will generate more accurate and more complete invariant sets than those generated by random testing. Along with this total, the number of invalid invariants can also be considered. Because we cover more variation of the state space in our test cases, we expect fewer spurious invariants to be inferred by E_{full} than by $E_{partial}$ during the entire process.

In this pilot study, we have access to the full set of known requirements, and the performance of the different experimental set-ups can also be assessed in terms how many of these are discovered. Also, we can measure the reproducibility of the output, i.e. the similarity of the outputs of any run to any other run within the same configuration. To assess how similar any particular invariant set is to another, we use set a set-similarity statistic, the Jaccard coefficient [11]. Often used in clustering and other applications where similarity scores are needed [19], this metric is a measurement of the overlap of two sets, with a score of 0 (lowest) signifying no overlap, and a score of 1 (highest) signifying set equivalence. We compute these similarity scores between all pairs of runs within each configuration. We expect to observe a higher similarity between pairs of individual E_{full} experiments than the similarity between pairs of individual $E_{partial}$ experiments.

4.4   Invariant Refinement through Iteration

The second hypothesis we wish to test is that iterating our procedure produces more accurate and complete sets of invariants. To assess this, following the validation phase of each of the previous experiments, we perform the entire process again. For E_{full}, we use as a new test suite the suite generated during the previous validation step together with the original test suite used for invariant-generation. For $E_{partial}$, we generate another suite of randomly selected test cases. We refer to the configuration and results of the E_{full} experiments after only one iteration as $E_{full}^{(1)}$ (which corresponds to exactly the configuration discussed in Section 4.3), and results of these experiments extending over two iterations to be $E_{full}^{(2)}$. A similar scheme applies to $E_{partial}$, where we refer to $E_{partial}^{(1)}$ and $E_{partial}^{(2)}$. It should be noted that although the validation phases for $E_{partial}^{(2)}$ involves generating test suites guided by coverage criterion, we discard this when producing new data for the second iteration, as we wish to preserve the "coverage-blindness" of the $E_{partial}$ test suites.

As before, five runs are performed using one of the second iteration configurations. For further analysis, we again report the number of valid invariants mined, as well as the pairwise Jaccard similarity measurements between experimental runs in belonging to the same configuration. We expect that the number of valid invariants to increase from results in $E_{full}^{(1)}$ to $E_{full}^{(2)}$, due to the increase in the amount of testing; the newly introduced test cases for the second iteration can potentially include counterexamples and other new portions of the state space that were not well represented in the first iteration. For this reason, the number of valid invariants detected by $E_{partial}^{(2)}$ is also expected to exceed the number found by $E_{partial}^{(1)}$, but again because no structural guidance is given, the likelihood of counter examples and other unexplored portions of the state machine being encountered is lower, so the increase should not be as significant.

5   Experimental Results

This section presents the results of our empirical study on $\mathcal{D}$. Table 1 shows the results of running $E_{full}^{(1)}$ and $E_{full}^{(2)}$ experiments, while Table 2 shows the results for the $E_{partial}^{(1)}$ and $E_{partial}^{(2)}$ configurations.

The data in the tables supports both hypotheses made in Sections 4.3 and 4.4. In particular, in the first iteration of the structural-coverage method, the accuracy ratios (proportion of proposed invariants that the validation step determines are indeed invariant) are in the range $0.69 - 0.82$, with an average over the 5 runs of 0.76; the corresponding figures for the first iteration of the randomly generated method are $0.42 - 0.76$, with an average of 0.54. Thus, about $\frac{3}{4}$ of the invariants inferred from full-coverage test data are valid in the first iteration, on average, while only just over $\frac{1}{2}$ are using randomly generated data. The differences in completeness (ratio of net invariants to total number of known invariants, based on requirements documentation) is also pronounced, with coverage test-data yielding numbers in the range $0.43 - 0.67$ (average of 0.57) and random test data producing results in the range $0.19 - 0.45$ (average of 0.31).

These differences are accentuated when the results of the second iteration are considered. In the structural-coverage case (Table 1) the accuracy and completeness ratios rise to 0.97 and 0.92, respectively, while in the random case the corresponding figures are 0.67 and 0.51. Structural-coverage test data yields a negligible number of incorrect invariants and infers 92% of the total invariants, while $\frac{1}{3}$ of the invariants produced from random test data are determined to be invalid in the second iteration and just over $\frac{1}{2}$ of known invariants are discovered.

Table 1. Results from $E^{(1)}_{full}$ and $E^{(2)}_{full}$. The "Putative" columns reports the total number of potential invariants mined after the inference phase, but before validation. "Invalid" reports the number of invariants that were found to be spurious in the validation phase. "Net" reports the number of validated invariants. "Acc." is the accuracy ratio: the ratio of "Net" to "Putative". "Comp." is the completeness ratio: the ratio of "Net" to the 42 total invariants contained in the original specification. The average of each column is reported in the last row.

Run #	$E^{(1)}_{full}$					$E^{(2)}_{full}$				
	Putative	Invalid	Net	Acc.	Comp.	Putative	Invalid	Net	Acc.	Comp.
1	26	8	18	0.69	0.43	40	1	39	0.97	0.93
2	34	6	28	0.82	0.67	40	2	38	0.95	0.90
3	30	9	21	0.70	0.50	38	1	37	0.97	0.88
4	33	7	26	0.79	0.62	42	1	41	0.98	0.98
5	34	7	27	0.79	0.64	38	0	38	1.00	0.90
Avg	31.4	7.4	24.0	0.76	0.57	39.6	1.0	38.6	0.97	0.92

Table 2. Results from $E^{(1)}_{partial}$ and $E^{(2)}_{partial}$. The columns are the same as in Table 1.

Run #	$E^{(1)}_{partial}$					$E^{(2)}_{partial}$				
	Putative	Invalid	Net	Acc.	Comp.	Putative	Invalid	Net	Acc.	Comp.
1	19	11	8	0.42	0.19	29	13	16	0.55	0.38
2	22	11	11	0.50	0.26	27	10	17	0.63	0.40
3	26	12	14	0.54	0.33	34	9	25	0.74	0.60
4	26	13	13	0.50	0.31	32	15	17	0.53	0.40
5	25	6	19	0.76	0.45	35	3	32	0.91	0.76
Avg	23.6	10.6	13.0	0.54	0.31	31.4	10.0	21.4	0.67	0.51

The data in these tables also supports the second hypothesis: that iteration of the process yields more accurate and more complete sets of invariants. In the structural-coverage case, the average accuracy ratio increases from 0.76 to 0.97, and the average completeness ratio rises from 0.57 to 0.92. The corresponding figures for the random-test case show a similar (but less substantial) improvement: from 0.54 to 0.67 (accuracy), and from 0.31 to 0.51 (completeness).

Table 3 and Table 4 present the Jaccard pairwise similarities between individual runs of the same type. The average Jaccard similarity for $E^{(1)}_{partial}$ is 0.51, and it increases to 0.58 when a second iteration is added in $E^{(2)}_{partial}$. The structurally-guided coverage testing shows better results. The average for $E^{(1)}_{full}$ is 0.65, which increases to 0.87 when adding a second iteration. These findings, coupled with the completeness-ratio results from Table 1 and Table 2, support our hypothesis, showing that randomly guided test cases lead to both fewer invariants being detected, as well as high variation in the set of those that are detected, when compared to test cases satisfying coverage criteria.

Table 3. Jaccard similarity scores for $E_{full}^{(1)}$ and $E_{full}^{(2)}$. The minimum, average, and maximum values are also given.

$E_{full}^{(1)}$	1	2	3	4	5
1	1	0.53	0.86	0.52	0.67
2		1	0.63	0.64	0.72
3			1	0.62	0.71
4				1	0.61
5					1

$E_{full}^{(2)}$	1	2	3	4	5
1	1	0.88	0.85	0.90	0.83
2		1	0.92	0.88	0.81
3			1	0.86	0.83
4				1	0.88
5					1

	Min	Avg	Max
$E_{full}^{(1)}$	0.52	0.65	0.87
$E_{full}^{(2)}$	0.81	0.87	0.92

Table 4. Jaccard similarity scores for $E_{partial}^{(1)}$ and $E_{partial}^{(2)}$

$E_{partial}^{(1)}$	1	2	3	4	5
1	1	0.46	0.47	0.62	0.35
2		1	0.47	0.60	0.58
3			1	0.59	0.43
4				1	0.52
5					1

$E_{partial}^{(2)}$	1	2	3	4	5
1	1	0.74	0.52	0.74	0.50
2		1	0.45	0.70	0.48
3			1	0.56	0.63
4				1	0.48
5					1

	Min	Avg	Max
$E_{partial}^{(1)}$	0.35	0.51	0.62
$E_{partial}^{(2)}$	0.45	0.58	0.74

Regarding the effort needed to conduct these experiments, space limitations prevent us from reporting fully. However, it should be noted that no run of Reactis or Magnum Opus ever required more than 3.5 minutes to complete on the commercial laptops used in the study. The data suggest obvious time savings for validating invariants over manual inspection.

6   Related Work

In *specification mining* [3, 5, 9, 10, 16, 20, 23], the interaction behavior of running programs is extracted [14] by machine-learning algorithms [15] wherein a state machine, which is supposed to represent a model of the program's specification, is constructed and analyzed using a variety of static techniques [4]. Our approach, in contrast, concentrates on deriving individual requirements rather than constructing a total specification of the system. In addition, our approach is distinguished by its provisions of guarantees regarding coverage of behavior.

We also use Magnum Opus for its easy setup and its support for association rules, but other tools could also be used to mine the invariants.

The Weka project[24] is a toolkit for performing data-mining-related tasks and includes the Apriori algorithm [2], one of the earliest algorithms used for association rule mining. The particular types of association rules mined are similar to Magnum Opus in that they do not support invariants involving ranges.

The Daikon system proposed by Ernst *et al.* [8] performs dynamic detection of "likely invariants" in programs written in C, C++, Java, and Perl. An early step in the approach uses code instrumenters to obtain trace data that is passed into its inference algorithm. This trace data does not guarantee good coverage over the program under inspection; Ernst *et al.* note that multiple runs may be required by the program under inspection and combined. The invariants proposed by Daikon are checked for redundancy, but it is difficult to validate invariant correctness for test cases other than those given by the presented trace data. Through the use of Reactis, our framework only will produce test cases with a specified coverage level (able to be set by the user). Also, by converting invariants into monitor models and validating them, we can provide stronger assurances in the correctness of our final invariant set.

Hangal *et al.*'s IODINE framework [12] dynamically mines low-level invariants on hardware designs. Rather than employ a machine-learning approach, they use *analyzers* that monitor signals in the design and report observations that are of interest, such as equality between signals, mutual exclusion between signals, etc. In contrast to our work, the observations / invariant types that are discoverable are determined by the analyzers selected, which can be difficult to identify if one is searching for invariants that are either unknown or otherwise not considered. In our case, test cases are generated through the same general framework regardless (using structural coverage), and the data-mining tool employed is the determining factor of what types of invariants are discovered.

Mesbah *et al.* [13] proposed a method of automatic testing of the user interfaces of AJAX-based applications. Their approach reveals invariants of an AJAX application and constructs a state machine of the application, over which other invariants (which they equate to requirements) are identified. The notion of differing states in their context corresponds to the various paths of action events that can be taken through user interactions such as button clicks. Their work focuses on using these invariants to detecting faults for testing purposes, rather than attempting to construct a well-covered set of invariants which corresponds to a largely complete view of the state machine, as our work does.

Cheng *et al.* [7] use data-mining techniques to extract putative invariants over a program's dynamic execution, and augment an existing bounded model checker that uses SAT formulations of the code statically. This approach is shown to speed up software verification when compared to performing bounded model checking without the invariants obtained from the data mining. In contrast, our work infers a largely complete set of such invariants that could characterize the model itself over the variety of dynamic executions that could possibly occur.

7 Conclusions and Future Work

This paper has presented a framework for requirements reconstruction from executable software artifacts, such as control software, that follow a read-compute-write behavior model. The method relies on the application of data-mining techniques to test data that structurally cover the artifact to derive proposed requirements in the form of invariants expressing relationships between inputs and outputs. The method then uses an automated validation step to identify spurious invariants. The method was piloted on a production automotive lighting-control application modeled in Simulink; the experimental data indicate that using full-coverage test data yields better invariant sets than random test data, and that iteratively applying the approach further improves these invariants.

As future work, we wish to experiment further with the method, using other automotive-related Simulink models. We also would like to study the impact that the use of different coverage criteria — decision coverage, MC/DC, etc. — have on the quality of invariant sets. Finally, the invariants that were studied in this work lack a temporal aspect; we are interested in pursuing requirement-generation strategies that permit the inference of requirements that contain a time element (e.g. "if a happens then b must happen within x time units").

References

[1] Ackermann, C., Ray, A., Cleaveland, R., Heit, J., Shelton, C., Martin, C.: Model-based design verification: A monitor based approach. In: SAE WC (2008)

[2] Agrawal, R., Imieliński, T., Swami, A.: Mining association rules between sets of items in large databases. In: SIGMOD 1993, pp. 207–216. ACM, New York (1993)

[3] Ammons, G., Bodík, R., Larus, J.R.: Mining specifications. SIGPLAN Not. 37(1), 4–16 (2002)

[4] Ball, T., Rajamani, S.K.: Automatically validating temporal safety properties of interfaces. In: Dwyer, M.B. (ed.) SPIN 2001. LNCS, vol. 2057, pp. 103–122. Springer, Heidelberg (2001)

[5] Biermann, A.W., Feldman, J.: On the synthesis of finite-state machines from samples of their behavior. IEEE Trans. Computers, 592–597 (1972)

[6] Charette, R.N.: This car runs on code (February 2009),
http://www.spectrum.ieee.org/green-tech/advanced-cars/
this-car-runs-on-code

[7] Cheng, X., Hsiao, M.S.: Simulation-directed invariant mining for software verification. In: DATE 2008, pp. 682–687. ACM, New York (2008)

[8] Ernst, M.D., et al.: The Daikon system for dynamic detection of likely invariants. Science of Computer Programming 69(1-3), 35–45 (2007)

[9] Gabel, M., Su, Z.: Symbolic mining of temporal specifications. In: ICSE 2008, pp. 51–60. ACM, New York (2008)

[10] Goues, C., Weimer, W.: Specification mining with few false positives. In: Kowalewski, S., Philippou, A. (eds.) TACAS 2009. LNCS, vol. 5505, pp. 292–306. Springer, Heidelberg (2009)

[11] Hamers, L., et al.: Similarity measures in scientometric research: the jaccard index versus salton's cosine formula. Inf. Process. Manage. 25(3), 315–318 (1989)

[12] Hangal, S., et al.: Iodine: a tool to automatically infer dynamic invariants for hardware designs. In: DAC 2005, pp. 775–778. ACM, New York (2005)

[13] Mesbah, A., van Deursen, A.: Invariant-based automatic testing of ajax user interfaces. In: ICSE 2009, Washington, pp. 210–220. IEEE, Los Alamitos (2009)

[14] Michael, C.C., Ghosh, A.: Using finite automata to mine execution data for intrusion detection. In: Debar, H., Mé, L., Wu, S.F. (eds.) RAID 2000. LNCS, vol. 1907, pp. 66–79. Springer, Heidelberg (2000)

[15] Raman, A., Patrick, J., North, P.: The sk-strings method for inferring pfsa. In: ICML 1997 (1997)

[16] Ramanathan, M.K., Grama, A., Jagannathan, S.: Static specification inference using predicate mining. SIGPLAN Not. 42(6), 123–134 (2007)

[17] Raz, O.: Helping everyday users find anomalies in data feeds. PhD thesis, Pittsburgh, PA, USA, Chair-Shaw, Mary (2004)

[18] Raz, O., Koopman, P., Shaw, M.: Semantic anomaly detection in online data sources. In: ICSE 2002, pp. 302–312. ACM, New York (2002)

[19] Romesburg, H.C.: Cluster Analysis for Researchers. Lulu Press, North Carolina (2004)

[20] Shoham, S., et al.: Static specification mining using automata-based abstractions. In: ISSTA 2007, pp. 174–184. ACM, New York (2007)

[21] Webb, G.I.: Efficient search for association rules. In: KDD 2000, pp. 99–107. ACM, New York (2000)

[22] Webb, G.I.: Discovering significant patterns. Mach. Learn. 68(1), 1–33 (2007)

[23] Weimer, W., Necula, G.C.: Mining temporal specifications for error detection. In: Halbwachs, N., Zuck, L.D. (eds.) TACAS 2005. LNCS, vol. 3440, pp. 461–476. Springer, Heidelberg (2005)

[24] Witten, I.H., Frank, E.: Data Mining: Practical machine learning tools and techniques, 2nd edn. Morgan Kaufmann, San Francisco (2005)

Code Contracts for .NET: Runtime Verification and So Much More

Mike Barnett

Microsoft Research, Redmond, WA, USA
mbarnett@microsoft.com

The project *Code Contracts for .NET* [1] comes from the Research in Software Engineering (RiSE) group [5] at Microsoft Research. We took the lessons we learned from the Spec# project [3,4] and have applied them in a setting available to all .NET programmers without the need for them to adopt an experimental programming language or the Spec# programming methodology. It has been available since early 2009 with a commercial use license on the DevLabs [7] web site. Since then there have been about 20,000 downloads, with an active forum of users.

The central concepts are method pre- and postconditions and object invariants. These are specified using ordinary method calls defined in the class `Contract` which has been introduced into the Base Class Library in .NET 4.0[1]. Contracts can be specified for interface methods (including abstract methods) and can refer to "old" values and return values (in method postconditions).

A library-based approach allows all .NET programmers to use Code Contracts, whether from C#, VB, F#, or any of the other .NET languages. By using a library instead of a separate programming language we trade off "beauty" for "usability": there is no barrier to incrementally adding contracts to an existing codebase, no change is needed in existing build environments, and all existing IDE features are leveraged while authoring and maintaining both the code and the specifications. It also means that we get — for free — a concrete semantics against which the soundness of static analyses can be evaluated.

The current download contains tools for runtime verification, static checking, documentation generation, and editor extensions, as well as Visual Studio integration. We also have a set of reference assemblies for most of the libraries in the Base Class Library. A *reference assembly* provide contracts for external references. Our reference assemblies have been produced as part of a continuing collaboration with the .NET product group.

All of our tools operate on the compiled binary produced by each compiler. Since the contracts occur within the code, it is important to provide infrastructure for extracting and manipulating contracts. This functionality is available through CCI [6], an open-source project. We hope that this allows an ecosystem to develop for many different tools that are interested in leveraging specifications. The infrastructure performs contract inheritance and well-formedness checks (e.g., special rules govern what can appear within a contract), which all of our tools make use of.

---

[1] Earlier versions of .NET can use the Code Contracts tools by referencing a separate library — supplied with the tools — that defines this class.

G. Roşu et al. (Eds.): RV 2010, LNCS 6418, pp. 16–17, 2010.

In the runtime checker, contract failures are completely customizable, either via an event-based hook or else by user-supplied methods that replace the built-in error handlers. Runtime checks are injected for method contracts at method entry and exit, while object invariants are enforced at the end of public constructors and all public methods. Invariant checks occur only for the outermost method on the call stack and method contracts include a recursion guard. Preconditions can also be injected at call-sites for programming against a runtime assembly that is not itself instrumented for runtime checking, but for which a reference assembly exists. Source context information is preserved in the instrumented assemblies for debugging. Runtime checking also interacts with other tools; most notably with Pex [8,2], a white-box test generation tool.

Code Contracts for .NET aims for an entire development experience centered around code specifications: runtime checking is just one facet. It is crucial to have contracts appear during code authoring and maintenance. They must be present in printed and on-line documentation. Other tools, such as code optimizers and static analyses, should be able to take advantage of them.

Acknowledgements

None of this would have been possible without all of the team members, past and present: Melitta Andersen, Sheldon Blauman, Manuel Fähndrich, Brian Grunkemeyer, Katy King, Francesco Logozzo, Vipul Patel, Justin van Patten, Herman Venter, and Daryl Zuniga.

References

1. Barnett, M., Fähndrich, M., Logozzo, F.: Embedded contract languages. In: SAC 2010: Proceedings of the ACM Symposium on Applied Computing, Lausanne, Switzerland. ACM Press, New York (2010)
2. Barnett, M., Fähndrich, M., de Halleux, P., Logozzo, F., Tillmann, N.: Exploiting the synergy between automated-test-generation and programming-by-contract. In: Beckert, B., Hähnle, R. (eds.) ICSE 2009, 31th International Conference on Software Engineering, pp. 401–402. IEEE, Los Alamitos (2009)
3. Barnett, M., Leino, K.R.M., Schulte, W.: The Spec# programming system: An overview. In: Barthe, G., Burdy, L., Huisman, M., Lanet, J.-L., Muntean, T. (eds.) CASSIS 2004. LNCS, vol. 3362, pp. 49–69. Springer, Heidelberg (2005)
4. Spec# developer community. Spec# web site. Microsoft Research (2006),
   http://research.microsoft.com/specsharp/
5. Research in Software Engineering. Rise web site. Microsoft Research (2010),
   http://research.microsoft.com/rise/
6. Common Compiler Infrastructure. CCI web site. CodePlex (2010),
   http://ccisamples.codeplex.com/
7. Microsoft Visual Studio. Devlabs web site. Microsoft Corporation (2010),
   http://msdn.microsoft.com/en-us/devlabs/
8. Tillmann, N., de Halleux, J.: Pex – white box test generation for .NET. In: Beckert, B., Hähnle, R. (eds.) TAP 2008. LNCS, vol. 4966, pp. 134–153. Springer, Heidelberg (2008)

Visual Debugging for Stream Processing Applications

Wim De Pauw, Mihai Leţia, Buğra Gedik, Henrique Andrade*, Andy Frenkiel,
Michael Pfeifer, and Daby Sow

IBM T.J. Watson Research Center
Hawthorne NY 10532, USA
{wim,mletia,bgedik,afrenk,pfeifer,sowdaby}@us.ibm.com

Abstract. Stream processing is a new computing paradigm that enables continuous and fast analysis of massive volumes of streaming data. Debugging streaming applications is not trivial, since they are typically distributed across multiple nodes and handle large amounts of data. Traditional debugging techniques like breakpoints often rely on a stop-the-world approach, which may be useful for debugging single node applications, but insufficient for streaming applications. We propose a new visual and analytic environment to support debugging, performance analysis, and troubleshooting for stream processing applications. Our environment provides several visualization methods to study, characterize, and summarize the flow of tuples between stream processing operators. The user can interactively indicate points in the streaming application from where tuples will be traced and visualized as they flow through different operators, without stopping the application. To substantiate our discussion, we also discuss several of these features in the context of a financial engineering application.

Keywords: Visualization, debugging, streaming applications, performance analysis, tracing.

1 Introduction

Stream processing is a new emerging computing paradigm with applications in various areas such as environment monitoring, financial trading, business intelligence and healthcare [1]. This paradigm enables continuous and immediate analysis of massive volumes of streaming data. In contrast with traditional data analysis approaches, stream computing does not require data to be persisted before being analyzed. It allows for data to be analyzed *while in motion*, by going through a mostly static set of long-standing queries that constitute the core of stream processing applications.

While data stream processing systems are substantially different from traditional database-centric analysis systems, developers are confronted with familiar challenges and goals, i.e. the identification of the causes for incorrect or missing results, the identification of errors in the input data, the understanding of performance degradation issues, including exhaustion of resources, and the coping with design flaws, among

---

* Currently working at Goldman Sachs. Henrique can be reached at
henrique.c.m.andrade@gmail.com

G. Roşu et al. (Eds.): RV 2010, LNCS 6418, pp. 18–35, 2010.
© Springer-Verlag Berlin Heidelberg 2010

others. However, the nature of streaming applications prevents classical debugging approaches to fully achieve these debugging goals. Indeed, typical streaming applications can be highly distributed to handle large data throughput and low latency requirements. This distribution of computation yields numerous possible data paths in an application thus complicating the identification of causes of problems.

Furthermore, in a streaming environment where data is constantly in motion, it is quite hard, if not impossible, to capture a complete and globally consistent view of the input data streams and the application state. While breakpoints may be useful for debugging single node applications, they are insufficient for streaming applications for the following reasons. First, the cause and the manifestation of an error may be situated at different locations. Second, halting the execution on one node often has a "train wreck" effect on streaming applications, disturbing the relative order of events throughout the application. Finally, the large amounts of data that are typically processed in streaming applications make manual inspections of individual tuples sent across operators quite impractical and difficult without proper tooling.

This paper presents a new visual and analytic environment to support large-scale application understanding, including specific features for debugging, performance analysis, and troubleshooting. Our environment consists of several visualization methods to study, characterize, and summarize the flow of tuples between streaming operators as part of System S [2], a large-scale stream-processing platform developed at IBM Research.

We demonstrate several techniques for tracing and visualizing the data flow of streaming applications that enable the developer to understand the application's runtime behavior and more effectively locate and diagnose typical problems. The proposed environment allows the user to recreate these data flows in a temporally accurate fashion. The user can also interactively indicate points in the streaming application from where tuples will be traced and visualized as they flow through different operators, without stopping the application.

The tracing and visualizations described here are intended to be used in concert with the existing debugging techniques described in our earlier work [3, 4, 5], thereby enabling the developers to apply the existing techniques when they can be the most effective. To substantiate our discussion, we organize the presentation of the features of our visualization tool in the context of a simple, yet real-world inspired financial engineering application.

In Section 2, we describe the programming model used by System S, the distributed stream computing platform on which we have implemented our visual debugging concepts. After a comparison with related work in Section 3, we propose the fundamental model of the data dependencies in Section 4. We describe the visual syntax of our tool in Section 5. Section 6 illustrates the new features with real-world debugging scenarios. Section 7 highlights major design points in our prototype and we conclude with Section 8.

2   SPADE and System S in a Nutshell

SPADE [6] is the programming language used for developing stream processing applications on System S [2], a distributed stream processing platform developed by IBM Research. We briefly describe some of the programming language features, focusing on the aspects that are directly related to the visualization capabilities described in this work:

Flow composition: The SPADE language provides composition capabilities that are used to create *data flow graphs* out of basic analytical units called *operators*. Operators are composed into data flow graphs via stream connections. This is called *static flow composition*, where the topology of the data flow graph is constructed at application development time and does not change at runtime. The language also supports *dynamic flow composition*, where connections are established at runtime, based on conditions specified at development time and availability of matching streams at runtime. In addition to these, SPADE also supports hierarchical flow composition via *composite operators*. A composite operator encapsulates a data flow graph as an operator, which enables development of large-scale streaming applications.

Flow manipulation: SPADE provides a type system and an expression language. They provide the basic constructs for expressing flow manipulations as custom functions and operators. A standard set of operators that are parameterizable using SPADE expression language, as well as a large set of built-in functions are also provided. The standard set of operators include basic relational manipulations such as selection, projection, aggregation, join, and sort, as well as common utilities such as buffering, throttling, splitting, merging, etc. Fundamental abstractions, such as windowing, punctuations, output functions, and operator parameters, among others are provided to facilitate flexible and powerful flow manipulations. The language also provides a set of *edge adapters* to connect operators to external sources and sinks, for ingesting external stream data and producing results to be consumed by external applications, respectively.

Extensible analytics: The SPADE language supports extensibility through *toolkits*. A toolkit is a set of reusable operators and functions [7]. The language can be extended with new operators, written in general-purpose programming languages, such as C++ and Java. Such operators can be type generic and parametrizable. In other words, they can potentially operate on any type (as in a Projection operator in relational algebra) and can be customized using SPADE's expression language (as in defining a match condition for a relational *Join* operator). This enables third parties to provide cross-domain as well as domain-specific toolkits of operators and functions, which encapsulate various streaming analytics from a wide range of application domains [1].

Distributed execution: The SPADE language provides various configuration options that influence the mapping of the logical data flow graph to a physical one, which can be deployed on a set of distributed hosts. For instance, the language can be used to express operator fusion constraints, which influence how operators are grouped into partitions that map to OS processes. Similarly, it can be used to specify partition placement constraints, which influence how processes representing the partitions are mapped to hosts. Ex-location and isolation constraints at the partition and host-level are also supported. These constraints can be used to express detailed requirements [8] in terms of how an application executes on the distributed platform. The SPADE language can also be used to specify threading and queueing configurations, controlling the data processing behavior within an operator and of an input port, respectively.

System S provides the runtime platform on which SPADE applications run. It provides management services such as scheduling, security, job management and monitoring, fault-tolerance services, dynamic stream traffic routing, to name a few. It also provides a high-performance communication substrate for SPADE applications, which makes available highly efficient transport capabilities for cross-process and cross-node communication; including some of the capabilities we make use of for visualization purposes, such as exposed performance metrics and tuple tagging.

3 Related Work

There are several bodies of literature related to this work, ranging from debugging systems to streaming data provenance tracking systems. Causeway [9] is a debugging system that allows developers to debug message-passing distributed systems. Using Causeway, the developer can observe the connection between the function call stack and the message passing mechanism. However, debugging is done postmortem, by processing offline traces that have been generated at runtime. Our tool allows live debugging and is able to reconfigure the tracing, based on intermediate results, which might already have attracted the attention of a developer. The authors of Causeway state that their system generates large quantities of debugging data, but they do not tackle the problem of narrowing the tracing space. Our tool uses execution slices to only trace the part of the system that is under observation, as we will describe later. Causeway is able to capture dependencies between an incoming message and one or more outgoing messages that were caused by it, but does not support the model where several incoming messages are aggregated into an outgoing message. Our debugging environment is able to aggregate tuples from the same or different input ports to output a single resulting tuple. To present the results, the Causeway tool uses text-based representations, comparable to the ones found in traditional debuggers while our tool provides the user with graphical models of entities in System S and their interactions.

Finding causalities between input and output data has been the focus of research in data provenance. In the context of stream computing, data provenance has received only a limited amount of attention, such as in the work of Vijayakumar et al. [10] Their work focuses on identifying and storing dependencies among streams (by encoding, as a tree, the IDs of ancestor streams of a derived stream), rather than the data dependencies for individual stream tuples. In our earlier work [11, 12] we proposed efficient techniques to track data and explored a model-based solution for data provenance in stream computing platforms. In a nutshell, our approach compresses the meta-data needed to track data provenance into a set of rules capturing input-output dependencies. The system that we developed is limited to backward provenance queries. Furthermore, the capture of provenance meta-data is severely limited by the capacity of the underlying storage system where the traces are persisted.

Our previous work in problem determination for Web Services uses message tagging [13] as well as semantic correlations between messages [14] to discover the data flow in business applications. Aguilera et al. [15] propose a method that treats the distributed components as black boxes. They infer causal paths from the observed messages by finding nested calls for RPC-style communication or by applying signal processing techniques that rely on the time variance between request and response messages. However, all these techniques that help with problem determination in distributed debugging are hard to apply to stream processing, because the volume ingested streaming data makes the implementation of these techniques impractical, if not impossible.

The Streams Debugger [5] enables a developer to inspect individual tuples in a SPADE application, by setting breakpoints and tracepoints on an operator's input or output ports. At a breakpoint, the flow of tuples on the stream connection is suspended, enabling the developer to examine, and optionally update, the contents of the tuple traversing the port. Tracepoints are similar to breakpoints, but trace the tuple without stopping the data flow. While the Streams Debugger has demonstrated utility for understanding and diagnosing the behavior of individual operators, it is not adequate when used to locate problems related to a long sequence of transformations that are characteristic of larger stream processing applications. In part, the techniques described in this paper are motivated by the observation that the Streams Debugger will benefit from an integration with our new visual environment that lets the developer reason about the end-to-end data flows of streaming applications.

4 Basic Model for Tracing Streaming Applications

As mentioned in Section 1, finding the cause of unexpected or incorrect results in streaming applications can be challenging since cause and effect can be located in different operators of the distributed application and be disjoint in time. For example, a particular operator might have a computational bug, which is noticed only when an incorrect output tuple generated by that operator is processed further downstream by another operator. Moreover, massive amounts of fast moving data in streaming applications can make it difficult for a user to isolate and retrieve the causal paths, in particular, because of the interweaving patterns created by correlation and aggregation operators. On the one hand, correlations computed by a join operation will take two (or more streams) and use incoming tuples from both input ports to compute the results. On the other hand, aggregations will compute an output tuple based on a collection of input tuples aggregated over a window. Hence, one can infer that the *provenance* of intermediate and final results can be clouded by operations like joins and aggregations. In other words, the outcome of an operator can be impacted by the preceding control flow, data flow, or by side effects, for example, occurring via out-of-band communication with other non-stream applications (via files, sockets, interactions through a database, etc.).

In this paper, we will focus primarily on dependencies caused by the regular stream data flow. The complexity of data dependencies can grow quickly for any non-trivial streaming application. The key to our visual debugging techniques is to trace and process information that allows the reconstruction and filtering of the data dependency paths that are of interest to the user. In addition, we will also describe how carving out a subset in the execution space limits the amount of traced information to manageable proportions.

4.1 Establishing Data Dependency Relationships

Developers of stream processing applications often want to see how data tuples are flowing between and through the operators of an application as well as inspect their content. In many cases, developers want to trace back to tuples that were employed to perform computations inside an operator and, ultimately, produced this operator's outgoing tuples. Tuples are generated by the output port of an operator, transported by a stream connection, and routed to one or more operators, where they are received via an operator's input port. On receiving a tuple, an operator will generally perform computational steps that may or may not yield an immediate output tuple. For example, a filter operator might simply discard an input tuple whose properties do not satisfy the filtering predicate. As we discussed before, more complex data dependencies might arise when more than a single tuple gives rise to the creation of an outgoing tuple, e.g., in a *join* operator.

In this context, data dependencies in stream processing applications can be decomposed into two types of causality corresponding to *inter-* and *intra-operator* data flows (Figure 1). In either case, the main capability required to aid developers with understanding and debugging their applications consists of appropriately capturing and tagging these flows.

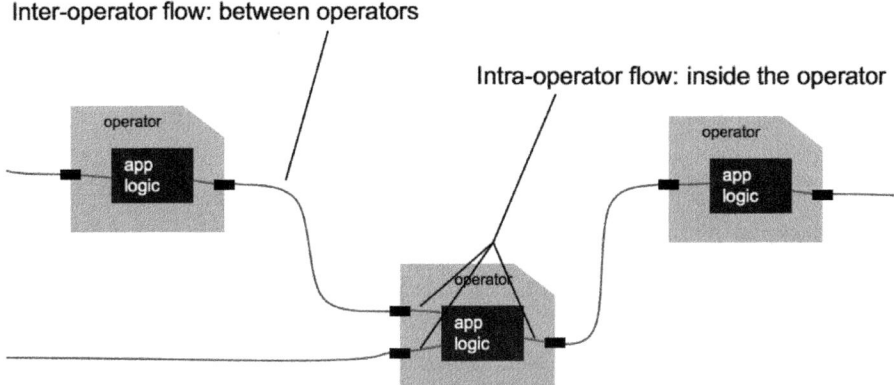

Fig. 1. Inter- and intra-operator data flow in a streaming application

Inter-Operator Data Flow

Recording the flow of tuples between operators is relatively straightforward. Typically, an operator producing a tuple tags it with a unique ID. This ID is carried with the tuple at the middleware level and is invisible at the application level. In fact, for performance reasons, such tagging can be completely disabled, when running an application in production mode. When the tuple arrives at the consuming operator(s), the ID and other contextual information, such as timestamps, are logged for future use by our tool.

Intra-Operator Data Flow

Intra-operator data flows are substantially more complex to capture. While in the simplest case, an operator might (or might not) forward a tuple based on a filter predicate, the causality relationship between an incoming and an outgoing tuple can be considerably more intricate than the one-to-one relationship defined by filtering. In a slightly more complex case, an output tuple is created out of a single incoming tuple, by preserving certain fields, dropping others, or computing new fields, effectively performing a *projection* operation (from relational algebra).

More often than not, multiple tuples are involved in the creation of a new outgoing tuple. As we alluded to before, a *join* or an *aggregate* operator may produce a new tuple, based on a condition that takes into account multiple incoming tuples. As an extreme example, an aggregation operation may take an average across the last one thousand incoming tuples. In this case, there is a data dependency between the outgoing tuple and these one thousand incoming tuples.

As expected, intra-operator data dependencies are defined by the internal processing logic of an operator, and therefore, are less straightforward to capture accurately in an automated fashion. In our current implementation, rather than relying on (sometimes inaccurate) heuristics or more sophisticated but accurate static analysis, we provide an API for operator developers to define the intra-operator data dependency. This approach meshes well with the extensibility framework afforded by the code generation infrastructure that underlies the SPADE language [7]. Nevertheless, we are also looking into static analysis to automatically establish these relationships. While our existing approach might be a burden in the general case, System S comes with a large library of pre-built operators, relieving developers of worrying about this task, except for operators that developers themselves might add to the application.

4.2 Narrowing the Execution Space with Execution Slices

After the inter- and intra-operator data dependencies have been established for individual tuples, our visualization tool can use the raw tracing information to infer the graph that represents the detailed data flows observed at runtime from a stream processing application.

Due to the high-data volumes and large-scale characteristics of production level stream processing applications, simply recording the inter- and intra-operator tuple flow is not always practical. First, tracing data flows in an application causes substantial perturbation on the system under study, which can impact its external behavior and in some cases change the results. Second, tracing every single data flow in the entire application for any extended period typically generates enormous amounts of trace data to be processed by the visualization tool. Third, and perhaps more importantly, even if enough computing power were available to generate the trace data, preprocess, and ingest this data, the results would most likely cause cognitive overload to the human analyst for any realistic application.

In our visualization framework, we make use of *execution slices* as a means to declutter and focus the analysis on the relevant data. This concept has been successfully employed as a clutter-reducing strategy in the area of dynamic program analysis (e.g. by Wong et al. [16]). Similarly, in our context, we can carve out a portion of the execution space by limiting tracing in the application topology (i.e., by activating tracing only in a portion of the dataflow graph) and in time (i.e., by allowing the tracing to be activated during user-defined time windows, interactively).

Furthermore, our tool makes use of static analysis on the SPADE program-generated dataflow graph, to automatically determine the set of operator nodes in the application that are upstream from an operator where anomalies have been observed. Alternatively, it is also possible to limit the set of operators to be traced downstream of a given operator, if the user's intention is to evaluate the impact of tuples coming from a certain stream connection created by that operator.

Finally, our tool can also limit the amount of trace data by only recording enough tuple events per operator's input port subjected to a cap defined in terms of a maximum count or a maximum time interval.

5   Visualizing Data Flows

Our visualization tool allows developers to inspect tuple flows passing through the operators. Developers are also able to control the tracing options and focus on specific sites of the application by selecting the parts of the application that are of immediate interest to the task at hand (e.g., debugging or analyzing a specific part of the flow).

The visualization tool is fully integrated with System S' Streamsight visualization environment [3, 4]. In the present tool, however, the main focus has been on mechanisms to tease apart and analyze specific data flows, on establishing the provenance for final and intermediate results, and on additional capabilities to drill down and look at properties associated with the multiplexed tuple flows coexisting in the same stream connection, providing powerful application understanding and debugging functions to developers. As will be seen, these additional capabilities nicely complement (and, therefore, are naturally integrated with) the original Streamsight tool.

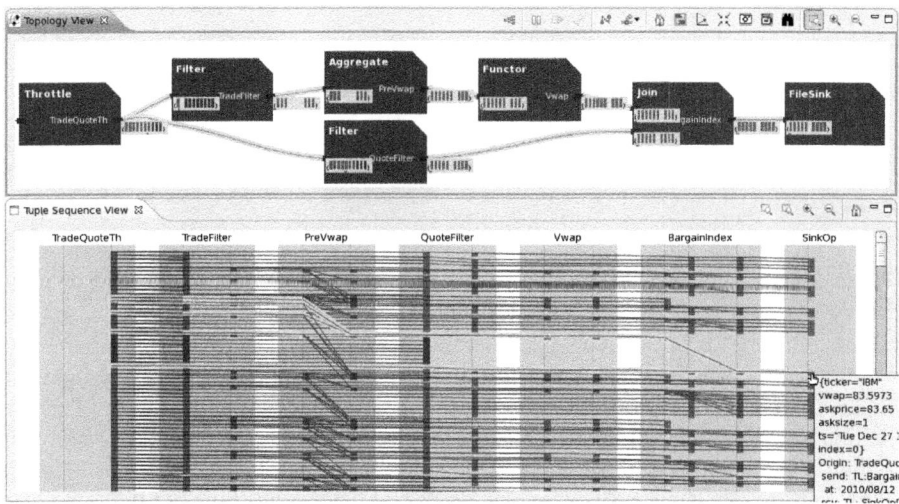

Fig. 2. The visualization tool has two views. The Topology view, at the top, shows data flowing through the operators (in green) from left to right; tuple log widgets near the input and output ports show individual tuples. The Tuple Sequence view, at the bottom, shows the tuples as small dots (in this example, in blue and red), organized vertically by time and horizontally by the input and output ports of operators, shown as light blue vertical lanes. Clicking on a tuple in either view will highlight (in yellow) the tuples forward and backward data dependencies.

Figure 2 shows the visualization tool with two views, the Topology view at the top and the Tuple Sequence View at the bottom. The Topology view renders operators, which contain the processing logic expressed in the SPADE language, as green rectangles with a slanted corner. In this example, data is being generated by the leftmost operator (*TradeQuoteTh*) and sent to operators to the right. An operator can have zero or more input ports (shown as small red rectangles on an operator's left border) and zero or more output ports (shown as red small rectangles on an operator's right border). Data in the form of individual tuples is sent from output ports to input ports across stream connections, shown as the connection splines in the Topology view. The original Streamsight tool provided the user with dynamic aggregate information such as the tuple rates on specific streams, but did not capture individual tuple information as currently done with the new tool.

In our new tool, we allow developers to observe individual tuples at specific input or output ports as well as their data dependencies across the application. Building on these features, we constructed a powerful application understanding and debugging methodology. The following scenario illustrates these features.

A developer can turn on tracing either for a particular port, a subset of application operators, or for the whole application. As a result, small scrolling tuple log widgets will appear next to the respective ports as depicted in the upper part of Figure 2. Figure 3 shows one such tuple log widget in detail. A limited number (ten, in this example) of tuples is visible, while additional tuples (if available) can be made visible by scrolling left or right. Moving the mouse over a tuple will bring up a tooltip, which displays the complete tuple content. As seen in the figure, a tuple is a collection of attributes; both the attribute name and the associated value are shown.

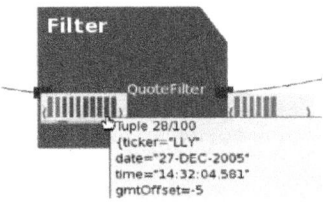

Fig. 3. A tuple log widget next to a port allows the user to browse through the tuples and their contents that have been received by an input port or sent by an output port

Clicking on a tuple highlights it locally, but more importantly also highlights all tuples upstream and downstream that have a data dependency to this tuple. This operation also highlights all the data flow paths throughout the application, as shown in Figure 2 and illustrated in Section 6.3. In addition, the corresponding tuples and data flow paths in the Tuple Sequence view described below and shown in the lower part of Figure 2 are highlighted. From an application understanding standpoint, this new capability can be useful to track the provenance and the impact of specific tuples on the results an application generates. From a debugging standpoint, this capability provides the fundamental answer to the question of "where did this (incorrect) result come from?".

Further extending this capability, the tool also allows the user to automatically color tuples according to the content of a certain attribute in the tuple. This capability, while simple in concept, is extremely useful in allowing individual subflows multiplexed in the same stream to be teased apart and made visible based on specific properties of the data traffic. In the example shown in Figures 2 and 3, we depict a particular stock trading application (which we will describe in more detail later). In this case, each tuple is colored according to the value of the "ticker" attribute, allowing us to separate transactions related to particular companies whose shares are publicly traded in the stock market.

While the Topology view allows the developer to monitor how tuples are flowing through the application, it does not provide the user with any insight into the specific timing or ordering of the tuples. The Tuple Sequence view, shown in the lower part of Figure 2, addresses this issue by laying out the tuples horizontally, by operator, and vertically, by time. The light blue vertical lanes represent each of the application operators under inspection. Inside each operator lane, the light gray vertical rails represent input ports (to the left) and output ports (to the right). Tuple instances are rendered as small rectangles. Their y-coordinates reflect the time that they were observed at the port; their x-coordinates represent the operator and port locations where they were observed. The dark red lines between the tuples show the inter-operator dependencies (i.e., the transmission of tuples between operators), whereas the green lines show the intra-operator dependencies. Operators in this view are sorted horizontally based on the their topological order from source to sink (and, if needed, on their vertical order, when adjacent horizontal paths might exist) in the Topology view. This ensures that, in most cases, the flow of most tuples goes from left to right, similar to the flow in the Topology view. Note also that, the information depicted in this view slides downwards, as time progresses.

A user can hover over a tuple to see its content and timing information. Clicking on a tuple or a connection in this view highlights the data path(s) going into and out of this tuple as defined by the inter- and intra-operator data dependencies and the computed tuple provenance. Clicking on tuples in either the Topology or the Tuple Sequence view will highlight these tuples and their data paths in both views, to help the user situate the specific flow in the context of the overall application view. To decrease the amount of clutter, the user can choose to focus only on a specific highlighted path, triggering the tool to hide the now irrelevant elements. For example, isolating the (yellow) highlighted path shown in Figure 2 will result in the user seeing the view shown in Figure 9.

6 Usage Scenarios

Our tool is fully functional and seamlessly integrated with our earlier visualization tool, System S' Streamsight [3, 4]. To discuss and demonstrate the dataflow debugging capabilities as well as the large-scale application understanding features available in our tool, we will briefly describe the Bargain Discovery stream processing application [17]. We will employ this application to motivate several real-world problems faced in the context of much larger stream processing applications [1].

6.1 The Bargain Discovery Application

Our sample application emulates a scenario where a securities trading firm makes money by quickly spotting *bargains* in trading transactions in the stock market. To identify a bargain, a hypothetical firm first needs to acquire data to build a model for pricing all (or some of) the securities that are being traded in the market. Once a security is priced (let's call it the security's *fair* price), the firm can assess whether *ask* quotes are *mispriced*. That is, the application can determine whether a seller is willing to sell that security (or a bundle of them) for a price that is lower than the *fair* price as predicted by the pricing model.

The incoming *primal* stream to this application carries all the information necessary for performing such computation, i.e., the market feed, including quote and trade transactions [18]. In our implementation, trade transactions (where a security is actually sold) are used by the pricing model to compute the security's real-time fair price (in this case, by employing a simple moving volume-weighted average of recent trade transactions) to score quote transactions (where a security is simply being quoted by another party).

The top view of Figure 2 shows a Streamsight data flow graph of this application. Here, the top flow corresponds to the implementation of the pricing model. The notable part there is the use of an *aggregate* operator, which computes the volume weighted moving averages for each different stock symbol seen in the stock market feed. The bottom flow, which filters only quote transactions, is used to transport these transactions to a *join* operator, where quotes are scored against the pricing model. Finally, the potential bargains spotted by the application are scaled, ranked, and communicated to an external sink that, in the real world, would be connected to a trading execution application, which would take care of acting on these bargains.

6.2 Detecting an Incorrect Parameter in an Aggregate Operator

The following debugging scenario describes a problem that is hard to spot by the sole examination of the output data, since the impact on the results can be rather subtle, at least in relatively short timespans. However, in the long term, the bug can potentially cause a significant financial loss. In this case, the implementation of the application does not match one key aspect of the requirements laid out by a quantitative analyst who designed the Bargain Discovery application.

On performing an application validation test, the developer starts by examining all operators and their interconnections, and subsequently samples the incoming and outgoing tuples in the Topology view of our tool. In principle, everything seems to look fine. To verify the behavior of the application over time, the developer now turns to the Tuple Sequence view. There the developer observes that the data flow going through the *PreVwap Aggregate* operator exhibits the pattern shown in Figure 4a. From this pattern, it appears that this operator consumes four new input tuples before it produces an output tuple. However, the original application specification required that an output tuple be created with the weighted average of the last four tuples, after every new incoming tuple arrives at the operator. Clearly, the *PreVwap Aggregate* has been incorrectly deployed with a "tumbling window" parameter (i.e., the window state is *reset* every time an aggregation is produced), while the specification demanded a "sliding window" average (i.e., the window state is *updated* on arrival of new tuples, by discarding older ones). From an application design standpoint, using a sliding window in this operator allows for a smoother function constantly indicating the fair value prices for each stock symbol.

After redeploying the application with the corrected parameter in the configuration of the *Aggregate* operator, the developer can observe the new (and now compliant) behavior depicted by Figure 4b. As can be seen, about four times as many output tuples are now created in the same time span.

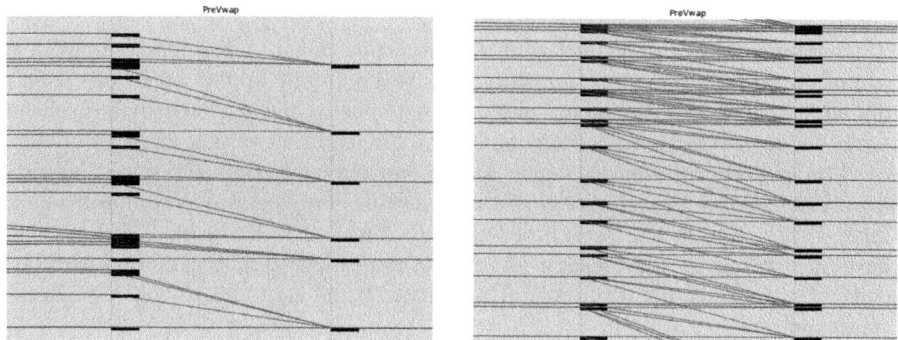

Fig. 4a (left) and **4b** (right). Time moves downwards, tuples are shown as small black rectangles, and the green lines represent intra-operator dependencies. In the incorrect implementation, on the left side, the *PreVwap Aggregate* operator creates an output tuple (on the second vertical rail) each time four new input tuples (on the first vertical rail) have arrived to (supposedly) calculate the weighted moving average value for the stock price. Here it can be seen that an incoming tuple contributes to only one outgoing tuple, which is an indication of a problem, as this pattern is not consistent with computing a *moving* metric. In the corrected version, on the right side, the *PreVwap Aggregate* operator uses a sliding window to calculate the average value over the four last incoming tuples, thus creating an output tuple after every incoming tuple. It can be seen here that an incoming tuple contributes to four outgoing tuples (in this case, the sliding window was configured to hold four tuples at any given point in time and uses these tuples to produce the moving average).

6.3   Tracking Down the Locus of a Calculation Error

Figure 5 shows the content of a tuple at the sink operator. A tuple with a positive *index* field, like the one shown here, indicates a trading bargain and the specific value indicates the magnitude of the bargain for ranking purposes (i.e., a *bigger* bargain should be acted on first, due to its higher profit making prospect).

However, the tuple shown in this figure as well as other tuples seen at the input port suggest that the system has spotted bargains, although, surprisingly, the ask price seems to be higher than the *VWAP* or fair price value predicted by the pricing model, opposite to what the definition of a bargain is. This is a clear sign that something went wrong, leaving the question of where the problem actually originated.

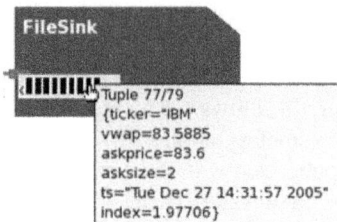

Fig. 5. Hovering over one of the result tuples shows an (incorrect) tuple with an ask price higher than the fair price (*VWAP*)

In order to retrieve the *lineage* of this incorrect result, a developer can click on one of the tuples with incorrect results. This will highlight all the tuples, upstream in the application, whose contents might have impacted the outcome of the selected tuple. Moving to the left, from the tuple with the incorrect values, the developer can quickly spot the contributing tuples at the *join* operator. Both the fair *value tuple* (received from the *Vwap* operator and used for this computation) as well as the *quote* tuple (received from the *QuoteFilter* operator) turn out to be correct. This leads the developer to take a closer look at the *BargainIndex* operator. Examining the SPADE code[1] then leads to the discovery of a "greater than" sign that should have been a "less than" sign.

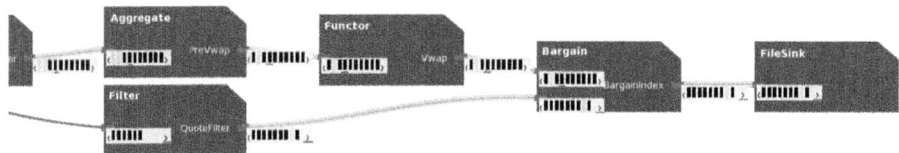

Fig. 6. Selecting the tuple with the incorrect value in the result operator on the right highlights its lineage, showing the upstream tuples potentially contributing to the error

6.4 Investigating the Absence of a Result

The incorrect behavior in an application sometimes manifests itself by the absence of an expected result. For example, automated unit tests set in place to ensure an application gets validated before deployment are typically built with pre-determined inputs that will lead to an *expected* output. Finding out why we did *not* observe an outcome is often more difficult than investigating an incorrect outcome.

In the following debugging scenario, a developer observes that no tuples are received at the sink, as shown in Figure 7. However, the same figure also shows that all operators in front of the sink operator did receive tuples.

---

[1] System S provides an integrated environment that allows developers to conveniently jump from the dataflow graph representation to the specific segment of source code implementing that segment and vice-versa [3, 5].

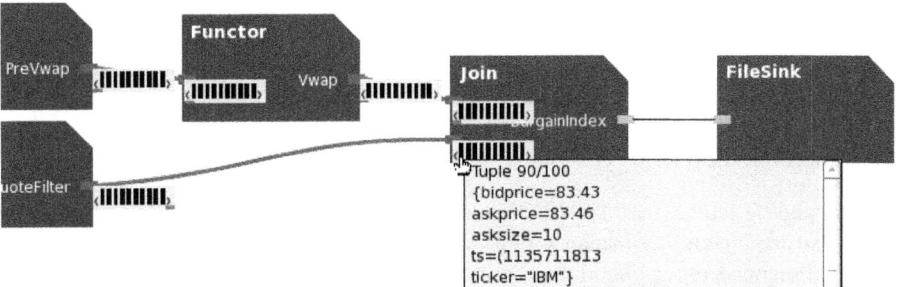

Fig. 7. The sink operator, to the right, does not receive any tuples (as seen by the absence of a tuple log widget). Nevertheless, tuples are arriving at preceding operators, but none are produced by the output port of the *join* operator. Hovering the tooltip over one of the input queues in the *join* operator reveals the ticker symbols for the tuples that have been received so far.

The first suspicion is that there is a problem in the *BargainIndex join* operator. Examining a few individual tuples at both inputs of the *BargainIndex* reveals that the lower port seems to receive only tuples with the ticker symbol "IBM" (shown by the tooltip in the Figure 7), whereas the upper port seems to receive only tuples with a ticker symbol "LLY" (not shown). This suggests that the *join* operator works correctly, but simply did not find tuples with matching ticker symbols, required to evaluate and potentially indicate the existence of a *bargain*.

The next step is to go upstream and look at the distribution of ticker symbols in the tuples flowing through the application. The visualization tool can color the tuples according to the content of an attribute belonging to the schema that defines a stream and its tuples, at the request of the user. For example, Figure 8 shows the tuples flowing through the operators in this application colored by the content of the "ticker" attribute. Each value for the ticker attribute is automatically hashed into a color. The figure shows that tuples with ticker symbol "LLY" are rendered in red, whereas tuples containing "IBM" are rendered in blue. It also reveals that the *TradeFilter* operator (second from the left) only forwards LLY tuples and that the *QuoteFilter* operator (at the bottom) only forwards IBM tuples. The solution for this problem was to change the parameterization of the *TradeFilter* operator, so that it also forwards IBM tuples. In this case, the problem stemmed from an (incorrectly implemented) effort at parallelizing the application [17]. Specifically, the filter condition in the Trade part of the graph was not the same as the condition in the *Quote* part of the graph. With this parallelization approach, the space of stock ticker symbols (around 3,000, for the

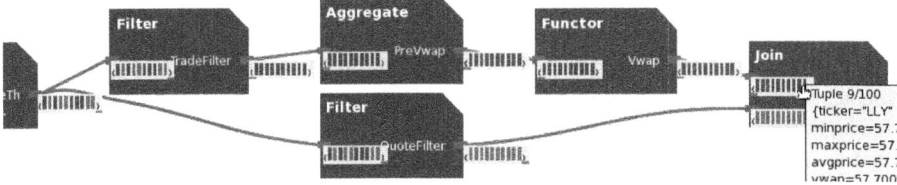

Fig. 8. Tuples are colored by the *ticker* attribute: tuples containing "LLY" are rendered in red, "IBM" tuples are (appropriately) in blue. The *TradeFilter* only forwards "LLY" tuples, the *QuoteFilter* only allows "IBM" tuples, preventing the *join* operator to make matches.

New York Stock Exchange) was partitioned into ranges (e.g., from A to AAPL, from C to CIG, etc) so that replicas of the bargain discovery segment could operate on different input data concurrently, yielding additional parallelism and allowing the application to process data at a much higher rate.

6.5 Latency Analysis

Understanding latency is a key challenge in streaming applications, in particular, for those that have rigid performance requirements, as is the case, for example, of many financial engineering applications. To assess latency, we must first establish what the latency metrics represent. Latency can be defined in many different ways, depending on the particular path of interest within the flow graph as well as the set of tuples involved. Second, manually capturing latency via application-level time-stamps imposes a heavy burden on the developer and often complicates the application logic. As a result, system and tooling support for analyzing latency are a critical requirement for stream processing systems. This requirement addresses the need for providing comprehensive application understanding, especially from the perspective of user-friendly performance analysis.

As an example, consider the Bargain Discovery application, discussed earlier, and the following measures of latency that are relevant to application understanding:

A. Given a tuple that indicates that a bargain has been spotted, the time between (i) the arrival of the *quote* tuple that triggered the spotting of that new bargain and (ii) the generation of the bargain tuple itself is *one* of the latency metrics of interest. This latency measure helps in understanding how quickly the bargains are spotted based on the arrival of new quotes.

B. Given a tuple representing a volume weighted average price (VWAP), the time between (i) the arrival of the trade tuple that triggered the price and (ii) the generation of the VWAP tuple itself is another latency metric of interest. This latency measure helps in understanding how quickly new trades are reflected in the current VWAP fair value price, which impacts the freshness of the pricing model and in turn the accuracy of the discovery (or not) of the bargains.

C. Given a tuple representing a trade, the time between (i) the arrival of the trade tuple itself and (ii) the generation of the last bargain tuple that was impacted by the trade tuple in question is another latency metric of interest. This latency measure helps in understanding the duration of the impact of given trade tuple to the pricing model.

It is interesting to note that the above listed use cases can be broadly divided into two categories. These categories are determined by the anchor tuple used for defining the latency, which impacts the type of workflow involved in the visual analysis of the latency. We name these categories as *result-anchored* and *source-anchored* latencies. A result-anchored latency is defined using the downstream result tuple as an anchor. It is visually analyzed by first locating the result tuple and then using the result tuple's provenance to locate the source tuple. Use cases A and B above fall into this category, as illustrated by Figure 9, produced by our visualization tool.

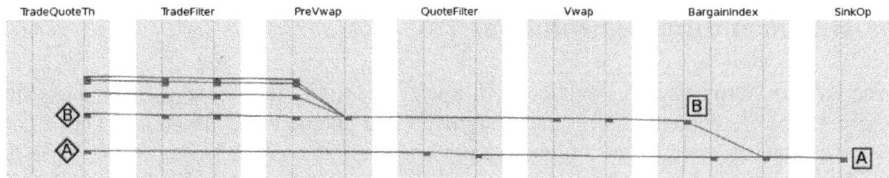

Fig. 9. Visualization of the result-anchored latencies from the use cases A and B, showing the provenance of a bargain tuple and the start and end points for the computation of the result-anchored latencies

In this figure, we mark the source tuples using a diamond shape and the result tuples using a square shape. For use cases A and B, we first locate the result tuple and use it as an anchor point to take the provenance. For use case A, the bargain tuple is our anchor point, whereas for use case B, the VWAP tuple is our anchor point. We then locate the source tuple in the lineage of the result tuple. For use case A, the source tuple is the *quote* tuple, whereas for use case B, the source tuple is the last *trade* tuple that is in the lineage of the result tuple. Once the source and target tuples are located, the latency can be retrieved easily.

A source-anchored latency is defined using the upstream source tuple as the anchor. It can be visually analyzed by first locating the source tuple and then using the source tuple's downstream lineage to locate the result tuple. Use case C above falls into this category, as illustrated by the Figure 10.

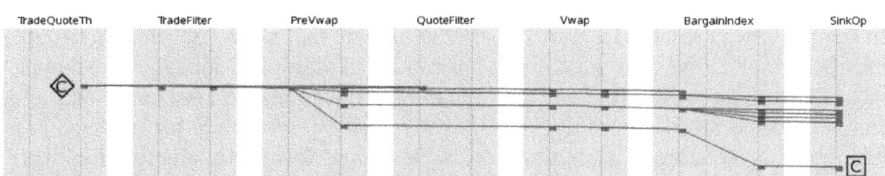

Fig. 10. Visualization of the source-anchored latency from the use case C, showing a downstream lineage of a trade tuple and the start and end points for the computation of the source-anchored latency

For use case C, we first locate the source tuple and use it as an anchor point to take the downstream lineage. The *trade* tuple is our anchor point in this case. We then locate the target tuple in the lineage of the source tuple. In this case, the result tuple of interest is the last bargain tuple produced downstream that is in the lineage of the source tuple. Once the source and target tuples are located, the latency can be retrieved easily.

Finally, it should be pointed out that the average latencies and outliers can also be of interest, rather than the instantaneous latencies of specific tuples. Given that our tool has access to various samples for a given type of provenance or lineage, simple pattern analyses techniques can be used to compute average values as well as outliers for the desired latencies. For instance, the latency defined in use case A can be averaged over all the bargain tuples in the history to compute an average value. While our tool does not provide this capability yet, this represents a simple and straightforward extension.

7 Design and Implementation

The System S runtime was enhanced to track inter-tuple dependencies by intercepting tuples as they leave output ports and assigning them unique tuple identifiers. These identifiers enable the receiver of a tuple to learn about the immediate origin of the tuple. To track intra-tuple dependencies, a provenance tag is added to each tuple. The provenance tag is maintained by the System S runtime based on a lightweight API exposed to application developers for specifying dependencies of output tuples to input ones.

The System S runtime maintains one-step dependency only, which captures inter- and intra-operator dependencies, but does not include the complete provenance information, which contributes to lowering the amount of overhead imposed by tracing operations.

The visualization tool is used to reconstruct the complete provenance information from one-step data dependency information collected from multiple operator ports. The new visualization features for debugging and data flow analysis are implemented as an Eclipse plug-in and are fully integrated into System S' Streamsight visualization environment [3, 4]. In our current prototype we use a mix of CORBA calls and files for the two-way communication between the System S runtime and the visualization. We designed the tool so that it can process and reflect near-live information from the runtime system. In particular, the data models that contain the tuple and data dependency information can be populated incrementally. Similarly, the visual front-end is able to render the new information almost immediately.

8 Conclusion

In this paper we presented a new, visual environment that allows developers to debug, understand, and fine-tune streaming applications. Traditional debugging techniques, like breakpoints, are insufficient for streaming applications because cause and effect can be situated at different locations. Development environments for message-based distributed or concurrent systems offer the developer insight by aligning the distributed events with the messages that were exchanged. However, even these techniques tend to be impractical for debugging streaming applications because of the sheer volume of data that they produce.

Our new environment allows the developer to limit the tracing information to execution slices, defined in time and in space. It organizes the traced tuples based on their data dependencies. This offers a natural way for the user to navigate the distributed execution space in terms of provenance and lineage. We offer two new views to the developer. The Topology view projects the execution information, i.e. the tuples, their contents and their mutual data dependencies, on the application topology graph. The Tuple Sequence view organizes tuples by time and by operator. The combination of these two views offers a natural way for a developer to explore causal paths during problem determination, as well as to carry out performance analysis.

References

1. Turaga, D., Andrade, H., Gedik, B., Venkatramani, C., Verscheure, O., Harris, D., Cox, J., Szewczyk, W., Jones, P.: Design Principles for Developing Stream Processing Applications. Software: Practice & Experience Journal (to appear, 2010)

2. Amini, L., Andrade, H., Bhagwan, R., Eskesen, F., King, R., Selo, P., Park, Y., Venkatramani, C.: SPC: A distributed, scalable platform for data mining. In: Workshop on Data Mining Standards, Services and Platforms, DMSSP, Philadelphia, PA (2006)
3. De Pauw, W., Andrade, H.: Visualizing large-scale streaming applications. Information Visualization 8, 87–106 (2009)
4. De Pauw, W., Andrade, H., Amini, L.: Streamsight: a visualization tool for large-scale streaming applications. In: Proceedings of the 4th ACM Symposium on Software Visualization, SoftVis 2008, Ammersee, Germany, September 16 - 17, pp. 125–134. ACM, New York (2008)
5. Gedik, B., Andrade, H., Frenkiel, A., De Pauw, W., Pfeifer, M., Allen, P., Cohen, N., Wu, K.-L.: Tools and strategies for debugging distributed stream processing applications. Software: Practice & Experience 39(16) (2009)
6. Gedik, B., Andrade, H., Wu, K.-L., Yu, P.S., Doo, M.: SPADE: The System S Declarative Stream Processing Engine. In: International Conference on Management of Data, ACM SIGMOD (2008)
7. Wang, H.Y., Andrade, H., Gedik, B., Wu, K.-L.: A Code Generation Approach for Auto-Vectorization in the SPADE Compiler. In: International Workshop on Languages and Compilers for Parallel Computing, pp. 383–390 (2009)
8. Khandekar, R., Hildrum, K., Parekh, S., Rajan, D., Wolf, J., Andrade, H., Wu, K.-L., Gedik, B.: COLA: Optimizing Stream Processing Applications Via Graph Partitioning. In: Bacon, J.M., Cooper, B.F. (eds.) Middleware 2009. LNCS, vol. 5896, pp. 308–327. Springer, Heidelberg (2009)
9. Stanley, T., Close, T., Miller, M.S.: Causeway: A message-oriented distributed debugger. Technical report, HPL-2009-78, HP Laboratories (2009)
10. Vijayakumar, N., Plale, B.: Towards Low Overhead Provenance Tracking in Near Real-Time Stream Filtering. In: Moreau, L., Foster, I. (eds.) IPAW 2006. LNCS, vol. 4145, pp. 46–54. Springer, Heidelberg (2006)
11. Blount, M., Davis, J., Misra, A., Sow, D., Wang, M.: A Time-and-Value Centric Provenance Model and Architecture for Medical Event Streams. In: ACM HealthNet Workshop, pp. 95–100 (2007)
12. Misra, A., Blount, M., Kementsietsidis, A., Sow, D., Wang, M.: Advances and Challenges for Scalable Provenance in Stream Processing Systems. In: Moreau, L., Foster, I. (eds.) IPAW 2006. LNCS, vol. 4145. Springer, Heidelberg (2006)
13. De Pauw, W., Lei, M., Pring, E., Villard, L., Arnold, M., Morar, J.F.: Web Services Navigator: Visualizing the execution of Web Services. IBM Systems Journal 44(4) (2005)
14. De Pauw, W., Hoch, R., Huang, Y.: Discovering Conversations in Web Services Using Semantic Correlation Analysis. In: International Conference on Web Services 2007, pp 639–646 (2007)
15. Aguilera, M.K., Mogul, J.C., Wiener, J.L., Reynolds, P., Muthitacharoen, A.: Performance debugging for distributed systems of black boxes. In: Proceedings of the Nineteenth ACM Symposium on Operating Systems Principles, SOSP 2003, Bolton Landing, NY, USA, October 19 - 22, pp. 74–89. ACM, New York (2003)
16. Wong, W.E., Qi, Y.: An Execution Slice and Inter-Block Data Dependency-Based Approach for Fault Localization. In: Proceedings of the 11th Asia-Pacific Software Engineering Conference, pp. 366–373 (2004)
17. Andrade, H., Gedik, B., Wu, K.-L.: Scale-up Strategies for Processing High-Rate Data Streams in System S. In: International Conference on Data Engineering, IEEE ICDE (2009)
18. Zhang, X.J., Andrade, H., Gedik, B., King, R., Morar, J., Nathan, S., Park, Y., Pavuluri, R., Pring, E., Schnier, R., Selo, P., Spicer, M., Venkatramani, C.: Implementing a High-Volume, Low-Latency Market Data Processing System on Commodity Hardware using IBM Middleware. In: Workshop on High Performance Computational Finance (2009)

Runtime Verification in Context: Can Optimizing Error Detection Improve Fault Diagnosis?

Matthew B. Dwyer[1], Rahul Purandare[1], and Suzette Person[2]

[1] Department of Computer Science and Engineering, University of Nebraska,
Lincoln NE 68588-0115, USA
{dwyer,rpuranda}@cse.unl.edu
[2] NASA Langley Research Center, Hampton, VA 23681, USA
suzette.person@nasa.gov

Abstract. Runtime verification has primarily been developed and evaluated as a means of enriching the software testing process. While many researchers have pointed to its potential applicability in online approaches to software fault tolerance, there has been a dearth of work exploring the details of how that might be accomplished.

In this paper, we describe how a component-oriented approach to software health management exposes the connections between program execution, error detection, fault diagnosis, and recovery. We identify both research challenges and opportunities in exploiting those connections. Specifically, we describe how recent approaches to reducing the overhead of runtime monitoring aimed at error detection might be adapted to reduce the overhead and improve the effectiveness of fault diagnosis.

1 Introduction

The past decade has witnessed a growing interest in relating program executions to rich correctness properties as a way to increase the observability of software system behavior and thereby enhance the software testing process. The foundations of runtime verification have been well established. Researchers have developed sophisticated specification notations for expressing properties to be checked at runtime, e.g., [1,2], devised techniques for synthesizing efficient monitors to check those properties, e.g., [3], and produced powerful frameworks that allow monitors to be incorporated into programs, e.g., [4,5].

Early runtime verification systems, e.g., UPenn's MaC [2] and NASA's Java Path Explorer [6], focused on using monitoring to enhance program testing. While enhanced test oracles offer significant value, it seems clear that even in the early years of research on runtime verification, researchers envisioned using it in a broader context. For example, the authors of both the MaC and Java Path Explorer papers identify exploring monitoring in a broader context as future work in stating "Our current system is geared towards the detection of faults. It would be desirable in the future to build monitors that can steer a system to a correct state." [2] and asking "How can missions be made safer in the face of errors occurring during flight that survived tests?" [6].

G. Roşu et al. (Eds.): RV 2010, LNCS 6418, pp. 36–50, 2010.

Research towards those goals has been modest, at least in part because it is a very difficult challenge. In recent years, however, there has been a concerted effort to understand how one might construct *software health management* (SHM) subsystems [7]. Building on decades of work in systems and vehicle health management, SHM seeks to accommodate the nature of software faults, e.g., that arise as discontinuities relative to their input domain, and provide an overall framework into which different *error detection*, *fault diagnosis*, and *recovery* techniques can be incorporated to achieve greater tolerance to software errors in fielded systems.

We believe that the broader context of SHM provides a number of significant challenges and opportunities for the runtime verification research community, which has focused primarily on error detection techniques. More specifically, we believe there is a need to consider the connections between error detection and other elements of SHM solutions. In this paper, we consider one such connection, between error detection and fault diagnosis, in light of recent efforts to mitigate the runtime overhead of error detection.

One of the key challenges to widespread use of runtime verification, especially monitoring of rich properties, i.e., monitors that check non-trivial predicates over program data state and monitors that reason about sequences of program states, is runtime overhead. Recent studies of the performance of state-of-the-art algorithms for monitoring typestate properties [8] on Java program executions [5,9,10] have revealed rather bimodal findings in terms of performance; for many combinations of programs and properties, the overhead is negligible– less than 5% –but there are combinations that incur significant overhead– more than 100%.

Monitor overhead is determined by a number of factors: the number of program locations that must be observed, the extent to which different data values require the need for multiple copies of a monitor, and the cost of updating monitor state and checking for violations. In the case of monitoring a typestate property, i.e., using a finite-state automaton (FSA) that expresses constraints on the legal ordering of operations called on an instance of a given type, monitoring can incur significant overhead. For example, to monitor the *HasNext* property on the *bloat* benchmark, one of the DaCapo benchmarks [11] that was studied in [5], over 211 million operations, spread across one million iterator instances, are processed during monitoring.

Given such a large overhead to monitor a single property, work to optimize this type of property monitor is needed and has become an active area of research in recent years, e.g., [10,12]. The results thus far are quite promising, however, in all of the work to date, there is no consideration of how optimization might impact the broader context in which the monitor is deployed. For example, both error detection and fault diagnosis must observe program behavior. How are those observations related to one another? Can optimizing error detection also optimize fault diagnosis? Will such optimization preserve the information needed by fault diagnosis?

In this paper, we begin to explore some of these questions, and more broadly, to consider the connections that arise from considering runtime verification in an SHM context. Our study offers some insights into how those connections might be exploited to produce better SHM systems, and suggests principles that must be observed when designing an error detection techniques for SHM.

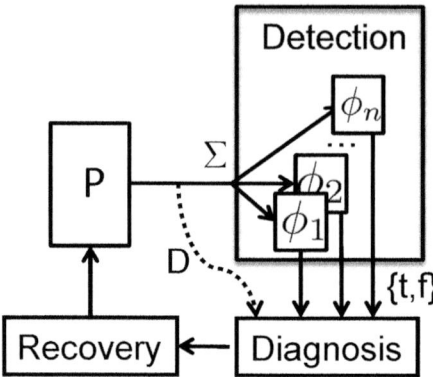

Fig. 1. Conceptual architecture for software health management

The paper is organized as follows. Section 3 describes one recent strategy for optimizing runtime monitors for typestate properties and describes the property preservation requirements developed for that optimization. Section 4 considers the impact of applying that optimization strategy on three techniques for online fault diagnosis that have been proposed recently. We present, in Section 5, a series of research challenges and opportunities related to how runtime verification fits into SHM solutions that we believe the research community is well-positioned to advance in the near future. We begin with a discussion of existing research that forms the background for our study.

2   Background and Related Work

We provide background on the application of runtime monitoring for error detection, survey approaches to software health management, and outline a few recent approaches to software fault localization.

2.1   Runtime Monitoring for Error Detection

Monitoring the execution of a software system might be performed for a variety of reasons, e.g., to assess performance, to enforce security policies, or to provide test coverage information. The runtime verification community has focused, primarily, on monitoring the conformance of program executions relative to a formally specified correctness property. This type of monitoring can extend the set of errors that can be observed during system execution compared to a traditional test oracle which evaluates predicates on output values. Moreover, since such monitors typically observe the internal state of a software system they are capable of detecting errors *before* they give rise to system-level failures, such as outputting an incorrect value.

The top portion of Figure 1 depicts the relationship between a program, P, and an error detection capability realized through runtime monitoring. A set of correctness properties, ϕ_i, are defined and those properties together define the set of *observations*

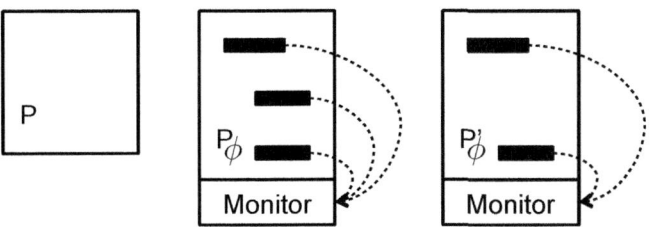

Fig. 2. Monitor instrumentation and optimization

of program behavior that is necessary to make judgments about the satisfaction or falsification of each of the ϕ_i; this set is denoted Σ–the alphabet of program observations. As the program executes, it reaches locations at which an observation, or symbol, in Σ is generated and that observation is communicated to the monitor associated with each property. Each monitor tracks the sequence of observations and renders a boolean judgment about the conformance of the program execution with respect to its property.

This conceptual architecture for monitoring can be instantiated using a wide range of property monitoring approaches. For example, monitoring *assertion properties* relies on observations that query the data state of the program. In this case, a single observation is all that is required to render a judgment of $\neg\phi$, and if all observations satisfy ϕ then a satisfying judgment is produced on program exit. Monitoring *temporal or sequencing properties* relies on observation of a set of program locations along with data values, e.g., indications of calls and returns to methods of a given class coupled with the identity of the receiver object. For such properties, the processing of an observation updates the monitor state and judgments are rendered when an object's lifetime ends or the property enters a *trap state*, i.e., a state for which no subsequent observations can prevent the property from being falsified.

The identification of observations during program execution and their communication to the property monitor can be achieved in a variety of ways. In recent years, the runtime verification community appears to have converged on the use of program instrumentation, realized by sophisticated aspect weaving technologies, as being a particularly effective means of integrating the generation of observations into programs [4,13]. To illustrate, consider the three versions of program P shown in Figure 2. On the left is the original, uninstrumented, version of P. In the middle is P_ϕ, an instrumented version of P that produces observations relevant to ϕ. We discuss the rightmost version in Section 3. When the instrumentation in P_ϕ is executed, sophisticated data structures are used to route observations [5] to monitors that are synthesized from high-level property specifications [3,14]. This monitoring code is incorporated in the deployed program, e.g., as the added module shown at the bottom of Figure 2, so that it can be invoked as needed during runtime.

2.2 Software Health Management

For at least three decades, there has been a recognition that the challenges of constructing correct software are so significant that deployed systems will contain faults and that cost-effective techniques for tolerating faults at runtime would be extremely valuable. Many techniques have been proposed, but no technique has emerged as one that can be widely applied in practice–some techniques have been shown to be ineffective [15,16].

More recently, forms of software fault tolerance have been explored under the names autonomic, recovery-oriented, failure-oblivious, self-healing, self-adaptive and re-configurable systems. Even more recently, the term *software health management* (SHM) has emerged in the safety-critical systems community and we adopt that term here to encompass the general class of software fault tolerance approaches.

Rather than surveying the significant literature in these areas, we present, in Figure 1, a conceptual architecture for SHM that includes three capabilities that are incorporated into the subject program: error *detection*, fault *diagnosis*, and system *recovery*.

As described above, as program P executes it is monitored for properties, ϕ_i. Runtime monitoring *detects* property violations, i.e., errors, that indicate a potential need for system recovery. In an SHM solution, error detection communicates the identity of the violated property to a fault *diagnosis* capability. Fault diagnosis is a very different problem than error detection. Its goal is to identify the system component whose behavior initiated the erroneous behavior that was ultimately detected–the faulty component. Information from the faulty component may be separated both temporally and structurally within the code from the component that exhibited the error. Consequently, additional diagnostic information, D, is recorded during program execution to aid fault diagnosis. While Σ and D may overlap or be generated from common locations in the program, that need not be the case. Once diagnosis completes, it passes an indication of the faulty component(s) to the *recovery* capability which may reconfigure, restart, remove or replace those component(s).

This architecture can be instantiated in a wide variety of ways. For example, the Pinpoint system [17] provides for SHM of web-services by instrumenting portions of the service implementations and J2EE infrastructure to capture data for error detection and fault diagnosis, which then triggers rather rudimentary component reboot for recovery [18]. Other approaches skip fault diagnosis altogether [19,20] and instead simply repair data structures at the point of failure as a means of recovering from immediate system failure. The FLORA [21] system allows an application to be refactored into isolated recovery units that are rebootable, and allows different error detection and fault diagnosis approaches to be incorporated–we discuss one such approach below.

None of these solutions seems appropriate in a safety-critical context. For such systems, SHM approaches are typically much more integral to overall system development and are not regarded as an *add on*. Approaches like [22] take a holistic approach and consider the possibility that faults might also exist within detection, diagnosis, and recovery algorithms–their approach is to prove those algorithms correct.

Researchers and developers will undoubtedly continue to evolve SHM solutions from individual application domains to more general settings, from coping with individual types of of faults to broad classes of faults, and between different levels of criticality. As they do, there will be opportunities for results from runtime verification to be incorporated as long as those results are designed to *fit* into the broader SHM context.

2.3 Software Fault Localization

Over the past decade, the software engineering research community has developed a rich literature on techniques for identifying the root cause of a program failure, i.e., the fault. Most of the techniques that have been developed are intended to support human developers by narrowing their attention to parts of the program that are more likely to be faulty. In doing this, they may produce a ranking of program elements, e.g., statements, methods, classes, from *most likely to be faulty* to *least likely*. A developer starts at the top of the list and works their way down and, if the localization technique is effective, they save time in finding the fault and can then proceed with fixing it.

In recent years, several researchers have investigated the adaptation of fault localization techniques to online fault diagnosis. While many different fault localization approaches might be used for this purpose, here we describe two classes of approaches that use very different types of recorded information.

Spectrum-based fault localization [23]. This technique records information about which system components are executed during a run of the system. This information is captured prior to deployment as the system undergoes its final round of testing. The information recorded includes the coverage or execution frequency of each component.

Let the set of system components be $c_1, \ldots, c_m$, then the *hit spectrum*, hs, is an array of m values drawn from $\{0, 1\}$ where $hs[i] = 1$ indicates that component c_i was executed in a program run. The *count spectrum*, cs, is an array of m natural numbers where $cs[i]$ indicates the number of times component c_i was executed in a program run. Rather than accumulate this information across a test suite, as is done in test adequacy calculations, the spectra are stored for each of n runs thereby forming an $n \times m$ *activity matrix*. An additional row stores a boolean value indicating whether an error was detected during the run.

Studies have shown that spectrum-based on-line fault localization can narrow the location of a fault to a set of components comprising between 10% and 25% of the system components across a range of software systems with injected faults [24,25]. The system achieves good localization performance when given spectra for at least 10 error-free executions, and, surprisingly, without spectra for runs with errors the technique is able to eliminate 75% of the components from consideration. For these reasons, in recent work, spectrum-based fault localization has been incorporated as an on-line diagnosis technique in the FLORA system [26].

Sequence-based fault localization [27]. This technique records information about the *order* in which system components are executed during a run of the system. Intuitively, this technique should provide richer information when compared with spectra, which are order-independent, and the study presented in [27] confirms this intuition at least with respect to hit spectra.

It can be very costly to record the entire component execution sequence for any given program run. Consequently, the approach of Dallmeier et al. [27] uses several techniques to reduce the cost of capturing and storing sequence information. The most aggressive technique stores all sub-sequences of component invocations of length k. This results in the recording of a *sequence set* for each program run.

As with spectrum-based localization, sequence sets are accumulated for both erroneous and error-free runs. The sequence sets for a set of runs are processed to produce a ranking of components – from *most likely to be faulty* to *least likely*. A case study applied sequence-based localization to multiple faulty versions of a non-trivial software system with $k = 8$. They explored varying numbers of error-free runs together with a single error run. The faulty component was ranked first 36% of the time and in the top two 47% of the time. On average, the faulty component fell in the top 21% of the ranking which is comparable to the accuracy achieved by spectrum-based diagnosis.

3   Optimizing Monitor Overhead

We begin with some definitions that will permit us to explain monitor optimization in sufficient detail. For the purposes of illustration, we discuss monitoring of properties expressed as deterministic *finite state automaton* (FSA) [28]. An FSA is a tuple $\phi = (S, \Sigma, s_0, \delta, A)$ where: S is a set of states, Σ is an alphabet of symbols that encode program observations, $s_0 \in S$ is the initial state, $\delta: S \times \Sigma \to S$ is the state transition function, and $A \subseteq S$ are the accepting states. We use $\Delta: S \times \Sigma^+ \to S$ to define the composite state transition for a sequence of symbols from Σ; we refer to such a sequence as a *trace* and denote it π. We lift the transition function from traces to sets of traces, Π, and define $\Delta(s, \Pi) = \{s'|\exists \pi \in \Pi : \Delta(s, \pi) = s'\}$[1], i.e., the set of states reached from s via any trace in Π. We define an *error* state as err $\in S$ such that $\neg \exists \pi \in \Sigma^* : \Delta(\text{err}, \pi) \in A$. A property defines a *language* $L(\phi) = \{\pi \mid \pi \in \Sigma^* \wedge \Delta(s_0, \pi) \in A\}$.

FSA monitoring generally involves instrumenting a program to detect each occurrence of an observation, $a \in \Sigma$. A *simple* runtime monitor stores the current state, $s_c \in S$, which is initially s_0, and at each occurrence of an observation a, it updates the state to $s_c = \delta(s_c, a)$ to track the progress of the FSA in recognizing the trace of the program execution. We say that a program execution *violates* a property, ϕ, if the generated trace, π, ends in a non-accepting state, i.e., $\Delta(s_0, \pi) \notin A$; violations can be detected as soon as the monitor enters an error state, i.e., $s_c = err$.

3.1   Monitor Correctness

Definition 1 (Monitor Correctness for Error Detection). *A runtime monitor for property ϕ observing execution trace π is* **sound** *if it reports a violation if $\pi \notin L(\phi)$, and* **complete** *if it reports a violation only if $\pi \notin L(\phi)$. A runtime monitor is correct in the context of error detection if and only if it is sound and complete.*

Soundness guarantees that no observed violation will be missed, whereas completeness guarantees that false reports of violations will not occur. We note in the context of error detection systems soundness is associated with the absence of *false negatives*. In other words, an error detection system is sound if and only if not reporting an error means

---
[1] Δ inside the set comprehension corresponds to the composite state transition for a sequence of symbols from Σ.

the absence of errors in the system [29]. For runtime monitoring, the notions of soundness and completeness are relative to the trace generated by observations of program behavior. In general, runtime monitoring would be complete, but unsound since it is impractical to observe all program behavior. Hence, soundness in Definition 1 is defined relative to just the observed behavior.

While it might seem obvious to require sound and complete monitoring, this requirement can incur greater overhead than approaches that sacrifice one or the other. For example, researchers have explored a variety of sampling techniques that assure completeness of monitoring [30,31,32], but sacrifice soundness. This means that there may exist a trace of the program that violates ϕ, but no error is reported. The advantage of sacrificing soundness is the potential to maintain very low-levels of runtime overhead, e.g., below 10%. When using runtime monitoring for the purpose of error detection, i.e., to enrich existing test oracles, such a tradeoff may be appropriate however, sacrificing soundness is undesirable when monitoring is used in the context of SHM.

3.2   Transforming Loops to Optimize Monitoring

Over the past several years several researchers explored approaches to statically optimizing the overhead of runtime monitoring [9,10,12,33]. In principle, these techniques work much like compiler optimizations. They first perform static analyses to calculate information about how a program and property relate to each other. Then, as depicted on the right side of Figure 2, they use the results of those analyses to eliminate or modify monitor-related instrumentation within the program, to produce P'_ϕ, so as to reduce its runtime cost.

To illustrate how such optimizations interact with online fault diagnosis techniques, we provide a brief overview of the optimization described in [12]. This optimization targets loops that involve observations related to a property being monitored. The goal of the analysis is to determine whether the loop's iteration space, i.e., the series of executions of a loop's body that arise when executing a loop, can be partitioned into a prefix and a suffix as follows.

The loop prefix is comprised of a fixed number of iterations, such that after monitoring the observations in those iterations the property monitor is guaranteed to reach a common state regardless of the monitor state on entry to the loop. More formally, if π is a non-empty regular expression encoding all possible sequences of observations in a single loop iteration and d is the number of iterations in the prefix, then the loop is said to *stutter* at distance d for property ϕ if

$$\forall s \in S : \forall s' \in \Delta(s, \pi^d) : \Delta(s', \pi) = \{s'\}$$

We have found that for many properties and programs, the minimum stutter distance is 1. This means that only a single iteration of the loop must be monitored. Instrumentation related to property monitoring can be eliminated from the loop suffix. Consequently, monitoring a loop for a property defined as an FSA requires only constant overhead – the overhead does not vary with the number of iterations of the loop.

As an example, we consider the property $StartStart$ described by the FSA in Figure 3. This property states that "on a stopwatch, do not call start twice without calling

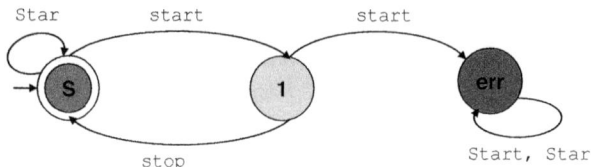

Fig. 3. Property StartStart

```
int b = 0;
while (b < n) {
    ...
    sw . start ()*;
    ...
    sw . stop ()*;
    ...
}
sw . reset ();
```

```
int b = 0;
while (b < n) {
    ...
    sw . start ()*;
    ...
    sw . stop ()*;
    ...
    break;
}
while (b < n) {
    ...
    sw . start ();
    ...
    sw . stop ();
    ...
}
sw . reset ();
```

Fig. 4. Example from SciMark 2.0 FFT: original (left) and optimized (right)

stop in between" [9]. The snippet of code in Figure 4 resembles the code in class FFT from the benchmark SciMark 2.0 [34]. The optimization described above transforms the code as shown in Figure 3. This loop stutters at unit distance, and only the first iteration of the loop needs to be monitored. The instrumented statements are marked by an asterisk in the figure, which shows that observable statements only in the predecessor loop are monitored. If during the program execution the original loop is required to be executed k times before exiting it, the monitor optimized using this technique will only observe 2 events instead of 2*k that will be observed by an unoptimized monitor.

In evaluating this optimization, we have found that it can yield significant reductions in runtime overhead. For example, for the Bloat DaCapo [11] benchmark and a property that requires the strict alternation of hasNext() and next() calls on iterators the number of observations that require processing is reduced by two orders of magnitude which yields a factor of 4 reduction in runtime overhead. This significant optimization benefit comes at no cost to the quality of error detection when monitoring since, for programs that are free of certain forms of uncaught unchecked exceptions, the optimized monitors are guaranteed to preserve both soundness and completeness provided the corresponding unoptimized monitor preserves them.

Optimization of monitoring must preserve the correctness of the original monitor.

Definition 2 (Correctness of Monitor Optimization for Error Detection). *A runtime monitor M' for property ϕ, is correctly optimized with respect to an unoptimized runtime monitor M for error detection if and only if for every trace π that would have been observed by M, it observes π', where $|\pi'| \leq |\pi|$ and M' reports a violation for π' if and only if M would have reported a violation for π.*

3.3 Preserving Diagnostic Information

In the context of SHM, one must consider the possibility that the optimization of error detection impacts the information collected for fault diagnosis. If Σ and D, from Figure 1, are completely distinct then there is no danger that optimizing error detection will impact fault diagnosis. In general, we expect that these two information sources may overlap, $\Sigma \cap D \neq \emptyset$. For example, the set of observations for error detection of typestate properties are exactly what are needed to form sequence sets for the fault localization in [27].

While it may be permissible for optimization to degrade D in some way without impacting the output of fault diagnosis, we define a more conservative property here that suffices as long as fault diagnosis is deterministic relative to its input.

Definition 3 (Diagnostic Information Preservation of Monitor Optimization for Error Detection). *An optimized runtime monitor M' for property ϕ, preserves diagnostic information, D, relative to an unoptimized runtime monitor M, if for every trace π that would have been observed by M, M' observes π', and $D \cap \pi = D \cap \pi'$.*

4 Adapting Monitor Optimization to Diagnosis

Overhead and resource constraints are important considerations when designing runtime monitors. These considerations are equally important when designing diagnosis capabilities. In this section, we consider the potential for adapting several optimization techniques for monitoring aimed at error detection to optimize the recording of information for diagnosis.

Stutter-optimization and hit-spectra present a clear opportunity for optimizing the recording of diagnosis information. Recall that stutter-optimization clones a loop prefix which contains instrumentation to support error detection, and leaves an uninstrumented loop suffix. From a diagnosis point of view, the bodies of the loop prefix and suffix are identical. Loop execution will remain in the prefix until all of the behavior relevant to error detection is covered thereby computing a hit-spectra for the prefix. For all paths through the loop that involve error detection instrumentation, this prefix hit-spectra is guaranteed to be the hit-spectra for the original loop. Consequently, diagnosis related instrumentation that records hit-spectra from the loop suffix can be safely removed.

Stutter-optimization and count-spectra require diagnosis related instrumentation in the loop suffix be preserved. This is because each execution of a block of code that is relevant for diagnosis must be recorded, and there is no way to infer the length of the loop suffix from the analysis performed for stutter-optimization of error detection monitors.

Stutter-optimization and sequence sets present a more subtle opportunity for optimizing the recording of diagnosis information. Recall that stutter-optimization preserves error detection whenever the prefix has at least a minimum stutter distance d. The optimization will instrument d iterations of the loop, i.e., the loop prefix, and on each iteration the non-empty string π is generated. The loop prefix is thus guaranteed to generate a sequence of at least length $d * |\pi|$. Prefixes and suffixes of that sequence will be combined with sequences occurring before and after the loop.

By setting the sequence length to k, one can apply stutter-optimization to a loop using a distance of $\max(d, \lceil k/|\pi| \rceil)$, which will ensure an adequate stutter distance and a sufficiently long sequence of symbols from the loop prefix to generate all k-length subsequences. Using this distance, the diagnosis related instrumentation in the loop suffix may be removed.

In this section, we have seen that for hit spectra and sequence set based fault diagnosis, stutter-optimization of error detection is diagnostic information preserving.

5   Challenges and Opportunities

In this section, we identify challenges and opportunities in runtime monitoring that we believe to be worth exploring in the broader context of software health management. The connections that arise from runtime verification in this context not only provide new requirements for designing error detection techniques, but also create new opportunities to improve the efficiency and effectiveness of fault detection and diagnosis, and produce better SHM systems.

Property Selection and Specification. One of the main reasons for using runtime monitors is to check properties that cannot easily be verified prior to deployment using static analysis techniques. While considerable progress has been made with respect to specification of rich correctness properties amenable to runtime monitoring, various challenges and opportunities remain in this area. For example, care must be taken in developing property specifications such that sufficient information is captured for both detection and diagnosis. For an expressive path-property, the property specification required for detection may suffice as an input for diagnosis; however, for a less expressive state-property the diagnosis module may require a more elaborate specification to correctly identify the faulty component(s). For example, when checking the state property *divide-by-zero*, in addition to the point where the error was detected, the diagnosis module may require a trace of instructions that generated, propagated and wrote a value of zero at the location of interest. This diagnosis can be very challenging due to arbitrarily large number of observations and real-time constraints.

Implicit Constraints. Property specifications form the primary requirements for runtime monitor operation; however, because monitors operate as a component of a larger system, checking properties of the system under observation, and interfacing with the diagnosis component, they are subject to implicit constraints resulting from constraints on the system and on the diagnosis component. Moreover, the nature of the system, e.g., highly-dependable, real-time, distributed, fault-tolerant, can also be a source of implicit constraints. For example, many of the systems being developed in the context of SHM are real-time embedded systems operating on precise schedules. This implies that the scheduling constraints must not be compromised by the addition of detection and diagnosis. For critical systems, one must also assure that the detection, diagnosis, and recovery implementations do not themselves introduce faults lest the overall dependability of the system be decreased.

Placement of Observations. The points at which program behaviors are observed to detect property violations affect not only the efficiency and proper functioning of the error detection capability, but they can also affect the efficiency and effectiveness of the diagnosis component to accurately identify the faulty component(s). We suggest that a static analysis that is geared towards improving the efficiency of monitors and the effectiveness of diagnosis can be developed and employed in order to identify an appropriate set of program points for instrumentation. For example, there are many cases where the same instrumentation can be used to generate observations for error detection and diagnostic information. It may also be possible to coalesce data from multiple instrumentation points when it can be proved that error detection will not occur during some region of program execution, e.g., [33]. Clearly opportunities for *piggybacking* both observation and diagnostic data collection should be exploited.

Exploiting Efficiency. If error detection and the collection of fault diagnosis information can be made more efficient, then the time gained might be exploited to gather alternate forms of diagnostic information that could improve diagnosis precision.

The cost of error detection and the collection of fault diagnostics is spread throughout execution, but once an error is detected the system should execute recovery actions very quickly. This argues for minimizing the cost of executing diagnostic algorithms, which seems to run counter to the goal of making precise fault diagnoses. Here again efficiency improvements can be leveraged for improved diagnoses by shifting some diagnostic processing to the point at which diagnosis information is collected. This effectively amortizes diagnostic cost across the entire program execution, rather then concentrating it between error detection and recovery.

Exploiting Diagnosis Algorithms. In our presentation, we adopted a conservative approach to optimizing error detection. With more information about the structure of diagnostic data and how a diagnosis algorithm processes that information it may be possible to achieve greater degrees of optimization of both error detection and of diagnostic data collection. For example, knowledge about redundancy of diagnostic data could be exploited. To illustrate, consider hit count spectra – one can easily optimize hit count data collection with removable instrumentation as has been done for test coverage data collection.

Predictive Error Detection. As discussed above the latency between error detection and recovery is a critical design constraint for SHM systems. One approach to relaxing this constraint is to shift error detection earlier in time. This can be achieved, for example, by migrating probes earlier in the code, e.g., the earliest point that is post-dominated by the original probe location, or by performing static analyses to calculate predicates on data values that when true guarantee that a path with probes leading to an error will be taken. This would allow a longer period of time for diagnosis to operate, and thereby produce a more precise result, or allow recovery to begin earlier. If an error is predicted long enough in advance, then program execution might be modified to avoid the failure thereby eliminating the need for recovery.

Acknowledgments

The ideas in this paper have been influenced over the course of many wide-ranging conversations about dynamic analysis and monitor optimization with our colleague Sebastian Elbaum. We also thank our colleague Paul Miner for his helpful insights on software fault-tolerance and software health management. Finally, we thank Natasha Neogi who asked "What information is lost during monitor optimization?" during a talk we gave–her question inspired us to think more deeply about these issues. This work was supported in part by the National Science Foundation through awards CCF-0747009 and CCF-0915526, the National Aeronautics and Space Administration under grant number NNX08AV20A, and the Air Force Office of Scientific Research through award FA9550-09-1-0129.

References

1. Barringer, H., Goldberg, A., Havelund, K., Sen, K.: Program monitoring with ltl in eagle. In: Parallel and Distributed Processing Symposium, International, vol. 17, p. 264 (2004)
2. Kim, M., Viswanathan, M., Ben-Abdallah, H., Kannan, S., Lee, I., Sokolsky, O.: Formally specified monitoring of temporal properties. In: Proceedings of the 11th Euromicro Conference on Real-Time Systems, pp. 114–122 (1999)
3. Havelund, K., Roşu, G.: Synthesizing monitors for safety properties. In: Katoen, J.-P., Stevens, P. (eds.) TACAS 2002. LNCS, vol. 2280, pp. 257–268. Springer, Heidelberg (2002)
4. Avgustinov, P., Tibble, J., de Moor, O.: Making trace monitors feasible. In: Conf. on Obj. Oriented Prog. Sys. Lang. and App., pp. 589–608 (2007)
5. Chen, F., Roşu, G.: Mop: an efficient and generic runtime verification framework. In: Conf. on Obj. Oriented Prog. Sys. Lang. and App., pp. 569–588 (2007)
6. Havelund, K., Roşu, G.: Monitoring java programs with java pathexplorer. In: Proc. 1st Workshop on Runtime Verification (2001)
7. NASA Aeronautics Research Mission Directorate, Aviation Safety Program: Integrated Vehicle Health Management Technical Plan, Version 2.03 (2009),
http://www.aeronautics.nasa.gov/nra_pdf/ivhm_tech_plan_c1.pdf
8. Strom, R.E., Yemini, S.: Typestate: A programming language concept for enhancing software reliability. IEEE Trans. Softw. Eng. 12, 157–171 (1986)
9. Bodden, E., Lam, P., Hendren, L.: Finding programming errors earlier by evaluating runtime monitors ahead-of-time. In: Int'l Symp. on Found. of Soft. Eng., New York, NY, USA, pp. 36–47 (2008)
10. Bodden, E.: Efficient hybrid typestate analysis by determining continuation-equivalent states. In: Int'l. Conf. on Soft. Eng. (2010)
11. Blackburn, S.M., Garner, R., Hoffman, C., Khan, A.M., McKinley, K.S., Bentzur, R., Diwan, A., Feinberg, D., Frampton, D., Guyer, S.Z., Hirzel, M., Hosking, A., Jump, M., Lee, H., Moss, J.E.B., Phansalkar, A., Stefanović, D., VanDrunen, T., von Dincklage, D., Wiedermann, B.: The DaCapo benchmarks: Java benchmarking development and analysis. In: Proc. of the 21st ACM SIGPLAN Conf. on Object-Oriented Programing, Systems, Languages, and Applications, pp. 169–190 (2006)

12. Purandare, R., Dwyer, M.B., Elbaum, S.: Monitor optimization via stutter-equivalent loop transformation. In: ACM Conf. on Obj. Oriented Prog. Sys. Lang. and App. (2010)
13. Seyster, J., Dixit, K., Huang, X., Grosu, R., Havelund, K., Smolka, S.A., Stoller, S.D., Zadok, E.: Aspect-oriented instrumentation with gcc. In: Rosu, G., Sokolsky, O. (eds.) RV 2010. LNCS, vol. 6418, pp. 405–420. Springer, Heidelberg (2010)
14. Chen, F., Meredith, P.O., Jin, D., Rosu, G.: Efficient formalism-independent monitoring of parametric properties. In: International Conference on Automated Software Engineering, pp. 383–394 (2009)
15. Knight, J.C., Leveson, N.G.: An experimental evaluation of the assumption of independence in multi-version programming*. IEEE Transactions on Software Engineering 12, 96–109 (1986)
16. Eckhardt, D.E., Caglayan, A.K., Knight, J.C., Lee, L.D., McAllister, D.F., Vouk, M.A., Kelly, J.J.P.: An experimental evaluation of software redundancy as a strategy for improving reliability. IEEE Trans. Softw. Eng. 17, 692–702 (1991)
17. Chen, M.Y., Kiciman, E., Fratkin, E., Fox, A., Brewer, E.: Pinpoint: Problem determination in large, dynamic internet services. In: DSN 2002: Proceedings of the 2002 International Conference on Dependable Systems and Networks, pp. 595–604. IEEE Computer Society, Los Alamitos (2002)
18. Candea, G., Kawamoto, S., Fujiki, Y., Friedman, G., Fox, A.: Microreboot — a technique for cheap recovery. In: OSDI 2004: Proceedings of the 6th conference on Symposium on Operating Systems Design & Implementation, pp. 31–44 (2004); Adopts the philosophy of converting all failures to crashes and then focuses on reboot of crashed components as the only recovery strategy. Downside is that this sacrifices any opportunity to do effective fault localization to better target the recovery. Upside is it is simple
19. Tang, Y., Gao, Q., Qin, F.: Leaksurvivor: towards safely tolerating memory leaks for garbage-collected languages. In: ATC 2008: USENIX 2008 Annual Technical Conference on Annual Technical Conference, USENIX Association, pp. 307–320 (2008)
20. Bond, M.D., McKinley, K.S.: Tolerating memory leaks. In: OOPSLA 2008: Proceedings of the 23rd ACM SIGPLAN conference on Object-oriented programming systems languages and applications, pp. 109–126. ACM, New York (2008)
21. Sözer, H., Tekinerdoğan, B., Akşit, M.: Flora: a framework for decomposing software architecture to introduce local recovery. Softw. Pract. Exper. 39, 869–889 (2009)
22. Walter, C.J., Lincoln, P., Suri, N.: Formally verified on-line diagnosis. IEEE Trans. Softw. Eng. 23, 684–721 (1997)
23. Abreu, R., Zoeteweij, P., van Gemund, A.J.C.: Spectrum-based multiple fault localization. In: ASE 2009: Proceedings of the, IEEE/ACM International Conference on Automated Software Engineering, pp. 88–99. IEEE Computer Society, Los Alamitos (2009)
24. Abreu, R., Zoeteweij, P., van Gemund, A.J.C.: On the accuracy of spectrum-based fault localization. In: TAICPART 2007: Proceedings of the Testing: Academic and Industrial Conference Practice and Research Techniques, pp. 89–98. IEEE Computer Society, Los Alamitos (2007)
25. Abreu, R., Zoeteweij, P., Golsteijn, R., van Gemund, A.J.C.: A practical evaluation of spectrum-based fault localization. J. Syst. Softw. 82, 1780–1792 (2009)
26. Sözer, H., Abreu, R., Akşit, M., van Gemund, A.J.C.: Increasing system availability with local recovery based on fault localization. In: Proc. of 10th International Conference on Quality Software, pp. 276–281 (2010)
27. Dallmeier, V., Lindig, C., Zeller, A.: Lightweight defect localization for java. In: Black, A.P. (ed.) ECOOP 2005. LNCS, vol. 3586, pp. 528–550. Springer, Heidelberg (2005)
28. Hopcroft, J.E., Ullman, J.D.: Introduction to Automata Theory, Languages and Computation. Addison-Wesley, Reading (1979)

29. Xie, Y., Naik, M., Hackett, B., Aiken, A.: Soundness and its role in bug detection systems. In: Proc. of the Workshop on the Evaluation of Software Defect Detection Tools (2005)
30. Bodden, E., Hendren, L.J., Lam, P., Lhoták, O., Naeem, N.A.: Collaborative runtime verification with tracematches. In: Sokolsky, O., Taşiran, S. (eds.) RV 2007. LNCS, vol. 4839, pp. 22–37. Springer, Heidelberg (2007)
31. Dwyer, M.B., Diep, M., Elbaum, S.G.: Reducing the cost of path property monitoring through sampling. In: Int'l. Conf. on Aut. Soft. Eng., pp. 228–237 (2008)
32. Arnold, M., Vechev, M., Yahav, E.: Qvm: An efficient runtime for detecting defects in deployed systems. In: Conf. on Obj. Oriented Prog. Sys. Lang. and App., pp. 143–162 (2008)
33. Dwyer, M., Purandare, R.: Residual dynamic typestate analysis. In: Int'l. Conf. on Aut. Soft. Eng., pp. 124–133 (2007)
34. Pozo, R., Miller, B.: Scimark 2.0. (2004), http://math.nist.gov/scimark

Contracts for Scala

Martin Odersky

École Polytechnique Fédérale de Lausanne (EPFL)
1015 Lausanne, Switzerland
martin.odersky@epfl.ch

Contracts are partial specifications that can be added to program code. They are checked by compilers or other tools, or, more commonly, by runtime checks. Languages such as Eiffel[8], JML[7], or Spec#[1] support contracts natively. Scala [11] does not. Instead, Scala provides flexible syntax that helps in writing high-level libraries which can often mimic true language extensions. An interesting question is to what degree this syntactic flexibility supports the embedding of contracts.

This note reviews some of the notations for contracts and other specifications that have been implemented in Scala, along with some more hypothetical extensions and alternatives.

Contracts as Code

Currently, the standard approach to writing specification-like statements in Scala relies on four operations, all defined in Scala's standard `Predef` object, which is imported by default. They are:

`assert(cond)`	Throws an `AssertionError` if the given condition cond is false.
`assume(cond)`	Like assert, but is treated as an assumption (pre-condition) rather than an assertion (post-condition) for program verifiers.
`require(cond)`	Throws an `IllegalArgumentException` if the given condition cond is false.
`expr ensuring pred`	Applies boolean-valued function `pred` to `expr`. If the result is `true`, the value of `expr` is returned; otherwise an `AsserttionError` is thrown.

There are also versions of these operators that take an additional argument indicating which error message to produce in case of failure.

Here is a small example using `require` and `ensuring`.

```
def sqrt(x: Double) = {
  require(x >= 0)
  newtonRaphson(x, 1.0)
} ensuring { result =>
  (result * result - x).abs < epsilon
}
```

G. Roşu et al. (Eds.): RV 2010, LNCS 6418, pp. 51–57, 2010.
© Springer-Verlag Berlin Heidelberg 2010

Note that `ensuring` takes a closure { `result` => ... } as argument which binds the method's result in its parameter. Since all of Scala's "contract operations" are pure library code, there is no good way to introduce "ghost-variables" such as `result` for a function's result. The closure binding syntax is a lightweight substitute.

Here is how these methods are implemented in the `Predef` object. The implementation of the `assert` method is straightforward:

```
@elidable(ASSERTION)
def assert(assertion: Boolean, message: => Any) {
   if (!assertion) throw new java.lang.AssertionError(message)
}
```

The `@elidable` annotation causes calls to `assert` to be suppressed on the `ASSERTION` elision level, which can be specified by a compiler option. Note that the `message` argument is a call-by-name parameter. This means that the price of constructing elaborate messages need to be paid only if the assertion is `false`.

The implementations of `assume` and `require` are analogous to `assert`, except that a different exception is thrown in case of failure. The `ensuring` method is more interesting:

```
final class Ensuring[A](val x: A) {
   def ensuring(cond: Boolean): A = { assert(cond); x }
   def ensuring(cond: A => Boolean): A = { assert(cond(x)); x }
   // two more variants that take error messages
}
implicit def any2Ensuring[A](x: A): Ensuring[A] = new Ensuring(x)
```

Note the *implicit conversion* `any2Ensuring` that maps any Scala value to an instance of the Ensuring class. This class acts as a wrapper that takes a Scala value and offers an `ensuring` method in four variants on it. When faced with an expression such as

```
expr ensuring cond
```

the Scala compiler will treat this as a method call

```
expr.ensuring(cond)
```

and attempt to make this expression typecheck by adding the implicit conversion any2Ensuring. This gives

```
any2Ensuring(expr).ensuring(cond)
```

and explains why `ensuring` can seemingly be applied to any Scala value.

The use of these specification methods has some advantages. First, being pure library code, they can be extended and customized as needed. Second, since the methods are plain Scala code, the binding of parameters and local variables work as expected.

On the other hand, there are also some shortcomings and difficulties to be overcome. One problem is that common specification notation for a function's result or an old value of a variable are not natively supported and have to be simulated using explicit bindings through local variables or closure parameters.

Another shortcoming is that only assertions applying to precisely one program point are currently supported. It would be nice to have invariants that apply to all entry and exit points of methods of a given class, for instance. In fact, with a little bit of work such functionality can also be provided in the libraries, by means of trait Invariants that can be mixed into classes. Here is a possible definition of such a trait:

```scala
trait Invariants {
  private var invs = new ListBuffer[() => Boolean]
  def invariant(cond: => Boolean) = invs += (() => cond)
  def step[T](body: => T): T = {
    for (inv <- invs) assert(inv())
    val result = body
    for (inv <- invs) assert(inv())
    result
  }
}
```

The trait offers two public methods, invariant and step. The invariant method adds a given condition (passed as a by-name parameter) to a private buffer. The step method brackets the execution of a given body with a check of all installed invariant conditions. Typically, step is used to enclose a computation that is supposed to maintain the class invariants. This trait has to be mixed in by any class that wants to use the invariant and step methods. As an example, here is an implementation of a stack that maintains a list of elements and a length field. The invariant in this case is that the value of the length field corresponds to the length of the list elems.

```scala
class Stack[T] extends Invariants {
  private var length = 0
  private var elems = List[T]()

  invariant(length == elems.length)

  def push(elem: T): Unit = step {
    elems = elem :: elems
    length += 1
  }

  def pop(): T = step {
    require(length > 0)
    val first :: rest = elems
    elems = rest
    length -= 1
    first
  }
}
```

The third shortcoming of using predefined operations for contracts is that, being code, these operations cannot be attached to abstract methods. However, the problem can be alleviated by defining an operation unimplemented that stands for an unimplemented value:

```
def unimplemented[T]: T = throw new UnimplementedOperationException
```

Using unimplemented, an "abstract" version of the sqrt function above could be defined as follows.

```
def sqrt(x: Double) = {
  require(x >= 0)
  unImplemented[Double]
} ensuring { result =>
  (result * result - x).abs < epsilon)
}
```

Unfortunately, this is still more verbose than what one might hope for. Also, this solution would make the formerly abstract method sqrt concrete for the purposes of type-checking. This means that missing implementations of sqrt in subclasses would no longer be flagged as static errors. It's quite conceivable that one could recover this static safety by means a Scala compiler plugin [9].

On the other hand, contracts as code also offer new possibilities that are hard to get in other specification notations. In particular, one can make use of Scala's flexible composition mechanisms for traits to elegantly separate specifications from implementations.

As an example, consider again the square-root function, but now split into three versions: a type signature, a specification, and an implementation. Each version is defined in a separate trait.

```
trait Math {
  def sqrt(x: Double): Double
}

trait MathSpec extends Math {
  protected def epsilon: Double
  abstract override def sqrt(x: Double): Double = {
    require(x >= 0)
    super.sqrt(x)
  } ensuring { result =>
    (x * x - result).abs < epsilon
  }
}

trait MathImpl extends Math {
  protected def epsilon: Double
  def sqrt(x: Double): Double = newtonRaphson(x, 1.0)
}
```

Note that the specification of `sqrt` in trait `MathSpec` invokes the (at this point unknown) implementation through a `super` call. The static supertrait of `MathSpec` is `Math`, which has an abstract definition of `sqrt`, but no concrete implementation. The `abstract override` annotation on the `sqrt` method in `MathSpec` says that this is OK, an implementation will be provided at the time of mixin composition (and this is checked by the compiler).

Here is a possible final assembly of the `Math` functionality.

```
class MathFinal extends MathImpl with MathSpec {
  val epsilon = 1.0e-15
}
```

By extending both `MathImpl` and `MathSpec`, class `MathFinal` pulls together implementation and specication. Its definition of the `epsilon` constant fills in at the same time an implementation variable that guides the termination of the square root approximations and a specification variable that guarantees the accuracy of the result.

It is also possible to combine several specifications which each capture some aspect of the problem domain. The specifications can be stacked through super calls and can be linked through mixin composition.

Alternatives and Complements

Here are some of the alternatives that have been explored for expressing contracts in Scala.

Comments. One could embed contracts with pre- and post-conditions in comments, analogous to what is done in JML, for example. However, there would then be no language-level help in abstracting and composing contracts.

Annotations. A slightly more structured approach is to express contracts as annotations. Typically, one assumes `@pre`, `@post`, and `@invariant` annotations that can take expressions of the host language as arguments. At first glance, annotations are attractive because they separate specifications from code. The downside is that it becomes difficult to link expressions in annotations to the right context. For instance, a `@pre` annotation of a method cannot simply refer to a parameter of this method. So the following would not compile:

```
@pre(x >= 0) // 'x' not visible here!
def sqrt(x; Double) = ...
```

Refinement Types. One could envision an extension of Scala with refinement types [4,2]. A refinement type augments a base type with a predicate that further characterizes legal values of the type. Refinement types are a good basis for static verification [12,5]. On the other hand, more work is needed to achieve with refinement types a clean separation of specification and implementation along the lines of the square root example above.

Property Specifications. Testing frameworks take a different approach to the specification of properties, separating tests from the tested code. The ScalaCheck tool [10] can produce test cases automatically based on the types of the specified properties. ScalaCheck is modelled after the QuickCheck tool for Haskell [3]. Here is an example of a specification of square root using ScalaCheck.

```
def sqrtOK =
  forAll ((x: Double) => if (x >= 0) {
    val r = sqrt(x)
    (r * r - x).abs < epsilon
  }
```

An advantage to this specification approach is that properties involving several methods can be expressed easily. For instance:

```
def pushPopOK[T] =
  forAll (x: T, s: Stack[T]) => s.pop(s.push(x)) == s
```

This form of property specifications complements the contracts as code approach well. A possible downside is that it tends to complicate static analysis because of the additional quantifiers.

Synthesis. Program synthesis makes specifications executable and therefore bridges the gap between specifications and implementations. Program synthesis extends standard programming with a non-deterministic choice operator, choose. A program synthesis tool for a range of constraint domains has been implemented for Scala by Kuncak et.al.[6]. For example, here is an implementation of a `secondsToTime` function that splits a given number of seconds into a time value consisting of hours, minutes and seconds:

```
def secondsToTime(totalSeconds: Int) : (Int, Int, Int) =
  choose { (h: Int, m: Int, s: Int) =>
    h * 3600 + m * 60 + s == totalSeconds &&
    h >= 0 &&
    m >= 0 && m < 60 &&
    s >= 0 && s < 60
  }
```

The non-deterministic choose expression is converted by a Scala compiler plugin into inline code.

Synthesis fits well with a contracts-as-code approach. Essentially, one can simply replace an unimplemented ensuring { ... } construct by the corresponding choose { ... }, provided the given predicate is expressible as a constraint for which a synthesis method exists.

Conclusion

This short note has presented and assessed some common approaches to express contracts in Scala. In conclusion, the contracts as code approach currently provided by Scala's library is attractive despite some notational inconveniences because it integrates well with the component abstractions of the base language and provides a natural fit for program synthesis. This note has proposed library abstractions for class invariants and an `unimplemented` marker as lightweight mechanisms that extend the applicability of the approach further.

References

1. Barnett, M., DeLine, R., Fähndrich, M., Jacobs, B., Leino, K.R.M., Schulte, W., Venter, H.: The spec# programming system: Challenges and directions. In: Meyer, B., Woodcock, J. (eds.) VSTTE 2005. LNCS, vol. 4171, pp. 144–152. Springer, Heidelberg (2008)
2. Bengtson, J., Bhargavan, K., Fournet, C., Gordon, A.D., Maffeis, S.: Refinement types for secure implementations. In: CSF 2008: Proceedings of the 2008 21st IEEE Computer Security Foundations Symposium, Washington, DC, USA, pp. 17–32. IEEE Computer Society, Los Alamitos (2008)
3. Claessen, K., Hughes, J.: Quickcheck: a lightweight tool for random testing of haskell programs. In: ICFP, pp. 268–279 (2000)
4. Flanagan, C.: Hybrid type checking. In: POPL 2006: Conference record of the 33rd ACM SIGPLAN-SIGACT symposium on Principles of programming languages, pp. 245–256. ACM, New York (2006)
5. Kawaguchi, M., Rondon, P.M., Jhala, R.: Type-based data structure verification. In: Hind, M., Diwan, A. (eds.) PLDI, pp. 304–315. ACM, New York (2009)
6. Kuncak, V., Mayer, M., Piskac, R., Suter, P.: Complete functional synthesis. In: Zorn, B.G., Aiken, A. (eds.) PLDI, pp. 316–329. ACM, New York (2010)
7. Leavens, G.T., Baker, A.L., Ruby, C.: Preliminary design of jml: a behavioral interface specification language for java. ACM SIGSOFT Software Engineering Notes 31(3), 1–38 (2006)
8. Meyer, B.: Eiffel: The Language. Prentice Hall, Hemel Hempstead (1992)
9. Nielsen, A.B.: Scala compiler phase and plug-in initialization (2008), http://lampsvn.epfl.ch/svn-repos/scala/lamp-sip/compiler-phase-init/sip-00002.xhtml
10. Nilsson, R.: Scalacheck user guide (2008), http://code.google.com/p/scalacheck/wiki/UserGuide
11. Odersky, M., Spoon, L., Venners, B.: Programming in Scala. Artima (2008)
12. Rondon, P.M., Kawaguchi, M., Jhala, R.: Liquid types. In: Gupta, R., Amarasinghe, S.P. (eds.) PLDI, pp. 159–169. ACM, New York (2008)

Runtime Analysis and Instrumentation for Securing Software*

R. Sekar

Department of Computer Science, Stony Brook University

Abstract. The past decade has witnessed an explosive increase in the
scale, intensity and sophistication of cyber attacks. While software ven-
dors have significantly increased their efforts on security, they are almost
always playing "catch up." As a result, security-conscious organizations
and individuals have come to expect their system administrators to deploy an array of tools and techniques to stay a step ahead of the hackers.
While developer-oriented security tools rely mainly on static analysis,
runtime analysis and policy enforcement are the mechanisms of choice
in administrator-oriented tools. Runtime techniques offer increased automation and precision over static analysis, thus addressing the needs of
administrators who don't have the time or resources needed to acquire
extensive knowledge about the internals of a software system.

In this talk, I will begin by summarizing some of the significant advances that have been achieved in the past few years in the context
of software vulnerability mitigation, including buffer overflow defenses,
and more recently, the impressive results that have been achieved using dynamic information-flow analysis for blocking the most popular exploits today, including SQL and command injection and cross-site scripting. I will then proceed to describe dynamic analysis and enforcement
techniques aimed at another high-profile security problem faced today,
namely, malware defense. Our initial target in this regard has been on
dynamic analysis techniques for extracting high-level models of program
behavior. These models could be used in a variety of applications such
as intrusion detection, vulnerability analysis and security policy verification. More recently, interesting advances have been made in the context
of security policy development, where a combination of static and dynamic analysis techniques have been developed to synthesize low-level,
enforceable policies that achieve a high-level goal such as protecting system integrity. Finally, I will conclude the talk with a discussion of some
research opportunities and challenges in software security.

---

* This work was funded in part by ONR grants N000140110967 and N000140710928,
and NSF grants CCF-0098154, CCR-0205376, CNS-0208877, CNS-0627687 and
CNS-0831298.

Run-Time Verification of Networked Software

Cyrille Valentin Artho

Research Center for Information Security (RCIS),
National Institute of Advanced Industrial Science and Technology (AIST),
Tokyo, Japan
c.artho@aist.go.jp

Abstract. Most applications that are in use today inter-operate with other applications, so-called peers, over a network. The analysis of such distributed applications requires that the effect of the communication with peers is included. This can be achieved by writing or generating stubs of peers, or by including all processes in the execution environment. The latter approach also requires special treatment of network communication primitives.

We also present an alternative approach, which analyzes a networked application by recording and caching its communication with peers. Caching becomes useful when several traces of the application are analyzed. It dispenses with the need of generating a new peer application execution for each different execution of the main application. Such a caching framework for input/output has been implemented on the Java PathFinder platform, which can be used to verify executions of non-deterministic applications at run-time.

1 Introduction

Most of the software written today does not implement a stand-alone system, but communicates with other software. Testing such networked software requires that either all necessary applications be running, or that applications outside the scope of the analysis be replaced by an open environment, or stubs. An open environment non-deterministically returns all possible outcomes of a given function, and is often used for analysis on a more abstract level. In model checking, approaches exist that iteratively narrow down the scope of an open environment, to generate a result that mirrors actual executions more closely [7,12,13]. Nonetheless, such techniques may not always generate over-approximations that are precise enough to analyze complex systems.

Run-time verification takes a different approach to analysis, executing the actual system under test (SUT) rather than an approximation. This has the benefit that observed execution failures always correspond to actual system failures. However, the analysis of a few execution traces may miss certain defects if a system is not fully deterministic. In particular, concurrent systems suffer from this problem: The thread schedule is not controlled by the application, and may vary between executions. Classical testing invariably covers only a subset of all possible schedules and may miss defects.

G. Roşu et al. (Eds.): RV 2010, LNCS 6418, pp. 59–73, 2010.

For concurrent software, run-time verification provides several means of extending classical testing. Approaches exist that analyze the detailed behavior of software, for example, its lock usage, in addition to its output [27]. Other approaches observe several execution traces that are generated in a way as to maximize the potential of finding faults [9,18]. For smaller systems, the coverage of possible execution schedules may even be exhaustive [22,30]. Exhaustive techniques are at the boundary between model checking and run-time verification, analyzing concrete executions while striving to cover all possible outcomes.

If one attempts to apply such techniques to networked software, the challenge of orchestrating the execution of a distributed system arises. Multiple executions may be achieved by restarting the SUT, or by backtracking it to a previous state. In either case, after the SUT has been backtracked or restarted, its state may not be logically consistent anymore with the state of its peer processes. Distributed systems can therefore not be directly executed when using backtracking.

1.1 Overview

This tutorial presents several approaches for verifying networked software [4]:

1. Stubs. Stubs summarize the behavior of the environment, replacing it with a simpler model. The model may be written manually, or recorded from a previous execution to represent the behavior of the environment for a given test case [8].
2. Multi-process analysis. The execution environment may be augmented in order to keep the state of multiple processes in sync, for example, by backtracking multiple processes simultaneously [13,19]. Alternatively, multiple processes may be transformed into a stand-alone system, requiring several program transformations to retain the original semantics [2,29].
3. Caching. Communication between the SUT and its environment is observed, and a model of observed communication traces is generated. This model can then be used to replay communication on demand for subsequent repeated executions of the SUT [3]. Caching yields major performance benefits if different outcomes of the SUT are analyzed by backtracking, thus replaying subsets of the full execution many times [5]. Challenges in this approach include tracking message boundaries while having only an incomplete knowledge of peer processes [3], and handling non-deterministic input/output of the SUT [5].

1.2 Outline

This text is organized as follows: Section 2 shows how software model checking relates to run-time verification. Problems arising with distributed systems are covered in Section 3. The three approaches presented in this tutorial are covered in Sections 4, 5, and 6. Section 7 concludes.

2   Run-Time Verification and Software Model Checking

Model checking [14] explores the entire behavior of a system by investigating each reachable system state. In classical model checker, both the system and the properties to be checked are translated into finite state machines. The properties are negated in the process, such that the analysis of the state space can detect whether undesired states are reachable. The system starts in an initial state, from where iteration proceeds until an error state is reached, or no further states are to be explored. This iteration can also be performed in the reverse manner, where iteration starts from the set of error states and proceeds backwards, computing whether one of these error states is reachable from an initial state.

Model checking is commonly used to verify algorithms and protocols [23]. However, more recently, model checking has been applied directly to concrete software systems [6,7,12,15,17,19,30]. Software model checking investigates the effects of all non-deterministic choices in the SUT, and in particular, all possible interleavings between threads and processes involved. The number of interleavings is exponential in the number of operations and threads, resulting in a *state space explosion* for any non-trivial system. For a more efficient system exploration, a number of partial-order reduction techniques have been proposed. They have in common that they do not analyze multiple independent interleavings when it can be determined that their effect is equivalent [11,23].

Properties typically verified in model checking include temporal properties, typically expressed in linear temporal logics [26] or similar formalisms such as state machines [10]. For software, typically checked constructs include pre- and post-conditions such as specified by contracts [25] and assertions. Furthermore, software model checkers for modern programming languages typically regard uncaught exceptions and deadlocks as a failure.

In software verification, model checking has the advantage that it can automatically and exhaustively verify systems up to a certain size. If the state space of the SUT becomes too large, a possible solution is to prioritize the search of the state space towards states that may more likely uncover defects. User-defined heuristics guide the state space search towards such states. This type of analysis may be implemented in a software model checker framework [21] or in the standard run-time environment, by choosing a heuristic that likely uncovers new thread schedule with each program execution [9,28].

In this sense, the two domains have much in common. Both software model checking and other run-time verification tools analyze the actual implementation of the SUT (or a derived version of it that preserves the original run-time behavior). Both techniques cover a set of execution traces that characterizes a large part of the behavior of the SUT, but not necessarily the entire state space.

In this paper, the term *backtracking* will denote the restoration of a previous state, even if that state is not a predecessor state of the current state. This definition allows the term "backtracking" to be used for search strategies other than depth-first search, and for techniques where a previous system state is restored by re-executing the SUT again from its initial state with the same input (and thread schedule) up to the given target state.

3   Distributed Applications

The analysis of multiple execution traces of a SUT becomes challenging if the SUT communicates with external processes. Backtracking the SUT allows the restoration of a previous state without having to execute the system again up to a given state. However, when backtracking the SUT, external (peer) processes are not affected. As a consequence of this, the states of the SUT is likely no longer consistent with the states of peer processes. From this inconsistency, two problems arise [3]:

1. The SUT will re-send data after backtracking, which interferes with peers.
2. After backtracking, the SUT will expect the same external input again. However, a peer does not re-send previously transmitted data.

Some run-time environments may be able to control the states of multiple processes at the same time. For example, a hypervisor can execute the entire operating system inside a virtual machine, and store and restore any state. However, such tools are, at the time of writing, slow for the usage of state space exploration because of the large size of each system state (consisting of an entire operating system at run-time). Furthermore, processes running on external systems cannot be handled on this way. We therefore focus on dealing with distributed (networked) software executing on verification tools that support one process at a time. In this context, the SUT will denote the process to be verified, and a *peer process* denotes another application running outside the scope of the verification tool. The *environment* of the SUT consists of several peer processes, and other resources used by the SUT, such as communication links to peers.

4   Modeling External Processes as Stubs

If an external process cannot be controlled by an analysis tool, a possible approach is to exclude it from analysis, and replace it with an open model that represents all its possible behaviors. Such an abstract environment model has been successfully used in software model checking [7,12,16]. When targeting complex applications, though, an open model may include too many behaviors of the environment to make analysis tractable. Furthermore, for run-time verification, concrete executions of environment processes are needed, as the SUT cannot be executed against an open model at run-time.

In the case of networked programs, any interaction between the SUT and its environment occurs through the application programming interface (API) providing network access. Responses of an environment process are also retrieved through this API. This allows a replacement of the API with a light-weight skeleton, or *stub,* which only returns the appropriate response of the environment process, without actually communicating with it. The open model is therefore closed with a specialized implementation that is tailored to one particular verification run (or a limited number of tests). Compared to the actual environment process, the implementation of the stub can usually be simplified significantly, removing operating system calls and inter-process communication. The implementation of such a stub is often simple enough to be written manually. For larger projects, frameworks exist that implement some of the common aspects of network APIs [8]. Another approach is to record a communication trace between the SUT and its environment for a given test run, and then generate a stub that implements the recorded responses [8].

In some cases, not all responses from a peer process may be fully deterministic. Network communication involves inherent non-determinism: Even during the verification of a concrete execution with deterministic input, it is possible that network communication is severed due to transmission problems. The reason for this lies in possible transmission problems and is not visible in the SUT. From the point of view of software, communication failures may be regarded as a non-deterministic decision of the environment. As a result, an exception indicating the loss of connectivity may be thrown at run-time, as an alternative outcome to the expected response.

Such exceptions cannot always be tested easily using conventional unit or system tests. A stub is quite suitable for modeling such outcomes, though. In the stub model, one execution for the successful case and another execution for the failure case can be covered. For verification, one can either use a software model checker that interprets such non-determinism as two related test executions, backtracking when necessary [30], or use a run-time verification tool that analyzes execution traces and then selectively implements fault injection, covering both outcomes [1].

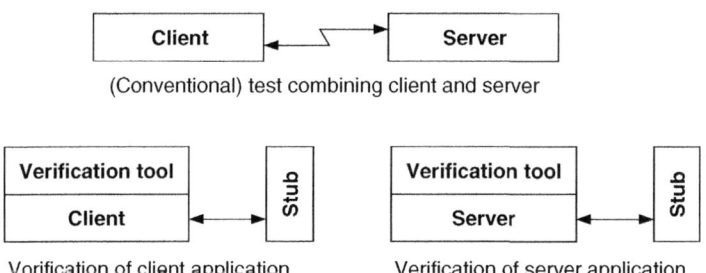

Fig. 1. Verification using stubs

Finally, an approach using stubs for peers is unlikely to find defects in peer processes. When using stubs to analyze a distributed system, one system is analyzed at a time (see Figure 1). It is therefore advisable to alternate the roles of SUT and stubs. Even then, a stub that replaces the other processes during verification may not reflect all possible outcomes of a peer process, especially when a stub is synthesized from recording one sample execution. This limits the degree of confidence gained. Nonetheless, stub-based verification is an elegant and efficient way of analyzing a distributed system, and works especially well when the target is concurrency within the SUT, and fault injection for the interaction between the SUT and the environment. The simplification of peers usually removes interleavings between the SUT and peers, which can be regarded as a partial-order reduction. The performance gained by this abstraction enables the usage of techniques such as fault injection or software model checking, in cases when they may not scale up to multi-process systems in their entirety.

5   Centralization

Many existing software analysis tools can only explore a single process and are not applicable to networked applications, where several processes interact. More often than not, extending the capabilities of these systems towards multiple processes would take considerable effort. It is often easier to reverse the problem, and transform multiple processes into a single process that behaves the same as the original (distributed) application. This approach is called *centralization* [29].

For centralization, processes are converted into *threads* and merged into a single process. Networked applications can then run as one multi-threaded process. Figure 2 illustrates the idea: All applications are run inside the same process, as threads. I/O between applications has to be virtualized, i. e., modeled such that it can be performed inside the execution environment. In the remainder of this section, the term "centralized process" will denote all threads of a given process that was part of a distributed system. In that terminology, three processes are centralized in the example in Figure 2, and converted into one physical process.

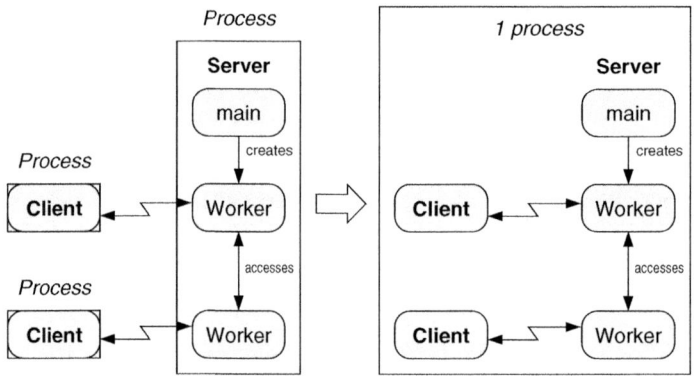

Fig. 2. Centralization

In the remainder of this section, we discuss the treatment of Java [20] programs. The ideas presented here can be readily generalized to other platforms. Centralization of a Java program involves four issues [2,29]:

1. Wrapping applications (processes) as threads, and starting them as such.
2. Keeping the address space of each process separate. In object-oriented languages, this is not a problem for normally created instances, as they are created separately for each application. Therefore, this problem is reduced to

the management of global variables, which are contained in the data segment of C or C++ programs, and in static fields in Java. In Java, each static field is unique and globally accessible by its class name. This uniqueness applies per class and thus per VM. In the centralized version, field accesses to static fields are shared between centralized processes, must be disambiguated. In addition to that, access to environment variables may have to be wrapped to present a distinct environment to each centralized process.

3. Static synchronized methods. In Java, instance-level synchronization is performed implicitly by the VM whenever a method is synchronized. For static methods, synchronization accesses a class descriptor that should again be unique for each centralized process. In programming languages that have no built-in concurrency constructs, like C or C++, global locks are already transformed in the previous step.

4. Shutdown semantics. When a process is shut down, its run-time environment closes open sockets and files before exiting. Furthermore, background (daemon) threads are killed. These actions do not occur if just a thread terminates. After centralization, such clean-up actions therefore do not occur automatically anymore, unless all centralized processes have terminated.

Likewise, actions that terminate an entire process would end up terminating all centralized processes in the centralized version; this has to be prevented to retain the original semantics.

Figure 2 illustrates the overall approach on a typical client-server example. Clients are single-threaded and communicate with the server. The server uses one main thread to accept requests, and one worker thread per request to handle accepted requests. Worker threads on the server side share a global state, such as the number of active connections. Centralization transforms the given processes into one process. In most cases, this transformation results in an additional wrapper thread that launches the main thread of each process involved.

Once all applications have been centralized, the effects of network communication have to be internalized, such that they can be analyzed entirely within the memory space of the centralized program. In this transformation, blocking and unblocking calls, and bidirectional communication, have to be modeled such that their semantics are preserved. The remainder of this section covers the necessary program transformations to address the four points listed above, and the treatment of network communication in the resulting transformed program.

5.1   Program Transformations for Centralization

The four points above address two underlying problems: combining all processes into a single process, and adapting the resulting single-process system such that it exhibits the same behaviors as the original multi-process system.

The first challenge of the required program transformation is to wrap the main method of each centralized process in its own thread (see Figure 3). The wrapper code constructs an instance of CentralizedProcess, which extends the built-in thread class with a virtual process ID. This process ID is used later on to distinguish the address spaces of the centralized processes [29]. Each application is called with its original arguments and receives a distinct process ID. In Figure 3, the exact arguments to main, and the code that ensures that the server is ready to accept incoming client requests, are elided.

```
1 /* Wrapper for running a process inside a thread */
  public class CentralizedProcess extends Thread {
    public int pid;

5   public CentralizedProcess (int procId) {
      super();
      pid = procId;
  } }

10 /* Wrapper for combining all processes */
  public class LaunchProcesses {
    public static final void main(...) {
      new CentralizedProcess(0) {
        public void run() {
15        Server.main(server_args);
      }}.start();

      // wait for server to be ready

20    for (int i = 1; i <= N; i++) {
        new CentralizedProcess(i) {
          public void run() {
            Client.main(client_args);
        }}.start();
25 } } }
```

Fig. 3. Wrapping and launching centralized processes

Second, in the implementation of the SUT, access to global data has to be changed. Code belonging to distinct applications must not (inadvertently) access the same memory location when centralized. Such a disambiguation of data accesses can be achieved by changing each global variable to an array, using the virtual process ID as an index to that array [29]. This transformation can be automated by tools that rewrite source code or byte code [2,29]. For complex data structures in Java, care has to be taken that code to initialize the resulting arrays is generated. For example, an integer field is set to 0 by default in Java, but an array is not created without corresponding code to create it. The initialization of array entries to 0 is again automatic in Java.

Third, it is possible in Java to use class descriptors for locking. Class descriptors can only exist once in each run-time environment, so the approach described above to replicate normal data structures is not applicable in this case. The solution is to use *proxy locks* instead of a class descriptor [29]. One array of proxy locks is created for each class descriptor used for locking. Proxy locks are accessed by virtual process ID as described above. Care has to be taken that class descriptors are not replaced when they are used for the purpose of reflection. In that case, the actual class descriptor, which is unique even in the centralization version of the program, has to be used. The distinction of the two cases, followed by code transformation, can usually be made by data flow analysis [2,29].

Finally, the semantics of program shutdown should be reflected accurately. There are two sides of this problem: On the one hand, a call to exit terminates only one process in the original application, but all centralized processes in the centralized program. On the other hand, resources such as files or network connections should be closed in the centralized version even if the run-time environment has not terminated yet.

In Java, the first aspect of shutdown semantics can be addressed by changing calls to System.exit to throwing an instance of ThreadDeath, which terminates the active thread. Complex cases may need code that manages the number of active child threads per centralized process, as this necessary to determine when a process has terminated. This is not always trivial in a centralized program, and an automatic transformation may not always be possible; for example, in Java, there is no direct way to kill one thread from another thread [20].

The second aspect, the automated release of shared resources, can be implemented by writing a custom shutdown handler, which is invoked whenever the last thread belonging to a centralized process terminates. Both aspects of the shutdown semantics require extensive run-time data structures to keep track of the status of each process, and are work in progress [2].

5.2   Networking for the Centralized Program

Distributed applications need communication mechanisms to interact. Such communication includes the usage of files or shared buffers. These can be modeled using a shared global array in the centralized version. More typically, though, communication takes place over a network. Inter-process communication mechanisms involve low-level operating system calls and are often outside the scope of run-time verification tools. While centralization itself makes multiple processes visible to a single-process analysis tool, it is also necessary to make inter-process communication transparent. This can be achieved by providing a communication model library. The library takes advantage of centralization, and provides the original communication API while sending messages between threads rather than (possibly remote) processes. Using this model library instead of the default library, inter-process communication takes place entirely within the memory of one application.

While this section only describes network communication in detail, the principles described are also applicable to other types of inter-process communication. The common aspects are as follows:

1. In an initial phase, applications set up a communication link. This usually involves one process waiting (listening) for another process to connect. Within each process, both actions are blocking, and will suspend the current thread performing this action until the action has completed.

   In the centralized program, blocking system calls that require a response from another process are modeled with inter-thread signals. In Java,

wait/notify pairs in both threads involved, model the "handshake protocol" between centralized processes.
2. Once communication is established, a bidirectional channel is available for
   the transmission of messages. Data that is communicated between applications can be modeled with constructs that share data between threads, such
   as arrays or inter-thread pipes.

For simplicity, network communication is described here as an interaction between two centralized processes, a *client* and a *server*. The server accepts incoming connections at a certain port. The client subsequently connects to that port.
After a connection is established, a bidirectional communication channel exists
between the client and the server. Communication can then be performed in an
asynchronous manner: Underlying transport mechanisms (commonly TCP/IP)
ensure that sent messages arrive eventually (if a connection is available), but
with some delay. This applies to messages in both directions. A connection can
be closed by the client or the server, terminating communication.

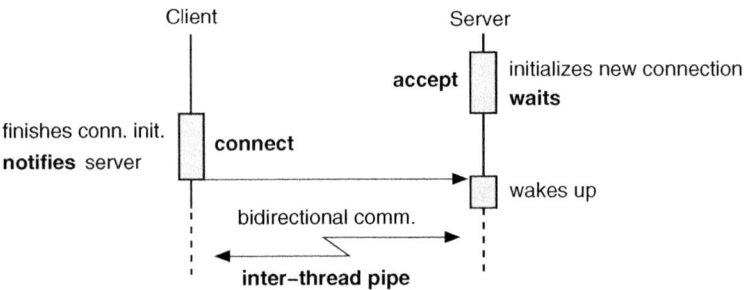

Fig. 4. Client-server communication

For establishing the network connection, we use a two-step initialization (see
Figure 4). In the first step, the accept call of the server, the server sets up its part
of the connection and then blocks (waits) on a common semaphore, which exists
in the network model code. When the client calls connect, it completes its part
of setting up the connection, and then unblocks (notifies) the server. This ensures
that the sequence of each original application passing through blocking library calls
is preserved in the centralized version. Upon connection, two unidirectional inter-
thread pipes are set up, as available through java.io.PipedInputStream and
java.io.PipedOutputStream. They model the underlying network communication normally provided by system libraries, replacing inter-process communication by inter-thread communication [2].

Once the network model for the centralized application is available, the code
that starts the centralized clients after the server is ready, can be provided (see
Figure 3). By inspecting the state of the connection hand-shake, the wrapper
code sees if the server has partially initialized its first connection, and is able to
accept an incoming client request. At that point, the execution of the wrapper
code can continue, and the clients can be launched [2].

To summarize, centralization of networked software consists of program transformation, and a network model library. The resulting centralized application can be executed by any run-time environment, making the approach very versatile for verification. While the complexity of all processes combined may be exceed the capabilities of a heavy-weight analysis tool, centralization is a promising technique for light-weight run-time verification algorithms, extending the scope of single-process tools (such as debuggers) to multiple processes.

6   Input/Output Caching

Unlike approaches that execute multiple (possibly transformed) processes inside the analysis tool, it is possible to execute only one process in the analyzer, and mitigate the effects of backtracking by caching the input/output (I/O) of the SUT. This *I/O cache* approach only runs a single process using the verification tool. Other processes run in their normal environment, perhaps even on remote hosts that are not controlled by the test setup. If multiple communication traces of the SUT are generated by backtracking the state of the SUT, followed by a different scheduling choice, then the state of peer processes has to be kept consistent with the SUT. Without enforcing consistency after backtracking, the state of the SUT would no longer correspond to the state of the communication protocol, as communication has taken place in the physical world and cannot be backtracked.

This discrepancy between the state of the SUT and the physical world can be overcome by caching communication data. A special I/O cache hides backtracking operations, and subsequent repeated communication, from external processes (see Figure 5). Communication with external processes is physically executed on the host until backtracking occurs. After backtracking, previously observed communication data is fetched from the cache [3]. This idea requires an execution environment that is capable of enumerating, storing, and restoring program states; software model checkers that virtualize the execution environment provide this functionality [30].

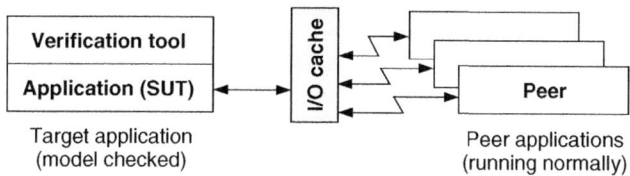

Fig. 5. Verification using I/O caching

The I/O cache keeps track of data that has already been sent to or received from the network. It determines if an I/O operation occurs for the first time; if so, data is physically transmitted; otherwise, data is simply read from the cache. Figure 6 illustrates the principle of the caching approach. Communication data is kept persistent by the cache, in conjunction with a mapping of (1) program states to stream positions, and (2) requests to responses [3]. The first mapping allows a reconstruction of the exact stream state upon backtracking; the second mapping determines the size of a response that corresponds to a particular request. After backtracking, the cache replays duplicate responses from memory. It also verifies that duplicate requests are consistent. If a different request is sent, because a different interleaving of threads generates a different output, cached data is no longer valid for the diverging communication trace [3].

Program state   **I/O Cache**

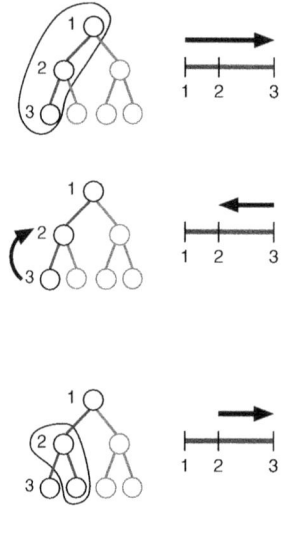

New state: I/O data is stored globally. The program state is mapped to the positions of each stream. The size of each message is also stored in a persistent data structure.

Backtracking: The current read/write positions in each stream are restored in accordance to the program state, but stream data is kept persistently. This can be regarded as rewinding the position of the stream without erasing it.

Continued exploration: Cached data of previous I/O operations is replayed. Output data is compared to previously cached data. Whenever communication data differs from cached data, or exceeds it, a new instance of the peer process is created. Previously cached data is replayed up to the given point, after which a new branch in the data cache is created (not shown in this figure).

Fig. 6. Mapping program states to communication data

Communication diverges in cases where requests depend on a global program state, for example, when the value of a global counter is sent over the network. When communication diverges after backtracking, the state of peer processes is no longer consistent with the state of the SUT. In such cases, peer processes have to be reset to a state that is equivalent to the state of the backtracked SUT. An equivalent peer state can be obtained by sending the new (diverging) input to a peer process, starting from the state at which communication diverged. This requires a new copy of the peer program, running from the point where communication diverges.

An extended cache model starts a new peer process in such cases, and replays communication data up to the point before the trace diverged. This results in a tree structure of communication traces. Despite the need to restart peer processes occasionally, the cache-based solution is still far more efficient than approaches where the peer processes are restarted each time after backtracking [5]. Work is in progress to replace restarting peer processes with restoring a recorded snapshot of all peers, by using virtualization tools [24].

The I/O caching approach analyzes one application in a distributed framework at a time. The other applications run normally. When analyzing a client, the service it requests may even be hosted on a remote machine that is controlled by the verification setup. When analyzing a server, the verification environment has to be able to execute a client on demand, to allow the server to receive requests. In either case, peer processes are not aware that the SUT is not executing serially, but subject to backtracking. Peer processes can therefore be executed in their normal test environment. The cache enables the verification tool to use backtracking to verify the outcome of non-deterministic decisions of the SUT, without always having to restart all peer processes involved after backtracking. As only the SUT is subject to backtracking, the caching technique ignores non-determinism in peer processes. Therefore, the technique is potentially unsound, but this unsoundness comes at a vast improvement in scalability compared to sound approaches such as centralization [3].

7   Conclusion

Distributed applications consist of several processes interacting over a network. Many existing analysis tools are designed to explore the state space of only a single process. Luckily, there exist several ways to adapt a multi-process program to a single-process analysis tool.

One approach is to treat each application separately. Interactions with other applications can be simulated by *stubs*, which replace the original function call and return a value suitable for testing. Stubs can be written manually or synthesized from data recorded in a sample execution. The resulting system is simpler than the original program. For concurrent peer processes, stubs generated from sample executions provide unsound but efficient verification.

To fully verify a distributed system in a single-process environment, multiple processes can be *centralized,* converted into a single process. In such a conversion, distinctive features of separate processes, in particular, their separate address spaces, have to be preserved. Finally, a new implementation of the network API is needed for the centralized program, where inter-process communication is replaced by inter-thread communication. The resulting program is fully self-contained, and all effects of communication are visible inside a single process.

As another alternative, network communication can be captured and replayed on the fly. This requires a *caching system* that provides transparent interaction between the system under test and external processes. The cache has to be integrated in the analysis tool, though, and the approach may be unsound. However, it provides the performance advantage of stubs without requiring code synthesis.

Input/output caching requires a special run-time environment, but it has the advantage of providing a virtual network environment that can communicate with external peers. The other approaches can be used without requiring adaptations of the verification tools, making it possible to verify multi-process systems on tools that handle only one process by themselves.

References

1. Artho, C., Biere, A., Honiden, S.: Exhaustive testing of exception handlers with enforcer. In: de Boer, F.S., Bonsangue, M.M., Graf, S., de Roever, W.-P. (eds.) FMCO 2006. LNCS, vol. 4709, pp. 26–46. Springer, Heidelberg (2007)
2. Artho, C., Garoche, P.: Accurate centralization for applying model checking on networked applications. In: Proc. 21st Int. Conf. on Automated Software Engineering (ASE 2006), Tokyo, Japan, pp. 177–188. IEEE Computer Society, Los Alamitos (2006)
3. Artho, C., Leungwattanakit, W., Hagiya, M., Tanabe, Y.: Efficient model checking of networked applications. In: Robinet, B. (ed.) Proc. TOOLS EUROPE, Zurich, Switzerland. LNBIP, vol. 19, pp. 22–40. Springer, Heidelberg (1974)
4. Artho, C., Leungwattanakit, W., Hagiya, M., Tanabe, Y.: Tools and techniques for model checking networked programs. In: Proc. SNPD 2008, Phuket, Thailand. IEEE, Los Alamitos (2008)
5. Artho, C., Leungwattanakit, W., Hagiya, M., Tanabe, Y., Yamamoto, M.: Cache-based model checking of networked applications: From linear to branching time. In: Proc. 24th Int. Conf. on Automated Software Engineering (ASE 2009), Auckland, New Zealand, pp. 447–458. IEEE Computer Society, Los Alamitos (2009)
6. Artho, C., Schuppan, V., Biere, A., Eugster, P., Baur, M., Zweimüller, B.: JNuke: Efficient Dynamic Analysis for Java. In: Alur, R., Peled, D.A. (eds.) CAV 2004. LNCS, vol. 3114, pp. 462–465. Springer, Heidelberg (2004)
7. Ball, T., Podelski, A., Rajamani, S.: Boolean and Cartesian Abstractions for Model Checking C Programs. In: Margaria, T., Yi, W. (eds.) TACAS 2001. LNCS, vol. 2031, pp. 268–285. Springer, Heidelberg (2001)
8. Barlas, E., Bultan, T.: Netstub: a framework for verification of distributed Java applications. In: Proc. 22nd Int. Conf. on Automated Software Engineering (ASE 2007), Atlanta, USA, pp. 24–33. ACM, New York (2007)
9. Ben-Asher, Y., Eytani, Y., Farchi, E.: Heuristics for finding concurrent bugs. In: Proc. Workshop on Parallel and Distributed Systems: Testing and Debugging (PADTAD 2003), Nice, France, p. 288a (2003)
10. Börger, E., Stärk, R.: Abstract State Machines — A Method for High-Level System Design and Analysis. Springer, Heidelberg (2003)
11. Bruening, D.: Systematic testing of multithreaded Java programs. Master's thesis, MIT (1999)
12. Chaki, S., Clarke, E., Groce, A., Jha, S., Veith, H.: Modular verification of software components in C. IEEE Transactions on Software Engineering 30(6), 388–402 (2004)
13. Chandra, S., Godefroid, P., Palm, C.: Software model checking in practice: an industrial case study. In: Proc. 24th Int. Conf. on Software Engineering (ICSE 2002), pp. 431–441. ACM Press, New York (2002)
14. Clarke, E., Grumberg, O., Peled, D.: Model checking. MIT Press, Cambridge (1999)
15. Corbett, J., Dwyer, M., Hatcliff, J., Pasareanu, C., Robby, Laubach, S., Zheng, H.: Bandera: Extracting finite-state models from Java source code. In: Proc. 22nd Int. Conf. on Software Engineering (ICSE 2000), Limerick, Ireland, pp. 439–448. ACM Press, New York (2000)
16. Dingel, J.: Computer-assisted assume/guarantee reasoning with VeriSoft. In: Proc. 25th Int. Conf. on Software Engineering (ICSE 2003), Washington, USA, pp. 138–148. IEEE Computer Society, Los Alamitos (2003)

17. Dwyer, M., Hatcliff, J., Hoosier, M., Robby: Building your own software model checker using the Bogor extensible model checking framework. In: Etessami, K., Rajamani, S.K. (eds.) CAV 2005. LNCS, vol. 3576, pp. 148–152. Springer, Heidelberg (2005)

18. Farchi, E., Nir, Y., Ur, S.: Concurrent bug patterns and how to test them. In: Proc. 20th IEEE Int. Parallel & Distributed Processing Symposium (IPDPS 2003), Nice, France, p. 286. IEEE Computer Society Press, Los Alamitos (2003)

19. Godefroid, P.: Model checking for programming languages using VeriSoft. In: Proc. 24th ACM Symposium on Principles of Programming Languages (POPL 1997), Paris, France, pp. 174–186. ACM Press, New York (1997)

20. Gosling, J., Joy, B., Steele, G., Bracha, G.: The Java Language Specification, 3rd edn. Addison-Wesley, Reading (2005)

21. Groce, A., Visser, W.: Heuristics for model checking Java programs. Int. Journal on Software Tools for Technology Transfer 6(4), 260–276 (2004)

22. Havelund, K., Pressburger, T.: Model checking Java programs using Java PathFinder. Int. Journal on Software Tools for Technology Transfer (STTT) 2(4), 366–381 (2000)

23. Holzmann, G.: Design and Validation of Computer Protocols. Prentice-Hall, Englewood Cliffs (1991)

24. Leungwattanakit, W., Artho, C., Hagiya, M., Tanabe, Y., Yamamoto, M.: Introduction of virtualization technology to multi-process model checking. In: Proc. 1st NASA Formal Methods Symposium, Moffett Field, USA, pp. 106–110 (2009)

25. Meyer, B.: Object-Oriented Software Construction, 2nd edn. Prentice-Hall, Englewood Cliffs (1997)

26. Pnueli, A.: The temporal logic of programs. In: Proc. 17th Annual Symposium on Foundations of Computer Science (FOCS 1977), Rhode Island, USA, pp. 46–57. IEEE Computer Society Press, Los Alamitos (1977)

27. Savage, S., Burrows, M., Nelson, G., Sobalvarro, P., Anderson, T.: Eraser: A dynamic data race detector for multithreaded programs. ACM Transactions on Computer Systems 15(4), 391–411 (1997)

28. Stoller, S.: Testing concurrent Java programs using randomized scheduling. In: Proc. 2nd Int. Workshop on Run-time Verification (RV 2002), Copenhagen, Denmark. ENTCS, vol. 70(4), pp. 143–158. Elsevier, Amsterdam (2002)

29. Stoller, S., Liu, Y.: Transformations for model checking distributed Java programs. In: Dwyer, M.B. (ed.) SPIN 2001. LNCS, vol. 2057, pp. 192–199. Springer, Heidelberg (2001)

30. Visser, W., Havelund, K., Brat, G., Park, S., Lerda, F.: Model checking programs. Automated Software Engineering Journal 10(2), 203–232 (2003)

Clara: Partially Evaluating
Runtime Monitors at Compile Time[*]
Tutorial Supplement

Eric Bodden[1] and Patrick Lam[2]

[1] Technische Universität Darmstadt, Germany
[2] University of Waterloo, Ontario, Canada
eric.bodden@cased.de

Abstract. CLARA is a novel static-analysis framework for partially evaluating finite-state runtime monitors at compile time. CLARA uses static typestate analyses to automatically convert any AspectJ monitoring aspect into a residual runtime monitor that only monitors events triggered by program locations that the analyses failed to prove safe. If the static analysis succeeds on all locations, this gives strong static guarantees. If not, the efficient residual runtime monitor is guaranteed to capture property violations at runtime. Researchers can use CLARA with most runtime-monitoring tools that implement monitors as AspectJ aspects.

In this tutorial supplement, we provide references to related reading material that will allow the reader to obtain in-depth knowledge about the context in which CLARA can be applied and about the techniques that underlie the CLARA framework.

1 Introduction

It is challenging to implement runtime-verification tools that are expressive, nevertheless induce only little runtime overhead. It is now widely accepted that, to be expressive enough, runtime-verification tools must be able to track the monitoring state of different objects or even combinations of objects separately. Maintaining these states at runtime is costly, especially when the program under test executes monitored events frequently.

Even worse, to be reasonably confident that a program does not violate the monitored property, programmers must monitor many different program runs. The more code locations a program contains at which the program may violate the monitored property, the more test cases one may need to execute to appropriately cover all possible execution paths through these code locations. Paired with potentially slow runtime monitors, this goal may be hard if not impractical to achieve.

We therefore developed the CLARA [9] framework to partially evaluate runtime monitors at compile time. Partial evaluation brings two main benefits:

---

[*] This work was supported by CASED (www.cased.de).

G. Roşu et al. (Eds.): RV 2010, LNCS 6418, pp. 74–88, 2010.
© Springer-Verlag Berlin Heidelberg 2010

1. The partially evaluated monitors usually induce a much smaller runtime overhead than monitors that are fully evaluated at runtime.
2. The partial evaluation can drastically reduce the number of code locations that one needs to consider when looking for code that may cause a property violation. This helps programmers to tell apart useful from useless test cases.

As we show in our accompanying research paper [17], CLARA's partial-evaluation algorithms can often prove that a given program can never violate the monitored property. In these cases, monitoring becomes entirely obsolete.

CLARA was designed such that it poses minimal restrictions on the runtime-verification tool that generates the runtime monitor. CLARA works with virtually all tools that generate runtime monitors in the form of AspectJ aspects.

In this paper we recapitulate CLARA's architecture, explain its major design decisions and give pointers to further in-depth reading material.

2   Architecture of Clara

CLARA targets two audiences: researchers in (1) runtime verification and (2) static typestate analysis. CLARA defines clear interfaces to allow the two communities to productively interact. Developers of runtime verification tools simply generate AspectJ aspects annotated with semantic meaning, in the form of so-called "Dependency State Machines". Static analysis designers can then create techniques to reason about the annotated aspects, independent of the monitor's implementation strategy.

Figure 1 gives an overview of CLARA. A software engineer first defines (top right of figure) finite-state properties of interest, in some finite-state formalism for runtime monitoring, such as Extended Regular Expressions or Linear-Temporal Logic, e.g. using JavaMOP [18] or tracematches [1]. The engineer then uses some specification compiler such as JavaMOP or the AspectBench Compiler [4] (abc) to automatically translate these finite-state-property definitions into AspectJ monitoring aspects. These aspects may already be annotated with appropriate Dependency State Machines. we extended abc to generate annotations automatically when transforming tracematches into AspectJ aspects. Other tools, such as JavaMOP, should also be easy to extend to generate these annotations. If the specification compiler does not yet support Dependency State Machines, the programmer can easily annotate the generated aspects by hand.

CLARA then takes the resulting annotated monitoring aspects and a program as input. CLARA first weaves the monitoring aspect into the program. The Dependency State Machine defined in the annotation provides CLARA with enough domain-specific knowledge to analyze the woven program. The accompanying research paper [17] summarizes Clara's predefined analyses; further details can be found in previous work [10, 11, 14] and the first author's dissertation [9]. The result is an optimized instrumented program that updates the runtime monitor at fewer locations. Sometimes, CLARA optimizes away all updates, which proves that the program cannot violate the monitored property.

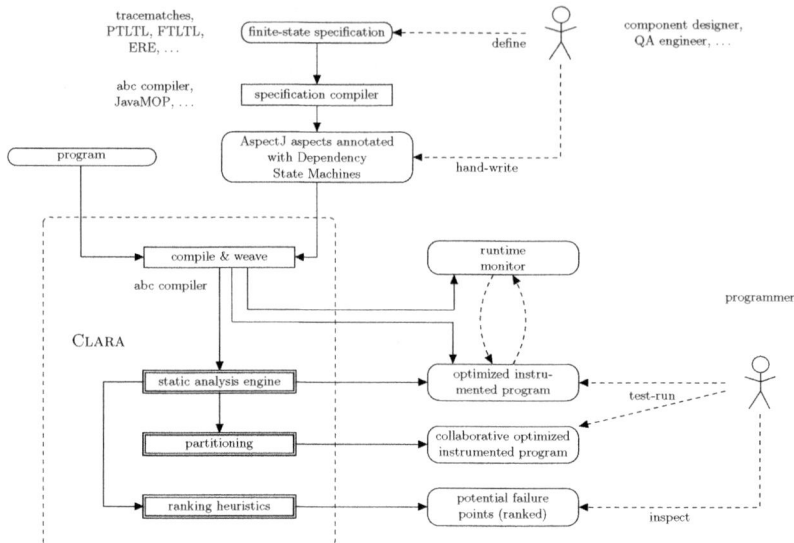

Fig. 1. Overview of CLARA

In addition, CLARA supports Collaborative Runtime Verification [13]. In Collaborative Runtime Verification, users execute differently-configured versions of the program under test; each version only contains partial monitoring code. Collaborative Runtime Verification interacts smoothly with the static analyses.

Finally, CLARA includes a set of built-in ranking heuristics [15]. These heuristics rank all program points that CLARA reports as "potential point of failure" according to a computed confidence value. This confidence value enables CLARA to prioritize program points where the program most likely violates the stated typestate property. Program points at which a violation is still possible, but not likely, will show up further down the ranked list. In addition, CLARA associates with each potentially property-violating program point all other program points that may have contributed to this violation, enabling programmers to easily inspect the context of the violation.

CLARA is available as open-source software at http://bodden.de/clara/, along with extensive documentation, the first author's dissertation [9], which describes CLARA in detail, and benchmarks and benchmark results.

In the following sections we discuss further reading on CLARA, explain how CLARA relates to existing approaches to runtime monitoring and static typestate analysis.

3   Further Reading on Clara and Its Analyses

CLARA started out as an extension to the AspectBench Compiler [4] that was specific to one single specification formalism for runtime monitors, called tracematches [1]. At ECOOP 2007, we presented a set of three static analyses that attempt to statically optimize tracematches at compile time [14]. The three analyses presented there are similar to the three analysis stages that CLARA contains today, however they were all bound to tracematches; they did not generalize to any other monitoring tool. Further, the third analysis stage from the ECOOP paper, the "Active-shadows Analysis", is entirely different from today's Nop Shadows Analysis. The former analysis did not work at all: too coarse-grained abstractions resulted in both bad performance and bad precision.

In 2007, we presented an approach to Collaborative Runtime Verification [12]. In this approach, runtime monitors are spread accross multiple users; every user only monitors a subset of the original instrumentation points. It is non-trivial to select subsets of instrumentation points that (1) still have the potential of causing, in combination, a property violation, and (2) will not cause any false warnings at runtime. In our approach, we present an algorithm to select such subsets. We further present an algorithm that enables certain subsets only from time to time. This trades recognition power for runtime: the program runs faster but may not detect all property violations. Our results showed that this approach scales very well. A journal version of this work appeared in 2008 [13]. CLARA contains an option to enable Collaborative Runtime Verification.

In 2008, we presented [15] a replacement for the ineffective Active-shadows Analysis. This new analysis improves on the Active-shadows Analysis:

- It uses intra-procedural must-alias information to allow for strong updates. In many situations it helps to know that two variables *must* point to the same object. Similarly, the new analysis now uses may-alias information that is flow-sensitive on the intra-procedural level (opposed to being flow-insensitive everywhere). We use a novel pointer abstraction, called Object Representatives [16], to transparently combine the different sources of alias information. The original Active-shadows Analysis had no access to such information, it only used flow-insensitive may-alias information.
- While the Active-shadows Analysis performed a flow-sensitive analysis of the entire program, the novel analysis inspects one method at a time. While the analysis analyzes this method flow-sensitively, it models outgoing method calls flow-insensitively. This trades precision for analysis time, speeding up the analysis significantly.

Further, we presented a novel ranking and filtering approach that aids programmers in finding "true warnings" in a set of potentially false warnings. For program points at which the static analyses issue a warning, the analyses collect information about possible sources of imprecision. If there are many such sources, then the warning is assigned a low probability of being a "true warning", otherwise a higher probability. The CLARA framework contains these filtering and ranking heuristics as well.

In 2009, in joint work with Feng Chen and Grigore Roşu [11], the developers of JavaMOP [18], we generalized the analyses from ECOOP so that they were applicable to AspectJ aspects in general, and to monitors generated by JavaMOP in particular. The analyses presented in this novel work are generalizations of the first two analysis stages from the ECOOP paper, however include also the following improvements:

- The Quick Check in [14] can only detect cases in which a monitor cannot reach a final state as a whole. The improved Quick Check from [11], on the other hand, considers individual paths to final states. This can yield advantages in case of complicated specifications.
- The Orphan Shadows Analysis in [11] is highly optimized. In [14], the analysis algorithm explicitly enumerated all possible combinations, i.e., subsets of instrumentation points. With 1000 or more points, there can be up to 2^{1000} subsets. While we only observed a few pathological cases where this exponential blow-up happened in practice, the novel implementation of the Orphan Shadows Analysis circumvents this problem through a new algorithm that requires no such enumeration.

Also in 2009, for the first author's dissertation [9], we extended the analysis approach to be a proper framework, CLARA, that can be easily extended by others. For the first time, CLARA provides a uniform way to (1) specify runtime monitors as annotated AspectJ aspects, and (2) integrate novel static typestate analyses. During the process, we discovered that the flow-sensitive analysis presented in 2008 [15] was incorrect: in certain cases it could occur that the analysis yielded optimized runtime monitors that give false warnings at runtime. (see [10] for an example) Interestingly, in the meantime Naeem and Lhoták had published [36] an improved version of our analysis from 2008 that contained the same mistake. In 2010, we published [10] a modified version of the analysis, called the Nop Shadows Analysis, which is the final version of the flow-sensitive analysis that CLARA contains today. Opposed to the original analysis attempts, this new analysis now contains a backwards-analysis pass that computes for every instrumentation point information about all continuations of the control flow from this point. It was this crucial piece of information that the original analysis was missing. The first author's dissertation [9] proves this analysis (and the analyses [11] from 2009) sound.

4 Runtime Monitoring Tools

In the following we discuss a number of monitoring tools that influenced the design and implementation of CLARA. We also discuss whether programmers could use these tools in combination with CLARA.

4.1 Stolz and Huch

Our work was originally motivated by Stolz and Huch's work [38] on runtime-verifying concurrent Haskell programs. The authors specify program properties using linear-temporal-logic formulae. Such formulae are generally evaluated over a propositional event trace: a formula refers to a finite set of named propositions and any of the propositions can either hold or not hold at a given event. Stolz and

Huch implemented a runtime library that would generate a propositional event trace at runtime and update a linear-temporal-logic formula according to the monitored propositional values. The library reports a property violation when the formula reduces to **false**. The formulas that Stolz and Huch allow for can be parameterized by different values, similar to the object-to-variable bindings that CLARA supports.

4.2   J-LO

We ourselves developed J-LO, the Java Logical Observer [8], a tool for runtime-checking temporal assertions in Java programs. J-LO follows Stolz and Huch's approach in large parts, however the propositions in J-LO's temporal-logic formulae carry AspectJ pointcuts as propositions. The J-LO tool accepts linear-temporal-logic formulae with AspectJ pointcuts as input, and generates plain AspectJ code by modifying an abstract syntax tree. J-LO extends the AspectBench Compiler, which allows it to then subsequently weave the generated aspects into a program under test. Pointcuts in J-LO specifications can be parameterized by variable-to-object bindings. While the implementation of J-LO is effective in finding seeded errors in small example programs, it causes a runtime overhead that is too high to allow programmers to use J-LO on larger programs. Nevertheless, one could annotate the J-LO-generated aspects with dependency information and then use CLARA's static analyses to remove some of this overhead.

4.3   Tracematches

Allan et al. [1] are the creators of tracematches. Tracematches share with J-LO the idea of generating a low-level AspectJ-based runtime monitor from a high-level specification that uses AspectJ pointcuts to denote events of interest. Nevertheless, the tracematch implementation generates runtime monitors that are far superior to those that J-LO generates. Avgustinov et al. [6] perform sophisticated static analyses of the tracematch-induced state machine to determine an optimal monitor implementation that satisfies three main goals:

1. The monitor implementation should be correct.
2. The monitor should allow parts of its internal state to be garbage-collected whenever possible without jeopardizing correctness.
3. The monitor should implement an indexing scheme that allows the monitor, at any event that binds a variable v to an object o, to quickly look up all state-machine instances for the binding $v = o$.

As Avgustinov et al. show, reclaiming memory (2) and indexing of partial matches (3) are both necessary to achieve a low runtime overhead in the general case. In all the experiments that we conducted with tracematches in our work, these optimizations were already enabled. Hence our experiments show that, while these optimizations are necessary, they may not always be sufficient on their own. However, in combination with CLARA's analysis, the runtime overhead will be low in most cases. Another difference between Allan et al.'s analyses and ours is that Allan et al. only analyze the state machine, while we analyze both the state machine and the program. This allows us to disable instrumentation at program points where this is sound, hence making it easier to check the program for potential property violations already at compile time. Allan et al.'s analyses do not analyze or modify the program under test.

4.4 Tracecuts

Walker and Viggers developed tracecuts [41], an approach that monitors programs with respect to a specification given as a context-free grammar over AspectJ pointcuts. Context-free grammars are strictly more expressive than the finite-state patterns that we consider in CLARA: the first author's dissertation [9, Chapter 2] shows that some properties exist that finite-state formalisms cannot express but that could be expressed as a context-free language. However, most interesting program properties are in fact finite-state properties.

It is unclear how much runtime overhead tracecuts induce. In previous work [5], we tried to compare the relative efficiency of J-LO, tracematches, tracecuts and another tool called PQL (see below). As we reported there, there is an implementation of tracecuts, but it is immature, and while its authors kindly gave us private access to their executables, they did not feel it was appropriate for us to use their prototype for our experiments.

4.5 JavaMOP

JavaMOP provides an extensible logic framework for specification formalisms [18]. Via logic plug-ins, one can easily add new logics into JavaMOP and then use these logics within specifications. As we already showed in this thesis, JavaMOP has several specification formalisms built-in, including extended regular expressions (ERE), past-time and future-time linear temporal logic (PTLTL/FTLTL), and context-free grammars. JavaMOP translates specifications into AspectJ aspects using the rewriting logic Maude [19]. JavaMOP aims to be a generic framework that should support multiple specification languages. Therefore, the designers of JavaMOP are careful when it comes to making assumptions about the specifications used with their framework.

To make JavaMOP compatible with CLARA, Feng Chen extended [11] the JavaMOP implementation so that it would perform some limited analysis of the specification, so that JavaMOP could annotate the generated monitors with dependency information that CLARA can use to partially evaluate these monitors at compile time.

4.6 PQL

The Program Query Language [35] by Martin at al. resembles tracematches in that it enables developers to specify properties of Java programs, where each property may bind free variables to runtime heap objects. PQL supports a richer specification language than tracematches: it uses stack automata rather than finite state machines, which yields a language slightly more expressive than context-free grammars. Martin et al. propose a flow-insensitive static-analysis approach to reduce the runtime overhead of monitoring programs with PQL. This approach inspired us to implement our Orphan Shadows Analysis. As the authors show and as we confirm in our work, such an analysis can be very effective in ruling out impossible matches. However, we also showed that a flow-sensitive analysis can yield additional optimization potential. PQL instruments the program under test manually, using the BCEL [20] bytecode engineering toolkit. If PQL used AspectJ instead, then is should be possible to optimize the generated monitor with Clara, similar to tracecuts. PQL was published as an open-source project, available for download at http://pql.sourceforge.net/. However, it appears that the project is no longer maintained.

4.7   PTQL

Goldsmith et al. [30] proposed PTQL, the Program Trace Query Language, which provides an SQL-like language for querying properties of program traces at runtime. The authors also provide "partiqle", a compiler for this language. The compiler instruments the program that is to be queried so that the program notifies monitoring code about the appropriate events at runtime. The monitor itself uses indexing trees to associate the monitor's internal state with the appropriate objects. It may be possible to evaluate parts of a program query at compile time, for instance when comparing a method name to a constant string. Partiqle resolves such parts of a query already during compilation. This is the same as the partial evaluation of pointcuts that happens in standard AspectJ compilers: these compilers also insert runtime checks only for parts of a pointcut that the compilers cannot determine at compile time. Partiqle resorts to a table-based approach to evaluate the remainder of the query at runtime. Because PTQL uses its own compiler, and is not based on AspectJ, one cannot currently use Clara to evaluate PTQL queries ahead of time. Even if PTQL did generate aspects for its monitoring needs, one would have to take into account that the PTQL language is very expressive and probably Turing complete. Hence it remains unclear whether one could effectively determine dependencies within a query at compile time, so that Clara could exploit these dependencies to optimize PTQL monitors.

4.8   Sub-alphabet Sampling

Dwyer, Diep and Elbaum propose a novel mechanism to guaranteeing low runtime overhead even in the presence of multiple monitoring properties and in cases where programs need to update the internal state of monitors for these properties very frequently [23]. The authors first propose to combine multiple properties over objects of the same class into one large "integrated" property. As the work shows, monitoring of this integrated property can be more efficient than monitoring of the individual original properties. Then second, the authors propose to project the monitor for this integrated property onto multiple sub-alphabet monitors, where each monitor monitors exactly one subset of the original alphabet Σ of events. These sub-alphabet monitors form a lattice that is isomorphic to the power-set lattice of Σ. By the way in which Dwyer et al. define their state-machine semantics, each individual monitoring automaton in this lattice is sound, i.e., cannot report any false positives. The authors show that programmers can gain fine-grained control over the perceived monitoring overhead by selecting a subset of monitors from the lattice. Further, the authors present several heuristics that attempt to select reasonable subsets automatically. As the results show, the sub-alphabet lattice allows for a flexible selection of monitors that gives programmers fine-grained control over their overhead. We therefore believe that the authors' technique is a valuable addition to our own efforts of reducing the runtime-monitoring overhead, in particular to CLARA's component for Collaborative Runtime Verification.

4.9   QVM

Arnold, Vechev and Yahav present QVM, the "Quality Virtual Machine", an extension of IBM's J9 Java Virtual Machine that implements a set of techniques that aim at aiding programmers to debug their programs [3]. QVM comes equipped with support for virtual-machine-level monitoring of single-object typestate properties. Programmers can use a simple syntax to define typestate properties for any given Java class. QVM then instruments instances of such classes to track the instances' typestate at runtime. Once QVM detects and report that a typestate property was violated, it starts sampling method calls that the program issues on objects that are allocated at the same allocation site as the object for which the violation occurred. Naturally, the calling sequences for both objects are not necessarily the same. Yet, the authors argue that in most cases these sequences will be similar enough such that the sampled trace will help the programmers pinpoint the actual problem on the violating sequence and hence fix the bug in their program code. QVM's techniques are complementary to all of the static techniques that Clara provides and it would be interesting to integrate both tools into a common solution.

5   Typestate Analysis

In the previous section we have described several approaches to runtime-verifying program properties through monitoring. Many of these properties are finite-state properties, i.e., one can express the properties using finite-state machines. In the scientific literature, there is a large body of work that attempts to determine finite-state properties of program already at compile time. In this literature, finite-state properties are often called typestate properties, and the related static analyses are called typestate analysis.

5.1 Typestate by Strom and Yemini

In their original paper on typestate [39], Strom and Yemini first describe the idea of having a value's type depend on an internal state, the typestate, associated with that value. Certain operations can change a value's type by transitioning from one typestate to another. Strom and Yemini used state charts [32] to describe the possible state transitions for a class of objects.

In the description by Strom and Yemini, typestate properties are restricted to describing the state of single objects. For example, their model does not allow the state of an iterator i to change when the iterator's collection c is modified. This is because the authors' model has no means of associating i with c. Recently, typestate properties have been enjoying renewed interest, and many current analyses, including ours, do support the analyses of such "generalized" typestate properties.

5.2 Fink et al.

Fink et al. present a static analysis of typestate properties [26]. Their approach, like ours, uses a staged analysis which starts with a flow-insensitive pointer-based analysis, followed by flow-sensitive checkers. The authors' analyses allow only for specifications that reason about a single object at a time. This prevents programmers from expressing multi-object properties such as FailSafeIter. Like us, Fink et al. aim to verify properties fully statically. However, our approach nevertheless provides specialized instrumentation and recovery code, while their approach only emits a compile-time warning. Also, CLARA supports a range of input languages so that developers can conveniently specify the properties to be verified, while Fink et al. do not say how developers might specify their properties.

5.3 Bierhoff and Aldrich

Bierhoff and Aldrich [7] recently presented an intra-procedural approach that enables the checking of typestate properties in the presence of aliasing. The authors' approach aims at being modular, and therefore abstains from potentially expensive whole-program analyses like the ones that CLARA uses. To be able to reason about aliases nevertheless, Bierhoff and Aldrich associate references with special access permissions. Their abstraction is based on linear logic, and using access permissions it can relate the states of one object (e.g. an iterator) with the state of another object (e.g. a collection). These permissions classify how many other references to the same object may exist, and which operations the type system allows on these references. The authors use reference counters to reclaim permissions to help their type system to accept more valid programs. In their approach, they assume that every method is annotated with information about how access permissions and typestates change when this method is executed. Of course this does not necessarily imply that it has to be the programmer who adds these annotations. Many approaches exist [2, 25, 27–29, 31, 33, 34, 37, 42] that can infer program properties. Some can even infer typestate properties. All of these tools operate under the assumption that programs are "mostly correct": by observing mostly correct program runs, the tools can infer which behavior is "usual". Deviations from this usual behavior can then be encoded as typestate properties.

In comparison to Fink et al., Bierhoff and Aldrich's approach has the advantage of being modular: given appropriate annotations it can analyze any method, class or package on its own. CLARA on the other hand needs the whole program to be present, and in particular expects a complete but nevertheless sufficiently precise call graph. When the whole program is available, and can be analyzed, then CLARA gives programmers the advantage that it does not require any program annotations. CLARA only requires annotations that describe error situations, not the program, and then automatically analyzes the program to see whether such error situations can occur. We have found that worst-case assumptions coupled with coarse-grained side-effect information are surprisingly effective.

Bierhoff and Aldrich define typestate properties via a textual representation of statecharts. Hence, programmers can conveniently model behavioral subtyping, as in the original typestate-checking methodology that Strom and Yemini proposed.

Because Bierhoff and Aldrich's work defines a type system and not a static checker like CLARA, the workflow that a programmer has to follow in Bierhoff and Aldrich's approach is slightly different than it is in the case of using CLARA. CLARA allows the programmer to define a program that may violate the given safety property. CLARA then tries to verify that the program is correct, and when this verification fails it delays further checks until runtime. Bierhoff and Aldrich's approach defines a type checker, and hence the idea is that the programmer is prevented from compiling a potentially property-violating program in the first place. This gives the advantage of strong static guarantees. After all, if the program does compile then the programmer knows that the program must fulfill the stated property. On the other hand, the type checker may reject useful programs that appear to violate the stated property but will not actually violate the property at runtime.

5.4   DeLine and Fähndrich

DeLine and Fähndrich's approach [21] is similar in flavor to Bierhoff and Aldrich's. The authors implemented their approach in the Fugue tool for specifying and checking typestates in .NET-based programs. Fugue checks typestate specifications statically, in the presence of aliasing. The authors present a programming model of typestates for objects with a sound modular checking algorithm. The programming model handles typical features of object-oriented programs such as down-casting, virtual dispatch, direct calls, and sub-classing. The model also permits subclasses to extend the interpretation of typestates and to introduce additional typestates, similar to the statecharts-based approach by Strom and Yemini. As in Bierhoff and Aldrich's approach, DeLine and Fähndrich assume that a programmer (or tool) has annotated the program under test with information about how calls to a method change the typestate of the objects that the method references. One fundamental difference between the two approaches is the treatment of aliasing. While Bierhoff and Aldrich used access permissions to reason about aliases, Fugue's type system tracks objects merely as "not aliased" or "maybe aliased". Objects typically remain "not aliased" as long as they are only referenced by the stack. The respective objects can change state only during this period. Once they become "maybe aliased", Fugue forbids any state-changing operations on these objects. This makes Fugue's type system less permissive than the system that Bierhoff and Aldrich describe: in the latter type system objects can change states even when they are aliased.

5.5   Dwyer and Purandare

Dwyer and Purandare use existing typestate analyses to specialize runtime monitors [24]. Their work identifies "safe regions" in the code using a simple static typestate analysis similar to [22]. Safe regions can be methods, single statements or compound statements (e.g. loops). A region is safe if its deterministic transition function does not drive the typestate automaton into a final state. A special case of a safe region would be a region that does not change the automaton's state at all. The authors call such a region an identity region. For regions that are safe but no identity regions, the authors summarize the effect of this region and change the program under test to update the typestate with the region's effects all at once when the region is entered, instead of at the individual shadows that the region contains. This has the advantage that the analyzed program will execute faster because it will execute fewer transitions at runtime. One possible disadvantage of such summary transitions may be that one loses the connection between the places in the code that perform a state transition and the places that actually cause these transitions. This makes it harder for programmers to investigate these program places manually to decide for themselves whether this part of the program could or could not violate the property at hand. Our static analysis does not attempt to determine regions; we instead decide if each single shadow is a nop-shadow. Dwyer and Purandare's analysis should be easily implementable in CLARA and we encourage such an implementation.

6   Conclusion

In this work, we have described the general architecture of CLARA and have given pointers to related work from the literature, work both by ourselves and others. CLARA is available as open source at `http://bodden.de/clara/` and we encourage researchers to use it and extend it. The website also includes a mailing list, on which we will be happy to answer any questions that may arise.

Acknowledgements. We thank everybody who contributed to the design and implementation of CLARA, including the developers and maintainers of Soot [40] and abc [4], but in particular Laurie Hendren, Grigore Roşu, Feng Chen, Oege de Moor, Pavel Avgustinov, Julian Tibble, Ondřej Lhoták and Manu Sridharan.

References

1. Allan, C., Avgustinov, P., Christensen, A.S., Hendren, L., Kuzins, S., Lhoták, O., de Moor, O., Sereni, D., Sittampalam, G., Tibble, J.: Adding Trace Matching with Free Variables to AspectJ. In: OOPSLA, pp. 345–364 (October 2005)
2. Ammons, G., Bodík, R., Larus, J.R.: Mining specifications. In: Symposium on Principles of Programming Languages (POPL), pp. 4–16 (January 2002)
3. Arnold, M., Vechev, M., Yahav, E.: QVM: an efficient runtime for detecting defects in deployed systems. In: OOPSLA, pp. 143–162. ACM Press, New York (2008)
4. Avgustinov, P., Christensen, A.S., Hendren, L., Kuzins, S., Lhoták, J., Lhoták, O., de Moor, O., Sereni, D., Sittampalam, G., Tibble, J.: abc: An extensible AspectJ compiler. In: AOSD, pp. 87–98 (March 2005)
5. Avgustinov, P., Tibble, J., Bodden, E., Lhoták, O., Hendren, L., de Moor, O., Ongkingco, N., Sittampalam, G.: Efficient trace monitoring. Tech. Rep. abc-2006-1 (March 2006),
   http://www.aspectbench.org/
6. Avgustinov, P., Tibble, J., de Moor, O.: Making trace monitors feasible. In: OOP-SLA, pp. 589–608 (October 2007)
7. Bierhoff, K., Aldrich, J.: Modular typestate checking of aliased objects. In: OOP-SLA, pp. 301–320 (October 2007)
8. Bodden, E.: J-LO - A tool for runtime-checking temporal assertions. Master's thesis, RWTH Aachen University (November 2005), http://www.bodden.de/pubs/
9. Bodden, E.: Verifying finite-state properties of large-scale programs. Ph.D. thesis, McGill University (June 2009), available through ProQuest,
   http://www.bodden.de/pubs/
10. Bodden, E.: Efficient hybrid typestate analysis by determining continuation-equivalent states. In: ICSE 2010: Proceedings of the 32nd ACM/IEEE International Conference on Software Engineering, pp. 5–14. ACM, New York (2010)
11. Bodden, E., Chen, F., Roşu, G.: Dependent advice: A general approach to optimizing history-based aspects. In: AOSD, pp. 3–14 (March 2009)
12. Bodden, E., Hendren, L.J., Lam, P., Lhoták, O., Naeem, N.A.: Collaborative runtime verification with tracematches. In: Sokolsky, O., Taşıran, S. (eds.) RV 2007. LNCS, vol. 4839, pp. 22–37. Springer, Heidelberg (2007)
13. Bodden, E., Hendren, L.J., Lam, P., Lhoták, O., Naeem, N.A.: Collaborative runtime verification with tracematches. Journal of Logics and Computation (November 2008), doi:10.1093/logcom/exn077
14. Bodden, E., Hendren, L.J., Lhoták, O.: A staged static program analysis to improve the performance of runtime monitoring. In: Ernst, E. (ed.) ECOOP 2007. LNCS, vol. 4609, pp. 525–549. Springer, Heidelberg (2007)
15. Bodden, E., Lam, P., Hendren, L.: Finding Programming Errors Earlier by Evaluating Runtime Monitors Ahead-of-Time. In: Symposium on the Foundations of Software Engineering (FSE), pp. 36–47 (November 2008)
16. Bodden, E., Lam, P., Hendren, L.: Object representatives: a uniform abstraction for pointer information. In: Visions of Computer Science - BCS International Academic Conference. British Computing Society (September 2008),
   http://www.bcs.org/server.php?show=ConWebDoc.22982
17. Bodden, E., Lam, P., Hendren, L.: Clara: a Framework for Statically Evaluating Finite-state Runtime Monitors. In: Rosu, G., Sokolsky, O. (eds.) RV 2010. LNCS, vol. 6418, pp. 74–88. Springer, Heidelberg (2010)

18. Chen, F., Roşu, G.: MOP: an efficient and generic runtime verification framework. In: OOPSLA, pp. 569–588 (October 2007)
19. Clavel, M., Eker, S., Lincoln, P., Meseguer, J.: Principles of maude. Electronic Notes in Theoretical Computer Science (ENTCS) 4 (1996)
20. Dahm, M.: BCEL, http://jakarta.apache.org/bcel
21. DeLine, R., Fähndrich, M.: Typestates for objects. In: Odersky, M. (ed.) ECOOP 2004. LNCS, vol. 3086, pp. 465–490. Springer, Heidelberg (2004)
22. Dwyer, M.B., Clarke, L.A., Cobleigh, J.M., Naumovich, G.: Flow analysis for verifying properties of concurrent software systems. ACM Transactions of Software Engineering and Methodolology (TOSEM) 13(4), 359–430 (2004)
23. Dwyer, M.B., Diep, M., Elbaum, S.: Reducing the cost of path property monitoring through sampling. In: ASE, Washington, DC, USA, pp. 228–237 (2008)
24. Dwyer, M.B., Purandare, R.: Residual dynamic typestate analysis: Exploiting static analysis results to reformulate and reduce the cost of dynamic analysis. In: ASE, pp. 124–133 (May 2007)
25. Ernst, M.D., Cockrell, J., Griswold, W.G., Notkin, D.: Dynamically discovering likely program invariants to support program evolution. IEEE Transactions on Software Engineering (TSE) 27(2), 99–123 (2001)
26. Fink, S., Yahav, E., Dor, N., Ramalingam, G., Geay, E.: Effective typestate verification in the presence of aliasing. In: International Symposium on Software Testing and Analysis (ISSTA), pp. 133–144 (July 2006)
27. Flanagan, C., Leino, K.R.M.: Houdini, an annotation assistant for ESC/Java. In: Oliveira, J.N., Zave, P. (eds.) FME 2001. LNCS, vol. 2021, pp. 500–517. Springer, Heidelberg (2001)
28. Gabel, M., Su, Z.: Javert: fully automatic mining of general temporal properties from dynamic traces. In: Symposium on the Foundations of Software Engineering (FSE), pp. 339–349 (November 2008)
29. Gabel, M., Su, Z.: Online inference and enforcement of temporal properties. In: ICSE 2010: Proceedings of the 32nd ACM/IEEE International Conference on Software Engineering, pp. 15–24. ACM, New York (2010)
30. Goldsmith, S., O'Callahan, R., Aiken, A.: Relational queries over program traces. In: OOPSLA, pp. 385–402 (October 2005)
31. Hangal, S., Lam, M.S.: Tracking down software bugs using automatic anomaly detection. In: ICSE, pp. 291–301 (May 2002)
32. Harel, D.: Statecharts: A visual formalism for complex systems. Science of Computer Programming 8(3), 231–274 (1987)
33. Li, Z., Zhou, Y.: PR-Miner: automatically extracting implicit programming rules and detecting violations in large software code. In: Symposium on the Foundations of Software Engineering (FSE), pp. 306–315 (September 2005)
34. Lo, D., Maoz, S.: Specification mining of symbolic scenario-based models. In: Workshop on Program analysis for software tools and engineering (PASTE), pp. 29–35 (November 2008)
35. Martin, M., Livshits, B., Lam, M.S.: Finding application errors using PQL: a program query language. In: OOPSLA, pp. 365–383 (October 2005)
36. Naeem, N.A., Lhoták, O.: Typestate-like analysis of multiple interacting objects. In: OOPSLA, pp. 347–366 (October 2008)
37. Pradel, M., Gross, T.R.: Automatic generation of object usage specifications from large method traces. In: ASE, pp. 371–382. IEEE Computer Society, Washington (2009)
38. Stolz, V., Huch, F.: Runtime verification of concurrent haskell programs. Electronic Notes in Theoretical Computer Science (ENTCS) 113, 201–216 (2005)

39. Strom, R.E., Yemini, S.: Typestate: A programming language concept for enhancing software reliability. IEEE Transactions on Software Engineering (TSE) 12(1), 157–171 (1986)
40. Vallée-Rai, R., Co, P., Gagnon, E., Hendren, L., Lam, P., Sundaresan, V.: Soot - a Java bytecode optimization framework. In: CASCON, p. 13. IBM Press (1999)
41. Walker, R., Viggers, K.: Implementing protocols via declarative event patterns. In: Symposium on the Foundations of Software Engineering (FSE), pp. 159–169 (October 2004)
42. Wasylkowski, A., Zeller, A., Lindig, C.: Detecting object usage anomalies. In: Symposium on the Foundations of Software Engineering (FSE), pp. 35–44 (September 2007)

You Should Better Enforce Than Verify*

Yliès Falcone

INRIA, Rennes - Bretagne Atlantique, France
Ylies.Falcone@inria.fr

Abstract. This tutorial deals with runtime enforcement and advocates its use as an extension of runtime verification. While research efforts in runtime verification have been mainly concerned with detection of misbehaviors and acknowledgement of desired behaviors, runtime enforcement aims mainly to circumvent misbehaviors of systems and to guarantee desired behaviors. First, we propose a comparison between runtime verification and runtime enforcement. We then present previous theoretical models of runtime enforcement mechanisms and their expressive power with respect to enforcement. Then, we overview existing work on runtime enforcement monitor synthesis. Finally, we propose some future challenges for the runtime enforcement technique.

Runtime verification [1,2] is a well established technique which consists in using a monitor to supervise, at runtime, the execution of an underlying program against a set of expected properties. A monitor is a decision procedure with an output function (*e.g.*, a state machine when dealing with regular properties) processing (step by step) an execution sequence of the monitored program, and producing a sequence of verdicts (truth values of a truth-domain) indicating fulfillment or violation of a property. Whilst the detection might sometimes be a sufficient assurance for some systems, the occurrence (resp. non-occurrence) of property violations (resp. validations) might be unacceptable for others.

Runtime enforcement [3,4,5,6] of the desired property is a possible solution to ensure expected behaviors and avoid misbehaviors. Within this technique the monitor not only observes the current program execution, but also modifies it. It uses an internal memorisation mechanism, in order to ensure that the expected property is fulfilled: it still reads an input sequence but now produces a new sequence of events in such a way that the property is enforced. The precise and formal relation between input and output sequences is usually ruled by two constraints: soundness and transparency. From an abstract point of view, those constraints entail the monitor to minimally modify the input sequence in order to ensure the desired property. When the program behaves well, the enforcement monitor lets the program execute with the least influence. If the program behavior is about to exhibit a deviation w.r.t. the expected property, the monitor uses its internal memorization mechanism to prevent the misbehavior.

Practical applications of runtime enforcement. There have been many practical applications of the theory of runtime enforcement (*e.g.*, in [7,8,9] for program safety, or

---

* A longer version with more results and examples is available on the author's webpage.

G. Roşu et al. (Eds.): RV 2010, LNCS 6418, pp. 89–105, 2010.

in [10,11] for access control policies). Most of them are built on Schneider's model of security automata. Although in this tutorial we will see an ideational difference between enforcement and verification, in practice there is not always a clear distinction between these disciplines. As so, even early runtime verification frameworks were often designed to, say, "execute some code" when a property is violated; hence modifying the initial program execution. For instance, when a property gets violated:

- JPAX [12], RMOR [13] allow to specify call-back functions that get called;
- Temporal Rover [14] allows to specify a bunch of code to be executed;
- MOP [15] augments monitors with exception handlers.

Nevertheless, reactions to errors are seldom used or at least lacks a systematic and formal study. Furthermore, it is clear that preventing bad behaviors would be more desirable than providing reactions to them ("better safe than sorry").

Tutorial outline. This tutorial focuses on the efforts towards building a theory of runtime enforcement which is, as we believe, emerging as a new activity. We advocate its use as an important complementary activity to runtime verification.

1   Underlying Concepts

Given an alphabet E, a sequence σ on E is a total function $\sigma : I \to E$ where I is either the interval $[0, n]$ for some $n \in \mathbb{N}$, or $\mathbb{N}$ itself. The empty sequence is denoted by ϵ. We denote by E^* the set of finite sequences over E and by E^ω the set of infinite sequences over E. $E^* \cup E^\omega$ is noted E^∞. We will assume some familiarity with the notions of sequence, prefix, and continuation. We will use $\sigma_{...n}$, for $n \in \mathbb{N} \setminus \{0\}$, to denote the prefix of σ of length n.

Execution Sequences. In runtime verification and enforcement techniques, as we are not aware of the program specification, the monitored program is often regarded as a generator of sequences. Thus, the runtime activity focuses on a restricted alphabet Σ_c of concrete events or operations the program can perform. Such sequences can be made of *e.g.*, resource-access events on a secure system, or kernel operations on an operating system. In a software context, these events may represent a relevant subset of instructions (*e.g.*, variable modifications or procedure calls). These operations determine the truth value of properties. Thus, in order to compare program's executions with the property, these concrete events should be abstracted in a finite set of *abstract events* Σ_a. This abstraction is an underlying correspondence $\Sigma_c \leftrightarrow \Sigma_a$, mapping every occurrence of a concrete event to the occurrence of an abstract event[1]. To simplify notations, in this tutorial we will talk uniformly about *execution sequences*, and use a unified alphabet Σ. Execution sequences, *i.e.*, possibly non-terminating runs, range over Σ^∞.

Policies vs. Properties. As often referred in the verification literature, a property is a set of *single* execution sequences, *i.e.*, a property partitions the set

---

[1] This is exactly the purpose of program instrumentation (cf. Section 2.1). Note also that the problem might be slightly more complex when dealing with *parametric events*, events that also depend of concrete execution values (see [16] for instance).

of possible execution sequences. Schneider [3] distinguishes properties from policies. A policy is defined over sets of execution sequences, *i.e.*, a policy partitions the set of sets of execution sequences. Properties thus represent a subset of the set of policies. Only properties are suitable for a monitoring approach since they can be decided on single executions; through a predicate applying on execution sequences *in isolation*. On the contrary, policies which are not properties cannot be monitored since they would require information from other executions. For instance [3], forbidding information flow from two variables in a program is a policy and not a property since checking it would require many executions to determine if values are correlated. Moreover, in this tutorial, as we are dealing with runtime techniques, we will consider only properties defined on linear executions, excluding specific properties defined on branching execution sequences [17]. Runtime frameworks have considered properties on finite, infinite, or both finite and infinite sequences. We will note Π the property under scrutiny and $\Pi(\sigma)$ when the sequence σ belongs to Π.

1.1   Classification of Properties

In the validation community, two classifications of properties have been mainly used: the *Safety-Liveness* and the *Safety-Progress* classifications.

The Safety-Liveness Dichotomy. Noticing that different properties lead to different kinds of proofs on programs, Lamport suggested in [18] that two classes of properties should be distinguished:

safety [18] properties stating that something bad does not happen (*e.g.*, deadlock-freedom, partial correction, FIFO ordering);

liveness [19] properties stating that a good thing eventually happens (*e.g.*, starvation-freedom, program termination).

From an abstract point of view, the difference between these properties is as follows. When safety properties are falsified it is always by a finite sequence. However, liveness properties cannot be falsified by finite sequences. That is to say, for a liveness property, any finite sequence is the prefix of an infinite one satisfying the property. For more results detailing the organization of properties within this class, we refer the reader to [19,20,21,22].

The Safety-Progress Hierarchy. Pnueli et al. introduced the Safety-Progress classification of properties [23,24], as a hierarchy between regular (linear time) properties defined as sets of *infinite* execution sequences. Unlike the Safety-Liveness dichotomy, the Safety-Progress classification is a hierarchy, and provides a finer-grain classification in a uniform way according to four views [25]: a language-theoretic one (seeing properties as sets of sequences), a logical one (seeing properties as LTL formulas), a topological one (seeing properties as open or closed sets), and an automata one (seeing properties as accepted words of Streett automata [26]). Connections between the various views endow this classification with means to translate and see a given property differently.

The Safety-Progress classification first defines basic classes over infinite execution sequences. Classes are informally defined as follows. *Safety* properties are the properties for which whenever a sequence satisfies a property, *all its prefixes* satisfy this property. *Guarantee* properties are the properties for which whenever a sequence satisfies a property, *there are some prefixes* (at least one) satisfying this property (*e.g.*, total correctness, program termination). *Response* properties are the properties for which whenever a sequence satisfies a property, *an infinite number of its prefixes* satisfy this property (*e.g.*, success of all processes entering critical section or weak fairness). *Persistence* properties are the properties for which whenever a sequence satisfies a property, *all but finitely many* of its prefixes satisfy this property (*e.g.*, entering nominal regime).

Furthermore, two extra classes can be defined as (finite) Boolean combinations (union and intersection) of basic classes. *Obligation* properties are combinations of safety and guarantee properties (*e.g.*, exceptions). *Reactivity* properties are combinations of response and persistence properties (*e.g.*, strong fairness). This latest is the most general class containing all linear temporal properties [23]. See [25,27] for more details.

2   Runtime Verification vs. Runtime Enforcement

In this section, we compare runtime verification and runtime enforcement. We first give an abstract picture of runtime verification and its main concepts. These concepts are mostly shared with runtime enforcement. Second, we introduce runtime enforcement and exhibit differences between the two fields.

2.1   Runtime Verification

We shall now introduce runtime verification at an abstract level. For more details, the reader may refer to surveys [1,2]. A candidate definition of "runtime verification" may be formulated as follows:

Definition 1 (Runtime Verification). *Runtime Verification is the discipline of computer science dedicated to the analysis of system executions (possibly leveraged by static analysis) by studying specification languages and logics, dynamic analysis algorithms, system instrumentation, and system guidance.*

However, the following definition has been the most admitted one [2]:

> *"Runtime verification is the discipline [...] that allows to determine whether a run of a system satisfies or violates a given correctness property."*

This definition leaves aside the topic of program guidance that runtime verification took into account early in its scope [28]. However, we believe that this definition is representative of the research efforts in the past decade: determining how a run of the system under scrutiny gives information about a property.

Flavors of runtime verification. Two kinds of approaches are usually distinguished in runtime verification [29]:

Detection of concurrency errors: Debugging is hard to achieve on multi-threaded
   systems due to the large numbers of possible behaviors and the difficulty
   to establish causality between events. Runtime verification techniques for
   concurrency errors extract information from the run of the system in order
   to determine if such transient errors may happen on other executions (even if
   the current execution exhibited no errors). For instance, several methods and
   tools were proposed to detect data races (*e.g.*, [30,31]), deadlocks (*e.g.*, [32]),
   or atomicity errors (*e.g.*, [33]).
Verification of user-provided specifications: It consists in checking whether or
   not the system satisfies a given specification. Several approaches were proposed from verification of simple assertions at a single location in the program
   to the verification of temporal assertions at several locations in the program.
   We refer to [1] for a study and a classification of existing approaches.

Basic Concepts. As one can notice from examining Definition 1, and as several authors [2,4,34] pointed out, runtime verification has been *only concerned
with sequence recognition*. Let us now elaborate more on the basic principles of
runtime verification by depicting its ingredients.

Trace. In order to analyze a program at runtime, its concrete execution needs to
be abstracted. In this perspective, the program under scrutiny is instrumented
so as to produce a sequence of concrete events, a *trace*. An hypothesis is that the
vocabulary of concrete events Σ_c should match with the vocabulary Σ_a in which
the property is expressed. Program instrumentation then consists in inserting
code at relevant places in the program to capture the occurrence of events in Σ_c
and associate each of them with an event in Σ_a. The various locations in the
program, where events are picked up, are named *locations*. Determining these
locations relies on an analysis of the program, either manual or automatic. When
manual, it consists in manually inserting monitor's code in relevant places in the
program. When automatic, the instrumentation relies on an analysis that can be
either static, dynamic, or both. Several approaches for program instrumentation
were considered (*e.g.*, manually in [12], with Aspect-Oriented Programming [35],
or byte-code insertion [36]). All these methods share the common objective to
be simple, efficient, with limited impact to program's performance. Moreover,
instrumentation may be realized on source code or on object code.

The monitor and its placement. Once settled, the trace is fed to one of the central concept in runtime verification: the *verification monitor*. There are various
alternatives for monitor placement wrt. the program [37]. Usually the monitor
runs in the same memory space as the program: *inline* placement. In this case,
the monitor's code can be inserted within program's code either at observation
points or by routine calls. In the second case, the monitor is placed in another
memory space: *outline* placement (*e.g.*, in a thread or different process).

   The monitor may also analyze the program in different ways, in a *lock-step*
manner or a *posteriori*, *i.e.*, a verdict is either incrementally produced (*online*
analysis) or once the program is terminated (*offline* analysis).

The monitor's purpose. The monitor behavior amounts to translate an execution
sequence $\sigma \in \Sigma^\infty$ into a sequence of verdicts $\omega \in \mathbb{B}^\infty$, for a truth domain $\mathbb{B}$.

events → | Verification Monitor | → verdicts

$\sigma \in \Sigma^\infty$
$\sigma \models \Pi?$

$\omega \in \mathbb{B}^\infty$

A monitor, for a property Π, behaves as a function $[\![\Pi]\!]_{\mathbb{B}}(\cdot) : \Sigma^\infty \to \mathbb{B}^\infty$ that provides an evaluation $\omega = [\![\Pi]\!]_{\mathbb{B}}(\sigma)$ for an execution sequence σ in the truth-domain $\mathbb{B}$ under consideration. Thus, one of the problems to be addressed is that each partial evaluation $[\![\Pi]\!]_{\mathbb{B}}(\sigma_{\dots n}) = \omega_{\dots n}$ of a *finite* sequence should not only give some relevant information on $\Pi(\sigma_{\dots n})$, but also possibly on $\Pi(\sigma)$. In this context, the principle expressing whether or not it is worth monitoring a property, *i.e.*, *monitorability*, get raised several definitions.

What is monitorable - definitions of monitorability. The first characterization of monitorable properties was given by Viswanathan and Kim in [38]. Monitorable properties were characterized as a strict subset of safety properties. The authors showed that, due to the undecidability of some problems, a verification monitor is limited by some computability constraints. Monitorable properties are precisely defined as the safety decidable properties[2].

Pnueli *et al.* gave a more general notion of monitorable properties [39] relying on the notion of verdict determinacy for an *infinite* sequence.

Definition 2 (Monitorability [39]). *Considering a finite sequence $\sigma \in \Sigma^*$, a property $\Pi \subseteq \Sigma^\infty$ is negatively determined (resp. positively determined) by an execution sequence σ if σ and each of its possible extension does not satisfy (resp. does satisfy) Π. Then, Π is σ-monitorable, i.e., monitorable after reading σ, if σ has an extension s.t. Π is negatively or positively determined by this extension. Finally, Π is monitorable, if it is σ-monitorable for every $\sigma \in \Sigma^*$.*

The idea is that it becomes unnecessary to continue the execution of a Π-monitor after reading σ if Π is not σ-monitorable. In [40], Bauer et al. gave a first under-approximation of monitorable properties following this definition. They noticed that, in the Safety-Liveness classification, safety and co-safety[3] properties are monitorable according to this definition. Later in [41,27], Falcone et al. tackled the question of monitorability within the Safety-Progress classification of properties. They established a characterization of monitorable properties as a super-set of obligation properties. Furthermore, they provided a syntactic criterion on Streett automata to determine whether or not the property recognized by an automaton is monitorable.

Noticing that the classical definition of monitorability may lead to inconsistencies, Falcone et al. proposed an *alternative* definition of monitorability [27,41]. Indeed, following the classical definition of monitorability, for some obligation properties, some correct and incorrect execution sequences would not be distinguishable. They proposed a definition of monitorability, parameterized by a truth-domain $\mathbb{B}$, allowing to discard properties leading to ambiguities in $\mathbb{B}$.

Definition 3 (Monitorability [41]). *A property Π is said to be monitorable with the truth-domain $\mathbb{B}$ iff $\forall \sigma_{good} \in \Pi, \forall \sigma_{bad} \notin \Pi : [\![\Pi]\!]_{\mathbb{B}}(\sigma_{good}) \neq [\![\Pi]\!]_{\mathbb{B}}(\sigma_{bad})$.*

---

[2] A non-decidable safety property is a safety property for which the test used to decide whether a given sequence belongs to the property is not computable.

[3] A property Π is a co-safety property if its negation $\neg\Pi$ is a safety property.

A property Π is monitorable wrt. the truth-domain $\mathbb{B}$, if it possible to distinguish correct from incorrect sequences within this truth domain. In other words, a property is monitorable, for a truth-domain, if it is possible to build a monitor that would not produce the same verdict for incorrect and correct sequences.

Synthesis of Runtime Verification Monitors. Generally, runtime verification monitors are generated from LTL-based specifications, as seen in [15,42]. Alternatively, ω-regular expressions have been used as a basis for generating monitors, as for example in [43]. To the author's knowledge, RuleR [44] is the system accepting the most expressive specification formalism. In RuleR, specifications are written as a set of rules and are then translated into an automaton-like language. An exhaustive list of works on monitor synthesis is far beyond the scope of this tutorial. We refer to [1,2,28] for more information on this topic.

Summary. All in all, runtime verification is a technique mainly used to detect expected or unexpected behaviors of a program at runtime. It consists in instrumenting the underlying program in order to be able to observe relevant events. These events are then fed to a decision procedure, a monitor, that states a verdict regarding property fulfilment or violation.

2.2 Runtime Enforcement

Runtime enforcement [3,4,5,6] is an extension of runtime verification that aims at answering the following questions, which are often left unanswered during a runtime verification process[4]:

- What happens when the property is violated ?
- Is it possible to *prevent* program's misbehaviors?

We propose a definition of runtime enforcement:

Definition 4 (Runtime Enforcement). *Runtime enforcement is technique dedicated to* ensure *that a run of a system satisfies a given desired property.*

Basic Concepts. Runtime verification and runtime enforcement share many concepts together. The concepts of trace, monitor placement, previously presented in Section 2.1, still apply for runtime enforcement. The main conceptual differences lie in the monitor and his purpose.

The used mechanism is an *enforcement monitor*. It shares the same features with a verification monitor. In particular, it is also dedicated to a property Π, but it is augmented with a memorisation mechanism $\mathcal{M}$. It still reads an input sequence $\sigma \in \Sigma^\infty$ but outputs a new sequence $o \in \Sigma^\infty$.

---

[4] Reaction to specification violation was originally in the scope of runtime verification [28]. Our point is that not much attention has been given to perform reactions in a completely formal and systematic way.

To do so, the monitor is endowed with a set Op of enforcement primitives that, by operating on the memorisation mechanism $\mathcal{M}$, are used to suppress or insert actions using the memory content and the current input, *i.e.*, each $op \in Op$ is a function $op : \mathcal{M} \times \Sigma^* \to \mathcal{M} \times \Sigma^*$. The upshot is that the monitor behaves as a function $[\![\Pi]\!]_{Op}(\cdot) : \Sigma^\infty \to \Sigma^\infty$ providing $o = [\![\Pi]\!]_{Op}(\sigma)$ when input σ.

Property Enforcement. The relation between input and output sequences should adhere the two following constraints that were enunciated in the work of Schneider, Bauer, Ligatti, and Walker:

soundness: the output sequences should be correct wrt. the property;
transparency: the input correct sequences should not be modified.

Thus, the enforcement monitor and its use of the memorization mechanism should be designed so as to guarantee those constraints. According to how an enforcement monitor transforms input sequences, several definitions of property enforcement[5] were proposed [4,45,34,46]. We shall now present them with the unified view of an enforcement monitor as a function that transforms sequences.

Definition 5 (Property enforcement). *An enforcement monitor dedicated to a property Π, abstracted as a function $[\![\Pi]\!]_{Op}(\cdot) : \Sigma^\infty \to \Sigma^\infty$ is said to enforce Π conservatively when (1), precisely when (2), delayed-precisely when (3), effectively wrt. the equivalence relation $\approx$ when (4); where (1), (2), (3), (4) are defined, for all $\sigma \in \Sigma^\infty$, as follows:*

$$\exists o \in \Sigma^\infty : [\![\Pi]\!]_{Op}(\sigma) = o \wedge \Pi(o) \tag{1}$$

$$(1) \wedge \Pi(\sigma) \Rightarrow \sigma = o \wedge \forall i < |\sigma| : \quad [\![\Pi]\!]_{Op}(\sigma_{\cdots i}) = \sigma_{\cdots i} \tag{2}$$

$$(1) \wedge \Pi(\sigma) \Rightarrow \sigma = o \wedge \forall i < |\sigma|, \exists j \leq i : [\![\Pi]\!]_{Op}(\sigma_{\cdots i}) = \sigma_{\cdots j} \tag{3}$$

$$(1) \wedge \Pi(\sigma) \Rightarrow \sigma \approx o \tag{4}$$

An enforcement monitor enforces a property:

- *conservatively* when it adheres only to soundness;
- *precisely* when it follows soundness, transparency, and it produces outputs in a lock-step manner with the input sequence and stops outputting actions as soon as the current input deviates from the property;
- *delayed-precisely* when it follows soundness, transparency, and it produces outputs in a lock-step manner with the input sequence and it can suppress actions and later insert them (when becoming correct again);
- *effectively* when it follows soundness and transparency related to an equivalence relation $\approx$.

Note that, when the considered equivalence relation is the equality, effective enforcement amounts to delayed-precise enforcement, except that effective enforcement relaxes the constraints on the output sequence when input an incorrect sequence which does not have any correct continuation.

In the remainder of this tutorial, we will discuss some questions presented for runtime verification in the scope of runtime enforcement. We first present the

---

[5] Property enforcement amounts to monitorability in runtime verification.

models of enforcement monitors. Then we will review known result in the study of enforceable properties that corresponds to the study of the monitorability of properties in runtime verification. We will also present some enforcement monitor synthesis approaches.

3 Models of Enforcement Monitors

We first present the main models[6] of enforcement monitors. Then we present derived models that take memory limitation into account.

3.1 General Models

We shall give a perspective on the main models of runtime enforcement monitors.

Security Automata. In his seminal work [3], Schneider introduced Security Automata (SA) as the first runtime mechanisms dedicated to property enforcement. SA are a variant of Büchi automata that execute in parallel with the underlying program. These automata are endowed with the ability to stop the underlying program as soon as a violation of the considered property is detected.

Edit-Automata. Ligatti et al. [4,47] later introduced Edit-Automata (EA). They noticed that, by only halting the program, Schneider's SA were too restricted. According to its current input and its control state, an EA can either:

- **insert** an action (by either replacing the current input or inserting it), or
- **suppress** the current input (possibly *memorized in the control state* for later).

Variants of EA have been defined: Insertion Automata (only inserting actions), Suppression Automata (only suppressing inputs). In EA-like enforcement mechanisms, memorization of events (*i.e.*, suppression) is realized using control states.

A hierarchy of Edit-Automata. Bielova and Masacci [34] noticed that edit-automata generated by Ligatti et al. with the provided algorithm in [47] are of a restricted form. While EA have no restrictions on the order of enforcement operations they can perform, Bielova and Masacci noticed that EA generated by Ligatti's construction run their enforcement operations in such a way that, when they are input an incorrect execution sequence, they always output the longest correct prefix. Following this observation, [34] built a hierarchy of EA according to the enforcement ability they are endowed (*i.e.*, how enforcement operations can be performed). Delayed-Automata are constrained Edit-Automata that always output a prefix of their input. In other words, they can only insert previously suppressed actions. All-or-Nothing automata are a more constrained form of EA, *i.e.*, they are constrained Delayed-Automata. On each transition they can only either output all suspended events or suppress the current event. The kind of automata actually synthesized by Ligatti are named Ligatti's Automata by the authors of [34]. These automata are All-or-Nothing automata that always produce the longest correct prefix of the input.

---

[6] We only give informal pictures of the various models we introduce. These models will be formally presented during the tutorial presentation.

Generic Enforcement Monitors. In [6,46], independently from [34], Falcone et al. proposed the mechanism of Generic Enforcement Monitors (GEMs) as an alternative to EA. Contrary to EA, their memorization is realized through a specific memory mechanism completed with a set of operations. Moreover, the proposed automata differ in several points by offering novel features regarding enforcement monitoring. We recall some of them.

First, finding and encoding an enforcement mechanism using edit-automata is not an intuitive operation. As exposed in [34], synthesized automata using the transformation proposed in [48] may produce unexpected results for bad sequences. Second, compared to EA, GEMs propose a clear distinction between control states (used for property recognition) and the sequence memorization (when the current execution deviates from the property) in the memory device for potential replay (if the execution meets the property again). Edit-Automata use a potentially infinite number of control states for property recognition and sequence memorization. Thus, even for a simple guarantee property *e.g.*, "eventually b" an edit-automaton needs an infinite number of states to memorize the potential incorrect sequence of events built on $\Sigma \setminus \{b\}$. Furthermore, one can notice that the size of an EA is hardly dependent on the vocabulary Σ under consideration. Hence such a mechanism is easier to implement, as they are given a restricted set of control states. Meanwhile, linking the proposed mechanism to their implementation is more compatible with formal reasoning. This provides more confidence in the implementation of such mechanisms.

3.2   Models Taking into Account Memory Constraints

While previously presented models of enforcement monitors provide good basis for the design of enforcement mechanisms, they are supposed to be able to memorize an unbounded number of events: through a potentially infinite number of control states for EA and its derivatives, with an unbounded-size memory in GEMs. In order to get more insights on the suitability of such mechanisms for practical purposes, several models were derived.

Shallow-History automata. Fong [49] studied the effect of restraining the capacity of the runtime execution monitor using an information-based approach. Shallow History Automata (SHA) keep as history a set of access events the underlying program made and do not keep any information about the order of their arrival. Then, Fong generalized the result by using abstraction by an homomorphism α on a variant of Schneider's automata. Fong defined the notion of α-SA that intuitively abstracts previously accepted events at each transition it performs. It raised up an information-based lattice of enforcement mechanisms. At the top of this lattice are the $\alpha^{\top}$-SA keeping history of all events ($\alpha^{\top}$ distinguishes all elements of Σ^*). At the bottom of this lattice are the "memory-less" $\alpha^{\perp}$-SA, not tracking the history ($\alpha^{\perp}$ does not distinguish any sequence of Σ^*, *i.e.*, they are one-state mechanisms that prohibit a given set of events). Furthermore, the class of SA built using the abstraction function α_{occ} that captures the occurrence of events in an execution sequence corresponds to the class of SHA.

Bounded History Automata. In [50], Talhi et al. proposed Bounded Security Automata (BSA) and Bounded Edit-Automata (BEA) as restricted versions of SA and EA. These models manipulate a bounded space to record a limited history. Given a fixed size to track histories, their states represent a bounded history of valid execution execution sequences. At each performed step, the transition function of a Bounded Security Automaton abstracts the current history (state) along with the read event in order to produce the next history (state). In Bounded Edit-Automata, states are refined into pairs distinguishing the accepted prefix and the suppressed suffix of the input sequence. Thus, the transition function abstracts the concatenation of the current accepted prefix with the supressed suffix along with the read event in order to produce the new state. A BSA (resp. BEA) whose the maximum size of a history is k is said to be a k-BSA (resp. k-BEA). As expected, enforcement power of Bounded History Automata raises up with the available memory (the maximum size of a history), *i.e.*, for $k, k' \in \mathbb{N}$, when $k < k'$: k'-BSA (resp. k'-BEA) are more powerful than k-BSA (resp. k-BEA).

Summary. We report comparisons [50] related to runtime enforcement mechanisms taking into account memory limitation in the figure below.

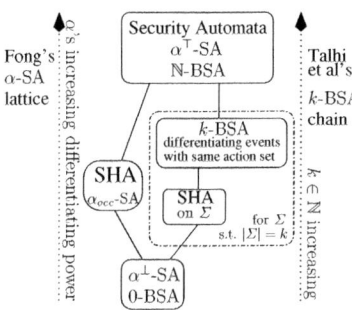

Classes of enforcement mechanisms are represented in a hierarchical manner. For any BSA, one can find an α-SA enforcing the same property. Moreover, for any α-SA, there exists a k-BSA s.t. k is the size used to encode the results of α. Moreover, for a given alphabet Σ of size k, k-BSA are more powerful than SHA. However, note that those limited-memory models assume an infinite number of states.

4   Enforcement Abilities of Enforcement Monitors

4.1   Power of General Runtime Enforcement Mechanisms

Security Automata and decidable safety properties. Schneider announced that the set of precisely enforceable properties with SA is the set of safety properties. Then in [5], Hamlen et al. refined the set of enforceable properties and showed that these SA were in fact restrained by some computational limits. Indeed, as Viswanathan noticed in [51], the class of enforceable properties is impacted by the computational power of enforcement monitors. As the enforcement mechanism can implement no more than computable functions, the enforceable properties are included in the decidable ones. Hence, authors of [5] showed that the set of safety properties is a strict upper limit of the power of enforcement monitors defined as SA (the unsatisfiable safety property is also not enforceable [45]).

Edit-Automata and infinite renewal properties. The properties effectively enforced wrt. the equality by edit-automata are called *infinite renewal* properties. They have been defined, in the Safety-Liveness classification, as the properties for which every infinite valid sequence has an infinite number of valid prefixes [4]. The set of renewal properties is a super set of safety properties and contains some liveness properties (but not all). Moreover, Ligatti et al. showed that insertion and suppression automata can enforce two different proper subsets of the set of enforceable properties by Edit-Automata.

Finite edit-automata and memory-bounded properties. In [52], Beauquier et al. studied the effective enforcement ability wrt. equality of finite-state edit automata. Focusing on regular languages, they proved that enforceable properties are *memory-bounded* properties. Furthermore, they provided a syntactic criterion on generalized Muller automata [53] to determine if the property recognized by a given automaton is memory-bounded and thus enforceable; this criterion is checkable in time $O(n^2)$, where n is the number of states in the automaton.

Generic enforcement monitors and response properties. In [46], Falcone et al. showed that GEMs, instantiated with a set of enforcement operations similar to insertion and suppression, can delayed-precisely enforce the set of response properties within the Safety-Progress classification of properties. Moreover, they proved that the set of response properties is the upper-bound for any enforcement mechanism with a finite number of states (but with an unbounded memory).

4.2   Power of Memory-Limited Runtime Enforcement Mechanisms

Shallow History Automata and an information-based lattice of enforceable policies. Fong showed in [49] that these automata can precisely enforce a set of properties strictly contained in the set of properties enforceable by SA. Regarding the lattice of enforcement monitors defined as α-SA, Fong showed that they give raise to a lattice on the space of all congruence relations over Σ^* which is ordered by the tracked information. Fong's classification has a practical interest by studying the effect of a practical programming constraint (limited memory) from an information point of view. It also shows that some classical security policies remain enforceable using such Shallow History Automata.

Bounded-History Automata and locally testable properties. In [50], Talhi et al. showed that there exists a taxonomy of effective enforceable properties wrt. equality based on the size limitation affecting the memory. As expected, for both BSA and BEA enforcement ability raises with the available space. Moreover, they related the enforcement ability of BHA to *locally testable properties*. Intuitively, a property is said k-locally testable if it can be recognized by an automaton with a finite memory and examining a sequence chunk of a fixed size k. According to which part of the sequence the chunk represents, several classes of locally testable properties can be defined. Intuitively, a property is prefix-testable (resp. suffix testable, prefix-suffix testable, strongly locally testable) if it is recognizable by examining a prefix (resp. suffix, both prefix and suffix, a factor) of limited size. Locally testable properties are linked to Bounded History Automata as follows:

– For BSA: prefix-closed k-prefix locally testable properties and k-strongly locally testable properties are enforceable with a memory of size k; suffix testable and prefix-suffix testable properties are not enforceable.

– For BEA: k-prefix locally testable properties are enforceable with a memory of size k; k-strongly locally testable are enforceable (no bound is given on the memory); suffix testable and prefix-suffix testable properties are not enforceable.

5   Synthesis of Runtime Enforcement Monitors

In [54], Martinelli and Matteucci tackle the synthesis of enforcement mechanisms as defined by Ligatti. More generally, the authors consider security automata and edit-automata. The monitor is modeled by an algebraic operator expressed in CCS. The program under scrutiny is then a term $Y \triangleright_K X$ where X is the target program, Y the controller program and $\triangleright_K$ the operator modeling the monitor where K is the kind of monitor (truncation, insertion, suppression or edit). The desired property for the underlying system is formalized using μ-calculus. In [55], Matteucci extends the approach in the context of real-time systems.

In [48], Ligatti et al. announced a construction of Edit-Automata from finitary properties defined using a predicate on finite sequences for effective enforcement. However, as shown by [34], this construction actually affords a Ligatti automaton that delayed-precise enforce the finitary property.

In [56,46], Falcone et al. defined class-specific transformations for the classes of enforceable properties within the Safety-Progress classification of properties. The monitor synthesis procedures were defined from Streett automata. Besides, due to the connections between the views in the classification, their transformation indirectly provides enforcement monitor synthesis from LTL formula and properties defined using language-based operators. In [27], the authors generalized the class-specific transformations in an independent one.

In [52], Beauquier et al. defined translation of generalized pruned Muller automata [53] (for memory-bounded properties) to finite edit-automata (*i.e.*, edit-automata whose set of states is finite).

In [57], Chabot et al. synthesize Schneider's security automata from properties expressed by Rabin automata [53]. Authors provide a construction from safety properties in the general case, and for more than safety when leveraged with static information gathered from the program. However, full expressiveness of Rabin automata is left aside for non prefix-closed properties.

6   Practical Problems and Future Challenges

We now describe some future challenges for runtime enforcement. Advances in runtime verification (see [1,2]) will also surely benefit to runtime enforcement.

6.1   Theoretical Open Questions

An open question is how static information on the program can leverage runtime enforcement. As suggested in [57], having a specification of the program under scrutiny allows to slightly increase the space of enforceable properties. However, the study has been conducted only for safety properties and security automata. Thus, it remains to study how static information on the program would leverage enforcement, for others classes than safety and using more powerful mechanisms.

As exposed in Section 4, effective enforcement abilities of Generic Enforcement Monitors and Edit-Automata is unknown. Moreover, as exposed in [34], provably correct synthesis of enforcement monitors, beyond safety properties, is only effective for delayed-precise enforcement, both for Edit-Automata and Generic Enforcement Monitors. A working direction is, in this respect, to find more expressive formalisms, and associated monitor synthesis techniques.

Another working direction would be to adapt runtime verification frameworks dedicated to detection of errors on multi-threaded programs and use the principle of runtime enforcement so as to provably prevent those errors.

Soundness and transparency along with precise and delayed-precise enforcement indicate exactly how good and bad sequences should be processed by an enforcement monitor. By contrast, effective enforcement leaves the monitor free to act on bad sequences. For this purpose, one should find relevant remedial actions to be taken, *e.g.*, completion of bad sequences into good ones.

6.2   Practical Challenges

A current working direction is to make the runtime enforcement technique more able to cope with practical limitations in order to deal with largescale examples. In particular it is likely that not all events produced by an underlying program can be freely *observed* and/or *controlled* by the enforcement mechanisms. Moreover, regarding the objective of limiting the resources consumed by the monitor, it might be interesting to study how to store in memory only an *abstraction* of the observed sequence of events for effective enforcement and a suitable equivalence relation. From a theoretical point of view, this means to define enforcement up to some *abstraction preserving trace equivalence relations.*

Similarly, it would be of interest to study the notion of enforcement when weakening the transparency constraint. In this case, the most general form of edit-automata and our generic EMs could be used. Their complete enforcement potentials remain to be studied. This perspective would involve to define other relations between the input and the output sequences; and thus define other enforcement primitives so as to enforce properties automatically. It seems to us that such alternative constraints should be motivated by practical needs.

Finally, most of the practical and effective approaches to runtime enforcement have been performed using security automata. Proposing a framework solving practical implementation issues and staging the most expressive forms of runtime enforcement mechanisms would certainly be an achievement.

Acknowledgement. This tutorial is partially built on previously published material by the author and his colleagues J.-C. Fernandez and L. Mounier. Also, the author is much in debt to K. Havelund for many enriching discussions on runtime verification. Moreover, the author would like to thank H. Marchand, C. Morvan, and S. Pinchinat for their comments on an early version of this tutorial.

References

1. Havelund, K., Goldberg, A.: Verify your runs. In: Meyer, B., Woodcock, J. (eds.) VSTTE 2005. LNCS, vol. 4171, pp. 374–383. Springer, Heidelberg (2008)
2. Leucker, M., Schallhart, C.: A brief account of runtime verification. Journal of Logic and Algebraic Programming 78, 293–303 (2008)
3. Schneider, F.B.: Enforceable security policies. ACM Transactions on Information and System Security 3 (2000)
4. Ligatti, J., Bauer, L., Walker, D.: Run-time enforcement of nonsafety policies. ACM Transaction Information System Security 12 (2009)
5. Hamlen, K.W., Morrisett, G., Schneider, F.B.: Computability classes for enforcement mechanisms. ACM Trans. Programming Lang. and Syst. 28, 175–205 (2006)
6. Falcone, Y., Fernandez, J.C., Mounier, L.: Enforcement monitoring wrt. the safety-progress classification of properties. In: SAC 2009: Proceedings of the ACM symposium on Applied Computing, pp. 593–600 (2009)
7. Dam, M., Jacobs, B., Lundblad, A., Piessens, F.: Security monitor inlining for multithreaded Java. In: Drossopoulou, S. (ed.) ECOOP 2009 – Object-Oriented Programming. LNCS, vol. 5653, pp. 546–569. Springer, Heidelberg (2009)
8. Aktug, I., Dam, M., Gurov, D.: Provably correct runtime monitoring. In: Cuellar, J., Maibaum, T., Sere, K. (eds.) FM 2008. LNCS, vol. 5014, pp. 262–277. Springer, Heidelberg (2008)
9. Erlingsson, U., Schneider, F.B.: SASI enforcement of security policies: a retrospective. In: NSPW 1999: Workhop on New Security Paradigms, pp. 87–95 (2000)
10. Cirstea, H., Moreau, P.E., de Oliveira, A.S.: Rewrite based specification of access control policies. Electron. Notes Theor. Comput. Sci. 234, 37–54 (2009)
11. de Oliveira, A.S., Wang, E.K., Kirchner, C., Kirchner, H.: Weaving rewrite-based access control policies. In: FMSE 2007: Proceedings of the ACM workshop on Formal Methods in Security Engineering, pp. 71–80 (2007)
12. Havelund, K., Rosu, G.: An overview of the runtime verification tool Java PathExplorer. Formal Methods in System Design 24 (2003)
13. Havelund, K.: Runtime verification of C programs. In: Suzuki, K., Higashino, T., Ulrich, A., Hasegawa, T. (eds.) TestCom/FATES 2008. LNCS, vol. 5047, pp. 7–22. Springer, Heidelberg (2008)
14. Drusinsky, D.: The Temporal Rover and the ATG rover. In: Havelund, K., Penix, J., Visser, W. (eds.) SPIN 2000. LNCS, vol. 1885, pp. 323–330. Springer, Heidelberg (2000)
15. Chen, F., Roşu, G.: MOP: An Efficient and Generic Runtime Verification Framework. In: OOPSLA 2007: Object-Oriented Programming, Systems, Languages and Applications, pp. 569–588 (2007)
16. Chen, F., Rosu, G.: Parametric trace slicing and monitoring. In: Kowalewski, S., Philippou, A. (eds.) TACAS 2009. LNCS, vol. 5505, pp. 246–261. Springer, Heidelberg (2009)
17. Emerson, E.A.: Temporal and modal logic. In: Handbook of Theoretical Computer Science, Volume B: Formal Models and Sematics (B), pp. 995–1072 (1990)
18. Lamport, L.: Proving the correctness of multiprocess programs. IEEE Transactions on Software Engineering 3, 125–143 (1977)
19. Alpern, B., Schneider, F.B.: Defining Liveness. Information Processing Letters 21, 181–185 (1985)
20. Manna, Z., Pnueli, A.: Adequate proof principles for invariance and liveness properties of concurrent programs. Sci. Comput. Program. 4, 257–289 (1984)

21. Owicki, S., Lamport, L.: Proving liveness properties of concurrent programs. ACM Transaction Programming Languages and Systems 4, 455–495 (1982)
22. Sistla, A.P.: On characterization of safety and liveness properties in temporal logic. In: PODC 1985: Proceedings of the 4th annual ACM symposium on Principles of distributed computing, pp. 39–48 (1985)
23. Manna, Z., Pnueli, A.: A hierarchy of temporal properties (invited paper, 1989). In: PODC 1990: Proceedings of the 9th annual ACM symposium on Principles of distributed computing, pp. 377–410 (1990)
24. Chang, E.Y., Manna, Z., Pnueli, A.: Characterization of temporal property classes. In: Kuich, W. (ed.) ICALP 1992. LNCS, vol. 623, pp. 474–486. Springer, Heidelberg (1992)
25. Chang, E., Manna, Z., Pnueli, A.: The Safety-Progress Classification. Technical report, Stanford University, Dept. of Computer Science (1992)
26. Streett, R.S.: Propositional Dynamic Logic of looping and converse. In: STOC 1981: Proceedings of the 13th Symp. on Theory Of computing, pp. 375–383. ACM, New York (1981)
27. Falcone, Y., Fernandez, J.C., Mounier, L.: What can you verify and enforce at runtime? Software Tools for Technology Transfer, special issue on Runtime Verification (2010), Invited Paper, under review. Preprint as Verimag TR-2010-5
28. Runtime Verification (2001-2009), http://www.runtime-verification.org
29. Colin, S., Mariani, L.: Run-time verification. In: Broy, M., Jonsson, B., Katoen, J.-P., Leucker, M., Pretschner, A. (eds.) Model-Based Testing of Reactive Systems. LNCS, vol. 3472, pp. 525–556. Springer, Heidelberg (2005)
30. Chen, F., Şerbănuţă, T.F., Roşu, G.: jPredictor: a predictive runtime analysis tool for Java. In: ICSE 2008: Proceedings of the 30th International Conference on Software Engineering, pp. 221–230 (2008)
31. Bodden, E., Havelund, K.: Racer: Effective race detection using AspectJ. IEEE Transactions on Software Engineering (2009)
32. Bensalem, S., Havelund, K.: Dynamic deadlock analysis of multi-threaded programs. In: Ur, S., Bin, E., Wolfsthal, Y. (eds.) HVC 2005. LNCS, vol. 3875, pp. 208–223. Springer, Heidelberg (2006)
33. Flanagan, C., Freund, S.N.: Atomizer: a dynamic atomicity checker for multi-threaded programs. In: POPL 2004: Proceedings of the 31st ACM SIGPLAN-SIGACT Symposium on Principles of Programming Languages, pp. 256–267 (2004)
34. Bielova, N., Massacci, F.: Do you really mean what you actually enforced? In: Degano, P., Guttman, J., Martinelli, F. (eds.) FAST 2008. LNCS, vol. 5491, pp. 287–301. Springer, Heidelberg (2009)
35. Kiczales, G., Lamping, J., Mendhekar, A., Maeda, C., Lopes, C.V., Loingtier, J.M., Irwin, J.: Aspect-oriented programming. In: Aksit, M., Matsuoka, S. (eds.) ECOOP 1997. LNCS, vol. 1241, pp. 220–242. Springer, Heidelberg (1997)
36. The Apache Jakarta Project: Byte Code Engineering Library (2009), http://jakarta.apache.org/bcel/
37. Delgado, N., Gates, A.Q., Roach, S.: A taxonomy and catalog of runtime software-fault monitoring tools. IEEE Trans. on Software Engineering 30, 859–872 (2004)
38. Viswanathan, M., Kim, M.: Foundations for the run-time monitoring of reactive systems - fundamentals of the MaC language. In: Liu, Z., Araki, K. (eds.) ICTAC 2004. LNCS, vol. 3407, pp. 543–556. Springer, Heidelberg (2005)
39. Pnueli, A., Zaks, A.: PSL model checking and run-time verification via testers. In: Misra, J., Nipkow, T., Sekerinski, E. (eds.) FM 2006. LNCS, vol. 4085, pp. 573–586. Springer, Heidelberg (2006)

40. Bauer, A., Leucker, M., Schallhart, C.: Comparing LTL semantics for runtime verification. Journal of Logic and Computation (2009)
41. Falcone, Y., Fernandez, J.-C., Mounier, L.: Runtime verification of safety-progress properties. In: Bensalem, S., Peled, D. (eds.) RV 2009. LNCS, vol. 5779, pp. 40–59. Springer, Heidelberg (2009)
42. Bauer, A., Leucker, M., Schallhart, C.: Runtime verification for LTL and TLTL. Technical Report TUM-I0724, Technische Universität München (2007)
43. d'Amorim, M., Roşu, G.: Efficient monitoring of ω-languages. In: Etessami, K., Rajamani, S.K. (eds.) CAV 2005. LNCS, vol. 3576, pp. 364–378. Springer, Heidelberg (2005)
44. Barringer, H., Rydeheard, D.E., Havelund, K.: Rule systems for run-time monitoring: From Eagle to RuleR. In: Sokolsky, O., Taşıran, S. (eds.) RV 2007. LNCS, vol. 4839, pp. 111–125. Springer, Heidelberg (2007)
45. Ligatti, J.A.: Policy Enforcement via Program Monitoring. PhD thesis, Princeton University (2006)
46. Falcone, Y., Mounier, L., Fernandez, J.C., Richier, J.L.: Runtime enforcement monitors: composition, synthesis, and enforcement abilities (2010), under revision at Formal Methods in System Design. Preprint as Verimag TR 2008-7
47. Ligatti, J., Bauer, L., Walker, D.: Enforcing non-safety security policies with program monitors. In: di Vimercati, S.d.C., Syverson, P.F., Gollmann, D. (eds.) ESORICS 2005. LNCS, vol. 3679, pp. 355–373. Springer, Heidelberg (2005)
48. Ligatti, J., Bauer, L., Walker, D.: Edit automata: Enforcement mechanisms for run-time security policies. Int. Journal of Information Security 4, 2–16 (2005)
49. Fong, P.W.L.: Access control by tracking shallow execution history. In: Proceedings of the 2004 IEEE Symposium on Security and Privacy, pp. 43–55 (2004)
50. Talhi, C., Tawbi, N., Debbabi, M.: Execution monitoring enforcement for limited-memory systems. In: PST 2006: Proceedings of the International Conference on Privacy, Security and Trust, pp. 1–12 (2006)
51. Viswanathan, M.: Foundations for the run-time analysis of software systems. PhD thesis, University of Pennsylvania, Philadelphia, PA, USA (2000)
52. Beauquier, D., Cohen, J., Lanotte, R.: Security policies enforcement using finite edit automata. Electr. Notes Theor. Comput. Sci. 229, 19–35 (2009)
53. Perrin, D., Pin, J.E.: Infinite Words, Automata, Semigroups, Logic and Games. Elsevier, Amsterdam (2004)
54. Martinelli, F., Matteucci, I.: Through modeling to synthesis of security automata. Electronic Notes in Theoritical Compututer Science 179, 31–46 (2007)
55. Matteucci, I.: Automated synthesis of enforcing mechanisms for security properties in a timed setting. Elec. Notes in Theoritical Comp. Science 186, 101–120 (2007)
56. Falcone, Y., Fernandez, J.C., Mounier, L.: Synthesizing enforcement monitors wrt. the safety-progress classification of properties. In: Sekar, R., Pujari, A.K. (eds.) ICISS 2008. LNCS, vol. 5352, pp. 41–55. Springer, Heidelberg (2008)
57. Chabot, H., Khoury, R., Tawbi, N.: Generating in-line monitors for Rabin automata. In: NordSec 2009: 14th Nordic Conf. on Secure IT Systems, pp. 287–301 (2009)

Runtime Verification for the Web
A Tutorial Introduction to Interface Contracts in Web Applications

Sylvain Hallé[1] and Roger Villemaire[2]

[1] Université du Québec à Chicoutimi, Canada
shalle@acm.org
[2] Université du Québec à Montréal, Canada
villemaire.roger@uqam.ca

Abstract. This tutorial presents an introduction to the monitoring of web applications. These applications run in a user's web browser and exchange requests and responses with a server in the background to update their display. A demo application, called the Beep Store, illustrates why complex properties on this exchange must be verified at runtime. These properties can be formalized using an extension of Linear Temporal Logic called LTL-FO$^+$. The tutorial concludes with the presentation of BeepBeep, a lightweight runtime monitor for web applications.

1   Introduction

In the past decade, numerous applications, such as Facebook and Google Mail, have become part of popular culture. These so-called "web" applications come into the scope of a programming paradigm called *cloud computing*, where the user's web browser is responsible for loading from a server and displaying the various elements of the application's page. The user can interact with some of these elements, which in turn trigger the browser to send further requests to the server, and update the display.

To be properly understood by their respective recipients, each request and each response is expected to follow a specific structure, where the possible operations, parameters and values are precisely defined. In many cases, the browser-server exchange also moves forward according to a protocol, where the validity of a request depends on past events.

The technologies over which web applications are built were not designed with complex interactions in mind. Consequently, they do not provide facilities to define or enforce such an "interface contract". Ensuring a correct match between the browser's and the server's behaviour is an open problem, currently left as the developer's sole responsibility. Recording the sequence of requests and responses, and providing a means of preventing contract violations from occurring is an appealing prospect in this regard.

The present tutorial summarizes our experiments in the enforcement of interface contracts in web applications. Its interest lies primarily in providing a

G. Roşu et al. (Eds.): RV 2010, LNCS 6418, pp. 106–121, 2010.

self-contained introduction to a domain that meets many favourable conditions for the application of runtime verification techniques. To this end, Section 2 presents a running web application typical of many real-world web services we studied in the past; Section 3 discusses the interface contract for this application. Section 4 introduces a formal language, LTL-FO$^+$, expressive enough for the constraints encountered, and describes how BeepBeep, a lightweight LTL-FO$^+$ runtime monitor, can be integrated into the initial application to effectively enforce the contract.

2   Anatomy of a Web Application: The Beep Store

For the purpose of this tutorial, we designed a simple web application called the Beep Store that will be used as a running example to illustrate web-based runtime verification concepts.

2.1   End-User Perspective

The Beep Store allows registered users to browse a fictional collection of books and music, and to manage a virtual shopping cart made of these elements. It runs out-of-the-box in any modern web browser pointed at the store's URL.[1]

Fig. 1. The Beep Store's web interface

Figure 1 shows a typical application screen. At any time, users can use the search box at the top right of the screen to type any keyword. Similarly, they can click on the "Search an item" menu element at the left to summon a more complete search pane, where they can restrict the search to a specific artist, a specific title, and split the result into pages of a fixed number of entries.

Pressing the "Go" button retrieves from the server the list of all relevant entries. Optionally, users have the option of adding an item from that list into

---

[1] http://beepbeep.sourceforge.net/examples/beepstore

a personal inventory called a "shopping cart". To do so, they must first log into the application (using the "Sign in" link at the top of the page) and provide their username and password. A shopping cart is automatically created when users add their first item into it.

Once a cart is created, a "Your Cart" button (not shown) appears at the right of the search box. Clicking this button opens the cart pane, which displays the list of all items currently in the user's cart, their quantity and total price. Buttons allow the user to edit the quantity for an item, or remove it altogether. Each action updates the cart's list on the fly.

Such a scenario is a purposefully condensed version of popular commercial web sites, such as Amazon or eBay. Indeed, although the Beep Store is a demo application, all its functionalities —and constraints on its use, as we shall see— have been found in at least one of the real-world web services we studied in the past [14]. This includes in particular the User-Controlled Lightpath Service [7], the Amazon e-Commerce Service [1], and the PayPal Express Checkout Service [2].

2.2   Internal Workings

Asynchronous JavaScript and XML (Ajax) refers to the collection of technologies used to develop such rich and interactive web applications. The execution of an Ajax application in a web browser is a straightforward process. First, the client's browser loads the application's page, `beepstore.html`. It uses it to render the page's content by interpreting its markup elements: text boxes, buttons, menu elements, headings, images. The header of this HTML file contains a link to a JavaScript document hosted in the same directory, called `beepstore.js`.

The JavaScript functions it contains are used for three purposes. First, it associates snippets of code to some page elements. For example, a button in the HTML file can be linked to a JavaScript function through the `onClick` event; any click on this button triggers the execution of the associated JavaScript function. Second, the web browser provides a JavaScript object, called `document`, whose methods can be used to access the HTML page's elements and modify their content and appearance dynamically. Hence, the button's `onClick` event can toggle the visibility of some page section that was previously hidden, producing an effect similar to a pop-up window. With proper coding, JavaScript can reproduce in the browser most of the look-and-feel of a traditional desktop application.

The last use of JavaScript is for the handling of requests and responses over the network. This is done through a standard object called `XMLHttpRequest`, also provided by the local browser.[2]

2.3   Interaction through XML

The second part of an Ajax application is a script running on the server side, and answering to requests initiated by the local browser's `XMLHttpRequest`

---

[2] An exception is Internet Explorer, which exposes the same functionalities under a different object called `MSXML`. Their differences are superficial.

object. In the case of the Beep Store, a PHP script called `beepstore.php` acts as the application's front door on the server. Data is exchanged using a standard markup called XML. Each XML document sent and received is called a *message*, and the communication between the browser and the server hence generates a message sequence.

Figure 2 shows the structure of two typical request-response pairs of messages sent by the Beep Store's application to its server. For instance, Figure 2(a) shows the message sent by the browser when a user clicks on the Login button: it includes an element called `Action` whose value indicates the name of the action to be executed by the server, and two additional parameters providing a `Username` and `Password`. The actual values inserted inside these two elements are dynamically fetched by the JavaScript function responsible for sending the Login message on the browser.

```
<Message>
 <Action>Login</Action>
 <Username>Sylvain</Username>
 <Password>banana</Password>
</Message>
```

(a) Login (request)

```
<Message>
 <Action>LoginResponse</Action>
 <SessionKey>123456</SessionKey>
</Message>
```

(b) Login (response)

```
<Message>
<Action>CartCreate</Action>
<SessionKey>123456</SessionKey>
<Items>
 <Item>
  <ItemId>123</ItemId>
  <Quantity>1</Quantity>
 </Item>
 ...
</Items>
</Message>
```

(c) Create a cart (request)

```
<Message>
 <Action>CartCreateResponse</Action>
 <SessionKey>123456</SessionKey>
 <CartID>789123</CartId>
 <Items>
  <Item>
   <ItemId>123</ItemId>
   <Quantity>1</Quantity>
   <Price>12.00</Price>
   <Author>The Beatniks</Author>
   <Title>Yelp!</Title>
  </Item>
  ...
 </Items>
</Message>
```

(d) Create a cart (response)

Fig. 2. Examples of XML messages for the Beep Store

The server's PHP script processes this request by checking that the name-password pair is contained in its user database. In such a case, it creates and records a new unique session key, and produces the response message shown in Figure 2(b). The JavaScript code on the client side parses it and keeps the session key in local memory for future requests.

Request and response messages for cart creation, shown in Figure 2(c)-(d), are more complex. In addition to the `Action` and `SessionKey`, the creation request includes a compound element, `Items`, itself made of one or more `Item` elements. Each item specifies an item ID (taken from the store's catalogue) and the quantity of this item to be included in the cart. The response returned by the server repeats that information, provides a unique ID to the newly created cart, and adds pricing, title and author information for each item, as obtained from the store's database.

2.4   The Beep Store as a Web Service

One can see how the exchange of XML messages outsources the application's core functionalities to the server over the network, leaving the client with only the lighter, GUI-related processing. For example, database search and cart manipulations are handled by the server, which only sends the results of these operations to the browser for proper display. This architecture is appealing, if only for practical reasons: a browser-side search for an item would involve downloading the whole store's catalogue on the client.

As a matter of fact, the server's functionality is not limited to this particular web client: it is made publicly available as an instance of a *web service*. Any third-party developer can produce a working pair of HTML/JavaScript files and send requests to the Beep Store's PHP script; provided that the requests are properly formed and sent in a reasonable sequence, the store's script will serve them.

Similarly, a different server, accepting the same messages as the Beep Store, could be used indifferently by the web client. A web service can even send requests to another service. Ultimately, the vision of web services is to separate functionalities into simple, stand-alone units, communicating over the network through standardized mechanisms such as XML messaging. A web application is a particular case of this scenario consisting of a single browser-server pair.

3   Interface Contracts in Web Applications

The appealing modularity of web services is the source of one major issue: how can one ensure the interaction between each application and each service proceeds as was intended by their respective providers? Without any clear and mutual understanding of the acceptable requests and responses, an Ajax client might try to send a message that the server does not recognize, and vice versa. A correct interoperation between a client and a service is only guaranteed if both partners follow a well defined and enforceable *interface contract*.

3.1   The Beep Store Interface Contract

The source for such an interface contract invariably comes from the service's documentation, intended for developers. The online documentation for the Beep Store[3] is modelled after that of real-world web services, in particular the Amazon E-Commerce Service.

---

[3] http://beepbeep.sourceforge.net/examples/beepstore/documentation

The first observable part of an interface contract that this documentation provides consists of the description of all the XML request and response messages for each operation, in a way similar to Figure 2. Any client and service must produce messages following the structure mentioned there.

In addition, accompanying text explains the semantics of each operation, and lists a number of conditions that must be fulfilled for each operation to be properly processed and return a response. Some of these constraints have been purposefully integrated into the Beep Store to faithfully reproduce behaviour found in some real-world web service we studied. Our prior work led us to divide these constraints into three categories:

Data Constraints. The first class of properties expresses constraints over the structure and values inside a single message at a time. For example, in the `ItemSearch` message:

P1. The element `Page` must be an integer between 1 and 20.
P2. The element `Page` is mandatory only if `Results` is present; otherwise it is forbidden.

These requirements go beyond the specification of a rigid XML structure: they also provide ranges for possible values, and even state that the presence of some element be dependent on the presence of another. Further data constraints could, for example, impose possible values for some element as a function of the value in another element —an example of such a constraint can be found in the Amazon E-Commerce Service [12].

Control-Flow Constraints. Other restrictions are related to the sequence in which operations are invoked. Any application introducing the concept of session, or manipulating persistent objects such as a shopping cart, includes control-flow constraints of that kind. For example:

P3. The `Login` request cannot be resent if its response is successful.
P4. All cart operations, such as `CartCreate`, must follow a successful `Login-Response`.

These constraints introduce the notion of *state* into the application: the possible future messages allowed depend on what has happened in the past. Indeed, it does not make sense for a user to try to login again after a successful login. Similarly, since shopping carts must be associated to a logged user, it is impossible to create such a cart without first logging in. An attempt at such operations hints at some programming flaw on the client side, and should be replied by an error message from the server.

Data-Aware Constraints. Furthermore, the Beep Store includes properties referencing data elements inside exchanged messages, such that these data elements are taken at two different moments in the execution and need to be compared. Properties having this characteristic have been dubbed "data-aware" temporal properties [15]. For example:

P5. There can be at most one active cart ID per session key.
P6. You cannot add the same item twice to the shopping cart.

Property 5 obviously forbids a client to involve a `CartCreate` operation twice. However, it also requires that at any time, the `CartId` value found in a message be the same for all subsequent messages. This must be respected both by the client (which cannot try to sneak information about another cart by simply providing a different ID) and the server (which cannot change a cart's ID after it has been communicated to the client).

Property 6, although seemingly counter-intuitive, has actually been found in the Amazon E-Commerce Service, as reported in [14]. The service requires that, to add one more of an existing item into a cart, the `CartEdit` operation be invoked on that item instead of repeating a `CartAdd` message. Therefore, this property entails that any `ItemId` appearing in a `CartAdd` message no longer appears in a future `CartAdd` (unless the item is found in a `CartRemove` message in between).

The reader is referred to the Beep Store documentation for a list of all constraints in the interface contract; further examples of constraints in other scenarios can be found in our earlier papers [13, 15, 14].

3.2   Issues with Current Technologies

The examples shown above represent a small portion of all the constraints imposed by the Beep Store. The interface contract for a typical web service is made of dozens of such properties. However, as numerous and well-documented as these properties are, the technologies over which web applications are built bring a number of issues when it comes to handling them.

Free-Form Messages. As such, there is no "web service protocol". The closest one gets to such a concept is with the Simple Object Access Protocol (SOAP) [20], itself built as a special case of the HTTP protocol that web browsers have been using for decades. A SOAP request is little more than a collection of HTTP headers, followed by an XML payload formed of two mandatory sections: `Head` and `Body` (the XML documents in Figure 2 are sent inside the `Body`). Apart from these conditions, SOAP regards the payload as a free-form document. This entails that the message structure —the web equivalent of types in a classical programming language— is not even checked.

Stateful Behaviour, Stateless Protocol. HTTP is also a *stateless* protocol, where each new request processed by the server is detached from previous ones, and unrelated to those that follow. At the time HTTP was designed, this characteristic was appealing for its simplicity of implementation and the limited resources it requires for processing a request. Yet, we have seen how the Beep Store, typical of many web applications, requires long-running interactions spanning multiple requests and responses, and where past requests determine current valid ones.

Since session logic is not carried transparently through the protocol, it must be explicitly handled by the application itself. This is why the Beep Store must simulate sessions through a sequence of individual request-response pairs, where a unique identifier created at the start of a session (the `SessionKey`) is repeated in each subsequent message. The session's state (shopping cart contents, user name) is written to persistent storage between requests and can be retrieved using this identifier.

No Standardized Contract Notation. It follows from these observations that most properties of an interface contract lie at a higher conceptual level than current web protocols. Their expression and enforcement should therefore be handled in an extra control layer on top of HTTP and SOAP.

The only part of interface contracts that made it to some form of standardization is the Web Service Description Language (WSDL) [9]. WSDL allows the creation of an auxiliary document that specifies the XML structure of each request and response accepted by a service. Existing software frameworks, such as Apache Axis [3], can generate template functions called *stubs* for each message. By communicating only through these auto-generated stubs, a client or server can be guaranteed to send only WSDL-compliant messages. The same stubs can also verify at runtime that any incoming message follows the WSDL specification.

If the generation of WSDL-based stubs and the runtime verification of message structures is now considered routine, the Beep Store shows that there is much more to interface contracts than checking XML message structures: WSDL runtime verification only traps violations of Property 1. No standardized language exists to express Properties 2-6; no framework helps building an application that complies with them, or traps their violations at runtime. A developer needs to peruse the service's natural language documentation, and check each constraint manually with a copious amount of tests.

To illustrate this fact, the Beep Store browser client can be turned into a deliberately faulty application. Its user interface contains a "Fault Parameters" pane, shown in Figure 3, that provides the complete list of constraints specified by the store's documentation. Normally, the client is robust and performs thorough checks of all these constraints before sending any message to the server. For example, once a shopping cart is created, it hides the "Create cart" button to avoid users creating a second one (see P5). Similarly, it hides the Login button once a user has successfully logged in (see P4). With the Fault pane, the user can tick the checkbox for any of these constraints, causing the application to bypass these measures and allow actions at inappropriate moments.

3.3 Particularities of Web Service Interface Contracts

Web service interface contracts bear many resemblances with temporal properties or contracts found in other domains. In object-oriented languages, some classes, such as Java's `File` or `Iterator`, also impose constraints on the sequence of method calls; these class contracts can be checked at runtime using tools such

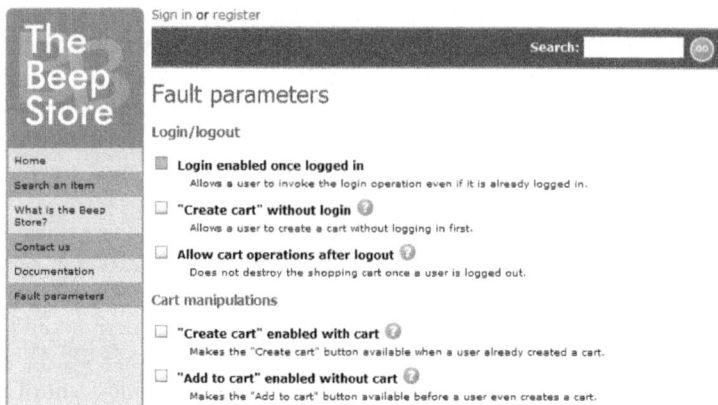

Fig. 3. The Beep Store's "Fault Parameters" pane allows the application to deliberately ignore some elements of its interface contract, causing the server to reply with an error message on purpose

as Java-MOP [8]. Similarly, research on trace validation applied to spacecraft test sequences unveiled constraints that correlate both data values and ordering of events [6]. This hints that existing solutions developed for other scenarios could be ported to the web service realm. However, web services exhibits a combination of characteristics that makes them unique.

Data-Aware Dependencies. Simplified versions of the contract properties could be verified using classical Petri nets, finite state automata or propositional linear temporal logic. However, many constraints can only be faithfully checked by taking into account dependencies between data parameters. Obviously, the data elements cannot be enumerated statically: Property 6 would have to be repeated for every item in the Beep Store's catalogue, which would be required to be known in advance.

Data-aware dependencies do not merely require the access to parameters inside a message; they also need such values to be kept, and compared at a later time with values inside another message. Moreover, the time separating these two messages is unknown in advance, and potentially unbounded; hence it does not suffice to keep a fixed-size window of past messages.

Complex Message Structure. Not only do most messages contain an action name and a set of data parameters, these parameters themselves are subject to a potentially complex XML structure. In the Beep Store, one cannot simply refer to "the" item ID in a shopping cart, as there can be multiple instances of the ItemId element in a message. A property can require that all, or only one of these item IDs fulfils a constraint, hence a form of quantification over message contents is required.

This is probably the single most distinguishing point with respect to other verification applications. Most verification solutions that take data dependencies into account work in a context where there is at most one instance of a parameter in a message (removing the need for quantification).

4   Runtime Verification of Interface Contracts

The previous sections described how the architecture of web applications, coupled with the state of current technologies, calls for a runtime verification solution of interface contracts. This section describes the authors' attempts at developing and running a possible solution. It first shows how the properties in Section 3 can be expressed in a formal language, called LTL-FO$^+$. It then presents BeepBeep, a Java-based runtime monitor for LTL-FO$^+$. BeepBeep can be integrated into the Beep Store described in Section 2, and enforce its interface contract at runtime.

4.1   Formalizing Contracts with LTL-FO$^+$

LTL-FO$^+$ is an extension of Linear Temporal Logic (LTL) developed to address the characteristics of web application interface contracts. Relating the expressiveness of this logic to other solutions has extensively been done in previous papers [15, 19].

Let Q be a set of queries, M a set of messages, and V a set of atomic values. A *query function* π is defined as $\pi : Q \times M \to 2^V$. Intuitively, $\pi(q, m)$ retrieves a set of values from a message m, given some "filtering criterion" q. We typically use as π the function that takes as query a path in an XML document (a slash-separated list of element names) and which returns all the values at the end of such a path in the current message. For example, in the following message m, we have $\pi(\text{"message/item"}, m) = \{A, B\}$.

```
<Message>
    <Item>A</Item>
    <Item>B</Item>
    <Client>10</Client>
</Message>
```

A *message trace* is a sequence $\overline{m} = m_1 m_2 \ldots$ such that $m_i \in M$ for $i \geq 1$; $\overline{m}^i$ denotes the suffix of $m_i m_{i+1} \ldots$.

Definition 1 (Syntax). *The language LTL-FO$^+$ (Linear Temporal Logic with Full First-order Quantification) is obtained by closing LTL under the following construction rules:*

1. *If x and y are variables or constants, then $x = y$ is a LTL-FO$^+$ formula;*
2. *If φ and ψ are LTL-FO$^+$ formulæ, then $\neg\varphi$, $\varphi \wedge \psi$, $\varphi \vee \psi$, $\varphi \to \psi$, $\mathbf{G}\,\varphi$, $\mathbf{F}\,\varphi$, $\mathbf{X}\,\varphi$, $\varphi\,\mathbf{U}\,\psi$, $\varphi\,\mathbf{V}\,\psi$ are LTL-FO$^+$ formulæ;*
3. *If φ is a LTL-FO$^+$ formula, x_i is a free variable in φ, $q \in Q$ is a query expression, then $\exists_q x_i : \varphi$ and $\forall_q x_i : \varphi$ are LTL-FO$^+$ formulæ.*

Definition 2 (Semantics). *We say a message trace* $\overline{m}$ *satisfies the LTL-FO$^+$ formula* φ, *and write* $\overline{m} \models \varphi$ *if and only if it respects the following rules: if* φ *is of the form* $\neg\psi$, $\psi \vee \psi'$, $\mathbf{F}\,\psi$, $\mathbf{X}\,\psi$ *and* $\psi\,\mathbf{U}\,\psi'$, *the semantics is identical to LTL's. Let* $q \in Q$ *be some query expression. The remaining cases are defined as:*

$$\overline{m} \models c_1 = c_2 \Leftrightarrow c_1 \text{ is equal to } c_2$$
$$\overline{m} \models \exists_q x_i : \varphi \Leftrightarrow \overline{m} \models \varphi[b/x_i] \text{ for some } b \in \pi(q, m_1)$$

We define the semantics of the other connectives with the usual identities: $\varphi \wedge \psi \equiv \neg(\neg\varphi \vee \neg\psi)$, $\varphi \rightarrow \psi \equiv \neg\varphi \vee \psi$, $\mathbf{G}\,\varphi \equiv \neg(\mathbf{F}\,\neg\varphi)$, $\varphi\,\mathbf{V}\,\psi \equiv \neg(\neg\varphi\,\mathbf{U}\,\neg\psi)$, $\forall_q x : \varphi \equiv \neg(\exists_q x : \neg\varphi)$.

Equipped with this language, it is possible to revisit the interface contract described earlier and formalize it with LTL-FO$^+$ formulæ. Properties 1 and 2 are data constraints; they only involve the temporal operator $\mathbf{G}$ to specify that the data constraint applies to all messages. If we define $q_1 = \texttt{Message/Action}$, $q_2 = \texttt{Message/Page}$ and $q_3 = \texttt{Message/Results}$, then Properties 1 and 2 become respectively equations 1 and 2 below:

$$\mathbf{G}\left(\forall_{q_1} a : a = \texttt{ItemSearch} \rightarrow (\forall_{q_2} p : p \geq 1 \wedge p \leq 20)\right) \qquad (1)$$
$$\mathbf{G}\left(\forall_{q_1} a : a = \texttt{ItemSearch} \rightarrow (\exists_{q_3} r : \top \leftrightarrow \exists_{q_2} p : \top)\right) \qquad (2)$$

The first property states that globally, if the message's action is $\texttt{ItemSearch}$, then for every $\texttt{Page}$ value p inside that message, p is in the range $[1, 20]$. Similarly, the second property states that any $\texttt{ItemSearch}$ message is such that for every $\texttt{Results}$ element, a $\texttt{Page}$ element must exist (π returns the empty set if no element with the specified path can be found in a message). The symbol $\top$ stands for "true"; $\exists_q x : \top$ is true whenever the path q exists.

In a similar way, control-flow properties P3 and P4 become formulæ 3 and 4 below:

$$\mathbf{G}\left(\forall_{q_1} a : a = \texttt{LoginResponse} \rightarrow (\mathbf{X}\,\mathbf{G}\,(\forall_{q_1} a' : a' \neq \texttt{LoginResponse}))\right) \quad (3)$$
$$(\forall_{q_1} a : a \neq \texttt{CartCreate}\,\mathbf{W}\,(\forall_{q_1} a' : a' \neq \texttt{LoginResponse}) \qquad (4)$$

Finally, by defining $q_4 = \texttt{Message/CartId}$, $q_5 = \texttt{Message/SessionKey}$ and $q_6 = \texttt{Message/Items/Item}$, data-aware properties 5 and 6 can be formalized into the following:

$$\mathbf{G}\left(\forall_{q_4} c : \forall_{q_5} k : \mathbf{G}\,(\forall_{q_4} c' : \forall_{q_5} k' : (k = k' \rightarrow c = c'))\right) \qquad (5)$$

$$\mathbf{G}\,(\forall_{q_1} a : a = \texttt{CartAdd} \rightarrow$$
$$(\forall_{q_6} i : \mathbf{X}\,\mathbf{G}\,(\forall_{q_1} a' : a' = \texttt{CartAdd} \rightarrow \forall_{q_6} i' : i \neq i'))) \quad (6)$$

Equation 5 states that in every message, the presence of a $\texttt{CartId}$ c and $\texttt{SessionKey}$ k entails that, from that point on, any other occurrences of a $\texttt{CartId}$ c' and $\texttt{SessionKey}$ k' are such that the same key imposes the same ID. This is equivalent to P5. The "data-awareness" of this constraint can be observed in the fact that two variables that have been quantified across temporal operators (such as c and c') are compared at a later point in the expression.

A particularity of LTL-FO$^+$ lies in its quantification mechanism: note in the definition how the values over which quantification applies are only those found in the *current* message, m_1. For example, in equation 6, variables i and i' both quantify over catalogue item IDs. If quantification did not depend on the current message, the previous formula would always be false, as any value c bound to i would also be admissible for i', making the assertion $i \neq i'$ false at least once. The previous formula rather states that at any time in the execution of the application, for any item ID i appearing in a `CartAdd` message, then from now on in any *future* `CartAdd` message, any item ID i' is different from i. Hence, it will be true exactly when no item appears more than once in any `CartAdd` message, which is consistent with Property 6.

LTL-FO$^+$ allows the Beep Store to publicize a formal version of its interface contract. To this end, an auxiliary file, `contract.txt`, is hosted along with the Beep Store's other files on the server. It contains the list of all LTL-FO$^+$ formulæ forming that contract, including equations (1)-(6) described above. Figure 4 shows a snippet of the contract file containing a text rendition of Property 1.

```
% The page element must be an integer between 1 and 20
; G ((([a /Message/Action] ((a) = ({ItemSearch}))) ->
     ([p /Message/Page] (((p) > ({1})) & ((p) < ({20})))))
```

Fig. 4. A sample contract specification. Each constraint is preceded by a caption.

4.2   The BeepBeep Runtime Monitor

Since LTL-FO$^+$ draws heavily on classical LTL, a runtime verification procedure can be obtained from an algorithm presented in [10], which creates the Büchi automaton for a given LTL formula. This algorithm performs on the fly and generates the automaton as the sequence of states unwinds. The LTL-FO$^+$ monitoring procedure, detailed in [15], is an extension of this algorithm, adapted for first-order quantification on message elements.

LTL-FO$^+$ monitoring can then be implemented into a lightweight tool for web applications. It suffices that incoming and outgoing messages be intercepted as "events" and fed to the monitor. The algorithm updates its internal state according to the processed event, and eventually blocks the actual transmission or reception if a violation is discovered.

Since a web application is inherently distributed, the location of this monitor leads to multiple architectural choices, shown in Figure 5. In client-side verification, shown in Figure 5(a), contract compliance is checked in the user's web browser before any message is allowed to be transmitted over the network: an outgoing message m is sent to a function δ monitoring a specification φ. Incoming messages are filtered in the same way before reaching the application's code. Server-side verification 5(b) works on the opposite. A third solution is to use a third-party protocol coordinator (not shown) as suggested by [5]. The coordinator ideally resides neither in the client's browser nor in the web server, and acts as a monitoring proxy for both ends of the communication. To illustrate monitoring on the client side, we developed BeepBeep, a lightweight, Java-based runtime monitor for Ajax web applications.[4]

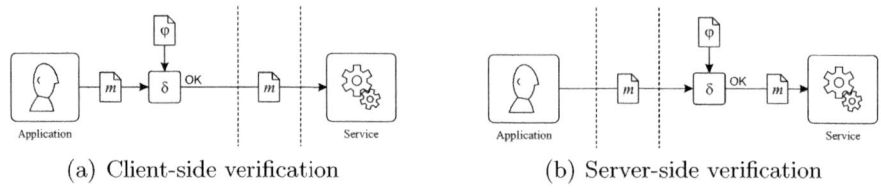

(a) Client-side verification   (b) Server-side verification

Fig. 5. Design choices for runtime verification of web applications

In classical (e.g. Java) programs, intercepting events generally requires instrumenting the code or resorting to mechanisms such as pointcuts [8]. In the present case, network operations converge to a single input-output point, the standard XMLHttpRequest object provided by the local browser. It becomes easy to interpose an extra layer of processing over that object, without resorting to any other form of instrumentation.

Including BeepBeep into an existing Ajax application is straightforward. It suffices to host BeepBeep's two files (beepbeep.jar, the Java applet, and beepbeep.js, an auxiliary JavaScript file) in the same directory as the Ajax application. BeepBeep is bootstrapped by adding a single line in the <head> portion of the application's HTML page.

When such a BeepBeep-enabled application is started, the procedure described in Section 2.2 is followed. BeepBeep's additional JavaScript include file dynamically appends the snippet of HTML code instructing the browser to load the Java applet implementing the LTL-FO$^+$ monitoring algorithm, which appears as a small rectangle at the bottom of the application's page. The specification passed to the applet is automatically retrieved from the contract.txt file hosted on the server.

The JavaScript code also overloads the methods of the standard XMLHttp-Request object. When the original application's JavaScript invokes the send method of XMLHttpRequest, it actually calls the method implemented by Beep-Beep first. This way, incoming and outgoing messages, before being actually sent (or returned), can be deviated to the applet for verification.

4.3   Wrapping Up

We can now return to the Beep Store application and perform runtime monitoring of its interface contract on the client side. Assuming that the store provides

---

[4] BeepBeep and its source code are available for download under a free software license: http://beepbeep.sourceforge.net

a contract file and hosts the two BeepBeep files, we can then modify its HTML code to include the additional JavaScript file, as described above.

The monitor-enabled Beep Store application can be started as usual in a standard browser. As previously, one can open the store's Fault parameters pane, and disable, for example, the internal enforcement of property 3 ("don't login twice"). This time, however, the rectangle at the bottom of the page tells us that BeepBeep successfully fetched a contract and is awaiting for incoming or outgoing XML messages.

The first login attempt can be executed as expected. BeepBeep's display updates, indicating that it indeed witnessed the corresponding messages, but let them through as they did not violate any constraint. After successfully logging in, as expected the faulty client fails to hide the Login link. Clicking on it a second time summons the Login pane, where one can enter the same credentials and press on the Login button. Like before, the client attempts to send a `Login` XML message; however, this time, BeepBeep intercepts the message, correctly discovers that it violates property 3, and skips the piece of code that would normally send it. It also pops a window alerting the user, showing the caption associated with the violated property in the contract file.

This scenario has also been experimented on a real-world web application for the Amazon E-Commerce Service [16]. Our findings indicate that on a low-end computer, monitoring LTL-FO$^+$ contract properties produces an average overhead of around 3% or 10 ms per message in absolute numbers. As a rule, the state of the network accounts for wider variations than the additional processing required by the monitor.

It shall be noted that BeepBeep is independent of any browser-server pair of applications. Its Java applet is self-contained, and the JavaScript auxiliary file can be included into any web page and load it at startup. It can correctly intercept and process any request as long as it is XML-based. Similarly, the contract to be monitored is hosted in a separate text file that is read each time the applet is loaded —hence the contract can be changed without changing the monitor. This way, BeepBeep is a runtime monitoring solution that can be applied to other scenarios than the Beep Store: it suffices to write an appropriate contract for the application under study.

5 Conclusion

This tutorial has highlighted the potential for the application of runtime verification techniques to the field of web services; yet several interesting questions have been left out from this presentation. For example, since events in web applications are sequences of XML messages, it is possible to treat a sequence of such events as one large XML "document" and leverage commercial XML query processors to perform an equivalent validation of message traces [18]. However, the monitoring of quantified formulæ presents a potential for unbounded resource consumption. The *forward-only fragment* of LTL is an ongoing attempt at providing a bounded subset of the logic suitable for limited environments [17].

Finally, if the goal of client-side monitoring is to relieve the server from the burden of dealing with faulty clients, how can one be certain that a client indeed monitors the contract? The concept of *cooperative runtime monitoring* [11] has recently been put forward to resolve such an issue.

Finally, it could be very well possible that application developers refrain from integrating more complex behaviours into their web applications precisely for lack of tools to deal with them in a systematic way. Hence even a modest contribution from runtime verification to the practitioner's toolbox could enhance the quality and ease of development of web applications. In this regard, we hope this tutorial will encourage researchers in the monitoring and validation community to consider web applications as a potential field of application to their work.

References

1. Amazon e-commerce service, http://solutions.amazonwebservices.com
2. Paypal web service API documentation, http://www.paypal.com
3. Apache Axis (2010), http://ws.apache.org/axis2
4. ASE 2010, 25th IEEE/ACM International Conference on Automated Software Engineering, Antwerp, Belgium, September 20-24. IEEE Computer Society, Los Alamitos (2010)
5. Alonso, G., Casati, F., Kuno, H., Machiraju, V.: Web Services, Concepts, Architectures and Applications, p. 354. Springer, Heidelberg (2004)
6. Barringer, H., Havelund, K., Rydeheard, D.E., Groce, A.: Rule systems for runtime verification: A short tutorial. In: Bensalem, S., Peled, D. (eds.) RV 2009. LNCS, vol. 5779, pp. 1–24. Springer, Heidelberg (2009)
7. Boutaba, R., Golab, W., Iraqi, Y., Arnaud, B.S.: Lightpaths on demand: A web-services-based management system. IEEE Communications Magazine, 2–9 (July 2004)
8. Chen, F., d'Amorim, M., Roşu, G.: Checking and correcting behaviors of java programs at runtime with Java-MOP. Electr. Notes Theor. Comput. Sci. 144(4), 3–20 (2006)
9. Christensen, E., Curbera, F., Meredith, G., Weerawarana, S.: Web services description language (WSDL) 1.1, W3C note (2001)
10. Gerth, R., Peled, D., Vardi, M.Y., Wolper, P.: Simple on-the-fly automatic verification of linear temporal logic. In: Dembinski, P., Sredniawa, M. (eds.) PSTV. IFIP Conference Proceedings, vol. 38, pp. 3–18. Chapman & Hall, Boca Raton (1995)
11. Hallé, S.: Cooperative runtime monitoring of LTL interface contracts. In: EDOC. IEEE Computer Society, Los Alamitos (to appear, October 2010)
12. Hallé, S., Bultan, T., Hughes, G., Alkhalaf, M., Villemaire, R.: Runtime verification of web service interface contracts. IEEE Computer 43(3), 59–66 (2010)
13. Hallé, S., Ettema, T., Bunch, C., Bultan, T.: Eliminating navigation errors in web applications via model checking and runtime enforcement of navigation state machines. In: ASE [4] (2010)
14. Hallé, S., Hughes, G., Bultan, T., Alkhalaf, M.: Generating interface grammars from WSDL for automated verification of web services. In: Baresi, L., Chi, C.-H., Suzuki, J. (eds.) ICSOC-ServiceWave 2009. LNCS, vol. 5900, pp. 516–530. Springer, Heidelberg (2009)
15. Hallé, S., Villemaire, R.: Runtime monitoring of message-based workflows with data. In: EDOC, pp. 63–72. IEEE Computer Society, Los Alamitos (2008)

16. Hallé, S., Villemaire, R.: Browser-based enforcement of interface contracts in web applications with BeepBeep. In: Bouajjani, A., Maler, O. (eds.) Computer Aided Verification. LNCS, vol. 5643, pp. 648–653. Springer, Heidelberg (2009)
17. Hallé, S., Villemaire, R.: Runtime monitoring of web service choreographies using streaming XML. In: Shin, S.Y., Ossowski, S. (eds.) SAC, pp. 2118–2125. ACM, New York (2009)
18. Hallé, S., Villemaire, R.: XML query evaluation in validation and monitoring of web service interface contracts. In: dvanced Applications and Structures in XML Processing: Label Streams, Semantics Utilization and Data Query Technologies, pp. 406–424. IGI Global (2010)
19. Hallé, S., Villemaire, R., Cherkaoui, O.: Specifying and validating data-aware temporal web service properties. IEEE Trans. Software Eng. 35(5), 669–683 (2009)
20. Mitra, N., Lafon, Y.: SOAP version 1.2 part 0: Primer, 2nd edn. (2007), http://www.w3.org/TR/2007/REC-soap12-part0-20070427

Statistical Model Checking: An Overview

Axel Legay[1], Benoît Delahaye[1], and Saddek Bensalem[2]

[1] INRIA/IRISA, Rennes, France
[2] Verimag Laboratory, Université Joseph Fourier Grenoble, CNRS, France

Abstract. Quantitative properties of stochastic systems are usually specified in logics that allow one to compare the measure of executions satisfying certain temporal properties with thresholds. The model checking problem for stochastic systems with respect to such logics is typically solved by a numerical approach [31,8,35,22,21,5] that iteratively computes (or approximates) the exact measure of paths satisfying relevant subformulas; the algorithms themselves depend on the class of systems being analyzed as well as the logic used for specifying the properties. Another approach to solve the model checking problem is to *simulate* the system for finitely many executions, and use *hypothesis testing* to infer whether the samples provide a *statistical* evidence for the satisfaction or violation of the specification. In this tutorial, we survey the statistical approach, and outline its main advantages in terms of efficiency, uniformity, and simplicity.

1   Introduction and Context

Quantitative properties of stochastic systems are usually specified in logics that allow one to compare the measure of executions satisfying certain temporal properties with thresholds. The model checking problem for stochastic systems with respect to such logics is typically solved by a numerical approach that iteratively computes (or approximates) the exact measure of paths satisfying relevant subformulas. The algorithm for computing such measures depends on the class of stochastic systems being considered as well as the logics used for specifying the correctness properties. Model checking algorithms for a variety of contexts have been discovered [2,13,8] and there are mature tools (see e.g. [25,7]) that have been used to analyze a variety of systems in practice.

Despite the great strides made by numerical model checking algorithms, there are many challenges. Numerical algorithms work only for special systems that have certain structural properties. Further the algorithms require a lot of time and space, and thus scaling to large systems is a challenge. Finally, the logics for which model checking algorithms exist are extensions of classical temporal logics, which are often not the most popular among engineers.

Another way to verify quantitative properties is to use a simulation-based approach. The key idea is to deduce whether or not the system satisfies the property by observing some of its executions with a monitoring procedure [1,19], and use *hypothesis testing* to infer whether the samples provide a *statistical*

G. Roşu et al. (Eds.): RV 2010, LNCS 6418, pp. 122–135, 2010.

evidence for the satisfaction or violation of the specification [42]. Of course, in contrast to a numerical approach, a simulation-based solution does not guarantee a correct result. However, it is possible to bound the probability of making an error. Simulation-based methods are known to be far less memory and time intensive than numerical ones, and are sometimes the only option [41].

The crux of the statistical model checking approach is that since sample executions of a stochastic system are drawn according to the distribution defined by the system, they can be used to get estimates of the probability measure on executions. Starting from time-bounded Probabilistic Computational Tree Logic properties [42], the technique has been extended to handle properties with unbounded until operators [33], as well as to black-box systems [32,37]. Tools based on this idea have been built [34,39], and they have been used to analyze many systems.

This approach enjoys many advantages. First, these algorithms only require that the system be executable (or rather, sample executions be drawn according to the measure space defined by the system). Thus, it can be applied to larger class of systems than numerical model checking algorithms including black-box systems and infinite state systems. Second the approach can be generalized to a larger class of properties, including Fourier transform based logics. Finally, the algorithm is easily parallelizable, which can help scale to large systems. However, the statistical approach also has some disadvantages when compared with the numerical approach. First, it only provides probabilistic guarantees about the correctness of the algorithms answer. Next, the sample size grows very large if the model checker's answer is required to be highly accurate. Finally, the statistical approach only works for purely probabilistic systems, i.e., those that do not have any nondeterminism. Furthermore, since statistical tests are used to determine the correctness of a system, the approach only works for systems that "robustly" satisfy a given property, i.e., the actual measure of paths satisfying a given subformula, is bounded away from the thresholds to which it is compared in the specification.

In this tutorial, we will overview existing statistical model checking algorithms and discuss their efficiency. We will also overview existing tools and case studies and discuss future work.

2   Our Objective

We consider a stochastic system $\mathcal{S}$ and a property ϕ. An *execution* of $\mathcal{S}$ is a possibly infinite sequence of states of $\mathcal{S}$. Our objective is to solve the *probabilistic model checking problem*, i.e., to decide whether $\mathcal{S}$ satisfies ϕ with a probability greater or equal to a certain threshold θ. The latter is denoted $S \models P_{\geq\theta}(\phi)$, where P is called a *probabilistic operator*. This paper will overview solutions to this problem. These solutions depend on the nature of $\mathcal{S}$ and ϕ. We consider three cases.

1. We first assume that $\mathcal{S}$ is a *white-box system*, i.e., that one can generate as much executions of the system as we want. We also assume that ϕ does

not contain probabilistic operators. In Section 3, we recall basic statistical algorithms that can be used to verify bounded properties (i.e., properties that can be monitored on fixed-length execution) of white-box systems.

2. In Section 4, we discuss extensions to the full probabilistic computation tree logic[8]. There, we consider the case where ϕ can also contain probabilistic operators and the case where it has to be verified on infinite executions.
3. In Section 5, we briefly discuss the verification of *black-box systems*, i.e. systems for which a part of the probability distribution is unknown.

In Section 6, we will present various experiments that show that (1) statistical model checking algorithms can be more efficient than numerical ones, and (2) statistical model checking algorithms can be applied to solve problems that are beyond the scope of numerical methods. Finally, Section 7 discusses our vision of the future of statistical model checking.

Remark 1. The objective of the tutorial is not to feed the reader with technical details, but rather to introduce statistical model checking, and outline its main advantages in terms of efficiency, uniformity, and simplicity.

Remark 2. There are other techniques that allow to estimate the probability for $\mathcal{S}$ to satisfy ϕ. These approaches (that are based on Monte-Carlo techniques) will not be covered in this paper. The interested reader is redirected to [17,20,26] for more details.

Remark 3. Statistical Model Checking also applies to non stochastic systems [17]. This topic will not be covered in this tutorial.

3 Statistical Model Checking : The Beginning

In this section, we overview several statistical model checking techniques. We assume that $\mathcal{S}$ is a white-box system and that ϕ is a bounded property. By bounded properties, we mean properties that can be defined on finite executions of the system. In general, the length of such executions has to be precomputed.

Let B_i be a discrete random variable with a Bernoulli distribution of parameter p. Such a variable can only take two values 0 and 1 with $Pr[B_i = 1] = p$ and $Pr[B_i = 0] = 1 - p$. In our context, each variable B_i is associated with one simulation of the system. The outcome for B_i, denoted b_i, is 1 if the simulation satisfies ϕ and 0 otherwise. To make sure that the above approach works, one has to make sure that one can get the result of any experiment in a finite amount of time. In general, this means that we are considering bounded properties, i.e., properties that can be decided on finite executions.

Remark 4. All the results presented in this section are well-known mathematical results coming from the area of statistics. As we shall see, these results are sufficient to verify bounded properties of a large class of systems. As those properties are enough in many practical applications, one could wonder whether the contribution of the computer scientist should not be at the practical level rather than at the theoretical one.

Before going further one should answer one last question: *"What is the class of models that can be considered?"* In fact, statistical model checking can be applied to any stochastic system and logic on which one can define a *probability space* for the property under consideration. Hence, the approach provides a uniform way for the verification of a wide range of temporal logic properties over various stochastic models, including Markov Chains or Continuous Timed Markov Chains [35,3,2]. In general, it is not necessary to make the hypothesis that the system has the Markovian property[1], except when working with nested formulas (see Section 4). It is worth mentioning that the technique cannot be applied to systems that combine both nondeterministic and stochastic aspects (such as Markov Decision Processes). Indeed, the simulation-based approach could not distinguish between the probability distributions that are sampled.

3.1   Qualitative Answer Using Statistical Model Checking

The main approaches [38,32] proposed to answer the qualitative question are based on *hypothesis testing*. Let $p = Pr(\phi)$, to determine whether $p \geq \theta$, we can test $H : p \geq \theta$ against $K : p < \theta$. A test-based solution does not guarantee a correct result but it is possible to bound the probability of making an error. The *strength* (α, β) of a test is determined by two parameters, α and β, such that the probability of accepting K (respectively, H) when H (respectively, K) holds, called a Type-I error (respectively, a Type-II error) is less or equal to α (respectively, β).

A test has *ideal performance* if the probability of the Type-I error (respectively, Type-II error) is exactly α (respectively, β). However, these requirements make it impossible to ensure a low probability for both types of errors simultaneously (see [38] for details). A solution to this problem is to relax the test by working with an *indifference region* (p_1, p_0) with $p_0 \geq p_1$ ($p_0 - p_1$ is the *size of the region*). In this context, we test the hypothesis $H_0 : p \geq p_0$ against $H_1 : p \leq p_1$ instead of H against K. If the value of p is between p_1 and p_0 (the indifference region), then we say that the probability is sufficiently close to θ so that we are indifferent with respect to which of the two hypotheses K or H is accepted. The thresholds p_0 and p_1 are generally defined in term of the single threshold θ, e.g., $p_1 = \theta - \delta$ and $p_0 = \theta + \delta$. We now need to provide a test procedure that satisfies the requirements above. In the next two subsections, we recall two solutions proposed by Younes in [38,43].

Single Sampling Plan. To test H_0 against H_1, we specify a constant c. If $\sum_{i=1}^{n} b_i$ is larger than c, then H_0 is accepted, else H_1 is accepted. The difficult part in this approach is to find values for the pair (n, c), called a *single sampling plan (SSP in short)*, such that the two error bounds α and β are respected. In practice, one tries to work with the smallest value of n possible so as to minimize the number of simulations performed. Clearly, this number has to be greater if α and β are smaller but also if the size of the indifference region is smaller. This results in

---

[1] The Markovian property ensures that the probability to go from a state s to a next state only depends on s, not on the states that have been visited before reaching s.

an optimization problem, which generally does not have a closed-form solution except for a few special cases [38]. In his thesis [38], Younes proposes a binary search based algorithm that, given p_0, p_1, α, β, computes an approximation of the minimal value for c and n.

Remark 5. There are many variants of this algorithm. As an example, in [33], Sen et al. proposes to accept H_0 if $\frac{(\sum_{i=1}^{n} b_i)}{n} \geq p$. Here, the difficulty is to find a value for n such that the error bounds are valid.

Sequential probability ratio test. The sample size for a single sampling plan is fixed in advance and independent of the observations that are made. However, taking those observations into account can increase the performance of the test. As an example, if we use a single plan (n, c) and the $m > c$ first simulations satisfy the property, then we could (depending on the error bounds) accept H_0 without observing the $n - m$ other simulations. To overcome this problem, one can use the *sequential probability ratio test (SPRT in short)* proposed by Wald [36]. The approach is briefly described below.

In SPRT, one has to choose two values A and B ($A > B$) that ensure that the strength of the test is respected. Let m be the number of observations that have been made so far. The test is based on the following quotient:

$$\frac{p_{1m}}{p_{0m}} = \prod_{i=1}^{m} \frac{Pr(B_i = b_i \mid p = p_1)}{Pr(B_i = b_i \mid p = p_0)} = \frac{p_1^{d_m}(1 - p_1)^{m-d_m}}{p_0^{d_m}(1 - p_0)^{m-d_m}}, \tag{1}$$

where $d_m = \sum_{i=1}^{m} b_i$. The idea behind the test is to accept H_0 if $\frac{p_{1m}}{p_{0m}} \geq A$, and H_1 if $\frac{p_{1m}}{p_{0m}} \leq B$. The SPRT algorithm computes $\frac{p_{1m}}{p_{0m}}$ for successive values of m until either H_0 or H_1 is satisfied; the algorithm terminates with probability 1 [36]. This has the advantage of minimizing the number of simulations. In his thesis [38], Younes proposed a logarithmic based algorithm SPRT that given p_0, p_1, α and β implements the sequential ratio testing procedure.

Discussion. Computing ideal values A_{id} and B_{id} for A and B in order to make sure that we are working with a test of strength (α, β) is a laborious procedure (see Section 3.4 of [36]). In his seminal paper [36], Wald showed that if one defines $A_{id} \geq A = \frac{(1-\beta)}{\alpha}$ and $B_{id} \leq B = \frac{\beta}{(1-\alpha)}$, then we obtain a new test whose strength is (α', β'), but such that $\alpha' + \beta' \leq \alpha + \beta$, meaning that either $\alpha' \leq \alpha$ or $\beta' \leq \beta$. In practice, we often find that both inequalities hold. This is illustrated with the following example taken from [38].

Example 1. Let $p_0 = 0.5$, $p_1 = 0.3$, $\alpha = 0.2$ and $\beta = 0.1$. If we use $A_{id} \geq A = \frac{(1-\beta)}{\alpha}$ and $B_{id} \leq B = \frac{\beta}{(1-\alpha)}$, then we are guaranteed that $\alpha' \leq 0.222$ and $\beta' \leq 0.125$. Through computer simulation (reproducing the same experiments 10000 of time), we observe that $\alpha' \leq 0.175$ and $\beta' \leq 0.082$. So the strength of the test is in reality better than the theoretical assumption.

3.2   Some Generalities Regarding Efficiency

The efficiency of the above algorithms is characterized by the number of simulations needed to obtain an answer as well as the time it costs to compute a simulation. The latter often depends on the property under verification. Both numbers are *expected numbers* as they change from executions to executions and can only be estimated (see [38] for an explanation). However, some generalities are known. For example, it is known that, except for some situations, SPRT is always faster than SSP. When $\theta = 1$ (resp. $\theta = 0$) SPRT degenerates to SSP; it is not a problem since SSP is known to be optimal for such values. Observe that the time complexity of statistical model checking is independent from the state-space and that the space complexity is of the order of the state space. Also, the expected number of simulations for SSP is logarithmic with respect to α and β and linear with respect to the indifference region; for SPRT, the number depends on the probability distribution p.

Remark 6. A very relevant discussion on complexity of statistical model checking can be found in Section 5.4 of [38].

4   Statistical Model Checking: Next Step

In the previous section, we have proposed statistical model checking algorithms for verifying bounded properties of white-box systems. In this section, we go one step further and consider three nontrivial extensions that are:

1. The nested case, i.e., the case where ϕ can also contain probabilistic operators. As an example, we can write the following property $P_{\geq \theta_1}(q \Rightarrow P_{\geq \theta_2}(\phi_2))$
2. The unbounded case, i.e., the case where ϕ cannot be decide on a finite execution. Here we will restrict ourselves to the until property. Given two formulas ϕ_1 and ϕ_2, the until operator ensures that ϕ_1 is true until ϕ_2 has been seen.
3. Boolean combinations of formulae, i.e., formulae of the form: $P_{\geq \theta_1}(\phi_1) \wedge P_{\geq \theta_2}(\phi_2)$.

We will only survey existing results and give pointers to the relevant papers.

4.1   The Unbounded Case: Until

We are now concerned with the verification of the *until property*. This property requires that a property ϕ_1 remains valid until a property ϕ_2 has been seen. The problem is that we do not know a priori the moment when ϕ_2 will be satisfied. Hence, one has to reason on infinite execution. There are two works on this topics, one by Sen et al.[33] and one more recent work by Pekergin et al. [30]. We will not give details on these works, but the reader should know that Sen works by extending the model with extra probabilities, which makes the solution extremely slow. Pekergin uses a new technique that is based on *perfect simulation*. According to [30], this technique is not only faster than Sen's one, but also more general as it allows to study the steady-state operator for continuous timed Markov Chains.

Remark 7. Contrary to the numerical results [35,5] the above results are not sufficient to verify properties of the form $P_{\geq\theta}(\phi)$, where ϕ is a property expressed in Linear Temporal Logic [29]. Incomplete results regarding the verification of these properties with simulation-based techniques can be found in [20,17].

4.2   Nested Probability Operators

We consider the problem of checking whether $\mathcal{S}$ satisfies ϕ with a probability greater or equal to θ. However, contrary to what we have been doing so far, we will now assume that ϕ cannot be decided on a single execution, i.e., we will assume that ϕ is of the form $P_{\geq\theta_1}\phi_1$. So, where is the difficulty? The difficulty is that ϕ cannot be model checked on a single execution, but rather depends on another test. Hence, we have to provide a way to nest tests. In his thesis, Younes proposed the following theorem.

Theorem 1. *Let $\psi = P_{\geq\theta}(\phi)$ be a property and assume that ϕ can be verified with Type-I error α' and Type-II error β', then ψ can be verified with Type-I error α and Type-II error β, assuming that the indifference region is of size at least $((\theta + \delta)(1 - \alpha'), (1 - (1 - (\theta - \delta)))(1 - \beta')$.*

Hence one has to find a compromise between the size of the indifference region of the inner test and the outer one. There are two interesting facts to know about nested operators:

1. Even for bounded properties, the above result (and in fact, any result in the literature [33,38,37,39]) only works for systems that have the Markovian property.
2. In practice, the complexity (in term of number of sampling) becomes exponential in the number of tests.

Remark 8. An interesting research direction would be to study the link with probabilistic testing [27].

4.3   Boolean Combinations

We have to consider two operations, namely conjunction and negation (as it is known that any Boolean combination reduces to combinations of these two operators). We recall some results provided by Younes. We start with conjunction.

Theorem 2. *Let ψ be the conjunction of n properties $\phi_1, \ldots, \phi_2$. Assume that each ϕ_i can be decided with Type-I error α_i and Type-II error β_I. Then ϕ can be decided with Type-I error $min_i(\alpha_i)$ and Type-II error $max_i(\beta_i)$.*

The idea behind the proof of the theorem is that

1. If we claim that the conjunction is not satisfied, this means that we have deduced that one of the operands is not.

2. If we claim that the conjunction is satisfied, this means that we have concluded that all the operands are satisfied. As we may have made mistakes in each individual verification, we get $\max_i(\beta_i)$.

For negation, the result is provided by the following theorem.

Theorem 3. *To verify a formula $\neg\psi$ with Type-I error α and Type-II error β, it is sufficient to verify ψ with Type-I error β and Type-II error α.*

5   Black-box Systems: A Note

Black-box Systems is an interesting class of stochastic systems whose treatment is beyond the scope of numerical techniques. Roughly speaking, a black-box systems is simply a system whose probability distribution (i.e., set of behaviors) is not totally known and cannot be observed. Hence, one can view a black-box system as a finite set of executions pre-computed and for which no information is available.

In the context of such systems, Type errors and indifference region cannot play a role. Indeed, those parameters influence the number of simulations that can be computed, but here the simulations are given and you cannot compute more!

A solution to this problem is to conduct a SSP test assuming that the parameter n is fixed to the number of simulations that are given in advance. The difficulty is to chose the constant c in such a way that it becomes roughly equal to accept H_0 or H_1 if $\theta = p$. In his thesis [38] and in [40], Younes proposed a solution to the problem. He also shown that a previous solution proposed by Sen [32] is not correct.

There are techniques to verify nested formulas over black-box systems. However, a technique for the verification of unbounded properties is still needed.

6   Tools and Experiments

Any statistical model checking toolset is build by combining 1) a monitoring procedure to decide whether a finite execution satisfies the property under consideration, 2) a statistical model checking algorithm, and 3) a tool that allows to describe a system and generate sets of executions.

The two firsts tools that implemented statistical model checking algorithms are *Ymer*[39] and *Vesta*[34]. *Vesta* implements a variation of the single sampling plan algorithm. The choice of implementing the SSP algorithm is motivated by the fact that it is easier to parallelize as the number of simulations to perform is known in advance. However, in his thesis, Younes showed that sequential algorithms are also easily parallelizable. *Ymer* is limited to bounded properties while *Vesta* also incorporate the unbounded until. In [22], the authors conducted several experiments that tend to show that (1) *Ymer* is faster than *Vesta* and (2) *Vesta* makes more false positive (selecting the bad hypothesis) than *Ymer*.

Regarding the unbounded case, it seems that *Vesta* is not very efficient and can make a lot of false positive. Both *Vesta* and *Ymer* have been applied to huge case studies. A comparison of *Ymer* and *Vesta* to established tools such as *PRISM* [25] can be found in [22].

Both *Ymer* and *Vesta* as well as their successors [23,24] focus on the verification of classical stochastic extension of temporal logics. In a series of recent work, we have shown that statistical model checking can also be used in other contexts that are clearly beyond the scope of existing tools. This topic is the subject of the next subsections.

6.1 Verifying Circuits

In [9,10], we applied SPRT to verifying properties of *mixed-signal circuits*, i.e., circuits for which there is an interaction between analog (continuous) and digital (discrete) values. Our first contribution was to propose a version of stochastic discrete-time event systems that fits into the framework introduced by Younes with the additional advantage that it explicitly handles analog and digital signals. We also introduced *probabilistic signal linear temporal logic*, a logic adapted to the specification of properties for mixed-signal circuits in the *temporal* domain and in the *frequency* domain. Our second contribution was the analysis of a $\Delta - \Sigma$ modulator. A $\Delta - \Sigma$ modulator is an efficient *Analog-to-Digital Converter circuit*, i.e., a device that converts analog signals into digital signals. A common critical issue in this domain is the analysis of the *stability* of the internal state variables of the circuit. The concern is that the values that are stored by these variables can grow out of control until reaching a maximum value, at which point we say that the circuit *saturates*. Saturation is commonly assumed to compromise the quality of the analog-to-digital conversion. In [14] and [18] reachability techniques developed in the area of hybrid systems are used to analyze the stability of a third-order modulator. Their idea is to use such techniques to guarantee that for *every* input signal in a given range, the states of the system remain stable. While this reachability-based approach is sound, it has important drawbacks such as (1) signals with long duration cannot be practically analyzed, and (2) properties that are commonly specified in the frequency domain rather than in the time domain cannot be checked. Our results show that a simulation-based approach makes it possible to handle properties and signals that are beyond the scope of the reachability-based approach. As an example, in our experiments, we analyze discrete-time signals with 24000 sampling points in seconds, while the approach in [14] takes hours to analyze signals with up to 31 sampling points. We are also able to provide insight into a question left open in [14] by observing that saturation does not always imply an improper signal conversion. This can be done by comparing the Fourier transform of each of the input analog signals with the Fourier transform of its corresponding digital signal. Such a property can easily be expressed in our logic and Model Checked with our simulation-based approach. We are unaware of other formal verification techniques that can solve this problem. Indeed, numerical techniques cannot reason on an execution at a time.

6.2   Systems Biology

In [11], we considered the verification of complex biological systems. we introduced a new tool, called BIOLAB, for *formally* reasoning about the behavior of stochastic dynamic models by integrating SPRT into the BIONETGEN [15,16] framework for rule-based modeling. We then used BIOLAB to verify the stochastic bistability of T-cell signalling. Our results have recently been extended to take prior knowledge on the model into account [6].

Remark 9. Statistical model checking techniques recently received a lot of attention in the area of systems biology. As an example, Carnegie Mellon University was awarded a \$10.000.000 grant for applying such techniques in the medical area [12].

6.3   Heterogeneous Applications

In [4], we have proposed to apply statistical model checking techniques to the verification of *heterogeneous applications*. Systems integrating multiple heterogeneous distributed applications communicating over a shared network are typical in various sensitive domains such as aeronautic or automotive embedded systems. Verifying the correctness of a particular application inside such a system is known to be a challenging task, which is often beyond the scope of existing exhaustive validation techniques.

In our paper, we proposed to exploit the structure of the system in order to increase the efficiency of the verification process. The idea is conceptually simple: instead of performing an analysis of the entire system, we proposed to analyze each application separately, but under some particular context/execution environment. This context is a *stochastic abstraction* that represents the interactions with other applications running within the system and sharing the computation and communication resources. The idea is to build such a context automatically by simulating the system and learning the probability distributions of key characteristics impacting the functionality of the given application. The abstraction can easily be analyzed with statistical model checking techniques.

The overall contribution of our study is an application of the above method on an industrial case study, the *heterogeneous communication system* (HCS for short) deployed for cabin communication in a civil airplane. HCS is an heterogeneous system providing entertainment services (ex : audio/video on passengers demand) as well as administrative services (ex: cabin illumination, control, audio announcements), which are implemented as distributed applications running in parallel, across various devices within the plane and communicating through a common Ethernet-based network. The HCS system has to guarantee stringent requirements, such as reliable data transmission, fault tolerance, timing and synchronization constraints. An important requirement is the *accuracy of clock synchronization* between different devices. This latter property states that the difference between the clocks of any two devices should be bounded by a small constant, which is provided by the user and depends on his needs (for example, to guarantee the fiability of another service). Hence, one must be capable to compute the smallest bound for which synchronization occurs and compare it with the bound expected by the user. Unfortunately, due to the large number of heterogeneous components that constitute the system, deriving such a bound manually from the textual specification is an unfeasible task. In this paper, we propose a formal approach that consists in building a formal model of the HCS, then we apply simulation-based algorithms to this model in order to deduce the smallest value of the bound for which synchronization occurs. We start with a fixed value of the bound and check whether synchronization occurs. If yes, then we make sure that this is the best one. If no, we restart the experiment with a new value.

We have been able to derive precise bounds that guarantee proper synchronization for all the devices of the system. We also computed the probability to satisfy the property for smaller values of the bound, i.e., bounds that do not satisfy the synchronization property with probability 1. Being able to provide such an information is of clear importance, especially when the best bound is too high with respect to user's requirements. We have observed that the values we obtained strongly depend on the position of the device in the network. We also estimated the average and worst proportion of failures per simulation for bounds that are smaller than the one that guarantees synchronization. Checking this latter property has been made easy because statistical model checking allows us to reason on one execution at a time. Finally, we have also considered the influence of clock drift on the synchronisation results. The experiments highlight the generality of our technique, which could be applied to other versions of the HCS as well as to other heterogeneous applications.

7   The Future of Statistical Model Checking

There are various directions for future research in the statistical model checking area. Here is a list of possible topics.

- Using efficient techniques for performing simulation is crucial to guarantee good performances for any statistical model checking algorithm. Unfortunately, the existing algorithms do not exploit efficient simulation techniques. It would thus be worth combining statistical model checking algorithms with such techniques (example : rare-event simulations, , ...). This is a huge implementation effort which also requires to define a methodology to select the good simulation technique to be applied.
- Statistical model checking algorithms have not yet been applied to the verification of multi-core systems, this area should be investigated.
- Statistical model checking algorithms do not apply to systems that combine both stochastic and non deterministic aspects. Extending the results to such systems is however crucial to perform verification of security protocols, networking protocols, and performance protocols.
- Statistical model checking algorithms reduce to decide between two hypothesis. In many areas, especially systems biology, we may have a prior knowledge on the probability to satisfy each hypothesis. Incorporating this prior

knowledge in the verification process may considerably reduce the number of simulations needed for the algorithm to terminate.

- Statistical model checking algorithms suppose that the property ϕ can be checked on finite executions of the system. There are however many situations where ϕ cannot be checked in a finite amount of time. This is for example the case when ϕ is a long-run average or a steady state property. In systems biology, we are clearly interested in the study of such properties.
- Verifying applications running within a huge heterogeneous system without is a challenging problem. In a recent work [4], the authors have proposed a new simulation-based technique for solving such problem. The technique starts by performing simulations of the system in order to learn the context in where the application is used. Then, it creates a stochastic abstraction for the application, which takes the context information into account. Up to know, there is no automatic way to learn the context and derive the stochastic context. However, what we have observed so far is that it often takes the form of properties that cannot be expressed in classical temporal logic. Hence, statistical model checking may be our last resort to analyze the resulting abstraction.
- Statistical model checking may help testers. In [28], Cavalli et al. proposed to use statistical techniques for conformance testing of timed stochastic systems. The technique should be automated. This could lead to new algorithms for verifying the so-called black-box systems.

Acknowledgments

We would like to thanks our collaborators on the statistical model checking project: Sumit Jha, and Marius Bozga.

References

1. Bauer, A., Leucker, M., Schallhart, C.: Monitoring of real-time properties. In: Arun-Kumar, S., Garg, N. (eds.) FSTTCS 2006. LNCS, vol. 4337, pp. 260–272. Springer, Heidelberg (2006)
2. Baier, C., Haverkort, B.R., Hermanns, H., Katoen, J.-P.: Model-checking algorithms for continuous-time markov chains. IEEE Trans. Software Eng. 29(6), 524–541 (2003)
3. Baier, C., Katoen, J.-P.: Principles of Model Checking. MIT Press, Cambridge (2008)
4. Basu, A., Bensalem, S., Bozga, M., Caillaud, B., Delahaye, B., Legay, A.: Statistical abstraction and model-checking of large heterogeneous systems. Technical report, INRIA (2010)
5. Bustan, D., Rubin, S., Vardi, M.Y.: Verifying omega-regular properties of markov chains. In: Alur, R., Peled, D.A. (eds.) CAV 2004. LNCS, vol. 3114, pp. 189–201. Springer, Heidelberg (2004)
6. Carnegie Mellon University. A Bayesian Approach to Model Checking Biological Systems (under submission, 2009)

7. Ciesinski, F., Baier, C.: Liquor: A tool for qualitative and quantitative linear time analysis of reactive systems. In: QEST, pp. 131–132. IEEE, Los Alamitos (2006)
8. Ciesinski, F., Größer, M.: On probabilistic computation tree logic. In: Baier, C., Haverkort, B.R., Hermanns, H., Katoen, J.-P., Siegle, M. (eds.) Validation of Stochastic Systems. LNCS, vol. 2925, pp. 147–188. Springer, Heidelberg (2004)
9. Clarke, E.M., Donzé, A., Legay, A.: Statistical model checking of mixed-analog circuits with an application to a third order delta-sigma modulator. In: HVC 2008. LNCS, vol. 5394, pp. 149–163. Springer, Heidelberg (2008)
10. Clarke, E.M., Donzé, A., Legay, A.: On simulation-based probabilistic model checking of mixed-analog circuits. Formal Methods in System Design (2009) (to appear)
11. Clarke, E.M., Faeder, J.R., Langmead, C.J., Harris, L.A., Jha, S.K., Legay, A.: Statistical model checking in biolab: Applications to the automated analysis of t-cell receptor signaling pathway. In: Heiner, M., Uhrmacher, A.M. (eds.) CMSB 2008. LNCS (LNBI), vol. 5307, pp. 231–250. Springer, Heidelberg (2008)
12. Cmacs, http://cmacs.cs.cmu.edu/
13. Courcoubetis, C., Yannakakis, M.: The complexity of probabilistic verification. Journal of the ACM 42(4), 857–907 (1995)
14. Dang, T., Donze, A., Maler, O.: Verification of analog and mixed-signal circuits using hybrid systems techniques. In: Hu, A.J., Martin, A.K. (eds.) FMCAD 2004. LNCS, vol. 3312, pp. 21–36. Springer, Heidelberg (2004)
15. Faeder, J.R., Blinov, M.L., Hlavacek, W.S.: Graphical rule-based representation of signal-transduction networks. In: SAC 2005: Proceedings of the 2005 ACM symposium on Applied computing, pp. 133–140. ACM, New York (2005)
16. Faeder, J.R., Blinov, M.L., Hlavacek, W.S.: Rule-based modeling of biochemical systems with BioNetGen. In: Maly, I.V. (ed.) Systems Biology. Methods in Molecular Biology. Humana Press, Totowa (2008)
17. Grosu, R., Smolka, S.A.: Monte carlo model checking. In: Halbwachs, N., Zuck, L.D. (eds.) TACAS 2005. LNCS, vol. 3440, pp. 271–286. Springer, Heidelberg (2005)
18. Gupta, S., Krogh, B.H., Rutenbar, R.A.: Towards formal verification of analog designs. In: ICCAD, pp. 210–217 (2004)
19. Havelund, K., Rosu, G.: Synthesizing monitors for safety properties. In: Katoen, J.-P., Stevens, P. (eds.) TACAS 2002. LNCS, vol. 2280, pp. 342–356. Springer, Heidelberg (2002)
20. Hérault, T., Lassaigne, R., Magniette, F., Peyronnet, S.: Approximate probabilistic model checking. In: Steffen, B., Levi, G. (eds.) VMCAI 2004. LNCS, vol. 2937, pp. 73–84. Springer, Heidelberg (2004)
21. Hermanns, H., Wachter, B., Zhang, L.: Probabilistic cegar. In: Gupta, A., Malik, S. (eds.) CAV 2008. LNCS, vol. 5123, pp. 162–175. Springer, Heidelberg (2008)
22. Jansen, D.N., Katoen, J., Oldenkamp, M., Stoelinga, M., Zapreev, I.S.: How fast and fat is your probabilistic model checker? an experimental performance comparison. In: Yorav, K. (ed.) HVC 2007. LNCS, vol. 4899, pp. 69–85. Springer, Heidelberg (2008)
23. Katoen, J.-P., Zapreev, I.S.: Simulation-based ctmc model checking: An empirical evaluation. In: Proc. of 6th Int. Conference on the Quantitative Evaluation of Systems (QEST), pp. 31–40. IEEE Computer Society, Los Alamitos (2009)
24. Katoen, J.-P., Zapreev, I.S., Hahn, E.M., Hermanns, H., Jansen, D.N.: The ins and outs of the probabilistic model checker mrmc. In: Proc. of 6th Int. Conference on the Quantitative Evaluation of Systems (QEST), pp. 167–176. IEEE Computer Society Press, Los Alamitos (2009)
25. Kwiatkowska, M.Z., Norman, G., Parker, D.: Prism 2.0: A tool for probabilistic model checking. In: QEST, pp. 322–323. IEEE, Los Alamitos (2004)

26. Laplante, S., Lassaigne, R., Magniez, F., Peyronnet, S., de Rougemont, M.: Probabilistic abstraction for model checking: An approach based on property testing. ACM Trans. Comput. Log. 8(4) (2007)
27. Larsen, K.G., Skou, A.: Bisimulation through probabilistic testing. Inf. Comput. 94(1), 1–28 (1991)
28. Merayo, M.G., Hwang, I., Núñez, M., Cavalli, A.R.: A statistical approach to test stochastic and probabilistic systems. In: Breitman, K., Cavalcanti, A. (eds.) ICFEM 2009. LNCS, vol. 5885, pp. 186–205. Springer, Heidelberg (2009)
29. Pnueli, A.: The temporal logic of programs. In: Proc. 18th Annual Symposium on Foundations of Computer Science (FOCS), pp. 46–57 (1977)
30. Rabih, D.E., Pekergin, N.: Statistical model checking using perfect simulation. In: Liu, Z., Ravn, A.P. (eds.) ATVA 2009. LNCS, vol. 5799, pp. 120–134. Springer, Heidelberg (2009)
31. Rutten, J., Kwiatkowska, M., Norman, G., Parker, D.: Mathematical Techniques for Analyzing Concurrent and Probabilistic Systems. In: Panangaden, P., van Breugel, F. (eds.) Mathematical Techniques for Analyzing Concurrent and Probabilistic Systems, P. Panangaden and F. van Breugel (eds.). CRM Monograph Series, vol. 23. American Mathematical Society, Providence (2004)
32. Sen, K., Viswanathan, M., Agha, G.: Statistical model checking of black-box probabilistic systems. In: Alur, R., Peled, D.A. (eds.) CAV 2004. LNCS, vol. 3114, pp. 202–215. Springer, Heidelberg (2004)
33. Sen, K., Viswanathan, M., Agha, G.: On statistical model checking of stochastic systems. In: Etessami, K., Rajamani, S.K. (eds.) CAV 2005. LNCS, vol. 3576, pp. 266–280. Springer, Heidelberg (2005)
34. Sen, K., Viswanathan, M., Agha, G.A.: Vesta: A statistical model-checker and analyzer for probabilistic systems. In: QEST, pp. 251–252. IEEE Computer Society, Los Alamitos (2005)
35. Vardi, M.Y.: Automatic verification of probabilistic concurrent finite-state programs. In: FOCS, pp. 327–338 (1985)
36. Wald, A.: Sequential tests of statistical hypotheses. Annals of Mathematical Statistics 16(2), 117–186 (1945)
37. Younes, H.L.S.: Probabilistic verification for "black-box" systems. In: Etessami, K., Rajamani, S.K. (eds.) CAV 2005. LNCS, vol. 3576, pp. 253–265. Springer, Heidelberg (2005)
38. Younes, H.L.S.: Verification and Planning for Stochastic Processes with Asynchronous Events. PhD thesis, Carnegie Mellon (2005)
39. Younes, H.L.S.: Ymer: A statistical model checker. In: Etessami, K., Rajamani, S.K. (eds.) CAV 2005. LNCS, vol. 3576, pp. 429–433. Springer, Heidelberg (2005)
40. Younes, H.L.S.: Error control for probabilistic model checking. In: Emerson, E.A., Namjoshi, K.S. (eds.) VMCAI 2006. LNCS, vol. 3855, pp. 142–156. Springer, Heidelberg (2005)
41. Younes, H.L.S., Kwiatkowska, M.Z., Norman, G., Parker, D.: Numerical vs. statistical probabilistic model checking. STTT 8(3), 216–228 (2006)
42. Younes, H.L.S., Simmons, R.G.: Probabilistic verification of discrete event systems using acceptance sampling. In: Brinksma, E., Larsen, K.G. (eds.) CAV 2002. LNCS, vol. 2404, pp. 223–235. Springer, Heidelberg (2002)
43. Younes, H.L.S., Simmons, R.G.: Statistical probabilistic model checking with a focus on time-bounded properties. Information and Computation 204(9), 1368–1409 (2006)

Runtime Verification with the RV System[*]

Patrick Meredith[1] and Grigore Roşu[2]

[1] Runtime Verification, Inc
[2] University of Illinois at Urbana-Champaign
{pmeredit,grosu}@illinois.edu

Abstract. The RV system is the first system to merge the benefits of Runtime Monitoring with Predictive Analysis. The Runtime Monitoring portion of RV is based on the successful Monitoring Oriented Programming system developed at the University of Illinois [6,7,9,21,5], while the Predictive Analysis capability is a vastly expanded version of the jPredictor System also developed at the University of Illinois [11,14].

With the RV system, runtime monitoring is supported and encouraged as a fundamental principle for building reliable software: monitors are automatically synthesized from specified properties and integrated into the original system to check its dynamic behaviors. When certain conditions of interest occur, such as a violation of a specification, user-defined actions will be triggered, which can be any code from information logging to runtime recovery. The RV system supports the monitoring of *parametric* properties that may specify a relationship between objects. Properties may be defined using one of several logical formalisms, such as: extended regular languages, context-free patterns, deterministic finite state machines, linear temporal logic, and past time linear temporal logic. The system is designed in such a way that adding new logical formalisms is a relatively simple task

The predictive capabilities allow any of these monitoring specifications to be extended to checking not just the actual runtime traces of program execution, but any trace that may be inferred from a constructed casual model. The Predictive Analysis also features built in algorithms for race detection and atomicity violations, that are both highly useful in concurrent system design and difficult to specify in terms of formal specification languages.

1   Introduction

This paper presents an introduction to the RV System, the first system to combine runtime monitoring and predictive analysis. Not only do these two components work in isolation to ease the testing and debugging of software, but they also work in conjunction: monitoring properties can be predicted against using the predictive analysis capabilities of the system.

[*] Supported in part by NSF grants CCF-0916893, CNS-0720512, and CCF-0448501, by NASA contract NNL08AA23C, by a Samsung SAIT grant, and by several Microsoft gifts.

G. Roşu et al. (Eds.): RV 2010, LNCS 6418, pp. 136–152, 2010.

Runtime monitoring allows one to check safety properties against the execution of a program during runtime. In the RV System, properties are *parametric*, which means they take into account the given objects that are related to a given property. For example, one may wish to state a property that an Enumeration from a given Vector in Java is not used after the Vector is updated. In this case the parameters will be a Vector and an Enumeration, and the property will be checked for every pair of Vector and Enumeration objects.

Predictive analysis allows one to check safety properties against all the *viable inferred* executions of a program that can be generated by creating a causal model from one run of the program. This is especially useful for checking safety properties that rely on the behavior of concurrent code, such as finding races and atomicity violations.

The remainder of this paper is as follows: Section 2 discusses a high level overview of the RV system. Section 3 provides an explanation of runtime monitoring, including an explanation of parametric slicing and several examples of how to use the monitoring portion of the RV system (referred to as RV-Monitor). Additionally, some performance results are given. Section 4 discusses the concepts necessary to understanding the predictive analysis of the RV system (RV-Predict), as well as explaining, at a high level, several of the algorithms used in prediction. As with monitoring, several examples and results are given.

2   System Overview

Fig. 1 shows the dependency diagram for the RV System. The RV System consists of two components, RV-Monitor and RV-Predict, which are further divided into sub-components. The arrows represent the direction of data flow. In the case of components that generate code, the generated code is treated as synonymous with the component that generates it in order to simplify the diagram.

1. **RV-Monitor**
   (a) **Runtime Monitoring** performs actual monitoring on a program under test. This is achieved by generating an AspectJ aspect that is weaved

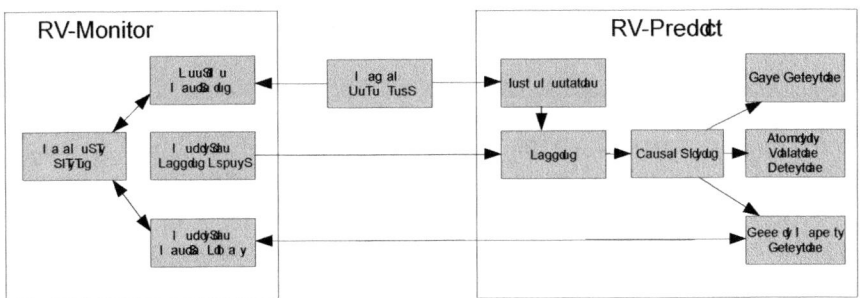

Fig. 1. System Overview

into the program under test, which is then run to collect monitoring results. This is discussed in detail in Section 3.

(b) **Prediction Logging Aspect** generates an aspect that is weaved into the program under test that causes the program to generate logging info for use in prediction of arbitrary properties. This is orthogonal to the **Instrumentation** component of **RV-Predict** described below, and used in conjunction with it. The logging aspect is automatically inferred from a specification designed for the **Runtime Monitoring** component.

(c) **Prediction Monitor Library** generates a library that communicates with the **Generic Property Detection** component of **RV-Predict**. The **Generic Property Detection** component sends events to the **Prediction Monitor Library** which reports monitoring results back to the **Generic Property Detection** component. The library is generated from a specification designed for the **Runtime Monitoring** component.

(d) **Parametric Slicing** slices a trace based on parameter instances. This component is used both by the **Runtime Monitoring** and **Prediction Monitor Library** in order to properly find violations and validations of *parametric* properties. This is explained in more detail in Section 3.1.

2. RV-Predict

(a) **Instrumentation** adds logging code to a program under test. This will cause important information about a run of the program under test, such as the creation of threads or the entry and exit of methods, to be output by the **Logging** component.

(b) **Logging** runs the program under test which has been instrumented with logging code via the **Instrumentation** component. If generic property detection is performed, the program under test will be weaved with the **Prediction Logging Aspect** generated aspect before logging commences.

(c) **Causal Slicing** performs casual slicing of the logged trace of the program using the concept of *sliced causality* first introduced in [11]. Causal slicing is able to reduce the amount of necessary information in a trace, which allows the various prediction steps to find more viable linearizations of the trace. It is described in detail in Section 4.1.

(d) **Race Detection** performs race detection. This is achieved by determining when to accesses to the same variable, at least one of which is a write, may be reordered while still preserving the causal dependences of the program. It is described in more detail in Section 4.2.

(e) **Atomicity Violation Detection** finds violations in the intended atomicity of a program. More detail on this can be found in [14].

(f) **Generic Property Detection** detects violations and validations of given generic specifications by discovering possible linearizations that are causally possible and feeding the events of these linearizations to a library generated by the **Prediction Monitor Library**. These specifications are written using the same syntax as those used by the **Runtime Monitoring** component. It is described in more detail in Section 4.2.

```
UnsafeMapIterator(Map m, Collection c, Iterator i){
    event create_coll after(Map m) returning(Collection c)} :
        (call(* Map.values()) || call(* Map.keySet())) && target(m) {}
    event create_iter after(Collection c) returning(Iterator i) :
        call(* Collection+.iterator()) && target(c) {}
    event use_iter before(Iterator i) : call(* Iterator+.next()) && target(i) {}
    event update_map after(Map m) : call(* Map.remove*(..)) || call(* Map.put*(..))
        || call(* Map.putAll*(..)) || call(* Map.clear())) && target(m) {}
    fsm: start [ create_coll -> s1 ]
         s1    [ update_map -> s1, create_iter -> s2 ]
         s2    [ use_iter -> s2, update_map -> s3 ]
         s3    [ update_map -> s3, uset_iter -> end ]
         end   []
         @end { System.out.println("fsm:  Accessed invalid Iterator!"); _RESET; }
    ere: create_coll update_map* create_iter use_iter* update_map+ use_iter
         @match { System.out.println("ere: Accessed Invalid Iterator!"); _RESET; }
    cfg: S -> create_coll Updates create_iter Nexts update_map Updates use_iter,
         Nexts -> Nexts use_iter | epsilon
         Updates -> Updates update_map | epsilon
         @match { System.out.println("cfg: Accessed Invalid Iterator!"); _RESET; }
    ftltl: <>(create_coll and <> (create_iter and <> (update_map and <> use_iter)))
         @validation { System.out.println("ftltl: Accessed Invalid Iterator!"); _RESET; }
    ptltl: use_iter ->
         ((<*> (create_iter and (<*> create_coll))) -> ((not update_map) S create_iter))
         @violation { System.out.println("prltl: Accessed Invalid Iterator!"); _RESET; }
}
```

Fig. 2. FSM, ERE, CFG, FTLTL, and PTLTL UnsafeMapIterator. Inset: graphical depiction of the property.

3   Runtime Monitoring

Monitoring executions of a system against expected properties plays an important role not only in different stages of software development, e.g., testing and debugging, but also in the deployed system as a mechanism to increase system reliability. This is achieved by allowing the monitors to perform *recovery* actions in the case that a specification is matched, or fails to match. Numerous approaches, such as [18,15,8,3,1,2,20,17,10], have been proposed to build effective and efficient monitoring solutions for different applications. More recently, monitoring of parametric specifications, i.e., specifications with free variables, has received increasing interest due to its effectiveness at capturing system behaviors, such as the one presented in Fig. 2, which encapsulates the proper use of Map Iterators.

It is highly non-trivial to monitor such parametric specifications efficiently. It is possible to see a tremendous number of parameter instances during the execution of a monitored program. For example, it is not uncommon to see hundreds of thousands of iterators in a program, which will generate hundreds of thousands of parameter instances in the UnsafeMapIterator specification in Fig. 2.

Several approaches have been introduced to support the monitoring of parametric specifications, including Eagle [3], Tracematches [1,2], PQL [20], and PTQL [17]. However, they are all limited in terms of supported specification formalisms. Other techniques, e.g., Eagle, Tracematches, PQL and PTQL, follow a formalism-dependent approach, that is, they have their parametric specification formalisms hardwired, e.g., regular patterns (like Tracematches), context-free patterns (like PQL) with parameters, etc., and then develop algorithms to generate monitoring code for the particular formalisms. Although this approach provides a feasible solution to monitoring parametric specifications, we argue that it not only has limited expressiveness, but also causes unnecessary complexity in developing optimal monitor generation algorithms, often leading to inefficient monitoring. In fact, the experiments summarized in Section 3.3 shows that RV-Monitor generates more efficient monitoring code than other existing tools.

Fig. 2 shows a RV-Monitor specification of the UnsafeMapIterator property. The idea of UnsafeMapIterator is to catch an intricate safety property of Java. There are several methods to create Collection (essentially sets) from Java Maps. One may then create Java Iterators to traverse these Collections. However, if the Map is updated, the Iterators are invalidated.

The specification uses five different formalisms: finite state machines (FSM), extended regular expressions (ERE), context-free grammars (CFG), future-time linear temporal logic (FTLTL), and past-time linear temporal logic (PTLTL). Because each of the properties in Fig. 2 is the same, five messages will be reported whenever an Iterator is incorrectly used after an update to the underlying Map. We show all five of them to emphasize the formalism-independence of our approach. Under normal circumstances a user would chose just one formalism.

On the first line, we name the specified property and give the parameters used in the specification. Then we define the involved events using the AspectJ syntax. For example, create_coll is defined as the return value of functions values and keyset of Map. We adopt AspectJ syntax to define events in RV-Monitor because it is an expressive language for defining observation points in a Java program. As mentioned, every event may instantiate some parameters at runtime. This can be seen in Fig. 2: create_coll will instantiate parameters m and c using the target and the return value of the method call. When one defines a pattern or formula there are implicit events, which must begin traces; we call them *monitor creation* events. For example, in a pattern language like ERE, the monitor creation events are the first events that appear in the pattern. We assume a semantics where events that occur before monitor creation events are ignored.

3.1   Parametric Slicing

RV-Monitor automatically synthesizes AspectJ instrumentation code from the specification, which is weaved into the program we wish to monitor by any standard AspectJ compiler. In this way, executions of the monitored program

#	Event	#	Event
1	create_coll$\langle m_1, c_1 \rangle$	7	update_map$\langle m_1 \rangle$
2	create_coll$\langle m_1, c_2 \rangle$	8	use_iter$\langle i_2 \rangle$
3	create_iter$\langle c_1, i_1 \rangle$	9	create_coll$\langle m_2, c_3 \rangle$
4	create_iter$\langle c_1, i_2 \rangle$	10	create_iter$\langle c_3, i_4 \rangle$
5	use_iter$\langle i_1 \rangle$	11	use_iter$\langle i_4 \rangle$
6	create_iter$\langle c_2, i_3 \rangle$		

Fig. 3. Possible execution trace over the events specified in UnsafeMapIterator

will produce traces made up of events defined in the specification, as those in Fig. 2. Consider the example eleven event trace in Fig. 3 over the events defined in Fig. 2. The # column gives the numbering of the events for easy reference. Every event in the trace starts with the name of the event, e.g., create_coll, followed by the parameter binding information, e.g., $\langle m_1, c_1 \rangle$ that binds parameters m and c with a map object m_1 and a collection c_1, respectively. Such a trace is called a *parametric trace* since it contains events with parameters.

Our approach to monitoring parametric traces against parametric properties is based on the observation that each parametric trace actually contains multiple *non-parametric trace slices*, each for a particular parameter binding instance. Intuitively, a slice of a parametric trace for a particular parameter binding consists of names of all the events that have identical or *less informative* parameter bindings. Informally, a parameter binding b_1 is identical or less informative than a parameter binding b_2 if and only if the parameters for which they have bindings agree, and b_2 binds either an equal number of parameters or more parameters: parameter $\langle m_1, c_2 \rangle$ is less informative than $\langle m_1, c_2, i_3 \rangle$ because the parameters they both bind, m and c, agree on their values, m_1 and c_2, respectively, and $\langle m_1, c_2, i_3 \rangle$ binds one more parameter. From here on we will simply say less informative to mean identical or less informative. Fig. 4 shows the trace slices and their corresponding parameter bindings contained in the trace in Fig. 3. The Status column denotes the monitor output category that the slice falls into (for ERE). In this case everything but the slice for $\langle m_1, c_1, i_2 \rangle$, which matches the property, is in the "?" (undecided) category. For example, the trace for the binding $\langle m_1, c_1 \rangle$ contains create_coll update_map (the first and seventh events in the trace) and the trace for the binding $\langle m_1, c_1, i_2 \rangle$ is create_coll create_iter update_map use_iter (the first, fourth, seventh, and eighth events in the trace).

Based on this observation, our approach creates a set of monitor instances during the monitoring process, each handling a trace slice for a parameter binding. Fig. 5 shows the set of monitor instances created for the trace in Fig. 3, each monitor labeled by the corresponding parameter binding. This way, the monitor *does not need to handle the parameter information* and can employ any existing technique for ordinary, non-parametric traces, including state machines and push-down automata, providing a formalism-independent way to check parametric properties. When an event comes, our algorithm will dispatch it to related monitors, which will update their states accordingly. For example, the seventh event in Fig. 3, update_map$\langle m_1 \rangle$, will be dispatched to monitors for $\langle m_1, c_1 \rangle$,

Instance	Slice	Status
$\langle m_1 \rangle$	update_map	?
$\langle m_1, c_1 \rangle$	create_coll update_map	?
$\langle m_1, c_2 \rangle$	create_coll update_map	?
$\langle m_2, c_3 \rangle$	create_coll	?
$\langle m_1, c_1, i_1 \rangle$	create_coll create_iter use_iter update_map	?
$\langle m_1, c_1, i_2 \rangle$	create_coll create_iter update_map use_iter	match
$\langle m_1, c_2, i_3 \rangle$	create_coll create_iter update_map	?
$\langle m_2, c_3, i_4 \rangle$	create_coll create_iter use_iter	?

Fig. 4. Slices for the trace in Fig. 3

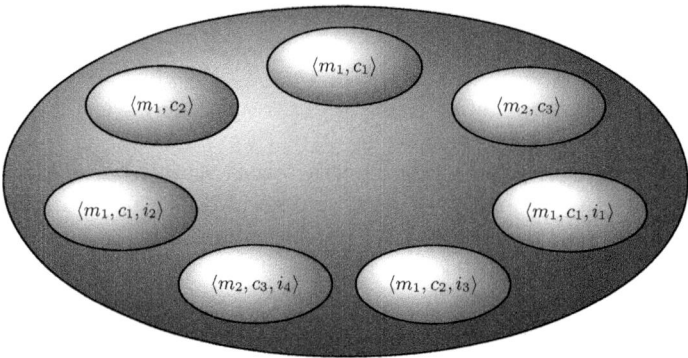

Fig. 5. A parametric monitor with corresponding parameter instance monitors

$\langle m_1, c_2 \rangle$, $\langle m_1, c_1, i_1 \rangle$, $\langle m_1, c_1, i_2 \rangle$, and $\langle m_1, c_2, i_3 \rangle$. New monitor instances will be created if the event contains new parameter instances. For example, when the third event in Fig. 3, create_iter$\langle c_1, i_1 \rangle$, is received, a new monitor will be created for $\langle m_1, c_1, i_1 \rangle$ by combining $\langle m_1, c_1 \rangle$ in the first event with $\langle c_1, i_1 \rangle$.

An algorithm to build parameter instances from observed events, like the one introduced in [12], may create many useless monitor instances leading to prohibitive runtime overheads. For example, Fig. 4 does not need to contain the binding $\langle m_1, c_3, i_4 \rangle$ even though it can be created by combining the parameter instances of update_map$\langle m_1 \rangle$ (the seventh event) and create_iter$\langle c_3, i_4 \rangle$ (the tenth event). It is safe to ignore this binding here because m_1 is not the underlying map for c_3, i_4. It is critical to minimize the number of monitor instances created during monitoring. The advantage is twofold: (1) that it reduces the needed memory space, and (2), more importantly, monitoring efficiency is improved since fewer monitors are triggered for each received event. RV-Monitor uses several algorithms in order to prevent the creation of instances that are known to be unneeded, as well as to remove those that become unneeded during execution.

3.2   Monitoring Example

Here we give a simple example of monitoring using RV-Monitor, consider the following Java program:

```
bash-3.2$ cat SafeEnum_1.java
import java.util.*;
public class SafeEnum_1 {
        public static void main(String[] args){
                Vector<Integer> v = new Vector<Integer>();
                v.add(1); v.add(2); v.add(4); v.add(8);
                Enumeration e = v.elements();
                int sum = 0;
                if(e.hasMoreElements()){
                        sum += (Integer)e.nextElement();
                        v.add(11);
                }
                while(e.hasMoreElements()){
                        sum += (Integer)e.nextElement();
                }
                v.clear();
                System.out.println("sum: " + sum);
        }
}
```

This program violates a basic multi-object protocol, namely that a vector should not be modified during enumeration. For performance reasons, the JVM does not perform this runtime check, so one can end up with a subtle, non-deterministic and hard to check error in one's program. Suppose now that one wants to monitor the program above using rv-monitor. All one needs to do is to create a subdirectory called mop and to place in this directory all the property specifications against which one wants to monitor the program. In our case,

```
bash-3.2$ cat mop/SafeEnum.mop
package mop;
import java.io.*;
import java.util.*;

SafeEnum(Vector v, Enumeration e) {
        event create after(Vector v) returning(Enumeration e) :
                call(Enumeration Vector+.elements())
            && target(v) {}
        event updatesource after(Vector v) :
                (call(* Vector+ remove*(..))
            || call(* Vector+.add*(..))
            || call(* Vector+.clear(..))
            || call(* Vector+.insertElementAt(..))
            || call(* Vector+.set*(..))
            || call(* Vector+.retainAll(..)))
            && target(v){}
        event next before(Enumeration e) :
                call(* Enumeration+.nextElement())
            && target(e){}

        ere : create next* updatesource updatesource* next
        @match {
            System.out.println("improper enumeration usage at " + __LOC);
            __RESET;
        }
}
```

Now one can call the rv-monitor program, which does a series of operations under the hood (compiles the program, compiles the specification, weaves the generated monitor with the program binary, then runs the resulting monitored program) and only shows the user the relevant information:

```
bash-3.2$ rv-monitor SafeEnum_1
-Processing ./mop/SafeEnum.mop
 SafeEnumMonitorAspect.aj is generated

SafeEnum_1.java
Executing your program:
improper enumeration usage at SafeEnum_1.java:23
sum: 26
Done
```

The message above makes it clear to the user that the program violates the specification.

3.3   Monitoring Results

Our previous work on monitoring, in particular [21,5] shows that, in general the overhead of monitoring is around 10%. However, some exceptionally intensive properties, such as iterator based properties in the bloat and pmd benchmarks from DaCapo [4] showed exceptionally large overheads. Recent advances have lowered these overheads considerably, as can be seen in Fig. 6 where JavaMOP is our earlier system and RV-Monitor is our current system.

	UnsafeMapIterator	
	JavaMOP	RV-Monitor
bloat	935%	194%
pmd	196%	74%

Fig. 6. JavaMOP Vs. RV-Monitor

4   Predictive Analysis

Concurrent systems in general and multithreaded systems in particular may exhibit different behaviors when executed at different times. This inherent non-determinism makes multithreaded programs difficult to analyze, test and debug. Predictive analysis is able to detect, correctly, concurrency errors from observing execution traces of multithreaded programs. By "correct" or "sound" prediction of errors we mean that there are *no false alarms*. The program is automatically instrumented to emit runtime events for use in the **Causal Slicing** component, and the various detection components on the right side of Fig. 1. The particular execution that is observed need *not* hit the error; yet, errors in other executions can be correctly predicted together with counter-examples leading to them.

There are several other approaches also aiming at detecting potential concurrency errors by examining particular execution traces. Some of these approaches aim at verifying general purpose properties [25,26], including temporal ones, and are inspired from debugging distributed systems based on Lamport's *happens-before* causality [19]. Other approaches work with particular properties, such as data-races and/or atomicity. [24] introduces a first lock-set based algorithm to detect data-races dynamically, followed by many variants aiming at improving its accuracy. For example, an ownership model was used in [23] to achieve a more precise race detection at the object level. [22] combines the lock-set and the happen-before techniques. The lock-set technique has also been used to detect atomicity violations at runtime, e.g., the reduction based algorithms in [16] and [27]. [27] also proposes a block-based algorithm for dynamic checking of atomicity built on a simplified happen-before relation, as well as a graph-based algorithm to improve the efficiency and precision of runtime atomicity analysis.

Previous efforts tend to focus on either soundness or coverage: those based on happens-before try to be sound, but have limited coverage over interleavings, thus missing errors; lock-set based approaches have better coverage but suffer from false alarms. RV-Predict aims at improving coverage without giving up soundness or genericity of properties. It combines *sliced causality* [11], a happen-before causality drastically but soundly sliced by removing irrelevant causalities using semantic information about the program obtained with an apriori static analysis, with *lock-atomicity*. Our predictive runtime analysis technique can be understood as a hybrid of testing and model checking. Testing because one runs the system and observes its runtime behavior in order to detect errors, and model checking because the special causality with lock-atomicity extracted from the running program can be regarded as an abstract model of the program, which can further be investigated exhaustively by the observer in order to detect potential errors.

4.1   Causal Slicing

We briefly describe our technique for extracting from an execution trace of a multithreaded system the sliced causality relation corresponding to some property of interest φ. Our technique is *offline*, in the sense that it takes as input an already generated execution trace (see Fig. 1); that is because causal slicing must traverse the trace backwards. Our technique consists of two steps: *(1)* all the irrelevant events (those which are neither property events nor events on which property events are dependant) are removed from the original trace, obtaining the *(φ)-sliced trace*; and *(2)* a *vector clock (VC)* based algorithm is applied on the sliced trace to capture the sliced causality partial order.

Extracting Slices. Our goal here is to take a trace ξ and a property φ, and to generate a trace ξ_φ obtained from ξ filtering out all its events which are irrelevant for φ. When slicing the execution trace, one must nevertheless keep all the property events. Moreover, one must also keep any event e with $e \ (\sqsubset_{ctrl} \cup \sqsubset_{data})^+ \ e'$ for some property event e'. This can be easily achieved by traversing the original trace backwards, starting with ξ_φ empty and accumulating in ξ_φ events that either are property events or have events depending on them already in ξ_φ. One can employ any off-the-shelf analysis tool for data- and control- dependence; e.g., RV-Predict uses termination-sensitive control dependence [13].

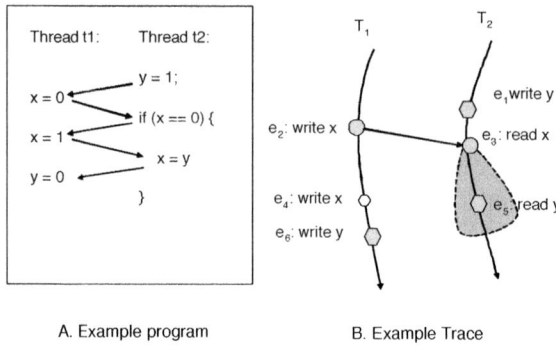

A. Example program   B. Example Trace

Fig. 7. Example for relevance dependence

To understand the process, consider the example in Fig. 7, threads T_1 and T_2 are executed as shown by the solid arrows (A), yielding the event sequence "$e_1, e_2, e_3, e_4, e_5, e_6$" (B). Suppose the property to check refers only to y; the property events are then e_1, e_5, and e_6. Events e_2 and e_3 are immediately marked as relevant, since $e_2 \sqsubset_{data} e_3 \sqsubset_{ctrl} e_5$. If only closure under control- and data-dependence were used to compute the relevant events, then e_4 would appear to be irrelevant, so one may conclude that "e_2, e_6, e_1, e_3, e_5" is a sound permutation; there is, obviously, no execution that can produce that trace, so one reported a false alarm if that trace violated the original property on y. Consequently, e_4 is also a relevant event and $e_3 \sqsubset_{rlvn} e_4$.

Unfortunately, one backwards traversal of the trace does not suffice to correctly calculate all the relevant events. Reconsider Fig. 7. When the backward traversal first reaches e_4, it is unclear whether e_4 is relevant or not, because we have not seen e_3 and e_2 yet. Thus a second scan of the trace is needed to include e_4. Once e_4 is included in ξ_φ, it may induce other relevance dependencies, requiring more traversals of the trace to include them. This process would cease only when no new relevant events are detected and thus resulting sliced trace stabilizes. If one misses relevant events like e_4 then one may "slice the trace too much" and, consequently, one may produce false alarms. Because at each trace traversal some event is added to ξ_φ, the worse-case complexity of the sound trace slicing procedure is square in the number of events. Since execution traces can be huge, in the order of billions of events[1], any trace slicing algorithms that is worse than linear may easily become prohibitive. For that reason, RV-Predict traverses the trace only once during slicing, thus achieving an approximation of the complete slice that can, in theory, lead to false alarms. However, our experiments show that this approximation is actually very precise in practice: we have yet to find a false alarm in any of our experiments.

---

[1] RV-Predict compresses traces to keep sizes manageable. Reversing the trace is done at logging time by outputting a buffer of events backwards into separate archives. The archives are then read by the trace slicer in reverse order.

Vector Clocking. Vector clocks [19] are routinely used to capture causal partial orders in distributed and concurrent systems. A VC-based algorithm was presented in [26] to encode a conventional multithreaded-system "happen-before" causal partial order on the unsliced trace. We next adapt that algorithm to work on our sliced trace and thus to capture the sliced causality. Recall that a vector clock (VC) is a function from threads to integers, $VC : T \to Int$. We say that $VC \leq VC'$ iff $\forall t \in T$, $VC(t) \leq VC'(t)$. The max function on VCs is defined as: $\max(VC_1, ..., VC_n)(t) = \max(VC_1(t), ..., VC_n(t))$ ([26]).

Before we explain our VC algorithm, let us introduce our event and trace notation. An *event* is a mapping of *attributes* into corresponding *values*. One event can be, e.g., $e_1 : (counter = 8, thread = t_1, stmt = L_{11}, type = write, target = a, state = 1)$, which is a write on location a with value 1, produced at statement L_{11} by thread t_1. One can include more information into an event by adding new attribute-value pairs. We use $key(e)$ to refer to the value of attribute key of event e. To distinguish different occurrences of events with the same attribute values, we add a designated attribute to every event, *counter*, collecting the number of previous events with the same attribute-value pairs (other than the *counter*). The trace for the vector clocking step is the φ-sliced trace ξ_φ obtained in Section 4.1.

Intuitively, vector clocks are used to track and transmit the causal partial ordering information in a concurrent computation, and are typically associated with elements participating in such computations, such as threads, processes, shared variables, messages, signals, etc. If VC and VC' are vector clocks such that $VC(t) \leq VC'(t)$ for some thread t, then we can say that VC' has newer information about t than VC. In our VC technique, every thread t keeps a vector clock, VC_t, maintaining information about all the threads obtained both locally and from thread communications (reads/writes of shared variables). Every shared variable is associated with two vector clocks, one for writes (VC_x^w) used to enforce the order among writes of x, and one for all accesses (VC_x^a) used to accumulate information about all accesses of x. They are then used together to keep the order between writes and reads of x. Every property event e found in the analysis is associated a VC attribute, which represents the computed causal partial order. We next show how to update these VCs when an event e is encountered during the analysis (the third case can overlap the first two; if so, the third case will be handled first):

1. $type(e) = write$, $target(e) = x$, $thread(e) = t$ (the variable x is written in thread t) and x is a shared variable. In this case, the write vector clock VC_x^w is updated to reflect the newly obtained information; since a write is also an access, the access VC of x is also updated; we also want to capture that t committed a causally irreversible action, by updating its VC as well: $VC_t \leftarrow VC_x^a \leftarrow VC_x^w \leftarrow \max(VC_x^a, VC_t)$.
2. $type(e) = read$, $target(e) = x$, $thread(e) = t$ (the variable x is read in t), and x is a shared variable. Then the thread updates its information with the write information of x (we do not want to causally order reads of shared variables!), and x updates its access information with that of the thread: $VC_t \leftarrow \max(VC_x^w, VC_t)$ and then $VC_x^a \leftarrow \max(VC_a^x, VC_t)$.

3. e is a property event and $thread(e) = t$. In this case, let $VC(e) := VC_t$. Then $VC_t(t)$ is increased to capture the intra-thread total ordering: $VC_t(t) \leftarrow VC_t(t) + 1$.

4.2   Race and Generic Property Detection

The basic idea of race detection is simple: check for accesses to the same variable with incomparable VCs. However, it is easy to note that this has quadratic worst case complexity, because each access must be compared against every other access. Clearly, when billions of accesses may occur in a trace, this is unacceptable. Not only would this be unbearable slow, but it would be impossible to even fit the accesses in memory to perform the comparisons.

To alleviate this, as well as to make it more easy to deal with streaming to and from the disk when memory is overfull, we use the idea of a window of comparisons, ignoring pairs of events that trivially cannot have incomparable vector clocks. If at some point we note the second access, $a_2^{T_1}$ in thread T_1 must occur after the fifth access, $a_5^{T_2}$, in thread T_2 we know that we do not need to check the $a_2^{T_1}$ against any further accesses in thread T_2 because all accesses in a given thread must be totally ordered (and the traces are backwards).

To implement this we use a set^2 of search states. Each search state abstracts the notion of checking accesses in two threads. Each search state keeps an iterator to the list of accesses representing one of its two given threads. The algorithm begins by keeping search states for each pair of threads in a set (actually not all threads are known immediately, but we will elide this detail for ease of understanding). Each state is advanced by considering the accesses pointed to by each of its iterators. If the iterators are incomparable, three new search states are added to the set. One state where one iterator is advanced, one where the other iterator is advanced, and one where both iterators are advanced. If the two accesses are incomparable and are not protected by a shared lock, a race is reported. If, one the other hand, the vector clocks of the two accesses in question are ordered, only one of the iterators is advanced, for example, if the access in thread t of the search state must take place before the access in thread t', the iterator pointing to the access from thread t is advanced, and no other states are generated.

This idea is easily extrapolated to generic property detection. One caveat, however, is that the iterators of the search states point to streams of monitoring events like those describes in Section 3 rather than accesses to shared variables. Also, rather than keeping iterators to only two threads in a search state, each search state keeps an iterator to every thread in the program. Each search state, additionally, keeps a reference to a monitor provided by the **Prediction Monitor Library** component of Fig. 1. When a search state is advanced, a new set of states is created and added to the overall set of states the same as for race detection, save that the advanced iterators are the subset of iterators with

---

^{2} We must use a set to avoid duplicate search states, or the algorithm can quickly explode.

incomparable *VCs*, and that states that end up with the same monitor state are collapsed immediately into one chosen representative search state. For each search state thus generated, the event uncovered by advancing one of the iterators is given to its monitor to check for property violation or validation. While this is exponential in the worst case, in practice most search states are collapsed because they have identical monitor states and positions in the event stream.

4.3   Prediction Example

Here we give a simple example of race prediction using RV-Predict:

```
bash-3.2$ cat simple/Simple.java
package simple;
public class Simple extends Thread {
   static public int i = 1;
   public static void main(String[] args) {
      (new Simple()).start();
      (new Simple()).start();
   }
   public void run() {
      i++;
      System.out.println(i);
   }
}
```

This program creates two threads, each incrementing the shared variable *i* and then printing it. This program has two dataraces, one on the variable *i* and one on the output. All one has to do is to compile this program with javac and then pass the binary to RV-Predict:

```
bash-3.2$ javac simple/Simple.java
bash-3.2$ RV-Predict simple.Simple
Instrumenting...
...Done
Executing the instrumented code...
 2
 3
...Done
Running Race Detection...
  Determining race candidates
  The following are our race candidates:
   | java.io.PrintStream (instance #657291792) | simple.Simple.i
  Predicting for race candidate: java.io.PrintStream (instance #657291792)

  /--- Race found on java.io.PrintStream (instance #657291792) ---\
  | Write at simple.Simple:10                                      |
  | Write at simple.Simple:10                                      |
  \---------------------------------------------------------------/

  Predicting for race candidate: simple.Simple.i

  /--- Race found on simple.Simple.i ---\
  | Read  at simple.Simple:10            |
  | Write at simple.Simple:9             |
  \-------------------------------------/

...Done
bash-3.2$
```

Both races were detected from one run of the program, even though the observed run behaved normally (the output was 2,3). The different components of RV-Predict from Fig. 1 can be seen in the above output. "Execution the instrumented code" corresponds to the **Logging** component. "Instrumenting" and "Race Detection" are self-evident.

4.4   Prediction Results

Fig. 8 summarizes the differences in real time and disk usage between the original jPredictor system first presented in [14] and RV-Predict for race prediction as measured on a system with two quad core Xeon E5430 processors running at 2.66GHz and 16 GB of 667 MHz DDR2 memory running Redhat Linux. On very small examples jPredictor occasionally outperforms RV-Predict, but on anything substantial RV-Predict is a vast improvement. Account, elevator, and tsp are actual programs used to benchmark parallel systems. Huge, medium, small, and the mixed locks examples are microbenchmarks that we designed to test particularly difficult aspects of race detection, such as millions of accesses to the same shared variable in huge.

		jPredictor		RV-Predict	
Name	Input	Real Time	Disk Usage	Real Time	Disk Usage
account	-	0:02.07	236K	0:04.31	360K
elevator	-	5:55.29	63M	1:20.31	864K
tsp	map4 2	5:30.87	16M	1:33.44	744K
tsp	map5 2	10:10.19	17M	2:20.95	868K
tsp	map10 2	8:25:04.00	442M	29:27.13	2.8M
huge	-	crash	crash	0:42.22	13M
medium	-	crash	crash	0:06.12	840K
small	-	crash	crash	0:05.99	292K
mixedlockshuge	-	8:13:40.00	250M	0:13.95	2.9M
mixedlocksbig	-	5:44.89	25M	0:07.03	496K
mixedlocksmedium	-	0:08.92	2.7M	0:07.25	308K
mixedlockssmall	-	0:05.46	1.5M	0:05.67	296K

Fig. 8. jPredictor Vs. RV-Predict

References

1. Allan, C., Avgustinov, P., Christensen, A.S., Hendren, L.J., Kuzins, S., Lhoták, O., de Moor, O., Sereni, D., Sittampalam, G., Tibble, J.: Adding trace matching with free variables to AspectJ. In: OOPSLA 2005, pp. 345–364. ACM, New York (2005)
2. Avgustinov, P., Tibble, J., de Moor, O.: Making trace monitors feasible. In: OOPSLA 2007, pp. 589–608. ACM, New York (2007)
3. Barringer, H., Goldberg, A., Havelund, K., Sen, K.: Rule-Based Runtime Verification. In: Steffen, B., Levi, G. (eds.) VMCAI 2004. LNCS, vol. 2937, pp. 44–57. Springer, Heidelberg (2004)

4. Blackburn, S.M., Garner, R., Hoffman, C., Khan, A.M., McKinley, K.S., Bentzur, R., Diwan, A., Feinberg, D., Frampton, D., Guyer, S.Z., Hirzel, M., Hosking, A., Jump, M., Lee, H., Moss, J.E.B., Phansalkar, A., Stefanović, D., VanDrunen, T., von Dincklage, D., Wiedermann, B.: The DaCapo benchmarks: Java benchmarking development and analysis. In: Object-Oriented Programming, Systems, Languages and Applications (OOPSLA 2006), pp. 169–190. ACM, New York (2006)

5. Chen, F., Meredith, P., Jin, D., Roşu, G.: Efficient formalism-independent monitoring of parametric properties. In: Automated Software Engineering (ASE 2009). IEEE, Los Alamitos (2009) (to appear)

6. Chen, F., D'Amorim, M., Roşu, G.: A formal monitoring-based framework for software development and analysis. In: Davies, J., Schulte, W., Barnett, M. (eds.) ICFEM 2004. LNCS, vol. 3308, pp. 357–372. Springer, Heidelberg (2004)

7. Chen, F., D'Amorim, M., Roşu, G.: Checking and correcting behaviors of Java programs at runtime with JavaMOP. In: Runtime Verification (RV 2006). ENTCS, vol. 144, pp. 3–20 (2006)

8. Chen, F., Roşu, G.: Towards monitoring-oriented programming: A paradigm combining specification and implementation. In: Runtime Verification (RV 2003). ENTCS, vol. 89 (2003)

9. Chen, F., Roşu, G.: Java-MOP: A monitoring oriented programming environment for Java. In: Halbwachs, N., Zuck, L.D. (eds.) TACAS 2005. LNCS, vol. 3440, pp. 546–550. Springer, Heidelberg (2005)

10. Chen, F., Roşu, G.: MOP: An efficient and generic runtime verification framework. In: OOPSLA 2007, pp. 569–588. ACM, New York (2007)

11. Chen, F., Roşu, G.: Parametric and Sliced Causality. In: Damm, W., Hermanns, H. (eds.) CAV 2007. LNCS, vol. 4590, pp. 240–253. Springer, Heidelberg (2007)

12. Chen, F., Roşu, G.: Parametric trace slicing and monitoring. In: Kowalewski, S., Philippou, A. (eds.) TACAS 2009. LNCS, vol. 5505, pp. 246–261. Springer, Heidelberg (2009)

13. Chen, F., Roşu, G.: Parametric and termination-sensitive control dependence - extended abstract. In: Yi, K. (ed.) SAS 2006. LNCS, vol. 4134, pp. 387–404. Springer, Heidelberg (2006)

14. Chen, F., Şerbănuţă, T.F., Roşu, G.: jPredictor: a predictive runtime analysis tool for Java. In: International Conference on Software Engineering (ICSE 2008), pp. 221–230. ACM, New York (2008)

15. Drusinsky, D.: Temporal Rover (1997–2009), http://www.time-rover.com

16. Flanagan, C., Freund, S.N.: Atomizer: a dynamic atomicity checker for multithreaded programs. In: Principles of Programming Languages, POPL 2004 (2004)

17. Goldsmith, S., O'Callahan, R., Aiken, A.: Relational queries over program traces. In: OOPSLA 2005, pp. 385–402. ACM, New York (2005)

18. Havelund, K., Roşu, G.: Monitoring Java programs with Java PathExplorer. In: Runtime Verification (RV 2001). ENTCS, vol. 55 (2001)

19. Lamport, L.: Time, clocks, and the ordering of events in a distributed system. Comm. of ACM 21(7), 558–565 (1978)

20. Martin, M., Livshits, V.B., Lam, M.S.: Finding application errors and security flaws using PQL: a program query language. In: OOPSLA 2007, pp. 365–383. ACM, New York (2005)

21. Meredith, P., Jin, D., Chen, F., Roşu, G.: Efficient monitoring of parametric context-free patterns. In: Automated Software Engineering (ASE 2008), pp. 148–157. IEEE, Los Alamitos (2008)

22. O'Callahan, R., Choi, J.D.: Hybrid dynamic data race detection. In: ACM SIGPLAN Symposium on Principles and Practice of Parallel Programming, PPoPP 2003 (2003)
23. von Praun, C., Gross, T.R.: Object race detection. In: Object Oriented Programming, Systems, Languages, and Applications, OOPSLA 2001 (2001)
24. Savage, S., Burrows, M., Nelson, G., Sobalvarro, P., Anderson, T.: Eraser: a dynamic data race detector for multithreaded programs. ACM Transaction of Computer System 15(4), 391–411 (1997)
25. Sen, A., Garg, V.K.: Detecting temporal logic predicates in distributed programs using computation slicing. In: Papatriantafilou, M., Hunel, P. (eds.) OPODIS 2003. LNCS, vol. 3144, pp. 171–183. Springer, Heidelberg (2004)
26. Sen, K., Roşu, G., Agha, G.: Runtime safety analysis of multithreaded programs. In: ACM SIGSOFT Symposium on Foundations of Software Engineering, FSE 2003 (2003)
27. Wang, L., Stoller, S.D.: Accurate and efficient runtime detection of atomicity errors in concurrent programs. In: ACM SIGPLAN Symposium on Principles and Practice of Parallel Programming, PPoPP 2006 (2006)

A Meta-Aspect Protocol
for Developing Dynamic Analyses

Michael Achenbach[1] and Klaus Ostermann[2]

[1] Aarhus University, Denmark
ma@cs.au.dk
[2] University of Marburg, Germany
kos@informatik.uni-marburg.de

Abstract. Dynamic aspect-oriented programming has been widely used for the development of dynamic analyses to abstract over low-level program instrumentation. Due to particular feature requirements in different analysis domains like debugging or testing, many different aspect languages were developed from scratch or by extensive compiler or interpreter extensions. We introduce another level of abstraction in form of a meta-aspect protocol to separate the host language from the analysis domain. A language expert can use this protocol to tailor an analysis-specific aspect language, based on which a domain expert can develop a particular analysis. Our design enables a flexible specification of the join point model, configurability of aspect deployment and scoping, and extensibility of pointcut and advice language. We present the application of our design to different dynamic analysis domains.

1   Introduction

Many dynamic analyses make use of program instrumentation tools to transform the abstract-syntax tree (AST) of analyzed code. This leads to a tight coupling between low-level language and analysis design. A designer needs expert knowledge of the language specification, evolution of the language makes analyses brittle, and the analysis code base includes many instrumentation details [5].

Aspect-oriented programming (AOP) has been used to overcome these problems [17, 25]. AOP allows high-level abstractions of program instrumentation using pointcut and advice, and facilitates rapid design of small analysis aspects, decoupled from language details. However, different dynamic analyses require different aspect language features and instrumentation techniques. A debugging tool might require a fine-grained instrumentation level (e.g., statement-based) [19], while a memory profiler might need only object-allocation instrumentation [24]. Often, domain-specific aspect languages (DSALs) are built from scratch or by extensive compiler extensions to fit particular requirements. A general-purpose AOP language that covers all possible features, however, induces unnecessary overhead and requires broader expert knowledge than a DSAL.

In object-oriented languages, metaobject protocols (MOPs) have been developed to access and adapt the language semantics from the programming level

G. Roşu et al. (Eds.): RV 2010, LNCS 6418, pp. 153–167, 2010.
© Springer-Verlag Berlin Heidelberg 2010

of the language itself [14]. In AOP, meta-aspect protocols (MAPs) have been suggested, where parts of the language semantics are like in MOPs controlled through a concrete interface [11]. This enables domain-specific extensions (DSX) without the requirement of a new compiler or interpreter. However, there exists no MAP known to the authors that covers the requirements of dynamic analyses.

We present a MAP that focuses in particular on the requirements of dynamic analyses in the setting of dynamically typed languages. It is based on a load-time program transformation that inserts hooks for dynamic aspect weaving and scoping. The join point model is based on a user-defined AST-transformation, so that every syntactic element can be included as a join point. The language interface facilitates the configuration of different dynamic deployment methods (global, per block, per reference) and scoping mechanisms (stack/reference propagation) [4,6,21], and the extension of pointcut and advice [1].

We present two DSXs based on our protocol focusing on the requirements of the domains debugging and testing, respectively. Based on these extensions, we develop two exemplary analysis aspects with a small code base.

The contributions of this work are as follows:

- We discuss several dynamic analyses that build on AOP. We point out particular dynamic AOP features that are required in certain analysis domains.
- We present a dynamic meta-aspect protocol that provides direct access to the aspect language semantics at runtime and allows the configuration of domain-specific extensions for particular dynamic analysis domains.
- We provide an implementation of our extensible language and evaluate its applicability by developing language extensions and analysis aspects for the domains debugging and testing.

We chose Ruby as implementation language, but the design could be applied to other dynamic languages like Groovy as well. We intend our MAP to be used for prototyping and developing analyses in domains like debugging and testing, which are not limited by strict performance requirements, since dynamic AOP comes with the cost of a certain runtime overhead.

The remainder of this paper is organized as follows: We analyze the requirements of dynamic analyses in Sec. 2 and discuss related AOP approaches. Section 3 presents the design of our meta-aspect protocol for dynamic analyses. We evaluate our protocol in Sec. 4 on two example applications, followed by our conclusion.

2 Motivation

In the following, we analyze the requirements of dynamic analysis regarding AOP, in order to build a flexible abstraction layer over program instrumentation. We then discuss related approaches that either lack flexibility or generality.

2.1 Interception Requirements of Dynamic Analyses

Dynamic analyses vary widely in their interception requirements. We structure the resulting design space in four dimensions: Join point model, aspect deployment, aspect scope, and pointcut and advice language.

Join Point Model. Different analyses require different kinds of access to the program structure or execution context in form of join points.[1] To analyze performance and relation of method calls or to analyze memory consumption, method execution and object allocation join points are typically sufficient [24]. These requirements are met by general-purpose AOP languages like AspectJ [13]. However, more advanced monitoring and debugging tools require instrumentation on the level of basic blocks [5] or statements like assignment [17]. The debugging approach of [19] also introduces line number join points. Data-race detection is based on field access join points [7]. No general-purpose AOP language known to the authors meets all these requirements.

Aspect Deployment. The entity on which an aspect is deployed differs among many dynamic analyses (e.g., on the whole program, on objects or methods). Bodden and Stolz suggest dynamic advice deployment (with a global deploy/undeploy functionality) and per object deployment as in Steamloom [6] to optimize temporal pointcuts over execution traces [8]. Toledo et al. also deploy security aspects in the dynamic scope of application objects [23]. In earlier work, we used deployment on a block of code like in CaesarJ [4] to separate design changing aspects used in different test cases [2]. Deployment on a block is particularly powerful in combination with expressive aspect scoping [21].

Aspect Scope. Dynamic analyses often require fine-grained control over the scope in which an aspect is active to determine what should be and what should not be analyzed. E.g., omniscient debuggers (that can step backward in time) rely on vast execution traces. Tanter suggests therefore a notion of partial traces defined by an expressive scoping strategy [22]. Toledo et al. embed web application code into the scope of a security aspect that monitors access attempts [23]. A so called *pervasive* scope ensures that neither method calls nor references escape the aspect.

Pointcut and Advice Language. Allan et al. introduce binding of free variables in pointcut expressions for trace matching [3]. Dinkelaker et al. integrate a 3-valued logic language into the advice language [10], which is advantageous for analyses that reason with boolean abstractions at runtime like Java PathFinder [26]. Aspects that augment a program for test generation could be extended with domain-specific constructs for non-deterministic choice [12]. The possibility to specify new keywords for pointcut and advice enables shorter, analysis-specific pointcut and advice definitions [1].

Our survey shows that certain classes of analyses require different AOP features. General-purpose AOP does not solve the problem. If it covered all necessary AOP features of all analysis domains, it would induce a lot of performance overhead for some domains. If it was specialized, some domains would lack important

---

[1] A join point is a point in the program text (static) or in the execution (dynamic), where an interception with aspects can take place. A join point model defines the set of possible join points and also the kind of interaction, e.g., if and how the program state or control-flow can be changed at the join point and how aspects interact.

features. Furthermore, the more features are covered, the more expert knowledge is required by the analysis developer. A DSAL, in contrast, allows for domain-specific abstractions of the respective analysis domain.

To avoid building a new DSAL for each class of dynamic analysis from scratch, we need another level of abstraction between language and analysis domain. This will allow a language expert to tailor a domain-specific extension that covers the features of a certain analysis type like debugging. Based on the DSX, a domain expert can rapidly prototype a dynamic analysis that is decoupled from host language details.

2.2   Related Work

There have been previous works on extensible AOP languages, but none of them meets the requirements for dynamic analyses in a satisfactory way. A meta-aspect protocol (MAP) has been developed for the dynamic language Groovy [11]. The join point model is configurable, based on the one of AspectJ [13], which, as illustrated above, is not sufficient for fine-grained instrumentation, e.g., on basic block level. The MAP facilitates both static and dynamic deployment, but does not provide configurable and expressive dynamic scoping concepts. There are also approaches that extend AspectJ by modifying its sources to include more fine-grained join points [9].

Javana is an instrumentation system for building customized dynamic analysis tools for the JVM [15]. The domain-specific Javana language, provides an AOP-like join point model over virtual machine events like object allocation, class loading, or method compilation. Unlike in our approach, the set of events and the language are fixed and can neither be extended nor reduced.

There are specialized approaches for particular analysis domains. Nusayr et al. suggest an AOP framework for runtime monitoring with basic block join points and pointcuts over time and space [17]. Nir-Buchbinder and Ur present a framework for concurrency-aware analysis tools [16]. Binder et al. develop profiler aspects based on the @J language, that supports basic block join points and inter advice communication [5]. Rakesh develops debuggers with line number pointcuts [19]. All these approaches lack generality by implementing fixed sets of features, focusing on the respective analysis domains.

3   The Meta-Aspect Protocol

A meta-aspect protocol (MAP) gives access to the aspect language semantics through a concrete interface on the program level [11]. From the discussion in Section 2.1 we can derive that a MAP for dynamic analysis requires variability in the following dimensions: We need a flexible join point model that allows every syntactical element to be a potential join point. We require different dynamic deployment methods and expressive dynamic scoping. Finally, pointcut and advice language should be extensible with domain-specific constructs.

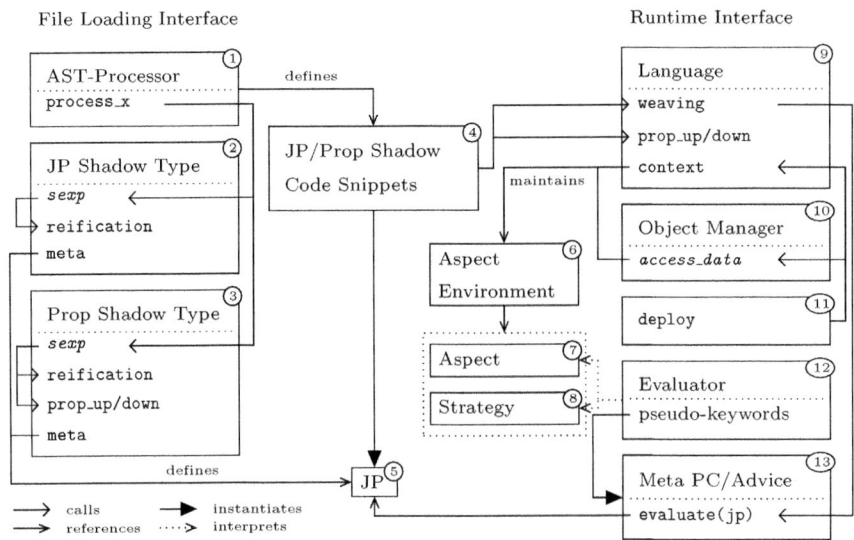

Fig. 1. Overview of the language interface and the main components. Courier fonts refer to actual source methods. Methods in italics are non-modifiable.

We provide a language interface that is instantiated with configurations and extensions of the aforementioned dimensions. We give an overview of the interface and the main components in Sec. 3.1. The join point model is defined by an AST transformation, which we explain in Sec. 3.2. Section 3.3 presents our extensible pointcut and advice language. We illustrate instantiations of different dynamic deployment methods in Sec. 3.4 and demonstrate the configurability of our language w.r.t. expressive aspect scoping in Sec. 3.5.

The features of all four dimensions can be selectively combined. We will instantiate distinguished sets of features to develop two example applications in Sec. 4. The implementation and all examples shown in this work are integrated into the TwisteR project, available at http://twister.rubyforge.org.

3.1 Language Interface

Figure 1 gives an overview of the language interface and the main components. We will briefly discuss each and go into more detail in the following sections. The interface is separated into a file loading and a runtime interface. The first comes into play when client code is loaded. The second contains callback methods and extensible classes used at runtime. Loaded code is transformed by a custom AST processor (1), which inserts join point and propagation shadows (4). A join point shadow is a code snippet placed at join points. It guides advice interaction through the `weaving` callback (9). Propagation shadows are code snippets that maintain the scope of aspects. They embed the original code at the point of insertion (e.g., a method call) and configure aspect propagation before and after the embedded code with the prop_up/down methods. These methods exist once globally (9) and once for each propagation shadow type (3).

Aspects (7) are associated with scoping strategies (8) and stored in an aspect environment (6). The environment is maintained via the global language interface (9) or through an object manager (10), which associates data with arbitrary runtime objects using reflection. At runtime, join and propagation points are reified through meta objects (5), on which context data is accessible. They are evaluated by meta objects for pointcut and advice (13), guided by the weaving callback. Pointcut and advice are instantiated through extensible evaluators (12), which interpret aspects and scoping strategies, for enabling the embedding of domain-specific pointcut and advice languages. Finally, aspect deployment is performed by a user-defined method at (11), which modifies the corresponding aspect environment.

3.2   AST-Based Join Point Model

We represent the AST of a program using S-expressions known from LISP. The join point model of a custom AOP language is defined by a transformer on this expression. The custom S-expression processor is part of the language interface and augments particular AST nodes with join point and propagation shadows for dynamic weaving and scoping.

S-Expressions. S-expressions are nested list-based data structures. In our implementation, we use external libraries for parsing code and translating S-expressions back to code written in Ruby [18, 20]. Each S-expression is represented by a function call s(...) listing nested elements as arguments. The list consists of a type symbol, followed by nested S-expressions or primitives like symbols, strings or numbers. We chose the S-expression representation dependent on the external libraries – transforming it into an AST data structure would be straightforward.

Processor for Join Point Generation. We distinguish two types of join point shadows: the first type encloses a piece of code, which we will call *interceptor* shadow, the second type only attaches statements to a sequence of code, which we will call *companion* shadow. While the first can change the entire control flow, the second can still access and change the state of the enclosing object.

At load-time, an AST-transformation, defined by a custom S-expression processor (see Fig. 1 (1)), is applied to the code. The transformer performs a traversal over the AST and calls visitor methods for each node type to insert join point shadows. Each join point type is represented by a singleton class (see Fig. 1 (2)) that builds the corresponding shadows. At runtime, each join point is represented by a reified meta object (see Fig. 1 (5)), accessible by pointcut and advice.

Figure 2 illustrates an S-expression processor that integrates method-execution and if-condition join points, which we will need for our testing application (see Sec. 4.1). The class CustomProcessor implements visitor methods process_x for each node type x that needs augmentation with join point shadows. The singleton

```
        class CustomProcessor              (5)  class AroundIfCond
            < JoinPointProcessor                    < InterceptorShadowType
 (1)    def process_if(exp)                      def self.reification ast_context
            oldc = process(exp.shift)                {:modifier=>:around}
            newc = AroundIfCond.sexp(oldc)        end
            return s(:if, newc, process(exp.shift),  def self.meta
                process(exp.shift))                  IfConditionJoinPoint
        end                                       end
        def process_defn(exp)                   end
            name = exp.shift
 (2)        ast_context[:name] = name        (6)  class BeforeMExec
            args = process(exp.shift)               < CompanionShadowType
            old = process(exp.shift)             def self.reification ast_context
            before = BeforeMExec.sexp               {:name=>ast_context[:name],
 (3)        cap = capture(:result, old)             ...}
            after = AfterMExec.sexp(capture)      end
 (4)        newb = s(:block, before, cap.sexp,   def self.meta
                after, cap.var)                     MethodExecutionJoinPoint
            return s(:defn, name, args, newb)    end
        end                                     end
        end
```

Fig. 2. Custom join point processor

classes that create the join point shadows are defined at (5) and (6) (`AfterMExec` not shown here). At (1), we augment the if-expression condition with an interceptor shadow that embeds the original code. We iterate over the subexpressions using `exp.shift` and process each recursively.

At method definitions (2), we add the actual method name to the context stack, which stores context information of each AST node and its parents. The original method body is transformed to capture its result in a fresh local variable at (3). The join point shadows are inserted into a sequence before and after the original method body at (4). The method evaluates to the captured result of the original block. Connecting the capturing class and `AfterMExec` enables access to the result through the reified meta join point.

The classes at (5) and (6) differ in their join point reification. The method `reification` defines how to reify the dynamic context at runtime and specifies how to instantiate the meta object that represents the join point. E.g., the method execution join point provides access to the name of the executing method, retrieved from the context stack. Each join point automatically provides access to the self reference of the surrounding object.

Hooks for Weaving. Each join point shadow defines the interaction with pointcut and advice. As a default, interceptor shadows introduce *around* advice application and embed the original code to be called if no advice can be applied or if the `proceed` method is called. Companion shadows introduce advice like

```
tracing = Aspect.new do                    around pc{jp.type == :if_cond} do
  before pc{jp.type == :execution} do        puts "Cond => #{res = proceed}"
    puts "Tracing #{jp.name}"                 res
  end                                        end
  after ...                                end
```

Fig. 3. Simple tracing aspect

before and *after* at discrete points in the program, so that the original control-flow is not modified.

3.3 Pointcut and Advice Language

In earlier work, we developed an extensible pointcut and advice language that we adopted in the current approach [1]. Figure 3 shows the instantiation of a simple aspect that traces method execution and condition evaluation. Aspects are first-class values, their definition is passed as a closure (between do..end) to the constructor (called by `Aspect.new`). The closure is interpreted on an extensible evaluator object (see Fig. 1 (12)) on which pseudo-keywords like `pc` are resolved as pretended method calls and property accesses [10]. Behind every keyword is a meta class that represents the construct, e.g., each pointcut is reflected by a meta pointcut with an evaluation function that takes the reified join point as an argument and returns `true` or `false` (see Fig. 1 (13)). The meta classes implement also operators that allow their composition and syntactic sugar (like the operators &,| and ! to compose pointcuts). The `before`, `around`, and `after` pseudo-keywords specify advice that will be executed at matching join points. The pseudo-keyword `jp` gives access to the reified meta join point. In [1], we presented extensions of this approach, e.g., the introduction of new pseudo-keywords, which enables an AspectJ-like syntax, or the simulation of `cflow`. Extensions could also comprise constructs that embed temporal logics or binding of free variables.

3.4 Deployment

In this section, we present different aspect deployment methods and their application. We first illustrate a simple global deployment mechanism, which we will use for our debugging application (see Sec. 4.2). Then we define a deployment of aspects on object references and deployment in the scope of a block of code, which we will apply in our testing application (see Sec. 4.1).

Global Deployment. Using the global deployment method, all deployed aspects have a global scope. Figure 4 shows the language interface and sample deployment. The aspect language `Global` subclasses `AspectLanguage`, which manages the registration of all language components. At (1), we initialize a global aspect environment that stores a list of deployed aspects (see Fig. 1 (6)). The methods at (2) define the language semantics. They are called during language

```
class Global < AspectLanguage                  (4)  def deploy aspect
  def initialize                                      LANG.context.add aspect
(1)  @context = AspectEnvironment.new              end
  end                                             def undeploy aspect
(2)  def processor; CustomProcessor end             LANG.context.remove aspect
  def context; @context; end                      end
  def weaving jp                                   # Example code:
    context.iterate_aspects{ |a|                  def get_sign x
      a.each_advice(jp){ |pc, ad|                   if x>0; ">0" else "<=0" end; end
      if pc.evaluate(jp)                          def sign x; puts get_sign(x); end
(3)       yield lambda{ad.evaluate(jp)}      (5)  deploy tracing
      end }}                                       sign(5)
  end                                             undeploy tracing
end
```

Fig. 4. Global deployment of the tracing aspect from Fig.3

initialization and from the join point shadows. We reuse the join point processor defined in Fig. 2. The `weaving` is performed at every join point shadow, it takes a meta join point and an anonymous block as arguments. The block guides advice application and is called with `yield` for each matching advice at (3). This abstracts as a co-routine over the actual weaving loop of both companion and interception types. Extensions of the weaving loop could comprise, e.g., advice precedence or optimizations that omit aspects at particular join points.

The deployment methods are defined at (4), and manipulate the global aspect environment (the aspect language is accessible via the global constant **LANG**). We deploy the tracing aspect from Fig.3 at (5) on a simple example. The application of the `sign` method causes tracing of `sign` and `get_sign` and of the evaluation of the condition in `get_sign`.

Per Object Deployment. The first column of Fig. 5 shows deployment in the scope of particular objects. Instead of a global aspect environment, we maintain an environment per object. The objects are augmented using a central object manager (see Fig. 1 (10)), initialized at (1). It can be accessed using the `objects` method of the language. At (2), the weaving process iterates over the object stored in the target field of the join point, which is, e.g., the receiver object at method calls or the `self` reference at an if-condition join point. The deployment method at (3) creates a new aspect environment and adds it to the corresponding object. Applying the example at (4) using the tracing aspect from Fig. 3 will trace the method call `to_s` of `date`, but no methods from other objects.

Per Block Deployment. The second column of Fig. 5 introduces deployment in the scope of a block of code. Instead of one global environment, an environment stack is initialized at (5) and maintained with the callback methods at (6). The deployment method at (7) takes an aspect, a (yet unused) scoping strategy and an anonymous block as arguments. It maintains the aspect environment stack around the call to the block (`yield`), so that the deployed aspect is active in the

```
     class PerObject < AspectLanguage
       def initialize
(1)      @objects = ObjMan.new(:env)
       end
       def weaving jp
(2)      if objects.augmented?(jp.target)
           env = objects.get_data(jp.target)
           env.iterate_aspects{ |a|
             ... }
         end
       end
     end

     def deploy_on object, a
(3)    env = AspectEnvironment.new
       env.add a
       LANG.objects.augment(object)
       LANG.objects.set_data(object, env)
     end

     # Example:
(4)  date = Date.new(15, 3)
     deploy_on date, tracing
     puts date.to_s
```

```
     class PerBlock < AspectLanguage
       def initialize
(5)      @context = [AspectEnvironment.new]
       end
(6)    def context; @context.last; end
       def prop_up env
         @context.push env
       end
       def prop_down
         @context.pop
       end
     end

(7)  def deploy a, s=nil
       env = LANG.context.clone
       LANG.prop_up(env)
       LANG.context.add a, s
       yield
       LANG.context.remove a, s
       LANG.prop_down
     end

     # Example:
(8)  deploy tracing do sign(5) end
```

Fig. 5. Per object and per block deployment of the tracing aspect

dynamic extent of this block. The example at (8) will apply tracing to everything in the control flow of the method call sign(5).

3.5 Scoping

Tanter generalized the scope of aspects with a set of propagation or scoping functions [21]. An aspect can, for example, be propagated over the call stack at particular join points or into object references to enable a so called *pervasive* scoping. Our design facilitates a lightweight integration of some or all of these scoping mechanisms as we will show in the following. A scoping strategy object stores the scoping functions and is associated with each aspect (shown in Fig. 5 at (7) as parameter s). It can be accessed at various points during weaving and propagation. Scoping functions have the same semantics as pointcuts in our language (see Sec 3.3) and can be extended in the same way. The propagation of aspects is performed by propagation shadows in the code. Those are inserted like join point shadows by the AST transformation. A propagation shadow embeds a piece of code like an interceptor shadow and inserts a propagation expression before and after the code. Possible expressions are filter(x), where the current aspect environment is filtered by function x, inject(x, f), where the aspect environment is filtered by x and stored in the actual join point using field f, and extract(f), where the aspect environment is restored from the actual join point using field f.

```
(1)  class AroundMExecProp              class CustomProcessor ...
       < PropagationShadowType            def process_defn(exp) ...
     def self.reification ast_context       return s(:defn, name, args,
       {:name => ast_context[:name]}  (2)      AroundMExecProp.sexp(body))
     end                                  end
     def self.meta ...                  end
     def self.prop_up
       filter(:c)                       # Example:
     end                                s = Strategy.new {
     end                          (3)   {:c => pc{jp.name != :get_sign}}}
                                         deploy tracing, s do sign(5) end
```

Fig. 6. Scoping strategy over the call stack

Call Stack Scope. Figure 6 defines the propagation of aspects over the call stack. The singleton class for propagation shadow creation (see Fig. 1 (3)) also has an associated meta join point for reification. We reuse the processor from Fig. 2 and the language `PerBlock` defined in Fig. 5, but augment method bodies with the propagation expression at (2). The propagation expression automatically calls the context propagation of the language (which we defined in Fig. 5 at (6)), so that the environment stack is extended in the context of the embedded code. Before the embedded code is executed, the propagation at (1) applies the filter method, which uses scoping function c of the scoping strategy associated with each aspect in the environment. The example at (3) defines a strategy that associates with function c a pointcut that prevents propagating the tracing beyond the dynamic extent of the `get_sign` method.

Delayed Evaluation Scope. In object-oriented languages, an object created in the scope of a dynamic aspect can escape this scope through a reference (which would be a flaw for a security aspect [23]). The propagation of aspects into references allows a richer and more pervasive scoping [21]. We reuse the language defined in Fig. 6, augmenting object creation sites with a propagation shadow that applies `inject(d, result)` after the embedded code, which will store the actual environment in the result (the created object) filtered by d. At method executions, we use propagation `extract(target)` to restore the aspect environment from the receiver. Now we can apply the language in the following example:

```
s = Strategy.new do {:d => True} end
deploy tracing, s do; date = Date.new 17,4; end
puts date.to_s
```

We associate the strategy function d with a constant pointcut that always returns `true`, which propagates the tracing aspect into the escaping reference `date`.

4   Applications

In the following, we present two instantiations of our MAP. They are used for the development of two different analyses that build on distinguished AOP features.

```
class TestLangProcessor ...
  def process_if(e)
    # From Fig. 2
  end
  def process_defn(exp)
    # From Fig. 6
  end
end

# Example:
def create_display color, refresh
  log "Create display"
  if color
    # Creates colored display...
    if refresh; # ...with refresh
    else; # ...without refresh
    end
  end
end
```

```
# Variant without lazy choice:
(1)  create_display(choice(true, false),
         choice(true, false))

# Variant with lazy choice:
lazy_choice = ExtAspect.new do
  around if_cond do
    case (result = proceed)
      when TVTrue then true
      when TVFalse then false
      when TVUnkn then
        choice(true, false)
      else result
    end; end; end

s = Strategy.new {
    {:c => !name(:log)}}}
(3)  deploy lazy_choice, s do
       create_display(TVUnkn, TVUnkn)
     end
```

Fig. 7. Aspect for lazy choice in testing with non-determinism

4.1   Explorative Testing

In earlier work, we presented a test exploration tool that reduces the size of test cases by applying a non-deterministic choice operator [2]. Such an operator has also been used for the generation of complex test input [12]. The authors of [12] suggest the application of lazy choice to avoid a combinatorial explosion of possible executions. In the following, we instantiate the MAP for integrating lazy choice with an aspect that delays choices to the evaluation of conditions.

The language components for instantiating the MAP are shown in Fig 7. We implement a 3-valued boolean abstraction with TVTrue, TVFalse and TVUnkn. We will reuse the stack propagation from Fig. 6 and the deployment on blocks from Fig. 5. Due to the direct evaluation of choice, the execution of the example at (1) will lead to four different execution paths of which two are identical. At (2), we define a lazy choice aspect that resolves 3-valued logic abstractions at the evaluation of conditions. Like that, the choice is delayed to the point were the *unknown* value flows into a condition. In the scope of the aspect, the test at (3) will yield only the three distinguished executions. For the sake of brevity, we omit caching of made choices in this example. With the deployment strategy s, we optimize the aspect's scope by avoiding propagation into logging methods of the program. While we saved only one execution, lazy choice becomes particularly important when generating more complex test input.

4.2   Debugging

In the following, we develop a debugging-specific extension of our protocol and then build a prototype debugger based on it. The first column of Fig. 8 shows

```
class AtStmt                              tracing = ExtAspect.new do
    < CompanionShadowType          (1)      before stmt & stype(:lasgn) do
  def self.reification ast_context            puts "Assignment to: #{var}"
  result = {:modifier => :before,           end
    :stype => ast_context[:stype]}        end
  if ast_context[:var]
   result[:var] =                         debugging = ExtAspect.new do
     ast_context[:var]                      around execution do
  end                                         puts "Entering: #{name}"
  return result                             print "Step [i|o|t|u]:"
 end                                         com = gets.chomp
 def self.meta ...                  (2)      deploy(tracing) if com =~ /t/
end                                          undeploy(tracing) if com =~ /u/
class CustomProcessor ...                    if com =~ /o/
 def process_if(exp)                (3)        undeploy debugging
  ast_context[:stype] = :if                    begin
  return s(:block,                               proceed
     AtStmt.sexp, s(:if,...))                   ensure
 end                                            deploy debugging
 def process_lasgn(exp)                         end
  ast_context[:stype] = :lasgn                else
  name = exp.shift                              proceed
  ast_context[:var] = name                    end
  return s(:block,                  (4)      end
     AtStmt.sexp, s(:lasgn,...))            before stmt ...
 end                                        end
end                                       end
                                          deploy debugging
                                          # Application code...
```

Fig. 8. Debugging language components and debugging aspect

an excerpt of the join point processor. We define a statement-based join point model that introduces join point shadows, e.g., at assignments, conditions, loop headers and bodies, method calls, etc. We reuse some language components like method execution join points defined in Fig. 2, the global deployment mechanism from Fig. 4 and some simplifying pointcut and advice expressions. We minimize the reified context information for the sake of brevity, but it is straightforward to include more data, e.g., about the static nesting of each statement.

The second column of Fig. 8 shows a simple debugging aspect. A statement advice enables stepping per statement at (4). We reuse the tracing aspect from Fig 4 extended with statement-based tracing, e.g., variable assignment at (1). The tracing can be toggled on and off during debugging with a command at (2). When tracing is off, the tracing aspect is not deployed and does not produce additional runtime overhead. The around advice intercepts method executions to facilitate a *step over* or *step into* functionality at (3). If the user chooses *step over*, the debugging aspect undeploys itself in the dynamic extent of the method's proceed.

The example shows the instantiation of a fine-grained join point model that goes beyond general-purpose AOP. Together with the testing example it demonstrates the selection and combination of distinct AOP features. We expect that analyses in other domains like profiling or security can also be rapidly developed through different instantiations of our meta-aspect protocol.

5   Conclusion

We presented a meta-aspect protocol for tailoring analysis-specific aspect languages. Our discussion of dynamic analyses showed distinguished requirements on AOP in different analysis domains. We illustrated a broad spectrum of dynamic AOP features that can be selectively combined. Analysis-specific instantiations configure join point model, deployment and scoping, based on which the actual analysis aspects can be rapidly prototyped. We discussed two example analyses in the domains debugging and testing to validate the usefulness of the approach. We demonstrated how to separate the work of language and domain expert, which will greatly ease the rapid development and the maintenance of dynamic analyses in different domains.

Acknowledgments

The authors would like to thank Christian Hofer and all the anonymous reviewers for their insightful comments and suggestions.

References

1. Achenbach, M., Ostermann, K.: Growing a dynamic aspect language in Ruby. In: Proceedings of the 2010 AOSD Workshop on Domain-Specific Aspect Languages. ACM, New York (2010)
2. Achenbach, M., Ostermann, K.: Testing object-oriented programs using dynamic aspects and non-determinism. In: Proceedings of the 1st ECOOP Workshop on Testing Object-Oriented Systems. ACM, New York (2010)
3. Allan, C., Avgustinov, P., Christensen, A.S., Hendren, L., Kuzins, S., Lhoták, O., de Moor, O., Sereni, D., Sittampalam, G., Tibble, J.: Adding trace matching with free variables to AspectJ. In: OOPSLA 2005, pp. 345–364. ACM, New York (2005)
4. Aracic, I., Gasiunas, V., Mezini, M., Ostermann, K.: An overview of CaesarJ. In: Rashid, A., Aksit, M. (eds.) Transactions on Aspect-Oriented Software Development I. LNCS, vol. 3880, pp. 135–173. Springer, Heidelberg (2006)
5. Binder, W., Villazón, A., Ansaloni, D., Moret, P.: @J: towards rapid development of dynamic analysis tools for the Java Virtual Machine. In: Proceedings of the Third Workshop on Virtual Machines and Intermediate Languages, pp. 1–9. ACM, New York (2009)
6. Bockisch, C., Haupt, M., Mezini, M., Ostermann, K.: Virtual machine support for dynamic join points. In: AOSD 2004, pp. 83–92. ACM, New York (2004)
7. Bodden, E., Havelund, K.: Racer: effective race detection using AspectJ. In: Proceedings of the 2008 International Symposium on Software Testing and Analysis, pp. 155–166. ACM, New York (2008)

8. Bodden, E., Stolz, V.: Efficient temporal pointcuts through dynamic advice deployment. In: Open and Dynamic Aspect Languages Workshop (2006)
9. Copty, S., Ur, S.: Multi-threaded testing with AOP is easy, and it finds bugs! In: Cunha, J.C., Medeiros, P.D. (eds.) Euro-Par 2005. LNCS, vol. 3648, pp. 740–749. Springer, Heidelberg (2005)
10. Dinkelaker, T., Mezini, M.: Dynamically linked domain-specific extensions for advice languages. In: Proceedings of the 2008 AOSD Workshop on Domain-Specific Aspect Languages, pp. 1–7. ACM, New York (2008)
11. Dinkelaker, T., Mezini, M., Bockisch, C.: The art of the meta-aspect protocol. In: AOSD 2009, pp. 51–62. ACM, New York (2009)
12. Gligoric, M., Khurshid, S., Gvero, T., Kuncak, V., Jagannath, V., Marinov, D.: Test generation through programming in UDITA. In: ICSE 2010, pp. 225–234. ACM, New York (2010)
13. Kiczales, G., Hilsdale, E., Hugunin, J., Kersten, M., Palm, J., Griswold, W.G.: An overview of AspectJ. In: Knudsen, J.L. (ed.) ECOOP 2001. LNCS, vol. 2072, pp. 327–353. Springer, Heidelberg (2001)
14. Kiczales, G., Rivieres, J.D., Bobrow, D.G.: The Art of the Metaobject Protocol. MIT Press, Cambridge (1991)
15. Maebe, J., Buytaert, D., Eeckhout, L., De Bosschere, K.: Javana: a system for building customized Java program analysis tools. In: OOPSLA 2006, pp. 153–168. ACM, New York (2006)
16. Nir-Buchbinder, Y., Ur, S.: ConTest listeners: a concurrency-oriented infrastructure for Java test and heal tools. In: Fourth International Workshop on Software Quality Assurance, pp. 9–16. ACM, New York (2007)
17. Nusayr, A., Cook, J.: AOP for the domain of runtime monitoring: breaking out of the code-based model. In: Proceedings of the 4th Workshop on Domain-Specific Aspect Languages, pp. 7–10. ACM, New York (2009)
18. Parse Tree and Ruby Parser, http://parsetree.rubyforge.org/
19. Rakesh, M.G.: A lightweight approach for program analysis and debugging. In: Proceedings of the 3rd India Software Engineering Conference, pp. 13–22. ACM, New York (2010)
20. Ruby2Ruby, http://seattlerb.rubyforge.org/ruby2ruby/
21. Tanter, É.: Expressive scoping of dynamically-deployed aspects. In: AOSD 2008, pp. 168–179. ACM, New York (2008)
22. Tanter, É.: Beyond static and dynamic scope. In: Proceedings of the 5th ACM Dynamic Languages Symposium, pp. 3–14. ACM, New York (2009)
23. Toledo, R., Leger, P., Tanter, É.: AspectScript: Expressive aspects for the Web. In: AOSD 2010, ACM, New York (2010)
24. Villazón, A., Binder, W., Ansaloni, D., Moret, P.: Advanced runtime adaptation for Java. In: GPCE 2009, pp. 85–94. ACM, New York (2009)
25. Villazón, A., Binder, W., Ansaloni, D., Moret, P.: HotWave: creating adaptive tools with dynamic aspect-oriented programming in Java. In: GPCE 2009, pp. 95–98. ACM, New York (2009)
26. Visser, W., Havelund, K., Brat, G., Park, S.: Model checking programs. In: Automated Software Engineering, pp. 3–11. IEEE, Los Alamitos (2000)

Behavior Abstraction in Malware Analysis*

Philippe Beaucamps, Isabelle Gnaedig, and Jean-Yves Marion

INPL - INRIA Nancy Grand Est - Nancy-Université - LORIA
Campus Scientifique - BP 239 F54506 Vandoeuvre-lès-Nancy Cedex, France
{Philippe.Beaucamps,Isabelle.Gnaedig,Jean-Yves.Marion}@loria.fr

Abstract. We present an approach for proactive malware detection working by abstraction of program behaviors. Our technique consists in abstracting program traces, by rewriting given subtraces into abstract symbols representing their functionality. Traces are captured dynamically by code instrumentation, which allows us to handle packed or self-modifying malware. Suspicious behaviors are detected by comparing trace abstractions to reference malicious behaviors. The expressive power of abstraction allows us to handle general suspicious behaviors rather than specific malware code and then, to detect malware mutations. We present and discuss an implementation validating our approach.

Keywords: Malware, behavioral detection, behavior abstraction, trace, string rewriting, finite state automaton, formal language, dynamic binary instrumentation.

1 Introduction

Detection techniques of computer malware have traditionally relied on a combination of static and dynamic analysis. A shortcoming of static analysis, however, is the general intractability of knowing in advance the entire program code as it may change dynamically. Packing and obfuscation techniques typically capitalize on this intractability to prevent the reconstruction of the program code. Structural and behavioral techniques, on the other hand, may be used to guard against code protection and code transformation and are consequently more robust and reliable. These techniques rely on the analysis of the program structure or its behavior rather than its binary code. This ensures an independence from basic syntactic modifications or from packing techniques.

Structural techniques analyze the control flow graph representing the program, by assuming that its structure remains untouched. They compare it to control flow graphs of known malware using static analysis [10], sub-graph isomorphism [9], tree automata [7] or similarity measures [12,4]. Unfortunately, these techniques are not resilient to functional polymorphism of behaviors, of which malware variants are a form, and which expresses that behaviors can

---

* This work has been partially supported by the High Security Lab of the LORIA in Nancy: http://lhs.loria.fr. A full version of this article can be found in [5].

G. Roşu et al. (Eds.): RV 2010, LNCS 6418, pp. 168–182, 2010.

be carried out in different ways, without their functionality being altered. This polymorphism often impacts the structure of the control flow graph.

Conversely, behavioral approaches, first introduced in Cohen's seminal work [11], monitor system calls and their arguments and have traditionally relied on the use of finite state machines [18,21]. Recent approaches [19] deal with functional polymorphism by preprocessing execution traces and transforming them into a high-level representation which captures their semantic meaning. But as these approaches deal with the execution trace being observed, they analyze a single behavior at a time. Subsequently, [16] proposed to use attribute automata but the cost is an exponential time complexity procedure.

Other behavioral approaches also use model checking techniques to track data [6,17,22]: they define behavioral signatures as temporal logic formulae, defined on a syntactic level. But none of these approaches considers functional polymorphism. Moreover they do not tackle either the problem of constructing a high-level view of a program, which limits their applicability.

Our goal here is to provide a generic framework for malware detection, abstract enough to be independent of the implementation of programs, resilient to variants and relying on general suspicious behaviors rather than on specific malware code. Unlike the approaches cited before, which only consider the detection scenario by working on one trace at a time, we intend to make our formalism more generally applicable to analysis and signature generation of unkown malware by working on a set of traces representing the whole behavior of a program.

For this purpose, we present an approach working on an abstract representation of the behavior of a program. We propose an original strong theoretical setting underpinned by the theory of formal languages and based on string rewriting systems and finite state automata. Abstraction is carried out with respect to behavior patterns defined by string rewriting systems. Behavioral detection is then carried out by automata intersection.

More precisely, execution traces of a program describe the capture of specific data such as program instructions, system calls with their arguments, or file system and network interactions. We represent a set of execution traces by an automaton called trace automaton. An abstraction of this trace automaton is then constructed, with respect to a set of predefined behavior patterns defined as regular languages and describing high-level properties or actions such as a file operation, a hook installation or a data leak. This gives a representation independent of the program implementation. Finally, the abstracted trace automaton is intersected with a malware database, composed of abstract signatures representing known malicious behaviors.

Our technique offers two detection scenarios: identifying a program as suspicious when it performs some malicious action like keylogging, or detecting an action sequence similar to the one of a known malware. The model we use, combining string rewriting systems and finite state automata, allows us to detect very efficiently malicious behaviors with high level descriptions, that is in linear time. Detection speed can be tuned by setting the right tier of abstraction level. So our behavioral detection model could be used inside a firewall for example.

After presenting the background in Section 2, we define behavior patterns in Section 3. Section 4 presents the abstraction mechanism of trace languages. Section 5 explains how to represent trace languages by trace automata and gives complexity bounds for computing abstractions. Section 6 formalizes the detection problem with its cost. Section 7 presents the implementation of our approach together with experiments. We conclude in Section 8.

2   Background

Let Σ be some finite alphabet. We denote by Σ^* the set of finite words on Σ. Subsets of Σ^* are called languages on Σ. The empty word is denoted by ϵ.

Let Σ' be some finite alphabet. The projection homomorphism which maps words of Σ^* to words of Σ'^* is denoted by $u|_{\Sigma'}$ for any $u \in \Sigma^*$ and is defined, for $a \in \Sigma$, by: $a|_{\Sigma'} = a$ if $a \in \Sigma'$ and $a|_{\Sigma'} = \epsilon$ otherwise. This definition is homeomorphically extended to languages on Σ, and the projection on Σ' of a language L on Σ is denoted by $L|_{\Sigma'}$.

A finite state automaton $\mathcal{A}$ on an alphabet Σ is a tuple (Q, δ, q_0, F) where Q is a finite set of states, $\delta : Q \times \Sigma \rightarrow Q$ is the transition relation, $q_0 \in Q$ is the initial state, and $F \subseteq Q$ is the set of final states. A run of $\mathcal{A}$ on a word $w = a_0 a_1 \cdots a_n$ is a sequence of states $r = q_0 q_1 \cdots q_{m \leq n+1}$ such that: $\forall i < m, q_{i+1} \in \delta(q_i, a_i)$. The run r is successful if $m = n + 1$ and $q_m \in F$; in this case, w is said to be recognized by $\mathcal{A}$. The set of words for which there exists a successful run of $\mathcal{A}$ is the language recognized by $\mathcal{A}$ and is denoted by $\mathcal{L}(\mathcal{A})$. Languages recognized by some finite state automaton $\mathcal{A}$ are called regular. The size of a finite state automaton A, denoted by $|A|$, is defined as the number of states of A.

For a given binary relation $\rightarrow$, we denote by $\rightarrow^*$ its reflexive transitive closure. A string rewriting system (SRS in short) is a triple $(\Sigma, V, \rightarrow)$, where V is a set of variables and $\rightarrow$ a binary relation on $(\Sigma \cup V)^*$. A regular SRS is a 4-tuple $(\Sigma, V, S, \rightarrow)$, where $S \in V$ and the relation $\rightarrow$ is generated by rules of the form $a \rightarrow A$, $aA \rightarrow B$ and $\epsilon \rightarrow A$, with $a \in \Sigma$, $A, B \in V$. The language recognized by a regular SRS is the set $\{u | u \in \Sigma^*, u \rightarrow^* S\}$. Languages recognized by regular SRS are exactly the regular languages. The size of a regular SRS R, denoted by $|R|$, is defined as the number of variables of V.

3   Behaviors

We now introduce a model of abstract machine from which we define notions of execution trace and behavior. An abstract machine $\mathcal{M}$ consists of the triple $(\mu_0, IP_0, \rightarrow)$ where (μ_0, IP_0) is an initial configuration of $\mathcal{M}$ and $\rightarrow$ is a transition function from Configurations to Configurations, where Configurations denotes the set of configurations of $\mathcal{M}$.

A configuration of $\mathcal{M}$ is a pair (μ, IP) where:

- $\mu : Addresses \rightarrow Data$ represents the memory of $\mathcal{M}$. Addresses is the set of addresses of $\mathcal{M}$ and Data is a set of values; both are subsets of $\mathbb{N}$;

- $IP \in Addresses$ is the instruction pointer.

Thus, we have $(\mu, IP) \to (\mu', IP')$ if the machine $\mathcal{M}$ executes the instruction at address IP of memory μ. The memory μ' is the memory obtained after executing this instruction and IP' is the address of the next instruction to execute. A program is a set of instructions. An *execution* of an abstract machine $\mathcal{M}$ is a finite sequence:

$$(\mu_0, IP_0) \to (\mu_1, IP_1) \to \ldots \to (\mu_n, IP_n).$$

In our scenario, the configuration (μ_0, IP_0) is the initial configuration. A program is loaded into μ_0 at the address pointed by the instruction pointer IP_0. So, at the beginning of an execution, a program is executed inside an initial environment (also) given by μ_0. Then, the program is run. At each step, we see interactions with the "outside" through the memory. Though our model of abstract machine can only represent single-threaded programs, this formalization of communications is enough for our purpose.

The reader will notice that we focus on abstract machines rather than on programming languages. There are several reasons for this. First of all, our model allows us to talk about programming languages at any level of abstraction. Second, in the context of malware, programs are generally self-modifying. Programs are treated as data objects and elements of *Data* are regarded as instructions. A program text is variable, which is not the usual point of view in semantics, see for example Gunter's textbook [15]. Moreover, low level instructions, like in the x86 case, are not of fixed size and a program can modifiy its code by instruction misalignment. So we think that our model of abstract machine is a right approach to underpin our study on malware behavior detection.

As said before, dynamic analysis and detection rely on capture and analysis of execution data. This data may be the sequence of instructions being executed, the sequence of system calls (i.e. calls to system code), etc. Other approaches may capture yet higher-level actions of a program, for instance network interactions, file system accesses, inter process communications (IPC), register usage statistics or any data that can be used to characterize a behavior. Our framework aims at dealing with any kind of the above data using an alphabet Σ.

We first formalize the capture of some execution data, represented by elements of Σ, in the machine $\mathcal{M}$.

Definition 1 (Capture operator). *A capture operator with respect to Σ is an operator $\pi : Configurations \to \Sigma \cup \{\epsilon\}$ which associates with some configuration the captured data if any, and ϵ otherwise.*

Note that in the general case, captured data of a configuration c_n may depend on the history of the execution i.e. on configurations $c_{i_1} \ldots c_{i_k}$ for $i_1 \ldots i_k \in [1..n-1]$ at previous times. This is needed for example to compute register usage statistics or to capture non atomic behaviors (for instance "smtp connection" which is the combination of a network connection and reception of the message "220 .* SMTP Ready"). For the sake of simplicity, for defining π, we do not consider $c_{i_1} \ldots c_{i_k}$.

From now on, in our examples, we consider more specifically the operator capturing library calls, including system calls.

Definition 2 (Execution trace). *Let M be a machine, $e = c_1 \ldots c_n$ an execution of M and π a capture operator with respect to Σ. Then $\pi(c_1) \ldots \pi(c_n) \in \Sigma^*$ is the* execution trace *of the execution e of M with respect to π, denoted $\pi(e)$.*

In the following, we will call trace language of a machine M with respect to the capture operator π, the set of execution traces of M with respect to π. We denote it by $Traces_\pi(M)$, or simply $Traces(M)$ when π is clear from the context. We can now formally define the notion of behavior we want to detect in a program, with respect to some capture operator.

Definition 3 (Behavior pattern). *A* regular behavior pattern B *is a regular language on Σ. We call* simple behavior pattern *an element of B.*

A behavior pattern does not necessarily describe a malicious behavior in itself. It can describe an innocuous behavior – e.g. creating a process, opening a file, sending a mail – or a relevant behavior sequence, possibly modulo shuffling of independent actions. It can also represent a more specific behavior which is shared by different malicious codes.

Example 1. Throughout this paper, we consider the example of the Allaple worm, a polymorphic network worm. A simplified excerpt of the code of its variant Allaple.A is given in [5]. It contains three behavior patterns: the ping of a remote host, the opening of a Netbios connection and the scanning of local drives. An example of execution trace of this excerpt is the following sequence of library calls:

`...GetLogicalDriveStrings.GetDriveType.FindFirstFile.`
`FindFirstFile.FindNextFile...`

This trace exhibits the behavior pattern which describes the scanning of local drives: `GetLogicalDriveStrings.GetDriveType.FindFirstFile`.

4   Trace Abstraction

Given some machine, recall that our goal is to abstract its execution traces, by replacing concrete behavior patterns by more abstract representations, expressing their functionality, in order to compare them to reference malicious behaviors.

In this section, we formally define the abstraction of a program trace with respect to behavior patterns. We start with a simple behavior pattern, then generalize abstraction to a regular behavior pattern and finally to a set of regular behavior patterns. We show that abstraction can be viewed as a string rewriting process where each behavior pattern is replaced by a new specific symbol.

4.1   Abstracting with Respect to a Simple Behavior Pattern

Let $t \in B$ be a simple behavior pattern for some B. Let M be a machine and $u \in Traces_\pi(M)$ an execution trace of M for some π. Identifying occurrences of the pattern t in the trace u amounts to matching t to some subword of u.

Let $\lambda \notin \Sigma$ be a new symbol denoting the abstraction of our pattern t. We define $\Sigma' = \Sigma \cup \{\lambda\}$. Trace abstraction of u with respect to pattern t of Σ^* is defined by rewriting u with the string rewriting system R on Σ'^*, where R is composed of a single rewrite rule: $R = \{t \to \lambda\}$.

Let $\to_t$ denote the rewriting relation induced by R, which rewrites substrings:

$$\forall u, v \in \Sigma'^*, u \text{ rewrites into } v, \text{ which is written } u \to_t v \text{ iff}$$
$$\exists u' \in \Sigma'^*, \exists u'' \in \Sigma'^*, \begin{cases} u = u' \cdot t \cdot u'' \\ v = u' \cdot \lambda \cdot u''. \end{cases}$$

A trace has been abstracted when every occurrence of the pattern t has been replaced by the abstract symbol λ. Thus abstraction of a trace is nothing but normalization of that trace with respect to the SRS R. Note that R is not confluent in general, so a trace may have several normal forms. Abstraction of a trace can be naturally generalized to a trace language.

Example 2. Returning to our excerpt of the Allaple worm, suppose we are interested in detecting the previously defined behavior of scanning local drives. Then $t = \texttt{GetLogicalDriveStrings.GetDriveType.FindFirstFile}$, and we define $\lambda = \texttt{SCAN\_DRIVES}$. The execution trace in Example 1 is thus abstracted into:
$\texttt{...SCAN\_DRIVES.FindFirstFile.FindNextFile...}$

Note that we consider normal forms instead of partially reduced ones. In other words, we require that every occurrence of a pattern that can be matched is eventually rewritten. This allows to ensure that the computation of the malicious behavior exhibited by a given malware is maximal. Also, this allows a more precise detection of behaviors of the type "A followed by B, without C in between": partially rewriting a trace acb into AcB would then lead to a positive detection, while the normal form ACB does not match the behavior.

4.2 Abstracting with Respect to a Regular Behavior Pattern

A behavior pattern can usually be achieved in different ways and malware writers may capitalize on this to perform functional polymorphism. For instance, creating a file may be processed using different sequences of instructions: detection will only be interested in the functionality expressed by these sequences, not in their implementation details. Thus, we now consider the case of a behavior pattern defined as a language, and more specifically as a regular language, as presented in Definition 3. Indeed, regular patterns allow to account for example for behaviors interleaved with other unrelated or irrelevant actions. For instance, file writes may often be interleaved with other interactions with the system, e.g. string manipulation functions.

Normalization now consists in rewriting a trace language with the rules transforming into λ any simple pattern of a behavior pattern $\mathcal{B}$, where $\mathcal{B}$ is a regular language on Σ^*. Since $\mathcal{B}$ may be infinite, we consider a regular SRS $(\Sigma, V, S, \to)$ recognizing $\mathcal{B}$ and we define relation $\to_{\mathcal{B}}$ on $(\Sigma' \cup V)^*$ as the rewriting relation induced by $\to \cup \{S \to \lambda\}$. Using the reflexive transitive closure of $\to_{\mathcal{B}}$, we define trace language abstraction with respect to a regular behavior pattern.

Definition 4 (Abstract trace language). *Let $\mathcal{B}$ be a regular behavior pattern, and $\rightarrow_{\mathcal{B}}$ its associated rewriting relation. The abstract form of the trace language L with respect to $\mathcal{B}$, denoted by $L \downarrow_{\mathcal{B}}$, is defined by:*

$$L \downarrow_{\mathcal{B}} = \{v \in \Sigma'^* \mid \exists u \in L, \ u \rightarrow_{\mathcal{B}}^* v \ \text{and} \ \nexists w \in \Sigma'^*, \ v \rightarrow_{\mathcal{B}} w\} \ .$$

The following theorem expresses that abstraction preserves regularity, which is a fundamental characteristic of our approach.

Theorem 1. *Let $\mathcal{B}$ be a regular behavior pattern and L a trace language. If L is regular, then so is $L \downarrow_{\mathcal{B}}$.*

Proofs of all theorems of the paper are given in [5].

Example 3. One could extend the previous pattern SCAN_DRIVES to account for alternative library calls, e.g. calling FindFirstFileEx instead of FindFirstFile: SCAN_DRIVES = GetLogicalDriveStrings.GetDriveType.(FindFirstFile +FindFirstFileEx). This corresponds to the following SRS:

$$\text{FindFirstFile} \rightarrow A$$
$$\text{FindFirstFileEx} \rightarrow A$$
$$\text{GetDriveType.}A \rightarrow B$$
$$\text{GetLogicalDriveStrings.}B \rightarrow \text{SCAN\_DRIVES} \ .$$

4.3   Abstracting with Respect to a Set of Regular Behavior Patterns

Finally, we generalize abstraction to a set of behavior patterns. Indeed, in practice, a suspicious behavior can be expressed as the combination of several behavior patterns $\mathcal{B}_i$, each of them abstracting into a distinct symbol λ_i.

Throughout this paper, we denote by Γ the set of symbols representing abstractions of our behavior patterns and we extend Σ' to $\Sigma \cup \Gamma$.

Let $\mathcal{C} = \{\mathcal{B}_i \mid \mathcal{B}_i \subseteq \Sigma^*\}_{1 \leq i \leq n}$ be a finite set of regular behavior patterns respectively associated with distinct symbols $\lambda_i \in \Gamma$.

As a relation $\rightarrow_{\mathcal{B}_i}$ is defined on $(\Sigma' \cup V_i)^*$, the relation $\rightarrow_{\mathcal{C}} = \bigcup_{1 \leq i \leq n} \rightarrow_{\mathcal{B}_i}$ is defined on $(\Sigma' \cup \bigcup_{1 \leq i \leq n} V_i)^*$. We extend trace language normalization to a set of regular behavior patterns, and the trace language L is now normalized with $\rightarrow_{\mathcal{C}}$ into the abstract trace language $L \downarrow_{\mathcal{C}}$.

Theorem 2. *Let $\mathcal{C}$ be a finite set of regular behavior patterns. If L is regular, then so is $L \downarrow_{\mathcal{C}}$.*

4.4   Projecting the Abstract Trace Language on Γ

Once a trace language has been normalized with respect to some set of behavior patterns, details that have not been processed by the normalization have to be pruned. A completely abstracted trace language is indeed expected to be defined on Γ, in order to be compared afterwards to reference abstract behaviors. This pruning operation is performed by projecting the abstract trace language on Γ.

Definition 5 (Γ-abstract trace language). *Let $\mathcal{C}$ be a set of regular behavior patterns. Let L be a trace language for some machine $\mathcal{M}$. $\widehat{L} = L \downarrow_{\mathcal{C}} |_{\Gamma}$ is called the Γ-abstract trace language of $\mathcal{M}$ with respect to $\mathcal{C}$.*

Once the abstraction is complete, the simplified traces describe functionality-related actions and are consequently more robust and less complex. As they represent several different implementations of the same behavior, they allow to deal with functional polymorphism.

We can then compare the language of Γ-abstracted traces to the behavior of some known malware or to some generic malicious behavior defined on Γ.

Finally, the whole abstraction process could be repeated, as in Martignoni et al's layered architecture [19]. A first layer would look up behavior patterns defined in terms of raw analysis data. A second layer would look up behavior patterns defined in terms of patterns from the first layer, and so on. However, this case is encompassed in our formalism. It suffices to define behavior patterns from the final layer directly in terms of the raw analysis data, by composition of the regular SRSs defining patterns of the different layers. The resulting patterns thereby remain regular on Σ, so our formalism can still be applied.

5   Trace Abstraction Using Finite State Automata

When considering a single trace, the associated trace language is trivially represented by an automaton. But when this trace language describes the set of traces $Traces\,(\mathcal{M})$ of some machine $\mathcal{M}$, this set is in general undecidable or at least non-regular, so no automaton can precisely represent it. Nevertheless, one may build a regular approximation of this trace language, which is usually twofold:

- the trace language is over-approximated, when replacing for instance $a^n \cdot b^n$ sequences (stemming from program loops for instance) by $a^* \cdot b^*$ sequences or when coping with obfuscation or dynamic analysis shortcomings. The resulting automaton then contains spurious traces (false positives).
  Formally, if $Traces\,(\mathcal{M})$ is over-approximated by L, then $Traces\,(\mathcal{M}) \subseteq L$.
- the trace language is under-approximated, when some hidden code path is not discovered or when some uninteresting path is discarded. The resulting automaton then misses some traces (false negatives).
  Formally, if $Traces\,(\mathcal{M})$ is under-approximated by L, then $L \subseteq Traces\,(\mathcal{M})$.

Thus a trace automaton represents a regular approximation of the trace language of some machine and can be defined as an automaton recognizing a part of the traces of $\mathcal{M}$.

Definition 6 (Trace automaton). *Given a machine $\mathcal{M}$, a trace automaton for $\mathcal{M}$ with respect to Σ is a finite-state automaton A on Σ such that:*

$$\exists S \subseteq \Sigma^*, S \subseteq Traces\,(\mathcal{M}) \wedge S \subseteq \mathcal{L}\,(A) \ .$$

In order to construct the trace automaton of a machine, one may either use a collection of captured traces or reconstruct the program machine code from its binary representation. In the first case, the automaton is built in such a way that the captured traces correspond to a path in the trace automaton. In the second case, the machine code of the program can be reconstructed using common techniques that combine static and dynamic analysis: it is then projected on the trace alphabet and the trace automaton is inferred from the code structure.

Example 4. Figure 1 shows a trace automaton for the Allaple.A excerpt representing the ping of a remote host and the scanning of local drives.

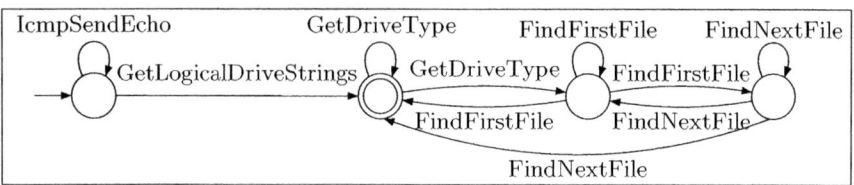

Fig. 1. Trace automaton for the Allaple. A excerpt.

By Theorem 2, the abstraction problem for a regular trace language now amounts to computing an automaton recognizing the abstraction of this language. Construction of this automaton, which we call abstract trace automaton, is described in the proofs of the following theorems and uses a method proposed by Esparza et al. [13]. It consists in modifying the initial trace automaton by adding new transitions using the left hand sides of the rewriting rules and then intersecting it with an automaton recognizing the words in normal form with respect to our rewrite system.

Thus, the abstract trace automaton may be more complex than the initial one, as shown by the Allaple worm example. Abstraction of the trace automaton with respect to patterns SCAN_DRIVES and PING, where PING = IcmpSendEcho describes the ping of a remote host, gives the automaton of Figure 2.

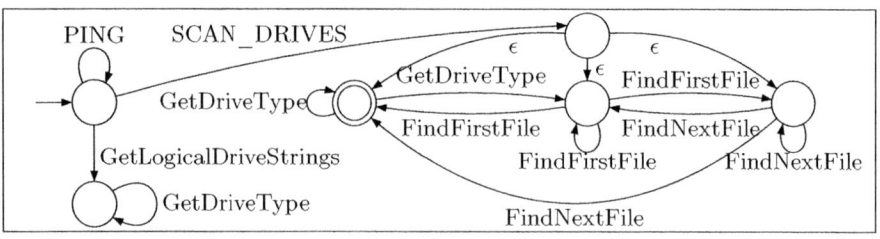

Fig. 2. Abstract trace automaton for the Allaple. A excerpt.

Theorem 3. *Let A be a trace automaton and $\mathcal{C} = \{\mathcal{B}_i\}_{1 \leq i \leq n}$ a set of behavior patterns recognized by regular SRSs $\{R_{\mathcal{B}_i}\}_{1 \leq i \leq n}$. Let $|\mathcal{C}| = \sum\limits_{1 \leq i \leq n} |R_{\mathcal{B}_i}|$.*

Then an automaton of size $O(|A|)$ recognizing $\mathcal{L}(A) \downarrow_{\mathcal{C}}|_{\Gamma}$ can be constructed in time $O\left(|A|^3 \cdot |\mathcal{C}|^2\right)$ and space $O\left(|A|^2 \cdot |\mathcal{C}|^2\right)$.

The final abstraction of the Allaple.A excerpt, for $\Gamma = \{\texttt{PING}, \texttt{SCAN\_DRIVES}\}$, is depicted in Figure 3.

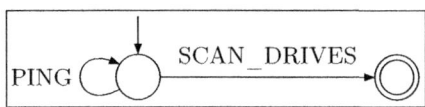

Fig. 3. Γ-abstract automaton for the Allaple. A excerpt.

6   Application to Malware Detection

Using the abstraction framework defined in Section 4, malware detection now consists in computing the abstract trace language of some machine and comparing it to a database of malicious behaviors defined on Γ. These malicious behaviors either describe generic behaviors, e.g. sending spam or logging keystrokes, or behaviors of specific malware. According to our abstraction formalism, malicious behaviors are sets of particular combinations of behavior patterns abstractions.

Definition 7. *A* malicious behavior *on Γ, or* signature, *is a language on Γ.*

More specifically, a malicious behavior describes combinations of patterns, possibly interleaved with additional patterns which are irrelevant in these combinations. For instance, we define the signature for the Allaple worm as the following regular language, which explicitly allows interleaving of patterns that do not match the upcoming pattern:

$$\texttt{LOCAL\_COM\_SERVER} \cdot (\Gamma \setminus \{\texttt{PING}\})^* \cdot \texttt{PING} \cdot$$
$$(\Gamma \setminus \{\texttt{NETBIOS\_CONNECTION}\})^* \cdot \texttt{NETBIOS\_CONNECTION}.$$

The automaton representing the signature of Allaple is given in Figure 4. Note that the $\texttt{SCAN\_DRIVES}$ pattern, which is present in the Γ-abstract trace automaton of the Allaple.A excerpt, does not appear here because the signature describes a common discriminating behavior exhibited by all samples of Allaple.

Definition 8. *Let L_m be a malicious behavior on Γ. A machine $\mathcal{M}$, with a Γ-abstract trace language $\widehat{L}$, exhibits the malicious behavior L_m iff there exists $v \in L_m$ and $u \in \widehat{L}$ such that $u = u_1 v u_2$, where $u_1, u_2 \in \Gamma^*$.*

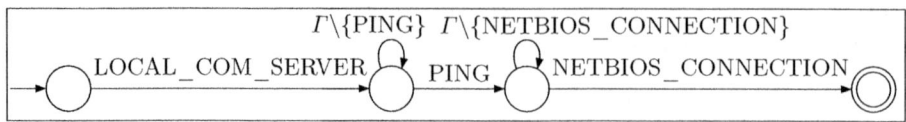

Fig. 4. Allaple signature

Thus, $\mathcal{M}$ exhibits the behavior L_m if some subword of an abstract trace of $\widehat{L}$ is in L_m. Our *malicious database* is then a set $\mathcal{D}$ of malicious behaviors. A machine $\mathcal{M}$ is *malicious* with respect to $\mathcal{D}$ if it exhibits some malicious behavior of $\mathcal{D}$.

$\widehat{L}$ can be constructed either from a single captured trace or from a whole trace language. In the first case, the detection process is lighter. In the second case, we get a better description of the program behavior, so detection is more reliable.

When $\widehat{L}$ is represented by an automaton A and L_m by an automaton A_m, $\mathcal{M}$ exhibits the behavior L_m when the following holds. Let A'_m be the automaton recognizing the set of words containing a subword in L_m: A'_m is constructed from A_m by adding loops labelled by symbols of Γ on the initial state and the final states of A_m. Then $\mathcal{M}$ exhibits the behavior L_m iff $\mathcal{L}(A) \cap \mathcal{L}(A'_m) \neq \emptyset$.

The malicious database is then represented by an automaton $A_{\mathcal{D}}$ which is the union of the automata A_m representing the signatures and may be minimized.

Theorem 4. *Let $\mathcal{D}$ be a set of regular malicious behaviors on Γ, recognized by an automaton $A_{\mathcal{D}}$. Let $\mathcal{M}$ be a machine, with a Γ-abstract trace language recognized by an automaton A. Then deciding whether $\mathcal{M}$ is malicious with respect to $\mathcal{D}$ takes time:* $O\left(|A_{\mathcal{D}}|^2 \cdot |A|^2\right)$.

Note that runtime detection could be efficiently implemented from these results, since all constructions (Γ-abstraction, automata intersection) are incremental.

Now, infection could be defined more intuitively and more generally in the following way: behavior patterns, instead of representing building blocks of a malicious behavior, could directly represent a malicious behavior, which would then be defined on Σ.

Definition 9. *Let $\mathcal{C}$ be a set of behavior patterns. Let $\mathcal{M}$ be a machine, with a trace language L. $\mathcal{M}$ is* malicious *if $L \downarrow_\mathcal{C} |_\Gamma \neq \{\epsilon\}$.*

With the above detection model, we lose the expressive power of abstraction and the robustness of our detection model. But on the other hand, detection is performed by the sole process of normalization.

7   Implementation and Experiments

We implemented the presented techniques in a tool which is able to capture execution traces of a given program, to build its trace automaton, to abstract it with respect to a set of predefined behavior patterns and to compare it to a malware database.

Setting up the detection environment. In order to avoid static analysis short-comings and to ignore unreachable code, we use dynamic analysis to construct a trace automaton for some program loaded into a machine. The program is instrumented using Pin [3], which allows us to collect library calls along with their arguments while the program is running. Other instrumentation tools, like Dynamorio [1], could have been utilized with similar results. Instrumentation allows us to perform low-level analysis of the execution and to have a tight control over the program. In particular, our instrumentation tool handles threads, child processes and hooks, and features a simple data flow analyzer which relates call arguments to previously used data. In order to reduce the size of captured traces and to capture the behavior of a program at a source code level, we only collect library calls directly made from the program code, ignoring calls originating from libraries themselves.

When an execution trace is captured, we construct a trace automaton by associating a state with each different instruction pointer responsible for making a library call. Threads are handled by associating a state with a set of instruction pointers. Additional execution traces can be used to complete the trace automaton. Automata are manipulated with the OpenFST library [2].

Behavior patterns are defined after observing malicious execution traces and extracting basic sequences likely to be part of a malicious behavior. These patterns often define usual interactions of the program with the system or the network. Once extracted, a sequence either defines a new behavior pattern or extends an existing pattern.

The malware database is a collection of malicious behaviors, which is built from a set of generic signatures along with signatures of known malware, constructed using their Γ-abstract trace automata. The resulting database automaton is minimized in order to speed up detection.

Experiments. To test our detection method, samples of malicious programs were collected using a honeypot[1] and identified using Kaspersky Antivirus.

We defined 40 behavior patterns, extended to allow data constraints expressing properties about the arguments of the calls (see [5]). These constraints are compatible with our formalism and amount to modify the trace automaton by adding transitions denoting the verification of a constraint. Examples of such patterns include writing to system files, persisting oneself in the Windows registry or browsing drives and files. A complete abstraction example for the Agent.ah worm is also given in [5].

Three experimentation scenarios were defined. In a first setting, we define signatures for given malware families, by analysis and Γ-abstraction of a few samples. Samples from different variants of each family are then compared to the signatures: several of these variants are new, i.e. they were not considered when defining the signatures. This allows us to test the applicability of our approach and its robustness against mutation. In a second setting, a more general signature is defined for a common malicious behavior encountered in different

---

[1] The honeypot of the Loria's High Security Lab: `http://lhs.loria.fr`

malware families. Several malicious samples are then tested, in order to find out which samples exhibit this behavior. This allows us to test the expressive power of behavior abstraction. In a third setting, sane applications are tested, to ensure that the rate of false positives is low.

We tested the above settings on known malware families, among which Allaple, Virut, Agent, Rbot, Afcore and Mimail. In particular, our honeypot shows that Allaple, Virut and Agent are currently among the most active worms, which makes their analysis particularly relevant.

In the first scenario, we constructed a signature for Allaple (Figure 4) and abstracted samples from the variants a, b, d and e. Three of them were successfully matched to the signature. The fourth variant made use of Windows services, which our instrumentation tool does not currently handle. The same scenario was repeated for Virut, with its variants ai, ak, ao, n, q and r. Detection was again successful for four of them, although another technical shortcoming was encountered, stemming from the inability of our tool to instrument injected code called in remote threads.

For the second scenario, the signature is a generic malicious behavior describing malware replication, defined by the following patterns: injection of its own code in foreign live processes, duplication on logical drives, duplication on network shares, creating a local COM server, and registering an OLE component.

We then analyzed 39 variants from 16 malware families, among which: Agent, Mimail, Avron, Drefir... Samples of these variants were abstracted and compared to the previous behavior. Twenty of them were successfully matched.

For the last scenario, we abstracted traces of common applications, among which: Notepad, Firefox, VLC... All of them failed to exhibit a malicious behavior from the previous experiments.

8   Conclusion and Future Work

In this paper, we have presented a new malware detection approach using abstract representations of malicious behaviors to identify malicious programs. Programs to analyze, represented as trace languages, are abstracted by rewriting with respect to elementary behavior patterns, defined as regular string rewriting systems. Abstractions are then compared to a database of abstract malicious behaviors, wich describe combinations of the former patterns.

Abstraction is the key notion of our approach. Providing an abstracted form of program behaviors and signatures allows us to be independent of the program implementation, to handle similar behaviors in a generic way and thus to be robust with respect to existing and future variants. The strength of our technique lies also in the fact that abstract malicious behaviors are combinations of elementary patterns: this allows us to efficiently summarize and compact the possible combinations likely to compose suspicious behaviors. Moreover, malicious behaviors are easy to update since they are expressed in terms of basic blocks. Behavior patterns themselves, as they describe basic functionalities, are easier to update than if they had described more complex ones.

Behavior abstraction may also prove useful in similarity analysis of malicious programs. Like for detection, the use of abstract representations of programs makes the analysis resilient to functional polymorphism and to minor changes.

We plan to extend our approach in several directions. The first one is concerned with data flow analysis. The behavior patterns we define are unable to express that the actions they match are actually related. Data flow information would allow to address this question. While this issue is not very relevant when matching local behaviors (eg. writing data to a file), it becomes more important when specifying wider behaviors which spread over large execution sequences. Work is in progress to handle data flow by using model checking with temporal logic formulae with parameters.

The second extension is concerned with interleaved behavior pattens. When two behavior patterns are interleaved in an execution trace, our approach can only match one pattern out of the two since, while rewriting the first one, the second will be consumed. Although interleaving does not occur very often in practice since common behavior patterns are small and not very prone to interleaving, we intend to propose non-consuming approaches to pattern abstraction.

Also, we would like to improve the construction of a trace automaton approximating a trace language. When it is built from execution traces, meaningless paths are created by interference between relevant paths. This increases the matching possibilities between the abstract trace automaton and the malicious signatures, which impacts the precision of the detection. A solution would be to duplicate function calls in the automaton when appropriate.

Lastly, captured traces do not give an exhaustive view of all possible executions and some interesting behaviors may only be observed when some conditions are met. We could use existing tools identifying these conditions. Sage [14] and BitScope [8] use symbolic execution to systematically discover new execution paths. Moser et al. [20] also address this problem in the malware context by monitoring how certain inputs impact the control flow and by instrumenting these inputs to drive the execution.

References

1. DynamoRIO, http://dynamorio.org
2. OpenFST, http://www.openfst.org/
3. Pin, http://www.pintool.org
4. Apel, M., Bockermann, C., Meier, M.: Measuring similarity of malware behavior. In: IEEE Conference on Local Computer Networks, pp. 891–898. IEEE, Los Alamitos (October 2009)
5. Beaucamps, P., Gnaedig, I., Marion, J.-Y.: Behavior Abstraction in Malware Analysis - Extended Version. HAL-INRIA Open Archive Number inria-00509486
6. Bergeron, J., Debbabi, M., Desharnais, J., Erhioui, M.M., Lavoie, Y., Tawbi, N.: Static detection of malicious code in executable programs. In: Symposium on Requirements Engineering for Information Security (2001)
7. Bonfante, G., Kaczmarek, M., Marion, J.-Y.: Architecture of a morphological malware detector. Journal in Computer Virology (2008)

8. Brumley, D., Hartwig, C., Liang, Z., Newsome, J., Song, D., Yin, H.: Automatically identifying trigger-based behavior in malware. Botnet Detection 36, 65–88 (2008)
9. Bruschi, D., Martignoni, L., Monga, M.: Detecting self-mutating malware using control-flow graph matching. In: Büschkes, R., Laskov, P. (eds.) DIMVA 2006. LNCS, vol. 4064, pp. 129–143. Springer, Heidelberg (2006)
10. Christodorescu, M., Jha, S., Seshia, S.A., Song, D., Bryant, R.E.: Semantics-aware malware detection. In: IEEE Symposium on Security and Privacy, pp. 32–46. IEEE Computer Society, Los Alamitos (2005)
11. Cohen, F.: Computer viruses: Theory and experiments. Computers and Security 6(1), 22–35 (1987)
12. Dullien, T., Rolles, R.: Graph-based comparison of executable objects. In: Symposium sur la Sécurité des Technologies de l'Information et des Télécommunications (2005)
13. Esparza, J., Rossmanith, P., Schwoon, S.: A uniform framework for problems on context-free grammars. Bulletin of the EATCS 72, 169–177 (2000)
14. Godefroid, P., Levin, M.Y., Molnar, D.: Automated whitebox fuzz testing. In: Network Distributed Security Symposium. Internet Society (2008)
15. Gunter, C.A.: Semantics of Programming Languages: Structures and Techniques. MIT Press, Cambridge (1992)
16. Jacob, G., Debar, H., Filiol, E.: Malware behavioral detection by attribute-automata using abstraction from platform and language. In: Balzarotti, D. (ed.) RAID 2009. LNCS, vol. 5758, pp. 81–100. Springer, Heidelberg (2009)
17. Kinder, J., Katzenbeisser, S., Schallhart, C., Veith, H.: Detecting malicious code by model checking. In: Julisch, K., Krügel, C. (eds.) DIMVA 2005. LNCS, vol. 3548, pp. 174–187. Springer, Heidelberg (2005)
18. Le Charlier, B., Mounji, A., Swimmer, M.: Dynamic detection and classification of computer viruses using general behaviour patterns. In: International Virus Bulletin Conference, pp. 1–22 (1995)
19. Martignoni, L., Stinson, E., Fredrikson, M., Jha, S., Mitchell, J.C.: A layered architecture for detecting malicious behaviors. In: Lippmann, R., Kirda, E., Trachtenberg, A. (eds.) RAID 2008. LNCS, vol. 5230, pp. 78–97. Springer, Heidelberg (2008)
20. Moser, A., Kruegel, C., Kirda, E.: Exploring multiple execution paths for malware analysis. In: IEEE Symposium on Security and Privacy, pp. 231–245. IEEE Computer Society, Los Alamitos (2007)
21. Sekar, R., Bendre, M., Dhurjati, D., Bollineni, P.: A fast automaton-based method for detecting anomalous program behaviors. In: IEEE Symposium on Security and Privacy, pp. 144–155. IEEE Computer Society, Los Alamitos (2001)
22. Singh, P.K., Lakhotia, A.: Static verification of worm and virus behavior in binary executables using model checking. In: Information Assurance Workshop, pp. 298–300. IEEE Press, Los Alamitos (2003)

Clara: A Framework for Partially Evaluating Finite-State Runtime Monitors Ahead of Time[*]

Eric Bodden[1], Patrick Lam[2], and Laurie Hendren[3]

[1] Technische Universität Darmstadt, Germany
[2] University of Waterloo, Ontario, Canada
[3] McGill University, Montreal, Quebec, Canada

Abstract. Researchers have developed a number of runtime verification tools that generate runtime monitors in the form of AspectJ aspects. In this work, we present CLARA, a novel framework to statically optimize such monitoring aspects with respect to a given program under test. CLARA uses a sequence of increasingly precise static analyses to automatically convert a monitoring aspect into a residual runtime monitor. The residual monitor only watches events triggered by program locations that the analyses failed to prove safe at compile time. In two-thirds of the cases in our experiments, the static analysis succeeds on all locations, proving that the program fulfills the stated properties, and completely obviating the need for runtime monitoring. In the remaining cases, the residual runtime monitor is usually much more efficient than a full monitor, yet still captures all property violations at runtime.

1 Introduction

Finite-state properties, also known as typestate [1] properties, constrain the set of acceptable operations on a single object or a group of objects, depending on the object's or group's history. Many formalisms allow programmers to easily express typestate properties, including linear temporal logic, regular expressions, message sequence charts and live sequence charts [2, Chapter 2]. Potential applications of runtime monitoring include the evaluation of arbitrary queries over the runtime program state and the enforcement of stated properties. For instance, a monitor could detect attempts to circumvent an access-control policy and then either log the attempt or stop the detected unauthorized access. Researchers have proposed and implemented runtime monitoring tools [3, 4, 5, 6, 7] which compile high-level temporal specifications into monitor implementations.

While runtime monitoring could be useful for finding violations in practice, it is subject to the same problems as software testing. Runtime monitoring gives no static guarantees: a particular program run can only prove the presence of property violations, not their absence. Hence, developers and testers must exercise judgment in deciding when to stop monitoring program runs, since exhaustive testing is generally infeasible. Furthermore, although significant advances have

---

[*] This work was supported by NSERC and CASED (www.cased.de)

G. Roşu et al. (Eds.): RV 2010, LNCS 6418, pp. 183–197, 2010.

been made [8, 9, 10], runtime monitors can still slow down monitored programs significantly, sometimes by several orders of magnitude.

In this paper we therefore propose CLARA, a framework for partially evaluating runtime monitors at compile time. Partial ahead-of-time evaluation addresses all of the problems mentioned above. CLARA specializes a given runtime monitor to a program under test. The result is a residual runtime monitor that only monitors events triggered by program locations that the analyses failed to prove safe at compile time. In our experiments, CLARA's analyses can prove that the program is free of program locations that could drive the monitor into an error state in 68% of all cases. In these cases, CLARA gives the strong static guarantee that the program can never violate the stated property, eliminating the need for runtime monitoring of that program. In many other cases, the residual runtime monitor will require much less instrumentation than the original monitor, therefore yielding a greatly reduced runtime overhead. In 65% of all cases that showed overhead originally, no overhead remains after applying the analyses.

CLARA's principal design goal is to provide a maximally general framework for statically analyzing runtime monitors. We anticipate that CLARA will appeal to researchers in runtime verification, as it supports a large variety of runtime monitoring tools. Researchers in static analysis, on the other hand, can easily extend CLARA with novel static analyses to understand and optimize runtime monitors even further. How do we achieve this generality? CLARA's design is based on the crucial observation that most current runtime-verification tools for Java share two common properties: (1) internally, they use a finite-state-machine model of the property, and (2) they generate runtime monitors in the form of AspectJ aspects [11]. Figure 1 shows a state-machine model for the "ConnectionClosed" property: a disconnected connection should not be written to, unless the connection is potentially reconnected at some later point. Figure 2 shows a monitoring aspect for this property. The remainder of the paper explains this aspect and its analysis in more detail. CLARA takes such monitoring aspects as input and weaves the aspects into the program under test. While weaving, CLARA conducts static analyses, suppressing calls to the monitoring aspect when it can statically prove that these calls are unnecessary.

To perform its static analysis, CLARA must understand the monitoring aspect's internal transition structure. Because every aspect-generating monitoring tool uses a different code-generation strategy, and we wish to be independent of that strategy, CLARA expects the monitoring aspect to carry an annotation

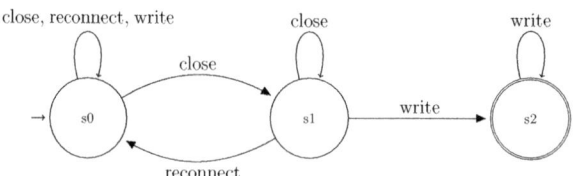

Fig. 1. "ConnectionClosed" typestate property: no write after close

```
1  aspect ConnectionClosed {
2      Set closed = new WeakIdentityHashSet();
3
4      dependent after close(Connection c) returning:
5          call(* Connection.disconnect()) && target(c) { closed.add(c); }
6
7      dependent after reconn(Connection c) returning:
8          call(* Connection.reconnect()) && target(c) { closed.remove(c); }
9
10     dependent after write(Connection c) returning:
11         call(* Connection.write(..)) && target(c) {
12         if(closed.contains(c))
13             error("May not write to "+c+": it is closed!"); }
14
15     dependency {
16         close, write, reconn;
17         initial s0: close  -> s0, write -> s0,  reconn -> s0, close -> s1;
18               s1: reconn -> s0, close -> s1, write -> s2;
19         final  s2: write -> s2;
20     } }
```

Fig. 2. "ConnectionClosed" aspect with Dependency State Machine

encoding the monitor's transition structure explicitly—a Dependency State Machine. Figure 2 shows this annotation in lines 15–20. Most runtime verification tools can easily generate such a state-machine annotation because they internally use a state-machine model of the monitored property. For our experiments, we extended the implementation of tracematches [3] to generate the annotations automatically; we are currently talking to the developers of JavaMOP about extending their tool to generate annotations, too.

In this paper we present the following original contributions:

- We present CLARA, an extensible open framework to evaluate AspectJ-based finite-state runtime monitors ahead of time.
- We explain the syntax and semantics of Dependency State Machines, CLARA's mechanism to interface with existing runtime-monitoring tools.

Further, we summarize CLARA's three predefined static analyses and show through a large set of experiments that, in many cases, these analyses can evaluate runtime monitors ahead of time, either largely reducing runtime overhead or entirely obviating the need for monitoring at runtime.

2   The Clara Framework

CLARA targets two audiences: researchers in (1) runtime verification and (2) static typestate analysis. CLARA defines clear interfaces to allow the two communities to productively interact. Developers of runtime verification tools simply

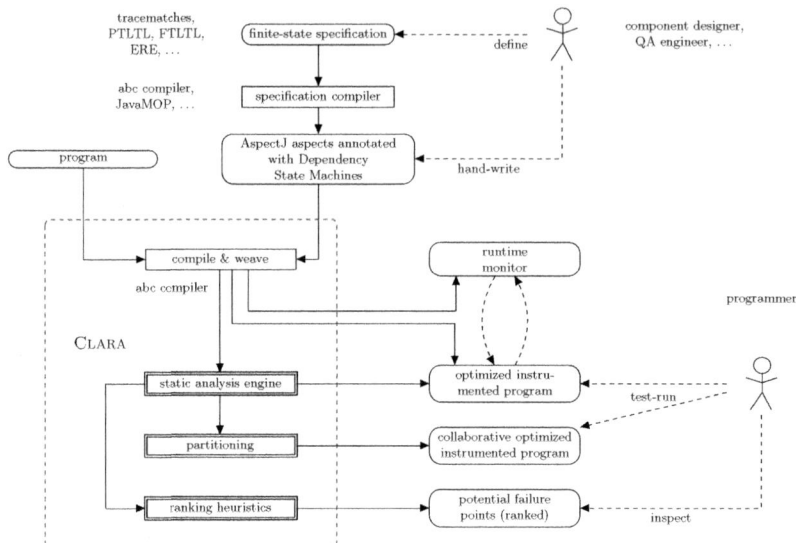

Fig. 3. Overview of CLARA

generate AspectJ aspects annotated with semantic meaning, in the form of Dependency State Machines. Static analysis designers can then create techniques to reason about the annotated aspects, independent of implementation strategy.

Figure 3 gives an overview of CLARA. A software engineer first defines (top right of figure) finite-state properties of interest, in some finite-state formalism for runtime monitoring, such as Extended Regular Expressions or Linear-Temporal Logic, e.g. using JavaMOP or tracematches. The engineer then uses some specification compiler such as JavaMOP or the AspectBench Compiler [12] (abc) to automatically translate these finite-state-property definitions into AspectJ monitoring aspects. These aspects may already be annotated with appropriate Dependency State Machines: we extended abc to generate annotations automatically when transforming tracematches into AspectJ aspects. Other tools, such as Java-MOP, should also be easy to extend to generate these annotations. If the specification compiler does not yet support Dependency State Machines, the programmer can easily annotate the generated aspects by hand.

CLARA then takes the resulting annotated monitoring aspects and a program as input. CLARA first weaves the monitoring aspect into the program. The Dependency State Machine defined in the annotation provides CLARA with enough domain-specific knowledge to analyze the woven program. We will further explain CLARA's predefined analyses in Section 4. The result is an optimized instrumented program that updates the runtime monitor at fewer locations. Sometimes, CLARA optimizes away all updates, which proves that the program cannot violate the monitored property.

CLARA also supports Collaborative Runtime Verification, which distributes instrumentation overhead among multiple users; and ranking heuristics, which aid programmers in inspecting remaining instrumentation manually [13] [2, Ch. 6 & 7]. Space limitations preclude us from discussing ranking and Collaborative Runtime Verification here.

CLARA is freely available as free software at `http://bodden.de/clara/`, along with extensive documentation, the first author's dissertation [2], which describes CLARA in detail, and benchmarks and benchmark results.

We next describe the syntax and semantics of Dependency State Machines, the key abstraction of CLARA. This abstraction allows CLARA to decouple runtime monitor implementations from static analyses.

3   Syntax and Semantics of Dependency State Machines

Dependency State Machines extend the AspectJ language to include semantic information about relationships between different pieces of advice. Runtime verification tools which generate AspectJ aspects can use this extension to produce augmented aspects. CLARA can reason about the augmented aspects to prove that programs never violate monitored properties or to generate optimized code.

3.1   Syntax

Our extensions modify the AspectJ grammar in two ways: they add syntax for defining Dependent Advice [14] and Dependency State Machines. The idea of Dependent Advice is that pieces of monitoring advice are often inter-dependent in the sense that the execution of one piece of advice only has an effect when executing before or after another piece of advice, on the same objects. Dependency State Machines allow programmers to make these dependencies explicit so that static analyses can exploit them. Our explanations below refer to the ConnectionClosed example in Figure 2.

The **dependent** modifier flags advice to CLARA for potential optimization; such advice may be omitted from program locations at which it provably has no effect on the state of the runtime monitor. Dependent advice must be named. Lines 4, 7 and 10 all define dependent advice.

The Dependency State Machines extension enables users to specify state machines which relate different pieces of dependent advice. Dependency State Machine declarations define state machines by including a list of edges between states and an alphabet; each edge is labelled with a member of the alphabet. CLARA infers the set of states from the declared edges. Line 16 declares the state machine's alphabet: {`disconn`, `write`, `reconn`}. Every symbol in the alphabet references dependent advice from the same aspect. Lines 17–19 enumerate, for each state, a (potentially empty) list of outgoing transitions. An entry "s1: t -> s2" means "there exists a t-transition from s1 to s2". Users can also mark states as **initial** or **final** (error states). Final states denote states in which the monitoring aspect "matches", i.e., produces an externally visible side effect like the error message in our example (line 13, Figure 2).

The first author's dissertation [2, page 134] gives the complete syntax for Dependency State Machines and also explains sanity checks for these annotations;

e.g., each state machine must have initial and final states. Note that these checks are minimal and support a large variety of state machines so that CLARA can support many different runtime verification tools. For instance, we allow multiple initial and final states and we allow the state machine to be non-deterministic.

3.2   Semantics

The semantics of a Dependency State Machine refine the usual advice-matching semantics of AspectJ [15]. In AspectJ, pieces of advice execute at "joinpoints", or intervals of program execution. Programmers use "pointcuts", predicates over joinpoints, to specify the joinpoints where advice should apply. In Figure 2, the expression **call**(∗ Connection.disconnect()) && **target**(c) is a pointcut that picks out all method calls to the disconnect method of class Connection. When the pointcut applies, it binds the target object of the call to variable c.

Let $\mathcal{A}$ be the set of all pieces of advice and $\mathcal{J}$ be the set of all joinpoints that occur on a given program run. We model advice matching in AspectJ as follows:

$$match: \quad \mathcal{A} \times \mathcal{J} \quad \rightarrow \quad \{\beta \mid \beta : \mathcal{V} \rightharpoonup \mathcal{O}\} \cup \{\bot\}.$$

Given advice $a \in \mathcal{A}$ and a joinpoint $j \in \mathcal{J}$, $match(a, j)$ is $\bot$ when a does not execute at j. If a does execute, then $match(a, j)$ yields a variable binding β, which maps a's formal parameters to objects.

Our formal semantics for Dependency State Machines will provide a replacement for $match$, called $stateMatch$, that determines the cases in which a dependent piece of advice needs to execute: informally, a dependent advice a must execute when (1) AspectJ would execute a and (2) when not executing a at j would change the set of joinpoints for which the Dependency State Machine reaches its final state for a binding compatible with β. (We define "compatible" later.) An optimal implementation, which determines exactly all cases in which a dependent advice does not need to execute, is un-computable, as it would have to anticipate the future behaviour (and inputs) of the program. The trick is therefore to implement statically computable approximations to $stateMatch$. At the end of this section, we will present a soundness condition for $stateMatch$. This condition uses the set of possible future behaviours to describe the permissible (sound) implementations of $stateMatch$.

Semantics by example. Figure 4 contains a small example program that helps explain the intuition behind our semantics. The program triggers joinpoints which the ConnectionClosed aspect monitors. AspectJ calls a program point that triggers a joinpoint j the "joinpoint shadow" of j, or just "shadow" [16] for short.

Formal semantics. Our semantics of Dependency State Machines describe the set of program traces which cause the state machines to reach their final states. Note, however, that there is a mismatch between the usual semantics for 1) state machines and 2) program traces: state machines are not aware of variable bindings. We will call the traces that arise from program executions *parameterized*

```
1  public static void main(String args[]) {
2    Connection  c1 = new Connection(args[0]),
3         c2 = new Connection(args[1]);
4    c1.write(args[2]); // write(c1): irrelevant shadow−stays in same state
5    c1.close ();       // close(c1)
6    c1.close ();       // close(c1): also  irrelevant
7    c1.write(args[2]); // write(c1): violation−write after close on c1
8    c1.close ();       // close(c1): irrelevant−no subsequent writes on c1
9    c2.write(args[2]); // write(c2): write, but on c2, hence incompatible with 8
10 }
```

Fig. 4. Example program

traces [17]. To apply Dependency State Machines to parameterized traces, we project a parameterized trace onto a set of ground traces, which the Dependency State Machine can process, obtaining one ground trace for every variable binding.

We will also define the semantics of Dependency State Machines in terms of "events", not joinpoints. A joinpoint describes a time interval, while an event is an atomic point in time. Events simplify reasoning by prohibiting nesting.

Event. Let j be an AspectJ joinpoint. Then j induces the pair of events j_{before} and j_{after}, which occur at the beginning and end of j. For any set $\mathcal{J}$ of joinpoints we define the set $\mathcal{E}(\mathcal{J})$ of all events of $\mathcal{J}$ as: $\mathcal{E}(\mathcal{J}) := \bigcup_{j \in \mathcal{J}} \{j_{before}, j_{after}\}$. We write $\mathcal{E}$ instead of $\mathcal{E}(\mathcal{J})$ when $\mathcal{J}$ is clear from context.

For any declaration of a Dependency State Machine, the list of dependent advice names forms an alphabet Σ. For instance, the alphabet for Connection-Closed from Figure 2 is $\Sigma = \{\text{disconn}, \text{write}, \text{reconn}\}$.

Parameterized events. Let $e \in \mathcal{E}$ be an event and Σ be the alphabet of advice references in the declaration of a Dependency State Machine. We define the parameterized event $\hat{e}$ as follows:

$$\hat{e} := \bigcup_{a \in \Sigma} \{(a, \beta) \mid \beta = match(a, c) \wedge \beta \neq \perp\}.$$

Here, $match(a, e)$ is AspectJ's matching function, lifted to events; it therefore maps advice/event pairs to variable bindings, returning parameterized events. We label the set of all possible parameterized events $\hat{\mathcal{E}}$. Projection maps parameterized event traces ($\hat{\mathcal{E}}^*$) to "ground traces" (Σ^*).

Projected event. For every parameterized event $\hat{e} \in \hat{\mathcal{E}}$ and binding β we may project $\hat{e}$ with respect to β:

$$\hat{e} \downarrow \beta := \{a \in \Sigma \mid \exists (a, \beta_a) \in \hat{e} \text{ such that } compatible(\beta_a, \beta)\},$$

where *compatible* means that β_1 and β_2 agree on their joint domains:

$$compatible(\beta_1, \beta_2) := \forall v \in (dom(\beta_1) \cap dom(\beta_2)) : \ \beta_1(v) = \beta_2(v).$$

In this predicate, $dom(\beta_i)$ denotes the domain of β_i, i.e., the set of variables where β_i is defined.

Parameterized and projected event trace. Any finite program run induces a finite parameterized event trace $\hat{t} = \hat{e}_1 \ldots \hat{e}_n \in \hat{\mathcal{E}}^*$. For any variable binding β we define a set of projected traces $\hat{t} \downarrow \beta \subseteq \Sigma^*$ as follows. $\hat{t} \downarrow \beta$ is the smallest subset of Σ^* for which:

$$\forall t = e_1 \ldots e_n \in \Sigma^* : \quad \text{if } \forall i \in \mathbb{N} \text{ with } 1 \leq i \leq n : e_i \in \hat{e}_i \downarrow \beta \text{ then } t \in \hat{t} \downarrow \beta$$

We call such traces t, which are elements of Σ^*, "ground" traces; parameterized traces are instead elements of $\hat{\mathcal{E}}^*$.

A Dependency State Machine will reach its final state (and the related aspect will have an observable effect, e.g., will issue an error message) whenever a prefix of one of the ground traces of any variable binding is in the language described by the state machine. This yields the following definition.

Set of non-empty ground traces of a run. Let $\hat{t} \in \hat{\mathcal{E}}^*$ be the parameterized event trace of a program run. Then we define the set $groundTraces(\hat{t})$ of non-empty ground traces of $\hat{t}$ as:

$$groundTraces(\hat{t}) := \left(\bigcup_{\beta \in \mathcal{B}} \hat{t} \downarrow \beta \right) \cap \Sigma^+$$

We intersect with Σ^+ to exclude the empty trace, which contains no events and hence cannot cause the monitoring aspect to have an observable effect.

The semantics of a Dependency State Machine. We define the semantics of Dependency State Machines as a specialization of the AspectJ-inspired predicate $match(a, e)$, which models the decision of whether or not the dependent advice $a \in \mathcal{A}$ matches at event $e \in \mathcal{E}$, and if so, with which variable binding. We call our specialization $stateMatch$ and define it as follows:

$$stateMatch : \quad \mathcal{A} \times \hat{\mathcal{E}}^* \times \mathbb{N} \quad \rightarrow \quad \{\beta \mid \beta : \mathcal{V} \rightharpoonup \mathcal{O}\} \cup \{\bot\}$$

$$stateMatch(a, \hat{t}, i) :=$$
$$\quad \text{let } \beta = match(a, e) \text{ in}$$
$$\quad \begin{cases} \beta & \text{if } \beta \neq \bot \wedge \exists t \in groundTraces(\hat{t}) \text{ such that } necessaryShadow(a, t, i) \\ \bot & \text{otherwise} \end{cases}$$

Note that $stateMatch$ considers the entire parameterized event trace $\hat{t}$, plus the current position i in that event trace. In particular, the trace $\hat{t}$ contains future events. The function $stateMatch$ is therefore under-determined. This is intentional. Even though it is impossible to pass $stateMatch$ all of its arguments, static analyses can approximate all possible future traces.

We have left a parameter $necessaryShadow$ in the definition of $stateMatch$. This parameter may be freely chosen, as long as it meets the soundness condition defined below. A static optimization for Dependency State Machines is *sound* if it meets the soundness condition.

Soundness condition. The soundness condition requires that an event be monitored if we would miss a match or obtain a spurious match by not monitoring the event. A Dependency State Machine $\mathcal{M}$ matches, i.e., causes an externally observable effect, after every prefix of the complete execution trace that is in $\mathcal{L}(\mathcal{M})$, the language that $\mathcal{M}$ accepts.

Matching prefixes of a word. Let $w \in \Sigma^*$ and $\mathcal{L} \subseteq \Sigma^*$. Then the matching prefixes of w (with respect to $\mathcal{L}$) are the set of prefixes of w in $\mathcal{L}$:

$$matches_{\mathcal{L}}(w) := \{p \in \Sigma^* \mid \exists s \in \Sigma^* \text{ such that } w = ps\} \cap \mathcal{L}$$

Soundness condition. For any sound implementation of *necessaryShadow* we require:

$$\forall t = t_1 \ldots t_i \ldots t_n \in \Sigma^+. \ \forall i \leq n \in \mathbb{N}.$$
$$matches_{\mathcal{L}(\mathcal{M})}(t_1 \ldots t_{i-1}t_it_{i+1} \ldots t_n) \neq matches_{\mathcal{L}(\mathcal{M})}(t_1 \ldots t_{i-1}t_{i+1} \ldots t_n)$$
$$\implies necessaryShadow(t_i, t, i)$$

The soundness condition hence states that, if we are about to read a symbol t_i, and the monitoring aspect hits the final state when processing the complete trace t but not when processing the partial trace which omits t_i, or the other way around, then we must monitor t_i.

Note that CLARA's semantics assume that the advice associated with Dependency State Machines implement the monitor's transition structure. In particular, any dependent advice which does anything beyond computing a state transition must be marked final. Tools which generate Dependency State Machines, or programmers who write them, must take this semantics into account.

4   Clara as a Framework

Version 1.0 of CLARA includes three sound static analyses which eliminate irrelevant shadows. Recall from Figure 3 that CLARA executes these analyses immediately after weaving; the analyses plug into its static analysis engine. Analyses may access all declared Dependency State Machines and the woven program. The analyses also receive a list of joinpoint shadows.

For every shadow s, CLARA exposes the following pieces of information:

- The dependent piece of advice a that s invokes, along with the name of a and a list of variables that a binds.
- The source code position of s.
- The dynamic residue of s, which abstractly represents the runtime check that determines whether a will actually execute. A static analysis can disable s by setting its residue to the constant "NeverMatch".
- A mapping from the variables that a binds at s to a points-to set [18] that models all objects that these variables could possibly point to.

CLARA comes pre-equipped with three analyses that all aim to determine "irrelevant shadows". Such shadows must return `false` for *necessaryShadow*; in other words, disabling an irrelevant shadow must preserve the behaviour of the runtime monitor. An analysis disables a shadow by modifying its dynamic residue to never match.

The **Quick Check** [14], CLARA's first analysis stage, quickly computes whether all shadows for a particular property are irrelevant because they do not suffice to reach a final state; if so, it removes all of the shadows for that property. The second analysis stage, the **Orphan Shadows Analysis** [14] takes pointer information into account to find more specific sets of shadows, related by pointer information, which can all be disabled. CLARA uses a flow-insensitive and context-sensitive, demand-driven, refinement-based pointer analysis [18] to determine which events may occur on which groups of compatible variable bindings. The third stage, the **Nop Shadows Analysis** [19], explicitly takes the program's control flow into account. Using a backwards pass, the Nop Shadows Analysis first determines for every shadow *s* a tri-partitioning of automaton states: states from which the remainder of the program execution will, may, or won't reach the final state. Next, the Nop Shadows Analysis uses a forward pass to determine the possible automaton states at *s*. If *s* may only transition between states in the same equivalence class, then the analysis can soundly disable *s*.

We described all of three analyses in earlier work in [2,14,19]; the dissertation also includes soundness proofs. In this paper, however, we describe for the first time the common framework that makes these analyses accessible to various AspectJ-based runtime monitoring tools.

Adding Analyses to CLARA

CLARA allows researchers to add their own static analyses to the static analysis engine at any point. The CLARA website provides an empty skeleton extension for researchers to fill in. Analyses execute, in sequence, immediately after weaving. CLARA executes the three default analyses in the order in which we described them above: quick ones first, more complex ones later. In many cases, even simple analyses like the Quick Check are already powerful enough to recognize all shadows as irrelevant, which obviously simplifies the task of the more complicated analyses.

Programmers can insert their own analysis at any point in the sequence, as a so-called re-weaving pass. As the name suggests, a pass participates in a process called re-weaving [20]: just after having woven the monitoring aspects into the program, the AspectBench Compiler that underlies CLARA executes the given sequence of passes. Each pass may modify the so-called "weaving plan", e.g., by modifying the residues of joinpoint shadows. After all passes have finished, the compiler then restores the original un-woven program version and re-weaves the program using this new plan, this time then with fewer joinpoint shadows when the analysis passes succeeded.

5   Experimental Results

In this section we explain our empirical evaluation and our experimental results. Due to space limitations, we can only give a summary of those results. The first author's dissertation [2] gives a full account.

Although one can apply CLARA to any AspectJ-based runtime monitor, we decided to restrict our experiments to monitors generated from tracematch specifications. This does not limit the generality of our results: in earlier work [14] we showed that the relative optimization effects of our static analyses are largely independent of the concrete monitoring formalism.

For our experiments we wrote a set of twelve tracematch [3] specifications for different properties of collections and streams in the Java Runtime Library. Table 1 gives brief descriptions for each of these properties. We selected properties of the Java Runtime Library due to the ubiquity of clients of this library. Our tracematch definitions are available at http://bodden.de/clara/benchmarks/.

Table 1. Monitored specifications for classes of the Java Runtime Library

property name	description
ASyncContainsAll	synchronize on d at calls to c.containsAll(d) for synchronized collections c, d
ASyncIterC	only iterate a synchronized collection c when owning a lock on c
ASyncIterM	only iterate a synchronized map m when owning a lock on m
FailSafeEnum	do not update a vector while iterating over it
FailSafeEnumHT	do not update a hash table while iterating over its elements or keys
FailSafeIter	do not update a collection while iterating over it
FailSafeIterMap	do not update a map while iterating over its keys or values
HasNextElem	always call hasMoreElements before calling nextElement on an Enumeration
HasNext	always call hasNext before calling next on an Iterator
LeakingSync	only access a synchronized collection using its synchronized wrapper
Reader	do not use a Reader after its InputStream is closed
Writer	do not use a Writer after its OutputStream is closed

We used CLARA to instrument the benchmarks of version 2006-10-MR2 of the DaCapo benchmark suite [21] with these runtime monitors. DaCapo contains eleven different workloads of which we consider all but eclipse. Eclipse uses reflection heavily, which Clara still has trouble dealing with. For our experiments, we used the HotSpot Client VM (build 1.4.2_12-b03, mixed mode), with its standard heap size on a machine with an AMD Athlon 64 X2 Dual Core Processor 3800+ running Ubuntu 7.10 with kernel version 2.6.22-14 and 4GB RAM. We summarize our results in Table 2.

As the table shows, instrumenting 109 out of the 120 cases require at least one instrumentation point for runtime monitoring. (We mark other cases with "-".) CLARA was able to prove ($\checkmark$) for 74 out of these 109 cases (68%) that the program cannot violate the property on any execution. In these cases, monitoring is unnecessary because CLARA removes all instrumentation. 37 of the original 109 combinations showed a measurable runtime overhead. After applying the static analysis, measurable overhead only remained in 13 cases (35%). These cases often show significantly less overhead than without optimization.

Table 2. Effect of CLARA's static analyses; numbers are runtime overheads in percent before and after applying the analyses; ✓: all instrumentation removed, proving that no violation can occur; >1h: run took over one hour

	antlr		bloat		chart		fop		hsqldb	
	before	after	before	after	before	after	before	after	before	after
ASyncContainsAll	-	-	0	0 ✓	0	0 ✓	-	-	-	-
ASyncIterC	-	-	140	0 ✓	0	0 ✓	5	0 ✓	0	0 ✓
ASyncIterM	-	-	139	0 ✓	0	0 ✓	0	0 ✓	0	0 ✓
FailSafeEnumHT	10	4	0	0 ✓	0	0 ✓	0	0 ✓	0	0
FailSafeEnum	0	0 ✓	0	0 ✓	0	0 ✓	0	0	0	0 ✓
FailSafeIter	0	0 ✓	>1h	>1h	8	8	14	0 ✓	0	0 ✓
FailSafeIterMap	0	0 ✓	>1h	22027	0	0	7	MEM	0	0 ✓
HasNextElem	0	0 ✓	0	0 ✓	-	-	0	0 ✓	0	0 ✓
HasNext	-	-	329	258	0	0	0	0 ✓	0	0 ✓
LeakingSync	9	0 ✓	163	0 ✓	91	0 ✓	209	0 ✓	0	0 ✓
Reader	30218	0 ✓	0	0 ✓	0	0 ✓	0	0 ✓	0	0
Writer	37862	36	229	228	0	0 ✓	5	0 ✓	0	0

	jython		luindex		lusearch		pmd		xalan	
	before	after	before	after	before	after	before	after	before	after
ASyncContainsAll	0	0	0	0 ✓	0	0 ✓	0	0 ✓	-	-
ASyncIterC	0	0	0	0 ✓	0	0 ✓	28	0 ✓	-	-
ASyncIterM	0	0	0	0 ✓	0	0 ✓	35	0 ✓	-	-
FailSafeEnumHT	>1h	>1h	32	0 ✓	0	0 ✓	0	0 ✓	0	0 ✓
FailSafeEnum	0	0	30	0 ✓	18	0 ✓	0	0	0	0 ✓
FailSafeIter	0	0	5	0 ✓	20	0 ✓	2811	524	0	0 ✓
FailSafeIterMap	13	13	5	0 ✓	0	0 ✓	>1h	>1h	0	0 ✓
HasNextElem	0	0	12	0 ✓	0	0 ✓	0	0	0	0
HasNext	0	0	0	0 ✓	0	0 ✓	70	64	-	-
LeakingSync	>1h	0	34	0 ✓	365	0 ✓	16	0 ✓	0	0 ✓
Reader	0	0	0	0 ✓	77	0 ✓	0	0	0	0 ✓
Writer	0	0	0	0 ✓	0	0 ✓	0	0	0	0 ✓

Jython causes trouble for CLARA because of its heavy use of reflection and dynamic class loading. Due to these features, the pointer analysis that CLARA uses has to make conservative assumptions, yielding imprecise results. CLARA also performs less well on Iterator-based properties than on others. Because Java programs usually create all iterator objects through the same **new** statement, CLARA requires context information to distinguish different iterators statically. Our pointer analysis sometimes fails to generate enough context information, leading to imprecision. For fop/FailSafeIterMap, our analysis ran out of memory, despite the fact that we allowed 3GB of heap space.

The first author's dissertation [2] presents detailed experiments and results.

6   Related Work

CLARA's static analyses can be considered to be typestate analyses. Strom and Yemini [1] were the first to suggest the concept of typestate analysis. Recently, researchers have presented several new approaches with varying cost/precision trade-offs. We next describe the approaches most relevant to our work. We distinguish work in type systems, static verification and hybrid verification.

Type-system based approaches. Type-system based approaches define a type system and implement a checker for that system. The checker prevents programmers from compiling potentially property-violating programs and gives strong static guarantees. However, the type checker may reject useful programs which statically appear to violate the stated property but never actually violate the property at runtime.

DeLine and Fähndrich [22] as well as Bierhoff and Aldrich [23] present type systems for object-oriented languages with aliasing. Bierhoff and Aldrich's type system is generally more permissive than DeLine and Fähndrich's. To enable modular analyses, both of these approaches require annotations in the target program indicating state transitions and aliasing relationships. We do not require annotations in the program; our approach infers state changes from advice.

Static analysis approaches. Unlike type systems, such approaches perform whole-program analysis and, unlike hybrid approaches, have no runtime component.

Fink et al. present a static analysis of typestate properties [24]. Their approach, like ours, uses a staged analysis which starts with a flow-insensitive pointer-based analysis, followed by flow-sensitive checkers. The authors' analyses allow only for specifications that reason about a single object at a time, while we allow for the analysis of multiple interacting objects. Fink et al.'s algorithms only determine "final shadows" that complete a property violation (like "write" in our example) but not shadows that initially contribute to a property violation (e.g. "close") or can prevent a property violation (e.g. "reconnect"). Therefore, their algorithms cannot generate residual runtime monitors.

Hybrid analysis approaches. Naeem and Lhoták present a fully context-sensitive, flow-sensitive, inter-procedural whole-program analysis for typestate-like properties of multiple interacting objects [25]. Naeem and Lhoták's analysis is fully inter-procedural. Unfortunately, Naeem and Lhoták based parts of their analysis on earlier work of ours [26] that turned out be unsound [19]. All of CLARA's analyses provides have been proven sound [2].

Dwyer and Purandare use existing typestate analyses to specialize runtime monitors [27]. Their work identifies "safe regions" in the code using a static typestate analysis. Safe regions can be single statements, compound statements (e.g. loops), or methods. A region is safe if its deterministic transition function does not drive the typestate automaton into a final state. For such regions, their analyses summarize the effect of this region and change the program under test to update the typestate with the region's effects all at once when the region is entered. Because these specializations change the points at which transitions occur, they can make it harder for programmers to understand monitor behaviour. Further, their approach cannot generally handle groups of multiple interacting objects, while ours can.

7   Conclusion

We have presented CLARA, a framework for partially evaluating finite-state runtime monitors ahead-of-time using static analysis. CLARA is compatible with any runtime monitor that is expressed as an AspectJ aspect. To make any such aspect analyzable by CLARA, users need only ensure that the aspect is annotated with a Dependency State Machine, a textual finite-state-machine representation of the property being verified. Dependency State Machines function as an abstract interface, allowing researchers in runtime verification to implement monitor optimizations on one side of this interface and static-analysis researchers to implement static analyses on the other side. This way, CLARA allows researchers from two communities to integrate their approaches with each other.We have presented the syntax and semantics of Dependency State Machines and CLARA's extensible static analysis engine, along with three analyses that we provide with CLARA. Through experiments with the DaCapo benchmark suite, we have shown that CLARA's static analysis approach can greatly reduce the amount of instrumentation necessary for runtime monitoring in most Java programs. Our experiments further revealed that this reduced amount of instrumentation yields a largely reduced runtime overhead in many cases.

CLARA is available as free, open-source software. We hope that other researchers will soon be joining us in using CLARA, and that its availability will foster progress in the field of typestate analysis.

References

1. Strom, R.E., Yemini, S.: Typestate: A programming language concept for enhancing software reliability. IEEE Transactions on Software Engineering (TSE) 12(1), 157–171 (1986)
2. Bodden, E.: Verifying finite-state properties of large-scale programs. PhD thesis, McGill University (June 2009) (available through ProQuest)
3. Allan, C., Avgustinov, P., Christensen, A.S., Hendren, L., Kuzins, S., Lhoták, O., de Moor, O., Sereni, D., Sittampalam, G., Tibble, J.: Adding Trace Matching with Free Variables to AspectJ. In: OOPSLA, pp. 345–364 (October 2005)
4. Bodden, E.: J-LO - A tool for runtime-checking temporal assertions. Master's thesis, RWTH Aachen University (November 2005)
5. Chen, F., Roşu, G.: MOP: an efficient and generic runtime verification framework. In: OOPSLA, pp. 569–588 (October 2007)
6. Maoz, S., Harel, D.: From multi-modal scenarios to code: compiling LSCs into AspectJ. In: Symposium on the Foundations of Software Engineering (FSE), pp. 219–230 (November 2006)
7. Krüger, I.H., Lee, G., Meisinger, M.: Automating software architecture exploration with M2Aspects. In: Workshop on Scenarios and state machines: models, algorithms, and tools (SCESM), pp. 51–58 (May 2006)
8. Avgustinov, P., Tibble, J., de Moor, O.: Making trace monitors feasible. In: OOPSLA, pp. 589–608 (October 2007)
9. Chen, F., Meredith, P., Jin, D., Roşu, G.: Efficient formalism-independent monitoring of parametric properties. In: ASE, pp. 383–394 (2009)
10. Dwyer, M.B., Diep, M., Elbaum, S.: Reducing the cost of path property monitoring through sampling. In: ASE, Washington, DC, USA, pp. 228–237 (2008)
11. AspectJ team: The AspectJ home page (2003), http://eclipse.org/aspectj/
12. Avgustinov, P., Christensen, A.S., Hendren, L., Kuzins, S., Lhoták, J., Lhoták, O., de Moor, O., Sereni, D., Sittampalam, G., Tibble, J.: abc: An extensible AspectJ compiler. In: AOSD, pp. 87–98 (March 2005)

13. Bodden, E., Hendren, L., Lam, P., Lhoták, O., Naeem, N.A.: Collaborative runtime verification with tracematches. Journal of Logics and Computation (November 2008), doi:10.1093/logcom/exn077
14. Bodden, E., Chen, F., Roşu, G.: Dependent advice: A general approach to optimizing history-based aspects. In: AOSD, pp. 3–14 (March 2009)
15. Hilsdale, E., Hugunin, J.: Advice weaving in AspectJ. In: AOSD, pp. 26–35 (March 2004)
16. Masuhara, H., Kiczales, G., Dutchyn, C.: A compilation and optimization model for aspect-oriented programs. In: Hedin, G. (ed.) CC 2003. LNCS, vol. 2622, pp. 46–60. Springer, Heidelberg (2003)
17. Chen, F., Roşu, G.: Parametric trace slicing and monitoring. In: Kowalewski, S., Philippou, A. (eds.) TACAS 2009. LNCS, vol. 5505, pp. 246–261. Springer, Heidelberg (2009)
18. Sridharan, M., Bodík, R.: Refinement-based context-sensitive points-to analysis for Java. In: Conference on Programming Language Design and Implementation (PLDI), pp. 387–400 (June 2006)
19. Bodden, E.: Efficient hybrid typestate analysis by determining continuation-equivalent states. In: ICSE 2010: Proceedings of the 32nd ACM/IEEE International Conference on Software Engineering, pp. 5–14. ACM, New York (2010)
20. Avgustinov, P., Christensen, A.S., Hendren, L., Kuzins, S., Lhoták, J., Lhoták, O., de Moor, O., Sereni, D., Sittampalam, G., Tibble, J.: Optimising AspectJ. In: Conference on Programming Language Design and Implementation (PLDI), pp. 117–128 (June 2005)
21. Blackburn, S.M., Garner, R., Hoffman, C., Khan, A.M., McKinley, K.S., Bentzur, R., Diwan, A., Feinberg, D., Frampton, D., Guyer, S.Z., Hirzel, M., Hosking, A., Jump, M., Lee, H., Moss, J.E.B., Phansalkar, A., Stefanovic, D., VanDrunen, T., von Dincklage, D., Wiedermann, B.: The DaCapo benchmarks: Java benchmarking development and analysis. In: OOPSLA, pp. 169–190 (October 2006)
22. DeLine, R., Fähndrich, M.: Typestates for objects. In: Odersky, M. (ed.) ECOOP 2004. LNCS, vol. 3086, pp. 465–490. Springer, Heidelberg (2004)
23. Bierhoff, K., Aldrich, J.: Modular typestate checking of aliased objects. In: OOPSLA, pp. 301–320 (October 2007)
24. Fink, S., Yahav, E., Dor, N., Ramalingam, G., Geay, E.: Effective typestate verification in the presence of aliasing. In: International Symposium on Software Testing and Analysis (ISSTA), pp. 133–144 (July 2006)
25. Naeem, N.A., Lhoták, O.: Typestate-like analysis of multiple interacting objects. In: OOPSLA, pp. 347–366 (October 2008)
26. Bodden, E., Lam, P., Hendren, L.: Finding Programming Errors Earlier by Evaluating Runtime Monitors Ahead-of-Time. In: Symposium on the Foundations of Software Engineering (FSE), pp. 36–47 (November 2008)
27. Dwyer, M.B., Purandare, R.: Residual dynamic typestate analysis: Exploiting static analysis results to reformulate and reduce the cost of dynamic analysis. In: ASE, pp.124–133 (May 2007)

Checking the Correspondence between UML Models and Implementation

Selim Ciraci[1], Somayeh Malakuti[1], Shmuel Katz[2], and Mehmet Aksit[1]

[1] Software Engineering Group
University of Twente
Enschede, The Netherlands
{s.ciraci,s.malakuti,m.aksit}@ewi.utwente.nl
[2] Department of Computer Science
The Technion
Haifa, Israel
katz@cs.technion.ac.il

Abstract. UML class and sequence diagrams are used as the basis for runtime profiling along with either offline or online analysis to determine whether the execution conforms to the diagrams. Situations where sequence diagrams are intended to characterize all possible executions are described. The approach generates an execution tree of all possible sequences, using a detailed collection of graph transformations that represent a precise operational semantics for sequence diagrams, including treatment for polymorphism, multiple activations, reference to other diagrams, and the use of frames in sequence diagrams. The sequence diagrams are also used to determine the information that should be gathered about method calls in the system. Aspects that can follow the flow of messages in a distributed system, are generated and the results of execution are recorded. The execution tree is used to automatically check the recorded execution to detect operations that do not correspond to any of the diagrams. These represent either new types of sequence diagrams that should be added to the collection, or implementation errors where the system is not responding as designed. In either case, it is important to identify such situations.

Keywords: runtime verification, UML class and sequence diagrams, execution semantics, graph transformation, aspect-oriented profiling.

1 Introduction

Software models are increasingly used in different phases of the software development life cycle. Here we consider class and sequence diagram models from the UML [1] suite of design models, and use them as the basis for run-time verification and analysis of implemented code. UML is a widely accepted/standardized modeling language for Object-Oriented (OO) systems. Although many diagrams exist, the two most popular are generally acknowledged to be class diagrams to describe the structure and interrelationships among the classes, and sequence diagrams to describe sequences of method calls among objects that together describe important usage scenarios.

G. Roşu et al. (Eds.): RV 2010, LNCS 6418, pp. 198–213, 2010.

Class diagrams list the fields and methods in each class, and show which classes use other classes, which inherit from others, and multiplicities of classes in various relationships with other classes. Sequence diagrams are commonly used for partially documenting the behavior of the software system as interaction patterns among objects. Due to polymorphism, conditional frames, and multiple activations, these diagrams can represent many possible execution sequences and complex interactions.

Other notations for describing constraints, such as temporal logic, or even state diagrams and the Object Constraint Language (OCL) notations within UML, suffer from low availability: they simply are not widely used in industrial contexts, and are less likely to be updated as the system evolves. For example, UML state diagrams further describe the behavior of a system by defining the internal states and transitions among them for the classes (and objects derived from them). They are sometimes used to describe abstract versions of key protocols. However, it is actually rare to provide a full set of state diagrams, since they are viewed as extraneous and considered to be low-level.

We need to make sure that the implementation is consistent with the diagrams. Since user intervention, reaction, and decision-making are often involved in the use of such reactive systems, runtime verification of conformance is needed, in addition to testing and formal verification of the code. As explained in more detail in the related work section, most other works on using UML to generate monitors concentrate on the class diagrams. Even the few that use sequence diagrams do not treat necessary and common features such as polymorphism, multiple activations, and tracing over multiple sequence diagrams where one diagram refers to another.

Sequence diagrams have traditionally been used as a source for test cases that can be executed on the implemented system to see whether an expected sequence of method calls and responses occurs. This is reasonable if the sequence diagrams are seen simply as describing some sample scenarios of interaction, that in no way prevent other uses and orderings of method calls in the system. Sometimes this is indeed the approach used by software developers to describe expectations from a particular class or method within it: the overall behavior is implicitly understood by describing typical, but by no means exhaustive, cases of its use.

However, there are many software systems with UML designs where the sequence diagrams are more exhaustive: each sequence diagram provides a transaction-like description of scenarios that once begun, should be completed, and the collection of sequence diagrams is intended to show the entire possible use of the system. For a banking system, for example, the provided user actions of initiating a cash withdrawal, a transfer of funds, a deposit, etc, must be followed by an entire sequence of method calls described in one of the sequence diagrams. In the Crisis Mangagement case study presented in the following section, the types of crisis (car accident, fire, etc.) are all assumed to have corresponding sequence diagrams that design the proper response after analyzing the needs. When a situation is encountered that does not correspond to any of the diagrams, either it is a new type of crisis, or the system is not responding as designed. In either case, it is important to identify such situations. Such a use of sequence diagrams is also supported by the extension to live sequence charts [2] where after a pre-sequence occurs, an instance of the main sequence must follow.

When the sequence diagrams are used in this way, they can be used to automatically generate run-time profiling aspects and offline or online analyzers that detect when the system is not being used in conformance with any of the sequence diagrams. As noted above, such detection could mean either that the collection of sequence diagrams is incomplete, and new scenarios need to be added, or indeed that the implemented system is reacting incorrectly, and some object does not respond as expected to a method call that is part of a scenario.

The approach taken here is to use the sequence diagrams directly to generate a state graph and then an execution tree of all possible abstract states and method calls in the system based on the available knowledge. Since the internal behavior of the methods in the objects is not available, we only check for key visible events, interleaved with internal events and possibly actions from other scenarios. The implemented code and the sequence diagrams are analyzed automatically to determine which information must be collected, and to generate run-time non-invasive aspects that log messages and relevant information, including tracking of the connections between threads in different processors that correspond to a single execution of a sequence diagram. For our implementation, the gathered information is automatically analyzed offline to detect non-conformance with the collection of scenarios, and provide helpful feedback. We also describe how to detect the deviations during execution, simply by sending the gathered information directly to an online version of the analyzer.

This paper introduces an additional automatic traceability and verification step to detect inconsistencies between specified UML sequence diagrams and the actual run-time behavior. One of the key difficulties of run-time verification is knowing what to check, and providing a practical way for users to express that. Since sequence diagrams are already widely used to specify what is possible in a system, their direct use for run-time verification is both natural and useful.

Our approach is fully automated with a set of integrated simulation, run-time verification and feedback generation tools. Furthermore, it can be applied to systems that are composed of a set of distributed sub-systems developed in multiple languages.

The remainder of this paper is organized as follows: In the following section, we present a motivating example on the design of a crisis management system (CMS) to illustrate the problem. Section 3 describes related work in greater detail. In Section 4, we provide an overview of the approach, while Sections 5, 6 and 7 detail the simulation of the sequence diagrams, the extraction of information to generate run-time monitors, and the automatic analysis to detect deviations. Section 8 has a summary of application to the motivating example, while Section 9 concludes the paper.

2 Motivating Example

Helping the victims of a crisis situation requires rigid management and allocation of resources. For example, the allocated resources should be accounted for and free resources should be assigned to a crisis by their location. The Crisis Management System (CMS) case study [3] provides requirements for designing and implementing a software system to manage the resources. In this section, we provide one design alternative to illustrate how our approach can help in finding inconsistencies between UML models and the implementation.

Our design alternative focuses on *coordination* of the crisis resolution process. To facilitate this, we added support for *scenarios* for recurring crises in our design. A scenario prescribes the actions that should be taken in order to resolve the specific crisis like a car accident. As the users become experienced with recurring crises, they may want to extend existing scenarios and/or add new scenarios to the system. Thus, we modularized the scenarios in our design. The scenarios can be viewed as reactive systems that act upon outside events about the state of the crisis, which are: crisis start, resource allocate, resource dispatch, initial report about the crisis, resolution failed and crisis resolved. Both the scenarios and the system framework that organizes them can be described using class and sequence diagrams.

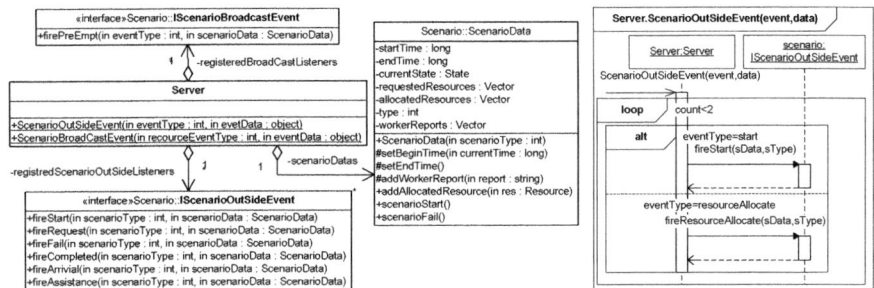

Fig. 1. The class diagram and a sequence diagram of the CMS

The event-based communication and the modularization of the scenarios can be supported by using the observer pattern. Here, the observer provides the interface of events to which the scenarios should react. Figure 1 illustrates the class diagram of the design with these patterns. Here, the class *Server* provides methods where the users (e.g., the user interface) communicate with the scenarios. The interface *IScenarioOutSideEvent* lists the events to which the scenarios should react. A scenario implements this interface and in each method, the actions it should take are specified. The class *ScenarioData* holds the data about the crisis, such as the allocated resources and the time the crisis started. Each crisis has a distinct type designated with the attribute *ScenarioData.type*.

The sequence diagram *Server.ScenarioOutSideEvent* in Figure 1 shows the Server looping through the list of scenarios and letting them know about the start of a crisis. Note that the call to the method *ScenarioOutSideEvent* is asynchronous; the class *Server* executes as a different process so that events arriving at the same time from different sources can be handled. The call to the method *fireStart* is polymorphic and any instance of a scenario can receive this call. Upon receiving an event, a scenario decides if it is interested in the crisis or not with the value of this attribute. This is illustrated with the sequence diagram *CarCrashScenario.fireStart()* in Figure 2.

The CMS has constraints essential for correct operation that emerge from the diagrams. For example, from the class diagrams it is clear that they should handle the list of events. The reactions to the events can be seen in the sequence diagrams of the scenarios. These constraints should be correctly reflected in the implementation, as a violation of a constraint may have catastrophic effects in CMS. In addition, scenarios

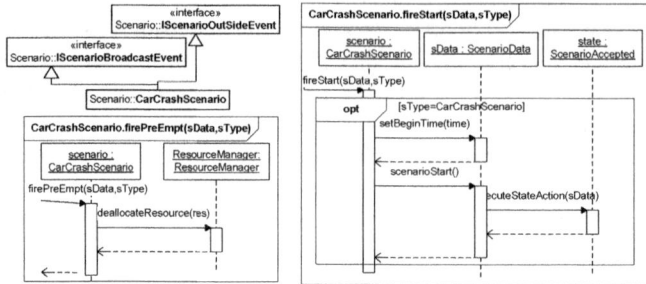

Fig. 2. The class *CarCrachScenario* and the sequence diagram showing the handling of the event *fireStart()*

may react to the same event and interfere with each other, which is considered additional source of complication.

As an example, assume that the CMS is deployed in an environment where only car accidents are managed. In due time, the users realize some accidents need prioritization. One such example is presidential emergencies coordinated by the class *PresidentialEmergency*. Prioritization then becomes a requirement, where a high priority scenario may require another scenario to release its resources. The design allows releasing of the resources through *scenario broadcast events*; a high-priority scenario asks the other scenarios to release resources by calling the method *Server.ScenarioOutSideEvent()*, which in turn calls the method *IScenarioOutSideEvent.firePreEmpt()*. The designer models the sequence diagrams showing the object *CarCrashScenario* handling the event *firePreEmpt*. Now assume that the developers do not correctly implement this previously unnecessary sequence diagram, so the resources are in fact not released.

As shown in Figure 3, the scenario *PresidentialEmergency* throws the broadcast event for releasing resources when it starts. Because the sequence diagram of *CarCrashScenario* responding to this event is not correctly implemented, it does not release the resources causing the coordination of the presidential emergencies to fail. The error is caused by the code not conforming to the sequence diagrams and, in the remaining sections of this paper, we describe how the approach proposed in this paper can capture such conformance errors.

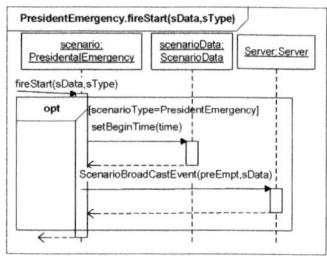

Fig. 3. Sequence diagram showing the scenario presidential emergency handling the event *fireStart*

3   Related Work

In the literature, the conformance checking of UML class diagram models with the implementation has been addressed in several ways. Code generation techniques [4] directly generate program skeletons (class declarations and lists of method headers) that can then be expanded to full systems and are guaranteed to satisfy the structural requirements of the class diagram. Mappings can be used to connect formal model elements to UML model elements using predicate logic [5], and runtime state observation can be used to check for consistent use [6]. These techniques only consider structural UML diagrams (class or object diagrams in particular) for conformance matching and do not address the conformance of the behavior/interactions specified using UML sequence diagrams.

A partial solution that does restrict the behavior is provided by adding class invariants or other assertions to the class diagram, using the OCL (Object Constraint Language) notation. Such assertions can then be verified for the implementation, either using static formal methods, or using well-known run-time verification approaches to check assertions about the state of the system. Unfortunately, such invariants are again not always provided in industrial uses of UML, and of course do not treat liveness or required sequences of actions.

Some approaches such as [7,8] aim at checking the behavioral correctness of software by utilizing state diagrams as their specification language. The problem with state diagram is the level of granularity depends on the employed language/tool for modelling. Thus UML state diagrams can only model the behavior within an object, and not inter-object behavior or message flow. Other languages such as Stateflow [9] focus on the modelling of the abstract behavior of software, without providing constructs to model objects and interactions within and among objects that realize the behavior. Therefore, it may be difficult, if not impossible, to use Stateflow for more fined-grained models of the software.

To overcome the shortcomings of state diagrams, [10,11,12] make use of UML sequence diagrams as their specification language to verify security policies and web-service interactions, respectively. Although a sequence diagram can include polymorphic calls, calls made by multiple threads of execution, or activate other sequence diagrams, those approaches cannot verify such advanced features of sequence diagrams. For example, in our case study, we would not be able to verify that the execution of *PresidentialEmergencyScenario* in one thread results in the release of resources that are acquired by another thread executing *CarCrashScenario*. The polymorphic nature of *fireStart* in the example is also beyond the capabilities of those tools.

There are several approaches [13,14,15,16] that make use of formalisms such as temporal logics and regular expressions for their specification language. One may try to express design conformance criteria as predicates in these formalisms and verify the implementation of software against these predicates. However, there are two difficulties. First, it is likely that most industrial developers are not expert in these formalisms, and would show resistance to using them [17]. Second, instead of reusing design models, separate specifications are used for the verification, which implies that the specifications must also be updated as the software evolves. In the development of complex software with strict time-to-market requirements, it is already a challenge to keep the design documents up-to-date [18], and having more documents (i.e. verification specifications) to update is a time-consuming and error-prone activity.

There are other works such as [19] which extend the message sequence charts of UML as their specification language. However, we believe that such customized versions of UML are not widely used in industrial environments.

4   Requirements and Overview of the Solution

In view of the shortcomings of existing techniques, we identify the following requirements for a conformance checking system based on class and sequence diagrams:

1) The ability to distinguish between polymorphic calls. As Figures 2 and 3 show, the invocations of *fireStart* and *firePrempt* on *Scenario* objects can be received by different scenarios. Here, according to the object on which the polymorphic methods are invoked, the conformance checking system must be able to match the execution trace with the corresponding sequence diagram.

2) The ability to check the conformance of sequences that span multiple sequence diagrams. For example, a sequence diagram may use a reference frame to include or activate another sequence diagram, as seen in the *PresidentialEmergency* diagram.

3) The ability to support multiple activations. In the implementation of our motivating example, multiple sources (running as different processes and threads) may trigger an event by calling the method *ScenarioOutSideEvent*. Here, the conformance checking system must be able to distinguish between the execution trace of each thread, and must check each trace against the corresponding sequence diagram.

In this paper, we describe an implemented conformance checking system that addresses the requirements above. To utilize sequence diagrams as the specification, we provide a simulator which constructs an execution tree from the sequence diagrams. The execution trees are later on used as specification for the conformance verification. The verification is done in an off-line manner, after the execution of the software terminates, which implies that the execution traces of software must be profiled for the off-line analysis. We make use of aspect-oriented programming to generate profiling aspects (i.e. observers) and insert the aspects into the implemented software code.

Figure 4 shows the three-phase architecture of our approach. In the compilation phase, a developer specifies the sequence and class diagrams, and the XML representation of the diagrams are input to the tools *UML to Graph Convertor* and *Translator*. The tool *UML to Graph Convertor* converts class and sequence diagrams to their equivalent graph representation. The generated graphs are input to the simulator called GROOVE [20], to which we added contains detailed graph transformation rules that closely mimic the actual OO execution of the operations described in the sequence diagrams. These are used to generate an execution tree of all possible executions that conform to the sequence diagrams (that we call a *simulation*).

In the right-hand side, for each specified sequence diagram, the tool *Translator* generates the *Profiling* aspect in the aspect-oriented language Compose* [21]. *Translator* checks the static structure of the software to extract a list of methods defined in the code. In addition, it receives information about the so-called activator method (i.e. the first method that is invoked in a sequence diagram) from each sequence diagram, and generates the *Profiling* aspects. The aspects log information about the methods that are invoked during the execution of an activator method. Since multiple invocations to an

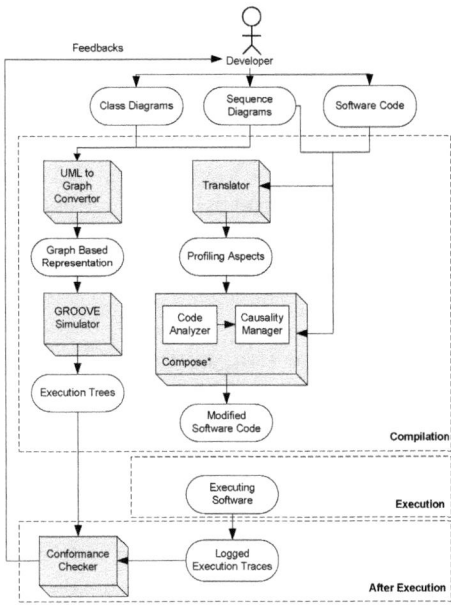

Fig. 4. The overall architecture of our solution

activator method may exist, the *Profiling* aspects distinguish among the invocations by associating a unique identifier, called *ActivationID*, to each of them. Consequently, separate log files are generated for each invocation of the activator method.

If during the execution of an activator method, a remote method is invoked in another process, the corresponding *ActivationID* must be passed to the target process and *ActivationID* must be preserved until the call returns to the caller process. This facilitates logging the information about all the local and remote invocations during the execution of an activator method. The *Profiling* aspects are input to the Compose* compiler which generates the executable codes for the aspects and inserts them in the software code. The module *Code Analyzer* within the Compose* compiler checks the software code to detect whether there is an inter-process communication (i.e. remote method invocation) within the context of an activator method. The analysis is done based on the available static information about the remote method invocations, for example, sockets or Java-RMI method invocations. If there is such an invocation, the module *Causality Manager* modifies the invocation in both caller and callee sides with one more parameter holding *ActivationID*. Both *Code Analyzer* and *Causality Manager* receive the name of activator methods as input from the sequence diagrams.

After the execution terminates, the tool *Conformance Checker* verifies the log file against the simulation and provides feedback to the developer. The feedback includes both where and in which sequence diagram a deviation is found, and the sequence of calls that led to the deviation including the inconsistent method call or other response.

Although in this work we focus on off-line conformance checking, it is relatively straightforward to accomplish an online checker as well. Here, we need to implement the tool *Conformance Checker* as another aspect which receives the required information from the *Profiling* aspects and checks the observed information against the already-generated execution trees.

As we will explain in the following sections, the sequence diagrams and generated execution models and states are independent from the implementation language of the software. Moreover, the Compose* language is also a language- and platform-independent aspect-oriented language; and the Compose* compiler can compile aspects for various language environments such as Java, .Net and C. This increases the applicability of our approach to software developed in various or even multiple languages.

5   From Class and Sequence Diagrams to Graph Transition System

The simulation of the class and sequence diagrams models are realized with graph-based state-space generation [20] by *i)* Defining a model for representing an OO-like runtime for the UML models with graphs, and *ii)* Modeling generic execution and exception handling semantics with graph-transformation rules over this model. The main reason for adopting graph-based state-space generation is that UML models can be transformed to graph models in a relatively straightforward manner. Also, the user is not requested to provide any other specifications than the UML class and sequence diagrams.

The simulation of the models resembles the execution of an OO software system. For this, we use Design Configuration Models (DCMs), whose meta-model is defined with Design Configuration Modeling Language (DCML), which includes a call stack, operation frames and program counters in addition to the UML elements. These models are represented as graphs since we defined the OO-like execution semantics with graph transformation rules.The DCMs are not defined to be a full semantic representation of OO software. They only include elements that can be modeled with class and sequence diagram models. A DCM is generated from one class diagram and at least one sequence diagram. We programmed a proof-of-concept converter for ArgoUML [22] and the interested readers are referred to [23] for a detailed description of the UML-to-DCML conversion.

The simulation starts from a user specified method we refer to as the *activator method*. It generates a state-space, called the Graph Transition System (GTS), showing all possible execution sequences that can be achieved by the invoke of the activator method. The state-space is a tree where each path from root to a leaf node is an execution sequence. The simulation is realized with a graph-production system, consisting of 57 graph transformation rules that model OO-like execution semantics for UML class and sequence diagrams (these rules can be downloaded from [24]). With these rules the following actions of the sequence diagrams is simulated:

Follow in the activation bars – DCML contains a program counter, which shows the action to be simulated. This program counter is advanced in the activation bar once the action simulation completes.

Call invocation – Allows the simulation of the call instances, self calls, super calls and calls to static methods. For example, the dispatch of a call to an instance method involves finding the receiver object, and then, traversing the inheritance hierarchy to find the latest implementation of the operation. If the object receiving the call implements the called operation, then the inheritance hierarchy is not traversed. If, on the other hand, the object does not implement the operation, the super-type of this object is traversed. After the method implementation is located, an operation frame for the method is created. The program counter of this operation frame points to the first action of the method (i.e. the first action in the activation bar). The newly created frame also contains a pointer (in the form of an edge) to the operation frame from which the call is made; in this way, a call stack is simulated. The semantics of the call to an instance is implemented with 5 graph transformation rules. These rules match when the program counter is a call action node whose receiver is an instance.

Asynchronous call invocation– These are presently allowed only as activator messages that initiate a sequence diagram. For asynchronous calls that are activator messages, before the call is invoked, a transformation rule increase the attribute *activationCount* of the operation frame. In this way, multiple invocations of the activator method can be distinguished in the state-space.

Parameter passing – is realized by going through the parameters specified in a call action and adding the necessary graph-edges so that the values/object of the parameters are accessible to the dispatched method: for *in* parameters these graph-edges simulate call-by-value and for *out/in-out* parameters they simulate call-by-reference.

Create operations – simulation of these creates a new object which represents the classifier receiving the create action in the sequence diagram.

Return from a method – is simulated in two steps when the program counter points to a return action. In the first step, if the returning method has a return value, it is copied to the previous (calling) operation frame. In the second step, a transformation rule "pops" the frame of the returning method from the call stack.

Return value assignments – After the pop of the operation frame, if a return value is copied to the top of the call stack, this return value is assigned to a variable specified in the call action. The assignment is also simulated in two steps: first the type compatibility of the returned value and the assigned variable is checked. Then, if this check succeeds, the variable gets the return value of a method.

Conditional execution – When the program counter is at an alternative frame with N frame fragments, the simulation continues in N branches: in each branch the actions within one of these fragments are simulated. For an optional frame, two branches are created, one activating the operational frame, and one ignoring it.

Loops – The simulation of a loop frame, requires the user to specify the desired number of iterations. Semantics of loops are modeled with 2 transformation rules, which match when the simulation reaches a loop frame node. One of these transformation rules arranges the program counter so that the simulation loops over the actions within the loop fragment. The second transformation rule tests whether the loop is repeated by the user-specified amount and, if so, it terminates the loop.

Figure 5 illustrates an excerpt of the GTS from the simulation of the sequence diagrams shown in Figures 1- 3. The sequence diagram $S1$ shows the operation frame and

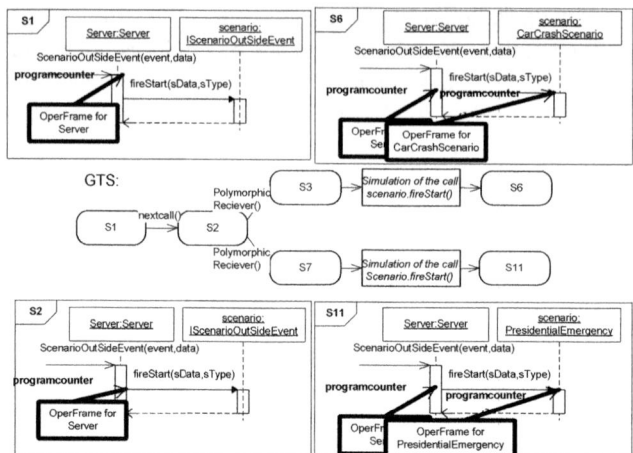

Fig. 5. An excerpt from the GTS of the simulation of the sequence diagrams Server.ScenarioOutSideEvent(), CarCrashScenario.fireStart(), and PresidentialEmergency.fireStart() depicted in Figures 1, 2 and 3

the program counter at state $S1$: the program counter is at the beginning of the activation bar of the classifier *Server* showing that the call *ScenarioOutSideEvent()* has just been dispatched. From state $S1$ the simulation moves to state $S2$ with the transition *nextcall*, which is the name of the graph transformation rule responsible for incrementing the program counter. Since at $S1$ the call *ScenarioOutSideEvent()* is dispatched, this rule matches and moves the simulation to the beginning of the next action. The sequence diagram $S2$ shows the program counter at state $S2$.

The call *fireStart* is a polymorphic call and can be received by the instance of classes that implement the interface *IScenarioOutSideEvent*. There are two such instances in the input sequence diagrams and, so, there are two outgoing transitions from the state $S2$. When the program counter is at a polymorphic call, the transformation rule *PolymorphicReceiver* has a match for each possible receiver. Each match picks one of the receivers and the application of the match arranges the picked instance as the receiver of the call. This multiple matching causes branching. After the arrangement of the receiver instance, the call is simulated. The sequence diagrams $S6$ and $S11$ corresponding to the states with the same name, show the operation frame after the call dispatched: at state $S6$ the call *fireStart* is received by the instance of the class *CarCrashScenario* and at state $S11$, it is received by the instance of the class *PresidentialEmergency*. Even though these receivers are in different sequence diagrams, the execution sequences where they respond to a call from the users (i.e. the call *ScenarioOutSideEvent()*) is generated.

The GTS also includes transitions that display which methods begin/end executing. These transitions are added by *parameterized transformation rules*; i.e, a rule specifies a set of node attributes that should be output instead of the parameters. For example, a label *executeMethod(activationCount, ClassifierID, ClassName, MethodName)* is added by the transformation rule *executeMethod* which matches when the program counter is at the beginning of an activation bar.

6   Runtime Observation

During the execution of software, upon the invocation of the activator method, the corresponding profiling aspect is activated, and consequently the runtime transitive effect of the activator method is logged. The output of the logger is the *observed execution sequence*, which is a a state machine where each state has at most one transition. The transitions are of the form $< action > ($ *activationID, ObjectID, ClassName, Method-Name*$)$. Here, the action can be *executeMethod* when the logger observers the start of a method or *returnMethod* when the logger observes the end of a method. To facilitate the conformance checking, the class name, object unique identifier ($ObjectID$), method name and arguments of the methods are logged. As we explained in Section 4, we distinguish between multiple invocations of an activator method by assigning a unique identifier called *activationID* to each invocation, and we log the execution trace initiated from each invocation in a separate logfile. Note that each logfile must eventually finish (be closed) in order to check for deviations. This can be guaranteed even for executions that do not perform expected events by, for example, building in an "error" operation that closes a log file whenever a time bound has passed with no activity in that log.

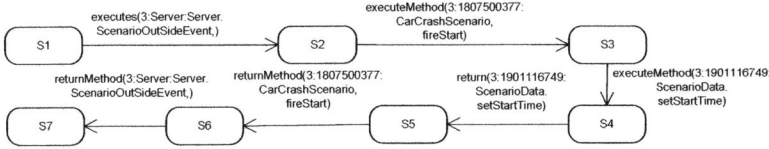

Fig. 6. An example observed execution sequence

In Figure 6 an example output of the logger is shown. Here, after the activator method *Server.ScenarioOutSideEvent()* starts execution, the car crash scenario executes and returns. The logging stops with the return of the activator method.

7   Verifying Runtime Observation with GTS

The verification is realized by tracing the GTS with the transitions of an observed execution sequence. However, before the tracing starts the GTS is converted to a non-deterministic automata, we refer to as an *abstract execution*. This automata is generated in the following steps: 1) all transitions except the ones added by the informative transformation rules are removed. 2) The states where a different invocation of the activator method occurs (i.e. states with different *activationCounts*) are connected to the start state with λ transitions. 3) a self transition labeled *, a wild

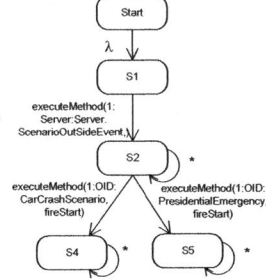

Fig. 7. The abstract execution automaton for the example GTS in Figure 5

card transition, is added to each state except the start state. The semantics of the wild-card transition is specified as follows:

Let ℓ_i be the labels of the all the outgoing transitions from state S_i and let U be the union of all transition labels from an observed execution sequence. The wildcard transition for S_i are all the input whose label belongs to $U - \ell_i$.

The wildcard transition allows us to abstract away from the observed execution sequence to the level of the sequence diagram: as a sequence diagram shows the sequence of important calls, the observed execution may contain calls that are not modeled in it. During the verification the wildcard transitions allows us to map these calls that are not in the sequence diagrams to *don't cares*. Figure 7 illustrates the abstract execution for the GTS presented in Figure 5. Here, there is only one λ transition because there is one invocation of the activator method *Server.ScenarioOutSideEvent()*.

The verification algorithm applies the transitions in the order they are seen from the observed execution sequence to the abstract execution, taking wildcard (irrelevant) operations into account. After applying these transitions, it checks if a final state or a state with a different *activationCount* in the abstract execution is reached. If such a state is not reached, then there are calls missing in the observed execution sequence which are in the sequence diagram. An important part of the verification is the binding of the identifiers. The classifier and the activation identifiers from the abstract execution are treated as variables, which are bound to actual values from the observed execution sequence. At a transition T_a of the abstract execution, if the method and the class names match to the next transition T_o from observed execution but the activation/classifier identifiers (*activationCount, classifierID*) are not bound, then the activation/classifier identifiers of T_a are set to the values of these identifiers at T_o.

We programmed an extension to GROOVE, that uses the output of the runtime ob-server and verifies it against the GTS generated from the simulation of UML models. Here, the verification step is repeated for each log file.

8   Case Study: Crisis Management System

In Section 2, we described an example inconsistency between the sequence diagrams of the CMS and an implementation, where the scenario car crash does not handle the request to preempt its resources correctly. Here, we show how our approach can de-tect this inconsistency. For simulation, we used the sequence diagrams showing the handling of the event *fireAllocate()* for the classes *CarCrashScenario* and *Presiden-tialEmergency* scenario, in addition to the class and sequence diagrams presented in Figures 1, 2 and 3. Each of these two additional sequence diagrams have 3 call ac-tions (and 3 return actions); the DCM generated from these diagrams contains 36 ac-tions. With these diagrams we simulated following scenario: the user interface making 4 outside events; these events are all different invocations of the activator method, and so, they are shown as asynchronous calls. The simulation of these diagrams generated 20075 states and 21007 transitions and completed in 2 minutes using 37Mb memory (with 2.2GHz Core Duo2 laptop running JRE 1.6_11). The simulation generated this many states because the GTS contains every possible execution of the sequence dia-grams. For example, an invocation of the method *ScenarioOutSideEvent()* generates 16 branches: 2 branches for the frame fragments of the alternative frame, 2 more branches due to the polymorphic call in each frame fragment adding 4 branches. In each of these 4 branches, another 4 branches is added due the loop frame. The number of transitions are higher then the number of states because of the build-in isomorphism detection mechanism of GROOVE. During simulation, GROOVE detects the isomorphic states in different branches of the GTS and merges them reducing the size of the GTS.

We implemented a prototype CMS in Java using the models presented in Section 2. We also added a sample user interface where the outside events can be sent to the server: the user interface and the class *Server* run in different threads. The implementation of the scenarios and server only consists of the calls presented in the models of Section 2 with the following exceptions: **i)** Upon receiving an event the scenarios call the method *ScenarioStatistics.addStatistic()*; this call is added to test the wildcard transitions. **ii)** To conform with the motivating example the method *ResourceManager.requestDeallocate()* used for releasing resources is not called by the car crash scenario upon receiving the preemption event. We ran this prototype with 2 user interface threads, where one user interface sends two start events and the other sends two allocate events. This run output 4 observed execution sequences, one for each invocation of the method *ScenarioOutSideEvent()*.

The 4 log files are then transfered into the GROOVE to verify the execution sequences. The verification of these state machines took 25 seconds, which includes the time for abstraction execution generation. For the resource allocation request sent by the second user interface thread to the presidential emergency scenario, the verification displayed the mismatch *executeMethod(2, PID, ResourceManager, requestDeallocate)*. This states that the car crash scenario did not in practice call the method to deallocate the resources; however, in the GTS from the sequence diagram this method is called.

This case study shows that it is possible check the UML-to-code conformance for sequence diagrams with polymorphic calls and for execution sequences spanning multiple sequence diagrams. Moreover, the runtime observer is able to trace sequences that originated from different sources and overlap.

9   Conclusion

Sequence and class diagrams can provide constraints that go beyond the assert statements commonly used to provide input for runtime monitoring and verification. This is especially true when the diagrams are intended to describe all possible types of usage for the system. Moreover, these diagrams are often readily available, when used as part of the design process of systems. No new notation has to be mastered, or kept updated as the system evolves, since most development processes anyway require updating the design for purposes of documentation and maintenance.

It may be argued that the conformance checking can be realized without generating all possible sequences (as is done here), where the conformance checker traces the sequence diagrams directly according to the logged execution. For situations where the number of logs to be checked is small, this is less costly than generating all possible executions in advance. However, direct tracing may become too expensive when the number of logs to be checked is large. Software systems, like CMS, are usually deployed at multiple sites and at each site many logs are sampled for consistency checking. Our approach is designed for such situations.

As future work, we are going to apply the approach to industrial software systems. In our previous studies, we have applied a similar simulation to the UML models of an industrial software system from the health care domain [23], where all possible uses of the software system are specified with sequence diagrams. We observed that the simulation generated execution sequences that are not explicitly modeled but are possible due to polymorphism. These execution sequences contained errors, showing the importance of considering the polymorphism in simulation. The application also showed that GROOVE and the simulation can scale to the industrial context.

Acknowledgements

This paper was written when Shmuel Katz visited the University of Twente for 6 months. This visit was partially supported by the NWO Grant no: 040.11.140.

References

1. UML: Unified modeling language, http://www.uml.org
2. Damm, W., Harel, D.: Lscs: Breathing life into message sequence charts. Formal Methods in System Design 19, 45–80 (2001)
3. Kienzle, J., Guelfi, N., Mustafiz, S.: Crisis Management Systems: A Case Study for Aspect-Oriented Modeling. Trans. on Aspect-Oriented Software Development 7, 1–22 (2010)
4. Harrison, W., Barton, C., Raghavachari, M.: Mapping uml designs to java. In: OOPSLA 2000, pp. 178–187. ACM, New York (2000)
5. Massoni, T., Gheyi, R., Borba, P.: A framework for establishing formal conformance between object models and object-oriented programs. Elec. Notes Theor. Comp. Sci. 195, 189–209 (2008)
6. Crane, M.L., Dingel, J.: Runtime conformance checking of objects using alloy. In: RV 2003, pp. 2–21. Springer, Heidelberg (2003)
7. Shing, M.T., Drusinsky, D.: Architectural design, behavior modeling and run-time verification of network embedded systems. In: Kordon, F., Sztipanovits, J. (eds.) Monterey Workshop 2005. LNCS, vol. 4322, pp. 281–303. Springer, Heidelberg (2007)
8. Drusinsky, D.: Semantics and runtime monitoring of tlcharts: Statechart automata with temporal logic conditioned transitions. In: RV 2004, pp. 3–21. Springer, Heidelberg (2005)
9. Stateflow, http://www.mathworks.com/products/stateflow/
10. Seehusen, F., Stolen, K.: A transformational approach to facilitate monitoring of high-level policies. In: Workshop on Policies for Distributed Systems and Networks, pp. 70–73 (2008)
11. Simmonds, J., Chechik, M., Nejati, S., Litani, E., O'Farrell, B.: Property patterns for runtime monitoring of web service conversations. In: Leucker, M. (ed.) RV 2008. LNCS, vol. 5289, pp. 137–157. Springer, Heidelberg (2008)
12. Kiviluoma, K., Koskinen, J., Mikkonen, T.: Run-time monitoring of architecturally significant behaviors using behavioral profiles and aspects. In: ISSTA 2006, pp. 181–190. ACM, New York (2006)
13. Malakuti, S., Bockisch, C., Aksit, M.: Applying the composition filter model for runtime verification of multiple-language software. In: ISSRE 2009, pp. 31–40. IEEE, Los Alamitos (2009)

14. Kim, M., Viswanathan, M., Kannan, S., Lee, I., Sokolsky, O.: Java-mac: a run-time assurance approach for java programs. Formal methods in system design 24 (2004)
15. Chen, F., Rosu, G.: Mop: an efficient and generic runtime verification framework. In: OOPSLA 2007. ACM, New York (2007)
16. Havelund, K., Rosu, G.: An overview of the runtime verification tool java pathexplorer. Formal methods in system design 24, 189–215 (2004)
17. Hatcliff, J., Dwyer, M.B.: Using the bandera tool set to model-check properties of concurrent java software. In: Larsen, K.G., Nielsen, M. (eds.) CONCUR 2001. LNCS, vol. 2154, pp. 39–58. Springer, Heidelberg (2001)
18. Gulesir, G.: Evolvable Behavior Specifications Using Context-Sensitive Wildcards. PhD thesis, University of Twente (2008)
19. Cook, T., Drusinsky, D., Shing, M.: Specification, validation and run-time monitoring of soa based system-of-systems temporal behaviors. In: ICSSE 2007, pp. 16–18 (2007)
20. Kastenberg, H., Rensink, A.: Model checking dynamic states in groove. In: Valmari, A. (ed.) SPIN 2006. LNCS, vol. 3925, pp. 299–305. Springer, Heidelberg (2006)
21. de Roo, A., Hendriks, M., Havinga, W., Durr, P., Bergmans, L.: Compose*: a language- and platform-independent aspect compiler for composition filters. In: WASDeTT 2008 (2008)
22. ArgoUML, http://argouml.tigris.org
23. Ciraci, S.: Graph Based Verification of Software Evolution Requirements. PhD thesis, Univ. of Twente, Enschede, CTIT Ph.D. thesis series no. 09-162 (2009)
24. GrACE: Graph-based adaptation, configuration and evolution modeling, http://trese.cs.utwente.nl/willevolve/

Compensation-Aware Runtime Monitoring*

Christian Colombo[1], Gordon J. Pace[1], and Patrick Abela[2]

[1] Dept. of Computer Science, University of Malta, Malta
[2] Ixaris Ltd, Malta
{christian.colombo,gordon.pace}@um.edu.mt, patrick.abela@ixaris.com

Abstract. To avoid large overheads induced by runtime monitoring, the use of asynchronous log-based monitoring is sometimes adopted — even though this implies that the system may proceed further despite having reached an anomalous state. Any actions performed by the system after the error occurring are undesirable, since for instance, an unchecked malicious user may perform unauthorized actions. Since stopping such actions is not feasible, in this paper we investigate the use of compensations to enable the undoing of actions, thus enriching asynchronous monitoring with the ability to restore the system to the original state in which the anomaly occurred. Furthermore, we show how allowing the monitor to adaptively synchronise and desynchronise with the system is also possible and report on the use of the approach on an industrial case study of a financial transaction system.

1 Introduction

The need for correctness of systems has driven research in different validation and verification techniques. One of the more attractive approaches is the use of monitors on systems to verify their correctness at runtime. The main advantage in the use of runtime verification over other approaches, is that it is a relatively lightweight approach and scales up to large systems — guaranteeing the observation of abnormal behaviour.

Even though monitoring of properties is usually computationally cheap when compared to the actual computation taking place, the monitors induce an additional overhead, which is not always desirable in real-time, reactive systems. In transaction processing systems, the additional overhead induced by each transaction can limit throughput and can cripple the user-experience at peak times of execution. One approach usually adopted in such circumstances, is that of evaluating the monitors asynchronously with the system, possibly on a separate address space. The overhead is reduced to the cost of logging events of the system, which will be processed by the monitors. However, by the time the monitor has identified a problem, the system may have proceeded further.

The problem is closely related to one found in long-lived transactions [14] — transactions which may last for too long a period to allow for locking of resources, but which could lead to an inconsistent internal state if the resources are released. To solve the

---

* The research work disclosed in this publication is partially funded by the Malta National Research and Innovation (R&I) Programme 2008 project number 052.

G. Roşu et al. (Eds.): RV 2010, LNCS 6418, pp. 214–228, 2010.

problem, typically one defines *compensations*, to undo partially executed transactions if discovered to be infeasible half way through. In the case of asynchronous monitoring, allowing the system to proceed before the monitor has completed its checks may lead to situations where the system should have been terminated earlier. As with long-lived transactions, we allow this run-ahead computation. We adopt the use of compensations in our setting to enable the undoing of system behaviour when an asynchronous monitor discovers a problem late, thus enabling the system to rollback to a sane state. Furthermore, in a setting such as transaction-processing systems, one can afford most of the time to run the monitors in synchrony with the system, falling back to asynchrony only when required due to high system load. Thus, we propose an architecture to enable loosely-coupled execution of monitors with the system, typically running synchronously, but allowing for de-synchronisation when required and re-synchronisation when desired.

In this paper, we present a framework to enable compensation-aware monitoring — and prove that the compensation triggering mechanism works as expected, resulting in similar behaviour as though we had run the monitor synchronously. Furthermore, we show that enabling the monitor to synchronise (and desynchronise) at will with the system does not change the behaviour. We have investigated the use of this approach on an industrial case study — dealing with financial transactions, and for which a compensation-based implementation was already in place.

The paper is organised as follows — in section 2 we present background necessary to reason about compensations, which we use to formally characterise compensation-aware monitoring in section 3. An architecture implementing this mode of monitoring is presented in section 4, and we illustrate its use on an industrial case study in section 5. Finally we discuss related work in section 6.

2   Compensations

Two major changes occurred which rendered traditional databases inadequate in certain circumstances [14,13]: on the one hand there was the advent of the Internet, facilitating the participation of heterogeneous systems in a single transaction, and on the other hand, transactions became longer in terms of duration (frequently, the latter being a consequence of the former). These changes meant that it was possible for a travel agency to automatically book a flight and a hotel on behalf of a customer without any human intervention — a process which may take time (mainly due to communication with third parties and payment confirmation) and which may fail. These issues rendered the traditional mechanism of resource locking for the whole duration of the transaction impractical since it may cause severe availability problems, and motivated the need for a more flexible way of handling transactions amongst heterogeneous systems while at the same time ensuring correctness. A possible solution is the use of compensations [14,13] which are able to deal with partially committed long-lived transactions with relative ease. Taking again the example of the flight and hotel booking, if the customer payment fails, the agency might need to reverse the bookings. This can be done by first cancelling the hotel reservation followed by the flight cancellation, giving the impression that the bookings never occurred. Although several notations supporting compensations have been proposed [5,4,3,15,21], little work [5,6] has been done to provide a mathematical basis for compensations. For simplicity, in the case of compensating CSP (cCSP) [5], to study the effect of the use of compensations, it is assumed that they are perfect cancellations of particular actions. This leads to the idea that executing an action followed by the execution of its compensation, is the same as if no action has been performed at all. In practice, it is rarely the case that two operations are perfect inverses of each other and that after their execution no trace is left. However, the notion of cancellation is useful as a check to the correctness of the formalism.

In this section we present the necessary background notions of cancellation compensations, based on [5].

2.1   Notation

To enable reasoning about system behaviour and compensations, we will be talking about finite strings of events. Given an alphabet Σ, we will write Σ^* to represent the set of all finite strings over Σ, with ε denoting the empty string. We will use variables a, b to range over Σ, and v, w to range over Σ^*. We will also assume action τ indicating internal system behaviour, which will be ignored when investigating the externally visible behaviour. We will write Σ_τ to refer to the alphabet consisting of $\Sigma \cup \{\tau\}$.

Definition 1. *Given a string w over Σ_τ, its external manifestation, written $w^{-\tau}$, is the same string but dropping instances of τ.*
Two strings v and w are said to be externally equal, written $v =_\tau w$, if their external manifestation is identical: $v^{-\tau} = w^{-\tau}$. This notion is extended to sets of strings.

External equivalence is an equivalence relation, and a congruence up to string catenation.

2.2   Compensations

For every event that happens in the system, we will assume that we can automatically deduce a compensation which, in some sense, corresponds to the action to be taken to make up for the original event. Note that executing the two in sequence will not necessarily leave the state of the system unchanged — a typical example being that of a person withdrawing a sum of money from a bank ATM, with its compensation being that of returning the sum but less bank charges.

Definition 2. *Corresponding to every event a in alphabet Σ, its compensation will be denoted by $\bar{a}$. We will write $\bar{\Sigma}$ to denote the set of all compensation actions. For simplicity of presentation, we will assume that the set of events and that of their compensations are disjoint[1]. Extending compensations to an alphabet enriched with the internal action τ, we assume that $\bar{\tau} = \tau$.*

---

[1] One may argue that the two could contain common elements — e.g. *deposit* can either be done during the normal forward execution of a system, or to compensate for a *withdraw* action. However, one usually would like to distinguish between actions taken during the normal forward behaviour and ones performed to compensate for errors, and we would thus much rather use *redeposit* as the name of the compensation of *withdraw*, even if it behaves just like *deposit*.

We also overload the compensation operator to strings over Σ_τ, in such a way that the individual events are individually compensated, but in reverse order: $\overline{\varepsilon} \overset{def}{=} \varepsilon$ and $\overline{aw} \overset{def}{=} \overline{w}\,\overline{a}$. For example, $\overline{abc} = \overline{c}\,\overline{b}\,\overline{a}$.

To check for consistency of use of compensations, the approach is typically to consider an ideal setting in which executing a, immediately followed by $\overline{a}$ will be just like doing nothing to the original state. Although not typically the case, this approach checks for sanity of the triggering of compensations.

Definition 3. *The compensation cancellation of a string simplifies its operand by (i) dropping all internal actions τ; and (ii) removing actions followed immediately by their compensation. We define cancel(w) to be the shortest string for which there are no further reductions of the form cancel($w_1 a \overline{a} w_2$) = cancel($w_1 w_2$).*

Since the sets of normal and compensation events are disjoint, strings may change under cancellation only if they contain symbols from both Σ and $\overline{\Sigma}$. Cancellation reduction is confluent and terminates.

Definition 4. *Two strings w and w' are said to be* cancellation-equivalent, *written $w =_c w'$, if they reduce via compensation cancellation to the same string: cancel(w) = cancel(w'). A set of strings W is said to be* included in set W' up-to-cancellation, *written $W \subseteq_c W'$, if for every string in W, there is a cancellation-equivalent string in W':*

$$W \subseteq_c W' \overset{def}{=} \forall w \in W \cdot \exists w' \in W' \cdot w =_c w'$$

Two sets are said to be equal up-to-cancellation, *written $W =_c W'$, if the inclusion relation holds in both directions.*

Cancellation equivalence is an equivalence relation, and is a congruence up to string (and language) catenation. Furthermore, a string followed by its compensation cancels to the empty string:

Proposition 1. *The catenation of a string with its compensation is cancellation equivalent to the empty string: $\forall w \cdot w\overline{w} =_c \varepsilon$.*

3   Compensations and Asynchronous Monitoring

We start by characterising synchronous and asynchronous monitoring strategies. In the synchronous version, it is assumed that the system and monitor perform a handshake to synchronise upon each event. In contrast, in the asynchronous approach, the events the system produces are stored in a buffer, and consumed independently by the monitor, which may thus lag behind the system. Based on the asynchronous semantics, we then define a compensation-aware monitoring strategy, which monitors asynchronously, but makes sure to undo any system behaviour which has taken place *after* the event which led to failure. Finally we show how enabling synchronisation and desynchronisation at will leaves the results intact.

3.1 Synchronous and Asynchronous Monitoring

We will assume a labelled transition system semantics over alphabet Σ for both systems and monitors. Given a class of system states S, we will assume the semantics $\longrightarrow_{sys} \subseteq S \times \Sigma \times S$, and similarly a relation $\longrightarrow_{mon}$ over the set of monitor states M. We also assume a distinct $\odot \in S$ identifying a stopped system, and $\otimes \in M$ denoting a monitor which has detected failure. Both $\odot$ and $\otimes$ are assumed to have no outgoing transitions.

Using standard notation, we will write $\sigma \xrightarrow{a}_{sys} \sigma'$ (resp. $m \xrightarrow{a}_{mon} m'$) as shorthand for $(\sigma, a, \sigma') \in \longrightarrow_{sys}$ (resp. $(m, a, m') \in \longrightarrow_{mon}$). For any transition relation $\xrightarrow{a}_X$ ($a \in \Sigma$), we will write $\xRightarrow{w}_X$ ($w \in \Sigma^*$) to denote its reflexive transitive closure.

Definition 5. *The transition system semantics of the synchronous composition of a system and monitor is defined over $S \times M$ using the rules given in Fig 1. The rule* SYNC *defines how the system and monitor can take a step together, while* SYNCERR *handles the case when the monitor discovers an anomaly. A state (σ, m) is said to be (i) suspended if $\sigma = \odot$; (ii) faulty if $m = \otimes$; and (iii) sane if it is not suspended unless faulty $(\sigma = \odot \implies m = \otimes)$.*

The set of traces generated through the synchronous composition of system σ and monitor m, written $\mathsf{traces}_\parallel(\sigma, m)$ *is defined as follows:*

$$\mathsf{traces}_\parallel(\sigma, m) = \{w \mid \exists(\sigma', m') \cdot (\sigma, m) \xRightarrow{w}_\parallel (\sigma', m')\}$$

Example 1. For example consider a simple system P over alphabet $\{a, b\}$ and a monitor A which consumes an alternation of a and b events starting with a i.e. $abab\ldots$ but breaks for any other input. The synchronous composition of such system and monitor takes a step if both the system and the monitor can take a step independently on the given input. Therefore, if the system performs event a: $(P, A) \xrightarrow{a}_\parallel (P', A')$. If system P performs a b instead, the system would break: $(P, A) \xrightarrow{b}_\parallel (\odot, \otimes)$.

Proposition 2. *A sequence of actions is accepted by the synchronous composition of a system and a monitor, if and only if it is accepted by both the monitor and the system acting independently. Provided that $m' \neq \otimes$, $(\sigma, m) \xRightarrow{w}_\parallel (\sigma', m')$, if and only if $\sigma \xRightarrow{w}_{sys} \sigma'$ and $m \xRightarrow{w}_{mon} m'$.*

In contrast to synchronous monitoring, asynchronous monitoring enables the system and the monitor to take steps independently of each other. The state of asynchronous monitoring also includes an intermediate buffer between the system and the monitor so as not to lose messages emitted by the system which are not yet consumed by the monitor.

Definition 6. *The asynchronous composition of a system and a monitor, is defined over $S \times \Sigma_\tau \times M$, in terms of the three rules given in Fig. 1. Rule* ASYNC$_S$ *allows progress of the system adding the events to the intermediate buffer, while rule* ASYNC$_M$ *allows the monitor to consume events from the buffer. Finally rule* ASYNCERR *suspends the system once the monitor detects an anomaly. Suspended, faulty and sane states are defined as in the case of synchronous monitoring by ignoring the buffer.*

The set of traces accepted by the asynchronous composition of system σ and monitor m, written $\mathsf{traces}_{|||}(\sigma, m)$ *is defined as follows:*

$$\mathsf{traces}_{|||}(\sigma, m) = \{w \mid \exists(\sigma', w', m') \cdot (\sigma, \varepsilon, m) \overset{w}{\Longrightarrow}_{|||} (\sigma', w', m')\}$$

Example 2. Taking the same example as before, upon each step of the system, an event is added to the buffer — if the system starts with an event b: $(P, \varepsilon, A) \overset{b}{\longrightarrow}_{|||} (P', b, A)$. Subsequently, the system may either continue further, or the monitor can consume the event from the buffer and fail: $(P', b, A) \overset{\tau}{\longrightarrow}_{|||} (P', \varepsilon, \otimes)$. At this stage the system can still progress further until it is stopped by the rule AsyncErr.

Proposition 3. *The system can always proceed independently when asynchronously monitored, adding events to the buffer, while the monitor can also proceed independently, consuming events from the buffer: (i) if* $\sigma \overset{w}{\Longrightarrow}_{sys} \sigma'$, *then* $(\sigma, w', m) \overset{w}{\Longrightarrow}_{|||} (\sigma', w'w, m)$; *and (ii) if* $m \overset{w}{\Longrightarrow}_{mon} m'$, *then* $(\sigma, ww', m) \overset{\tau^*}{\Longrightarrow}_{|||} (\sigma, w', m')$.

Synchronous Monitoring

$$\text{SYNC} \quad \frac{\sigma \overset{a}{\longrightarrow}_{sys} \sigma', \ m \overset{a}{\longrightarrow}_{mon} m'}{(\sigma, m) \overset{a}{\longrightarrow}_{||} (\sigma', m')} \ m \neq \otimes \qquad\qquad \text{SYNCERR} \quad \frac{\sigma \overset{a}{\longrightarrow}_{sys} \sigma', \ m \overset{a}{\longrightarrow}_{mon} \otimes}{(\sigma, m) \overset{a}{\longrightarrow}_{||} (\odot, \otimes)}$$

Asynchronous Monitoring

$$\text{ASYNC}_S \quad \frac{\sigma \overset{a}{\longrightarrow}_{sys} \sigma'}{(\sigma, w, m) \overset{a}{\longrightarrow}_{|||} (\sigma', wa, m)} \qquad\qquad \text{ASYNC}_M \quad \frac{m \overset{a}{\longrightarrow}_{mon} m'}{(\sigma, aw, m) \overset{\tau}{\longrightarrow}_{|||} (\sigma, w, m')}$$

$$\text{ASYNCERR} \quad \frac{}{(\sigma, w, \otimes) \overset{\tau}{\longrightarrow}_{|||} (\odot, w, \otimes)} \ \sigma \neq \odot$$

Compensation-Aware Monitoring

$$\text{COMP} \quad \frac{}{(\odot, wa, \otimes) \overset{\bar{a}}{\longrightarrow}_C (\odot, w, \otimes)}$$

Adaptive Monitoring

$$\text{RESYNC} \quad \frac{}{(\sigma, \varepsilon, m) \overset{\tau}{\longrightarrow}_A (\sigma, m)} \qquad\qquad \text{DESYNC} \quad \frac{}{(\sigma, m) \overset{\tau}{\longrightarrow}_A (\sigma, \varepsilon, m)}$$

Fig. 1. Semantics of different monitoring schemas

3.2   Compensation-Aware Monitoring

The main problem with asynchronous monitoring is that the system can proceed beyond
an anomaly before the monitor detects the problem and stops the system. We enrich
asynchronous monitoring with compensation handling so as to 'undo' actions which
the system has performed after an error is detected.

Definition 7. *Compensation-aware monitoring uses the asynchronous monitoring rules,
together with an additional one* COMP *which performs a compensation action of actions still lying in the buffer once the monitor detects an anomaly. The rule is shown
in Fig. 1.*

   The set of traces generated through the compensation-aware composition of system
σ *and monitor m, written* traces $_C(\sigma, m)$*, is defined as follows:*

$$\text{traces}_C(\sigma, m) = \{w \mid \exists(\sigma', m') \cdot (\sigma, \varepsilon, m) \overset{w}{\Longrightarrow}_C (\sigma', \varepsilon, m')\}$$

Sane, suspended and faulty states are defined as in asynchronous monitoring.

Example 3. Consider the previous example with:

$$(P, \varepsilon, A) \overset{b}{\longrightarrow}_C (P', b, A) \overset{b}{\longrightarrow}_C (P'', bb, A) \overset{\tau}{\longrightarrow}_C (P'', b, \otimes) \overset{a}{\longrightarrow}_C (P''', ba, \otimes) \overset{\tau}{\longrightarrow}_C (\odot, ba, \otimes)$$

   At this stage, compensation actions are executed for the actions remaining in the
buffer in reverse order:

$$(\odot, ba, \otimes) \overset{\bar{a}}{\longrightarrow}_C (\odot, b, \otimes) \overset{\bar{b}}{\longrightarrow}_C (\odot, \varepsilon, \otimes)$$

Proposition 4. *States reachable (under synchronous, asynchronous and compensation-
aware monitoring) from a sane state are themselves sane. Similarly, for suspended and
faulty states.*

Strings accepted by compensation-aware monitoring follow a regular pattern.

Lemma 1. *For an unsuspended state* (σ, ε, m)*, if* $(\sigma, \varepsilon, m) \overset{w}{\Longrightarrow}_C (\odot, v, \otimes)$*, then there
exist some* $w_1, w_2 \in \Sigma^*$ *such that the following three properties hold: (i)* $w =_\tau w_1 v w_2 \bar{w}_2$*;
(ii)* $m \overset{w_1}{\Longrightarrow}_{mon} \otimes$*; (iii)* $\exists \sigma'' \cdot \sigma \overset{w_1 v w_2}{\Longrightarrow}_{sys} \sigma''$*.*

   Similarly, for an unsuspended state (σ, ε, m)*, if* $(\sigma, \varepsilon, m) \overset{w}{\Longrightarrow}_C (\sigma', v, m')$ *(with* $\sigma' \neq
\odot$*), then there exists* $w_1 \in \Sigma^*$ *such that the following three properties hold: (i)* $w =_\tau w_1 v$*;
(ii)* $m \overset{w_1}{\Longrightarrow}_{mon} m'$*; (iii)* $\sigma \overset{w_1 v}{\Longrightarrow}_{sys} \sigma'$*.*

Proof. The proof of the lemma is by induction on the derivation string w.
For the base case, with $w = \varepsilon$*, we consider the two possible cases separately:*

 - *Given that* $(\sigma, \varepsilon, m) \overset{\varepsilon}{\Longrightarrow}_C (\odot, v, \otimes)$*, it follows immediately that* $\sigma = \odot$*,* $v = \varepsilon$ *and
   $m = \otimes$. By taking* $w_1 = w_2 = \varepsilon$*, all three statements follow immediately.*
 - *Alternatively, if* $(\sigma, \varepsilon, m) \overset{\varepsilon}{\Longrightarrow}_C (\sigma', v, m')$*, it follows immediately that* $\sigma = \sigma'$*,* $v = \varepsilon$
   and $m = m'$*. By taking* $w_1 = \varepsilon$*, all three statements follow immediately.*

Assume the property holds for a string w*, we proceed to prove that it holds for a string*
wa*.*
*By analysis of the transition rules, there are four possible ways in which the final tran-
sition can be produced:*

(a) Using the rule ASYNCERR: $(\sigma, \varepsilon, m) \overset{w}{\Rightarrow}_C (\sigma', v, \otimes) \overset{\tau}{\rightarrow}_C (\odot, v, \otimes)$.

(b) Using the rule COMPB: $(\sigma, \varepsilon, m) \overset{w}{\Rightarrow}_C (\odot, va, \otimes) \overset{\bar{a}}{\rightarrow}_C (\odot, v, \otimes)$.

(c) Using the rule ASYNC$_S$: $(\sigma, \varepsilon, m) \overset{w}{\Rightarrow}_C (\sigma'', v, m') \overset{a}{\rightarrow}_C (\sigma', va, m')$.

(d) Using the rule ASYNC$_M$: $(\sigma, \varepsilon, m) \overset{w}{\Rightarrow}_C (\sigma', av, m'') \overset{\tau}{\rightarrow}_C (\sigma', v, m')$.

The proofs of the four possibilities proceed similarly. Consider the possibility (b):

$$(\sigma, \varepsilon, m) \overset{w}{\Rightarrow}_C (\odot, va, \otimes) \overset{\bar{a}}{\rightarrow}_C (\odot, v, \otimes)$$

By the inductive hypothesis, it follows that there exist w_1' and w_2' such that (i) $w =_\tau$ $w_1' vaw_2' \overline{w}_2'$; (ii) $m \overset{w_1'}{\Rightarrow}_{mon} \otimes$; (iii) $\exists \sigma'' \cdot \sigma \overset{w_1' vaw_2'}{\Rightarrow}_{sys} \sigma''$.
We require to prove that there exist w_1 and w_2 such that: (i) $w\bar{a} =_\tau w_1 vw_2 \overline{w}_2$; (ii) $m \overset{w_1}{\Rightarrow}_{mon} \otimes$; (iii) $\exists \sigma'' \cdot \sigma \overset{w_1 vaw_2}{\Rightarrow}_{sys} \sigma''$.
Taking $w_1 = w_1'$ and $w_2 = aw_2'$ statement (i) can be proved as follows:

$$\begin{aligned}
&w\bar{a} \\
=_\tau \;&\{ \text{ by statement (i) of the inductive hypothesis } \} \\
&w_1' vaw_2' \overline{w}_2' \bar{a} \\
= \;&\{ \text{ by definition of compensation of strings } \} \\
&w_1' vaw_2' \overline{aw_2'} \\
= \;&\{ \text{ by choice of } w_1 \text{ and } w_2 \} \\
&w_1 vw_2 \overline{w}_2
\end{aligned}$$

Statement (ii) follows immediately from the statement (ii) of the inductive hypothesis and the fact that $w_1 = w_1'$. Similarly, from statement (iii) of the inductive hypothesis, $\sigma \overset{w_1' vaw_2'}{\Rightarrow}_{sys} \sigma'$, if follows by definition of w_1 and w_2, that $\sigma \overset{w_1 vw_2}{\Rightarrow}_{sys} \sigma'$.
The proofs of the other possibilities follow in a similar manner.

We can now prove that synchronous monitoring is equivalent to compensation-aware monitoring with perfect compensations. This result ensures the sanity of compensation triggering as defined in the semantics.

Theorem 1. *Given a sane system and monitor pair (σ, m), the set of traces produced by synchronous monitoring is cancellation-equivalent to the set of traces produced through compensation-aware monitoring: $\text{traces}_\parallel(\sigma, m) =_c \text{traces}_C(\sigma, m)$.*

Proof. To prove that $\text{traces}_\parallel(\sigma, m) \subseteq_c \text{traces}_C(\sigma, m)$, we note that every synchronous transition $(\sigma', m) \overset{a}{\rightarrow}_\parallel (\sigma'', m'')$, can be emulated in two steps by the compensation-aware transitions $(\sigma', v, m) \overset{a\tau}{\Rightarrow}_C (\sigma'', v, m'')$, leaving the buffer intact. Using this fact, and induction on string w, one can show that if $(\sigma, m) \overset{w}{\Rightarrow}_\parallel (\sigma', m')$, then $(\sigma, \varepsilon, m) \overset{v}{\Rightarrow}_C (\sigma', \varepsilon, m')$, with $w = v^{-\tau}$. Hence, $\text{traces}_\parallel(\sigma, m) \subseteq_c \text{traces}_C(\sigma, m)$.
Proving it in the opposite direction ($\text{traces}_C(\sigma, m) \subseteq_c \text{traces}_\parallel(\sigma, m)$) is more intricate.
By definition, if $w \in \text{traces}_C(\sigma, m)$, then $(\sigma, \varepsilon, m) \overset{w}{\Rightarrow}_C (\sigma', \varepsilon, m')$. We separately consider the two cases of (i) $\sigma' = \odot$ and (ii) $\sigma' \neq \odot$.

– *When the final state is suspended* ($\sigma' = \odot$):

$$(\sigma, \varepsilon, m) \overset{w}{\Longrightarrow}_C (\odot, \varepsilon, m')$$
$\Longrightarrow$ { *by sanity of initial state and proposition 4* }
$$(\sigma, \varepsilon, m) \overset{w}{\Longrightarrow}_C (\odot, \varepsilon, \otimes)$$
$\Longrightarrow$ { *by lemma 1* }
$$\exists w_1, w_2 \cdot w =_\tau w_1 w_2 \overline{w}_2 \wedge m \overset{w_1}{\Longrightarrow}_{mon} \otimes' \wedge \exists \sigma'' \cdot \sigma \overset{w_1}{\Longrightarrow}_{sys} \sigma''$$
$\Longrightarrow$ { *by proposition 2* }
$$\exists w_1, w_2 \cdot w =_\tau w_1 w_2 \overline{w}_2 \wedge \exists \sigma'' \cdot (\sigma, m) \overset{w_1}{\Longrightarrow}_\| (\sigma'', \otimes)$$
$\Longrightarrow$ { *by definition of* $traces_\|$ }
$$\exists w_1, w_2 \cdot w =_\tau w_1 w_2 \overline{w}_2 \wedge w_1 \in traces_\|(\sigma, m)$$
$\Longrightarrow$ { *by proposition 1* }
$$\exists w_1 \cdot w =_c w_1 \wedge w_1 \in traces_\|(\sigma, m)$$

– *When the final state is not suspended* ($\sigma' \neq \odot$):

$$(\sigma, \varepsilon, m) \overset{w}{\Longrightarrow}_C (\sigma', \varepsilon, m')$$
$\Longrightarrow$ { *by lemma 1* }
$$\exists w_1 \cdot w =_\tau w_1 \wedge m \overset{w_1}{\Longrightarrow}_{mon} m' \wedge \sigma \overset{w_1}{\Longrightarrow}_{sys} \sigma'$$
$\Longrightarrow$ { *by proposition 2* }
$$\exists w_1 \cdot w =_\tau w_1 \wedge (\sigma, m) \overset{w_1}{\Longrightarrow}_\| (\sigma', m')$$
$\Longrightarrow$ { *by definition of* $traces_\|$ }
$$\exists w_1 \cdot w =_\tau w_1 \wedge w_1 \in traces_\|(\sigma, m)$$
$\Longrightarrow$ { *by the alphabet of synchronous monitoring* }
$$\exists w_1 \cdot w =_c w_1 \wedge w_1 \in traces_\|(\sigma, m)$$

Hence, in both cases it follows that:
$$w \in traces_C(\sigma, m) \implies \exists w_1 \cdot w =_c w_1 \wedge w_1 \in traces_\|(\sigma, m)$$
From which we can conclude that:
$$traces_C(\sigma, m) \subseteq_c traces_\|(\sigma, m)$$

3.3 Desynchronising and Resynchronising

Despite compensation-awareness, in some systems it may be desirable to run monitoring synchronously with the system during critical sections of the code, only to desynchronise the system from the monitor again once control leaves the critical code section. In this section, we investigate a monitoring strategy which can run both synchronously or asynchronously in a non-deterministic manner. Any heuristic used to decide when to switch between modes corresponds to a refinement of this approach.

Definition 8. *The adaptive monitoring of a system, is defined in terms of the two additional (over and above synchronous and asynchronous monitoring) rules given in Fig. 1. Rule* RESYNC *allows the system to synchronise once the buffer is empty, while rule* DESYNC *allows the monitor to be released asynchronously. By also including the compensation rule* COMP, *we obtain adaptive compensation-aware monitoring* ($\longrightarrow_{AC}$).
    The set of traces generated through the adaptive composition of system σ and monitor m, written $traces_A(\sigma, m)$, *is defined as follows:*

$$traces_A(\sigma, m) \stackrel{def}{=} \{w \mid \exists (\sigma', w', m') \cdot (\sigma, m) \stackrel{w}{\Longrightarrow}_A (\sigma', w', m') \vee (\sigma, m) \stackrel{w}{\Longrightarrow}_A (\sigma', m')\}$$

The traces for compensation-aware adaptive composition $traces_{AC}(\sigma, m)$ *can be similarly defined.*

Theorem 2. *Asynchronous and adaptive monitoring are indistinguishable up to traces:* $traces_A(\sigma, m) = traces_{|||}(\sigma, m)$. *Compensation-aware adaptive monitoring is also indistinguishable from compensation-aware monitoring up to traces:* $traces_{AC}(\sigma, m) = traces_C(\sigma, m)$.

The theorems can be easily proved based on transition-relation inclusion. An immediate corollary of this last result, is that compensation-aware adaptive monitoring is cancellation-equivalent to synchronous monitoring.

It is important to note that the results hold about trace equivalence. In the case of adaptive monitoring, we are increasing the set of diverging configurations — since every state can diverge through repeatedly desynchronising and resynchronising. One would be required to enforce fairness constraints on desynchronising and resynchronising rules to ensure achieving progress in the monitored systems.

4   A Compensation-Aware Monitoring Architecture

LARVA [9] is a synchronous runtime verification architecture supporting DATEs [8] as a specification language. A user wishing to monitor a system using LARVA must supply a system (a Java program) and a set of specifications in the form of a LARVA script — a textual representation of DATEs. Using the LARVA compiler, the specification is transformed into the equivalent monitoring code together with a number of aspects which extract events from the system. Aspects are generated in AspectJ, an aspect-oriented implementation for Java, enabling automatic code injection without directly altering the actual code of the system. When a system is monitored by LARVA generated code, the system waits for the monitor before continuing further execution.

We propose an asynchronous compensation-aware monitoring architecture, cLARVA, with a controlled synchronous element. In cLARVA, control is continually under the jurisdiction of the system — never of the monitor. However, the system exposes two interfaces to the monitor: (i) an interface for the monitor to communicate the fact that a problem has been detected and the system should stop; and (ii) an interface for the monitor to indicate which actions should be compensated. Note that these correspond directly to rules ASYNCERR and COMP respectively. Therefore, the actual time of stopping and how the indicated actions are compensated are left for the system to decide.

Fig. 2 shows the four components of cLARVA and the communication links between them. The monitor receives system events through the events player from the log, while the system can continue unhindered. If the monitor detects a fault, it communicates with the system so that the latter stops. Depending on the actions the system carried out since the actual occurrence of the fault, the monitor indicates these actions for compensation. It is important to point out that the monitor can only compensate for actions of which it is aware — the monitor can never alert the system to compensate actions which have not been logged.

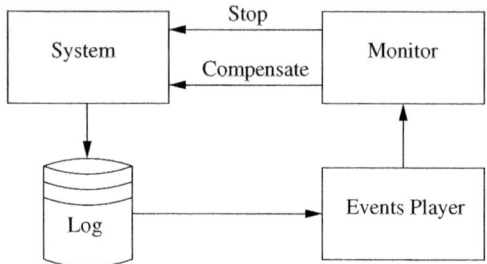

Fig. 2. The asynchronous architecture with compensations cLARVA

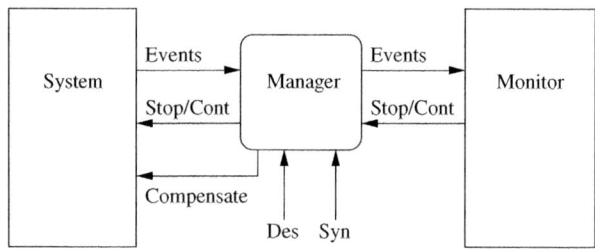

Fig. 3. The asynchronous architecture with synchronisation and desynchronisation controls

To support switching between synchrony and asynchrony, a *synchronisation manager* component is added as shown in Fig. 3. All connectors in the diagram are synchronous with the system not proceeding after relaying an event until it receives control from the manager. The following code snippet shows the logic of the synchronisation manager:

```
c = ok                   ;set default control to ok
while (c != stop)
  if (synch_mode)
    e = in_event()       ;read event from system
    c = out_event(e)     ;forward to monitor and get its resulting state
    out_control(c)       ;relay control to system
  else
    par                  ;parallel execution
      e1 = in_event()    ;read from system
      addToBuffer(e1)    ;store in buffer
      out_control(c)     ;return control to system
    with
      e2 = readFromBuffer() ;read from buffer
      c = out_event(e2)  ;forward to monitor and get its resulting state
end
```

The behaviour in which this architecture differs from cLARVA is that it can operate in both synchronous and asynchronous modes and can switch between modes. Switching from synchronous to asynchronous is trivial. The opposite requires that the manager waits for the monitor to consume all the events in the buffer and then allowing the system to proceed further. So far this has not been implemented, but we aim to implement it in the future as an improvement on cLARVA.

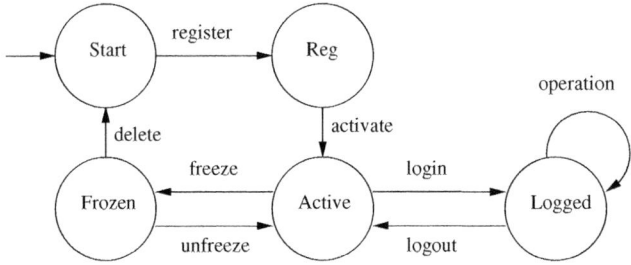

Fig. 4. The lifecycle property

In real-life scenarios it is usually undesirable to stop a whole system if an error is found. However, in many cases it is not difficult to delineate parts of the system to ensure that only the relevant parts of the system are stopped. For example, consider the case where a transaction is carried out without necessary rights. In such a case, the transaction should be stopped and compensated. However, if a user has managed to illegally login and start a session, then user operations during that session should be stopped and compensated.

5   Case Study

We have applied cLARVA on Entropay, an online prepaid payment service offered by Ixaris Systems Ltd[2]. Entropay users deposit funds through funding instruments (such as their own personal credit card or through a bank transfer mechanism) and spend such funds through spending instruments (such as a virtual VISA card or a Plastic Mastercard). The service is used worldwide and thousands of transactions are processed on a daily basis.

The advantage of applying the proposed architecture to EntroPay is that the latter already incorporates compensations in its implementation. The case study is further simplified by the fact that properties are not monitored globally but rather on a per user or per credit card basis. Therefore, when a problem is found with a particular user or card, only the compensations for that particular entity need to be triggered.

The case study implementation closely follows the architecture described above with two control connections: one with an interface for stopping EntroPay with respect to a particular user and another to the compensation interface of EntroPay, through which the monitor can cause the system to execute compensations.

In what follows, we give a classification of properties which were monitored successfully and how these are compensated in case of a violation detection.

Life cycle. A lot of properties in Entropay depend on which phase of the life-cycle an entity is in. Fig. 4 is an illustration of the user life-cycle, starting with registration and activation, allowing the user to login and logout (possibly carrying out a series of operations in between), and finally, the possibility of freezing/unfreezing/deleting a user in case of inactivity.

---

[2] www.ixaris.com

Implicitly, such a property checks that for a user to perform a particular operation and reach a particular state, the user must be in an appropriate state. If a life cycle property is violated, the user actions carried out after the violation is compensated and the user state is corrected. For example, if a user did not login and managed to carry out a transfer, then as soon as the monitor detects the violation, any ongoing user operations are stopped and the illegal transfer is compensated.

Real-time. Several properties in Entropay, have a real-time element. For example, a user account which is inactive for more than six months is frozen. If freezing does not take place, then, upon detection, the monitor issues a compensation for any actions carried out after the expected freezing and freezes the user account.

Rights. User rights are a very important aspect of Entropay's security. A number of transactions require the user to have the appropriate rights before a transaction is permitted. If a transaction is carried out without the necessary rights, it is compensated.

Amounts. There are various limits (for security reasons) on the frequency of certain transactions and the total amount of money which these transactions constitute. If a user is found to have carried out more transactions than allowed, then the excess transactions are compensated. Similarly, transaction amounts which go beyond the allowed threshold are compensated for.

The case study was successfully executed on a database of 300,000 users with around a million credit cards. A number of issues have been detected through the monitoring system: (i) certain logs were missing; (ii) some users were found to be in a wrong state, eg. should be in a frozen state but still active; (iii) the limit of the amount of money a user can spend was in some cases exceeded. Monitoring of the logs performed asynchronously ensured the identification of issues, and through the compensation mechanism, identification of actions to be taken to rollback the system to the point where the violation occurred. At that point, one can then either notify the operator of the issue, or trigger the system's own exception handling mechanism.

Although the current properties being monitored on Entropay are relatively light-weight and monitoring can be done relatively seamlessly, due to security issues, running the monitor synchronously is not an option — avoiding changes in the architecture of Entropay. The monitors are linked to the database of log entries to enable asynchronous monitoring, but giving feedback and compensation actions upon discovering issues.

6   Related Work

In principle, any algorithm used for synchronous monitoring can be used for asynchronous monitoring as long as all the information available at runtime is still available asynchronously to the monitor through some form of buffer. The inverse, however, is not always true because monitoring algorithms such as [19] require that the complete trace is available at the time of checking. In our case, this was not an option since our monitor has to support desynchronisation and resynchronisation at any time during the processing of the trace.

There are numerous algorithms and tools [2,7,1,19,20,12,16,11] which support asynchronous monitoring — sometimes also known as trace checking or offline monitoring. A number of these tools and algorithms [2,7,1,19] support only asynchrony unlike our approach which supports both synchronous and asynchronous approaches. Furthermore, although a number of approaches [12,16,20,11] support both synchronous and asynchronous monitoring, no monitoring approach of which we are aware is able to switch between synchronous and asynchronous monitoring during a single execution.

Although the idea of using rollbacks (or perfect compensations) as a means of synchronisation might be new in the area of runtime verification, this is not the case in the area of distributed games [17,18,10]. The problem of distributed games is to minimise the effects on the playing experience due to network latencies. Two general approaches taken are pessimistic and optimistic synchronisation mechanisms. The former waits for all parties to be ready before anyone can progress while the latter allows each party to progress and resolve any conflicts later through rollbacks.

The problem which we have addressed in this work is a simplified version of the distributed game problem with only two players: the system and the monitor. In a similar fashion to game synchronisation algorithms, the system rolls-back (or compensates) to revert to a state which is consistent with the monitor.

7   Conclusions and Future Work

In this paper, we have presented an adaptive compensation-aware monitoring architecture, and an implementation cLARVA. Combined with the notion of compensations where actions of a system can be 'undone' to somewhat restore a previous state, we reduce the effect of errors detected late (due to asynchronous monitoring) by compensating for additional events which the system may have performed in the meantime. We have demonstrated the use of this approach on a financial transaction handling software. The advantage of this case study is that compensations were already a well-defined concept from the developers perspective.

At the moment we are investigating the use of heuristics for desynchronisation and resynchronisation of the system and monitor. At the simplest level, one can simply trigger asynchronous monitoring when the system load reaches a certain level, and switch back to synchronous monitoring when it falls below the threshold. It would be interesting to explore further the development of smarter heuristics for this purpose — taking into account other issues, such as the trust in (or lack thereof) parties involved in the transaction and its monetary value.

A significant limitation of our work is the assumption that compensations are associated to individual actions. Apart from the fact that this might not always be the case, this approach is highly inflexible as one cannot simultaneously compensate for several actions, or commit a series of actions such that they cannot be compensated. In the future, we aim to lift this limitation by introducing a structured approach to compensations.

References

1. Andrews, J.H., Zhang, Y.: General test result checking with log file analysis. IEEE Trans. Softw. Eng. 29(7), 634–648 (2003)
2. Barringer, H., Groce, A., Havelund, K., Smith, M.: An entry point for formal methods: Specification and analysis of event logs. In: Formal Methods in Aerospace, FMA (2009)

3. Bruni, R., Melgratti, H., Montanari, U.: Theoretical foundations for compensations in flow composition languages. In: POPL 2005: Proceedings of the 32nd ACM SIGPLAN-SIGACT symposium on Principles of programming languages, pp. 209–220 (2005)
4. Butler, M.J., Ferreira, C.: An operational semantics for stac, a language for modelling long-running business transactions. In: De Nicola, R., Ferrari, G.-L., Meredith, G. (eds.) COORDINATION 2004. LNCS, vol. 2949, pp. 87–104. Springer, Heidelberg (2004)
5. Butler, M.J., Hoare, C.A.R., Ferreira, C.: A trace semantics for long-running transactions. In: 25 Years Communicating Sequential Processes, pp. 133–150 (2004)
6. Caires, L., Ferreira, C., Vieira, H.T.: A process calculus analysis of compensations. In: Kaklamanis, C., Nielson, F. (eds.) TGC 2008. LNCS, vol. 5474, pp. 87–103. Springer, Heidelberg (2009)
7. Chang, F., Ren, J.: Validating system properties exhibited in execution traces. In: Automated Software Engineering (ASE), pp. 517–520. ACM, New York (2007)
8. Colombo, C., Pace, G.J., Schneider, G.: Dynamic event-based runtime monitoring of real-time and contextual properties. In: Cofer, D., Fantechi, A. (eds.) FMICS 2008. LNCS, vol. 5596, pp. 135–149. Springer, Heidelberg (2009)
9. Colombo, C., Pace, G.J., Schneider, G.: Larva — safer monitoring of real-time java programs (tool paper). In: Software Engineering and Formal Methods (SEFM), pp. 33–37. IEEE Computer Society, Los Alamitos (2009)
10. Cronin, E., Kurc, A., Filstrup, B., Jamin, S.: An efficient synchronization mechanism for mirrored game architectures. Multimedia Tools Appl. 23(1) (2004)
11. D'Angelo, B., Sankaranarayanan, S., Sánchez, C., Robinson, W., Finkbeiner, B., Sipma, H.B., Mehrotra, S., Manna, Z.: Lola: Runtime monitoring of synchronous systems. In: Temporal Representation and Reasoning (TIME 2005). IEEE Computer Society Press, Los Alamitos (2005)
12. Ezust, S.A., Bochmann, G.V.: An automatic trace analysis tool generator for estelle specifications. In: Applications, technologies, architectures, and protocols for computer communication (SIGCOMM), pp. 175–184 (1995)
13. Garcia-Molina, H., Salem, K.: Sagas. In: SIGMOD 1987: Proceedings of the 1987 ACM SIGMOD international conference on Management of data, pp. 249–259 (1987)
14. Gray, J.: The transaction concept: Virtues and limitations (invited paper). In: Proceedings of 7th International Conference on Very Large Data Bases, Cannes, France, September 9-11, pp. 144–154 (1981)
15. Guidi, C., Lucchi, R., Gorrieri, R., Busi, N., Zavattaro, G.: SOCK: A calculus for service oriented computing. In: Dan, A., Lamersdorf, W. (eds.) ICSOC 2006. LNCS, vol. 4294, pp. 327–338. Springer, Heidelberg (2006)
16. Havelund, K., Roşu, G.: Synthesizing monitors for safety properties. In: Katoen, J.-P., Stevens, P. (eds.) TACAS 2002. LNCS, vol. 2280, p. 342. Springer, Heidelberg (2002)
17. Jefferson, D.: Virtual time. In: International Conference on Parallel Processing (ICPP), pp. 384–394. IEEE Computer Society, Los Alamitos (1983)
18. Mauve, M., Vogel, J., Hilt, V., Effelsberg, W.: Local-lag and timewarp: consistency for replicated continuous applications. IEEE Transactions on Multimedia 6(1), 47–57 (2004)
19. Roşu, G., Havelund, K.: Synthesizing dynamic programming algorithms from linear temporal logic formulae. Technical report, RIACS (2001)
20. Roşu, G., Havelund, K.: Rewriting-based techniques for runtime verification. Automated Software Eng. 12(2), 151–197 (2005)
21. Vaz, C., Ferreira, C., Ravara, A.: Dynamic recovering of long running transactions. In: Kaklamanis, C., Nielson, F. (eds.) TGC 2008. LNCS, vol. 5474, pp. 201–215. Springer, Heidelberg (2009)

Recovery Tasks: An Automated Approach to Failure Recovery

Brian Demsky[1], Jin Zhou[1], and William Montaz[2]

[1] University of California, Irvine
[2] Octo Technology, France

Abstract. We present a new approach for developing robust software applications that breaks dependences on the failed parts of an application's execution to allow the rest of the application to continue executing. When a failure occurs, the recovery algorithm uses information from a static analysis to characterize the intended behavior of the application had it not failed. It then uses this characterization to recover as much of the application's execution as possible.

We have implemented this approach in the Bristlecone compiler. We have evaluated our implementation on a multiplayer game, a web portal, and a MapReduce framework. We found that in the presence of injected failures, the recovery task version provided substantially better service than the control versions. Moreover, the recovery task version of the game benchmark successfully recovered from a real fault that we accidentally introduced during development, while the same fault caused the two control versions to crash.

1 Introduction

All too often, failures are caused by the propagation of errors through critical components of software applications. Current software development tools actually encourage the introduction of unnecessary dependences between conceptually unrelated components. These dependences introduce new error propagation pathways, which in turn can introduce new vulnerabilities. For example, many programming languages encourage developers to map otherwise independent software components onto the same thread. If one component fails, other components mapped onto the same thread will likely fail even though their only relationship with the original failure is artificially induced via the mapping of components to threads.

Our previous work on Bristlecone introduced a task-based language designed to eliminate artificial dependences that serve to propagate errors [8]. A shortcoming of Bristlecone is that it cannot prevent the propagation of failures through legitimate dependences. If a failure occurs, it can be desirable for tasks that legitimately depend on the failed part of the computation to operate in a degraded manner. For example, if a failure prevents rendering a web page frame, the web browser can still render the web page by simply rendering the frame as an empty box.

This paper extends our previous work on Bristlecone to manage failure propagation through legitimate dependences. The technique is based on the observation that although it is difficult to anticipate how applications may fail, there are often locations in an application in which it is straightforward to break dependences on data that is

G. Roşu et al. (Eds.): RV 2010, LNCS 6418, pp. 229–244, 2010.

missing because of a failure. For example, developing recovery routines for all possible failures of a web page rendering engine is likely to be impossible. However, a developer might reasonably write a rendering engine that can assemble frames into a web page even when some frames are missing because of a failure.

We extend Bristlecone with *recovery tasks*. Recovery tasks serve as software circuit breakers — they break legitimate data dependences in the event of a software error to mitigate the damage caused by that error. More precisely, a recovery task can function even if an error in another part of the computation causes some of the recovery task's input parameters to be unavailable. Note that the exact task that breaks a dependence chain is not important — the system simply needs a point in the dependence chain to halt the propagation of a failure.

Our approach uses static analysis to characterize the *intended behavior* of the failed part of a computation. We use the term intended behavior to refer to the behavior that a failed computation would have had if the failure had not occurred. For each possible failure point, this analysis computes which tasks the computation, had it not failed, would have executed. The analysis then identifies recovery tasks in these sets. The recovery algorithm then uses the recovery tasks to break data dependences on the failure and recover that part of the computation.

A failure will cause the application to skip some tasks. The analysis next determines which data structures these skipped task would have modified. The runtime uses these results to mark any data structures that the skipped part of the application may have modified as damaged. It then uses the recovery tasks to break the execution's dependence on the damaged data structures.

Our approach contains the following key components:

- **Language Extensions:** Developers use annotations to declare a set of recovery tasks that can execute even if a failure causes some of their parameter objects to be unavailable. The developer guards accesses to those parameter with checks that verify that the parameter is available before accessing it.
- **Static Analysis:** The compiler analyzes the application's code and task specifications to construct an abstract state transition graph for each class. These graphs abstract concrete objects' state with nodes that represent abstract states. We have developed a static analysis that reasons about the state transition graphs to characterize the intended behavior of the failed code.
- **Recovery Algorithm:** The runtime system uses static analysis results to reason about the intended behavior of the failed part of the computation. While it is in general impossible to determine the exact intended behavior of the failed part on the objects' states, our analysis can still generate constraints on the possible states of these objects. The recovery algorithm uses the results of the static analysis to determine which recovery tasks should be executed.

1.1   Comparison to Manual Recovery

Many programming languages, including Java, provide exception handling mechanisms that are designed to help applications recover from failures. Exception handling works best when recovery can be performed at a location that syntactically encloses the failure and the recovery action allows the application to return to completely normal execution. Unfortunately, effective error recovery can require addressing a wide range of consequences of an error, which may propagate through both the control and data dependences. In particular, the natural place to recover from an error that prevents the generation of a data structure can often be after several subsequent operations on the data. Moreover, it may not be possible to completely recover from an error at a single program point — the effects of the error may linger for some time and require that recovery actions be woven throughout the application.

Writing exception handlers can require the developer to write code that propagates failure recovery information to the points at which application can perform recovery. Our approach automatically reasons about an application to characterize the effects of error propagation through both data and control dependences. Our algorithm uses this information to generate a set of recovery actions for the application.

1.2 Contributions

This paper makes the following contributions:

- **Recovery Algorithm:** It presents a new recovery algorithm that manages the propagation of errors through legitimate dependences to recover applications from failures.
- **Analysis:** It presents a static analysis and a recovery algorithm that can reason about the intended behavior of the failed part of a computation.
- **Language Extensions:** It presents language extensions that developers can use to express high-level insight into how to modify an application's execution to break dependences that would otherwise serve to propagate failures.
- **Experience:** It presents an evaluation of the technique on several benchmarks. For each application, we report our experience developing the application and evaluate how robust the application is to injected failures relative to control versions.

2 Example

We present a web browser example that illustrates the recovery algorithm.

2.1 Classes

Figure 1 presents parts of the `Page`, `Frame`, and `FrameDescriptor` class declarations. When the example web browser parses a frame, it creates a new `Page` object to store the rendered web page. For each frame, the parser creates a `FrameDescriptor` object that describes where to place the frame and a `Frame` object that contains the information needed to render the frame. The `Frame` object will store the rendered frame.

Class declarations contain declarations for the class's abstract states. Bristlecone's abstract states support orthogonal classifications of objects: an object may simultaneously be in more than one abstract state. The runtime uses the abstract state of an object to determine which *tasks* to invoke on the given object. When a task exits, it can change the values of the abstract states of its parameter objects.

An abstract state is declared with the keyword flag followed by a name. The Frame class declaration contains three abstract state declarations: the plugin state, which indicates that rendering the frame object requires a plugin; the rendered state, which indicates that the browser has rendered the frame; and the processed state, which indicates that the browser has incorporated the rendered frame into the page.

```
1  public class Page {
2     flag rendered;
3     flag displayed;
4     ...
5  }
6
7  public class Frame {
8     flag plugin;
9     flag rendered;
10    flag processed;
11    ...
12 }
13
14 public class FrameDescriptor {
15    ...
16 }
```

Fig. 1. Class Definitions

2.2 Tasks

Figure 2 presents task definitions from the web browser example. A task definition consists of the task keyword, the task's name, the task's parameter declarations, and the task's body. A parameter declaration consists of a type, a parameter variable, and a guard expression. An object can serve as a task's parameter if it satisfies the parameter's guard expression. The runtime invokes a task when there exist parameter objects in the heap that satisfy all the parameter guard expressions for the task. We discuss some of the example task definitions below:

- **ParsePage Task:** The ParsePage task allocates a Page object to the web page, splits the page into individual frames, and then generates a Frame object and a FrameDescriptor object for each frame.

  Note that it is important that the Frame objects are associated with both the correct FrameDescriptor and Page objects. Otherwise, the web browser may place frames in the wrong pages. The ParsePage task groups these objects by using tags. It creates a new tag instance of type pagetag and then binds this tag to the Page and Frame objects.

- **RenderFrame Task:** The RenderFrame task renders a frame. Its parameter declaration indicates that the runtime can invoke this task on Frame objects in the heap and the parameter guard expression ! rendered indicates that the parameter object must not be in the rendered abstract state. When invoked, the task checks whether rendering this frame requires a plugin, and then it either executes a taskexit statement that transitions the object into the rendered abstract state to indicate that the frame is rendered or a taskexit statement that transitions the object into the plugin abstract state to indicate that a plugin is required to render the frame.

```
 1  task ParsePage (...) {
 2     ...
 3     tag pt=new tag(pagetag);
 4     Page p=new Page ()(add pt);
 5     ...
 6     while (moreFrames ()) {
 7        ...
 8        tag ft=new tag(frametag);
 9        FrameDescriptor fd=new FrameDescriptor () (add ft);
10        Frame f=new Frame ()(add pt, add ft);
11        ...
12     }
13  }
14
15  task RenderFrame(Frame f in !rendered && !plugin) {
16     if (needsplugin())
17        taskexit (f: plugin:=true);
18     ...
19     taskexit (f: rendered:=true);
20  }
21
22  task InvokePlugin (Frame f in plugin and !rendered) {
23     ...
24     taskexit (f: rendered:=true);
25  }
26
27  task AddFrameToPage (Page p in !rendered with pagetag pt, FrameDescriptor fd
28        with frametag ft, optional Frame f in rendered and !processed with
29        pagetag pt and frametag ft) {
30     if (isavailable(f)) {
31     //Add Frame to Page
32        ...
33     }
34     if (lastframe)
35        taskexit (f: processed:=true; p: rendered:=true);
36     else
37        taskexit (f: processed:=true);
38  }
39
40  task DisplayPage (Page p in rendered and !displayed) {
41     //Display Page
42     ...
43     taskexit (p: displayed:=true);
44  }
```

Fig. 2. Task Definitions

- **AddFrameToPage Task:** The `AddFrameToPage` task adds a rendered frame to the web page. Even if a software fault prevents a frame from being rendered, it is still possible to display the web page with that frame blanked. Therefore, we use the `optional` keyword to specify that the task can execute even if the `Frame` parameter is unavailable due to a failure. We call tasks that contain optional parameters recovery tasks. Recovery tasks use `isavailable` checks to verify that an optional parameter is available before accessing that parameter.

  Note that it is important that both the `FrameDescriptor` object corresponds to the `Frame` object and the `Frame` object is a frame for this specific `Page` object. The tag guard expression `with pagetag pt` in the first and third parameter declarations ensures that those parameter objects are bound to the same `pagetag` tag instance.

2.3   Error-Free Execution

We next discuss how the runtime would execute the example in an error-free execution:

1. **Parsing the Page:** The browser first executes the ParsePage task. This task creates a Page object to store the page, parses the web page, and creates both a Frame object and a FrameDescriptor object for each frame in the page.
2. **Processing Frames:** The browser next processes the frames by performing the following operations:

   A. **Render the Frame:** The browser executes the RenderFrame task to render the frame. If the frame requires a plugin to render, the runtime passes the frame to the InvokePlugin task.
   B. **Optionally Invoke a Plugin:** If a frame requires a plugin, the browser executes the InvokePlugin task to invoke the necessary plugin.
   C. **Add the Frame to the Web Page:** The AddFrameToPage task adds a rendered Frame object to the Page object. Once all frames have been rendered, this task marks the Page object as rendered.

3. **Displaying the Page:**   After the Page object has been rendered, the DisplayPage task displays the page.

2.4   Reasoning about Failures

In this example, the developer has provided a recovery task implementation of the AddFrameToPage task that can function even if a failure affects one of its parameter objects. If rendering a web page frame fails, this allows the runtime to break dependences on missing frames at the AddFrameToPage task. Breaking these dependences allows the web browser to recover from errors in processing and rendering web page frames and still display the affected web page.

If a failure occurs, the recovery algorithm must characterize how the computation would have proceeded in the absence of the failure. The recovery algorithm can then resume execution of the failed part of the application's execution if it can break the data dependences on failed part of the execution. Therefore, the recovery algorithm computes the set of recovery tasks that the computation was intended to execute.

If the example fails, an important question is whether the computation would have invoked the AddFrameToPage recovery task in the absence of a failure. We use static analysis of the abstract state transition graphs to determine the intended behavior of the failed part of the computation. A separate static analysis generates the abstract state transition graphs [8]. Figure 3 presents the abstract state transition graph for the Frame class. For every reachable object state, there is a node in this graph with the abstract state component of that state and an abstracted count of the tags of each type that are bound to the object. For example, the node labeled 2. plugin, frametag(1), pagetag(1) represents objects in the plugin abstract state and that are bound to exactly one instance of both a frametag tag and a pagetag tag. Edges represent the possible transitions an object's state may make during the execution of a task. Double boundaries indicates that new objects can be allocated with that state.

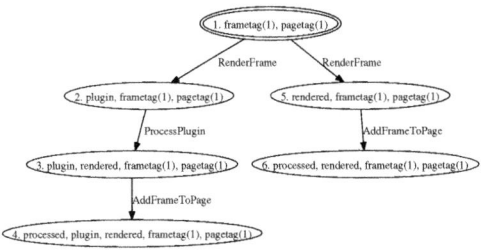

Fig. 3. Abstract State Transition Graph for the Frame Class

The recovery algorithm characterizes the intended behavior of the failed part of the computation. Note that the runtime plays a role in the execution of Bristlecone applications — it non-deterministically selects a task whose parameter guards are satisfied to invoke next. The analysis of the failed part of the execution can suppose that the runtime would have selected whichever schedule for the failed part of the computation that makes recovery easiest. Therefore for each reachable abstract object state, the static analysis computes the set of recovery tasks that the scheduler could cause the application to eventually execute with the object serving as an optional parameter. For each recovery task, it computes the possible states of the object when the task is invoked.

The analysis begins with the recovery tasks and then reasons backwards on the abstract state transition graph. The analysis operates as follows on the example:

1. It first analyzes the two base cases: objects in the state `5. rendered, frametag(1), pagetag(1)` can immediately serve as parameter objects for the optional parameter of the `AddFrameToPage` task. Similarly, objects in the state `3. plugin, rendered, frametag(1), pagetag(1)` can also immediately serve as parameter objects for the optional parameter of the `AddFrameToPage` task.

2. The analysis next reasons backwards and examines the state `2. plugin, frametag(1), pagetag(1)`. If a `FrameObject` reaches this state, the runtime can invoke the `processPlugin` task to place the object in the `3. plugin, rendered, frametag(1), pagetag(1)` state to which it can serve as a parameter object of the `AddFrameToPage` task.

3. The analysis finally examines the state `1. frametag(1), pagetag(1)`. The `RenderFrame` task can transition objects from this state into two different abstract states. Because the `AddFrameToPage` task can be executed from both final destination states, the runtime can cause objects in this state to serve as parameters of the `AddFrameToPage` task. Since the `RenderFrame` task decides the initial state transition, there remains uncertainty about the exact state of the recovery task's `Frame` parameter. We represent this uncertainty using the set {`3. plugin, rendered, frametag(1), pagetag(1)`, `5. rendered, frametag(1), pagetag(1)`} that includes both states.

2.5   Recovering from Failures

We use a hypothetical failure to illustrate the operation of the recovery algorithm. Suppose that the `RenderFrame` task dereferences a null pointer. The runtime first rolls back the `RenderFrame` task to return the heap to a consistent state. Then it performs the following steps to continue past the failure to render the web page:

1. **Determine the possible destination states for the failed task:** The runtime uses the static analysis results to determine that in the absence of the failure, this task would transition the `Frame` object into either the `2. plugin, frametag(1), pagetag(1)` state or the `5. rendered, frametag(1), pagetag(1)` state. Because the task failed, the runtime cannot determine which of these two states the `Frame` object would have transitioned.

2. **Compute the recovery tasks in the intended execution:** The runtime uses the static analysis results to determine a set of tasks for each state that the runtime could execute regardless of the application's behavior. The analysis results from the previous section show that the runtime could cause `Frame` objects in the `2. plugin, frametag(1), pagetag(1)` state to transition to the `3. plugin, rendered, frametag(1), pagetag(1)` state. In this state, they can serve as parameter objects for the optional parameter of the `AddFrameToPage` task. `Frame` objects in the `5. rendered, frametag(1), pagetag(1)` state can also serve as parameter objects for the optional parameter of the `AddFrameToPage` task.

3. **Compute the intersection:** Because the `RenderFrame` task failed, the runtime cannot determine the exact intended execution. However, if a recovery task appears on all paths, the runtime can still safely execute that task. The analysis computes the intersection of the recovery task results from step 2 to determine that the runtime can cause the `AddFrameToPage` task to be executed. Because the failure prevents the runtime from discovering the path taken by the `RenderFrame` task, the runtime does not know the exact abstract state that the `Frame` object would have been in when the `AddFrameToPage` task executed. So the runtime represents the object's state with the set of possible states $\{$ `3. plugin, rendered, frametag(1), pagetag(1)`, `5. rendered, frametag(1), pagetag(1)` $\}$.

4. **Execute the recovery task:** The runtime next executes the recovery task. Note that the `isavailable` predicate returns false indicating that the `Frame` object is not available because of a failure. The runtime marks the object as a *failed object*. The object's data is now inconsistent with its abstract state. Therefore, the data in that object can never be accessed. This means that the object cannot serve as a non-optional parameter object.

5. **Update the abstract states:** When the recovery task exits, the runtime updates the `Frame` object's set of states to $\{$ `4. processed, plugin, rendered, frametag(1), pagetag(1)`, `6. processed, rendered, frametag(1), pagetag(1)` $\}$. The execution of tasks on the `Frame` object is now complete. In general, the runtime would compute the intersection of the sets of recovery tasks for all of the possible states that the `Frame` object may be in. The runtime would then execute one of the tasks in the intersection.

3 Static Analysis

The goal of the static analysis is to determine a failed computation's intended behavior.

3.1 Abstract State Transition Graphs

The analysis operates on the abstract state transition graphs that we developed in previous work [8]. A *abstract state node* represents the abstract state and tag components of an object's state — each node contains the states of all the abstracted object's abstract states and a 1-limited count (0, 1, or at least 1) of the number of tag instances of each type that are bound to the object. The abstract state transition graph contains abstract state nodes for each reachable abstract state. The abstract state transition graph contains a set of edges that abstract the actions of tasks on objects. There is an edge between two abstract state nodes if a task can be invoked on an object in the abstract state corresponding to the source node and the task could transition the object into the abstract state corresponding to the destination node.

Abstract state nodes $n \in N$ abstract the reachable abstract states. The set T represents the set of tasks. The set $P \subseteq T \times \mathbb{N}$ represents the set of combinations of tasks and parameter indices for the invocation of a task on an object. The set of edges $E \subseteq N \times P \times N$ represents the possible transactions of an object's abstract state.

3.2 Analysis Abstraction

The analysis computes the *recovery function* $r : N \rightarrow 2^O$ that maps abstract state nodes to their corresponding *recovery set*. A recovery set is the set of recovery tasks invocations for which there exist a scheduling strategy that ensures that the computation will eventually invoke the task on the object abstracted by the state transition graph. $O \subseteq T \times \mathbb{N} \times 2^N$ is the set of recovery task invocations. Each recovery task invocation $o = \langle t, i, s \rangle \in O$ consists of a task t, the optional parameter index i, and the set s of parameter object abstract states at invocation. These states represent the possible states of the object at task invocation if the recovery task is invoked.

The dataflow lattice is the standard lattice for sets: the elements of these sets are sets of recovery task invocations, meet is set union, and the subset relation defines the partial order. The analysis is a fixed-point algorithm on the abstract state transition graph.

3.3 Transfer Function

We next describe the transfer function for computing the set of recovery task invocations for an abstract state node $n \in N$. There are two sources of uncertainty in the abstract state transition graph: (1) there is uncertainty in how a task's execution will change an object's state and (2) there is uncertainty in the task the runtime chooses to invoke. The Section *Results for a Single Task Invocation* describes how we handle the first type of uncertainty in detail. The Section *The Runtime's Choice of Task* describes how we handle the second type of uncertainty. We first describe the basic transfer functions. We later extend the basic analysis to support tags and multiple parameter tasks in Sections 3.4 and 3.5, respectively.

Results for a Single Task Invocation. We represent a task invocation on an object using the pair $\langle t, i \rangle \in P$ where t is the task and i is parameter that references the object. For each task invocation $p = \langle t, i \rangle \in P$ the algorithm computes the set of recovery task invocations that can break data dependences if the failed part of the computation includes p. We consider the following two possible cases:

Optional Parameter Case: If parameter i of task t is optional, the set of recovery task invocations for the invocation of the task-parameter pair p on the abstract state n is $\{\langle t, i, \{n\} \rangle\}$.

Normal Case: Otherwise, the algorithm computes the set of possible destination abstract states $N_{dst_n} = \{n_{dst} \mid \langle n, p, n_{dst} \rangle \in E\} = \{n_{dst_1}, ..., n_{dst_m}\}$. Because the runtime does not choose the destination state of a task, the set of recovery task invocations for p can only include combinations of recovery task t_{opt} and optional parameter i_{opt} that appear in the recovery sets of all destination states. The set of recovery task invocations for the task invocation p on n is therefore: $\{\langle t_{opt}, i_{opt}, s_1 \cup ... \cup s_m \rangle \mid \langle t_{opt}, i_{opt}, s_1 \rangle \in r(n_{dst_1}), ..., \langle t_{opt}, i_{opt}, s_m \rangle \in r(n_{dst_m})\}$. The recovery task invocation's set of abstract states is equal to the union of all the component sets of abstract states $\{s_1, ..., s_m\}$ because the analysis cannot determine the destination state of the task invocation p and therefore cannot determine the exact state that an object would be in when it serves as the i_{opt} parameter of the task t_{opt}.

The Runtime's Choice of Task. When an abstract state has more than one possible task invocation, the runtime can choose which task to invoke. To compute the set of recovery task invocations for the abstract state n, the analysis first computes the set of recovery task invocations for each pair of task t and parameter i that can be invoked on the abstract state n. The set of recovery task invocations for n is the union of these sets.

3.4 Multiple-Parameter Tasks

Tasks that operate on multiple-parameters pose extra challenges. Because the abstract state transition graph only characterizes the application's behavior with respect to a single object, the runtime must ensure that all other parameter object guards for a multiple-parameter task are satisfied. Moreover, a multiple-parameter task could potentially introduce inconsistencies in other object's states if the abstract states of some parameter objects were updated and another parameter object's abstract states were not. For example, if the abstract states of other parameter objects were updated without actually executing the multiple-parameter task, it would likely introduce inconsistencies between the other object's data and the states of its abstract states. If the runtime declared the other objects as failed, the recovery attempt could cause the loss of key data structures. To avoid these issues, the analysis conservatively omits multiple-parameter tasks that change the abstract states or tag bindings of other parameters. Note that omitting these tasks is safe, it simply reduces how much of the computation can be recovered.

We have extended the transfer function for multiple-parameter tasks to add predicates to recovery task invocations. These predicates verify that the heap contains objects that satisfy the guard expressions for the other parameters of the task. The runtime uses these predicates to check whether an execution path involving a multiple-parameter task is feasible, and therefore that the corresponding recovery task can be executed.

3.5   Tag Bindings

Another complication is that a task in the failed part of the execution may bind a new tag instance to an object. Because Bristlecone cannot determine the exact tag instance that would have been bound, the static analysis must conservatively handle this case. We have extended the transfer function to omit recovery task invocations if the current task binds a tag descriptor of the same type as the tag guards that appear either in the recovery task's guard expressions or in any tag guard predicates in the recovery task invocation. Note that omitting these invocations is safe, it simply reduces the set of possible recoveries that the system can generate.

4   Recovery Algorithm

The runtime should only invoke a recovery task on a failed object when the intended execution would have executed that task. Because the failure prevented part of the computation from executing, the analysis may not be able to determine the exact abstract state of the failed object, but only that the object's abstract state satisfies the recovery task's guard. There are two sources of uncertainty in the abstract state of a failed object:

- **Uncertainty from Failed Tasks:** A task can have multiple exits and therefore potentially transition its parameter objects into different abstract states. Because the runtime cannot determine which exit a failed task would have taken had it not failed, the runtime must conservatively assume that the task could take any of the exits. The recovery algorithm represents this uncertainty using a *possible abstract state set* $S_F = \{n_1, ..., n_j\} \subseteq 2^N$ that contains all possible abstract states that the tasks could have transitioned the parameter objects into. A recovery task can only be invoked on a possible abstract state set if it can be invoked on all of its component abstract states.
- **Uncertainty from the Runtime:** If the runtime would have had a choice between multiple tasks to invoke on an object in a failure-free execution, the runtime can use the same freedom to make recovery easier. Because the choice of which failed task the runtime executes does not have an immediate side-effect, the runtime can delay this choice. This delay gives the runtime extra flexibility in recovery and provides a beneficial source of uncertainty in an object's state. The recovery algorithm represents this uncertainty source with a *choice set* $C = \{S_{F_1}, ..., S_{F_m}\} \subseteq 2^{2^N}$ of choices between many possible abstract state sets. A recovery task can be invoked on a choice set if it could be invoked on at least one of the component possible abstract state sets. When a recovery task is invoked, its guards constrain the abstract states of the parameter objects and may force the runtime to commit to a specific choice of task scheduling for the failed part of the computation.

4.1   Task Invocation

Task invocation during normal execution is conceptually straightforward — the runtime maintains the current state of the objects and invokes tasks on these objects when the objects satisfy the task's guards. Our previous work describes efficient runtime techniques for task invocation. In this section, we extend this work to support recovery tasks by tracking the states of failed objects. We first describe how the runtime uses static analysis to compute the set of recovery tasks that can be executed on a failed task's parameter objects. We then describe how, after a recovery task completes execution on a failed object, the runtime uses the static analysis results to compute the set of recovery tasks it can execute next on the failed object.

Failed Tasks. This section describes the actions taken by the runtime when task t fails with its ith parameter object o in the state given by the choice set $C = \{\{n_{11}, ..., n_{1k_1}\}, ..., \{n_{j1}, ..., n_{jk_j}\}\}$.[1] The runtime first computes which recovery tasks could have been executed had task t not failed. It also characterizes the possible states of the object o at the time these recovery tasks would have been invoked.

The runtime computes the function $R \subseteq T \times \mathbb{N} \to 2^{2^N}$ that characterizes the set of possible recovery task invocations. We define the function $\mathcal{O} = T(t, i, n)$ to return the set of recovery task invocations $\mathcal{O}$ for a failure of task t on the ith parameter object in state n. The runtime uses the procedure described in Section 3.3 to compute T from the static analysis results.

The operator $\diamond$ models the effects of the uncertainty of the failed task's execution by conservatively combining the sets of recovery task invocations – a recovery task is in the combination only if it appears in both sets. Formally, we define $\mathcal{O}_1 \diamond \mathcal{O}_2 = \{\langle t', i', S\rangle \mid \langle t', i', S_1\rangle \in \mathcal{O}_1 \land \langle t', i', S_2\rangle \in \mathcal{O}_2, S = S_1 \cup S_2\}$. We use the $\diamond$ operator to compute the set of possible recovery task invocations for an object in the possible abstract state $S_F = \{n_1, ..., n_j\} \subseteq 2^N$ that served as parameter i during a failure of task t as $T(t, i, n_1) \diamond ... \diamond T(t, i, n_j)$. We use the set union operator to extend this computation to choice sets — the algorithm computes the set of possible recovery task invocations $\mathcal{C} = (T(t, i, n_{11}) \diamond ... \diamond T(t, i, n_{1k_1})) \cup ... \cup (T(t, i, n_{j1}) \diamond ... \diamond T(t, i, n_{jk_j}))$. We define $R(t, i) = \{S \mid \langle t, i, S\rangle \in \mathcal{C}\}$. The function R gives for each possible recovery task invocation $\langle t, i\rangle$ that can be enqueued, the choice set that characterizes the failed object's state. Note that the object remains enqueued in any previous task queues.

Recovery Tasks on Failed Objects. This section describes the actions the runtime takes to execute a recovery task on a failed parameter object. The runtime starts the task's execution with the object in the state computed in the previous section for the task invocation. When the task exits, the runtime updates each of the object's possible states with the abstract states and tag changes from the `taskexit` statement. The runtime then removes the parameter objects from all task queues. If the parameter object is in a non-failed state, the runtime enqueues the object in the task queues. Otherwise, for a failed parameter object in the state given by the choice set $C = \{\{n_{11}, ..., n_{1k_1}\}, ..., \{n_{j1}, ..., n_{jk_j}\}\}$ the algorithm uses the recovery function r to compute $\mathcal{C} = (r(n_{11}) \diamond ... \diamond r(n_{1k_1})) \cup ... \cup (r(n_{j1}) \diamond ... \diamond r(n_{jk_j}))$. We define $R(t, i) = \{S \mid \langle t, i, S\rangle \in \mathcal{C}\}$. The algorithm then uses R to determine, for each possible recovery task invocation $\langle t, i\rangle$ that can be enqueued, the corresponding choice set.

---

[1] A non-trivial choice set can appear after a failure of a recovery task invocation during the process of recovery. The recovery algorithm continues to try to break other data dependences at future recovery tasks that access the object. Note that the parameter objects of a normal failed task will be in a trivial choice set $C = \{\{n_{11}\}\}$.

5   Experience

We next discuss our experiences using recovery tasks to develop three robust software applications: a multiplayer game, a web portal, and a simplified MapReduce framework. We have implemented the enhanced recovery algorithm with support for recovery tasks in the Bristlecone compiler and runtime. The source code for the compiler, runtime, and benchmarks is available at `http://demsky.eecs.uci.edu/software.php`.

For each benchmark, we developed three versions: a recovery task version, a standard Bristlecone version without recovery tasks, and a Java version.

We used randomized failure injection to simulate the effects of software faults. The compiler inserts failure injection code after every instruction in the generated code. We inject exactly one failure into each execution at a random instruction. The failures we injected simulate the entire class of software faults that cause failures in the same task that contains the fault. This fault class includes illegal memory accesses, failed assertions, failed data structure consistency checks, library errors, and arithmetic exceptions.

We developed this randomized failure injection strategy to avoid biases that hand-selected faults may introduce. Note that our randomized failure injection strategy likely represents an unrealistically harsh metric — it may inject faults that are extremely difficult to recover from, but are unlikely to occur in practice. For example, it sometimes injects failures into simple, completely deterministic startup code. While such injected failures cause the Bristlecone versions to fail to recover because the entire application depends on the startup code, they are unlikely to occur in practice as they would have been caught the first time the application was executed.

5.1   Multiplayer Game

The multiplayer game benchmark is a simplified version of larger scale multiplayer on-line games. Software bugs have been a recurring problem for many of these games. Our game consists of a world with both humans and monsters. Humans try to escape through exits while monsters try to capture the humans. The game contains AI components that use search algorithms to plan the moves for both monsters and humans. The recovery task version uses a recovery task to collect the players' moves and update the map.

In the process of developing the AI code, which is shared across all versions, we made an unintentional coding mistake that could cause an out-of-bounds array access under certain circumstances. The recovery task version recovered from this bug while the other two versions crashed. While this experience is only a single anecdote, we found it to be an encouraging validation of the approach.

Our workload was running the game with all players controlled by the AI. We performed 100 trials of the experiment on each of the three versions. We found that using recovery tasks enabled the recovery task version of the game to survive the injected failure in all 100 trials. We found that in the presence of errors, the standard Bristlecone and Java versions were unable to continue the game.

5.2   Web Portal

The web portal models a category of applications that perform independent computations, combine the results, and then display some aggregation to the user. When a web browser requests the portal page, the web portal generates requests for the current weather conditions, stock prices, and the Google home page. Finally, the web portal combines the results from the individual responses into a single page and serves this page to the browser. The recovery task version enhances the data combination phase to enable recovery from failures that make parts of the information unavailable.

Our workload consisted of using a web browser to view the portal web page. We performed 20 trials of the experiment on each of the three versions. We found that using recovery tasks enabled the web portal to serve the unaffected parts of the web portal page in 17 of the 20 trials. We found that in the presence of errors, the standard Bristlecone and Java versions were unable to serve the portal web page. However, all three versions were able to isolate errors to a single request — all versions of the web portal were able to serve future page requests after a failure.

5.3 MapReduce Framework

MapReduce provides an abstract programming model for parallel computations on large data sets [7]. Users specify the computation in terms of a map function and a reduce function and MapReduce automatically parallelizes the computation across machines.

We implemented a simplified MapReduce framework. The implementation partitions the input, invokes the map function, aggregates intermediate results, invokes the reduce function, and aggregates the final results. The recovery task version uses recovery tasks for aggregating the map and reduce results.

Our workload counts the occurrences of each word in a text file. We performed 100 trials on each of the three versions. For each trial, we recorded whether the final output was generated. Without failure injection, all of the versions generated the final output. With the injected failures, the recovery task version produced the final output in 93 trials while the other two versions failed in all trials. When the recovery task version failed, it warned the user that the word counts could potentially be low. We expect that users will often find the output useful as it represents a lower bound on word counts.

We divide the injected failures into three categories: (1) failures that affect map workers, (2) failures that affect reduce workers, and (3) failures that affect the tasks that coordinate the computation. We observed 86 executions in the first category. The effect of these errors was to cause word counts to be low or missing — in these executions the counts were low by an average of 5%. We observed 7 executions in the second category. The effect of these errors was to cause word counts for some words to be missing. We observed that 86 words out of 6,213 total words were missing on average from these executions. The 7 failed executions fall in the third category.

5.4 Discussion

We measured the execution time of both the recovery task version and the Java version of the multiplayer game and MapReduce benchmarks. We omit a performance evaluation for the web portal because of the difficulty of measuring its performance given that the portal accesses remote web servers. The Bristlecone version of the MapReduce benchmark running on a RAM disk took 0.63 seconds to execute while the Java version took 0.58 seconds. The recovery task version of the multiplayer game benchmark took 0.94 seconds to execute while the Java version took only 0.63 seconds.

In general, we have found writing Bristlecone applications to be straightforward — most of the code was shared with the Java version. The Bristlecone versions of the benchmarks were comparable in length to the Java versions. The recovery task version of MapReduce framework contains 20% fewer lines of code than the Java version, the recovery task version of multiplayer game contains 5% more lines of code, and the recovery task version of web portal contains 6% more lines of code of which about one third were simply abstract state declarations.

6   Related Work

Recovery blocks [1] and N-version programming [3] are two classic approaches to fault tolerance. These approaches add significant software development costs. Bristlecone is designed to provide fault tolerance for applications that cannot afford the development costs associated with these classic techniques.

Backward recovery uses a combination of checkpointing and acceptance tests to prevent a software system from entering an incorrect state [5]. Forward recovery uses multiple copies of a computation to recover from transient errors [11]. Unfortunately, it can be difficult to handle deterministic failures with these methods as the same error will likely cause the software system to repeatedly fail.

The Recovery-Oriented Computing project has explored systems out of a set of individually rebootable components [4]. Researchers have used retry with reconfiguration to address configuration issues [13]. Contract-based data structure repair [15] is an alternative approach to tolerating failed components.

A key component of Bristlecone is decoupling unrelated conceptual operations and tracking data dependences between these operations. Dataflow computations also keep track of data dependences between operations so that the operations can be parallelized [12]. Errors in a dataflow computation could easily cause key data structures to be lost. Bristlecone's abstract state and tag constructs allow data structures to passively persist across failures.

Tuple-space languages, such as Linda [9], decouple computations to enable parallelization. The threads of execution communicate through primitives that manipulate a global tuple space. However, these language were not designed to address software errors — software errors can permanently halt threads of execution in these languages causing the system to eventually fail.

Orc [6] and Oz [14] are other examples of task-based languages. This work is largely orthogonal as they are not designed for fault tolerance. Actors are a concurrent programming paradigm in which applications are architected as several actors that communicate through messages [10]. Actors are note designed for fault tolerance and failures may cause actors to drop messages and corrupt or lose their state.

Erlang has been used to implement robust systems using a software architecture containing a set of supervisors and a hierarchy of increasingly simple implementations of the same functionality [2]. Bristlecone is complementary to the supervisor approach — while the supervisor approach gives the developer complete control over recovery, it requires the developer to manually develop multiple implementations of the same functionality. Bristlecone requires only minimal additional development effort.

7   Conclusion

We have presented an analysis that reasons about the effects of potential failures and a recovery algorithm that uses the analysis results to determine how to recover the application from the failure. Our experience shows that the new technique recovers significantly better from failures for our benchmarks. Moreover, we found it straightforward to use this technique to develop applications, and that it did not significantly affect either the complexity or length of the benchmarks.

Acknowledgments. This research was supported by the National Science Foundation under grants CCF-0846195 and CCF-0725350. We would like to thank the anonymous reviewers for their helpful comments.

References

1. Anderson, T., Kerr, R.: Recovery blocks in action: A system supporting high reliability. In: ICSE (1976)
2. Armstrong, J.: Making Reliable Distributed Systems in the Presence of Software Errors. PhD thesis, Swedish Institute of Computer Science (November 2003)
3. Avizienis, A.: The methodology of N-version programming (1995)
4. Candea, G., Fox, A.: Recursive restartability: Turning the reboot sledgehammer into a scalpel. In: HotOS-VIII (2001)
5. Chandy, K.M., Ramamoorthy, C.: Rollback and recovery strategies. IEEE Transactions on Computers C-21(2), 137–146 (1972)
6. Cook, W.R., Patwardhan, S., Misra, J.: Workflow patterns in Orc. In: Ciancarini, P., Wiklicky, H. (eds.) COORDINATION 2006. LNCS, vol. 4038, pp. 82–96. Springer, Heidelberg (2006)
7. Dean, J., Ghemawat, S.: MapReduce: Simplified data processing on large clusters. In: OSDI (2004)
8. Demsky, B., Sundaramurthy, S.: Bristlecone: Language support for robust software applications. To Appear in TSE (2010)
9. Gelernter, D.: Generative communication in Linda. TOPLAS 7(1), 80–112 (1985)
10. Hewitt, C., Baker, H.G.: Actors and continuous functionals. Technical report, Massachusetts Institute of Technology, Cambridge, MA, USA (1978)
11. Huang, K., Wu, J., Fernandez, E.B.: A generalized forward recovery checkpointing scheme. In: FTPDS (April 1998)
12. Johnston, W.M., Hanna, J.R.P., Millar, R.J.: Advances in dataflow programming languages. ACM Computing Surveys 36(1) (2004)
13. Qin, F., Tucek, J., Sundaresan, J., Zhou, Y.: Rx: Treating bugs as allergies—a safe method to survive software failures. In: SOSP (2005)
14. Smolka, G.: The Oz programming model. In: Orłowska, E., Alferes, J.J., Moniz Pereira, L. (eds.) JELIA 1996. LNCS, vol. 1126, p. 251. Springer, Heidelberg (1996)
15. Zaeem, R.N., Khurshid, S.: Contract-based data structure repair using alloy. In: D'Hondt, T. (ed.) ECOOP 2010 – Object-Oriented Programming. LNCS, vol. 6183, pp. 577–598. Springer, Heidelberg (2010)

Formally Efficient Program Instrumentation

Boris Feigin and Alan Mycroft

Computer Laboratory, University of Cambridge
{Boris.Feigin,Alan.Mycroft}@cl.cam.ac.uk

Abstract. The term "instrumentation" refers to modification of a program or its runtime environment to make hidden details of execution visible. Instrumentation can severely compromise program execution speed. Frameworks like DTrace (Sun Microsystems) and VProbes (VMware) offer practical ways of addressing performance concerns, but there has been no formal understanding of what it means for instrumentation to be efficient. To fill this gap, we propose a criterion based on that of Popek and Goldberg for virtual machines and on our previous work relating this to Jones optimality of program specializers. We further suggest linguistic constraints on instrumentation code to enable more aggressive static optimization of dynamically instrumented programs.

1 Introduction

There is a wealth of literature on the subject of program instrumentation, and many tools are used in practice. Implementation methods range from manually adding `printf` calls to purpose-built frameworks with virtual machines and JIT compilers. Historically, instrumentation was seen as a debugging aid, unsuitable for use in production systems primarily because the runtime overhead of instrumentation can slow down a program by orders of magnitude. This traditional view is challenged by modern, lightweight dynamic binary instrumentation frameworks—of which DTrace (developed by Sun Microsystems) is perhaps the best-known example—that allow instrumentation code to be selectively enabled and disabled at runtime. The performance implications of an instrumentation framework largely determine its adoption. Although there is broad informal agreement that only those parts of the program that are being instrumented should incur a performance penalty, no formal criteria exist. The present paper begins to address this shortcoming. Section 2 introduces AL, an assembly language, and IL, an instrumentation script loosely based on DTrace's "D" language. As a form of augmented execution, instrumentation shares many similarities with virtualization. Our efficiency criterion (Section 3) is inspired by one of Popek and Goldberg's [10] requirements for virtual machine monitors. This addresses explicit overheads, but implicit overheads remain: compiler optimization opportunities lost to allow potential instrumentation. Section 4 suggests linguistic restrictions on IL scripts to recover such lost ground.

Technical Preliminaries: Jones Optimality. A partial evaluator uses known input values to optimise a program. Let $\llbracket \cdot \rrbracket$ be an evaluation function and p a

G. Roşu et al. (Eds.): RV 2010, LNCS 6418, pp. 245–252, 2010.
© Springer-Verlag Berlin Heidelberg 2010

program with two inputs d_1 and d_2, then a partial evaluator *mix* satisfies the equation $[\![p]\!](d_1, d_2) = [\![[\![mix]\!](p, d_1)]\!](d_2)$. The output of *mix* is called the *residual* or *specialized* program. Specializing an interpreter for language L written in language M with respect to p, a program in L, has the effect of compiling p into M. This surprising fact is known as the first Futamura projection. Some specializers are better than others: for example, the trivial specializer does no useful work and merely splices its inputs into a predetermined program template. Jones optimality, due to Neil Jones [6], is intended to tell the good specializers from the bad. Let *sint* range over self-interpreters (a self-interpreter is an interpreter written in the same language that it interprets), then *mix* is Jones-optimal iff $\exists sint.\ \forall p.\ [\![mix]\!](sint, p) =_\alpha p$ where $=_\alpha$ is a decidable syntactic equality. Intuitively, this means that *mix* is capable of removing a layer of interpretational overhead. A later version of Jones optimality [8, Definition 6.4] specifies a weaker relation, defined over the running times of the computations.

2 AL and IL

We will use an assembly language called AL with syntax:

$$insn ::= \text{NOP} \mid \text{MOV } r_{\text{dst}}, a_{\text{src}} \qquad\qquad a ::= v \mid r \quad \text{where } v \in Val,\, r \in Reg$$
$$\mid \text{LOAD } r_{\text{dst}}, (a_{\text{src}}) \mid \text{STORE } (a_{\text{dst}}),\, a_{\text{src}} \mid \text{ALU}\langle op \rangle\, r_{\text{dst}}, a_{\text{src1}}, a_{\text{src2}}$$
$$\mid \text{CALL } a_{\text{loc}} \mid \text{RET} \mid \text{JZ } a_{\text{cond}}, a_{\text{loc}} \mid \text{HLT} \mid \text{OUT } r_{\text{src}} \mid \text{UPDATE} \mid \text{BRK} \mid \text{BRET} .$$

AL programs run on a finite CISC-style Harvard architecture: instructions and data are stored separately. The code store cannot be read or written to and the data store cannot be executed.[1]Most of the instructions are standard, and the destination operand comes before the source operand(s); OUT prints the contents of a register; BRK invokes the trap handler which resides at a well-known address inaccessible by means of a jump or call; BRET returns from the handler—both BRK and BRET are part of the instrumentation mechanism and may not occur in user programs; UPDATE terminates the program preserving the entire machine state. Since we will not be considering recursive instrumentation (i.e. "instrumentation of instrumentation code") the trap handler is not re-entrant. Instrumentation is added and removed when a program reaches an *update point* by executing UPDATE: we borrow the term from dynamic software updating. UPDATE can be thought of as transferring control to the operating system. The trace of an AL program is the sequence of operations that were executed together with their data-flow inputs and outputs. We further define a name erasure map over traces which discards the operand encoding information as well as register names and the target addresses of jumps and calls. A program to calculate the factorial of 5 and the first few operations in its original and erased traces are shown below. Outputs are enclosed in square brackets and the letters following the values (r or i) identify the opcode variant used.

---

[1] Similar constraints are often imposed on x86 code to allow reliable disassembly.

Program	Trace	Erased trace
fac5: MOV r1, 5	MOV [5]/r1, 5/i	MOV [5], 5
MOV r2, 1	MOV [1]/r2, 1/i	MOV [1], 1
loop: JZ r1, done	JZ 5/r1, 24/i	JZ 5
MUL r2, r1, r2	MUL [5]/r2, 5/r1, 1/r2	MUL [5], 5, 1
SUB r1, r1, 1	SUB [4]/r1, 5/r1, 1/i	SUB [4], 5, 1
JZ 0, loop	JZ 0/i, 8/i	JZ 0
done: OUT r2	JZ 4/i, 24/i	JZ 4
	. . .	. . .

Nethercote and Mycroft [9] argued that a dynamic data dependence graph built from a program trace represents the "essence" of a computation. The erased trace is an attempt to capture the same intuition with a more lightweight formalism.

IL is an instrumentation language in the spirit of "D" [3] with syntax:

$$exp ::= val \mid var \mid bvar \mid \mathsf{pc} \mid \mathsf{reg}(exp) \mid \mathsf{code}(exp) \mid \mathsf{data}(exp) \mid op \; exp^+$$
$$comm ::= comm; \; comm \mid \mathsf{if} \; exp \; \mathsf{then} \; comm \mid var \leftarrow exp \mid \mathsf{print} \; exp^+$$
$$pat ::= opcode \; bvar^+ \quad rule ::= pat \; \{ \; comm \; \} \quad script ::= rule^\star \; .$$

IL rules pattern-match on AL opcodes, binding variables (*bvars*) to the operands of the instruction. The UPDATE, BRK and BRET instructions are special and cannot be instrumented (see the next section). The order of the rules is not important; each instruction can only be instrumented once. Instrumentation code is executed before the instruction takes effect. A sample IL script is shown below:

$$\mathsf{STORE} \; (r_{\mathrm{dst}}), r_{\mathrm{src}} \quad \{ \; x \leftarrow \mathsf{data}(12345678); \; \mathsf{print} \; x; \; \}$$
$$\mathsf{JZ} \; r_{\mathrm{cond}}, r_{\mathrm{loc}} \quad \{ \; \mathsf{if} \; \mathsf{code}(\mathsf{reg}(r_{\mathrm{loc}})) = \mathsf{NOP} \; \mathsf{then} \; y \leftarrow y + 1; \; \mathsf{print} \; y; \; \} \; .$$

We further assume the existence of two auxiliary functions: $\mathcal{I}(t)$ maps an IL script t to an instrumented interpreter for AL which is itself written in AL. An instrumenting function $\mathcal{C}_t(p)$ augments an AL program p using script t, producing an instrumented AL program. Given any specializer *mix* for AL, one possibility is to define $\mathcal{C}_t(p)$ as $[\![mix]\!](\mathcal{I}(t), p)$.

3   Efficient Instrumentation

Jones [7] notes that original and specialised computations can—for reasonable specializers—be related by "execution order"-preserving maps. Previously we showed [5] that a version of Jones optimality built on this observation—which we called "Jones optimality for traces"—can capture Popek and Goldberg's [10] efficiency criterion. To provide isolation between individual virtual machines, a virtual machine monitor (VMM) must emulate privileged instructions: roughly, those that affect the operation of the CPU itself or other hardware. Popek and Goldberg's efficiency criterion states that non-privileged instructions must be executed directly by the hardware with no intervention by the VMM. This mirrors Cantrill et al.'s [3] claim that "when DTrace is not in use, the system is just as if DTrace were not present at all". The key point is that common-case performance—i.e. execution of unprivileged instructions for VMMs and non-instrumented execution for DTrace—should not degrade.

Assume programs p and p' yield erased traces tr and tr'. Then p is *(erased) trace-simulated* by p' $(p \preceq p')$ iff tr is a subsequence of tr', i.e. $\exists f. \forall i. tr(i) = tr'(f(i))$ where f is a strictly increasing function. An instrumenting function $\mathcal{C}$ should result in an instrumented program $\mathcal{C}_t(p)$ which executes all the instructions that the original program p does, interspersed with instrumentation code. We call $\mathcal{C}$ a *faithful instrumenting function* iff $\forall t. \forall p. p \preceq \mathcal{C}_t(p)$. Faithfulness limits the choice of instrumentation function $\mathcal{C}$ because of the intensional nature of $\preceq$. However, erased trace simulation is purposely a loose relation in the sense that it does not require an exact matching (as would a bisimulation) between the execution states under the standard and non-standard interpretations. The benefit is that erased trace simulation allows many sensible implementations of the instrumenting function. First, consider naive interpretation, i.e. $\mathcal{C}_t(p) = [\![mix_{\mathrm{triv}}]\!](\mathcal{I}(t), p)$ where mix_{triv} is the trivial specializer for AL. The simplest interpreter implements every instruction in terms of itself: an ADD with an ADD, a MOV with a MOV, etc.; this clearly gives faithful instrumentation. The dispatch mechanism used by the interpreter—a switch statement or threading—is not important here. Arguably interpretation is not a viable implementation strategy for a variety of reasons: DTrace and many other frameworks use in-place binary patching to substitute instrumented instructions with breakpoints. The breakpoint instruction provides rudimentary support for what the virtualization literature calls "trap-and-emulate" execution. It is educational to reconstruct breakpoints rationally starting from context-threaded (CT) interpretation [2], although AL contains explicit provision for trap-and-emulate. A CT interpreter replaces every non-jump instruction in its input program with a call to the procedure in the interpreter that implements the opcode. Once the resulting context threading table (CTT) is constructed, the interpreter jumps to the first instruction in the table. Note that, as a result, a CT interpreter cannot be implemented on a machine with no data execution capability. Instruction operands are retained in a separate table in data memory:

Original	CTT	(Operands)	Instrumented	(Operands)
MOV r1, 3	CALL doMOV	r1, 3	MOV r1, 3	N/A
ADD r2, r1, 5	CALL doADD	r2, r1, 5	CALL doADD	r2, r1, 5
OUT r2	CALL doOUT	r2	OUT r2	N/A

For a self-interpreter, we expect inlining followed by constant propagation on the CTT to recover the original program (cf. a Jones-optimal mix). Suppose instead we allow the ADD instruction to be instrumented; then doADD calls cannot be inlined since the specific interpretation of ADD is not known when the program is compiled, but all the other doXXX calls can! The instrumented program in the table above executes in a mixed compiled/interpreted mode—the bulk of the program runs natively, but the ADD instruction is interpreted. The Linux kernel implementation of paravirtualization provides a real-world example. The hypervisor fills in a pv_cpu_ops structure with pointers to functions (`clts`, `write_cr0`, etc.) that emulate privileged instructions. Instead of executing a privileged instruction directly, the kernel calls the corresponding function in the structure. Morally speaking, an instance of `pv_cpu_ops` is a non-standard interpreter for x86 machine code and the kernel is a CTT. The default, native `pv_cpu_ops` implementation acts directly on the hardware—i.e. it defines a self-interpreter. Indeed, written in Haskell, `pv_cpu_ops` would be a type class and each hypervisor an instance; dictionary passing replaces a global `pv_cpu_ops` variable. As an aside: this view of non-standard interpretation through context threading is closely related to Carette et al.'s [4] "final tagless" style.

Faithfulness places a *lower bound* on the number of instructions executed by the instrumented program. Efficient instrumentation is also bounded *from above*. Let tr be the erased trace of the original program. Let tr' be the erased trace of the instrumented program from which all instrumentation code has been removed (the BRK/BRET pair indicate where execution passes between program and instrumentation code). Define $dom(t)$, the domain of script t, as the set of opcodes for which there is a rule in t. For example, the domain of the sample script in Sec. 2, $dom(t) = \{\texttt{STORErr}, \texttt{JZrr}\}$ where the suffix `rr` selects a particular version of the opcode (in this case, one whose both operands are registers). Define a predicate h on sequence indices such that $h(tr, i)$ is true iff the instruction at index i in tr is bracketed by a BRK/BRET pair. This enables us to define, using $dom(t)$ and h, the script-specific relation $\preceq_t$ between the instrumented and original programs that disregards instrumentation code: $p \preceq_t p'$ means the same as $p \preceq p'$ modulo the contribution of t (i.e. code bracketed by BRK/BRET). Every instruction in the trace of p which is not part of instrumentation as well as exactly one instruction from every block of instrumentation code must also occur in the trace of p' in the correct order. We call $\mathcal{C}$ an *efficient instrumenting function* iff $\forall t. \forall p. \mathcal{C}_t(p) \preceq_t p$. Finally, we call $\mathcal{C}$ a *good instrumentation function* iff it is both faithful and efficient:

$$\forall t. \forall p. \quad p \preceq \mathcal{C}_t(p) \preceq_t p \ .$$

Notice that the instrumenting function must behave uniformly for all scripts: compare with Jones optimality which requires the existence of a single self-interpreter for which the specializer is able to remove an entire layer of interpretational overhead, but says nothing about the variability of results produced by the specializer from one interpreter to the next, giving rise to "cheating" specializers. Defining good instrumentation in two parts (faithfulness and efficiency) has advantages over straightforward erased trace equality because the efficiency relation can be independently refined. Instrumentation by naive interpretation is clearly not "good" in the sense above because for every unit of useful work in the program, the interpreter executes many housekeeping instructions. Unfortunately, our definition suffers from the same drawback as the original statement of Jones optimality: it does not allow $\mathcal{C}$ to optimize the program. This is not necessarily a deficiency since it could be argued that a distinct boundary between program and instrumentation is desirable. We leave a detailed examination of this issue to further work and for now assume that programs are optimized prior to being instrumented (which is frequently the case in practice).

4   Static Optimization of Dynamically Instrumented Code

Debugging is well-known to be antagonistic to program optimization. Optimization in the presence of dynamic instrumentation is challenging for much the same reasons: IL scripts can distinguish previously equivalent programs. Worse still, the compiler must forego profitable optimization in deference to potential future instrumentation which may never materialize. So much as removing a spurious NOP instruction may have an effect on the result of an instrumented run. In the general case, the unoptimized execution state—the state of the program as it would have been, had the program not been optimized—must be preserved or reconstructed both at update points (UPDATE) and prior to entering instrumentation code (BRK). We are interested in static, common-case optimization of dynamically instrumented programs, relying on these observations: (*i*) instrumentation can only be applied at UPDATE points, (*ii*) instrumentation is applied rarely (i.e. most of the time an UPDATE is a no-op), and (*iii*) only a small proportion of instructions are instrumented at any given time. The trade-offs for instrumentation of production systems and debugging are slightly different. So, rather than attempt to undo the effect of arbitrary program transformations on the execution state (a costly procedure), we propose to selectively ban overly invasive instrumentation. As an example, consider the programs and script below:

Program	Optimized
MOV r9, 3	—
MOV r9, 5	MOV r9, 5
MOV r7, 1	—
OUT r9	OUT r9

Instrumentation Script
MOV r, v { print reg(r); }
OUT r { print "r7 holds ", reg(7); }

The optimized program is obtained from the original by eliminating two dead assignments: the first and third MOVs. Running either program produces the output "5". But when instrumented this is preceded by "0 3 0 1" in the original program, and "0 0" in the optimized (assuming the machine initializes registers to zero). The basic issue is that the optimizer is semantics-preserving with respect to the standard AL interpretation, but not the non-standard interpretation defined by the script. Various authors (e.g. Tolmach and Appel [11]) have suggested adding instrumentation to the program prior to optimization. However, our proposed efficiency criterion requires a strict separation between program and instrumentation code.

Since every instruction is a potential candidate for instrumentation, the optimizer cannot perform even the simplest peephole rewrites. A possible workaround is to declare certain instructions—e.g. all arithmetic instructions—as exempt from instrumentation. However, the problem remains that execution state on entry into instrumentation code is altered as a result of optimization. We note that instrumentation code introduces additional dependencies not present in the program itself (for instance, the rule for OUT in the script above makes r7 "live" in the usual data-flow sense). Therefore, by limiting the dependence of instrumentation code on the execution state of the program, further optimizations become possible. To this end we will ascribe types to IL expressions[2] to capture their observational power (i.e. ability to distinguish execution states) as a partial equivalence relation (PER). The approach closely follows Benton's work [1] on program transformation for imperative languages using PERs to model the context in which a command or expression is executed. A PER is a binary relation that is symmetric and transitive, but, unlike a proper equivalence relation, not necessarily reflexive. The *domain* of a PER $P \subseteq X \times X$ is the subset of X where P is reflexive: $|P| = \{x \in X \mid x\ P\ x\}$. Every equivalence relation is a PER and every PER is an equivalence relation on its domain. It will be convenient to refer to these two equivalence relations by name: $All_X = X \times X$ and $Id_X = \{(x, x) \mid x \in X\}$. If P and Q are PERs over X and Y respectively, then $(P \times Q)$ and $(P \Rightarrow Q)$ are PERs over $X \times Y$ and $X \to Y$ respectively:

$$
\begin{aligned}
(x, y)\ \ (P \times Q)\ \ (x', y') \quad &\text{iff} \quad x\ P\ x'\ \text{and}\ y\ Q\ y' \\
f\ \ (P \Rightarrow Q)\ \ g \quad\quad &\text{iff} \quad x\ P\ x' \Longrightarrow (f\ x)\ Q\ (g\ x')\ .
\end{aligned}
$$

Further, given function Γ (which should be thought of as a typing context) from elements of X to PERs over Y, by a slight abuse of notation we will treat Γ as a relation over $X \to Y$ defined as follows: $f\ (\Gamma)\ g \iff \forall x \in dom(\Gamma).\ f(x)\ \Gamma(x)\ g(x)$. Assume $[\![e]\!]_{IL}^{exp} \in State \times VEnv \to Val$ is the evaluation function for IL expressions; *State* is the state of an AL program, a tuple (pc, R, D, C) where pc is the program counter, $R \in Reg \to Val$ is the register file, and $D, C \in Loc \rightharpoonup Val$ are the data and code memories respectively, mapping locations to values; the environment $VEnv \equiv Var \to Val$ holds bindings of IL variables. Let P and Q PERs over $(State \times VEnv)$ and *Val* respectively and define equivalence of expressions like so: $e_1 \sim_{P \Rightarrow Q} e_2 \iff [\![e_1]\!]\ (P \Rightarrow Q)\ [\![e_2]\!]$. We will write $e : P \Rightarrow Q$ as shorthand for $e \in |P \Rightarrow Q|$. Intuitively, the relation P reveals the dependence of the expression on the program state and the IL variable environment; Q describes how the value computed by the expression is going to be used by the surrounding context. Note that every expression e such that $e : All \Rightarrow Id$ necessarily conflates all execution states and variable environments, e.g. 42, reg(7) ∗ 0. Such expressions have the least impact on program optimization because they are extensionally constant. Suppose that, like in the example above, the compiler optimizes away a dead MOV to r7. In that case, no guarantee can be made about the contents of the target register, since it may have been written to by a preceding MOV or STORE. The optimization remains sound in the presence of instrumentation expression e so long as e does not depend on the value: this is easily modelled by a register context Γ_R such that $\Gamma_R(r7) = All$. Further refinement is possible: if an IL command interprets r7 as a boolean (i.e. "if reg(7) then ..."), only the truth (or falsity) of the value needs to be preserved by optimization. We posit per-program syntactic (or "type system"-like) restrictions on instrumentation code to enforce independence from parts of the program state. We plan to explore this direction in further work.

---

[2] We focus on IL expressions here, but equivalence of commands is defined similarly, taking care to handle print: we consider two commands equivalent only if they produce exactly the same output—i.e. the same values in the same order.

5   Conclusions and Further Work

This paper has started to apply programming language theory to an emerging class of instrumentation tools—like DTrace and VProbes—where the instrumentation code is written in a domain-specific language. We have specifically focused on performance guarantees, proposing a definition for efficient instrumentation adapted from a well-known virtualization efficiency criterion. We do not claim that our proposed criterion is applicable to all instrumentation frameworks and under all circumstances. Rather, it is a first attempt to capture a property that has hitherto received little attention in the literature. Malicious or incompetent instrumentation code can compromise security by—directly or indirectly—leaking values of secret variables. DTrace has a coarse-grained capability system governing *what* a given UNIX user can instrument. In addition to performance guarantees, we believe that pervasive instrumentation of production systems will require a finer, language-based permissions model.

Acknowledgements

We thank Kathy Gray for comments on draft versions of this paper. The first author gratefully acknowledges an EPSRC studentship.

References

1. Benton, N.: Simple relational correctness proofs for static analyses and program transformations. In: Proceedings of POPL, pp. 14–25 (2004)
2. Berndl, M., Vitale, B., Zaleski, M., Brown, A.D.: Context threading: A flexible and efficient dispatch technique for virtual machine interpreters. In: Proceedings of CGO, pp. 15–26 (2005)
3. Cantrill, B., Shapiro, M.W., Leventhal, A.H.: Dynamic instrumentation of production systems. In: Proceedings of USENIX ATC, pp. 15–28 (2004)
4. Carette, J., Kiselyov, O., Shan, C.: Finally tagless, partially evaluated: Tagless staged interpreters for simpler typed languages. Journal of Functional Programming 19(5), 509–543 (2009)
5. Feigin, B., Mycroft, A.: Jones optimality and hardware virtualization: a report on work in progress. In: Proceedings of PEPM, pp. 169–175 (2008)
6. Jones, N.D.: Challenging problems in partial evaluation and mixed computation. New Generation Comput. 6(2&3), 291–302 (1988)
7. Jones, N.D.: Transformation by interpreter specialisation. Science of Computer Programming 52, 307–339 (2004)
8. Jones, N.D., Gomard, C.K., Sestoft, P.: Partial Evaluation and Automatic Program Generation. Prentice-Hall, Englewood Cliffs (1993)
9. Nethercote, N., Mycroft, A.: Redux: A dynamic dataflow tracer. ENTCS vol. 89(2) (2003)
10. Popek, G.J., Goldberg, R.P.: Formal requirements for virtualizable third generation architectures. Communications of the ACM 17(7), 412–421 (1974)
11. Tolmach, A.P., Appel, A.W.: A debugger for standard ML. Journal of Functional Programming 5(2), 155–200 (1995)

Interval Analysis for Concurrent Trace Programs Using Transaction Sequence Graphs

Malay K. Ganai and Chao Wang

NEC Labs America, Princeton, NJ, USA

Abstract. Concurrent trace programs (CTPs) are slices of the concurrent programs that generate the concrete program execution traces, where inter-thread event order specific to the given traces are relaxed. For such CTPs, we introduce transaction sequence graph (TSG) as a model for efficient concurrent data flow analysis. The TSG is a digraph of thread-local control nodes and edges corresponding to transactions and possible context-switches. Such a graph captures all the representative interleavings of these nodes/transactions. We use a mutually atomic transaction (MAT) based partial order reduction to construct such a TSG. We also present a non-trivial improvement to the original MAT analysis to further reduce the TSG sizes. As an application, we have used interval analysis in our experiments to show that TSG leads to more precise intervals and more time/space efficient concurrent data flow analysis than the standard models such as concurrent control flow graph.

1 Introduction

Verification of multi-threaded programs is hard due to the complex and often unexpected interleaving between the threads. Exposing concurrency related bugs—such as atomicity violations and data races—require not only bug-triggering inputs but also bug-triggering execution interleavings. Unfortunately, testing a program for every interleaving on every test input is often practically impossible. Runtime-based program analysis [1–13] infer and predict program errors from an observed trace. Compared to static analysis [14–20], runtime analysis often result in fewer false alarms.

Runtime analysis can be broadly classified into three categories: *runtime monitoring*, *runtime prediction*, and *runtime model checking*. In the *first* category, analysis such as[1–6] monitor the observed trace events (such as shared memory accesses) and flag true or potential violations of intended atomic transactions. In the *second* category, the analysis can also predict violations in other interleavings of the events in the observed trace. Some of these approaches [7, 8] use data abstraction, and thereby report false alarms as the interleaving may not be feasible; while other approaches such as [21] use happens-before causal relation to capture only (but may not be all) the feasible interleavings, and thereby, report no bogus (but may miss some true) violations. The *third* category includes more heavy-weight approaches such as dynamic model checking [9–11] and satisfiability-based symbolic analysis [12, 13]. These methods search

G. Roşu et al. (Eds.): RV 2010, LNCS 6418, pp. 253–269, 2010.

for violations in all feasible alternate interleavings of the observed trace and thereby, report a true violation if and only if one exists.

In dynamic model checking, for a given test input, systematic exploration of a program under all possible thread interleavings is performed. Even though the test input is fixed, explicit enumeration of interleavings can still be quite expensive. Although partial order reduction techniques (POR) [9, 22] reduce the set of necessary interleavings to explore, the reduced set often remains prohibitively large. Some previous work used ad-hoc approaches such as perturbing program execution by injecting artificial delays at every synchronization points [23], or randomized dynamic analysis to increase the chance of detecting real races [24].

In trace-based symbolic analysis [12, 13], explicit enumeration is avoided via the use of symbolic encoding and decision procedures to search for violations in a concurrent trace program (CTP) [25]. A CTP corresponds to data and control slice of the concurrent program (unrolled, if there is a thread local loop), and is constructed from both the observed trace and the program source code. One can view a CTP as a *generator* for both the original trace and all the other traces corresponding to feasible interleavings of the events in the original trace.

In this paper, we present a light-weight concurrent data flow analysis which can be used as an efficient preprocessor to reduce the subsequent efforts of the more heavy-weight symbolic analysis for concurrency verification such as [12, 13]. Our primary focus is on a suitable graph representation of CTP to conduct more precise and scalable concurrent data flow analysis than the standard models such as concurrent control flow graph (CCFG). In the sequel, we use interval analysis as an example.

In a nutshell, our approach proceeds as follows: from a given CCFG (corresponding to a CTP), we construct a transaction sequence graph (TSG) denoted as $G(V, E)$ which is a digraph with nodes V representing thread-local control states, and edges E representing either transactions (sequences of thread local transitions) or possible context switches. On the constructed TSG, we conduct an interval analysis for the program variables, which requires $O(|E|)$ iterations of interval updates, each costing $O(|V| \cdot |E|)$ time. Our main contributions are two fold:

- Precise and effective interval analysis using TSG.
- Identification and removal of redundant context switches.

For construction of TSGs, we leverage our mutually atomic transaction (MAT) analysis [26]—a partial-order based reduction technique that identifies a subset of possible context switches such that *all* and *only* representative schedules are permitted. Using MAT analysis, we first derive a set of so-called *independent transactions*. (As defined later, an independent transaction is globally atomic with respect to a set of schedules.) The beginning and ending control states of each independent transaction form the vertices of a TSG. Each edge of a TSG corresponds to either an independent transaction or a possible context switch between the inter-thread control state pairs (also identified in MAT analysis). Such a TSG is much reduced compared to the corresponding CCFG, where possible context switches occur between every pair of shared memory accesses. Most prior work such as [15–19] apply the analysis directly on CCFGs. In contrast, we conduct interval analysis on TSGs which leads to more precise intervals, and more time/space-efficient analysis than doing on CCFGs.

We improve our original MAT analysis further by reducing the set of possible context switches, and at the same time guarantee that such a reduced set captures all necessary schedules. Such improvement is important because:

- It significantly reduces the size of TSG, both in the number of vertices and in the number of edges; this in turn, results in a more precise interval analysis with improved runtime performance.
- The more precise intervals reduce the size and the search space of decision problems that arise during the more heavy-weight symbolic analysis.

The outline of the rest of the paper is as follows: We provide formal definitions and notations in Section 2. In Section 3, we give an informal overview of our approach, and in Section 4, we present our approach formally. We present our experimental results in Section 5, followed by conclusions, related, and future work in Section 6.

2   Formal Definitions

A multi-threaded concurrent program P comprises a set of threads and a set of shared variables, some of which, such as locks, are used for synchronization. Let M_i ($1 \leq i \leq n$) denote a thread model represented by a control and data flow graph of the sequential program it executes. Let V_i be a set of local variables in M_i and $\mathcal{V}$ be a set of (global) shared variables. Let $\mathcal{S}$ be the set of global states of the system, where a state $s \in \mathcal{S}$ is valuation of all local and global variables of the system. A global transition system for P is an interleaved composition of the individual thread models, M_i.

A thread transition $t \in \rho$ is a 4-tuple (c, g, u, c') that corresponds to a thread M_i, where c, c' represent the control states of M_i, g is an enabling condition (or *guard*) defined on $V_i \cup \mathcal{V}$, and u is a set of update assignments of the form $v := exp$ where variable v and variables in expression exp belong to the set $V_i \cup \mathcal{V}$. As per interleaving semantics precisely one thread transition is scheduled to execute from a state.

A *schedule* of the concurrent program P is an interleaving sequence of thread transitions $\rho = t_1 \cdots t_k$. In the sequel, we focus only on sequentially consistent [27] schedules. An event e occurs when a unique transition t is fired, which we refer to as the *generator* for that event, and denote it as $t = gen(P, e)$. A *run* (or concrete execution trace) $\sigma = e_1 \cdots e_k$ of a concurrent program P is an ordered sequence of events, where each event e_i corresponds to firing of a unique transition $t_i = gen(P, e_i)$. We illustrate the differences between schedules and runs in Section 3.

Let $begin(t)$ and $end(t)$ denote the beginning and the ending control states of $t = \langle c, g, u, c' \rangle$, respectively. Let $tid(t)$ denote the corresponding thread of the transition t. We assume each transition t is atomic, i.e., uninterruptible, and has at most one shared memory access. Let T_i denote the set of all transitions of M_i.

A *transaction* is an uninterrupted sequence of transitions of a particular thread. For a transaction $tr = t_1 \cdots t_m$, we use $|tr|$ to denote its length, and $tr[i]$ to denote the ith transition for $i \in \{1, \cdots, |tr|\}$. We define $begin(tr)$ and $end(tr)$ as $begin(tr[1])$ and $end(tr[|tr|])$, respectively. In the sequel, we use the notion of *transaction* to denote an uninterrupted sequence of transitions of a thread as *observed* in a system execution.

We say a transaction (of a thread) is *atomic* w.r.t. a schedule, if the corresponding sequence of transitions are executed uninterrupted, i.e., without an interleaving of another thread in-between. For a given set of schedules, if a transaction is atomic w.r.t. all the schedules in the set, we refer to it as an *independent transaction* w.r.t. the set.[1]

Given a run σ for a program P we say e *happens-before* e', denoted as $e \prec_\sigma e'$ if $i < j$, where $\sigma[i] = e$ and $\sigma[j] = e'$, with $\sigma[i]$ denoting the ith access event in σ. Let $t = gen(P, e)$ and $t' = gen(P, e')$. We say $t \prec_\sigma t'$ iff $e \prec_\sigma e'$. We use $e \prec_{po} e'$ and $t \prec_{po} t'$ to denote that the corresponding events and the transitions are in thread program order. We extend the definition of $\prec_{po}$ to thread local control states such that corresponding transitions are in the thread program order.

Reachable-before relation ($\sqsubseteq$): We say a control state pair (a, b) is reachable-before (a', b'), where each pair corresponds to a pair of threads, represented as $(a, b) \sqsubseteq (a', b')$ such that one of the following is true: 1) $a \prec_{po} a', b = b'$, 2) $a = a', b \prec_{po} b'$, 3) $a \prec_{po} a', b \prec_{po} b'$.

Dependency Relation ($\mathcal{D}$): Given a set T of transitions, we say a pair of transitions $(t, t') \in T \times T$ is dependent, i.e. $(t, t') \in \mathcal{D}$ iff one of the following holds (a) $t \prec_{po} t'$, (b) (t, t') is conflicting, i.e., accesses are on the same global variable, and at least one of them is a write access. If $(t, t') \notin \mathcal{D}$, we say the pair is *independent*.

Equivalency Relation ($\simeq$): We say two schedules $\rho_1 = t_1 \cdots t_i \cdot t_{i+1} \cdots t_n$ and $\rho_2 = t_1 \cdots t_{i+1} \cdot t_i \cdots t_n$ are equivalent if $(t_i, t_{i+1}) \notin \mathcal{D}$. An equivalent class of schedules can be obtained by iteratively swapping the consecutive independent transitions in a given schedule. A *representative* schedule refers to one of such an equivalent class.

Definition 1 (Concurrent Trace Programs (CTP), Wang 09). *A concurrent trace program with respect to an execution trace* $\sigma = e_1 \cdots e_k$ *and concurrent program P, denoted as* CTP_σ, *is a partial ordered set* $(T_\sigma, \prec_{\sigma,po})$

- $T_\sigma = \{t \mid t = gen(P, e) \text{ where } e \in \sigma\}$ is the set of generator transitions
- $t \prec_{\sigma,po} t'$ iff $t \prec_{po} t' \exists t, t' \in T_\sigma$

Let $\rho = t_1 \cdots t_k$ be a schedule corresponding to the run σ, where $t_i = gen(P, e_i)$. We say schedule $\rho' = t'_1, \cdots, t'_k$ is an *alternate schedule* of CTP_σ if it is obtained by interleaving transitions of ρ as per $\prec_{\sigma,po}$. We say ρ' is a *feasible schedule* iff there exists a concrete trace $\sigma' = e'_1 \cdots e'_k$ where $t'_i = gen(P, e'_i)$.

We extend the definition of CTP over multiple traces by first defining a *merge* operator [13] that can be applied on two CTPs, CTP_σ and CTP_ψ as: $(T_\tau, \prec_{\tau,po}) \overset{def}{=} merge((T_\sigma, \prec_{\sigma,po}), (T_\psi, \prec_{\psi,po}))$, where $T_\tau = T_\sigma \cup T_\psi$ and $t \prec_{\tau,po} t'$ iff at least one of the following is true: (a) $t \prec_{\sigma,po} t'$ where $t, t' \in T_\sigma$, and (b) $t \prec_{\psi,po} t'$ where $t, t' \in T_\psi$. A merged CTP can be effectively represented as a CCFG with branching structure but no loop. In the sequel, we refer to such a merged CTP as a CTP.

---

[1] We compare the notion of atomicity used here, vis-a-vis previous works [2, 6, 8]. In our work, the atomicity of transactions corresponds to the observation of the system, which may not correspond to the user intended atomicity of the transactions. Previous work assume that the atomic transactions are system specification that should always be enforced, whereas we infer atomic (or rather independent) transactions from the given system under test, and intend to use them to reduce the search space of symbolic analysis.

3   Our Approach: An Informal View

In this section, we present our approach informally, where we motivate our readers with an example. We use that example to guide the rest of our discussion. In the later sections, we give a formal exposition of our approach.

Consider a system P comprising interacting threads M_a and M_b with local variables a_i and b_i, respectively, and shared (global) variables X, Y, Z, L. This is shown in Figure 1(a) where threads are synchronized with *Lock/Unlock*. Thread M_b is created and destroyed using fork-join primitives. Figure 1(b) is the lattice representing the complete interleaving space of the program. Each node in the lattice denotes a global control state, shown as a pair of the thread local control states. An edge denotes a shared event write/read access of global variable, labeled with $W(.)/R(.)$ or *Lock(.)/Unlock(.)*. Note, some interleavings are not feasible due to Lock/Unlock, which we crossed out ($\times$) in the figure. We also labeled all possible context switches with **cs**. The highlighted interleaving corresponds to a concrete execution (run) σ of program P

$$\sigma = R(Y)_b \cdot Lock(L)_a \cdots Unlock(L)_a \cdot Lock(L)_b \cdots W(Z)_b \cdot W(Y)_a \cdot Unlock(L)_b \cdot W(Y)_b$$

where the suffices a, b denote the corresponding thread accesses.

A thread transition $(1b, true, b_1 = Y, 2b)$ (also represented as $1b \overset{b_1=Y}{\to} 2b$) is a generator of access event $R(Y)_b$ corresponding to the read access of the shared variable Y. The corresponding schedule ρ of the run σ is

$$\rho = (1b \overset{b_1=Y}{\to} 2b)(1a \overset{Lock(L)}{\to} 2a) \cdots (4a \overset{Unlock(L)}{\to} 5a)(2b \overset{Lock(L)}{\to} 3b) \cdots (6b \overset{Y=b_1+b_2}{\to} Jb)$$

From σ (and ρ), we obtain a slice of the original program called concurrent trace program (CTP) [25]. A CTP can be viewed as a generator of concrete traces, where the inter-thread event order specific to the given trace are relaxed. Figure 1(c) show the CTP_σ of the corresponding run σ shown as a CCFG (This CCFG happens to be the

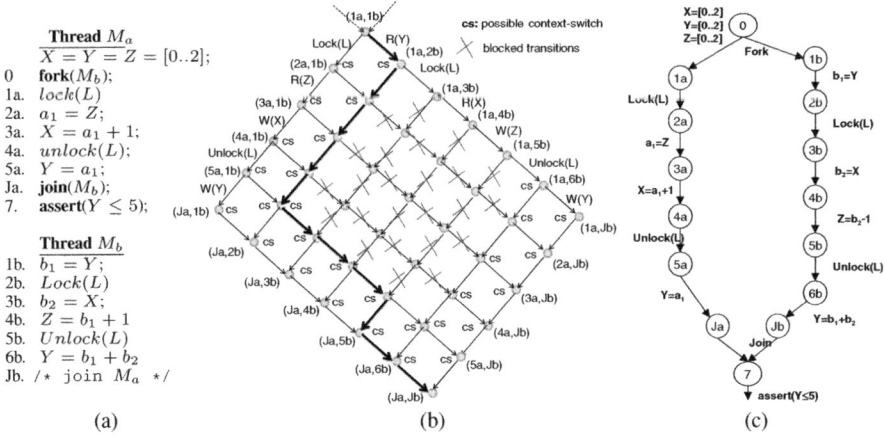

(a)   (b)   (c)

Fig. 1. (a) Concurrent system P with threads M_a, M_b and local variables a_i, b_i respectively, communicating with shared variable X, Y, Z, L. (b) lattice and a run σ (c) CTP_σ as CCFG.

same as P, although it need not be the case). Each node in CCFG denotes a thread control state (and the corresponding thread location), and each edge represents one of the following: thread transition, a context switch, a fork, and a join. To not clutter up the figure, we do not show edges that correspond to possible context switches (30 in total). Such a CCFG captures all the thread schedules of CTP_σ.

3.1   Transaction Sequence Graph

We now briefly describe the construction of TSG from the CCFG obtained above. Assuming we have computed—using MAT analysis (described in the next section)—independent transactions sets AT_a and AT_b and necessary context switches for threads M_a and M_b, where $AT_a = \{1a \cdots 5a, 5a \cdot Ja\}$, $AT_b = \{1b \cdot 2b, 2b \cdots 6b, 6b \cdot Jb\}$, and the context switching pairs are $\{(2b, 1a), (Ja, 1b)(6b, 1a)(5a, 2b), (Ja, 6b)(Jb, 1a)$ $(Ja, 2b)(Jb, 5a)\}$. The independent transactions are shown in Figure 2(a) as shaded rectangles.

Given such sets of independent transactions and context switching pairs, we construct a transaction sequence graph (TSG), a digraph as shown in Figure 2(b), as follows: the beginning and ending of each independent transaction forms nodes, each independent transaction forms a transaction edge (solid bold edge), and each context-switching pairs forms a context-switch edge (dash edge). We use V, TE, and CE to denote the set of nodes, transaction edges, and context-switch edges, respectively. Such a graph captures all and only the representative interleaving, where each interleaving is a sequence of independent transactions connected by directed edges. The number of nodes ($|V|$) and the number of transaction edges ($|TE|$) in TSG are linear in the number of independent transactions, and the number of context-switch edges ($|CE|$) is quadratic in the number of independent transactions. The TSG (in Figure 2(b)) has 7 nodes and 13 edges (= 5 transaction edges + 8 context-switch edges).

If we do not use MAT analysis, a naive way of defining an independent transaction would be a sequence of transitions such that only the last transition has a global access. This is the kind of graph representation used by most of the prior work in the literature [15–19]. In the sequel, we refer to a TSG obtained without MAT analysis as a CCFG. Such a graph would have 13 nodes, and 41 edges (=11 transaction edges + 30 context-switch edges).

Range Propagation on TSG. Although TSG may have cycles (as shown in Figure 2(b)), the sequential consistency requirement does not permit such cycles in any feasible path. A key observation is that any feasible path will have a sequence of transactions of length at most $|TE|$. As per the interleaving semantics, any schedule can not have two or more consecutive context switches. Thus, a feasible path will have at most $|TE|$ context switches. For example, path $Ja \cdot 2b \cdot 1a \cdot 5a$ involves two consecutive context switches, and therefore, can be ignored for range propagation. Clearly, one does not require a fixed point computation for range propagation, but rather a bounded number of iterations of size $O(|TE|)$.

Let $D[i]$ denote a set of TSG nodes reachable at BFS depth i from an initial set of nodes. Starting from each node in $D[i]$, we compute range along one transaction edge or along one context switch edge together with its subsequent transaction edge.

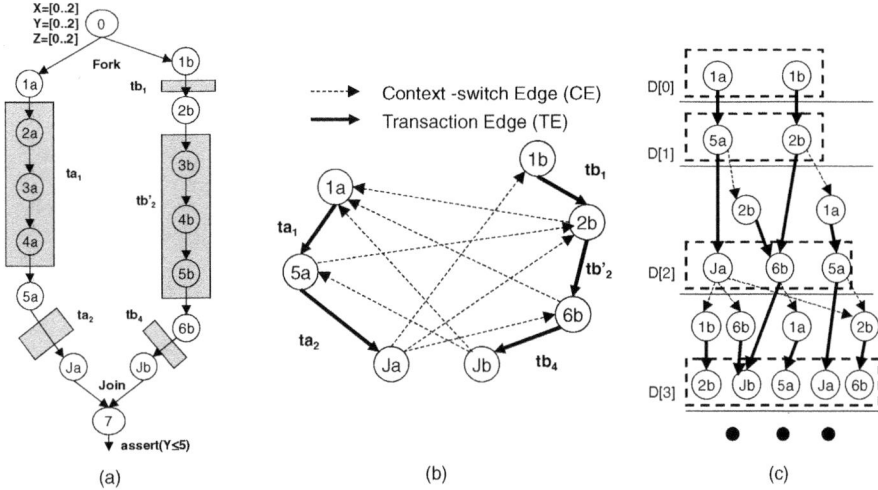

Fig. 2. (a) CCFG with independent transactions (b) TSG (c) Traversal on TSG

We show such a traversal on TSG in Figure 2(c), where dashed and solid edges correspond to context switch and transaction edges, respectively. The nodes in $D[i]$ are shown in dotted rectangles. As a transaction edge is associated with at most one context switch edge, a range propagation would require $O(|V| \cdot |TE|)$ updates per iteration.

3.2   MAT Analysis

We now discuss the essence of MAT analysis used to obtain TSG. Consider a pair (ta^{m_1}, tb^{m_1}), shown as the shaded rectangle m_1 in Figure 3(a), where $ta^{m_1} \equiv Lock(L)_a \cdot R(Z)_a \cdots W(Y)_a$ and $tb^{m_1} \equiv R(Y)_b$ are transactions of threads M_a and M_b, respectively. Note, we use an event to imply the corresponding generator transition.

From the control state pair $(1a, 1b)$, the pair $(Ja, 2b)$ can be reached by one of the two representative interleavings $ta^{m_1} \cdot tb^{m_1}$ and $tb^{m_1} \cdot ta^{m_1}$. Such a transaction pair (ta^{m_1}, tb^{m_1}) is *atomic pair-wise* as one avoids interleaving them *in-between*, and hence, referred as *Mutually Atomic Transaction*, MAT for short [26]. Note that in a MAT only the last transitions pair is dependent. Other MATs $m_2 \cdots m_7$ are similar. A MAT is formally defined as:

Definition 2 (Mutual Atomic Transactions (MAT), Ganai 09). *We say two transactions tr_i and tr_j of threads M_i and M_j, respectively, are mutually atomic iff except for the last pair, all other transitions pairs in the corresponding transactions are independent. Formally, a Mutually Atomic Transactions (MAT) is a pair of transactions, i.e., $(tr_i, tr_j), i \neq j$ iff $\forall k\ 1 \leq k \leq |tr_i|, \forall h\ 1 \leq h \leq |tr_j|, (tr_i[k], tr_j[h]) \notin \mathcal{D}$ ($k \neq |tr_i|$ and $h \neq |tr_j|$), and $tr_i[|tr_i|], tr_j[|tr_j|]) \in \mathcal{D}$.*

The basic idea of MAT-based partial order reduction [26] is to restrict context switching only between the two transactions of a MAT. A context switch can only occur from the

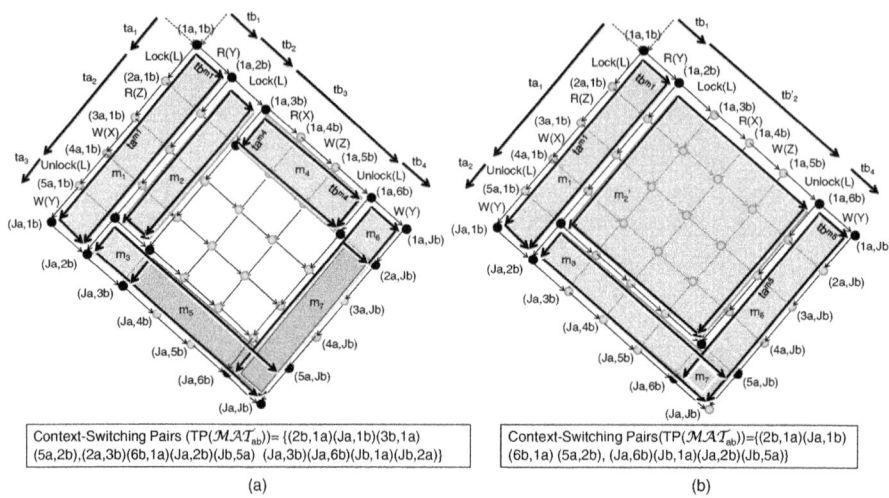

Context-Switching Pairs (TP($\mathcal{MAT}_{ab}$))= {(2b,1a)(Ja,1b)(3b,1a) (5a,2b),(2a,3b)(6b,1a)(Ja,2b)(Jb,5a) (Ja,3b)(Ja,6b)(Jb,1a)(Jb,2a)}	Context-Switching Pairs(TP($\mathcal{MAT}_{ab}$))={(2b,1a)(Ja,1b) (6b,1a) (5a,2b), (Ja,6b)(Jb,1a)(Ja,2b)(Jb,5a)}
(a)	(b)

Fig. 3. MATs m_i shown as rectangles, obtained using (a) GenMAT (b) GenMAT′

ending of a transaction to the beginning of the other transaction in the same MAT. Such a restriction reduces the set of necessary thread interleavings to explore. For a given MAT $\alpha = (f_i \cdots l_i, f_j \cdots l_j)$, we define a set $TP(\alpha)$ of possible context switches as ordered pairs, i.e., $TP(\alpha) = \{(end(l_i), begin(f_j)), (end(l_j), begin(f_i))\}$. Note that there are exactly two context switches for any given MAT.

Let TP denote a set of possible context switches. For a given CTP, we say TP is *adequate* iff for each feasible thread schedule of the CTP there is an equivalent schedule that can be obtained by choosing context switching only between the pairs in TP. Given a set $\mathcal{MAT}$ of MATs, we define $TP(\mathcal{MAT}) = \bigcup_{\alpha \in \mathcal{MAT}} TP(\alpha)$. A set $\mathcal{MAT}$ is called *adequate* iff $TP(\mathcal{MAT})$ is adequate. For a given CCFG, one can use an algorithm GenMAT [26] to obtain an adequate set of $\mathcal{MAT}$ that allows only representative thread schedules, as claimed in the following theorem.

Theorem 1 (Ganai, 2009). *GenMAT generates a set of MATs that captures all (i.e., adequate) and only (i.e., optimal) representative thread schedules. Further, its running cost is $O(n^2 \cdot k^2)$, where n is number of threads, and k is the maximum number of shared accesses in a thread.*

The GenMAT algorithm on the running example proceeds as follows. It starts with the pair $(1a, 1b)$, and identifies two MAT candidates: $(1a \cdots Ja, 1b \cdot 2b)$ and $(1a \cdot 2a, 1b \cdots 6b)$. By giving M_b higher priority over M_a, it selects the former MAT (i.e., m_1) uniquely. Note that the choice of M_b over M_a is arbitrary but is fixed through the MAT computation, which is required for the optimality result. After selecting MAT m_1, it inserts in a queue Q, three control state pairs $(1a, 2b), (Ja, 2b), (Ja, 1b)$ corresponding to the *begin* and the *end* pairs of the transactions in m_1. These correspond to the three corners of the rectangle m_1. In the next step, it pops out the pair $(1a, 2b) \in Q$, selects MAT m_2 using the same priority rule, and inserts three more pairs $(1a, 3b), (5a, 2b), (5a, 3b)$ in Q. Note that if there is no transition from a control state such as Ja, no MAT is generated from $(Ja, 2b)$. The algorithm terminates when all the pairs in the queue (denoted as • in Figure 3(a)) are processed. Note that the order of pair insertion can be arbitrary, but the same pair is never inserted more than once.

For the running example, a set $\mathcal{MAT}_{ab} = \{m_1, \cdots m_7\}$ of seven MATs is generated. Each MAT is shown as a rectangle in Figure 3(a). The total number of context switches allowed by the set, i.e., $TP(\mathcal{MAT}_{ab})$ is 12. The highlighted interleaving (shown in Figure 1(b)) is equivalent to the representative interleaving $tb^{m_1} \cdot ta^{m_1} \cdot tb^{m_3}$ (Figure 3(a)). One can verify (the optimality) that this is the only representative schedule (of this equivalence class) permissible by the set $TP(\mathcal{MAT}_{ab})$.

Reduction of MAT. We say a MAT is *feasible* if the corresponding transitions do not disable each other; otherwise it is *infeasible*. For example, as shown in Figure 3(a), MAT $m_2 = (ta^{m_2}, tb^{m_2})$ is infeasible, as the interleaving $tb^{m_2} \cdot ta^{m_2}$ is infeasible due to locking semantics, although the other interleaving $ta^{m_2} \cdot tb^{m_2}$ is feasible.

The `GenMAT` algorithm does not generate infeasible MATs when both the interleavings are infeasible. Such case arises when control state pairs such as $(2a, 3b)$ are simultaneously unreachable. However, it generates an infeasible MAT if such pairs are simultaneously reachable with only one interleaving of the MAT (while the other one is infeasible). For example, it generates MAT m_2 as $(5a, 3b)$ is reachable with only interleaving $Lock(L)_a \cdots Unlock(L)_a \cdot Lock(L)_b$ while the other one $Lock(L)_b \cdot Lock(L)_a \cdots Unlock(L)_a$ is infeasible. Such infeasible MAT may result in generation of other MATs, such as m_5 which may be redundant, and m_4 which may be infeasible. Although the interleaving space captured by $\mathcal{MAT}_{ab}$ is still adequate and optimal, the set apparently may not be "minimal" as some interleavings may be infeasible.

To address the minimality, we modify `GenMAT` such that only feasible MATs are chosen as MAT candidates. We refer to the modified algorithm as `GenMAT'`. We use additional static information such as lockset analysis [1] to obtain a reduced set $\mathcal{MAT}'_{ab}$ and later show (Theorem 2) that such reduction do not exclude any feasible interleaving. The basic modification is as follows: stating from the pair $(begin(f_i), begin(f_j))$, if a MAT $(f_i \cdots l_i, f_j \cdots l_j)$ is infeasible, then we select a MAT $(f_i \cdots l'_i, f_j \cdots l'_j)$ that is a feasible, where $end(l_i) \prec_{po} end(l'_i)$ or $end(l_j) \prec_{po} end(l'_j)$ or both.

With this modified step, `GenMAT'` produces a set $\mathcal{MAT}'_{ab} = \{m_1, m'_2, m_3, m_6, m_7\}$ of five MATs, as shown in Figure 3b. Note that infeasible MATs m_2 and m_4 are replaced with MAT m'_2. MAT m_5 is not generated as m_2 is no longer a MAT, and therefore, control state pair $(5a, 3b)$ is no longer in Q.

The basic intuition as to why m_5 is redundant is as follows: For m_5, we have $TP(m_5) = \{(Ja, 2b), (5a, Jb)\}$. The context switching pair $(Ja, 2b)$ is infeasible, as the interleaving allowed by m_5, i.e., $R(Y)_b \cdot Lock(L)_b \cdot Lock(L)_a \cdot W(Y)_a \cdot R(X)_a \cdots$ is an infeasible interleaving. The other context switching pair $(5a, Jb)$ is included in either $TP(m_3)$ or $TP(m_7)$, where m_3, m_7 are feasible MATs (Figure 3(b)). The proof that $TP(\mathcal{MAT}'_{ab})$ allows the same set of feasible interleavings as allowed by $TP(\mathcal{MAT}_{ab})$, is given in Section 4.

Independent Transactions. Given a set of MATs, we obtain a set of independent transactions of a thread M_i, denoted as AT_i, by splitting the pair-wise atomic transactions of the thread M_i as needed into multiple transactions such that a context switching (under

MAT-based reduction) can occur either to the beginning or from the end of such transactions. For the running example, the sets of independent transactions corresponding to $\mathcal{MAT}'_{ab}$ are $AT_a = \{1a \cdots 5a, 5a \cdot Ja\}$ and $AT_b = \{1b \cdot 2b, 2b \cdots 6b, 6b \cdot Jb\}$. These are shown in Figure 2(a) as shaded rectangles, and are shown as outlines of the lattice in Figure 3(b). The size of set of independent transaction determines the size of TSGs.

If we used $\mathcal{MAT}_{ab}$, we would have obtained $AT_a = \{1a \cdot 2a, 2a \cdots 5a, 5a \cdot Ja\}$ and $AT_b = \{1b \cdot 2b, 2b \cdot 3b, 3b \cdots 6b, 6b \cdot Jb\}$, as shown outlining the lattice in Figure 3(a). A TSG constructed using $\mathcal{MAT}_{ab}$ (not shown) would have 8 nodes and 17 edges (= 7 transaction edges + 10 context-switch edges). Note, out of the 12 context-switches, one can remove $(3b, 1a)$ and $(2a, 3b)$ as they are simultaneously unreachable.

4   Our Approach: TSG-Based Interval Analysis

We now present our approach formally. We first discuss MAT reduction step. Then we describe the construction of TSGs in Section 4.1, followed by interval analysis on TSG in Section 4.2. For comparison, we introduce a notion of interval metric in Section 4.3.

Given a CTP with threads $M_1 \cdots M_n$, and a dependency relation $\mathcal{D}$, we use algorithm GenMAT [26] to generate $\mathcal{MAT}_{ij}$ for each pair of threads M_i and M_j, $i \neq j$, and obtain $\mathcal{MAT} = \bigcup_{i \neq j} \mathcal{MAT}_{ij}$. Note that $\mathcal{D}$ may not include the conflicting pairs that are unreachable. We now define the feasibility of MAT to improve the MAT analysis.

Definition 3 (Feasible MAT). *A MAT $m = (tr_i, tr_j)$ is feasible such that both representative (non-equivalent) interleavings, i.e., $tr_i \cdot tr_j$ and $tr_j \cdot tr_i$, are feasible; otherwise it is infeasible. In other words, in a feasible MAT, the corresponding transitions do not disable each other.*

We modify GenMAT such that only feasible MATs are chosen as MAT candidates. We denote the modified algorithm as GenMAT′. The modified step is as follows: starting from the pair (f_i, f_j), if a pair $(l_i, l_j) \in \mathcal{D}$ is found that yields an infeasible MAT, then

- we select another pair $(l'_i, l'_j) \in \mathcal{D}$ such that $(l_i, l_j) \sqsubset (l'_i, l'_j)$ and $(f_i \cdots l'_i, f_j \cdots l'_j)$ is a feasible MAT, and
- there is no pair $(l''_i, l''_j) \in \mathcal{D}$ such that $(l_i, l_j) \sqsubset (l''_i, l''_j) \sqsubset (l'_i, l'_j)$ and $(f_i \cdots l''_i, f_j \cdots l''_j)$ is a feasible MAT.

where $\sqsubset$ is the reachable-before relation defined before. Interested readers may refer to the complete algorithm in the extended version [28].

Let $\mathcal{MAT}$ and $\mathcal{MAT}'$ be the set of MATs obtained using GenMAT and GenMAT′, respectively. We state the following MAT reduction theorem:

Theorem 2 (MAT reduction). $\mathcal{MAT}'$ *is adequate, and* $TP(\mathcal{MAT}') \subseteq TP(\mathcal{MAT})$.

The proof is provided in the extended version [28].

4.1   Transaction Sequence Graph

To build a TSG, we first identify independent transactions of each thread, i.e., those transactions that are atomic with respect to all schedules allowed by the set of MATs, as discussed in the following. Here we use $\mathcal{MAT}$ to denote the set of MATs obtained.

Identifying Independent Transactions. Given a set $\mathcal{MAT} = \bigcup_{i \neq j \in \{1,\cdots,n\}}$ $\mathcal{MAT}_{ij}$, we identify independent transactions, denoted as AT_i as follows:

- We first define a set of transactions $\mathcal{MAT}_i$ of thread M_i:

$$\mathcal{MAT}_i = \{tr_i | m = (tr_i, tr_j) \in \mathcal{MAT}_{ij} \; i \neq j \in \{1, \cdots, n\}\}$$

In other words, $\mathcal{MAT}_i$ comprises all transactions of thread M_i that are pairwise atomic with some other transactions. For the running example with the MAT set as shown in Figure 3(b), $\mathcal{MAT}_a = \{1a \cdots Ja, 1a \cdots 5a, 5a \cdot Ja\}$, and $\mathcal{MAT}_b = \{1b \cdot 2b, 2b \cdots 6b, 6b \cdot Jb\}$.

- Given two transactions $tr, tr' \in \mathcal{MAT}_i$, we say $begin(tr) \prec_{po} begin(tr')$ if $tr[1] \prec_{po} tr'[1]$. Using the set $\mathcal{MAT}_i$, we obtain a partial order set of control states S_i, referred as *transaction boundary* set, that is defined over $\prec_{po}$ as follows:

$$S_i \equiv \{begin(tr_{i,1}), begin(tr_{i,2}), \cdots, begin(tr_{i,m}), end(tr_{i,m})\}$$

where $tr_{i,k} \in \mathcal{MAT}_i$, and $tr_{i,m}$ denote the last transaction of the thread M_i. Note that due to conditional branching the order may not be total. For the running example, with the given sets $\mathcal{MAT}_a$ and $\mathcal{MAT}_b$, we obtain $S_a = \{1a, 5a, Ja\}$, and $S_b = \{1b, 2b, 6b, Jb\}$.

- Using the set S_i, we obtain a set of transactions AT_i of thread M_i as follows:

$$AT_i = \{t \cdots t' \mid c \xrightarrow{t \cdots t'} c' \text{ where } c \prec_{po} c' \text{ and } c, c' \in S_i \text{ and } t, \cdots, t' \in T_i \text{ and}$$
$$\text{there is no } c'' \in S_i \text{ such that } c \prec_{po} c'' \prec_{po} c'\}$$

Recall that T_i is the set of transitions in M_i. For the running example, we obtain AT_a and AT_b, as shown as shaded rectangles in Figure 2(a).

Proposition 1. *Each transaction $tr \in AT_i$ for $i \in \{1, \cdots, n\}$ is an independent transaction and is maximal, i.e., can not be made larger without it being an independent transaction. Further, for each transition $t \in T_i$, there exists $tr \in AT_i$ such that $t \in tr$.*

Constructing TSG. Given a set of context-switching pairs $TP(\mathcal{MAT})$, a set of independent transactions $\bigcup_i AT_i$, and a set of transaction boundaries $\bigcup_i S_i$, we construct a transaction sequence graph, a digraph $G(V, E)$ as follows:

- $V = \cup_i V_i$ is the set of nodes, where V_i denotes a set of thread local control states corresponding to the set S_i,
- $E = TE \bigcup CE$ is the set of edges, where

  - TE is the set of *transaction edges* corresponding to the independent transactions i.e., $TE = \{(begin(tr), end(tr)) \mid tr \in \bigcup_i AT_i\}$
  - CE is the set of *context switch edges* corresponding $TP(\mathcal{MAT})$ i.e., $CE = \{(c_i, c_j) \mid (c_i, c_j) \in TP(\mathcal{MAT})\}$

A TSG $G(V, E = (CE \cup TE))$, as constructed, has $|V| = O(\Sigma_i |AT_i|)$, $|TE| = (\Sigma_i |AT_i|)$, and $|CE| = (\Sigma_{i \neq j} |AT_i| \cdot |AT_j|)$, where $i, j \in \{1, \cdots, n\}$, and n is number of threads. In the worst case, however, $|V| = O(n \cdot k)$, $|TE| = O(n \cdot k)$, and $|CE| = O(n^2 \cdot k^2)$ where k is the maximum number of shared accesses in any thread.

Proposition 2. *TSG as constructed captures all and only the representative interleaving (of a given CTP), each corresponding to a total ordered sequence of independent transactions where the order is defined by the directed edges of TSG.*

4.2   Range Propagation on TSG

Range propagation uses data and control structure of a program to derive range information. In this work, we consider intervals for simplicity, although other abstract domains are equally applicable. For each program variable v, we define an interval $\langle l_v^c, u_v^c \rangle$, where l_v^c, u_v^c are integer-valued lower and upper bounds for v at a control location c. One can define, for example, the lower bound(L)/upper bound (U) of an expression $exp = exp_1 + exp_2$ at a control location c as $L(exp, c) = L(exp_1, c) + L(exp_2, c)$ and $U(exp, c) = U(exp_1, c) + U(exp_2, c)$, respectively (more details in [29]).

We say an interval $\langle l_v^c, u_v^c \rangle$ is *adequate* if value of v at location c, denoted as $val(v, c)$ is bounded in all program executions, i.e., $l_v^c \leq val(v, c) \leq u_v^c$. As there are potentially many feasible paths, range propagation is typically carried out iteratively along bounded paths, where the adequacy is achieved conservatively. However, such bounded path analysis can still be useful in eliminating paths that do not satisfy sequential consistency requirements. As shown in Figure 2(c), a sequence $5a \cdot 2b \cdot 6b \cdot 1a$ does not follow program order, and therefore, paths with such a sequence can be eliminated.

At an iteration step i of range propagation, let $r^{c,p}[i]$ denote the range information (i.e., a set of intervals) at node c along a feasible path p, and is defined as:

$$r^{c,p}[i] = \{\langle l_v^{c,p}[i], u_v^{c,p}[i] \rangle | \text{ interval for } v \text{ computed at node } c \text{ along path } p \text{ at step } i\}$$

One can merge $r^{c,p}[i]$ and $r^{c,p'}[i]$ conservatively as follows:

$$r^{c,p}[i] \sqcup r^{c,p'}[i] = \{\langle l_v^{c,p}[i], u_v^{c,p}[i] \rangle \sqcup \langle l_v^{c,p'}[i], u_v^{c,p'}[i] \rangle | \text{ interval for } v \text{ computed}$$
$$\text{at node } c \text{ along paths } p, p' \text{ at step } i\}$$

where the interval merge operator ($\sqcup$) is defined as:

$$\langle l, u \rangle \sqcup \langle l', u' \rangle = \langle min(l, l'), max(u, u') \rangle.$$

Let $r^c[i]$ denote the range information at node c at step i, i.e.,

$$r^c[i] = \{\langle l_v^c[i], u_v^c[i] \rangle \mid \text{ interval for } v \text{ computed at node } c \text{ at iteration step } i\}.$$

Let FP denote a set of feasible paths starting from nodes $D[i]$ of length $B \geq 1$, where B is a *lookahead* parameter that controls the trade off between precision and update cost. Given $r^{c,p}[i]$ with $p \in FP$, we obtain the range information at step i as $r^c[i] = \sqcup_{p \in FP} r^{c,p}[i]$ and cumulative range information at step i as $R^c[i] = \sqcup_{j=0}^{j=i} r^c[j]$.

We present a self-explanatory flow of our forward range propagation procedure, referred as RPT, for a given TSG $G = (V, E)$ in Figure 4(a). As observed in Section 3.1, in any representative feasible path, a transaction edge is associated with at most one context switch edge. Thus, the length of such a path is at most $2 \cdot |TE|$. At every iteration of range propagation, we compute the range along a sequence of $|B|$ transaction edges interleaved with at most $|B|$ context switch edges. Such a range propagation requires $\lceil |TE|/B \rceil$ iterations. The cost of range propagation at each iteration is $O(|V| \cdot |TE|^B)$. After RPT terminates, we obtain the final cumulative range information $R^c[i]$ at each node c, denoted as R^c.

Proposition 3. *Given a TSG $G = (V, E = (TE \cup CE))$ that captures all feasible paths of a CTP, the procedure RPT generates adequate range information R^c for each node $c \in V$, and the cost of propagation is $O(|V| \cdot |TE|^{B+1})$.*

We show a run of RPT in Figure 4(b) on the TSG shown in Figure 2(b). At each iteration step i, we show the range computed $r^c[i]$ (for each global variable) at the control states $1a, 5a, Ja, 1b, 2b, 6b, Jb$. Since there are 5 TE edges in the TSG, we require 5 iterations with $B = 1$. The cells with $\langle -, - \rangle$ correspond to no range propagation to those nodes. The cells in **bold** at step i correspond to nodes in $D[i]$. The final intervals at each node c, i.e., R^c, is equal to the data-union of the range values at c computed at each iteration $i = 1 \cdots 5$. We show the corresponding cumulative intervals obtained for the CCFG after 11 iterations (as it has 11 TE edges). Note that using TSG, RPT not only obtains more refined intervals, but also requires fewer iterations. Also observe that the assertion $Y \leq 5$ (line 7, Figure 1(a)) holds at Jb with the final intervals for Y obtained using TSG, while it does not hold at Jb when obtained using CCFG.

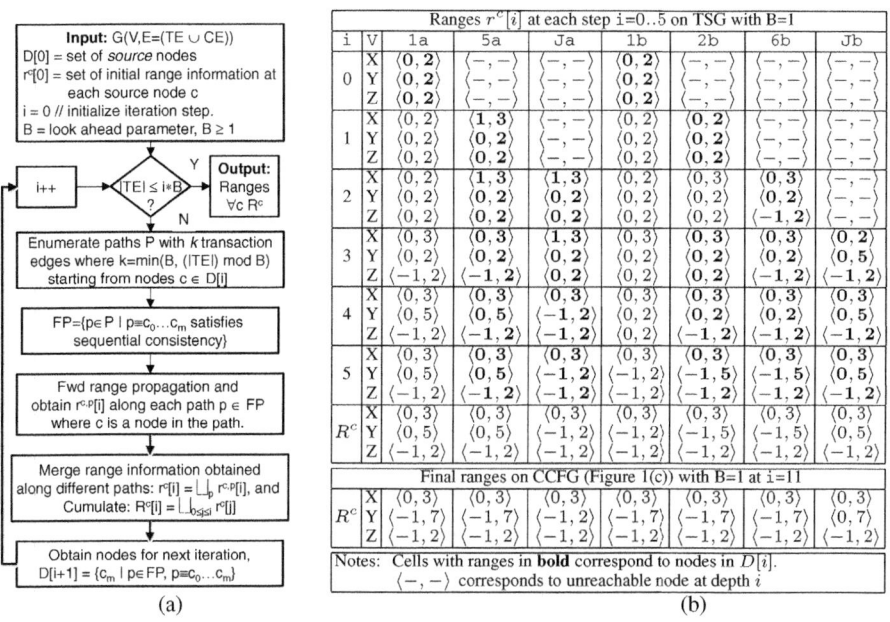

Fig. 4. (a) RPT: Range Propagation on TSG (b) A run of RPT on TSG (Figure 2) and CCFG

4.3 Interval Metric

Given the final intervals $\langle l_v^c, u_v^c \rangle \in R^c$, we use the total number of bits needed (the fewer the better) to encode each interval, as a metric to compare effectiveness of interval analysis on CCFG and TSGs. We refer to that as *interval metric*. It has two components: local (denoted as RB_l) and global (denoted as RB_g) corresponding to the total range bits of local and global variables, respectively.

The local component RB_l is computed as follows:

$$RB_l = \Sigma_{t \in \bigcup_i T_i} \Sigma_{v \in assgn_l(t)} \, \log_2(u_v^{end(t)} - l_v^{end(t)})$$

where $assgn_l(t)$ denotes a set of local variables assigned (or updated) in transition t.

For computing the global component RB_g, we need to account for context switching that can occur between global updates. Hence, we add a synchronization component, denoted as RB_g^{sync}, in the following:

$$RB_g = \Sigma_{t \in \bigcup_i T_i} \Sigma_{v \in assgn_g(t)} \log_2(u_v^{end(t)} - l_v^{end(t)}) + RB_g^{sync}$$

where $assgn_g(t)$ denotes a set of global variables assigned in transition t, and RB_g^{sync} is the synchronization component corresponding to a global state before an independent transaction begins, and is computed as follows:

$$RB_g^{sync} = \Sigma_{tr \in \bigcup_i AT_i} \Sigma_{v \in V} \log_2(u_v^{begin(tr)} - l_v^{begin(tr)})$$

where $v \in V$ is a global variable, and tr is an independent transaction.

For the running example, the interval metrics obtained are as follows: CCFG: $RB_l = 8, RB_g = 95$; TSG using $\mathcal{MAT}_{ab}$: $RB_l = 6, RB_g = 57$; TSG using $\mathcal{MAT}'_{ab}$: $RB_l = 6, RB_g = 43$.

5   Experiments

In our experiments, we use several multi-threaded benchmarks of varied complexity with respect to the number of shared variable accesses. There are 4 sets of benchmarks that are grouped as follows: simple to complex concurrent programs [26] (cp), our Linux/ Pthreads/C implementation [12] of atomicity violations reported in apache server [30] (atom), bank benchmarks [31] (bank), and indexer benchmarks [9] (index). Each set has concurrent trace programs (CTP) generated [25] from the runs of the corresponding concurrent programs. These benchmarks are publicly available at [32]. We used constant propagation algorithm [16] to preprocess these benchmarks in order to expose the benefits of our approach.

Our experiments were conducted on a linux workstation with a 3.4GHz CPU and 2GB of RAM, and a time limit of 20 minutes. From these benchmarks, we first obtained CCFG. Then we obtained TSG and TSG' after conducting MAT analysis on the CCFGs, using GenMAT and GenMAT', respectively, as described in Section 4.1. For all three graphs, we removed context switch edges between node pairs that are found unreachable using lockset analysis [1].

Comparison of RPT on CCFG, TSG, and TSG' are shown in Table 1 using lookahead parameter $B = 1$. The characteristics of the corresponding CTPs are shown in Columns 2-6, the results of RPT on CCFG, TSG and TSG' are shown in Columns 7-11, and Columns 12-17, and Columns 18-23, respectively. Columns 2-6 describe the following: the number of threads (n), the number of local variables (#L), the number of global variables (#G), the number of global accesses (#A), and the number of total transitions (#T), respectively. Columns 7-11 describe the following: the number of context switch edges (#CE), the number of transaction edges (#TE) (same as the number of iterations of RPT), the time taken (t, in sec), the number of local bits RB_l, and number of global bits RB_g, respectively. Columns 12-17 and 18-23 describe similarly for TSG and TSG' including the number of MATs obtained (#M). In case of CCFG, we obtained a transaction by combining sequence of transitions such that only the last transition has exactly one global access. The time reported includes MAT analysis (if performed) and run time of RPT.

Table 1. Comparison of RPT on CCFG, TSG and TSG'

Ex	Characteristics					CCFG					TSG						TSG'					
	n	#L	#G	#A	#T	#C	#TE	t(s)	RB_l	RB_g	#M	#C	#TE	t(s)	RB_l	RB_g	#M	#C	#TE	t(s)	RB_l	RB_g
cp1	3	4	3	41	28	90	24	<1	6	131	18	22	13	<1	6	82	9	14	9	<1	6	50
cp2	3	4	3	185	108	1562	88	<1	22	531	330	342	45	<1	22	354	121	222	25	<1	22	178
cp3	3	4	3	905	508	35802	408	13	102	2531	7650	7702	205	2	102	1714	2601	5102	105	1	102	818
atom1	3	1	2	27	25	44	16	<1	29	493	11	14	11	<1	29	300	6	9	8	<1	29	200
atom2	3	2	3	37	31	68	20	<1	30	647	14	19	13	<1	30	389	8	12	9	<1	30	245
atom3	3	2	11	412	243	4748	153	<1	61	10.5K	1321	1350	91	<1	61	6945	478	865	48	<1	61	3605
atom4	3	3	13	435	251	5336	160	1	32	12.4K	1344	1342	95	<1	32	7933	508	899	50	<1	32	4115
bank1	9	59	16	383	286	12.6K	180	10	855	22.8K	178	278	75	<1	808	10.6K	178	278	75	<1	808	10.6K
bank2	9	67	25	540	369	25.1K	231	63	818	35.9K	440	559	155	1	771	25.1K	277	409	115	<1	771	19K
bank3	9	67	26	599	386	24.8K	240	38	834	38.3K	384	454	147	<1	786	24.7K	212	320	99	1	786	16.6K
index1	9	11	24	229	168	7224	98	2	52	7653	6	12	12	<1	32	452	6	12	12	<1	32	452
index2	19	21	54	514	363	40.1K	213	51	154	43.5K	351	513	106	1	132	11.6K	225	366	64	1	132	6613
index3	31	33	184	2125	1490	627K	821	TO	NA	NA	2573	3386	496	40	883	399K	1399	2024	265	22	883	121K
index4	33	35	246	3914	2793	1.98M	1490	TO	NA	NA	29.6K	31.4K	922	822	1814	1M	10.8K	11.9K	479	275	1814	307K

Notes: n: num. of threads, #L: num. of local vars, #G: num. of global vars, #A: num. of global accesses, #T: num. of transitions, #CE: num. of context switch edges, #TE: num. of transaction edges (=num. of iterations), t(s): time in sec (TO: t > 1200s), #M: num. of MATs, RB_l: num. of local bits, RB_g: num. of global bits, $B = 1$ for the experiments

As we notice, RPT on TSG and TSG' (except index4) completes in less than a minute, and is an order of magnitude faster compared to that on CCFG. Also, the interval metric (RB_l, RB_g) for TSG and TSG' are significantly lower compared to CCFG. Further, between TSG' and TSG, the former generates tighter intervals.

We also evaluated reduction in the efforts of a heavy-weight trace-based symbolic analysis tool CONTESSA [13] using RPT results. For each benchmark, we selected a reachability property corresponding to a reachability of a thread control state. Using the tool, we then generated Satisfiability Modulo Theory (SMT) formula such that the formula is satisfiable if and only if the control state is reachable. We then compared the solving time of two such SMT formula, one encoded using the bit-widths of variables as obtained using RPT (denoted as ϕ_R), and other encoded using integer bit-width of 32 (denoted as ϕ_{32}). We observed that the solving on ϕ_R is faster than on ϕ_{32} by about 1-2 orders of magnitude. Further details are available in the extended version [28].

6   Conclusion, Related and Future Work

We presented an interval analysis for CTPs using the new notion of TSGs, which is often more precise and space/time efficient than using the standard CCFGs. We use a MAT analysis to obtain independent transactions and to minimize the size of the TSGs. We also propose a non-trivial improvement to the MAT analysis to further simplify the TSGs. Our work is related to the prior work on static analysis for concurrent programs such as [15-19], although such analysis were directly applied to the CCFG of a whole program. Our notion of TSG is also different from the transaction graph (TG) [20] and the task interaction concurrency graph (TICG) [14] that have been used in concurrent data flow analysis. Such graphs, i.e, TG and TICG, represent a product graph where nodes correspond to the global control states and edges correspond to thread transitions—such graphs are often significantly bigger in size than TSGs.

Although we have applied our TSG approach only to CTPs, in future we plan to generalize it for concurrent programs with loops. Such generalization would involve extending the MAT analysis to handle loops (e.g. by considering the loop back-edges during MAT generation) and introducing abstract domains to handle the interleaving of interacting loops (e.g. by considering independent transactions in a loop).

References

1. Savage, S., Burrows, M., Nelson, G., Sobalvarro, P., Anderson, T.: Eraser: a dynamic data race detector for multithreaded programs. ACM Trans. Comput. Syst. (1997)
2. Flanagan, C., Freund, S.N.: Atomizer: A dynamic atomcity checker for multithreaded programs. In: Proc. of IPDPS (2004)
3. Xu, M., Bodik, R., Hill, M.D.: A serializability violation detector for shared-memory server programs. In: Programming Language Design and Implementation (2005)
4. Wang, L., Stoller, S.D.: Runtime analysis of atomicity for multithreaded programs. IEEE Transactions on Software Engineering (2006)
5. Farzan, A., Madhusudan, P.: Monitoring atomicity in concurrent programs. In: Gupta, A., Malik, S. (eds.) CAV 2008. LNCS, vol. 5123, pp. 52–65. Springer, Heidelberg (2008)
6. Sadowski, C., Freund, S.N., Flanagan, C.: Singletrack: A dynamic determinism checker for multithreaded programs. In: Castagna, G. (ed.) ESOP 2009. LNCS, vol. 5502, pp. 394–409. Springer, Heidelberg (2009)
7. Farzan, A., Madhusudan, P.: Meta-analysis for atomicity violations under nested locking. In: Gupta, A., Malik, S. (eds.) CAV 2008. LNCS, vol. 5123. Springer, Heidelberg (2008)
8. Wang, L., Stoller, S.D.: Accurate and efficient runtime detection of atomicity errors in concurrent programs. In: Symposium on Principles and Practice of Parallel Programming (2006)
9. Flanagan, C., Godefroid, P.: Dynamic partial-order reduction for model checking software. In: Proc. of POPL (2005)
10. Musuvathi, M., Quadeer, S.: CHESS: Systematic stress testing of concurrent software. In: Puebla, G. (ed.) LOPSTR 2006. LNCS, vol. 4407, pp. 15–16. Springer, Heidelberg (2007)
11. Yang, Y., Chen, X., Gopalakrishnan, G.: Inspect: A Runtime Model Checker for Multithreaded C Programs. Technical Report UUCS-08-004, University of Utah (2008)
12. Wang, C., Limaye, R., Ganai, M., Gupta, A.: Trace-based symbolic analysis for atomicity violations. In: Esparza, J., Majumdar, R. (eds.) TACAS 2010. LNCS, vol. 6015, pp. 328–342. Springer, Heidelberg (2010)
13. Kundu, S., Ganai, M., Wang, C.: CONTESSA: CONcurrency TESTing Augmented with Symbolic Analysis. In: Touili, T., Cook, B., Jackson, P. (eds.) Computer Aided Verification. LNCS, vol. 6174. Springer, Heidelberg (2010)
14. Long, D.L., Clarke, L.A.: Task interaction graphs for concurrent analysis. In: International Conference on Software Engineering (1989)
15. Dwyer, M.B., Clarke, L.A.: Data flow analysis for verifying properties of concurrent programs. In: International Symposium on the Foundations of Software Engineering (1994)
16. Lee, J., Padua, D.A., Midkiff, S.P.: Basic compiler algorithms for parallel programs. Symposium on Principles and Practice of Parallel Programming (1999)
17. Farzan, A., Madhusudan, P.: Causal dataflow analysis for concurrent programs. In: Grumberg, O., Huth, M. (eds.) TACAS 2007. LNCS, vol. 4424, pp. 102–116. Springer, Heidelberg (2007)
18. Chugh, R., Voung, J.W., Jhala, R., Lerer, S.: Dataflow analysis for concurrent programs using datarace detection. In: Programming Language Design and Implementation (2008)
19. Lal, A., Touili, T., Kidd, N., Reps, T.: Interprocedural analysis of concurrent programs under a context bound. In: Ramakrishnan, C.R., Rehof, J. (eds.) TACAS 2008. LNCS, vol. 4963, pp. 282–298. Springer, Heidelberg (2008)

20. Kahlon, V., Sankaranarayanan, S., Gupta, A.: Semantic reduction of thread interleavings in concurrent programs. In: Kowalewski, S., Philippou, A. (eds.) TACAS 2009. LNCS, vol. 5505, pp. 134–138. Springer, Heidelberg (2009)

21. Chen, F., Roşu, G.: Parametric and sliced causality. In: Damm, W., Hermanns, H. (eds.) CAV 2007. LNCS, vol. 4590, pp. 240–253. Springer, Heidelberg (2007)

22. Gueta, G., Flanagan, C., Yahav, E., Sagiv, M.: Cartesian partial-order reduction. In: Bošnački, D., Edelkamp, S. (eds.) SPIN 2007. LNCS, vol. 4595, pp. 95–112. Springer, Heidelberg (2007)

23. Edelstein, O., Farchi, E., Goldin, E., Nir, Y., Ratsaby, G., Ur, S.: Framework for Testing Multi-threaded Java Programs. In: Concurrency and Computation: Practice and Experience (2003)

24. Sen, K.: Race directed random testing of concurrent programs. In: PLDI (2008)

25. Wang, C., Chaudhuri, S., Gupta, A., Yang, Y.: Symbolic pruning of concurrent program executions. In: ESEC-FSE (2009)

26. Ganai, M.K., Kundu, S.: Reduction of Verification Conditions for Concurrent System using Mutually Atomic Transactions. In: Păsăreanu, C.S. (ed.) SPIN Workshop. LNCS, vol. 5578, pp. 68–87. Springer, Heidelberg (2009)

27. Lamport, L.: How to make multiprocessor computer that correctly executes multiprocess programs. IEEE Transactions on Computers (1979)

28. Ganai, M. K.: Conference Notes,
    http://www.nec-labs.com/~malay/notes.htm

29. Rugina, R., Rinard, M.C.: Symbolic bounds analysis of pointers, array indices, and accessed memory regions. In: Programming Language Design and Implementation (2000)

30. Lu, S., Tuckt, J., Qin, F., Zhou, Y.: AVIO: detecting atomicity violations via access interleaving invariants. In: Architectural Support for Programming Languages and Operating Systems (2006)

31. Farchi, E., Nir, Y., Ur, S.: Concurrent bug patterns and how to test them. In: Parallel and Distributed Processing Symposium (2003)

32. System Analysis and Verification Team. NECLA SAV Benchmarks,
    http://www.nec-labs.com/research/system/systems_SAV-website/
    benchmarks.php

Causality Analysis in Contract Violation

Gregor Gössler[1], Daniel Le Métayer[1], and Jean-Baptiste Raclet[2]

[1] INRIA Grenoble – Rhône-Alpes, France
[2] IRIT, Toulouse, France

Abstract. Establishing liabilities in component-based systems is a challenging task, as it requires to establish convincing evidence with respect to the occurrence of a fault, and the causality relation between the fault and a damage. The second issue is especially complex when several faults are detected and the impact of these faults on the occurrence of the failure has to be assessed. In this paper we propose a formal framework for reasoning about logical causality between contract violations.

1 Introduction

Establishing liabilities in case of litigation is generally a delicate matter. It becomes even more challenging when IT systems are involved. Generally speaking, a party can be declared liable for a damage if a fault can be attributed to that party and that fault has caused the damage. The two key issues are thus to establish convincing evidence with respect to (1) the occurrence of the fault and (2) the causality relation between the fault and the damage. The first issue concerns the technique used to log the relevant events of the system and to ensure that the logs can be produced (and have some value) in court. The second issue is especially complex when several faults are detected in the logs and the impact of these faults on the occurrence of the failure has to be assessed. In this paper, we focus on this second issue and propose a formal framework for reasoning about causality. A system based on this framework could be used to provide relevant information to the expert, the judge, or the parties themselves (in case of amicable settlement) to analyze the origin of the failure of an IT system.

The notion of causality has been studied for a long time in computer science, but with very different perspectives and goals. In the distributed systems community, causality (following Lamport's seminal paper [11]) is seen essentially as a temporal property. In our context, the temporal ordering contributes to the analysis, but it is obviously not sufficient to establish the *logical causality* required to rule on a matter of liability: the fact that an event e_1 has occurred before an event e_2 does not imply that e_1 was the cause for e_2 (or that e_2 would not have occurred if e_1 had not occurred).

Causality has also been studied by logicians (e.g. in the framework of deontic logic or extensions of classical propositional logic), but in a very abstract way, without consideration for actual behaviors of software components or application to software traces. In this paper, we contribute to filling the gap between these two trends of work and provide ways to reason on component traces to establish

G. Roşu et al. (Eds.): RV 2010, LNCS 6418, pp. 270–284, 2010.

causality properties which go beyond temporal causality and can be used to assess the role of a fault in the occurrence of a failure.

In Section 2, we introduce our formal model of IT system based on components interacting according to well identified *interaction models*. Each component is associated with an individual *contract* which specifies its expected behavior. The system itself is associated with a *global contract* which is assumed to be implied by the composition of the individual contracts.

We first define several variants of logical causality in Section 3. The first variant, *necessary causality*, characterizes cases when the global contract would not have been violated if the local contract had been fulfilled. The second variant, *sufficient causality*, characterizes cases when the global contract would have been violated even if all the other components had fulfilled their contracts. In other words, the violation of its contract by a single component was sufficient to violate the global contract.

We further show that our definitions of causality are decidable in the introduced setting. We also provide conditions for decidability on trace suffixes. Such a possibility is of great practical significance because it makes it possible to analyze traces back to a given point in the past. Indeed, the analysis of liability in real cases can hardly assume that all traces of the past can always be produced and analyzed.

In Section 4, we sketch a case study, an adaptive cruise control system inspired from [1], and illustrate the definitions of Section 3 with different sets of execution traces giving rise to different combinations of causality.

In order to be able to trace the propagation of faults, we define in Section 5 *horizontal causality*, which relates prefixes of local traces of components on the same level of hierarchy. Horizontal causality allows to analyze causality among violations of component contracts.

Finally, Section 6 is devoted to a discussion of related work and Section 7 draws some conclusions and outlines perspectives for further work.

2   The Contract Framework

In this section we introduce a framework for reasoning about components and their interactions, contracts, and traces. We use labeled transition systems to model contracts.

Definition 1 (LTS). *A labeled transition system (LTS) over an action alphabet Σ is a tuple $B = (Q, q^0, \Sigma, \rightarrow)$ with Q a finite set of states, $q^0 \in Q$ an initial state, and $\rightarrow: Q \times \Sigma \times Q$ is transition relation.*

A component is an LTS. Throughout this paper, we make the assumption that components are black boxes whose traces of actions can be observed, whereas the internal behavior is unknown.

Composition of LTS is defined by a composition operation which is parametrized with an *interaction model*.

Definition 2 (Interaction model). *Given LTSs B_i with disjoint alphabets Σ_i, an interaction α over $\Sigma = \bigcup_i \Sigma_i$ is a non-empty subset of Σ of actions taking place simultaneously. An interaction model IM over the set of LTS is a set of interactions over Σ such that $\bigcup_{\alpha \in IM} \alpha = \Sigma$. We suppose that each action participates in exactly one interaction: $\forall \alpha_1, \alpha_2 \in IM : \alpha_1 \cap \alpha_2 \neq \emptyset \implies \alpha_1 = \alpha_2$.
For $\alpha \in IM$, let $\alpha(k) = \alpha \cap \Sigma_k$ be the actions of B_k participating in α.*

For simplicity, we write $a_1|a_2$ for the interaction $\alpha = \{a_1, a_2\}$.

Example 1. Consider the architecture of the system in Figure 3. Components are represented as boxes, actions as bullets, and interactions as lines connecting actions. For instance, we have $sld_o \in \Sigma_{SLD}$, $acc_i^s \in \Sigma_{ACC}$, and $sld_o|acc_i^s \in IM$. The latter interaction is a rendez-vous, modeling a hand-shake between SLD and ACC.

Definition 3 (Composition of LTS). *Given LTSs $B_i = (Q_i, q_i^0, \Sigma_i, \rightarrow_i)$, $i = 1, ..., n$, and an interaction model IM over $\bigcup_i \Sigma_i$, let their composition be the LTS $\|_{IM}\{B_i\} = (Q, q^0, IM, \rightarrow)$ where*

- *$Q = Q_1 \times ... \times Q_n$ and $q^0 = (q_1^0, \cdots, q_n^0)$;*
- *$(q_1, ..., q_n) \xrightarrow{\alpha} (q_1', ..., q_n')$ if for $i = 1, ..., n$, either $\alpha(i) = \emptyset$ and $q_i = q_i'$, or $q_i \xrightarrow{\alpha(i)}_i q_i'$.*

We extend the notion of interaction model to individual components, such that the interaction model of a component with action alphabet Σ is the set of singleton interactions $IM = \{\{a\} \mid a \in \Sigma\}$. This allows us to apply the following definitions both on the component and system level.

Definition 4 (Trace). *A trace tr over IM is a sequence of interactions in IM.*

Let IM^* and IM^ω denote the set of finite and infinite traces over IM, respectively. Let $tr[i..j]$ be the infix of tr between positions i and j and $tr[i]$ be the interaction occurring at position i. We suppose that each trace begins at position 1.

Definition 5 (Acceptance). *A trace tr over IM is accepted by an LTS $B = (Q, q^0, \Sigma, \rightarrow)$, noted $tr \models B$, if there exists a sequence of states $q_0, \cdots, q_i, \cdots$ of Q such that $q_0 = q^0$ and for all $i \geq 0$, $(q^i, tr[i+1], q^{i+1}) \in \rightarrow$.*

Given a *global* trace of $\|_{IM}\{B_i\}$, the component traces are obtained by projection.

Definition 6 (Projection). *The projection $\pi_k(tr)$ on B_k of a global trace $tr = \alpha_1.\alpha_2 \cdots \alpha_i \cdots$ over an interaction model IM is obtained by removing all empty interactions from the trace $\alpha_1(k).\alpha_2(k) \cdots \alpha_i(k) \cdots$.*

We use assume/guarantee-contracts (see e.g. [3]) to specify the expected behavior of black-box components interacting with each other, and conversely, limit the responsibility of a component if an assumption on its use is not satisfied.

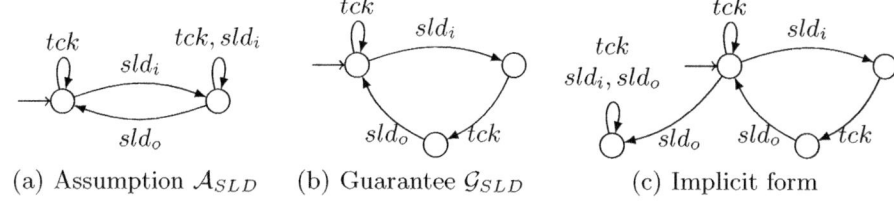

(a) Assumption $\mathcal{A}_{SLD}$ (b) Guarantee $\mathcal{G}_{SLD}$ (c) Implicit form

Fig. 1. A contract $\mathcal{C}_{SLD}$ for the SLD component

Definition 7 (Contract). *A contract over a component with interaction model IM is a pair $(\mathcal{A}, \mathcal{G})$ of deterministic LTSs over IM, where $\mathcal{A}$ is called* assumption *and $\mathcal{G}$* guarantee.

Example 2. We consider in Fig. 1 a contract $\mathcal{C}_{SLD}$ regarding the behavior of a *Speed Limit Detector* component (SLD) embedded in a car. It communicates with the environment though a sensor in order to get the speed limitation (sld_i) and is then able to forward this information (sld_o) in the system. Time is discretized with the tick (tck) action. According to Fig. 1(b), the component guarantees to forward each received input (sld_i) after one tick. The assumption of SLD is specified in Fig. 1(a): the guarantee will hold if the environment re-emits each input (sld_i) until it has been transmitted (sld_o).

Definition 8 (Satisfaction). *A trace tr over IM satisfies a contract $C = (\mathcal{A}, \mathcal{G})$, noted $tr \models C$, if for i the maximal position for which $tr[1..i] \models \mathcal{A}$ we have $tr[1..i] \models \mathcal{G}$.*

Example 3. The trace $tr_1 = sld_i.tck.sld_o.sld_i.tck.sld_o.tck.sld_i.tck.sld_o$ satisfies the contract in Fig. 1 whereas $tr_2 = sld_i.tck.sld_o.sld_i.tck.tck.sld_o.sld_i$ does not as $tr_2[6] \models \mathcal{A}_{SLD}$ but $tr_2[6] \not\models \mathcal{G}_{SLD}$.

The *implicit form* of a contract $\mathcal{C}$ is an LTS characterizing the set of traces satisfying $\mathcal{C}$.

Definition 9 (Implicit form). *Given a contract $C = (\mathcal{A}, \mathcal{G})$ over a component with interaction model IM, we call* implicit form *$\mathcal{IF}(C)$ of C the LTS $(Q_{\mathcal{A}} \times Q_{\mathcal{G}} \cup \{\top\}, (q_{\mathcal{A}}^0, q_{\mathcal{G}}^0), IM, \to)$ with the following transitions:*

- $(q_{\mathcal{A}}, q_{\mathcal{G}}) \xrightarrow{\alpha} (q_{\mathcal{A}}', q_{\mathcal{G}}')$ *if* $q_{\mathcal{A}} \xrightarrow{\alpha}_{\mathcal{A}} q_{\mathcal{A}}'$ *and* $q_{\mathcal{G}} \xrightarrow{\alpha}_{\mathcal{G}} q_{\mathcal{G}}'$
- $(q_{\mathcal{A}}, q_{\mathcal{G}}) \xrightarrow{\alpha} \top$ *if there is no transition labeled by α stemming from $q_{\mathcal{A}}$ in $\mathcal{A}$*
- $\top \xrightarrow{\alpha} \top$ *for all $\alpha \in IM$*

Example 4. The implicit form of the contract $\mathcal{C}_{SLD}$ is depicted in Fig. 1(c).

Proposition 1. $tr \models \mathcal{IF}(C) \iff tr \models C$

According to Proposition 1, satisfaction of a contract $\mathcal{C}$ can be verified by checking acceptance by the implicit form of $\mathcal{C}$.

Hypothesis 1. *Given a set of contracts C_i over components B_i, $i = 1, ..., n$, we require the contracts C_i to be consistent, that is, for all traces tr of $B = \|_{IM}\{B_i\}$,*

$$(\forall i : \pi_i(tr) \models C_i) \implies (\forall i : \pi_i(tr) \models G_i)$$

Similarly, for global contracts $(\mathcal{A}, \mathcal{G})$ over B, we assume that

$$(\forall i : \pi_i(tr) \models C_i) \implies tr \models \mathcal{G}$$

The satisfaction of this hypothesis can be effectively checked using results from [9].

In the remainder of this paper we consider a system with n components interacting together as described by a fixed interaction model *IM*. We suppose that the activity of each component is logged locally, yielding a trace of component actions.

3   Logical Causality

In contrast to the notion of precedence established by Lamport clocks [11] and vector clocks [8,13], we introduce stronger conditions for causality between the violation of a component contract and the subsequent violation of a global contract.

3.1   Definition

We define three notions of vertical causality (or causality for short): weak, necessary, and sufficient causality. Let $C_i = (\mathcal{A}_i, \mathcal{G}_i)$ be component contracts over components B_i, *IM* be an interaction model, and $C = (\mathcal{A}, \mathcal{G})$ be a global contract over $B = \|_{IM}\{B_i\}$. Let tr_i be a trace of B_i, $i = 1, ..., n$.

According to our hypothesis, the behavior at execution time is logged separately for each component. The obtained vector of local traces does not define a unique global trace, in general. Therefore, vertical causality is not defined as a relation between events of a local and a global trace, but as a predicate on the prefixes of local traces.

Weak causality formalizes the fact that the violation of a global guarantee is preceded (in the usual sense of causality in distributed systems) by the violation of the guarantee of a component contract.

Definition 10 (Weak causality). $tr_k[1..i]$ *is a potential cause of the violation of $\mathcal{G}$, written $tr_k[1..i] \nearrow_{C_k} \mathcal{G}$, if $tr_k[1..i] \not\models \mathcal{G}_k$, there exists a global trace $\mathbf{tr}$ over IM such that $\forall \ell : \pi_\ell(\mathbf{tr}) = tr_\ell$, and $\exists j : |\pi_k(\mathbf{tr}[1..j])| = i$, $\mathbf{tr}[j](k) \neq \emptyset$, and $j \leq \min\{m \mid \mathbf{tr}[1..m] \not\models \mathcal{G}\} < \infty$.*

Intuitively, the prefix $tr_k[1..i]$ is a potential cause of the violation of $\mathcal{G}$ if for some global trace $\mathbf{tr}$ having the observed projections, the position j of interaction $tr_k[i]$ in $\mathbf{tr}$ is between the violation of $\mathcal{G}_k$ and a subsequent violation of $\mathcal{G}$. Weak causality is illustrated in Figure 2.

Weak causality is complete in the sense that each violation of a global contract has a weak cause. The claim follows from Hypothesis 1.

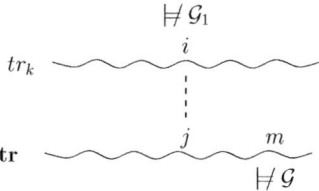

Fig. 2. Weak causality between prefix $tr_k[1..i]$ and a possible global trace **tr**

Definition 11 (Necessary causality). $tr_k[1..i]$ *is a necessary cause of the violation of* $\mathcal{G}$*, written* $tr_k[1..i] \nearrow^{n}_{\mathcal{C}_k} \mathcal{G}$*, if* $tr_k[1..i] \nearrow_{\mathcal{C}_k} \mathcal{G}$ *and*

$$\forall \mathbf{tr'} \in IM^* \ s.t. \ \left(|\pi_k(\mathbf{tr'})| \geq i \ \wedge \ \forall j \in \{1, ..., n\} \setminus \{k\} : \pi_j(\mathbf{tr'}) = tr_j \right) :$$
$$\left(\pi_k(\mathbf{tr'})[1..i] \models \mathcal{G}_k \implies \mathbf{tr'} \models \mathcal{G} \right)$$

That is, $tr_k[1..i]$ is a necessary cause of the violation of $\mathcal{G}$ if it is a weak cause, and replacing $tr_k[1..i]$ with a prefix $\pi_k(\mathbf{tr'})[1..i]$ satisfying $\mathcal{G}_k$ while keeping all other traces, would not have violated the global guarantee.

Given a set S of traces, we call a trace $tr \in S$ *maximal* if tr is not a strict prefix of some trace in S.

Definition 12 (Sufficient causality). $tr_k[1..i]$ *is a sufficient cause of the violation of* $\mathcal{G}$*, written* $tr_k[1..i] \nearrow^{s}_{\mathcal{C}_k} \mathcal{G}$*, if* $tr_k[1..i] \nearrow_{\mathcal{C}_k} \mathcal{G}$ *and* $\forall \mathbf{tr'} \in IM^* \cup IM^\omega:$

$$\left(\left(\forall p \in \{1, ..., n\} \setminus \{k\} : \pi_p(\mathbf{tr'}) \models \mathcal{C}_p \ \wedge \ \pi_k(\mathbf{tr'}) = tr_k \right) \right. \tag{1}$$
$$\left. \wedge \ \mathbf{tr'} \ \text{is maximal among the traces satisfying (1)} \right) \implies \mathbf{tr'} \not\models \mathcal{G}$$

Thus, $tr_k[1..i]$ is a sufficient cause of the violation of $\mathcal{G}$ if it is a weak cause, and replacing all traces except for tr_k with traces satisfying the component contracts, would also lead to a violation of the global guarantee. Maximality ensures $\mathbf{tr'}$ to be long enough for the effects of the violation of $\mathcal{G}_k$ to be propagated.

3.2   Decidability

We now discuss algorithmic procedures to test the different kinds of causality previously defined, in the context of the component framework introduced in Section 2.

Theorem 1. *Weak, sufficient, and necessary causality are decidable.*

Due to space limitations we only focus on the decision procedure for sufficient causality (Definition 12).

The first step consists in reconstituting the possible global traces of the system. For this, we define the composition of local traces and therefore consider the symbolic encoding of a trace as an LTS. A trace $tr_k = \alpha_1...\alpha_n$ of a component with alphabet Σ_k can be represented by the LTS $\mathcal{T}(tr_k) = (Q, q^0, \Sigma_k, \rightarrow)$ where $Q = \{q^0, \cdots, q^n\}$ and which has, for each interaction α_i, a transition (q^i, α_i, q^{i+1}). Then, the set of global traces $\mathbf{tr}$ whose projections coincide with observed local traces tr_i is characterized by the LTS $\|_{IM}\{\mathcal{T}(tr_i)\}$:

Proposition 2. $\mathbf{tr} \models \|_{IM}\{\mathcal{T}(tr_i) \mid i = 1, ..., n\} \iff \forall i = 1, ..., n : \pi_i(\mathbf{tr}) = tr_i$

To decide sufficient causality, the following sets of traces must be considered:

$$S_k = \{\mathbf{tr}' \in IM^* \text{ s.t. } \pi_k(\mathbf{tr}') = tr_k\} \tag{2}$$

$$S_j = \{\mathbf{tr}' \in IM^* \cup IM^\omega \text{ s.t. } \pi_j(\mathbf{tr}') \models C_j\}, \ j \in \{1, ..., n\} \setminus \{k\} \tag{3}$$

The LTS B_k characterizing S_k is given by $\mathcal{T}(tr_k)$. The LTS B_j for S_j is obtained by taking the implicit form $\mathcal{IF}(C_j)$ of C_j. Let $B = \|_{IM}\{B_i \mid i = 1, ..., n\}$.

It then suffices to tell if no maximal trace of B satisfies $\mathcal{G}$. This second step can be achieved via the following binary relation $\#$ on LTS called *inconsistency*. We call *sink state* a state of an LTS without any outgoing transition.

Definition 13 (Inconsistency). *Consider two LTS $S = (Q_S, q_S^0, IM, \rightarrow_S)$ and $T = (Q_T, q_T^0, IM, \rightarrow_T)$. Let $\preceq \subseteq Q_T \times Q_S$ be the greatest solution of*

$$\preceq = \{(q_T, q_S) \mid sink(q_T) \vee \exists \alpha \in IM. \exists q_T' \in Q_T. \exists q_S' \in Q_S :$$
$$q_T \xrightarrow{\alpha}_T q_T' \wedge q_S \xrightarrow{\alpha}_S q_S' \wedge q_T' \preceq q_S'\}$$

T is inconsistent with S (written $T\#S$) if $q_T^0 \npreceq q_S^0$.

Two LTS S and T are inconsistent if no maximal trace of T is accepted by S.

Proposition 3. $T\#S \iff (\forall tr : tr \text{ is a maximal trace of } T \implies tr \not\models S)$.

Thus, to decide sufficient causality, one has to check if no maximal trace of B satisfies $\mathcal{G}$, that is, whether $B\#\mathcal{G}$.

3.3   Causality Analysis on Bounded Past

The decision procedure described above requires, in the worst case, the local traces to be inspected entirely to determine causality between two traces. However, for systems that must guarantee a high degree of availability such as embedded and telecommunication systems, it is in general not be feasible to keep the full traces since the initialization of the system. Therefore we now discuss the stability of the definitions of causality when applied to suffixes of traces, in order to make causality analysis feasible in practice.

Consider a vector of traces (tr_i), and a suffix $tr_i' = tr_i[j_i..n_i]$ of each trace, with $n_i = |tr_i|$, such that the suffixes are obtained by the projection of some global trace: $\exists \mathbf{tr} \ \forall i : \pi_i(\mathbf{tr}) = tr_i'$, that is, the suffixes agree on the common interactions. We can now interpret the different definitions of causality over the suffixes tr_i' rather than tr_i. We have the following results:

Weak causality over suffixes is exact if the suffixes are sufficiently long to contain an interaction between the considered components.

The definitions of *necessary and sufficient causality* depend on the satisfaction of a contract and/or a guarantee by some prefix. As the simple assumption that they were satisfied by the missing prefix might be overly optimistic and compromise the legal value of the results, we suggest the following solution. For each contract $(\mathcal{A}, \mathcal{G})$, construct two observers $O(\mathcal{A})$ and $O(\mathcal{G})$ by adding to the LTS distinct $\perp$ states modeling that the observed trace does not satisfy the LTS, and transitions to $\perp$ so as to make the observer receptive to all possible traces. For each component, the log encompasses, in addition to the trace, a Boolean flag for each contract, indicating whether the contract was satisfied by the missing prefix, and the state of the observers at the end of the missing prefix. Therefore, the satisfaction of any contract, its assumption, and guarantee, can be computed exactly for each prefix of tr_i' from the log. The only remaining approximation is the matching of the projection of hypothetical traces $\pi_i(\mathbf{tr}')$ with tr_i, which we have to over-approximate by matching with the suffixes tr_i'.

It is now straight-forward to reformulate the definitions of causality using the bounded traces and observer states, and it can be shown that these approximated definitions are sound, in the sense that they under-approximate the exact definitions of causality.

4   Case Study: Adaptive Cruise Control

In this section, we illustrate our definitions of causality with a simple, but realistic, case study, an adaptive cruise control system inspired from [1]. The goal of the system, which is depicted in Fig. 3, is to automatically adjust the speed of a car in order to maintain a security distance with any front car and to comply with speed limitations. To this aim, the system includes two dedicated components, an *Object Recognition* component (OR) using a radar to provide the distance with the nearest object in front of the car and a *System Limit Detector* (SLD) communicating with road sign transmitters to get the current speed limit. The *Switch* component allows the driver to activate or deactivate the adaptive cruise control via a button on the *HMI* (Human Machine Interface) component. The core of the system is the *Adaptive Cruise Control* component (ACC) which decides from the speed limit, the distance with the object in front of the car, and the current speed, either to accelerate or to brake. The last two components are the *Throttle System* (TS) and the *Brake System* (BS) to activate the throttle and brake respectively.

The contracts of the components and the global contract of the system involve complex properties such as, for example, the conditions under which the SLD and OR components must send a new signal to the ACC component or the rules to be applied by ACC to determine the action to be taken. For the sake of conciseness, we focus on a single, but critical, aspect of the specifications in this section: timeliness. The issue of composing multiple contracts describing different aspects has been largely studied in [9].

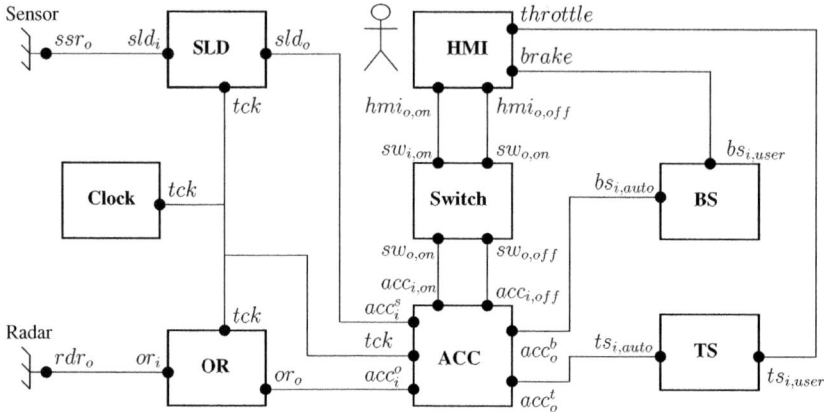

Fig. 3. Architecture of the cruise control system

Time is represented in the architecture through a *Clock* component which synchronizes with SLD, OR, and ACC through a rendez-vous on tck actions. Following the contract $\mathcal{C}_{SLD}$ in Fig. 1, exactly one clock tick action is allowed between an input sld_i and the corresponding output sld_o. We associate to OR a similar contract $\mathcal{C}_{OR}$ imposing also a delay of one tick between the occurrence of or_i and of or_o in $\mathcal{G}_{OR}$. For $\mathcal{G}_{ACC}$, there again the delay of reaction between the reception of input(s) acc_i^s and/or acc_i^o and the emission of the output acc_o^b or acc_o^t is fixed to 1. The assumption of $\mathcal{C}_{ACC}$ is the LTS accepting any traces in Σ_{ACC}^* for which any two occurrences of acc_i^s are separated by at least one tck.

Globally, in order to ensure the security of the car and compliance with speed regulations, the end-to-end throughput of the system must be less than three ticks. The guarantee of the global contract is then the LTS accepting the traces formed by the repetition of the sequence starting by any interleaving of $ssr_o|sld_i.sld_o|acc_i^s$ and $rdr_o|or_i.or_o|acc_i^o$ followed by $acc_o^b|bs_{i,auto}$ or $acc_o^t|ts_{i,auto}$ with at most three ticks in each sequence. It is easy to check that the set of local time constraints implies the global time constraint.

In the following, we consider successively scenarios involving failures within dependent (serial) components and independent (parallel) components. We use Δ, Δ_{SLD}, Δ_{OR} and Δ_{ACC} to denote the global delay and the delays observed for components SLD, OR, and ACC respectively. Local contracts impose that $\Delta_{SLD} = 1$, $\Delta_{OR} = 1$ and $\Delta_{ACC} = 1$, and the global guarantee requires that $\Delta \leq 3$.

4.1   Failures within Dependent Components

We first focus on failures involving serial components: the SLD and ACC components. The same scenarios can be transposed to any pair of dependent components (HMI and Switch, Switch and ACC, OR and ACC, etc.).

Two necessary causes. Let us consider first the following trace excerpts:

SLD: ... sld_i, tck, tck, sld_o, tck, tck, ...
ACC: ... tck, tck, acc_i^s, tck, tck, acc_o^b, ...

In these traces, both SLD and ACC violate their contracts ($\Delta_{SLD} = 2$, $\Delta_{ACC} = 2$), which leads to a violation of the global timing constraint ($\Delta = 4 > 3$). From the definition of Section 3, we obtain that both SLD and ACC failures are necessary causes for the global failure. Indeed, would any of them have been avoided, then the global delay would not have exceeded the threshold of 3.

One necessary and sufficient cause. We consider the following trace excerpts:

SLD: ... sld_i, tck, tck, tck, sld_o, tck, tck, ...
ACC: ... tck, tck, tck, acc_i^s, tck, tck, acc_o^t, ...

Again both SLD and ACC violate their contracts but SLD's violation is more serious ($\Delta_{SLD} = 3$, $\Delta_{ACC} = 2$). The definitions of Section 3 show that SLD's violation is a necessary and sufficient cause for the global failure but the violation of ACC is no longer a necessary cause. Similarly, the case where ACC's violation would be the most serious ($\Delta_{SLD} = 2$, $\Delta_{ACC} = 3$) would lead to identify ACC's violation as a necessary and sufficient cause.

Two sufficient causes. The following trace excerpts exhibit yet another causality pattern:

SLD: ... sld_i, tck, tck, tck, sld_o, tck, tck, tck ...
ACC: ... tck, tck, tck, acc_i^s, tck, tck, tck, acc_o^b, ...

Both SLD and ACC violate their contracts in the more serious way ($\Delta_{SLD} = 3$, $\Delta_{ACC} = 3$). Indeed, the definitions of Section 3 show that both violations are sufficient causes for the global failure.

4.2   Failures within Independent Components

To illustrate failures between independent components, we focus on cases involving the SLD and OR components. The same scenarios can occur between any pair of independent components (HMI and OR, Switch and SLD, etc.).

One necessary and sufficient cause. Consider first the following trace excerpts:

SLD: ... sld_i, tck, tck, tck, sld_o, tck, ...
OR: ... or_i, tck, tck, or_o, tck, tck, ...
ACC: ... tck, tck, acc_i^o, tck, acc_i^s, tck, acc_o^t, ...

Again both SLD and OR violate their contracts but SLD's violation is more serious ($\Delta_{sld} = 3$, $\Delta_{or} = 2$). Indeed, the definitions of Section 3 show that SLD's violation is a necessary and sufficient cause for the global failure.

Two sufficient causes. As a final example, consider the following trace excerpts:

SLD: $\ldots sld_i, tck, tck, tck, sld_o, tck, \ldots$
OR: $\ldots or_i, tck, tck, tck, or_o, tck, \ldots$
ACC: $\ldots tck, tck, tck, acc_i^o, acc_i^s, tck, acc_o^b, \ldots$

Both SLD and OR violate their contracts in the most serious way ($\Delta_{SLD} = 3$, $\Delta_{OR} = 3$) and the definitions of Section 3 show that both violations are sufficient causes for the global failure.

5   Horizontal Causality

As an extension of the framework we introduce horizontal causality, which relates prefixes of traces of components on the same level of hierarchy. If one is interested in the causality among violations of *local* contracts — for instance, in order to precisely establish the scenario leading to the violation of a global contract —, horizontal causality allows us to refine the analysis of vertical causality with further information about dependencies between contract violations.

Let $C_i = (\mathcal{A}_i, \mathcal{G}_i)$ be component contracts over components B_i, and $B = \|_{IM}\{B_i\}$. Let tr_i be a trace of B_i, $i = 1, ..., n$.

Definition 14 (Weak horizontal causality). *The prefix $tr_1[1..i]$ is a weak cause of the violation of $\mathcal{G}_2$ by $tr_2[1..j]$, written $tr_1[1..i] \rightarrow_{C_1,C_2} tr_2[1..j]$, if $tr_1[1..i] \not\models \mathcal{G}_1$, $tr_2[1..j] \not\models \mathcal{A}_2$, and there exists a global trace $\mathbf{tr}$ over IM such that $\forall \ell : \pi_\ell(\mathbf{tr}) = tr_\ell$, and $\exists k : |\pi_1(\mathbf{tr}[1..k])| = i$, $|\pi_2(\mathbf{tr}[1..k])| = j$, $\mathbf{tr}[k](1) \neq \emptyset$, $\mathbf{tr}[k](2) \neq \emptyset$, and $k \leq \min\{k' \mid tr_2[1..k'] \not\models \mathcal{G}_2\} < \infty$.*

Intuitively, $tr_1[1..i]$ is a potential cause of the violation of $\mathcal{G}_2$ by $tr_2[1..j]$ after k if there is an interaction between components 1 and 2 at position (i,j) after a violation of $\mathcal{G}_1$, $\mathcal{A}_2$ is violated at or before j, and $\mathcal{G}_2$ is subsequently violated.

In order to be able to trace the propagation of faults, we define *necessary* and *sufficient* horizontal causality. Intuitively, a contract violation would not have happened without collusion of a necessary cause. Conversely, a violation would also have occurred with only one sufficient cause, with all other components behaving correctly. Notice that we do not require the assumption of the downstream component to be satisfied up to the contract violation, in order to account for multiple causes.

Definition 15 (Necessary horizontal causality). *$tr_k[1..i]$ is a necessary cause of the violation of $\mathcal{G}_\ell$, written $tr_k[1..i] \rightarrow^{\mathbf{n}}_{C_k,C_\ell} tr_\ell[1..j]$, if $tr_k[1..i] \rightarrow_{C_k,C_\ell} tr_\ell[1..j]$ and*

$$\forall \mathbf{tr}' \in IM^* \text{ s.t. } \left(|\pi_k(\mathbf{tr}')| \geq i \wedge \forall p \in \{1, ..., n\} \setminus \{k, \ell\} : \pi_p(\mathbf{tr}') = tr_p \wedge$$
$$\pi_\ell(\mathbf{tr}')[1..j-1] = tr_\ell[1..j-1]\right) :$$
$$\left(\pi_k(\mathbf{tr}')[1..i] \models \mathcal{G}_k \wedge \pi_\ell(\mathbf{tr}') \models C_\ell \implies \pi_\ell(\mathbf{tr}') \models \mathcal{G}_\ell\right)$$

Definition 15 is illustrated in Fig. 4. Intuitively, $tr_k[1..i]$ is a necessary cause of the violation of $\mathcal{G}_\ell$ by $tr_\ell[1..j]$ if it is a weak cause, and replacing the faulty trace tr_k and the faulty suffix of tr_ℓ with correct traces ensures $\mathcal{G}_\ell$ to be respected.

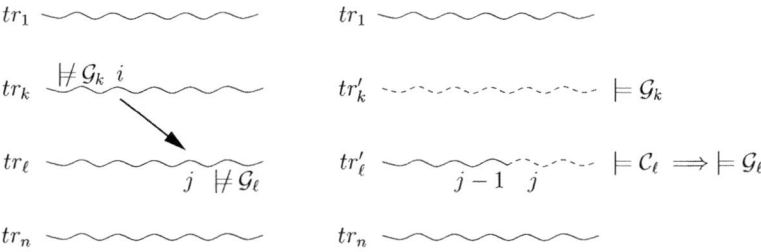

Fig. 4. Necessary horizontal causality $tr_k[1..i] \rightarrow^{\mathsf{n}}_{\mathcal{C}_k,\mathcal{C}_\ell} tr_\ell[1..j]$

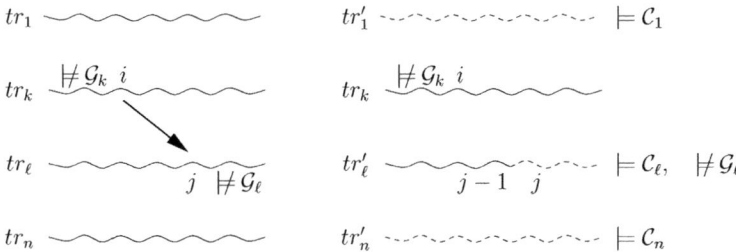

Fig. 5. Sufficient horizontal causality $tr_k[1..i] \rightarrow^{\mathsf{s}}_{\mathcal{C}_k,\mathcal{C}_\ell} tr_\ell[1..j]$

Definition 16 (Sufficient horizontal causality). $tr_k[1..i]$ *is a sufficient cause of the violation of* $\mathcal{G}_\ell$, *written* $tr_k[1..i] \rightarrow^{\mathsf{s}}_{\mathcal{C}_k,\mathcal{C}_\ell} tr_\ell[1..j]$, *if* $tr_k[1..i] \rightarrow_{\mathcal{C}_k,\mathcal{C}_\ell} tr_\ell[1..j]$ *and*

$$\forall \mathbf{tr}' \in IM^* \; s.t. \; \Big(\forall p \in \{1,...,n\} \setminus \{k\} : \pi_p(\mathbf{tr}') \models \mathcal{C}_p \; \wedge \; \pi_k(\mathbf{tr}') = tr_k \; \wedge$$

$$\pi_\ell(\mathbf{tr}')[1..j-1] = tr_\ell[1...j-1] \Big) : \pi_\ell(\mathbf{tr}') \not\models \mathcal{G}_\ell$$

Definition 16 is illustrated in Fig. 5. Intuitively, $tr_k[1..i]$ is a sufficient cause of the violation of $\mathcal{G}_\ell$ by $tr_\ell[1..j]$ if it is a weak cause, and replacing all local traces except for tr_k with correct traces still results in a violation of $\mathcal{G}_\ell$.

Example 5. Consider the scenario where SLD violates its local contract by sending an output twice, which violates ACC's assumption and causes ACC to stop producing outputs and violate its local guarantee and the global contract:

SLD: $sld_i, tck, sld_o, sld_o, tck, tck, tck, ...$
ACC: $tck, acc_i^s, acc_i^s, tck, tck, tck, ...$

According to Definition 12, the trace of SLD is considered as a sufficient cause for the violation of the global contract. The analysis of horizontal causality provides additional insights on the propagation of the failure: the trace of SLD is by Definition 15 a necessary cause and by Definition 16 a sufficient cause for the violation of $\mathcal{G}_{ACC}$.

6   Related Work

The research described here has been conducted in the context of a multidisci-
plinary project involving lawyers and computer scientists with the aim to put
forward a set of methods and tools (1) to define software liability in a precise
and unambiguous way and (2) to establish such liability in case of incident. On
the legal side, the notion of causality is essential in contractual liability as well
as tort law [6,18]. Among the crucial issues regarding the notion of causality are
the assertion of the existence of a causality relation between two events and the
treatment of multiple causes. A key condition for the existence of causality in
European tort law is the *conditio sine qua non*: "An activity or conduct is a
cause of the victim's damage if, in the absence of the activity, the damage would
not have occurred"[1], which is close to the so called "but for" test in British law
or the "proximate cause" in American law. This condition is captured by our
definition of necessary causality in Section 3.

The notion of causality appears directly or indirectly in different areas of computer science, with different flavors and for different purposes. On the theoretical
side, causality is usually seen as a temporal property in the distributed systems
community. In our context, the temporal ordering contributes to the analysis
(see the definition of weak causality in Section 3), but it is obviously not sufficient to establish the *logical causality* required to rule on a matter of liability:
the fact that an event e_1 has occurred before an event e_2 does not imply that e_1
was the cause for e_2 (or that e_2 would not have occurred if e_1 had not occurred).

The notions of faults, errors and failures have been studied extensively in the
areas of computer related risks and system dependability [14,2,12]. The dependencies between failures are often represented as fault trees [10] or FMEA (Failure Mode and Effect Analysis) tables or their FMECA (Failure Mode, Effects
and Criticality Analysis) extension [17]. A fault tree represents combinations of
events (based on AND and OR connectors) leading to a given failure. On the
other hand, an FMEA table identifies all potential effects of a given cause. In
other words, fault trees favor top-down approaches (from failures to their potential causes) when FMEA naturally leads to bottom-up analyses (from causes to
their consequences). In both cases however, the analysis is based on the exper-
tise of the designers of the system. The work presented here is complementary
to the fault tree and FMEA approaches in several ways: first, our analysis is
conducted a posteriori, based on real execution traces, and its results rely on a
formal model of the system. Therefore these results are well-founded and can be
used as evidence in case of dispute between the parties.

Causality has also been studied by logicians. For example, [7] explores different
notions of responsibility in a deontic setting. However, the modal operators are
characterized in a rather abstract way and no attempt is made to relate these
definitions to execution traces. In the classical logic setting, [4] proposes a logic
to reason about causes. The logic deals with transitivity of causes and allows for
predictive reasoning (deriving consequences from a cause) as well as abductive
reasoning (deriving the causes from the facts). Again, this trend of work takes

---

[1] Art. 3:101 of [6].

a fairly abstract point of view which is different from (and complementary to) the results presented in this paper.

Another related, but different area is model based diagnosis [5,15,16,19]. Diagnosis can be carried out either off-line or on-line with different cost and time constraints. Most of the contributions in this area focus on the possibility to detect the occurrence of a fault assuming certain observability properties. To our best knowledge however, the notion of logical causality as proposed here has not been considered in this context.

7   Conclusion

This paper contributes to filling the gap between the trends of work sketched in Section 6 and provides ways to reason on component traces to establish causality properties which go beyond temporal causality and can be used to assess the role of a fault in the occurrence of a failure.

A straightforward extension to this work which is not presented here for the sake of conciseness is the support for message passing within interactions and the generalization to *symbolic* components and contracts.

Another avenue for further work concerns the extension of our framework to alleviate over-approximations in the definitions of Section 3. One option to get more precise definitions of causality would be to involve the actual implementation of the components. For example, in the case of necessary causality, rather than considering the traces tr' equal to tr (except for component k), we could consider traces tr' produced by the implementations of the components (considering a correct behavior of component k). This approach introduces new issues though, such as the definition of a complete initial state for the execution of the implementations of the components.

Another useful extension concerns the notion of "group causality" which would apply to sets of actors rather than individual actors. In some cases, the information conveyed by group causality is strictly more precise than individual causality. For example, it may be the case that two events involving two actors satisfy together the criteria for necessary causality but none of them would satisfy these conditions individually. Collective (solidary or several) liability is also useful in a legal perspective [6].

Last but not least, it would also be interesting to introduce probabilities in the framework in order to reflect certain interpretations of causality in the legal sense, the differences between several causes being often considered with respect to their effects on the likeliness of the occurrence of the damage [6].

Acknowledgment. This work was supported by the French ANR project LISE number ANR-07-SESU-007.

References

1. Åkerholm, M., Carlson, J., Fredriksson, J., Hansson, H., Håkansson, J., Möller, A., Petterson, P., Tivoli, M.: The SAVE approach to component-based development of vehicular systems. The Journal of Systems and Software 80, 655–667 (2007)

2. Avizienis, A., Laprie, J.-C., Randell, B.: Fundamental concepts of computer system dependability. In: Proc. Workshop on Robot Dependability: Technological Challenge of Dependable Robots in Human Environments, pp. 21–22. IEEE, Los Alamitos (2001)

3. Benveniste, A., Caillaud, B., Ferrari, A., Mangeruca, L., Passerone, R., Sofronis, C.: Multiple viewpoint contract-based specification and design. In: de Boer, F.S., Bonsangue, M.M., Graf, S., de Roever, W.-P. (eds.) FMCO 2007. LNCS, vol. 5382, pp. 200–225. Springer, Heidelberg (2008)

4. Besnard, P., Cordier, M.-O., Moinard, Y.: Configurations for inference between causal statements. In: Lang, J., Lin, F., Wang, J. (eds.) KSEM 2006. LNCS (LNAI), vol. 4092, pp. 292–304. Springer, Heidelberg (2006)

5. Brandan-Briones, L., Lazovik, A., Dague, P.: Optimal observability for diagnosability. In: Proc. Principles of Diagnosis, DX 2008 (2008)

6. Busnelli, F.D., Comand, G., Cousy, H., Dobbs, D.B., Dufwa, B., Faure, M.G., Gilead, I., Green, M.D., Kerameus, K.D., Koch, B.A., Koziol, H., Magnus, U., Martn-Casals, M., Sinde Monteiro, J.F., Morteau, O., Neethling, J., Horton Rogers, W.V., Spier, J., Tichy, L., Widmer, P.: Principles of European Tort Law. Springer, Heidelberg (2005)

7. Cholvy, L., Cuppens, F., Saurel, C.: Towards a logical formalization of responsibility. In: Proc. ICAIL 1997, pp. 233–242. ACM Press, New York (1997)

8. Fidge, C.J.: Timestamps in message-passing systems that preserve the partial ordering. In: Raymond, K. (ed.) Proc. ACSC 1988, pp. 56–66 (1988)

9. Gössler, G., Raclet, J.-B.: Modal contracts for component-based design. In: Proc. SEFM 2009, pp. 295–303. IEEE Computer Society, Los Alamitos (2009)

10. Ericson II., C.A.: Fault tree analysis – a history. In: Proc. System Safety Conf. (1999)

11. Lamport, L.: Time, clocks, and the ordering of events in a distributed system. Communications of the ACM 21(7), 558–565 (1978)

12. Littlewood, B., Strigini, L.: Software reliability and dependability: a roadmap. In: Proc. ICSE 2000, pp. 175–188. ACM, New York (2000)

13. Mattern, F.: Virtual time and global states of distributed systems. In: Cosnard, M. (ed.) Proc. Workshop on Parallel and Distributed Algorithms, pp. 215–226. Elsevier, Amsterdam (1988)

14. Neumann, P.G.: Computer Related Risks. Addison-Wesley, Reading (1995)

15. Papadopoulos, Y.: Model-based system monitoring and diagnosis of failures using statecharts and fault trees. Reliability Engineering and System Safety 81, 325–341 (2003)

16. Picardi, C., Bray, R., Cascio, F., Console., L., Dague, P., Dressler, O., Millet, D., Rhefus., B., Struss, P., Valle, C.: integrating diagnosis in the design of automotive systems. In: Proc. ECAI 2002, pp. 628–632. IOS Press, Amsterdam (2002)

17. Picardi, C., Console, L., Berger, F., Breeman, J., Kanakis, T., Moelands, J., Collas, S., Arbaretier, E., De Domenico, N., Girardelli, E., Dressler, O., Struss, P., Zilbermann, B.: AUTAS: a tool for supporting FMECA generation in aeronautic systems. In: Proc. ECAI 2004. IOS Press, Amsterdam (2004)

18. von Bar, C.: Principles of European law, Non-contractual liability arising out of damage caused to another. Sellier (2009)

19. Yang, S., Hélouët, L., Gazagnaire, T.: Logic-based diagnosis for distributed systems. In: CRC Press (ed.) Perspectives in Concurrency Theory: A Festschrift for P. S. Thiagarajan (2009)

Reducing Configurations to Monitor in a Software Product Line

Chang Hwan Peter Kim[1], Eric Bodden[2], Don Batory[1], and Sarfraz Khurshid[1]

[1] Department of Computer Science and
Department of Electrical and Computer Engineering
The University of Texas at Austin, USA
{chpkim,batory}@cs.utexas.edu, khurshid@ece.utexas.edu
[2] Software Technology Group
Technische Universität Darmstadt, Germany
bodden@st.informatik.tu-darmstadt.de

Abstract. A software *product line* is a family of programs where each program is defined by a unique combination of features. Product lines, like conventional programs, can be checked for safety properties through execution monitoring. However, because a product line induces a number of programs that is potentially exponential in the number of features, it would be very expensive to use existing monitoring techniques: one would have to apply those techniques to every single program. Doing so would also be wasteful because many programs can provably never violate the stated property. We introduce a monitoring technique dedicated to product lines that, given a safety property, statically determines the feature combinations that cannot possibly violate the property, thus reducing the number of programs to monitor. Experiments show that our technique is effective, particularly for safety properties that crosscut many optional features.

1 Introduction

A *software product line ("SPL" or "product line" for short)* is a family of programs where each program is defined by a unique combination of *features*. By developing programs with commonalities and variabilities in a systematic way, SPLs help reduce both the time and cost of software development [17]. Unfortunately, SPLs also pose significant new challenges, as they involve reasoning about a family of programs whose cardinality may be exponential in the number of features.

In this paper, we consider the problem of runtime-monitoring SPLs for *safety property* [16] violation. We avoid monitoring every program of an SPL by statically identifying feature combinations (i.e., programs) that provably can never violate the stated property. These programs do not need to be monitored. Achieving this reduction is beneficial in at least two settings under which monitors are used. First, it can significantly speed up the testing process as these programs do not need to be run to see if the property can be violated. Second, if the

G. Roşu et al. (Eds.): RV 2010, LNCS 6418, pp. 285–299, 2010.
© Springer-Verlag Berlin Heidelberg 2010

monitor is used in production, it can speed up these programs because they are not monitored unnecessarily.

We accomplish this goal by starting with analyses that evaluate runtime monitors at compile time for *single* programs [5,6,7]. Our work extends these analyses by lifting them to understand features, making them aware of possible feature combinations. A programmer applies our analysis to an SPL once at each SPL release. The output is a bi-partitioning of feature combinations: (1) configurations that need to be monitored because violations may occur and (2) configurations for which no violation can happen.

To validate our work, we analyze two different Java-based SPLs. Experiments show we can statically rule out over half of the configurations for these case studies. Further, analyzing an entire SPL is not much more expensive than applying the earlier analyses to a single program.

To summarize, the contributions of this paper are:

- A novel static analysis to determine, for a given SPL and runtime-monitor specification, the feature combinations (programs) that require monitoring,
- An implementation of this analysis within the CLARA framework for hybrid typestate analysis [4], as an extension to Bodden et al.'s earlier whole-program analysis [6], and
- Experiments that show that our analysis noticeably reduces the number of configurations that require runtime-monitoring and thus saves testing time and program execution time for the programs studied.

2 Motivating Example

Figure 1 shows a simple example SPL, whose programs fetch and print data. There are different ways of representing a product line. In this paper, we use the *SysGen program* representation [13], where an SPL is an ordinary Java program whose members are annotated with the name of the introducing feature and statements are conditionalized using feature identifiers (in a manner similar to #ifdef).[1] Local data is fetched if the Local feature is selected (blue code), local data from a file is fetched if File is selected (yellow code) and internal contents of data are printed if Inside is selected (green code). Each member (class, field, or method) is annotated with a feature. In this example, every member is annotated with Base feature, meaning that it will be present in a program only if the Base feature is selected. A program (also referred to as a *configuration* or *feature combination*) in SysGen is instantiated by assigning a Boolean value for each feature and statically evaluating feature-conditionals and feature-annotations.

Every SPL has a *feature model* [2] that defines the legal combinations of features. The feature model for our SPL is expressed below as a context-sensitive grammar. Base is a required feature. Optional features (Inside, File, and Local) are listed in brackets.

---

[1] For presentation, we omit the class of field references in feature-conditionals and capitalize feature identifiers.

```
1    @BASE                              33   @BASE
2    class Program {                    34   class Util {
3      @BASE                            35     @BASE
4      List<String> data =             36     static String
5        new Vector<String>();         37           read(String file){...}
6                                       38
7      @BASE                            39     @BASE
8      void fetch(){                    40     static void
9        if(LOCAL)                      41           printHeader(){...}
10         fetchLocal();                42
11       data.add("done");             43     @BASE
12     }                                44     static void
13                                      45           print(List<String> data) {
14     @BASE                            46     if(INSIDE){
15     void fetchLocal(){               47       for(Iterator it =
16       if(FILE){                      48           data.iterator();
17         data.add(Util.read           49           it.hasNext();) {
18           ("secret.txt"));           50         System.out.println(it.next());
19       }                              51         System.out.println(it.next());
20       data.add(String.valueOf(       52       }
21             System.in.read()));      53     }
22     }                                54     System.out.println
23                                      55         ("size: " + data.size());
24     @BASE                            56     }
25     static void main(String args[])  57   }
26     {
27       Program p = new Program();
28       p.fetch();
29       Util.printHeader();
30       Util.print(p.data);
31     }
32   }
```

Fig. 1. Example Product Line

```
Example :: [Inside] [File] [Local] Base;
Inside or File or Local;
// Implementation constraints
(Inside implies Base) and (File implies Base) and (Local implies Base);
```

The model further requires at least one of the optional features to be selected (second line). In the last line, the feature model enforces additional implementation constraints that must hold for all programs in the product line to compile. For example, File implies Base because the code of the File feature references data (line 17, Figure 1) that belongs to Base (lines 3-5, Figure 1). A technique described elsewhere [18] can generate these implementation constraints automatically. In total, the feature model allows seven distinct programs (eight variations from three optional features then remove the case without any optional feature).

2.1   Example Monitor Specifications: ReadPrint and HasNext

Researchers have developed a multitude of specification formalisms for defining runtime monitors. As our approach extends the CLARA framework, it can generally apply to any runtime-monitoring approach that uses AspectJ aspects for monitoring. This includes popular systems such as JavaMOP [8] and tracematches [1]. For the remainder of this paper, we will use the tracematch notation because it can express monitors concisely. Figure 2(a) shows a simple example. ReadPrint prevents a print event after a read event is witnessed. In line 3 of Figure 2(a), a read symbol captures all those events in the program execution, known as *joinpoints* in AspectJ terminology, that are immediately *before* calls to Util.read*(..). Similarly, the symbol print captures joinpoints occurring immediately *before* calls to Util.print*(..). Line 6 carries the simple regular expression "read+ print", specifying that code body in lines 6–8 should execute whenever a print event follows one or more read events on the program's execution. Figure 2(b) shows a finite-state machine for this tracematch, where symbols represent transitions.

```
1  aspect  ReadPrint {
2      tracematch() {
3          sym read before:  call(* Util.read*(..));
4          sym print before:  call(* Util.print*(..));
5
6          read+ print {
7              throw new RuntimeException(''ReadPrint violation!'');
8          }
9      }
10 }
```

(a) ReadPrint Tracematch

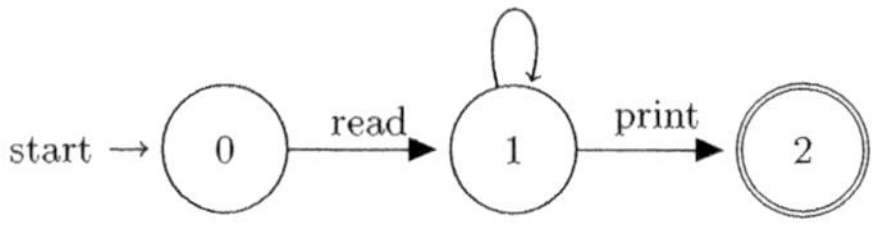

(b) Finite-State Machine

Fig. 2. ReadPrint Safety Property

Figure 3 shows another safety property, HasNext [6], which checks for iterators if next() is called twice without calling hasNext() in between. Note that this tracematch only matches if the two next() calls bind to the same Iterator object i, as shown in Figure 3(a), lines 2–4. When the tracematch encounters an event matched by a declared symbol that is not part of the regular expression, such as hasNext, the tracematch discards its partial match. Therefore, the tracematch would match a trace "next(i1) next(i1)" but not "next(i1) hasNext(i1) next(i1)", which is exactly what we seek to express.

A naive approach to runtime-monitoring would insert runtime monitors like ReadPrint and HasNext into every program of a product line. However, as we mentioned, it is often unnecessary to insert runtime monitors into some programs because these programs provably cannot trigger the runtime monitor.

```
1  aspect HasNext {
2    tracematch(Iterator i) {
3      sym next     before: call(* Iterator.next()) && target(i);
4      sym hasNext before: call(* Iterator.hasNext()) && target(i);
5
6      next next {
7        throw new RuntimeException(''HasNext violation!'');
8      }
9    }
10 }
```

(a) HasNext Tracematch

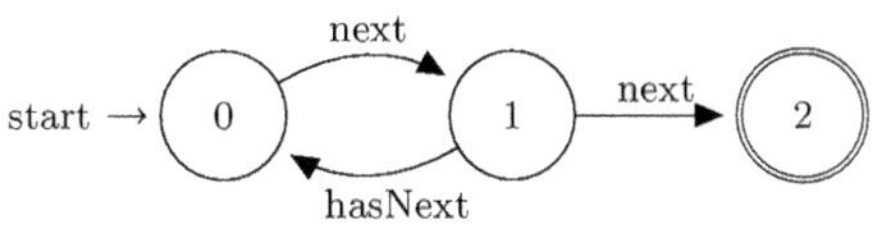

(b) Finite-state machine

Fig. 3. HasNext Safety Property [6]

2.2 Analysis by Example

Our goal is to statically determine the feature configurations to monitor, or conversely the configurations that cannot trigger the monitor. For our running example, let us first deduce these configurations by hand. For ReadPrint, both read and print symbols have to match, meaning that File (which calls read(..) in line 17) and Base (which calls print*(..) in lines 29 and 30) have to be present for the monitor to trigger. Also, Local needs to be present because it enables File's code to be reached. Therefore, the ReadPrint monitor has to be inserted if and only if these three features are present, which only holds for two out of the seven original configurations.

We represent the condition under which a monitor has to be inserted by treating a monitor, e.g. ReadPrint, as a feature itself and constructing its *presence condition*: ReadPrint iff (File and Local and Base). Similarly, the monitor for HasNext only has to be inserted iff Iterator.next() can be called, i.e., on the four configurations with Inside and Base present. The presence condition for HasNext is HasNext iff (Inside and Base). The goal of our technique is to extend the original feature model so that tracematch monitors are now features and the tracematch presence conditions are part of the revised feature model (the extension is shown in italics):

```
// ReadPrint and HasNext are now features themselves
Example :: [ReadPrint] [HasNext] [Inside] [File] [Local] Base;
// Implementation constraints
(Inside implies Base) and (File implies Base) and (Local implies Base);

// Tracematch presence conditions
ReadPrint iff (File and Local and Base);
HasNext iff (Inside and Base);
```

Note that, although a tracematch is itself a feature which can be selected or not, it is different from other features in that its selection status is determined *not* by the user, but instead by the presence or absence of other features.

2.3   The Need for a Dedicated Static Analysis for Product Lines

As mentioned earlier, there exist static analyses that improve the runtime performance of a monitor by reducing its instrumentation of a single program [5,6,7]. We will refer to these analyses as *traditional program analyses (TPA)*. There are two ways to apply such analyses to product lines. One way is inefficient, the other way imprecise. Running TPA against each instantiated program will be very inefficient because it will have to inspect every program of the product line separately. The other way is to run TPA against the product line itself. This is possible because a product line in a SysGen program representation can be treated as an ordinary program (recall that a SysGen program uses ordinary program constructs like if-conditionals, rather than pre-processor constructs like #ifdefs, to represent variability). However, this second way will be imprecise. For example, suppose we apply TPA on the ReadPrint and HasNext tracematches for our example SysGen program: both tracematches may match in the case in which all features are enabled. Being oblivious to the notion of features, the analysis will therefore report that the tracematches have to be present for every program of the product line. This shows that a static analysis, to be both efficient and effective on an SPL, has to be aware of the SPL's features.

3   Product Line Aware Static Analysis

Figure 4 displays an overview of our approach. First, for a tracematch, our analysis determines the symbols required for the tracematch to trigger ("Determine Required Symbols"). For each of these symbols, we use the aspect weaver to identify the statements that are matched ("Determine Symbol-To-Shadows"). We elaborate on these two steps in Section 3.1. Then, for each of the matched statements, we determine the feature combinations that allow the statement to be reachable from the program's main() method. This results in a set of *presence conditions*. We combine all these conditions to form the presence condition of the tracematch. We repeat the process for each tracematch ("Determine Presence Conditions") and add the tracematches and their presence conditions to the original feature model ("+"). We explain these steps in Section 3.2.

3.1   Required Symbols and Shadows

A safety property must be monitored for a feature configuration c if the code in c may drive the finite-state monitor from its initial state to its final (error) state. In earlier work [6], Bodden et al. described three different algorithms that try to determine, with increasing levels of detail, whether a single program

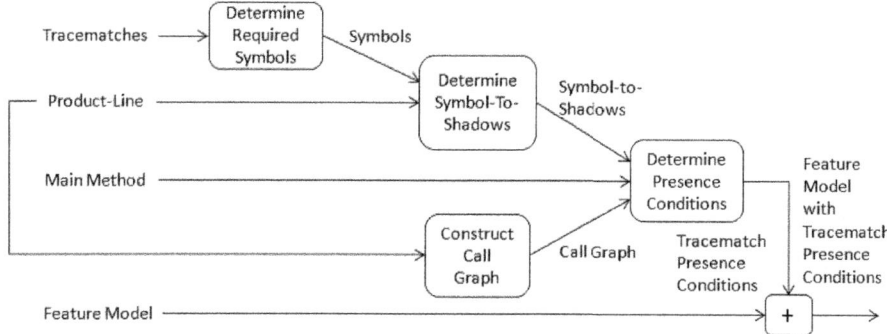

Fig. 4. Overview of Our Technique

can drive a monitor into an error state, and using which transition statements. The first, called *Quick Check*, rules out a tracematch if the program does not contain transition statements required to reach the final automaton state. The second, called *Consistent-Variables Analysis*, performs a similar check on every consistent variable-to-object binding. The third, called *Active-Shadows Analysis*, is flow-sensitive and rules out a tracematch if the program cannot execute its transition statements in a property-violating order.

In this paper, we limit ourselves to extending the Quick Check to SPLs. The Quick Check has the advantage that, as the name suggests, it executes quickly. Nevertheless, our results show that even this relatively pragmatic analysis approach can noticeably reduce the number of configurations that require monitoring. It should be possible to extend our work to the other analyses that Bodden et al. proposed, but doing so would not fundamentally alter our technique.

Required Symbols. A symbol represents a set of transition statements with the same label. Given a tracematch, we determine the *required symbols*, i.e., the symbols required to reach the error state, by fixing one symbol s at a time and checking whether removing all automaton edges labeled with s prevents the final state from being reached. For any given program p, if there exists a required symbol s for which p contains no s-transition, then p does not have to be monitored. For the `ReadPrint` property, the symbols `read` and `print` are required because without one of these, the final state in Figure 2(b) cannot be reached. For the `HasNext` property, only the symbol `next` is required. This is because one can reach the final state without seeing a `hasNext`-transition. If a tracematch has no required symbol, e.g. $a\,|\,b$ (either symbol will trigger the monitor, meaning that neither is required), it has to be inserted in all programs of the product line.[2]

---

[2] In practice, such a tracematch will be rare because the regular expression is generally used to express a sequence of events (meaning one of the symbols will be required), rather than a disjunction of events, which is typically expressed through a pointcut.

Symbol-to-Shadows. For each required symbol, we determine its *joinpoint shadows* (*shadows* for short), i.e., all program statements that may cause events that the symbol matches. We implemented our analysis as an extension of the CLARA framework. CLARA executes all analyses right after the advice-matching and weaving process has completed. Executing the analysis after weaving has the advantage that the analysis can take the effects of all aspects into account. This allows us to even handle cases correctly in which a monitoring aspect itself would accidentally trigger a property violation. A re-weaving analysis has access to the weaver, which in turn gives detailed information about all joinpoint shadows.

In the `ReadPrint` tracematch, the `read` symbol's only shadow is the `read-("secret.txt")` call in line 17 of Figure 1 and the `print` symbol's shadows are the calls `printHeader()` in line 29 and `print(p.data)` call in line 30. For the `HasNext` tracematch, the `next` symbol's shadows are the `next()` calls in lines 50 and 51, and the `hasNext` symbol's only shadow is the `hasNext()` call in line 49.

3.2   Presence Conditions

A tracematch monitor must be inserted into a configuration when each of the tracematch's required symbols is present in the configuration. The *presence condition (PC)* of a tracematch is thus the conjunction of the presence condition of each of its required symbols. In turn, a symbol is present if any one of its shadows is present. Thus, the PC of a symbol is the disjunction of the PC of each of its shadows. The PC of a shadow is the conjunction of features that are needed for that shadow to appear in an SPL program. A first attempt to computing the PC of a tracematch is therefore:

```
tracematch iff (pc(reqdSymbol_1) and ... and pc(reqdSymbol_n))
pc(symbol_i) = pc(shadow_i1) or ... or pc(shadow_im)
pc(shadow_j) = feature_j1 and ... and feature_jk
```

For example, Figure 5 shows how we determine the PC of the `ReadPrint` tracematch. The required symbols of this tracematch are `read` and `print`. `read` has one shadow in line 17 of Figure 1 and `print` has two shadows in lines 29 and 30. For the shadow in line 17 to be syntactically present in a program, the `if(FILE)` conditional in line 16 must be `true` and the `fetchLocal()` method definition (annotated with `BASE` in line 14) must be present. That is, `pc(line17) = [File and Base]`. Similarly, `pc(line29)` and `pc(line30)` are each expanded into `[Base]` because each of the shadows just requires `BASE`, which introduces the `Program` class and its `main`-method definition.

The solution in Figure 5 is imprecise in that it allows configurations where a shadow is syntactically present, but not necessarily reachable from the `main`

```
ReadPrint iff (pc(read) and pc(print))
ReadPrint iff ((pc(line17)) and (pc(line29) or pc(line30)))
ReadPrint iff (([File and Base]) and ([Base] or [Base]))
ReadPrint iff (File and Base)
```

Fig. 5. Computing ReadPrint's Presence Condition

method. For example, according to the algorithm, the read(..) shadow (line 17) is "present" in configurations {Base=true, Local=false, File=true, Inside=-DONT_CARE} even though it is not reachable from main due to Local being turned off. Based on this observation, the algorithm that we implemented can take into account the shadow's callers in addition to its syntactic containers. The algorithm therefore conjoins a shadow's imprecise PC with the disjunction of precise PC of each of its callers, recursively. For the line 17 shadow, which is called by line 10, which is in turn called by line 28, this precise algorithm would return:

```
pc(line17) = [enclosingFeatures and (pc(caller1) or ... or pc(caller_m))]
           = [enclosingFeatures and (pc(line10))]
           = [enclosingFeatures and
                 (enclosingFeaturesLine10 and (pc(line28)))]
           = [File and Base and (Local and Base and (Base))]
           = File and Local and Base
```

Substituting this in Figure 5, we get ReadPrint iff (File and Local and Base), which is optimal for our example and, as mentioned in Section 2.2, is what we set out to construct. Similarly, HasNext's presence condition is:

```
HasNext iff (pc(next))
HasNext iff (pc(line50) or pc(line51))
HasNext iff ([Inside and Base and (Base)] or [Inside and Base and (Base)])
HasNext iff (Inside and Base)
```

Note that, even though HasNext is more localized than ReadPrint, i.e., in one optional feature (Inside) as opposed to two optional features (File and Local), it is required in more configurations (4 out of 7) than ReadPrint (2 out of 7).[3] This is because the feature model allows fewer configurations with both Local=true and File=true than configurations with just Inside=true.

There may be shadows that can only be reached through a cyclic edge in a call-graph. Rather than including the features controlling the cyclic edge in the presence condition of such a shadow, for simplicity, we ignore the cyclic edge. This is not optimally precise but sound. For example, Util.read(..) call in Figure 6 is actually only present in an execution if the execution traverses the cyclic edge from c() to a(), which is possible only if X=true. Instead of adding this constraint on X to the presence condition of Util.read(..), we simply insert the monitor for both values of X.

3.3 Precision on a Pay-As-You-Go Basis

While considering the callers of a shadow makes its presence condition more precise, doing so is entirely optional for the following reason: without considering the callers, a shadow will simply be considered to exist both when a caller is present and when a caller is not present, which will insert a monitor even if a required symbol's shadow cannot be reached. For example, it would be sound,

---

[3] Base is a required feature according to the feature model.

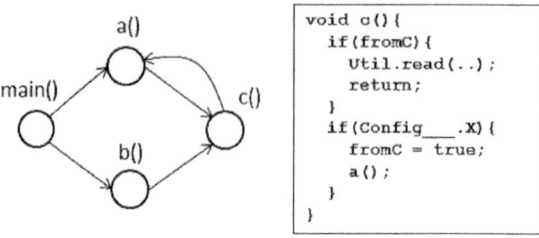

```
void c(){
    if(fromC){
        Util.read(..);
        return;
    }
    if(Config____.X){
        fromC = true;
        a();
    }
}
```

Fig. 6. Example of Computing a Presence Condition with Cycles in the Call-Graph

although not optimally precise, to return the imprecise presence condition of the shadow at line 17. But users of our approach can even go beyond that. Our analysis is pessimistic, i.e., starts from a sound but imprecise answer that ignores the call graph and then gradually refines the answer by inspecting the call graph. Therefore, our analysis can report a sound intermediate result at any time and after a certain number of call sites have been considered, we can simply stop going farther in the call-graph, trading precision for less computation time and resources. Being able to choose the degree of precision is useful especially because the call graph can be very large, which can make computing the presence condition expensive both time-wise and memory-wise. Our technique works with any kind of call graph. In our evaluation, we found that even simple context-insensitive call graphs constructed from *Spark* [14] are sufficient.

4   Evaluation

We implemented our analysis as an extension of the CLARA framework for hybrid typestate analysis [4] and evaluated it on the following SPLs: *Graph Product Line (GPL)*, a set of programs that implement different graph algorithms [15] and *Notepad*, a Java Swing application with functionality similar to Windows Notepad. We considered three safety properties for each SPL. For each property, we report the number of configurations on which the property has to be monitored and the time taken (duration) to derive the tracematch presence condition. We ran our tool on a Windows 7 machine with Intel Core2 Duo CPU with 2.2 GHz and 1024 MB as the maximum heap size.

Note that, although the product lines were created in-house, they were created long before this paper was conceived (GPL over 5 years ago and Notepad 2 years ago). Our tool, the examined product lines and monitors, as well as the detailed evaluation results are available for download [12].

4.1   Case Studies

Graph Product Line (GPL). Table 1 shows the results for GPL, which has 1713 LOC with 17 features and 156 configurations. The features vary algorithms and structures of the graph (e.g. directed/undirected and weighted/unweighted).

Table 1. Graph Product Line (GPL) Results

Lines of code	1713
No. of features	17
No. of configurations	156
DisplayCheck	
No. of configurations	55 (35%)
Duration	69.4 sec. (1.2 min.)
SearchCheck	
No. of configurations	46 (29%)
Duration	110.2 sec. (1.8 min.)
KruskalCheck	
No. of configurations	13 (8%)
Duration	69.8 sec. (1.2 min.)

The `DisplayCheck` safety property checks if the method for displaying a vertex is called outside of the control flow of the method for displaying a graph: a behavioral API violation. Instead of monitoring all 156 configurations, our analysis reveals that only 55 configurations, or 35% of 156, need monitoring. The analysis took 1.2 minutes to complete. The tracematch presence condition that represents these configurations is available on our website [12].

`SearchCheck` checks if the search method is called without first calling the `initialize` method on a vertex, which would make the search erroneous. Our analysis shows that only 29% of the 156 configurations need monitoring. The analysis took 1.8 minutes to complete.

`KruskalCheck` checks if the method that runs the Kruskal's algorithm returns an object that was not created in the control-flow of the method, which would mean that the algorithm is not functioning correctly. In 1.2 minutes, our analysis showed that only 8% of the GPL product line needs monitoring.

Notepad Table 2 shows the results for Notepad, which has 2074 LOC with 25 features and 144 configurations. Variations arise from permuting end-user features, such as saving/opening files, printing, and user interface support (e.g. menu bar or tool bar). The analysis, for all safety properties, takes notably longer than that for GPL because Notepad uses the Java Swing framework, which heavily uses call-back methods that increase by large amounts the size of the call graph that our analysis needs to construct and to consider.

Table 2. Notepad Results

Lines of code	2074
No. of features	25
No. of configurations	144
PersistenceCheck	
No. of configurations	72 (50%)
Duration	296.3 sec. (4.9 min.)
CopyPasteCheck	
No. of configurations	64 (44%)
Duration	259.9 sec. (4.3 min.)
UndoRedoCheck	
No. of configurations	32 (22%)
Duration	279.8 sec. (4.7 min.)

PersistenceCheck checks if java.io.File* objects are created outside of persistence-related functions, which should not happen. Our analysis completes in 4.9 minutes, reducing the configurations to monitor by 50%.

CopyPasteCheck checks if a paste can be performed without first performing a copy, an obvious error with the product line. The analysis completes in 4.3 minutes, reducing the configurations to monitor to 44% of the original number.

UndoRedoCheck checks if a redo can be performed without first performing an undo. The analysis takes 4.7 minutes and reduces the configurations to 22%.

4.2   Discussion

Cost-Benefit Analysis. As the Duration row for each product-line/tracematch pair shows, our analysis introduces a small cost. Most of the duration is from the weaving that is required to determine the required shadows and from constructing the inter-procedural call-graph that we then traverse to determine the presence conditions. Usually, monitors are used in testing. Then, the one-time cost of our analysis is worth incurring if it is less than the time it takes to test-run each saved configuration with complete path coverage (complete path coverage is required to see if a monitor can be triggered). Consider Notepad and PersistenceCheck pair, for which our technique is least effective as it takes the longest time, 4.1 seconds, per saved configuration (144-72=72 configurations are saved in 296.3 seconds of analysis time). The only way our technique would not be worth employing is if one could test-run a configuration of Notepad with complete path coverage in less than 4.1 seconds. Executing such a test-run within this time frame is unrealistic, especially in a UI-driven application like Notepad.

In another scenario where a monitor is used in production, our analysis allows developers to shift runtime-overhead that would incur on deployed systems to a development-time overhead that incurs through our static analysis.

Ideal (Product Line, Tracematch) Pairs. Our technique works best for pairs where the tracematch can only be triggered on few configurations of the product line. Ideally, a tracematch would crosscut many optional features or touch one feature that is present in very few configurations. This is evident in the running example, where the saving for ReadPrint, which requires two optional features, is greater than that for HasNext, which requires one optional feature. It is also evident in the case studies, where KruskalCheck and UndoRedoCheck, which are localized in a small number of features but requires other features due to the feature model, see better saving than their counterparts. Without any constraint, a tracematch requiring x optional features needs to be inserted on $1/(2^x)$ of the configurations (PersistenceCheck requires one optional feature, hence the 50% reduction). A general safety property, such as one involving library data structures and algorithms, is likely to be applicable to many configurations of a product line (if a required feature uses it, then it must be inserted in all configurations) and thus may not enable our technique to eliminate many configurations. On the other hand, a safety property crosscutting many optional features makes an ideal candidate.

5 Related Work

Statically Evaluating Monitors. Our work is most closely related to [6]. As mentioned in Section 2.3, this traditional static analysis is not suitable for product lines because it is oblivious to features. As mentioned in Section 3.1, the traditional static analysis proposes three stages of precision. Although we took only the first stage and extended it, there is no reason why the other stages cannot be extended in a similar fashion. Whether further optimization should be performed after running our technique remains an open question. Namely, it may be possible to take a configuration or a program that our technique has determined to require a monitor and apply the traditional program analysis on it, which could yield optimizations that were not possible in the SysGen program.

Testing Product Lines. The idea of reducing configurations for product line monitoring originated from our work on product line testing [13], which finds "sandboxed" features, i.e. features that do not modify other features' control-flow or data-flow, and treats such features as don't-cares to determine configurations that are identical from the test's perspective. But the two works are different both in setting and technique. In setting, in [13], only one of the identical configurations needs to be tested. In this paper, even if a hundred configurations are identical in the way they trigger a monitor (e.g. through the same feature), all hundred configurations need to be monitored because all hundred can be used by the end-user. In testing mode, it would be possible to run just one of the hundred configurations if our technique could determine that the configurations are identical in the way they trigger the monitor. However, this would require a considerably more sophisticated analysis and is beyond the scope of this paper. In technique, the static analysis employed in [13] is not suitable for our work because a sandboxed feature can still violate safety properties and cause a monitor to trigger. Thus the two works are complementary.

Model-Checking Product Lines. Works in model-checking product lines [9,10] are similar in intent to ours: using these techniques, programmers can apply model checking to a product line as a whole, instead of applying it to each program of the product line. In the common case, these approaches yield a far smaller complexity and therefore have the potential for speeding up the model-checking process. However, these approaches do not model-check concrete product lines. Instead, they assume a given abstraction, such as a transition system, of a product line. Because our technique works on *SysGen* and Java, we need to consider issues specific to Java such as the identification of relevant events, the weaving of the runtime monitor and the static computation of points-to information. Also, model-checking answers a different question than our analysis: model-checking a product line can only report the configurations that may violate the given temporal property. Our analysis further reports a subset of instrumentation points (joinpoint shadows) that can, in combination, lead up to such a violation. As we showed in previous work [3], identifying such shadows requires more sophisticated algorithms than those that only focus on violation detection.

Safe Composition. [18,11] collect implementation constraints in a product line that ensure that every feature combination is compilable or type-safe. Our work can be seen as a variant of safe composition, where a tracematch is treated as a feature itself that "references" its shadows in the product line and requires features that allow those shadows to be reached. However, our analysis checks a much stronger property, i.e. reachability to the shadows, than syntactic presence checked by the existing safe composition techniques. Also, collecting the referential dependencies is much more involved in our technique because it requires evaluating pointcuts that can have wildcards and control-flow constraints.

Relying on Domain Knowledge. Finally, rather than relying on static analysis, users can come up with a tracematch's presence condition themselves if they are confident about their understanding of the product line and the tracematch pair. However, this approach is highly error-prone as even a slight mistake in the presence condition can cause configurations that must be monitored to end up not being monitored. Also, our approach promotes separation of concerns by allowing a safety property to be specified independently of the product line variability.

6   Conclusion

A product line enables the systematic development of a large number of related programs. It also introduces the challenge of analyzing families of related programs, whose cardinality can be exponential in the number of features. For safety properties that are enforced through an execution monitor, conventional wisdom tells us that every configuration must be monitored. In this paper, we presented a static analysis that minimizes the configurations on which an execution monitor must be inserted. The analysis determines the required instrumentation points and determines the feature combinations that allow those points to be reachable. The execution monitor is inserted only on such feature combinations. Experiments show that our analysis is effective (often eliminating over one half of all possible configurations) and that it incurs a small overhead.

As the importance of product lines grows, so too will the importance of analyzing and testing product lines, especially in a world where reliability and security are its first and foremost priorities. This paper takes one of the many steps needed to make analysis and testing of product lines an effective technology.

Acknowledgement. The work of Kim and Batory was supported by the NSF's Science of Design Project CCF 0724979 and NSERC Postgraduate Scholarship. The work of Bodden was supported by CASED (www.cased.de). The work of Khurshid was supported by NSF CCF-0845628 and IIS-0438967.

References

1. Allan, C., Avgustinov, P., Christensen, A.S., Hendren, L.J., Kuzins, S., Lhoták, O., de Moor, O., Sereni, D., Sittampalam, G., Tibble, J.: Adding trace matching with free variables to aspectj. In: OOPSLA, pp. 345–364 (2005)

2. Batory, D.: Feature models, grammars, and propositional formulas. Technical Report TR-05-14, University of Texas at Austin, Texas (March 2005)
3. Bodden, E.: Efficient Hybrid Typestate Analysis by Determining Continuation-Equivalent States. In: ICSE 2010. ACM Press, New York (2010)
4. Bodden, E.: Clara: a framework for implementing hybrid typestate analyses. Technical Report Clara-2 (2009), http://www.bodden.de/pubs/tr-clara-2.pdf
5. Bodden, E., Chen, F., Rosu, G.: Dependent advice: a general approach to optimizing history-based aspects. In: AOSD 2009. ACM, New York (2009)
6. Bodden, E., Hendren, L., Lhoták, O.: A staged static program analysis to improve the performance of runtime monitoring. In: Ernst, E. (ed.) ECOOP 2007. LNCS, vol. 4609, pp. 525–549. Springer, Heidelberg (2007)
7. Bodden, E., Lam, P., Hendren, L.: Finding programming errors earlier by evaluating runtime monitors ahead-of-time. In: SIGSOFT 2008/FSE-16. ACM, New York (2008)
8. Chen, F., Roşu, G.: MOP: an efficient and generic runtime verification framework. In: OOPSLA 2007, pp. 569–588. ACM Press, New York (2007)
9. Classen, A., Heymans, P., Schobbens, P.-Y., Legay, A., Raskin, J.-F.: Model checking lots of systems: Efficient verification of temporal properties in software product lines. In: ICSE 2010. IEEE, Los Alamitos (2010)
10. Gruler, A., Leucker, M., Scheidemann, K.: Modeling and model checking software product lines. In: Barthe, G., de Boer, F.S. (eds.) FMOODS 2008. LNCS, vol. 5051, pp. 113–131. Springer, Heidelberg (2008)
11. Kästner, C., Apel, S.: Type-checking software product lines - a formal approach. In: Automated Software Engineering, ASE (2008)
12. Kim, C.H.P.: Reducing Configurations to Monitor in a Software Product Line: Tool and Results (2010), http://userweb.cs.utexas.edu/~chpkim/splmonitoring
13. Kim, C.H.P., Batory, D., Khurshid, S.: Reducing Combinatorics in Product Line Testing. Technical Report TR-10-02, University of Texas at Austin (January 2010), http://userweb.cs.utexas.edu/~chpkim/chpkim-productline-testing.pdf.
14. Lhoták, O., Hendren, L.: Scaling Java points-to analysis using Spark. In: Hedin, G. (ed.) CC 2003. LNCS, vol. 2622, pp. 153–169. Springer, Heidelberg (2003)
15. Lopez-herrejon, R.E., Batory, D.: A standard problem for evaluating product-line methodologies. In: Bosch, J. (ed.) GCSE 2001. LNCS, vol. 2186, pp. 10–24. Springer, Heidelberg (2001)
16. Schneider, F.B.: Enforceable security policies. ACM Trans. Inf. Syst. Secur. 3(1), 30–50 (2000)
17. Software Engineering Institute, CMU. Software product lines, http://www.sei.cmu.edu/productlines/
18. Thaker, S., Batory, D.S., Kitchin, D., Cook, W.R.: Safe composition of product lines. In: Consel, C., Lawall, J.L. (eds.) GPCE, pp. 95–104. ACM, New York (2007)

Runtime Instrumentation for Precise Flow-Sensitive Type Analysis

Etienne Kneuss, Philippe Suter, and Viktor Kuncak[*]

EPFL School of Computer and Communication Sciences, Lausanne, Switzerland
`firstname.lastname@epfl.ch`

Abstract. We describe a combination of runtime information and static analysis for checking properties of complex and configurable systems. The basic idea of our approach is to 1) let the program execute and thereby read the important dynamic configuration data, then 2) invoke static analysis from this runtime state to detect possible errors that can happen in the continued execution. This approach improves analysis precision, particularly with respect to types of global variables and nested data structures. It also enables the resolution of modules that are loaded based on dynamically computed information.

We describe an implementation of this approach in a tool that statically computes possible types of variables in PHP applications, including detailed types of nested maps (arrays). PHP is a dynamically typed language; PHP programs extensively use nested value maps, as well as 'include' directives whose arguments are dynamically computed file names. We have applied our analysis tool to over 50'000 lines of PHP code, including the popular DokuWiki software, which has a plug-in architecture. The analysis identified 200 problems in the code and in the type hints of the original source code base. Some of these problems can cause exploits, infinite loops, and crashes. Our experiments show that dynamic information simplifies the development of the analysis and decreases the number of false alarms compared to a purely static analysis approach.

1 Introduction

It is challenging to apply precise static analysis to realistic software applications; such applications often give results that are less precise than desired. The imprecision stems both from 1) the approximation that is necessary to ensure acceptable analysis performance, and 2) the absence of detailed information about the environment in which the application runs (such as the file system and user inputs). A common pattern that makes static analysis difficult is reading in configuration data from the external environment, then substantially changing the program behavior based on this data: turning certain features on or off, and loading external modules determined by the configuration. A static analysis typically gives very imprecise results in such cases; it can even fail to determine which files

---

[*] This research was supported in part by the Swiss National Science Foundation Grant #120433 "Precise and Scalable Analyses for Reliable Software".

G. Roşu et al. (Eds.): RV 2010, LNCS 6418, pp. 300–314, 2010.

to include in the application code base, making a conservative analysis entirely useless. Whereas a purely dynamic analysis for such software systems is useful, it may entirely miss opportunities for identifying errors by code inspection.

A hybrid approach. To address these difficulties we propose the following hybrid approach: 1) run the application in its environment as usual, in a deployment-like scenario, up to a user-specified point where most configuration data is expected to be known; 2) record the program state at this point; and 3) use the recorded state as the starting point for a static analysis. The values of many configuration variables thus effectively become constant. This improves the analysis, both of data structures and of control-flow, in some cases making the subsequent results vastly more precise.

We believe that such an hybrid analysis approach deserves more attention than it has received so far. Previous approaches in this spirit include symbolic execution from concrete state [12] and explicit-state model checking from concrete state [15]. In this paper, we show the benefits of this hybrid approach for data-flow analysis. We examine the problem of checking for *type errors* in applications written in PHP, a popular dynamically-typed scripting language.

PHP as the language of the web. PHP scripts are behind many web sites, including wikis, content management systems, and social networking web sites. It is notably used by major web actors, such as Wikipedia,Facebook[1] or Yahoo.[2] Unfortunately, it is very easy to write PHP scripts that contain errors. Among the PHP features that are contributing to this fact is the lack of any static system for detecting type or initialization errors.

Our analyzer. This paper presents PHANTM[3], a hybrid static and dynamic analyzer for PHP 5. PHANTM is an open-source tool written in Scala and available from `http://lara.epfl.ch/dokuwiki/phantm`. It contains a full parser that passes 10'000 tests from the PHP test suite, a static analysis algorithm for type errors, and a library to save and restore representations of concrete program states. PHANTM uses an abstract interpretation domain that approximates both simple and structured values (such as arrays and objects). PHANTM is flow-sensitive, handling initialization and supporting a form of typestate [13]. The motivation for this feature is that the same PHP variable can have different types at different program points. Moreover, the analyzer's notion of type also represents certain concrete values manipulated by the program. Flow sensitive analysis of structured values enables PHANTM to handle, e.g., frequently occurring code that uses untyped arrays with string keys as a substitute for records.

PHANTM supports a large number of PHP constructs in their most common usage scenarios, with the goal of maximizing the usefulness of the tool. It incorporates precision-enhancing support for several PHP idioms that we frequently encountered and for which our initial approach was not sufficiently precise. PHANTM reports some other features of PHP, such as generic error

---

[1] `http://wiki.github.com/facebook/hiphop-php/`

[2] `http://public.yahoo.com/~radwin/talks/php-at-yahoo-mysqluc2006.ppt`

[3] PHp ANalyzer for Type Mismatch.

handlers for undefined methods, as bad practice instead of attempting to abstract the complex behavior of the PHP interpreter. Based on our experience as PHP programmers, we believe that this is a reasonable design decision.

PHANTM analyzes each function separately by default but uses PHP documentation features to allow users to declare types of function arguments. It also comes with detailed type prototype information for a large number of standard library functions, and can be very helpful in annotating existing code bases. By providing additional flexibility in annotation and analysis, going beyond simple type systems, we expect PHANTM to influence future evolutions of the language and lead to more reliable applications. PHANTM also supports context-sensitive analysis of non-recursive functions without annotations.

Leveraging runtime information. PHANTM ships with a library that can be used to instrument the analyzed code and thereby improve the precision of error detection. Programs can be annotated to indicate that the static analysis should start at a given execution point, or to collect a trace of dynamically included files. The collected information is then read by the static analysis component which can use it to, for instance, conclude that certain parts of the program are never executed under a given initial configuration, to detect which function declarations are active, and to refine possible types and values of variables.

Experience. We have applied PHANTM to three substantial PHP applications. The first application is a webmail client used by several thousand users. The second is the popular DokuWiki software,[4] and the third is the feed aggregator SimplePie.[5] Using PHANTM, we have identified a number of errors in these applications.

2   Example

PHP has a dynamic typing policy: types are not declared statically, and variables can adopt various types at different times, depending on the values assigned to them. The basic types are booleans, integers, floating point numbers, strings, arrays and objects. There is also a null type for undefined values and a special type for external resources such as file handlers or database connections. Variables are not declared. Reading from an uninitialized variable results in null.

The *arrays* in PHP are essentially maps from integers and strings to arbitrary values; we thus use the terms *array* and *map* interchangeably. For instance, the following is a valid definition:

$arr = **array**("one" $\Rightarrow$ 1, -1 $\Rightarrow$ "minus one", 3 $\Rightarrow$ 3.1415);

After this assignment, $arr is an array defined for the keys "one", -1 and 3. Contrary to many programming languages, PHP arrays are passed by value and not aliased on assignments.

Handling typestate and nested data types. We illustrate some of the challenges in type analysis of PHP programs and show how PHANTM tackles them. Consider the following code:

```
$inputFile = "template.txt";
$conf["readmode"] = "r";
$conf["file"] = fopen($inputFile, $conf["readmode"]);
$content = fread($conf["file"]);
echo $content;
fclose($conf["file"]);
```

First, note that several values of different type are stored in an array. To check that the call to the library function **fopen** is correctly typed, we need to establish that the value stored in $conf['readmode'] is a string. This immediately points to the fact that our analyses cannot simply abstract the value of $conf as "any array", as the mapping between the keys and the types of the value needs to be stored. On this code, PHANTM correctly concludes that the entry for the key "readmode" always points to a string.

The function **fopen** tries to open a file in a desired mode and returns a pointer to the file (a resource, in PHP terminology) if it succeeded, or the value **false** otherwise. To properly handle this fact, PHANTM encodes the result of the call as having the type "any resource *or* **false**". Because **fread** expects a resource only, PHANTM will display the following warning message:

```
Potential type mismatch. Expected: Array[file => Resource, ...], found:
Array[file => Resource or False, ...]
```

This warning indicates that the developer did not handle the case when the file could not be opened. Note that **fclose** also expects only a resource, but PHANTM does not emit a second warning for the fourth line. The reason is that whenever PHANTM detects a type mismatch, it applies *type refinement* on the problematic variable, assuming that the intended type was the one expected rather than the one found. In many cases, this eliminates or greatly reduces the number of warnings for the same variable.

We can change the code to properly handle failures to open the file as follows:

```
$inputFile = "template.txt";
$conf["readmode"] = "r";
$conf["file"] = fopen($inputFile, $conf["readmode"]);
if($conf["file"]) {
  $content = fread($conf["file"]);
  echo $content;
  fclose($conf["file"]);
}
```

Now that the calls to **fread** and **fclose** are guarded by a check on $conf["file"], PHANTM determines that their argument will never evaluate to **false** and therefore accepts the program as type correct.

As a special case, PHANTM also detects uninitialized variables and array entries.[6] If we omit the first line in the source above, PHANTM will warn that the first argument of **fopen** is uninitialized, which could be used by an attacker to reveal the content of arbitrary accessible file on the server.

---

[6] These errors were a major source of vulnerabilities in past PHP versions, because the register_globals server configuration option was activated by default.

Using runtime instrumentation. PHP allows the inclusion of dependencies using dynamic paths. The following example, inspired by DokuWiki code, illustrates how such dynamic features rapidly result in a lot of false alarms when analyzed purely statically:

```php
$conf = array('version' => '1.2.3',
                'path_images' => 'images/',
                'canWrite' => is_writeable("data/"),
                'path_modules' => is_dir('local/') ? 'local/' : 'default/');
include 'config.php';
if (empty($modules)) { // default modules
    $modules = array('smiley' => array('inc/smiley.inc', 'inc/smiley2.inc'),
                    'acronyms' => array('inc/acronyms.inc'), ); }
foreach($modules as $files) {
    foreach($files as $file) {
        include getFullPath($conf, $file); } }
phantm_collect_state(get_defined_vars()); // record runtime state
function log_msg($msg) {
    global $conf;
    if ($conf['canWrite']) {
        file_put_contents("data/log", $msg, FILE_APPEND); } }
function displaySmiley() {
    global $conf;
    echo $conf['path_images'].$conf['smiley']['image'][':)']; }
```

In this example, the list of modules is configuration-dependent. Also, based on that list of modules, the code includes their associated files using a non-trivial indirection to resolve the path via getFullPath(). Later on, the displaySmiley() function accesses global and module-dependent configuration settings, assuming that they are defined. Such code would be extremely difficult to analyze purely statically without emitting any false positive. In order to analyze the rest of the application, it is crucial to know the exact state of the program after all the modules are initialized. Runtime instrumentation is a natural and convenient way to obtain this information.

Benefits of hybrid analysis in program understanding. Note that with runtime instrumentation, PHANTM will inform the user that the call to file_put_contents() is unreachable, if run in an environment where the data/ directory is not writeable. As another example, consider the following code:

```php
if (is_debug()) { $debug = true; } else { $debug = false; }
phantm_collect_state(get_defined_vars());
...
if ($debug) { ... }
```

PHANTM detects that the final **if** branch is unreachable when the code runs in a non-debug environment. Such warnings help the user understand which regions of code are relevant in a given environment.

3   Data-Flow Analysis for Flow-Sensitive Type Inference

We first outline the data-flow analysis that we use to infer types. Our description applies regardless of whether the analysis starts from the initial program state or from the dynamically recorded state captured as described in Section 4.

Concrete states.   As a first step in providing the meaning of our analysis representation, we present our model of runtime values, which are elements of disjoint sets corresponding to the possible types (see Figure 1). A concrete program state contains 1) a map from a set of constant strings (variable names) to values, and 2) a heap. A heap maps object references to object states, where an object state is a map from a set of constant strings (field names) to values.

Analysis representation and abstraction function.   Our abstract domain is presented in Figure 2. We use $\bot$ to denote an empty set of elements of $V^{\sharp}$. Figure 3 describes the meaning of abstract type elements using function β that abstracts the values of values of individual variables. The analysis abstracts boolean, string and integer constants by their precise value when it is known, for instance when

$$
\begin{aligned}
V &= \{\mathsf{True}, \mathsf{False}, \mathsf{Null}\} \cup \mathsf{Ints} \cup \mathsf{Floats} \cup \mathsf{Strings} & \text{values} \\
&\quad \cup \mathsf{Maps} \cup \mathsf{Objs} \cup \mathsf{Resources} \\
\mathsf{Maps} &= (\mathsf{Ints} \cup \mathsf{Strings}) \hookrightarrow V & \text{maps} \\
\mathsf{Tags} &= \{\mathsf{StdClass}, \text{all classes defined in the program}\} \\
H &= \mathsf{Objs} \hookrightarrow (\mathsf{Tags} \times (\mathsf{Strings} \hookrightarrow V)) & \text{heap states} \\
S &= (\mathsf{Strings} \hookrightarrow V) \times H & \text{program states}
\end{aligned}
$$

Fig. 1. Characterization of the concrete states. $A \hookrightarrow B$ denotes all partial functions from A to B.

$$
\begin{aligned}
\mathsf{DV}^{\sharp} &= \{\mathsf{True}^{\sharp}, \mathsf{False}^{\sharp}, \mathsf{Null}^{\sharp}, \mathsf{Int}^{\sharp}, \mathsf{Float}^{\sharp}, \mathsf{String}^{\sharp}, & \text{defined values} \\
&\quad \mathsf{Resource}^{\sharp}\} \cup \mathsf{Maps}^{\sharp} \cup \mathsf{Objs}^{\sharp} \cup \mathsf{Ints} \cup \mathsf{Floats} \cup \mathsf{Strings} \\
\mathsf{AV}^{\sharp} &= \{\mathsf{Undef}^{\sharp}\} \cup \mathsf{DV}^{\sharp} & \text{all values} \\
\mathsf{V}^{\sharp} &= \mathcal{P}_{\mathsf{fin}}(\mathsf{AV}^{\sharp}) \cup \{\top\} & \text{finite unions and top} \\
\mathsf{Maps}^{\sharp} &- (\mathsf{Ints} \sqcup \mathsf{Strings} \sqcup \{?\}) \hookrightarrow \mathsf{V}^{\sharp} & \text{abstract maps} \\
H^{\sharp} &= \mathsf{Objs}^{\sharp} \hookrightarrow (\mathsf{Tags} \times (\mathsf{Strings} \hookrightarrow \mathsf{V}^{\sharp})) & \text{abstract heap states} \\
S^{\sharp} &= (\mathsf{Strings} \hookrightarrow \mathsf{V}^{\sharp}) \times H^{\sharp} & \text{abstract program states}
\end{aligned}
$$

Fig. 2. Definition of the abstract domain

$$
\begin{aligned}
\beta(\mathsf{Null}) &= \mathsf{Null}^{\sharp}, \quad \beta(\mathsf{False}) = \mathsf{False}^{\sharp}, \quad \beta(\mathsf{True}) = \mathsf{True}^{\sharp} \\
\beta(i \in \mathsf{Ints}) &= i, \quad \beta(s \in \mathsf{Strings}) = s, \quad \beta(f \in \mathsf{Floats}) = f \\
\beta(o \in \mathsf{Objs}) &= o^{\sharp} \in \mathsf{Objs}^{\sharp} \text{ where } o \text{ was allocated at site } o^{\sharp} \\
\beta(m \in \mathsf{Maps}) &= \beta_2(m^{\sharp}, 0) \\
\beta_2(m \notin \mathsf{Maps}, i) &= \beta(m) \\
\beta_2(m \in \mathsf{Maps}, i < 5) &= \{(\beta(k) \mapsto \beta_2(v, i+1)) \mid (k \mapsto v) \in m\} \\
\beta_2(m \in \mathsf{Maps}, i \geq 5) &= (? \mapsto \mathsf{AV}^{\sharp})
\end{aligned}
$$

Fig. 3. Abstraction β of variable values used to define the abstraction function α

they serve as keys in a map. We refer to such precise values as *singleton scalar types*. In maps, we use the special value ? to denote the set of keys that are not otherwise represented by a constant. For example, to denote all maps where the key "x" is mapped to an integer and all other keys are undefined we use the abstract value $\mathsf{Map}^\sharp["x" \mapsto \mathsf{Int}^\sharp, ? \mapsto \mathsf{Undef}^\sharp]$. We use allocation-site abstraction [3] for objects. Whereas Objs represents the set of possible memory addresses in the heap, $\mathsf{Objs}^\sharp$ represents the set of program points where objects can be created.

PHP does not distinguish between variables that have never been assigned and variables that have been assigned to the value null. However, using null as a value can convey an intended meaning, while reading from an unassigned variable is generally an error. To distinguish between these two scenarios, our analysis uses two different abstract values for these two cases and handles them differently in the transfer function. Our analysis thus incorporates a limited amount of history-sensitive semantics.

Our goal is to approximate the set of types a variable can admit at a given program point. To do so, we consider for our abstract domain not only the values representing a specific type (such as $\mathsf{Int}^\sharp$) and specific values (such as constant strings), but also their combinations. We refer to such combinations of abstract values as *union types*, and we use the symbol τ to denote such a type. Even though we could in principle consider arbitrary union of arrays (i.e. maps), for termination and efficiency reasons we chose to simplify them by computing them point-wise,

$$\mathsf{Map}^\sharp[k_1^\sharp \mapsto \tau_1, k_2^\sharp \mapsto \tau_2, \dots, ? \mapsto \tau_D] \sqcup \mathsf{Map}^\sharp[k_1^\sharp \mapsto \tau_1', k_3^\sharp \mapsto \tau_3', \dots, ? \mapsto \tau_D'] =$$
$$\mathsf{Map}^\sharp[k_1^\sharp \mapsto \tau_1 \cup \tau_1', k_2^\sharp \mapsto \tau_2 \cup \tau_D', k_3^\sharp \mapsto \tau_D \cup \tau_3', \dots, ? \mapsto \tau_D \cup \tau_D'].$$

The set of union types forms a lattice where the partial order corresponds to the notion of subtyping. We denote type unions by the symbol $\cup$, which is the exact version of $\sqcup$. We define subtyping for unions by $\tau \sqsubseteq (\tau_1 \cup \tau_2) \iff \tau \sqsubseteq \tau_1 \vee \tau \sqsubseteq \tau_2$ and $(\tau_1 \cup \tau_2) \sqsubseteq \tau \iff \tau_1 \sqsubseteq \tau \wedge \tau_2 \sqsubseteq \tau$. We define the subtype relation point-wise for array types:

$$\mathsf{Map}^\sharp[k_1 \mapsto \tau_1, k_2 \mapsto \tau_2, \dots, ? \mapsto \tau_D] \sqsubseteq \mathsf{Map}^\sharp[k_1 \mapsto \tau_1', k_3 \mapsto \tau_3', \dots, ? \mapsto \tau_D']$$
$$\iff \tau_1 \sqsubseteq \tau_1' \wedge \tau_2 \sqsubseteq \tau_D' \wedge \tau_D \sqsubseteq \tau_3' \wedge \dots \wedge \tau_D \sqsubseteq \tau_D'$$

Therefore, $\mathsf{Map}^\sharp[? \mapsto \bot]$ and $\mathsf{Map}^\sharp[? \mapsto \top]$ are respectively the subtype and the supertype of all array types. Our approach relies on the fact that arrays in PHP, contrary to arrays in e.g. Java, are not objects and do not introduce a level of reference indirection.

3.1   Transfer Functions

For space reasons we only highlight less standard aspects of our abstract transfer functions. A compact description of the transfer functions of our analysis in Scala is given in around 1000 lines of Scala source code.[7]

---

[7] Please consult the file `src/phantm/types/TypeTransferFunction.scala` in the repository at `http://github.com/colder/phantm/`

Type refinement. Since the PHP language allows programs with little to no type annotations, it is often the case that types of values are completely unknown before they are used. To reduce the number of false positives generated by consecutive uses of such values, it is crucial that their types get refined along the way. For example, the code $b = $a + 1; $c = $a + 2; generates only one notice in PHANTM. Namely, after the first statement PHANTM assumes that $a is a valid operand for mathematical operations, and refines its type to $\text{Int}^\sharp \cup \text{Float}^\sharp$. To achieve this in the general case, PHANTM computes the lattice meet between the type lattice elements corresponding to the current and the expected variable types. For example, a typical computation of the intersection of array types gives

$$\text{Map}^\sharp[k_1^\sharp \mapsto \tau_1, k_2^\sharp \mapsto \tau_2, \ldots, ? \mapsto \tau_D] \sqcap \text{Map}^\sharp[k_1^\sharp \mapsto \tau_1', k_3^\sharp \mapsto \tau_3', \ldots, ? \mapsto \tau_D'] =$$
$$\text{Map}^\sharp[k_1^\sharp \mapsto \tau_1 \sqcap \tau_1', k_2^\sharp \mapsto \tau_2 \sqcap \tau_D', k_3^\sharp \mapsto \tau_D \sqcap \tau_3', \ldots, ? \mapsto \tau_D \sqcap \tau_D']$$

Such type refinement corresponds to applying an **assume** statement that is a consequence of successful execution of an operation.

Conditional filtering. PHANTM also applies type refinement for assume statements implied by control structures. Note that PHP allows values of every type to be used as boolean conditions, and gives different boolean values to inhabitants of those types. This allows PHANTM to do refinement on the types of values used as boolean conditions. For example, the type **null** can only evaluate to false, whereas integers may evaluate to either true or false (true unless the value is 0). This is especially useful for booleans, for which we also define **true** and **false** as types. We can precisely annotate a function returning false on error, and a different type on successful execution. PHANTM can then use type refinement to verify code that invokes a function and checks for errors in the invocation. If the representation of the value becomes $\bot$ during the refinement, PHANTM concludes that the branch cannot be taken, detecting unreachable code.

Enforcing Termination. Given our allocation-side model for handling the heap, we identify two remaining potential sources of an infinite-height lattice: nested arrays and unions of singleton scalar types. For arrays, we limit the array nesting depth to a constant (five, in the current implementation). For singleton scalar types, we make sure that new singleton scalar types cannot be generated except when abstracting a literal or a run-time state value. Any operation handling singleton scalar types will either have one of them as a result type, or have a more general, widened type. We have found this approach to work well in practice (see Figure 4 for analysis performance).

3.2   Reporting Type Errors Using Reconstructed Types

When the analysis reaches its fixpoint, it has effectively reconstructed the possible types for all variables at all program points. At this point, PHANTM makes a final pass over the program control-flow graph and reports type mismatches. Because transfer functions already perform type refinement, they contain all the necessary information to report type mismatches, and we reuse them to report type errors. PHANTM reports a type mismatch whenever the computed type at a given program point is not a subtype of the expected type. PHANTM has a number of options to control the verbosity of its warnings and errors.

4   Runtime Instrumentation

Many PHP applications can be separated into two parts: the bootstrapping code and the core functionality of the application. The bootstrapping code is responsible for handling configuration settings, loading external libraries, loading sessions or including the appropriate definitions. Because this part of the code strongly depends on the configuration of the environment at hand, it usually cannot be analyzed statically. Compounding the problem of imprecision is that these configuration values that are approximated imprecisely tend to be used often in the rest of the code. To overcome this problem, PHANTM includes a PHP library to instrument the analyzed application; one uses it to define a milestone in the code at which multiple aspects of the runtime state should get inspected. Using the state captured at this program point as the alternative starting point for static analysis, PHANTM can use information that goes beyond the source code and produce an overall better output.

4.1   State Recovery

The runtime information that PHANTM extracts includes: 1) all defined variables and constants and their associated values 2) a trace of function and class definitions, including the location in the code where the definition occurs, and 3) a trace of all included files. The library function used to mark the milestone and to collect the runtime information is called phantm_collect_state. It takes an array of variables as an argument, and is typically invoked as

```
phantm_collect_state(get_defined_vars());
```

When phantm_collect_state is called, the runtime state and the list of active definitions are stored into a file. This file can then be imported back into PHANTM using the --importState option.

PHANTM then loads the information and applies the following steps:

1. Attach the source of all included files to the AST of the main file.
2. Collect the function and class declarations that match the trace.
3. Create an abstract state s from the stored values for variables and constants.
4. Locate in the AST the program point p with the call to phantm_collect_state, and attach s to that program point.
5. Apply the static analysis starting from p.

In the reconstructed abstract state s, all scalar variables are associated to a singleton type that precisely describes the value from the collected state. A fresh, virtual, allocation site is associated to each object that was known at instrumentation time, and arrays are reconstructed with the correct set of keys and values (up to a bounded array nesting depth). The only limitation in practice is that resources cannot be reconstructed, because they typically cannot be serialized.

Summary of runtime analysis benefits. In our experience, runtime information improves the precision of our analyzer in the following ways:

Global variables. Projects like DokuWiki make an extensive use of global variables, e.g. to store configuration settings and database connections. Global variables are difficult to analyze in a purely static approach. Because they are typically defined in an initialization phase, our runtime instrumentation can capture their value; PHANTM can then use it in the static analysis phase.

Increased and precise definition coverage. PHANTM records the files that have been included during execution. Often all necessary libraries are included at the time of the phantm_collect_state indications, which means that all necessary functions are defined. When such dependencies are dynamic, they are not resolved with purely static analysis, resulting in warnings about undefined functions and results that are either useless or unsound (depending on whether missing the functions are assumed to perform arbitrary changes or no changes).

5   Evaluation

We evaluated PHANTM on three PHP applications. The first one is an email client which we will call WebMail, similar in functionality to IMP.[8] It has been in production for several years. There are currently over 5000 users registered to the service. WebMail was written in PHP 4.1 and has not evolved much since its launch. The source code is not public but has kindly been made available to us by the development team. Our second application is the popular open source wiki project DokuWiki and the third application is SimplePie, an open source library to manage the aggregation of RSS and Atom news feeds.

We first summarize the results of our evaluation without runtime instrumentation in Figure 4. "Warnings" is the number of warnings PHANTM emitted with normal verbosity, while "Filtered Warnings" is using a special mode which focuses on most relevant errors. "Problems" is the number of problems identified, including actual bugs, dangerous implicit conversions, statements that could issue notices in PHP, and errors in annotations. We see that even for large code bases, the time required by the analysis remains reasonable.

In the sequel we show how runtime instrumentation helped improve these results. Finally, we describe a number of issues discovered with PHANTM.

We evaluated the impact of runtime instrumentation on DokuWiki and WebMail. The code of of both projects is structured as a loading phase followed by code that uses the configuration data. Consequently, the benefits of runtime information are considerable. We illustrate the impact of runtime information for DokuWiki in Figure 5, listing several functions among those for which runtime instrumentation brought the most significant improvement. Note that a comparison of the total number of warnings is not sensible, because using instrumentation can add code to the analysis that cannot be discovered statically.

---

[8] http://www.horde.org/imp/

	Lines of code	Warnings	Filtered Warnings	Problems	Analysis Time
DokuWiki	31486	1232	270	76	244s
WebMail	3621	272	59	43	11s
SimplePie	15003	881	327	84	21s
Total	*50110*	*2385*	*656*	*203*	*276s*

Fig. 4. Summary of evaluation results without runtime instrumentation

	Lines	Without	With	Δ	Reduction
updateprofile	62	19	0	19	100%
act_resendpwd	90	16	5	11	69%
check	143	14	4	10	71%
auth_ismanager	70	12	6	6	50%
auth_login	49	10	4	6	60%

Fig. 5. Effects of runtime instrumentation on DokuWiki. "Without" is the number of warnings emitted by PHANTM without runtime instrumentation. "With" is the number of warnings emitted by PHANTM with the information from runtime instrumentation about global variables and the type of arguments. In both cases, the function body is analyzed entirely.

Observe that we obtain a substantial reduction in the case, for example, of updateprofile. This is explained by the fact that this function primarily deals with global variables, user-provided form elements, and the current logged user, which is runtime-dependent. In essence, such functions illustrate the limitations of purely static analyses, and show how helpful runtime instrumentation was in overcoming these limitations.

Overall, for functions analyzed both with and without runtime information, 109 warnings (12%) were eliminated when using runtime information for DokuWiki and 18 (12%) for WebMail. Using the instrumentation had no notable impact on the analysis time; the overhead was only in the one-time loading of the saved state, which takes around one second in our implementation.

5.1   Issues Identified by Phantm

We now describe a small selection of issues in the three applications that we identified by inspecting the warnings emitted by PHANTM.

WebMail bug 1). In a function handling the conversion from one string format to another, PHANTM emitted a warning on the following line:

```
$newchar = substr($newcharlist, strpos($charlist, $char), 1);
```

The warning indicates that **substr()** expects a string as its second argument, but that in this case the type False $\cup$ String was found. The developers were assuming that $charlist would always contain $char even though it was not always the case. Because of this bug, some of the passwords were improperly stored, potentially resulting in email accounts being inaccessible from WebMail and thus compromising WebMail's core functionality.

WebMail bug 2). In several places, two distinct functions were called with too many arguments. This was apparently the result of an incomplete refactoring during the development. Although these extra arguments did not cause any bug (they are silently ignored by the PHP interpreter), they were clearly errors and could have led to new bugs as the code evolves further.

WebMail bug 3). In a file containing definitions for the available languages, PHANTM reported a warning on the second of the following lines:

```
$dict["en"]["fr"]="anglais";
$dist["en"]["de"]="englisch";
```

The first line is well formed and stores the translation for "English" in French. The second line is accepted by the standard PHP interpreter even though $dist is undefined in the program; it contains a typographic error preventing the desired value from being stored in the array $dict.

WebMail bug 4). The tool identified several warnings for code such as $i = $str * 1, which casts a string into an integer using the implicit conversion triggered by the multiplication. Although it is not incorrect, it is flagged as bad style.

DokuWiki bug 1). We found multiple instances where the code relied on implicit conversions. Even though this is a commonly used feature of PHP, relying on them often highlights programming errors. For example, the following line

```
$hid = $this→_headerToLink($text,'true');
```

calls the method _headerToLink which is defined to take a boolean as its second argument, not a string. This code is not wrong per se, as the string "true" evaluates to true, however, "false" would evaluate to true as well!

DokuWiki bug 2). Keeping code documentation synchronized with the code itself is often problematic. As an illustration of this fact, PHANTM uncovered over 25 errors in the existing annotations of arguments and return values.

DokuWiki bug 3). We found a potential bug resulting from an unchecked file operation in the following function:

```
function bzfile($file) {
    $bz = bzopen($file,"r");
    while (!feof($bz)){ $str = $str . bzread($bz,8192); }
    bzclose($bz);
    return $str;
}
```

If **bzopen** fails to open the file denoted by $file, it will return **false** and as a consequence the call to **feof** will always return **false**, resulting in an infinite loop.

SimplePie bug 1). The following line of code assumes different operator precedence rules than those used by PHP:

if (... && !($file→method & SP_FILE_SRC_REMOTE === 0 ...))

The code first compares the constant SP_FILE_SRC_REMOTE to 0, which always results in **false**, and then computes the bitwise conjunction, while the goal is clearly to check whether a flag is set in $file→method. PHANTM finds the error by reporting that the right-hand side of **&** is a boolean value, and that an integer was expected.

SimplePie bug 2). PHANTM flags the following code as type incorrect:

if (... && strtolower(trim($attribs[''][‘mode’])) == ‘base64’))

An inspection of the statement shows that the right parenthesis of the call to **strtolower** is misplaced, in effect computing the lower case version of a boolean. As a result, the computation is incorrect when base64 is spelled with a capital "b", for instance.

6   Related Work

Data-flow analysis for type inference. Our work performs type inference using an abstract interpretation, resulting in a flow-sensitive static analysis. A systematic analysis of type analyses of different precision is presented in [4].

Static analysis of PHP. Existing work on statically analyzing PHP is primarily focused on the specific task of detecting security vulnerabilities and preventing attacks. PIXY [10] is a static analysis tool checking for vulnerabilities such as cross site scripting (XSS) or SQL injections, which remain the main attack vectors of PHP applications. Wassermann and Su [14] present work on statically detecting SQL injections using grammar-based specifications. Huang et al. [7] present a technique to conservatively prevent, rather than detect, similar attacks. They use a combination of code instrumentation, to automatically secure PHP scripts, and a static taint analysis, to reduce the number of additional checks. All these approaches focus on one analysis domain and make use of specific techniques and annotations. PHANTM on the other end ambitions to be useful in improving the quality of arbitrary PHP code and code documentation, while it can also serve to detect vulnerabilities, as illustrated in Section 5.1.

It is only recently that some work have been focusing on static analysis of types in PHP applications. Notably, the Facebook HIPHOP project[9] is relying on a certain amount of type analysis in order to optimize the PHP runtime. In essence, HipHop tries to find the most specific type used in order to map it to a native C++ type. In case such a type cannot be inferred, it simply falls back to a generic type.

---

[9] http://github.com/facebook/hiphop-php/

The recently released tool PHPLINT[10] aims to detect bugs through type errors. Even though its goal is close to the present work, PHANTM has a much more precise abstract domain, and therefore reports many fewer spurious warnings. For instance, PHPLINT fails to analyze precisely the initial example in Section 2 because it does not support arrays containing mixed types. Furthermore, it does not have union types, so many PHP functions will not be represented both soundly and precisely enough to 1) detect defects such as the Dokuwiki bug 3 of Section 5.1 and the **fopen** example of Section 2, while 2) avoiding false warnings when the developer correctly checks for return codes.

Type inference for other languages. Researchers have also considered flow-sensitive type inference in other languages. Soft typing approach has been explored primarily in functional languages [5, 1]. It supports first class functions, but is not flow-sensitive and does not support value-array types.

In [11] researchers present an analysis of Cobol programs that recovers information corresponding to tagged unions. The work on the C programming language [9, 2] deals with a language that allows subtle pointer and address arithmetic manipulations, but already contains significant static type information. PHP is a dynamically type safe language in that the run-time system stores dynamic type information, which makes e.g. ad-hoc tagged unions often unnecessary. On the other hand, PHP by itself provides no static type checking, which makes the starting point for analysis lower. In addition to considering a different language, one of the main novelties of our work is the support for not only flat types but also heterogeneous maps and arrays.

In [8] the authors present a type analysis for JavaScript also based on data-flow analysis. The abstract domain for array types presented in our paper goes beyond what is supported in [8]. On the other hand, the support for interprocedural analysis and pointer analysis in [8] is more precise than in the present paper. The main difference, however, is that we demonstrate the potential of combining dynamically computed program states with data-flow analysis.

Combining static and dynamic analysis. Combining static and dynamic analysis arises in a number of approaches. Our approach is closest to [12] and [15]. Promising approach have been developed that combine testing, abstraction, theorem proving [16] or combine may and must analysis [6]; these approaches compute a sound overapproximation, in contrast to our runtime information that performs a sample of an early stage of the execution to estimate properties of a dynamic environment.

7   Conclusion

Our experience with over 50000 lines of PHP code showed our tool to be fast enough and effective in identifying serious issues in code such as exploits, infinite loops, and crashes. The use of runtime information was shown to be helpful in reducing the number of false alarms in the tool and focusing the attention on true

---

[10] http://www.icosaedro.it/phplint/

errors. We therefore believe that it is well-worthwhile to build into future static analyses tools the ability to start the analysis from a recorded concrete program state. This approach overcomes several limitations of purely static approach while preserving certain predictability that help interpret the results that it computes. Our tool PHANTM is available for download and evaluation, and we report verifiable experimental results on significant code bases, including popular software whose source code is publicly available.

References

1. Aiken, A., Wimmers, E.L., Lakshman, T.K.: Soft typing with conditional types. In: POPL (1994)
2. Chandra, S., Reps, T.: Physical type checking for C. In: Workshop on Program analysis for software tools and engineering, PASTE (1999)
3. Chase, D.R., Wegman, M., Zadeck, F.K.: Analysis of pointers and structures. In: PLDI (1990)
4. Patrick Cousot. Types as abstract interpretations. In *POPL*, 1997.
5. Fagan, M.: Soft Typing: An Approach to Type Checking for Dynamically Typed Languages. PhD thesis, Rice University (1992)
6. Godefroid, P., Nori, A.V., Rajamani, S.K., Tetali, S.: Compositional must program analysis: unleashing the power of alternation. In: POPL (2010)
7. Huang, Y.-W., Yu, F., Hang, C., Tsai, C.-H., Lee, D.T., Kuo, S.-Y.: Securing web application code by static analysis and runtime protection. In: WWW (2004)
8. Jensen, S.H., Møller, A., Thiemann, P.: Type analysis for JavaScript. In: Palsberg, J., Su, Z. (eds.) Static Analysis. LNCS, vol. 5673, pp. 238–255. Springer, Heidelberg (2009)
9. Jhala, R., Majumdar, R., Xu, R.-G.: State of the union: Type inference via craig interpolation. In: Grumberg, O., Huth, M. (eds.) TACAS 2007. LNCS, vol. 4424, pp. 553–567. Springer, Heidelberg (2007)
10. Jovanovic, N., Kruegel, C., Kirda, E.: Pixy: A static analysis tool for detecting web application vulnerabilities. In: IEEE Symp. Security and Privacy (2006)
11. Komondoor, R., Ramalingam, G., Chandra, S., Field, J.: Dependent types for program understanding. In: Halbwachs, N., Zuck, L.D. (eds.) TACAS 2005. LNCS, vol. 3440, pp. 157–173. Springer, Heidelberg (2005)
12. Pasareanu, C.S., Mehlitz, P.C., Bushnell, D.H., Gundy-Burlet, K., Lowry, M.R., Person, S., Pape, M.: Combining unit-level symbolic execution and system-level concrete execution for testing NASA software. In: ISSTA (2008)
13. Strom, R.E., Yemini, S.: Typestate: A programming language concept for enhancing software reliability. In: IEEE TSE (January 1986)
14. Wassermann, G., Su, Z.: Sound and precise analysis of web applications for injection vulnerabilities. In: PLDI (2007)
15. Yabandeh, M., Knežević, N., Kostić, D., Kuncak, V.: Predicting and preventing inconsistencies in deployed distributed systems. ACM Transactions on Computer Systems 28(1) (2010)
16. Yorsh, G., Ball, T., Sagiv, M.: Testing, abstraction, theorem proving: better together? In: ISSTA, pp. 145–156 (2006)

Trace Recording for Embedded Systems: Lessons Learned from Five Industrial Projects

Johan Kraft[1], Anders Wall[2], and Holger Kienle[1]

[1] Mälardalen University, Box 883, 72123, Västerås, Sweden
{johan.kraft,holger.kienle}@mdh.se
[2] ABB AB, Corporate Research, Västerås, Sweden
anders.wall@se.abb.com

Abstract. This paper presents experiences from five industry collaboration projects performed between 2004 – 2009 where solutions for embedded systems trace recording have been developed and evaluated; in four cases for specific industrial systems and in the last case as a generic solution for a commercial real-time operating system, in collaboration with the RTOS company. The experiences includes technical solutions regarding efficient instrumentation and logging, technology transfer issues and evaluation results regarding CPU and RAM overhead. A brief overview of the *Tracealyzer* tool is also presented, a result of the first project (2004) which still is used by ABB Robotics and now in commercialization.

Keywords: embedded-systems, scheduling, tracing, trace-recording, monitoring, experiences, case-studies, overhead.

1 Introduction

Trace recording, or tracing, is a commonly used technique useful in debugging and performance analysis. Concretely, trace recording implies *detection* and *storage* of relevant events during run-time, for later off-line analysis. This work targets *embedded* computer systems, i.e., specialized control systems used in many industrial products, for instance cars, trains, robotics and telecom systems. Embedded systems come in all sizes, from single-chip 8-bit computers with a few KB of RAM to 32-bit computers with features and performance comparable to PCs. Embedded systems are often *real-time* systems, meaning that the correctness also depends on response time, i.e., the latency from an input to the corresponding output. This must not exceed a specified requirement, the *deadline*. Embedded systems are typically implemented on multi-tasking real-time operating systems, where *tasks* (threads) share the CPU using *fixed-priority scheduling* [3,5].

Trace recording for embedded systems can be performed at different abstraction levels and can be accomplished using software solutions, hardware solutions, such as Lauterbach Trace32[1], or hybrid hardware/software solutions such as the

---

[1] www.lauterbach.com

G. Roşu et al. (Eds.): RV 2010, LNCS 6418, pp. 315–329, 2010.

RTBx product of Rapita Systems[2]. A software-based approach means to add code instrumentation which logs the desired information in a software recorder module. This is typically performed without changing the application code but implies an overhead on CPU and RAM usage which for embedded systems can be of significance. Hardware solutions however require large, expensive equipment, mainly intended for lab use, while software solutions can remain active also in post-release use. This can be very valuable for reproducing customer problems, such as transient timing problems which only occur under rare circumstances.

The type of trace recording discussed in this paper is software-based trace recording for embedded systems, focusing on scheduling events, inter-process communication (IPC) events and relevant operating system calls. This is a higher abstraction level compared to, e.g., the work by Thane et al. [8] on replay debugging. However, our approach often gives sufficient information to pinpoint the cause of an error. If more information is necessary, this facilitates a detailed analysis using a debugger. In return, such recording is easy to integrate in existing systems since no application code instrumentation is required and the run-time overhead is very low, which allows for having the recording active also post-release. Many RTOS developers, including Wind River[3], ENEA[4] and Green Hills Software[5], provide tracing tools for their specific platform, but they typically never reveal any details or overhead measurements regarding their solutions. The main contribution of this paper is a synthesis of our experiences from five industry collaboration projects where trace recording solutions have been developed, including technical solutions used as well as results from recording overhead measurements.

2   Software Trace Recording

Software trace recorders typically operate by storing relevant events in a circular RAM buffer, as binary data in fixed-size records. In this manner, the recorder always holds the most recent history. In all implementations presented in this paper, a single ring-buffer is used for storing all types of events.

It is possible to detect scheduling events on most real-time operating systems, either by registering callbacks (hooks) on system events like task-switches, task creation and termination, or by modifying the kernel source code. The callback approach is possible on at least VxWorks (from Wind River) and OSE (from ENEA). Operating systems with available kernel source code, e.g., Linux and RTXC Quadros[6], can be modified to call the trace recorder module on relevant events. Åsberg et al. [2] has shown that for Linux (2.6 kernel), the only kernel modification required is to remove the "const" keyword from a specific function pointer declaration. It is however possible to realize Linux trace recording without kernel modifications, if using a custom scheduler like RESCH [1].

---

[2] www.rapitasystems.com
[3] www.windriver.com
[4] www.enea.com
[5] www.ghs.com
[6] www.quadros.com

In our approach we abstract from the context-switch overhead posed by the operating system and consider the task-switches as instantaneous actions. Only a single time-stamp is stored for each task-switch event and the OS overhead is instead accounted to the execution time of the tasks. Each task-switch event corresponds to exactly one *execution fragment*, i.e., the interval of uninterrupted execution until the next task-switch event. The rest of this section will discuss the information necessary for task-switch recording, the "what", "when" and "why". Due to space constraints, we focus of techniques for recording of task-switch events. Recording of IPC and operating system calls are however very similar.

2.1 Task Identity (The "What")

Most operating systems use 32-bit IDs for tasks, even though many embedded system only contain a handful of tasks. It is therefore often a good idea to introduce a short task ID, *STID*, using only 8 bits or 16 bits in order to make the task-switch events less memory consuming.

The STIDs needs to be allocated on task creation and quickly retrieved when storing task-switch events. This can be implemented by storing the STIDs in a data area associated with the task, for instance the task control block (TCB) in VxWorks, where there are unused "spare" field. In OSE there is a "user area" associated with each process, which can be used for this purpose.

Complex embedded systems with event-triggered behavior, such as telecom systems, often create and terminate tasks dynamically. In that case it is important to recycle the STIDs to avoid that they run out. This means that the termination of tasks must be registered in order to mark the particular STID as no longer in use. An STID may however not be reused for newly created tasks as long as there are references to a particular STID in the event ring-buffer.

2.2 Time-Stamping (The "When")

Obtaining a time-stamp is normally a trivial operation, but standard libraries typically only allow for getting clock readings with a resolution of maximum 1 or even 10 milliseconds, depending on the tick rate of the OS. This is too coarse-grained for embedded systems timing analysis, since many tasks, and especially interrupt routines, have execution times measured in microseconds. Fortunately, embedded systems usually have hardware features for getting more accurate time-stamps, such as real-time clocks (RTC). In other cases, if the CPU frequency is constant, it is possible to use a CPU instruction counter register.

In order to reduce the memory usage when storing the events, a good method is to encode the time-stamps in a relative manner, i.e., to only store the time passed since the previously stored event, i.e., the durations of the execution fragments. If the absolute time of the last stored event is kept, it is possible to recreate absolute time-stamps during off-line analysis. This allows for correlating the trace recording with other time-stamped logs created by the system.

The relative time-stamp encoding allows for using fewer bits for storing time-stamps, typically between 8 – 16 bits per event. A problem however occurs in cases where the duration of an execution fragment exceeds the capacity of the time-stamp field, i.e., 255 or 65535 time units. Handling the overflow issue for relative time-stamps introduces a tradeoff between memory usage and recorder-induced jitter (i.e., predictability). The most reliable but least efficient solution is to use enough bits for this purpose so that the overflow does not occur. A more efficient solution is to reduce the number of time-stamp bits to better fit the typical fragment duration, and instead introduce an alternative handling of the few cases where the number of time-stamp bits are insufficient. In this case, an extra "XTS" event (eXtended Time-Stamp) is inserted before the original event, carrying the time-stamp using enough (32) bits. This however introduces a control branch in the task switch probe, which might cause timing jitter in the recorder overhead and thereby additional timing jitter in the system as a whole, which can be bad for testability and predictability. We however believe that this jitter is negligible compared to other sources of jitter, such as execution time variations. The XTS approach is used in all five recorder implementations presented in this paper. Storing time-stamps of higher resolution (e.g., nanoseconds instead of microseconds) results in higher RAM usage due to either a wider time-stamp field or more frequent XTS events. However, if using a too low time-stamp resolution (e.g., milliseconds), some execution fragments may get a zero duration and thus becomes "invisible" in off-line visualization and analysis.

2.3   Task-Switch Cause (The "Why")

In preemptive fixed-priority scheduling [3,5] a task-switch may occur for several reasons: the running task might have been blocked by a locked resource, it might have suspended itself, terminated, or a task of higher priority might have preempted the task. This information is necessary to record in order to allow grouping of execution fragments into task *instances*, also known as task jobs. A task instance corresponds to one logical execution of the task, i.e., the processing of one work-package. The end of an instance is referred to as the *instance finish*, and corresponds to the termination of the task, i.e., exit from main function, or for non-terminating tasks when the task has performed one iteration of the main loop and enters a blocked or waiting state awaiting the next task activation, i.e., the start of the next instance.

From a trace perspective, a task instance corresponds to one or several consecutive execution fragments of the same task, possibly interleaved by execution fragments of other tasks, where the last fragment is ended by the instance finish, and where any previous fragments of the same instance is ended by preemption or blocking. The concepts of instances and execution fragments are illustrated by Figure 1, using an example with three tasks, where task H has the most significant priority and task L the least significant priority. Each execution fragment is labeled $T_{i,f}$, where T is the task name, i the instance number and f the execution fragment number within the instance. The upper row indicates the task-switch cause: preemption (P) or termination (T) (i.e., instance finish).

What counts as an instance finish for non-terminating tasks is system specific and depends on the software architecture. For non-terminating tasks there are

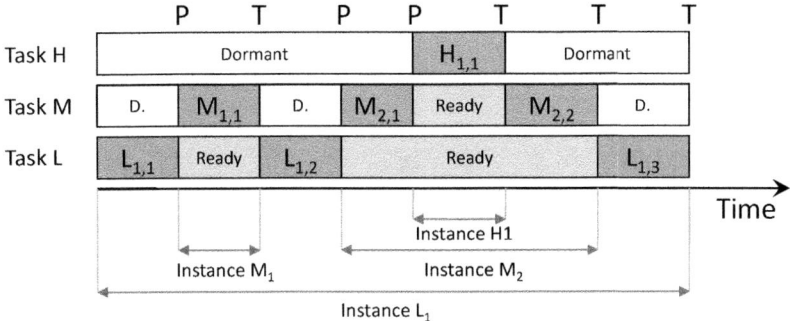

Fig. 1. Execution fragments and task instances

two options for detecting instance finish: using the scheduling status or using code instrumentation. If a certain scheduling status can be unambiguously associated with the inactive state of a task, a task-switch due to this scheduling status can be regarded as the instance finish. The next execution fragment of this task is thereby the start of the next instance. This approach is however difficult if the task may be blocked for other reasons (other semaphore or message queues), since the scheduling status at best tells the type of resource causing the blocking, but not the identity of the specific resource. A pragmatic solution is to add code instrumentation in the task main loop, immediately before the operating system call corresponding to the instance finish. A problem with code instrumentation in the application code is that the application developer has to be aware of the recorder solution, maintain the instrumentation points properly and also adding such instrumentation when adding new tasks to the system.

3   The Tracealyzer Tool

The Tracealyzer is a visualization tool with analysis capabilities for various timing and resource usage properties. The first version of the Tracealyzer was developed in 2004, in the project described in Section 4.1 in collaboration with ABB Robotics.

The main view of the tool displays a task trace using an novel visualization technique. Other trace visualization tools, such as the Wind River WindView, uses a trace visualization technique similar to a logic analyzer or Gantt-style charts, where the status of every task is displayed at all times, with one row or column per task. Such visualizations become hard to comprehend when zooming out to overview a longer scenario and the user may need to scroll in two dimensions.

In contrast, the visualization used by the Tracealyzer focuses on the task preemption nesting and only shows the currently active tasks, as depicted by Figure 2. This makes the trace easier to overview, especially long and complex scenarios with many tasks involved. The tool also provides a CPU load view

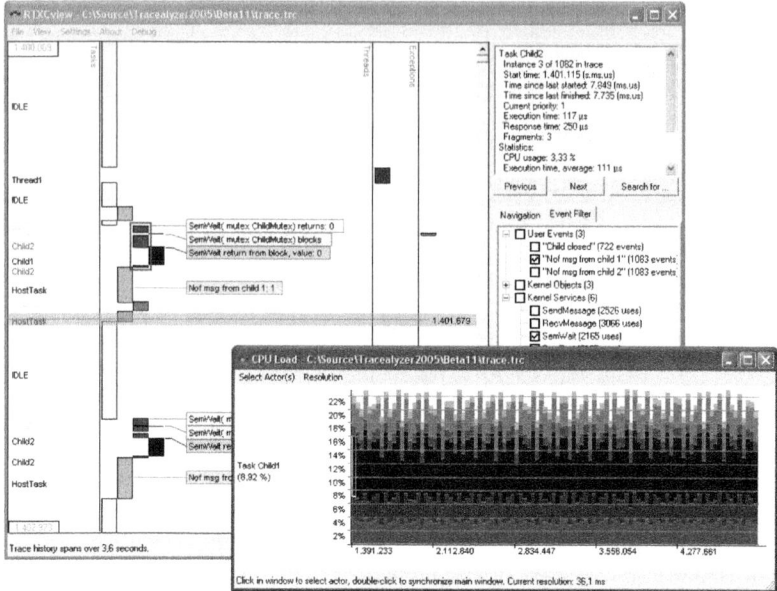

Fig. 2. The Tracealyzer (version 2.0)

over the entire trace. The two views are synchronized; the time window display in the main window is indicated in the CPU load overview and by clicking in the CPU load overview the trace view displays the corresponding time window. The tool has advanced features for searching, with several filters, and can also generate a report with detailed timing statistics for each task. The tool also allows for exporting timing data regarding tasks and other events to text format. More information about the tool is available at www.percepio.se where a demo version can be downloaded.

The Tracealyzer tool is since 2009 in commercialization by Percepio AB in collaboration with Quadros Systems, Inc. who develops the real-time operating system RTXC Quadros. A Quadros version will soon be marketed by Quadros Systems, under the name RTXCview.

4   Five Industrial Trace Recorder Projects

Starting 2004, five industry collaboration projects have been performed by the main author where trace recorders have been implemented for different existing systems. Four of these projects have included evaluation with respect to CPU and RAM usage. Three of the projects have lead to industrial deployment of the results, in one case as the coming official tracing tool for a commercial real-time operating system. The purpose of these projects have varied slightly, but all have included trace recording and visualization using the Tracealyzer, described in Section 3. The research motivation for these projects have been to verify the applicability of custom (third party) trace recording on common platforms for embedded systems. The motivation of the industrial partners where mainly to investigate the suitability of the Tracealyzer tool, which served as a "low-hanging fruit" for collaboration.

4.1   The RBT Project

ABB develops a control system for industrial robots, IRC 5. This is a large and complex embedded software system, consisting of around 3 million lines code. The operating system used is VxWorks, and the hardware platform is an Intel-based Industry PC. At the time of the evaluation, this system used an Intel Pentium III CPU and had 256 MB of RAM. It moreover has a flash-based hard drive, a network connection and an onboard FTP server.

Since VxWorks has features for registering callbacks on task-switch, task creation and task deletion, these events could be captured without kernel modifications. The task-switch callback function receives pointers to the task control blocks (TCBs) of both the previously executing task and for the task that is about to start. The developed recorder uses 8-bit STIDs, stored in an available "spare" field in the TCB by the task create callback routine. The task names are stored at creation time in a list of tasks, indexed by the STID.

All types of events are stored in a single ring buffer, using a fixed event size of 6 bytes. This required the use of bit-wise encoding in order to fit the desired information into the 48 bits available. The two first bytes are used to store two pieces of information in an asymmetric manner, where 2 bits are used for the event code and 14 bits for a relative time-stamp, obtained from an instruction counter of the Intel CPU used by this system. Since the time-stamp resolution used in this recorder is 1 μs, this solution allows for a execution fragment duration up to 2^{14} μs (16.4 ms). This is typically more than enough for this system; there are usually several task-switch events every millisecond. However, in some system modes, such as during system startup, the task-switch rate is much lower and the 14 bits may then be insufficient. As a precaution, an additional "XTS" event (eXtended Time-Stamp) is stored if the relative time-stamp does not fit in 14 bits. The XTS event stores the relative time-stamp using 32 bits and overrides the time-stamp field of the associated (following) event.

Recording inter-process communication events was considered important and this was accomplished by adding code instrumentation in the OS isolation layer. Semaphore operations are however not instrumented; they are very frequent in this system and it was feared that monitoring these would cause a major additional recording overhead. The event rate of the ABB system when recording task scheduling and IPC operations was found to be around 10 KHz. A ring buffer capacity of 100 000 events (600 000 bytes) therefore gives a trace history of around 10 seconds. The runtime of a recorder probe was found to be on average 0.8 μs, which at the typical event-rate of 10 KHz translates into a CPU overhead of 0.8 %.

As mentioned, ABB Robotics personnel decided after this project to integrate the recorder in their control system IRC 5 and to keep it active by default, also in the production version. The Tracealyzer is today used systematically at ABB Robotics for troubleshooting and for performance measurements. The recorder is triggered by the central error handling system, so whenever a serious problem occur a trace file is automatically stored to the system's hard drive. A trace file is in this case only about 600 KB and can therefore easily be sent by e-mail for quick analysis, e.g., if a customer experiences a problem.

4.2   The ECU Project

The system in focus of this project was the software of an ECU, i.e., a computer node in a vehicular distributed system developed by Bombardier Transportation[7]. Since also this system used VxWorks a similar recorder design could be used as in the RBT project. The company developers were mainly interested in the CPU usage per task, as well as for interrupt routines, during long-term operation of the vehicle. The hardware platform was a Motorola[8] PowerPC 603 running at 80 MHz.

In initial experiments using the Tracealyzer tool, the main problem was the endianness; the Motorola CPU uses big endian encoding, while the Tracealyzer expected little-endian encoding. In the first experiments in using the Tracealyzer for this system, the solution was a recorder design where all data is stored in little-endian format during run-time, by assigning each byte explicitly. This is far from optimal with respect to the CPU overhead of the recording and should be avoided. The latest version of the Tracealyzer assumes that the recorder writes the data to a binary file in native format and therefore detects the endianness, and converts if necessary, while reading the trace file. The endianness is detected by using a predefined 32-bit value, where the four bytes have different values, which is written to a predefined file location by the recorder, typically in the very beginning. An off-line analysis tool can then find the endianness from the order of these values.

Unlike the RBT project, this project included recording of interrupt routines. The operating system VxWorks does not have any callback functionality or similar for interrupts, but the interrupt controller of the CPU allowed for this. Interrupt routines could thereby be recorded as high-priority tasks, by adding task-switch events to the main ring buffer in the same way as for normal tasks.

An interesting requirement from Bombardier was that the recorded information should survive a sudden restart of the system and be available for post-mortem analysis. This was accomplished by using a hardware feature of the ECU; the event buffer was stored in Non-Volatile RAM (NVRAM). During the startup of the system, the recorder recovers any trace data stored in the NVRAM and writes it to a file, thereby allowing for post-mortem analysis. The ECU was equipped with 4 MB of NVRAM which is plenty since the company only needed a 2.5 second trace history. Since it was only desired to log task-switch events in this project, i.e., no IPC events like in the RBT case, it was possible to reduce the event size from six to four bytes per event.

---

[7] www.bombardier.com

[8] Now Freescale.

A recorder and a company-specific analysis tool was developed in a Master's thesis at Bombardier[4], but the Tracealyzer was not used after the initial tests leading to the thesis project. One of the Masters students was however employed by the company after the thesis project.

4.3   The WLD Project

This system is also an ECU-like computer, although not in the vehicular domain and the company is anonymous in this case. The computer system in focus is a node in a distributed system, with the overall purpose of automated welding for production of heavy industrial products. The computer in focus controls an electrical motor and is connected to a set of similar computer nodes over a field bus. The CPU used was an Infineon XC167, a 16-bit CPU running at only 20 MHz. The operating system used was RTXC Quadros.

Since the kernel source code of RTXC Quadros is available for customers, the recorder could be integrated in a custom version of the kernel. It was however not trivial to find the right location where to add the kernel instrumentation, especially for the task-switch events, since parts of the context-switch handling is written in assembly language. Time-stamps were obtained from the real-time clock (RTC) feature of the Infineon XC167 CPU and stored in a relative manner in the same way as in the previous cases.

There was no need for using short task IDs (STIDs) for reducing memory usage, since RTXC Quadros already uses 8-bit task handles. However, dynamic creation of tasks required an indirect approach, involving a lookup table, as the task handles of the operating system are reused. The lookup table contains a mapping between the RTXC task ID and the index of the task in an recorder-internal list of tasks, which is included in the generated trace file. The recorder task list contains the name and other information for up to 256 tasks. On task creation, the list is searched in order to find a matching task, so repeated dynamic creations of a single task only generates a single entry. However, there was no "garbage collection" in the recorder task list, so tasks which are no longer in the trace history still occupy an entry. This issue is however solved in the latest recorder implementation, described in Section 4.5. Interrupt routines were recorded by adding two probes in every interrupt service routine (ISR). Task-switch events are stored in the beginning and in the end of the ISR, using the interrupt code to look up a "faked" task entry, specified in a static table containing all interrupts. Nested interrupts are supported using a special purpose stack, holding the identity of the preempted ISRs, as well as the currently executing task.

The CPU overhead of the recording was measured and found higher than in previous cases, although still acceptable. The event rate was found to be around 500 Hz, i.e., about ten times less than in the ABB system, but the slow, low-end CPU (16-bit, 20 MHz) caused relatively high probe execution times, around 60 μs. This is 75 times longer than the probe execution times in the ABB system (0.8 μs). With a 500 Hz event rate, this translates into a CPU overhead of 3 %, which is significant, but probably not a serious issue compared to the potential benefits of trace recording. However, this recorder was not optimized for CPU usage; it was rather a first prototype on this platform. Several optimizations/fixes are possible in order to reduce the CPU usage of this recorder solution, as discussed in Section 4.6.

In a first evaluation by developers at the company, the welding system recorder was used together with the Tracealyzer tool in order to pinpoint the cause of a transient error which they previously had not been able to find. By studying a recorded trace in the Tracealyzer tool they could find that the error was caused by a wrongly placed "interrupt disable" instruction, which allowed for interrupts occurring during a critical section where interrupts should have been disabled. The company did however not integrate the developed recorder solution on a permanent basis, but has used the solution later for similar purposes. On those occasions, they have created a custom build using the instrumented RTXC Quadros kernel. This can lead to probe effect [7] problems, i.e., that the activation (or deactivation) of recording changes the system behavior.

4.4   The TEL Project

This project was performed together with an anonymous company in the telecom industry, which develops products based on the operating system OSE from ENEA. The particular system studied used a high-end PowerPC CPU, running at 1 GHz and with 256 MB of RAM. This project had the goal of providing means for exact CPU load measurements. Previously they had used a tool which sampled the currently executing task at randomly selected times and in that way got an approximate picture of the CPU usage of the various tasks. This was however considered too inaccurate. A Master's thesis project was initiated in 2008 in order to develop a recorder for this system [6].

A recorder for the Tracealyzer tool was developed and evaluated using standard performance tests of the system. The recorder used the "kernel hooks" feature of OSE, which is similar to the callback features in VxWorks, and 16-bit STIDs for tasks (*processes* in OSE terminology), stored in the "user area" of the process. The main problem was that OSE did not allow direct access to the kernel memory, for reading the process control block. It was thereby not possible to get the scheduling status of the tasks, which is necessary in order to identify task instances. A workaround was implemented, the Tracealyzer was modified for this case, so that priorities were used instead of status. This assumes that the priorities are static since the recorder cannot read them at the task-switch events, only at task creation. The resulting recorder was evaluated in the company lab using their normal test-cases for load testing. The CPU overhead of the recorder was found to be 1.1 % at an event rate of 18 KHz and a CPU load of 30 %. This result has to be considered as most acceptable, especially since the recorder was not optimized for CPU usage.

The project was successful in meeting the requirements, i.e., providing means for exact CPU load measurement, but the Tracealyzer could not be used to its full potential due to security restrictions in the OSE operating system, which prevented direct access to the process control blocks. The CPU overhead of the recorder was measured under realistic conditions and found to be relatively low despite a high event rate. The company did however not use the resulting recorder since it was not mature enough for industrial deployment, which requires a very robust solution, and since there was no obvious receiver at the company who could take over the recorder development and verification.

4.5 The RTOS Project

In 2009 the thesis author was contacted by a representative of Quadros Systems, Inc. who expressed interest in a collaboration aiming at developing a new trace tool for their operating system. This resulted in the development of the second generation Tracealyzer, along with a special version for Quadros Systems named *RTXCview*. This project also included the development of a whole new recorder design, in close collaboration with the chief engineer at Quadros Systems.

This recorder has little in common with the previous four versions. A major difference is that this recorder is designed for logging of generic operating system services without any hard-coded information in the recorder design. The recorder contains no assumptions on the operating system services that should be logged, this is configured through kernel instrumentation and using a configuration file of the Tracealyzer/RTXCview. All information needed by the off-line tool is stored in a single block of data which is statically initialized during compile-time. This eliminates the need for calling a recorder initialization routine at system startup, which was necessary in the previous versions. This design reduces the startup time of the system and makes it easy to retrieve the trace recording, e.g., if the system has stopped on a breakpoint using a debugger. This recorder does not use any bit-wise manipulations, which should reduce its CPU usage significantly. To achieve this, a larger event size was necessary, using eight bytes per event instead of four or six bytes.

In this design, there is no explicit task-list, as in other earlier recorders, but instead there is a generic symbol table which contains the names of tasks, user events, semaphores, and other named objects. A string added to this symbol table returns a 16-bit reference, the byte index of the string in the symbol table. If an identical string already exists in the symbol table, a reference to the existing string is returned instead of creating a new entry. This is therefore memory efficient and solves the issue of repeatedly created dynamic tasks. The symbol table lookup is fast since all symbol names which share a 6-bit checksum are connected in a linked list, as depicted by Figure 3. This however requires two extra bytes per symbol name, for storing the index of the next symbol with the same checksum, and an array holding 64 16-bit values, the linked-list heads. If a longer checksum (i.e., more checksum bits) is used, the look-up time is reduced, but the amount of memory required for the array of linked-list heads doubles for every extra checksum bit. For systems with plenty of memory, an 8-bit checksum should however not be any problems, since it only requires 512 bytes.

On task-switch events, the 8-bit RTXC task handles are stored without bothering about possible later reuse of the handle, which then might change the meaning of the currently stored handles. This is instead resolved off-line. The names of the currently active tasks are stored in a "dynamic object" table which

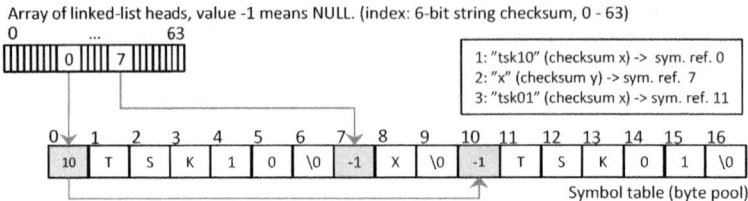

Fig. 3. The Symbol Table

is updated on task creation. When a task is terminated ("closed" in Quadros terminology), the name from the dynamic object table is stored in the symbol table and the resulting reference is stored, together with the RTXC task handle, in a special "close" event, which informs the off-line analysis tool that this mapping was valid up until this point. The off-line analysis can then find the correct task names of each execution fragment by reading the event trace backwards, starting at the trace end, and for each close event update the current mapping between RTXC task handle and name.

The described approach for handling reuse of dynamic task handles is used for all types of dynamically created kernel objects in RTXC Quadros, i.e., tasks, semaphores, mailboxes, alarms, etc. Time-stamps are stored in a relative manner, using 8, 16 or 32 bits per event, depending on the number of bytes available for each event type. Like in the other projects, XTS events are inserted when the normal time-stamp field is insufficient. The time unit of the time-stamps does not have to be microseconds as the time-stamp clock rate is specified in the recorder and provided to the off-line analysis tool, which converts into microseconds. It is thereby possible to use the hardware-provided resolution directly without run-time conversion into microseconds. Another time-related aspect is that absolute time-stamps are maintained also if the recording is stopped abruptly, e.g., due to a crash or breakpoint. The absolute time of the last stored event is kept updated in the recorder's main data structure and is thereby available for the off-line analysis. From this information and the relative time-stamps of the earlier events it is possible to recreate the absolute time-stamps of all events in the trace.

A prototype of this recorder has been implemented and delivered to Quadros Systems, who at the moment (Spring 2010) are working on integration of the recorder in their kernel. There are no big problems to solve; it is mainly a question of the limited development resources of Quadros Systems. No evaluation regarding the CPU overhead of this recorder has yet been performed. Developing and verifying a trace recorder for an operating system is much harder than for a specific embedded system, since an operating system recorder has to work for all hardware platforms supported by the operating system.

4.6   Summary of Recording Overhead Results

This section summarizes the measured recording overhead imposed by the recorders in the four cases where such measurements have been made, i.e.,

Table 1. Measured recording overheads in four industrial cases

Case	OS	CPU	F (MHz)	ES (bytes)	ET (μs)	ER (KHz)	CPU OH (%)	RAM OH (KB/s)
RBT	VW	P. III	533	6	0.8	10.0	0.8	60.0
ECU	VW	PPC 603	80	4	2.0	0.8	0.2	3.1
WLD	RTXC	XC167	20	4	60.0	0.5	3.0	2.0
TEL	OSE	PPC 750	1000	4	0.6	18.0	1.1	72.0

all cases except for the RTOS case (Section 4.5). The results are presented in Table 1.

In Table 1 "ES" means Event Size, i.e., the number of bytes used per event. ET means average probe execution time, ER means average event rate, in a typical recording. CPU OH means the corresponding CPU overhead and RAM OH means the corresponding number of (event buffer) bytes used per second. Note the relatively long probe execution time in the WLD case: 60 μs. The next faster ET, for ECU, was 30 times shorter even though the clock frequency was only four times higher in this case. This is probably due to the difference in CPU hardware architecture, the CPU in the WLD case is a 16-bit micro-controller, while more powerful 32-bit CPUs were used in the other cases.

Note that the four evaluated recorders were for low RAM usage, on the expense of higher CPU usage. It therefore possible to reduce the CPU overhead significantly by instead optimizing for CPU overhad, e.g., by increasing event size in order to avoid bit-wise encoding. Other possible optimizations are to move as much functionality as possible off-line (e.g., time-stamp conversion) and by using "inline" functions and macros instead of C functions. The latest recorder design, presented in Section 4.5, includes these improvements and should thereby give significantly lower CPU overhead, although not yet confirmed by experiments.

5   Lessons Learned

An important consideration is choosing an appropriate level of detail for the trace recording, e.g., should the recording include interrupt routines, or semaphore operations? This is a trade-off between the value of the information, with respect to the purpose of the recording, compared to the consequences of the associated recording overhead, such as a reduction in system performance, or increased unit cost if compensating the overhead with better but more expensive hardware. Including too little information may however also lead to increased costs if quality assurance becomes harder.

A related consideration is the trade-off between CPU usage and memory usage implied by using more advanced storage techniques, such a bit-wise encoding or data compression, which are more memory efficient but also more CPU demanding. We however believe that such techniques should generally be avoided in order to prioritize lower CPU overhead, since there is often unused RAM available, for a larger recording buffer, and if not so, a shorter trace history might be acceptable. A lower CPU overhead however improves system responsiveness and also reduces the risk of probe effects. One exception could be low-end embedded systems with very little RAM where a long trace history is very important, more important than CPU overhead. No type of system matching this description is however known to the authors.

Another consideration is whether the recorder should be integrated in the system on a permanent basis, or only activated when necessary. A permanent integration means that the CPU and memory overhead of the trace recording becomes permanent and may therefore reduce the system performance as experienced by customers. We however recommend this approach for several reasons: (1) the risk for probe effects is eliminated since the recording becomes an integrated and tested part of the system, (2) a trace is always available for diagnostic purposes, (3) the availability of a trace lowers the threshold for developers to begin using the trace recorder, (4) the recording cost in terms of CPU and memory usage is typically very small and therefore well motivated by the benefits. An exception to this recommendation would be systems which are highly focused on average-case performance and where the unit cost is a major issue, such as low-end multimedia devices.

The authors recommend that all types of events are stored in a single ring-buffer with fixed-size entries. This way, the chronological order of events is maintained. More advanced solutions using multiple buffers and/or variable-sized events may reduce memory usage, but leads to higher recorder complexity, higher risk of errors in the recorder and higher CPU overhead.

A good strategy is to store the information in a single data structure, which is statically allocated and initiated. This way, the recorder does not need a special initialization routine, but is recording directly at startup. Moreover, using this approach, the data can be easily fetched, e.g., using a debugger when stopped on a breakpoint, without having to execute a special "save" routine. As file format for the off-line tool, use a binary image of the run-time data structure. Differences in endian encoding can be resolved when reading the file.

A recommendation is to design trace recorders as simple and robust as possible and instead place the "intelligence" in the off-line tool. For instance, time-stamps should not be converted during run-time, bit-wise encoding should be avoided and startup initialization routines should be replaced by static initialization. A simple recorder design is also important if the recorder is to be trusted and maintained by the target system development organization. In that case, make sure there is an explicit receiver, a developer or lower level manager, which can take over the responsibility for the developed solution. This is believed to be the key success factor in the projects which led to industrial use.

6   Conclusions

This paper has presented experiences from five industry collaboration projects performed between 2004 – 2009 where solutions for embedded systems trace recording have been developed and evaluated. Several technical solutions and trade-off considerations have been presented and discussed. The CPU overhead of trace recording can be expected to be below 1 % on most systems using 32-bit CPUs, although it could reach about 3.6 % in the telecom system case if extrapolating the event rate up to 60 KHz at maximum CPU load. This is however an extreme case with respect to event rate. Implementation of trace recorder was possible as a third party developer on all three operating systems, although one required a different approach due to kernel security restrictions.

References

1. Åsberg, M., Kraft, J., Nolte, T., Kato, S.: A loadable task execution recorder for Linux. In: Proceedings of the 1st International Workshop on Analysis Tools and Methodologies for Embedded and Real-time Systems (July 2010)
2. Åsberg, M., Nolte, T., Perez, C.M.O., Kato, S.: Execution Time Monitoring in Linux. In: Proceedings of the Work-In-Progress session of 14th IEEE International Conference on Emerging Techonologies and Factory (September 2009)
3. Audsley, N.C., Burns, A., Davis, R.I., Tindell, K.W., Wellings, A.J.: Fixed priority pre-emptive scheduling: An historical perspective. Real-Time Systems Journal 8(2/3), 173–198 (1995)
4. Johansson, M., Saegebrecht, M.: Lastmätning av CPU i realtidsoperativsystem. Master's thesis, Mälardalen University, Västerås, Sweden (2007)
5. Liu, C.L., Layland, J.W.: Scheduling Algorithms for Multiprogramming in hard-real-time environment. Journal of the Association for Computing Machinery 20(1), 46–61 (1973)
6. Mughal, M.I., Javed, R.: Recording of Scheduling and Communication Events on Telecom Systems. Master's thesis, Mälardalen University, Västerås, Sweden (2008)
7. Schutz, W.: On the Testability of Distributed Real-Time Systems. In: Proceedings of the 10th Symposium on Reliable Distributed Systems, Pisa, Italy. Institut f. Techn. Informatik, Technical University of Vienna, A-1040, Austria (1991)
8. Thane, H., Hansson, H.: Using Deterministic Replay for Debugging of Distributed Real-Time Systems. In: 12th Euromicro Conference on Real-Time Systems (ECRTS 2000), pp. 265–272. IEEE Computer Society, Los Alamitos (June 2000)

Verification of an AFDX Infrastructure Using Simulations and Probabilities*

Ananda Basu[1], Saddek Bensalem[1], Marius Bozga[1], Benoît Delahaye[2],
Axel Legay[2], and Emmanuel Sifakis[1]

[1] Verimag Laboratory, Université Joseph Fourier Grenoble, CNRS
[2] INRIA/IRISA, Rennes, France

Abstract. Until recently, there was not a strong need for networking inside aircrafts. Indeed, the communications were mainly cabled and handled by Ethernet protocols. The evolution of avionics embedded systems and the number of integrated functions in civilian aircrafts has changed the situation. Indeed, those functionalities implies a huge increase in the quantity of data exchanged and thus in the number of connections between functions. Among the available mechanisms provided to handle this new complexity, one find Avionics Full Duplex Switched Ethernet (AFDX), a protocol that allows to simulate a point-to-point network between a source and one or more destinations. The core idea in AFDX is the one of Virtual Links (VL) that are used to simulate point-to-point communication between devices. One of the main challenge is to show that the total delivery time for packets on VL is bounded by some predefined value. This is a difficult problem that also requires to provide a formal, but quite evolutive, model of the AFDX network. In this paper, we propose to use a component-based design methodology to describe the behavior of the model. We then propose a stochastic abstraction that allows not only to simplify the complexity of the verification process but also to provide quantitative information on the protocol.

1 Introduction

Until recently, there was not a strong need for networking inside aircrafts. Digital technologies were initially introduced at the control platform of the aircrafts with the fly-by-wire technologies.

The evolution of avionics embedded systems and the number of integrated functions in civilian aircrafts implied a huge increase in the quantity of data exchanged and thus in the number of connections between functions. The Aircraft Data Networks used until now had either point to point connections, which incurred a high cost in aircraft production as well as increase of weight, or mono transmitter buses with very low performances (100Kbits/s). The innovation of *Avionics Full Duplex Switched Ethernet (AFDX)* [2] was to use an open standard such as Ethernet and take advantage of its high bandwidth, 100Mbps, and

---

* This work has been supported by the Combest EU project.

G. Roşu et al. (Eds.): RV 2010, LNCS 6418, pp. 330–344, 2010.

the use of cheap COTS components. AFDX also offers the capability to easily extend the avionic network with new devices, as well as to reduce the wiring.

For a network to be suitable for use in critical applications, it must be reliable and deterministic. In AFDX reliability is achieved with redundancy while determinism with the definition of Virtual Links (VL), which put constraints on the allowed traffic. A network is deterministic if we can guarantee an upper bound for the time a message needs to be delivered to its destination. For AFDX such upper bounds can be provided with analytical methods [10]. The bounds obtained are over approximations of the worst case and the analysis can only be performed on very abstract models [8]. There is thus the need for new methods that will guarantee more realistic upper bounds on more realistic models.

In a very recent work [6], we suggested *stochastic abstraction*. This technique can ease the verification process of large heterogeneous systems by abstracting some of the components of the system with probability distributions. The ability to add stochastic information can also be used to compute a probability for the system to satisfy the property. The latter can efficiently be done with *Statistical Model Checking* (SMC) [12,19,21] that has recently been proposed as an alternative to avoid an exhaustive exploration of the state-space of the model. The core idea of SMC is to conduct some simulations of the system and then use results from the statistic area in order to decide whether the system satisfies the property. Statistical model checking techniques can also be used to estimate the probability with which a system satisfies a given property [12,11]. Of course, in contrast with an exhaustive approach, a simulation-based solution does not guarantee a correct result. However, it is possible to bound the probability of making an error. Simulation-based methods are known to be far less memory and time intensive than exhaustive ones, and are sometimes the only option [22,14]. Statistical model checking gets widely accepted in various research areas such as systems biology [9,15] or software engineering, in particular for industrial applications. The technique in [6], which combines statistical model checking and stochastic abstraction, was capable of verifying properties of a model with more than 2^{3000} states in a few minutes.

In this experimental paper, we propose to apply the stochastic abstraction principle on AFDX networks. Our contributions are twofolds:

1. **Model of the network.** In this paper, we propose a BIP model for AFDX architecture. BIP [5] is a tool for specifying components and component interactions. One of the very attractive features of BIP is its ability to generate executions of composite systems. This is required to compute the stochastic abstraction as well as to apply statistical model checking. Another advantage of BIP is that it permits to give a very detailed description of each component. Also, components can be developed by independent teams, which decrease the complexity of the design.

2. **Verification.** We then examine the *latency requirements* property in AFDX, i.e., we check that the total delivery time for packets on virtual links is smaller than some predefined values. The difficulty is that our model of AFDX is constituted of many BIP components – this is needed to obtain an accurate

model of the network. Combining these components lead to a system that is too big (in terms of states) to be analyzed by classical verification techniques such as model checking. In order to overcome the problem, we suggest to abstract some of these components with probability distributions, hence producing another BIP model of the network that is a stochastic abstraction of the original one. We then apply statistical model checking to estimate a value of the bound for which the requirement is satisfied with probability 1. This is an important feature as correct upper bounds are mandatory for certification. We also show that one can use our approach to compute the probability that the latency requirement is satisfied for a given value of the bound. This latest feature is of interest to adapt/reconfigure the network for better average performances.

We believe that our work is interesting as it proposes (1) a very detailed and accurate model of an AFDX network that is obtained by a component-based design methodology (this also illustrate the advantages of the BIP toolset), and (2) an efficient formal technique for verifying properties and provide quantitative informations on this model.

Structure of the paper. Section 2 introduces BIP and SMC while Section 3 is dedicated to AFDX. In Section 4, we propose our compositional design methodology to generate formal models of AFDX networks. Section 5 focuses on a stochastic abstraction and presents our experiments. Finally, Section 6 concludes the paper and discuss related works.

2   Preliminaries

In this section, we briefly introduce the BIP framework that is used to define components and component interactions. BIP has the ability to simulate execution of composite systems. We then introduce statistical model checking that is a technique used to estimate/or validate the probability for a stochastic system to satisfy some given property. Statistical model checking requires the ability to simulate the model, which is exactly what BIP can provide.

2.1   The BIP Framework

The BIP framework, introduced in [5], supports a methodology for building systems from *atomic components*. It uses *connectors*, to specify possible interaction patterns between components, and *priorities*, to select amongst possible interactions. In BIP, data and their transformations can be written directly in C. Atomic components are finite-state automata extended with variables and ports. Ports are action names, and may be associated with variables. They are used for synchronization with other components. Control states denote locations at which the components await for synchronization. Variables are used to store local data. Composite components allow defining new components from sub-components (atomic or composite). Components are connected through flat or hierarchical *connectors*, which relate ports from different sub-components.

Connectors represent sets of *interactions*, that are, non-empty sets of ports that have to be jointly executed. They also specify guards and transfer functions for each interaction, that is, the enabling condition and the exchange of data across the ports of the interacting components. *Priorities* are used to select amongst simultaneously enabled interactions. They are a set of rules, each consisting of an ordered pair of interactions associated with a condition. When the condition holds and both interactions of the corresponding pair are enabled, only the one with higher-priority can be executed.

BIP is supported by an extensible tool-set which includes functional validation, model transformation and code generation features. Actually, code generation targets both simulation and implementation models (e.g., distributed, multi-threaded, real-time, etc.). In particular, simulation is driven by a specific middleware, *the BIP engine*, which allows to generate, explore and inspect execution traces corresponding to BIP models.

2.2   Statistical Model Checking

Consider a stochastic system $\mathcal{S}$ and a property ϕ. *Statistical model checking* refers to a series of simulation-based techniques that can be used to answer two questions : (1) **Qualitative** : Is the probability for $\mathcal{S}$ to satisfy ϕ greater or equal to a certain threshold θ? and (2) **Quantitative** : What is the probability for $\mathcal{S}$ to satisfy ϕ? Let B_i be a discrete random variable with a Bernoulli distribution of parameter p. Such a variable can only take 2 values 0 and 1 with $Pr[B_i = 1] = p$ and $Pr[B_i = 0] = 1 - p$. In our context, each variable B_i is associated with one simulation of the system. The outcome for B_i, denoted b_i, is 1 if the simulation satisfies ϕ and 0 otherwise.

Qualitative Answer using Statistical Model Checking. The main approaches [21,19] proposed to answer the qualitative question are based on *hypothesis testing*. Let $p = Pr(\phi)$, to determine whether $p \geq \theta$, we can test $H : p \geq \theta$ against $K : p < \theta$. A test-based solution does not guarantee a correct result but it is possible to bound the probability of making an error. The *strength* (α, β) of a test is determined by two parameters, α and β, such that the probability of accepting K (respectively, H) when H (respectively, K) holds, called a Type-I error (respectively, a Type-II error) is less or equal to α (respectively, β). A test has *ideal performance* if the probability of the Type-I error (respectively, Type-II error) is exactly α (respectively, β). However, these requirements make it impossible to ensure a low probability for both types of errors simultaneously (see [21] for details). A solution is to use an *indifference region* $[p_1, p_0]$ (with θ in $[p_1, p_0]$) and to test $H_0 : p \geq p_0$ against $H_1 : p \leq p_1$. We now very briefly sketch an hypothesis testing algorithm that is called the *sequential probability ratio test (SPRT in short)* [20]. Our intention is not to give too much details on SPRT – the interested reader will read [20].

In SPRT, one has to choose two values A and B $(A > B)$ that ensure that the strength (α, β) of the test is respected. Let m be the number of observations that have been made so far. The test is based on the following quotient:

$$\frac{p_{1m}}{p_{0m}} = \prod_{i=1}^{m} \frac{Pr(B_i = b_i \mid p = p_1)}{Pr(B_i = b_i \mid p = p_0)} = \frac{p_1^{d_m}(1-p_1)^{m-d_m}}{p_0^{d_m}(1-p_0)^{m-d_m}}, \tag{1}$$

where $d_m = \sum_{i=1}^{m} b_i$. The idea behind the test is to accept H_0 if $\frac{p_{1m}}{p_{0m}} \geq A$, and H_1 if $\frac{p_{1m}}{p_{0m}} \leq B$. The SPRT algorithm computes $\frac{p_{1m}}{p_{0m}}$ for successive values of m until either H_0 or H_1 is satisfied; the algorithm terminates with probability 1[20]. This has the advantage of minimizing the number of simulations. In his thesis[21], Younes proposed a logarithmic based algorithm SPRT that given p_0, p_1, α and β implements the sequential ratio testing procedure. When one has to test $\theta \geq 1$ or $\theta \geq 0$, it is better to use *Single Sampling Plan* (SSP) (see [21,17,19] for details) that is another hypothesis testing algorithm whose number of simulations is pre-computed in advance. In general, this number is higher than the one needed by SPRT, but is it known to be optimal for the above mentioned values. More details about hypothesis testing algorithms and a comparison between SSP and SPRT can be found in [17].

Quantitative Answer using Statistical Model Checking. In [12,16] Peyronnet et al. propose an estimation procedure to compute the probability p for $\mathcal{S}$ to satisfy ϕ. Given a *precision* δ, Peyronnet's procedure, which we call PESTIMATION, computes a value for p' such that $|p' - p| \leq \delta$ with *confidence* $1 - \alpha$. The procedure is based on the *Chernoff-Hoeffding bound*[13]. Let $B_1 \ldots B_m$ be m discrete random variables with a Bernoulli distribution of parameter p associated with m simulations of the system. Recall that the outcome for each of the B_i, denoted b_i, is 1 if the simulation satisfies ϕ and 0 otherwise. Let $p' = (\sum_{i=1}^{m} b_i)/m$, then Chernoff-Hoeffding bound [13] gives $Pr(|p' - p| > \delta) < 2e^{-\frac{m\delta^2}{4}}$. As a consequence, if we take $m \geq \frac{4}{\delta^2} \log(\frac{2}{\alpha})$, then $Pr(|p' - p| \leq \delta) \geq 1 - \alpha$. Observe that if the value p' returned by PESTIMATION is such that $p' \geq \theta - \delta$, then $\mathcal{S} \models Pr_{\geq \theta}$ with confidence $1 - \alpha$.

Playing with Statistical Model Checking Algorithms. The efficiency of the above algorithms is characterized by the number of simulations needed to obtain an answer. This number may change from executions to executions and can only be estimated (see [21] for an explanation). However, some generalities are known. For the qualitative case, it is known that, except for some situations, SPRT is always faster than SSP. PESTIMATION can also be used to solve the qualitative problem, but it is always slower than SSP [21]. If θ is unknown, then a good strategy is to estimate it using PESTIMATION with a low confidence and then validate the result with SPRT and a strong confidence.

3   The Avionics Full Duplex Switched Ethernet

AFDX [2] is a standard developed by Airbus for building highly reliable, time deterministic aircraft data networks (ADNs) based on commercial, off-the shelf Ethernet technology.

The first standard defined for ADNs has been ARINC 429 [1]. This standard, developed over thirty years ago and still widely used today, has proven

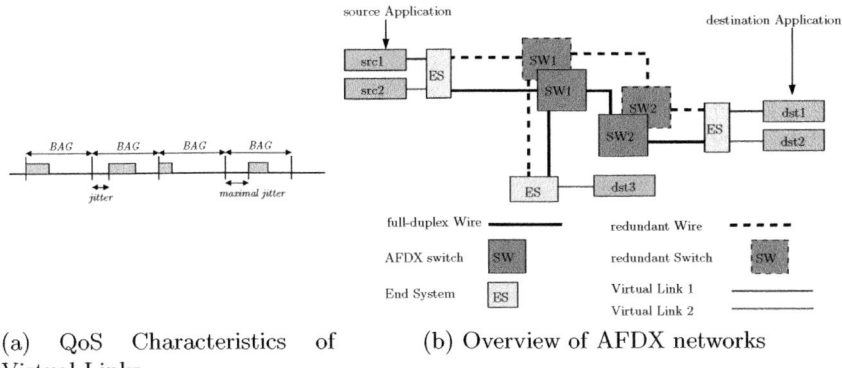

(a)   QoS   Characteristics   of   (b) Overview of AFDX networks
Virtual Links

Fig. 1. Details of AFDX

to be highly reliable in safety critical applications. It relies on point-to-point unidirectional bus with single transmitter and up to twenty receivers. Consequently, ARINC 429 networks need a significant amount of wiring and imply a non-negligible aircraft weight increase.

ARINC 664 has been defined as the next-generation ADNs standard. It is based upon IEEE 802.3 Ethernet and uses commercial off-the-shelf hardware thereby reducing costs and development time. AFDX is formally defined in Part 7 of the ARINC 664 specification [2]. It has been developed by Airbus Industries for the A380 and since then, it has been accepted by Boeing and used on the Boeing 787 Dreamliner. AFDX bridges the gap on reliability of guaranteed bandwidth from the original ARINC 664 standard. It features a star topology network of up to 24 end-systems connected to a switch, where each switch can be bridged together to other switches on the network. Based on this topology, AFDX is able to significantly reduce wire runs thus reducing overall aircraft weight. Additionally, AFDX provides dual link redundancy and Quality of Service (QoS).

Virtual Links. AFDX offer to avionics engineers the capability to think in terms of point-to-point connections of their applications at design time, just as they did in the past with ARINC 429. This capability is provided through the notion of *virtual links* (VL), that are, logical unidirectional connections from one transmitter end-system to one or many receiver end-systems. Moreover, virtual links are used to define and control the QoS within AFDX networks. They are annotated with non-functional characteristics including (i) the *bandwidth allocation gap* (BAG), the time interval allocated for the transmission of one packet, (ii) the *minimum* and *maximum packet size* and (iii) the *jitter* allowed for transmission, with respect to the beginning of the BAG. These characteristics can be visualized in figure 1a.

End Systems. The end-systems are the entry points on AFDX networks. They realize the interface between the application software and the network infrastructure. They mainly perform three tasks: traffic regulation, scheduling and redundancy management. First, *traffic regulation* transforms arbitrary (not regulated) flows of packets sent by applications such that they meet their corresponding virtual links characteristics. More precisely, stores packets and delivers them with the correct rate i.e., exactly one packet per BAG, without jitter. Second, *scheduling* organize the global flow obtained from several virtual links before their delivery on the channel. Packets coming from the traffic regulator and corresponding to different virtual links are interleaved in order to ensure QoS characteristics such as bounded delivery time or bounded jitter. Third, *redundancy management* enforces dual redundancy. On transmission side, packets are indexed, duplicated and sent towards destination on two distinct channels. On reception side, a *first valid wins* policy is applied, that is, the first valid packet received is delivered to the destination application, whereas the second is silently discarded.

Switches. AFDX switches are the core elements of AFDX networks. They perform tasks such as frame filtering, traffic policing, switching, and monitoring. *Frame filtering* discards invalid packets according to various integrity rules (concerning packet size, sequence numbers, incoming path, etc). In a similar way, *traffic policing* maintains the traffic for each virtual link within its (statically) declared characteristics i.e., avoid fault propagation such as network flooding because of faulty end-systems or switches. The *switching* functionality performs the routing of packets towards their destination(s). The routes are statically defined for every virtual link. Finally, *monitoring* realizes various logging and other administrative operations.

Requirements. The use of AFDX in safety-critical systems is usually subject to extra requirements. In particular, there are *latency requirements*, that are, the total delivery time for packets on virtual links must be smaller than some predefined values. For example, such requirements are mandatory when AFDX is used to transport data needed for navigation and control applications running on board. They usually have to be formally verified as part of the certification process. Nevertheless, their verification is difficult since they are system-level properties depending both on the network topology (physical infrastructure) and on the whole set of virtual links (application traffic) deployed on it.

4   A BIP Model for AFDX Systems

We have developed a systematic way to construct accurate functional models of AFDX networks in BIP. Network models are structural, that is, they are interconnected assemblies of models of AFDX entities (end-systems and switches), following the physical connections and reflecting the static deployment on virtual links. This construction arises naturally given the BIP modeling principles and enforces a clear separation between functional (behavior) and architectural (connection) elements. Moreover, it allows the development of models for real-sized AFDX networks, of arbitrary complexity with no difficulty.

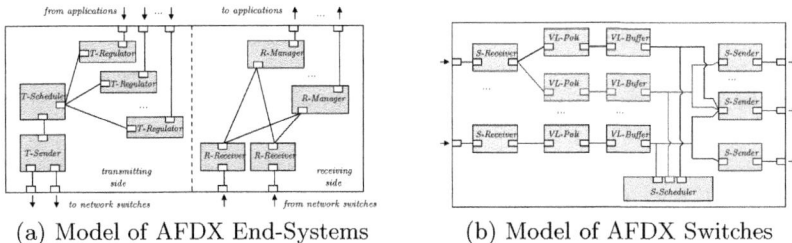

(a) Model of AFDX End-Systems   (b) Model of AFDX Switches

Fig. 2. Details of the modeling of AFDX in BIP

The BIP components modeling AFDX end-systems and switches are parametric and can accommodate arbitrary but statically fixed numbers of virtual links. Their inner architecture reflects the functional decomposition established by the AFDX standard [2]. For example, the BIP model for end-systems is composed of traffic regulator(s), scheduler, sender, receiver(s) and redundancy manager(s) sub-components, inter-connected as shown in figure 2a.

All sub-components are atomic and have been explicitly modeled using discretized timed automata. As an example, we provide the model of the atomic traffic regulator component in figure 3. The BIP component representing AFDX switches has been constructed in a similar way. Its inner architecture is shown in figure 2b. The switch model includes atomic sub-components implementing traffic classification, traffic policing, in packet buffering for each virtual link, scheduling and finally, out packet buffering, for each outgoing connection.

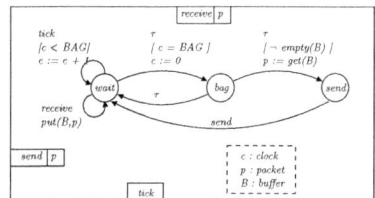

Fig. 3. Model of Traffic Regulator

In particular, let us remark that the AFDX standard leaves open the scheduling algorithms to be used within end-systems and switches. Nevertheless, our BIP models provide concrete implementations, that is, round-robin on incoming virtual links. We made this choice since, while being very easy to implement, it introduces relatively low jitter for multiplexing regulated flows of packets incoming on several virtual links. Still, the model can be easily changed to use other scheduling policy, if needed. We have identified nine types of atomic components in BIP necessary to model any AFDX system (excluding the application atomic components). As an example, a switch model with two input (each having ten Virtual Links) and one output, contains twenty-four atomic components. An end system generating ten Virtual Links is modeled by twenty-two atomic components.

BIP components interact using two categories of connectors. First, there are *data* connectors, as illustrated in figures 2a or 2b, which transport (abstractions of) data packets between various components. These connectors have an unique *sender* port and one or many *receiver* ports. At any interaction an abstract packet (a data structure containing the virtual link id, size, sequence numbers, etc.) is transferred simultaneously from the sender to all the receivers. Second, there is a global *tick* connector (not illustrated) which realizes the time synchronization within the whole model. This connector synchronizes all the *tick* ports, occuring within all the atomic components. Whenever a tick interaction takes place, it correspond to a discrete progress of time by one time unit. Since all components participate, the progress of time is therefore *synchronously* observed/followed by all of them. The time step has been chosen as 1 μs (microsecond) in order to correspond to the magnitude for sending frames on 100Mbps Ethernet networks. That is, the transmission duration for an Ethernet frame takes between 5 and 117 time units (i.e., microseconds).

5   Verification Methodology and Experiments

In this section, we present the experiments we conducted using our BIP model of the AFDX infrastructure. We are interested in verifying the latency requirement property introduced in Section 3. The problem with our model is that, as we have seen, switches are complex components, providing multiples functionalities. This complexity, which is needed to obtain a realistic model of the system, may prevent the use of classical model checking algorithms (state-space explosion). This is especially the case for AFDX systems made of many (e.g., tens) switches and supporting many (e.g., hundreds or thousands) virtual links. However, in order to reason on the latency requirement, we are only interested in the time needed for a message to go through the switch. We suggest to exploit this observation in order to reduce the complexity of the verification process.

More precisely, our idea (which is similar to the one we recently introduced in [6]) is to abstract switch complexity by replacing the switches with probability distributions on the delays for a message to cross them. We thus obtain a *stochastic abstraction* of our AFDX model. We can then use statistical model checking techniques to verify the end-to-end delay properties.

As a running example, let us consider the AFDX network given in Figure 5a. This network is constituted of three switches, five source end-systems, and one destination end system. The source end-systems are connected to the destination end system with several virtual links. For such a network with ten Virtual Links per end-system, the BIP model contains 213 atomic components. As we shall see in the next section, the number of virtual links going out from an end-system and the size of the BAGs may vary from experiments to experiments.

Our idea is to replace each switch by several probability distributions, one for each Virtual link. The result will be a BIP model in where the switches are replaced by several automata generating the distribution; an example is given in Figure 4. One can again simulate this model and then use statistical model checking algorithms to verify its

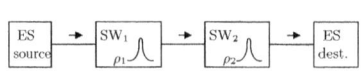

Fig. 4. Abstract stochastic model obtained for a designated virtual link VL_0

properties. As we shall see, these automata can directly be encoded in the BIP engine, which simplify the structure of the model.

We first give details on how to compute the probability distributions and then we discuss the experimental results for several scenarios, each of them depending on the number of virtual links and size of BAGs.

5.1   Stochastic Abstraction

In this section, we briefly describe our approach to learn the probability distributions that abstract switches behaviors.

For each switch and each virtual link, we try to estimate a probability distribution on the delay for a packet to cross the switch. This is done by running the BIP model corresponding to architecture of Figure 5a. For example, let assume that we made 33 measures on a given switch, i.e. the virtual links has sent 33 packets through the switch. The result will be a series of delay values and, for each value, the number of times it has been

Table 1. Simulation times in seconds

VL's per End System	Switch	Time
10	2	0:08:49
	1	0:36:14
20	2	0:19:24
	1	1:34:36
30	2	0:31:57
	1	2:03:22

observed. As an example, delay 5 has been observed 3 times, delay 19 has been observed 30 times. The probability distribution is represented with a table of 33 cells. In our case, 3 cells of the table will contain the value 5 and 30 will contain the value 19. The BIP engine will then select a value in the table in a uniform way.

According to our observation, 1000 simulations are enough to obtain an accurate estimation of the probability distribution. However, for confidence reasons, we have conducted 4000 experiments. Table 1 reports on the time needed to conduct these simulations switch by switch.

5.2   Experiments

We now report on our experiments. We are mainly interested in estimating a bound on the total delivery time for packets on virtual links. We are also interested in computing the probability that the total delivery time for packets is smaller than a given bound. This bound may be a requirement provided by the user. Verifying these properties is only illistrations of what we can do with our stochastic abstraction.

We consider the AFDX architecture given in Figure 5a, but our methodology applies to any AFDX architecture. We assume that the switches are replaced by probability distributions computed as explained in Section 5.1. As we have seen in the previous section, the number of virtual links and the size of the BAGs and the frames may vary. It is important to study the influence of these variation on the latency requirement. This will be done with the following scenarios.

Scenario 1. In this scenario, each source end-system (E.S. 1 to 5) is connected to the destination end-system (E.S. 6) with a single virtual link. Each of these

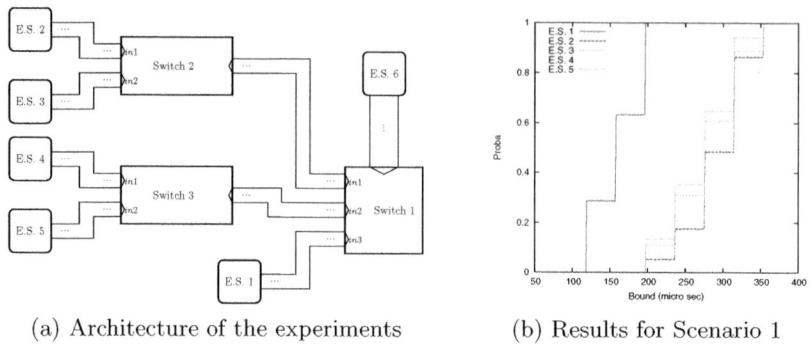

(a) Architecture of the experiments   (b) Results for Scenario 1

Fig. 5. Architecture of the Experiments and results for Scenario 1

five virtual links have the same parameters, that are BAG=4 ms, frame size=500 Bytes. Our first experiment was to compute, for each link, the probability that the total delivery time for packets is smaller than a given bound, until we reach probability one. We were using the ESTIMATION algorithm with a precision of of 0.01 and a confidence of 0.01 to estimate probabilities for bounds between 1 and 400 micro seconds. The results, which were obtained in less than 2 seconds, are given in Figure 5b. It is not surprising that End-system 1 gets a better behavior as it is only connected to one switch. In the next scenarios we shall see that these results can be validated with higher precision and confidence by using SPRT and SSP.

Scenario 2. In this scenario, we consider an increasing number of virtual links: 10, 20, and 30 links. All the virtual links have the same characteristics: BAG = 4ms, and frame size varying between 100 and 500 octets (which is different from the previous experiment in where this number was fixed). Our first experiment was the same as for Scenario 1, except that we had to consider bigger values of the bound in order to reach probability 1. The results are given in Figures 6a, 6b and 7a for respectively $X = 10$, $X = 20$ and $X = 30$ links. We shall observe that the bound varies between $0\mu s$ and $2000\mu s$ for $X = 10$, between $0\mu s$ and $3000\mu s$ for $X = 20$ and between $0\mu s$ and $3500\mu s$ for $X = 30$.

The second and third experiment consisted in validating the results we obtained in the first experiment using SPRT and SSP. Those algorithms cannot be used to check for an exact probability ($= \theta$) but for a bound on the probability ($\geq \theta$ or $\leq \theta$ with a simple modification of the algorithm [21]). This is not a problem. Indeed, if ESTIMATION told us that the probability is x for a given bound, then it means then it is also greater or equal to x. As outlined in Section 2.2, working with SSP and SPRT allows us to validate the results with a higher confidence. More precisely, we worked with a precision of 10^{-7} and confidence of 10^{-10} instead of 10^{-2}. The results are given in Table 2 for $X = 10$.

Finally, we have measured the minimum and maximum delay and the jitter (difference between these delays) for one of the virtual link of each End-system. This is a proportion computed on a fixed number of simulations, here $2.3 * 10^9$.

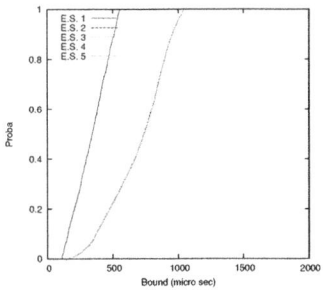
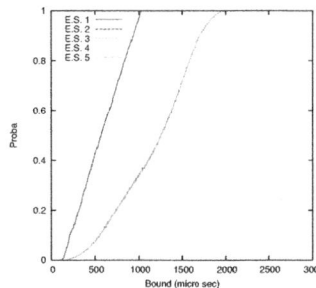

(a) Probability of having a delay lower than a given bound as a function of the bound for $X = 10$ for Scenario 2

(b) Probability of having a delay lower than a given bound as a function of the bound for $X = 20$ for Scenario 2

Fig. 6. Illustration of results for Scenario 2

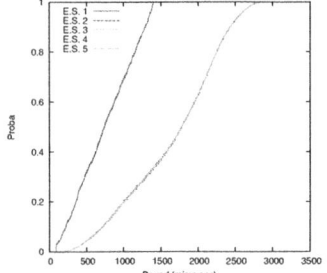
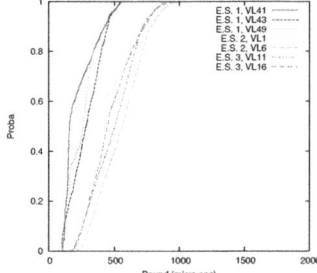

(a) Probability of having a delay lower than a given bound for $X = 30$ for Scenario 2

(b) Probability of having a delay lower than a given bound for Scenario 3

Fig. 7. Illustration of results for Scenario 2 and 3

We obtained, a jitter of 915 with a maximum delay of 1032 and a minimum delay of 117 for a virtual link between End-system 1 and End-system 6 with $X = 20$. As the number of simulations is quite high, we believe that our results are quite accurate. This show the interest of working with an executable model.

Scenario 3. In this scenario, we use a fixed number of ten virtual links. Those links have different BAGS, and the packets size still varies between 100 and 500 octets. Figures 8a and 8b represents the repartition of the virtual links in Switches 1 and 2 respectively. Switch 3 has the same repartition of virtual links as Switch 2. We conducted the same experiments as for Scenario 2.

We first measure the probability of having a delay lower than a given bound, varying between $0\mu s$ and $2000\mu s$. The results are given in Figure 7b. We then applied SPRT and SSP. The results are reported in Table 3. All the results are obtained in less than 10 seconds. Finally, we have measured the minimum delay, the maximum delay and the jitter for one virtual link of each group of virtual

Table 2. Results of SPRT and SSP experiments for $X = 10$ for Scenario 2

End-system	Bound	Estimated proba	Algorithm	Checked against	Result	NSimulations
1	479	$P = 0.831975$	SPRT	$P \geq 0.8$?	Y	1.210^{10}
			SPRT	$P \geq 0.85$?	N	1.510^{-10}
	564	$P = 1$	SSP	$P \geq 1$?	Y	2.310^{9}
2	859	$P = 0.730221$	SPRT	$P \geq 0.7$?	Y	1.610^{10}
			SPRT	$P \geq 0.5$?	Y	2.510^{9}
	1064	$P = 1$	SSP	$P \geq 1$?	Y	2.310^{9}
3	760	$P = 0.532258$	SPRT	$P \geq 0.5$?	Y	1.910^{10}
			SPRT	$P \geq 0.3$?	Y	2.110^{9}
	1064	$P = 1$	SSP	$P \geq 1$?	Y	2.310^{9}
4	977	$P = 0.931101$	SPRT	$P \geq 0.9$?	Y	6.810^{9}
			SPRT	$P \geq 0.5$?	Y	1.310^{9}
	1064	$P = 1$	SSP	$P \geq 1$?	Y	2.310^{9}
5	512	$P = 0.231049$	SPRT	$P \geq 0.2$?	Y	1.210^{10}
			SPRT	$P \geq 0.1$?	Y	1.610^{9}
	1064	$P = 1$	SSP	$P \geq 1$?	Y	2.310^{9}

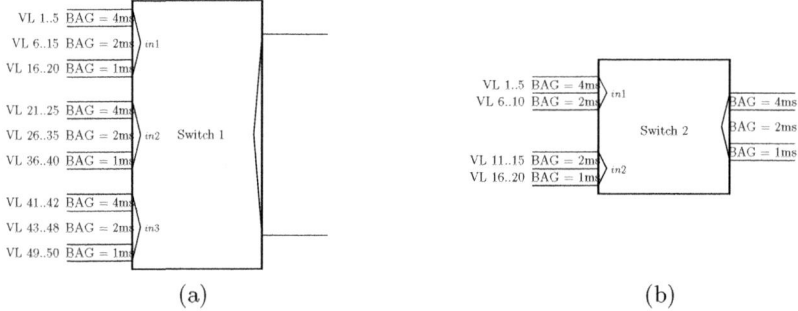

(a)   (b)

Fig. 8. Repartitions of the virtual links in the switches for Scenario 3

Table 3. Results of SPRT and SSP experiments Scenario 3

End-system-VL	Bound	Estimated proba	Algorithm	Checked against	Result	NSimulations
1-41	345	0.801593	SPRT	$P \geq 0.8$	Y	$1.3 \cdot 10^{9}$
	566	1	SSP	$P \geq 1$	Y	$2.3 \cdot 10^{9}$
1-43	403	0.804363	SPRT	$P \geq 0.8$	Y	$9.2 \cdot 10^{8}$
	561	1	SSP	$P \geq 1$	Y	$2.3 \cdot 10^{9}$
1-49	347	0.805792	SPRT	$P \geq 0.8$	Y	$9.2 \cdot 10^{8}$
	556	1	SSP	$P \geq 1$	Y	$2.3 \cdot 10^{9}$
2-1	751	0.901582	SPRT	$P \geq 0.9$	Y	$1.1 \cdot 10^{9}$
	1044	1	SSP	$P \geq 1$	Y	$2.3 \cdot 10^{9}$
2-6	785	0.902106	SPRT	$P \geq 0.9$	Y	$1.1 \cdot 10^{9}$
	1051	1	SSP	$P \geq 1$	Y	$2.3 \cdot 10^{9}$
3-11	505	0.504159	SPRT	$P \geq 0.5$	Y	$1.7 \cdot 10^{9}$
	932	1	SSP	$P \geq 1$	Y	$2.3 \cdot 10^{9}$
3-16	446	0.502088	SPRT	$P \geq 0.5$	Y	$3.1 \cdot 10^{9}$
	994	1	SSP	$P \geq 1$	Y	$2.3 \cdot 10^{9}$

links with the same characteristics. As an example, we obtain, a jitter of 451
with a maximum delay of 556 and a minimum delay of 105 for VL 49 between
End-system 1 and End-system 6.

6   Conclusion and Related Work

This paper proposes a model of the AFDX network based on the compositional design approach as well as a verification technique based on statistical model checking. To the best of our knowledge, this is the first complete, fully operational and timing accurate, model of AFDX developed using a formal framework. Other models are either performance models built within network simulators or timed automata models, restricted to few functionalities or describing very simple network configuration. The work of [4] focused on redundancy management and identified several issues occuring in the presence of particular network faults. Alternatively, [7,8,18] deal with computing bounds for end-to-end delays in AFDX networks. The papers [7,8] report experiments using three analysis methods: network calculus, stochastic simulation using QNAP2 and timed model-checking using Uppaal. The results confirm the well-established knowledge about these methods. Network calculus[10] provides pessimistic, unreachable bounds. Network stochastic simulation provide reachable bounds, however, these bounds hardly depend on the simulation scenario considered and can be too optimistic. Timed model-checking[3] provide exact bounds, however, it suffers for state explosion and cannot scale to realistic networks. Finally, the work in [18] provides a method for compositional analysis of end-to-end delays. It is shown that, to measure delays for a given virtual link, it is enough to consider only the traffic generated by the virtual links influencing, i.e., which share paths within the network. This observation is exploited to reduce the complexity of any forthcoming analysis. However (1) our global model is more detaillel and easier to extend/modify due to the use of the component-based design approach, (2) we are capable to retreive stochastic informations, (3) our approach is adaptive, and (4) we exploit simulations to ease the verification process.

References

1. ARINC 429, Aeronautical Radio Inc. ARINC specification 429. Digital Information Transfer Systems (DITS) part 1,2,3 (2001)
2. ARINC 664, Aircraft Data Network, Part 7: Avionics Full Duplex Switched Ethernet (AFDX) Network (2005)
3. Alur, R., Dill, D.: A Theory of Timed Automata. Theoretical Computer Science 126, 183–235 (1994)
4. Anand, M., Dajani-Brown, S., Vestal, S., Lee, I.: Formal modeling and analysis of afdx frame management design. In: ISORC, pp. 393–399. IEEE, Los Alamitos (2006)
5. Basu, A., Bozga, M., Sifakis, J.: Modeling Heterogeneous Real-time Systems in BIP. In: SEFM 2006, Pune, India. pp. 3–12 (September 2006)
6. Basu, A., Bensalem, S., Bozga, M., Caillaud, B., Delahaye, B., Legay, A.: Statistical abstraction and model-checking of large heterogeneous systems. In: Hatcliff, J., Zucca, E. (eds.) FORTE 2010. LNCS, vol. 6117, pp. 32–46. Springer, Heidelberg (2010)

7. Charara, H., Fraboul, C.: Modelling and simulation of an avionics full duplex switched ethernet. In: Proceedings of the Advanced Industrial Conference on Telecommunications/ Service Assurance with Partial and Intermittent Resources Conference/E-Learning on Telecommunication Workshop. IEEE, Los Alamitos (2005)

8. Charara, H., Scharbarg, J.L., Ermont, J., Fraboul, C.: Methods for bounding end-to-end delays on AFDX network. In: ECRTS. IEEE Computer Society, Los Alamitos (2006)

9. Clarke, E.M., Faeder, J.R., Langmead, C.J., Harris, L.A., Jha, S.K., Legay, A.: Statistical model checking in biolab: Applications to the automated analysis of t-cell receptor signaling pathway. In: Heiner, M., Uhrmacher, A.M. (eds.) CMSB 2008. LNCS (LNBI), vol. 5307, pp. 231–250. Springer, Heidelberg (2008)

10. Cruz, R.: A calculus for network delay. IEEE Transactions on Information Theory 37(1), 114–141 (1991)

11. Grosu, R., Smolka, S.A.: Monte carlo model checking. In: Halbwachs, N., Zuck, L.D. (eds.) TACAS 2005. LNCS, vol. 3440, pp. 271–286. Springer, Heidelberg (2005)

12. Hérault, T., Lassaigne, R., Magniette, F., Peyronnet, S.: Approximate probabilistic model checking. In: Steffen, B., Levi, G. (eds.) VMCAI 2004. LNCS, vol. 2937, pp. 73–84. Springer, Heidelberg (2004)

13. Hoeffding, W.: Probability inequalities. Journal of the American Statistical Association 58, 13–30 (1963)

14. Jansen, D.N., Katoen, J.-P., Oldenkamp, M., Stoelinga, M., Zapreev, I.S.: How fast and fat is your probabilistic model checker? an experimental performance comparison. In: Yorav, K. (ed.) HVC 2007. LNCS, vol. 4899, pp. 69–85. Springer, Heidelberg (2008)

15. Jha, S.K., Clarke, E.M., Langmead, C.J., Legay, A., Platzer, A., Zuliani, P.: A bayesian approach to model checking biological systems. In: Degano, P., Gorrieri, R. (eds.) Computational Methods in Systems Biology. LNCS, vol. 5688, pp. 218–234. Springer, Heidelberg (2009)

16. Laplante, S., Lassaigne, R., Magniez, F., Peyronnet, S., de Rougemont, M.: Probabilistic abstraction for model checking: An approach based on property testing. ACM Trans. Comput. Log. 8(4) (2007)

17. Legay, A., Delahaye, B.: Statistical model checking : An overview. CoRR abs/1005.1327 (2010)

18. Scharbarg, J.L., Fraboul, C.: Simulation for end-to-end delays distribution on a switched ethernet. In: ETFA. IEEE, Los Alamitos (2007)

19. Sen, K., Viswanathan, M., Agha, G.: Statistical model checking of black-box probabilistic systems. In: Alur, R., Peled, D.A. (eds.) CAV 2004. LNCS, vol. 3114, pp. 202–215. Springer, Heidelberg (2004)

20. Wald, A.: Sequential tests of statistical hypotheses. Annals of Mathematical Statistics 16(2), 117–186 (1945)

21. Younes, H.L.S.: Verification and Planning for Stochastic Processes with Asynchronous Events. Ph.D. thesis, Carnegie Mellon (2005)

22. Younes, H.L.S., Kwiatkowska, M.Z., Norman, G., Parker, D.: Numerical vs. statistical probabilistic model checking. STTT 8(3), 216–228 (2006)

Copilot: A Hard Real-Time Runtime Monitor

Lee Pike[1], Alwyn Goodloe[2], Robin Morisset[3], and Sebastian Niller[4]

[1] Galois, Inc.
leepike@galois.com
[2] National Institute of Aerospace
alwyn.goodloe@nianet.org
[3] École Normale Supérieure
robin.morisset@ens.fr
[4] Technische Universität Ilmenau, Germany
sebastian.niller@stud.tu-ilmenau.de

Abstract. We address the problem of runtime monitoring for hard real-time programs—a domain in which correctness is critical yet has largely been overlooked in the runtime monitoring community. We describe the challenges to runtime monitoring for this domain as well as an approach to satisfy the challenges. The core of our approach is a language and compiler called *Copilot*. Copilot is a stream-based dataflow language that generates small constant-time and constant-space C programs, implementing embedded monitors. Copilot also generates its own scheduler, obviating the need for an underlying real-time operating system.

1 Introduction

Safety-critical control systems, such as avionics and drive-by-wire systems, are well-tested, sometimes certified, and perhaps even formally verified. Yet undetected errors or incorrect environmental assumptions can cause failures resulting in the loss of life—as these control systems become more complex and pervasive, the risk of software failure grows. Hence, this domain begs for the application of runtime monitoring.

Hard real-time systems are ones in which correctness depends on execution occurring within a fixed period of time [GR04]. Surprisingly, most previous research in runtime monitoring focuses either on non real-time programs or *soft real-time* systems, in which occasionally missing deadlines is tolerated. To partially redress this deficiency in the literature, we address the problem of monitoring the class of hard real-time systems: in particular, we develop a monitoring framework for periodically-scheduled hard real-time systems.

In designing our monitoring framework, we apply four guiding principles we believe are fundamental constraints for any monitoring approach treating this domain:

1. *Functionality*: Monitors cannot change the functionality of the observed program unless a failure is observed.
2. *Schedulability*: Monitors cannot alter the schedule of the observed program.

G. Roşu et al. (Eds.): RV 2010, LNCS 6418, pp. 345–359, 2010.

3. *Certifiability*: Monitors must minimize the difficulty in re-validating the observed program; in particular, we make it our goal to avoid modifying the observed program's source code.
4. *SWaP overhead*: Monitors must minimize the additional overhead required including size, weight, and power (SWaP).

To satisfy these objectives, we have developed a simple stream language called *Copilot* that compiles into small constant-time and constant-space (i.e., no dynamic memory allocation) C programs. The language follows a sampling-based monitoring strategy in which global variables of the observed program (or programs) are periodically sampled; Copilot provides mechanisms for controlling when to observe the variables. Furthermore, using the Atom compiler [Haw08] as a back-end, Copilot automatically generates its own periodic schedule, allowing for easy integration into the periodic schedule of the observed program. By generating its own schedule, the monitor obviates the need for a real-time operating system (RTOS) for scheduling and concurrency control and so can be executed on minimal embedded hardware. The language is implemented as an embedded domain-specific language (eDSL) in the popular functional language Haskell [Jon02].

Outline. The remainder of the paper is organized as follows. Related work is described in Section 2. We describe and defend the use of state-variable sampling as our monitoring approach in Section 3. In Section 4, we present the syntax, types, and semantics for our Copilot language. We then present a lower-level semantics of the language with respect to logical time in Section 5; we also discuss our scheduling assumptions in more detail there. In Section 6, we present a synthesis (or compilation) algorithm for transforming a Copilot specification into a state-machine and briefly describe the implementation. We make concluding remarks and point to future work in Section 7.

2   Related Work

Monitoring and Checking (MaC) [KLKS04] and Monitor Oriented Programming (MOP) [CDR04] represent the state-of-the-art in monitoring frameworks, but are targeted at Java applications that are not hard real-time systems (a version of MaC targeted at C programs is also under development). The Requirement Monitoring and Recovery (RMOR) [Hav08] framework is (one of the first monitoring frameworks) targeting C programs. RMOR differs from our approach in that it requires that probes, built using aspect-oriented techniques, be inserted in the code at each location where state is updated, and it does not address the issues of monitoring real-time programs. Recent work on time-aware instrumentation applies static analysis techniques and novel algorithms to calculate an instrumentation that, when possible, satisfies the time budget [FL09]. Although its focus is on soft real-time systems, predictable runtime monitoring defines a monitor budget restricting the resources allowed to the monitor so that the composed system can perform in a predictable fashion [ZDG09]. We have taken an alternative approach that does not require modifying the monitored program (see Section 3). Pellizzoni *et al.* have constructed no-overhead monitors in which the monitors are implemented on FPGAs; the framework targets properties of a PCI bus [PMCR08].

The Copilot language is influenced by functional and stream-based languages. The syntax and semantics of infinite Haskell lists influence the syntax and the untimed semantics (see Section 4.3) of Copilot [Jon02]. The languages Lustre [HCRP91], μCryptol [PSM06], and Lola [DSS$^+$05] are all stream-based languages that influence the design of Copilot; in particular, Lustre and μCryptol are designed for use on embedded microprocessors.

As explained in detail in Section 6.2, Copilot is a domain specific language (DSL) that is embedded in the functional programming language Haskell. Similar DSLs used to generate embedded C code include Feldspar [ACD$^+$10], used for digital signal processing, and Atom [Haw08], used for embedded control system design. Indeed, Copilot uses Atom as a "back-end" in the compiler.

3   Sampling-Based Monitoring

Monitoring based on sampling state-variables has largely been disregarded as a runtime monitoring approach, for good reason: without the assumption of synchrony between the monitor and observed software, monitoring via sampling may lead to false positives and false negatives [DDE08]. For example, consider the property $(0; 1; 1)^*$, written as a regular expression, denoting the sequence of values a monitored variable may take. If the monitor samples the variable at the inappropriate time, then both false negatives (the monitor erroneously rejects the sequence of values) and false positives (the monitor erroneously accepts the sequence) are possible. For example, if the actual sequence of values is $0, 1, 1, 0, 1, 1$, then an observation of $0, 1, 1, 1, 1$ is a false negative by skipping a value, and if the actual sequence is $0, 1, 0, 1, 1$, then an observation of $0, 1, 1, 0, 1, 1$ is a false positive by sampling a value twice.

However, in a hard real-time context, sampling is a suitable strategy. Under the assumption that the monitor and the observed program share a global clock and a static periodic schedule, while false positives are possible, false negatives are not. A false positive is possible, for example, if the program does not execute according to its schedule but just happens to have the expected values when sampled. If a monitor samples an unacceptable sequence of values, then either the program is in error, the monitor is in error, or they are not synchronized, all of which are faults to be reported.

Most of the popular runtime monitoring frameworks described in Section 2 inline monitors in the observed program to avoid the aforementioned problems with sampling. However, in the domain of embedded real-time systems, that approach suffers the following problems, recalling our four criteria from Section 1. First, inlining monitors changes the real-time behavior of the observed program, perhaps in unpredicable ways. In a sampling-based approach, the monitor can be integrated as a separate scheduled process during available time-slices (this is made possible by generating efficient constant-time monitors). Indeed, sampling-based monitors may even be scheduled on a separate processor (albeit doing so requires additional synchronization mechanisms), ensuring time and space partitioning from the observed programs. Such an architecture may even be necessary if the monitored program is physically distributed. Another shortcoming of inlining monitors is that certified code (e.g., DO-178B for avionics [Inc92]) is common in this domain. Inlining monitors could necessitate re-certifying the observed program. We cannot claim our approach would obviate the need for re-certification, but it is a more modular approach than one based on instrumenting the source code of the observed program, which may result in a less onerous re-certification process.

4   The Copilot Language

In this section, we overview the syntax, type system, and semantics of Copilot.

4.1   Syntax

The Copilot language is a synchronous language described by a set of *stream equations*. A *stream* is an infinite sequence of values from some type. A *stream index* i is a non-negative integer; for stream σ, $\sigma(i)$ is the stream's value at index i. It is assumed that the value stored in stream index zero $\sigma(0)$ is an initial value.

To get a feel for the Copilot language, consider the following property of an engine controller:

If the temperature rises more than 2.3 degrees within 0.2 seconds, then the engine is immediately shut off.

Assume the period at which the temperature variable *temp* is sampled is 0.1 seconds, and the shut-off variable is *shutoff*. Then the property can be specified as follows in Copilot:

$$temps = [0,\ 0,\ 0] +\!\!+ extF\ temp\ 1$$
$$overTempRise = drop\ 2\ var\ temps > const\ 2.3 + var\ temps$$
$$trigger = (var\ overTempRise)\ \text{implies}\ (extB\ shutoff\ 2)$$

When the stream *trigger* becomes false, the property has failed.

A Copilot *monitor specification* is a nonempty set of stream equations defining typed *monitor variables* $m_0, m_1, \ldots, m_n$ of the form $m_i = EXP$ where EXP is an expression built from the BNF grammar in Figure 1. (We slightly simplify the grammar from our implementation, omitting expression terminals and type declarations.) In the grammar, the terminal $<Identifier>$ is a valid C99 variable name, and $<n>$ is a non-negative integer. Streams of Boolean values are used as triggers, signalling a property succeeding or failing.

Informally, the intended semantics for Copilot is the semantics of lazy streams, like in Haskell [Jon02]. In particular, the operation $+\!\!+$ is lazy list-append, and

stream definition	EXP	$= VAR \mid CVAR \mid APP \mid DROP \mid FUN \mid CONST$
monitor variable	VAR	$= var\ <Identifier>$
sample expression	$CVAR$	$= CTYPE\ <Identifier>\ <n>$
typed program variable	$CTYPE$	$= extB \mid extI8 \mid extI16 \mid extI32 \mid extI64 \mid extW8 \mid$
		$\quad extW16 \mid extW32 \mid extW64 \mid extF \mid extD$
stream drop	$DROP$	$= drop\ <n>\ e$
		$\quad$ where $e = VAR \mid CVAR \mid DROP \mid CONST$
stream append	APP	$= l \mathbin{+\!\!+} EXP$
		$\quad$ where l is a finite list of constants
function application	FUN	$= f(e_0,\ e_1,\ \dots,\ e_n)$, where
		$\quad e_i = VAR \mid CVAR \mid DROP \mid FUN \mid CONST$
constant stream	$CONST$	$= const\ c$
		$\quad$ where c is a constant

Fig. 1. Simplified Copilot Grammar

appends a finite list onto a stream. The operation $drop\ s\ n$ drops the first n indexes from stream s.

Besides monitor variables, the other class of variables in Copilot are *program variables*. Program variables reference global variables being sampled. Program variables can be any shared state accessible by the compiled C program monitor, including hardware registers or other C program variables. In a sampling expression, e.g., $extW64\ v\ 3$, the integer refers to the *phase* (or offset) into the periodic schedule at which v is to be sampled (see Section 5). In $CTYPE$ expressions, the 'ext' in the constructor denotes 'external', 'W denotes 'word', 'I denotes 'int', 'F' denotes 'float', and 'D' denotes 'double'. An expression containing no program variables is a *closed expression*; otherwise it is an *open expression*. Monitors are defined by open expressions, but closed expressions are useful as "helper streams"—e.g., counters to create new clocks [HCRP91]—for other definitions.

An expression $const\ 3$ denotes a stream of the value 3.

The functions of the language include the usual arithmetic operators (e.g., $+$, $-$, $*$, $/$, *modulo*, $==$, $<$ and the other comparison operators), and the logical operators *not, and, or, implies*. Other operators can be easily added to the language.

The append operator binds more weakly than function application, which binds more weakly than the drop operator. Variable operators bind most tightly.

Example 1 (Closed Monitor Expressions). We present simple closed monitor expressions below along with their intended semantics.

Monitor	Intended semantics
$m_0 = [\mathbf{T},\ \mathbf{F}] \mathbin{+\!\!+} var\ m_0$	$\mathbf{T}, \mathbf{F}, \mathbf{T}, \mathbf{F}, \dots$
$m_1 = [\mathbf{T}] \mathbin{+\!\!+} const\ \mathbf{F}$	$\mathbf{T}, \mathbf{F}, \mathbf{F}, \mathbf{F}, \dots$
$m_2 = drop\ 1\ (var\ m_3)$	$1, 2, 1, 2, \dots$
$m_3 = [0,\ 1,\ 2] \mathbin{+\!\!+} var\ m_2$	$0, 1, 2, 1, 2, \dots$
$m_4 = [0,\ 1] \mathbin{+\!\!+} var\ m_4 + drop\ 1\ (var\ m_4)$	$0, 1, 1, 2, 3, \dots$

Note that m_4 generates the Fibonacci sequence.

One design choice with the language is to disallow stream append expressions to appear within the context other operators. For example, the expressions $drop\ 1\ ([0,\ 1]\ +\!+\ var\ m)$ and $([0,\ 1]\ +\!+\ var\ m) + (const\ 3)$ are ill-formed. This decision ensures there are no "anonymous streams" in the language—i.e., each newly-constructed stream is either constant (*const*) or a function of streams assigned to a monitoring variable. The choice provides better control over the memory usage required by the monitor (it is a linear function of each monitor variable defined; see Section 6).

Example 2 (Embedding past-time LTL). The past-time LTL (ptLTL) operators are past-time analogues of the standard LTL operators. The ptLTL operators include previously ($\mathcal{P}$), has always been ($\mathcal{A}$), eventually previously ($\mathcal{E}$), and since ($\mathcal{S}$). Given their semantics defined in [MP92], they are defined in Copilot as follows (assume the appropriate *cType* and fixed phases n and l):

$$
\begin{aligned}
\mathcal{P}p &\equiv m_0 = [\mathbf{F}] +\!+ cType\ p\ n \\
\mathcal{A}p &\equiv m_1 = var\ m_2 \wedge cType\ p\ n,\ \text{where} \\
&\quad m_2 = [\mathbf{T}] +\!+ var\ m_2 \wedge cType\ p\ n \\
\mathcal{E}p &\equiv m_3 = var\ m_4 \vee cType\ p\ n,\ \text{where} \\
&\quad m_4 = [\mathbf{T}] +\!+ var\ m_4 \vee cType\ p\ n \\
p_0\mathcal{S}p_1 &\equiv m_5 = cType\ p_1\ n \vee (cType\ p_0\ l \wedge m_6),\ \text{where} \\
&\quad m_6 = [\mathbf{F}] +\!+ m_6
\end{aligned}
$$

4.2   Types

Copilot is statically and strongly typed—i.e., type-checking is done at compile-time, and type-incorrect function application is not possible. In our implementation, Copilot types are embedded into Haskell's type system (see Section 6.2). Copilot specifications lift C types to streams. The C types lifted are the C types corresponding to $CTYPE$ in Figure 1.

In the following, let $\overrightarrow{T}$ denote the type T lifted to the type of an infinite stream of values of type T. We denote that "expression exp has type T" by $exp :: T$. The type of an expression is the smallest relation satisfying the following:

- If m is a monitor variable of type $\overrightarrow{T}$, then $(var\ m) :: \overrightarrow{T}$.
- For a program variable expression, $(cType\ v\ n) :: \overrightarrow{T}$, where T is the type corresponding to the operator $ctype$.
- If $c :: T$ for each constant c in the list l and $exp :: \overrightarrow{T'}$, then $(l +\!+ exp) ::$ $(\overrightarrow{T} \cup \overrightarrow{T'})$.
- If $exp :: \overrightarrow{T}$, then $drop\ i\ exp :: \overrightarrow{T}$.
- If f is a n-ary function such that $f :: T_0,\ T_1,\ \ldots,\ T_n \rightarrow T$, and $exp'_0 ::$ $\overrightarrow{T_0},\ exp'_1 :: \overrightarrow{T_1},\ \ldots,\ exp'_n :: \overrightarrow{T_n}$, then $f(exp'_0,\ exp'_1,\ \ldots,\ exp'_n) :: \overrightarrow{T}$.
- If $c :: T$, then $(const\ c) :: \overrightarrow{T}$.

If $exp :: \overrightarrow{T}$ and $\overrightarrow{T_0}, \overrightarrow{T_1} \subseteq \overrightarrow{T}$ and $T_0 \neq T_1$, then the expression is *type incorrect*.

4.3   Untimed Semantics

Due to space considerations, we do not provide a formal semantics for Copilot. Following [DSS+05], Copilot's untimed semantics is defined in terms of *evaluation models*. Informally, an evaluation model is the n-tuple of streams denoted by a monitor specification, assuming a fixed set of streams denoting the values of program variables. Evaluation models are constructed inductively over the syntax of the specification assuming a fixed set of program variable values. A specification is said to be *well defined* if the values of the monitor variables at time t are uniquely defined by the values of the monitored variables at times $0 \ldots t$.

For example, well-definedness rules out specifications of the form $m = \neg(var\ m)$ no value for m can statisfy that equation. Well-definedness also rules out specifications of the form $m = drop\ 1\ (var\ m)$ since it admits several different solutions (e.g., both of the streams **T**, **T**, ... and **F**, **F**, ...).

Monitor specifications can be restricted syntactically to ensure they are well-defined. Define a *dependency graph* to be a directed, weighted, graph $(V,\ E)$ such that the vertexes V are the monitor and program variables. The edges E are constructed as follows: for variables v and v', $v \xrightarrow{w} v' \in E$ if and only if v' appears in some subexpression in the right-hand side of the stream equation for v (note that program variables are only sinks in the graph), and $w = weight(v)$, where

$$weight(exp) = \text{case } exp \text{ of}$$

$$
\begin{aligned}
l \mathbin{+\!\!+} e & \quad\rightarrow\quad weight(e) - length(l) \\
drop\ i\ e & \quad\rightarrow\quad i + weight(e) \\
f(e_0,\ e_1,\ \ldots,\ e_n) & \quad\rightarrow\quad max(weight(e_0),\ \ldots,\ weight(e_n))_i \\
var\ v' & \quad\rightarrow\quad 0 \\
cType\ v'\ n & \quad\rightarrow\quad 0 \\
const\ c & \quad\rightarrow\quad -\infty
\end{aligned}
$$

A *walk* of a dependency graph is a finite sequence of variables $v_0,\ v_1,\ \ldots,\ v_n$ such there exists an edge from v_i to v_{i+1}, for each v_i of the sequence. Variable v_i *depends* on v_j if v_i and v_j both appear in some walk, and $i < j$. A *loop* is a walk $v_0,\ v_1,\ \ldots,\ v_n$ such that $v_0 = v_n$. A *closed walk* is a walk $v_0,\ v_1,\ \ldots,\ v_n$ such that $v_i = v_n$ for some $0 \le i < n$. The *weight* of a walk $v_0,\ v_1,\ \ldots,\ v_n$ is the sum of the weights in the sequence.

Example 3. The dependency graphs for m_2, m_3, and m_4 in Example 1 are depicted below.

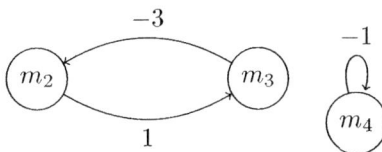

We make two restrictions to ensure that specifications are well-defined; one constrains the dependencies between program variables, and one constrains the dependencies of monitor variables on program variables. For the first constraint, we preclude circular dependencies on future values in stream definitions. For example, $m = drop\ 1\ (var\ m)$, has a circular dependency on its own future values, and in

$$m_0 = drop\ 1\ (var\ m_1)$$
$$m_1 = var\ m_0$$

m_0 and m_1 depend on each others' future values. Both specifications are not well-defined. A sufficient condition is to require the weight of loops in the dependency graph to be less than zero.

The second restriction is analogous but ensures a specification does not attempt to reference future program values: the weight of a walk terminating in a program variable must be less than or equal to zero. Thus, we have the following definition:

Definition 1 (Well-Formed Specification). *A monitor specification is* well-formed *if there exists*

– *No loop with a non-negative walk weight.*
– *No walk with a positive weight terminating in an external variable.*

Theorem 1 (Well-Formedness Theorem). *Every well-formed specification is well-defined.*

As noted in [DSS$^+$05], the converse of the theorem does not hold:

$$m_0 = (var\ m_0) \vee \mathbf{T}$$
$$m_1 = [0,\ 1]\ +\!\!+\ \text{if}\ \mathbf{F}\ \text{then}\ drop\ 1\ (cType\ p\ n)\ \text{else}\ var\ m_1$$

Both specifications are well-defined but not well-formed.

In addition to the well-formedness constraints, we introduce two minor additional constraints in Section 6 for the purpose of reducing the worst-case execution time and memory usage in our implementation.

5   Scheduling Semantics

In Section 4.3, we described an untimed semantics for Copilot. In this section, we describe the semantics of a Copilot implementation with respect to logical time [Lam78]. That is, we assume a *global clock* is the sequence of non-negative integers, and every stream shares the global clock. A *(clock) tick* is a value from the global clock sequence. We assume synchronization with respect to the abstract global clock, so every stream agrees on the time, but we do not assume an order of execution *within* a clock tick. Thus, one stream cannot depend on another stream having computed its next-state value during the current tick.

Not assuming an order of execution within a tick provides flexibility in implementing a monitor; for example, a monitor might be distributed on separate processors with the guarantee that synchronization is only required up to the global clock [HCRP91]. The compiler ensures the same behavior regardless of the order in which state variables are updated in the same tick (see Section 6).

We follow a standard model of hard real-time scheduling [GR04]. A monitor is a collection of recurring *tasks* (in our setting, C functions) that obtain inputs and compute output in a statically-bounded amount of time. We assume tasks are *periodic* and have a round-robin non-preemptive schedule. Consequently, all tasks have the same priority and run to completion without interrupts. The global clock is an abstraction of the hardware clock; the duration of each tick of the global clock is expected to be sufficiently long to account for the worst-case execution time (WCET) of all possible computation that occurs within a tick. A tick is triggered by sampling the hardware clock.

Typically, we assume the monitored program also has these scheduling characteristics. In this case, the monitor can be integrated into the round-robin schedule of the observed program, provided WCET constraints are met. However, the monitor can also be scheduled as a single high-priority task that manages its own sub-tasks (e.g., sampling) according to the schedule it generates. Care must be taken that the monitor's temporal assumptions are met under this framework.

At the ticks at which a state variable is scheduled to be assigned a new value, we say the variable *fires*; otherwise, we say the variable *idles*. A variable's schedule can be succinctly stated in terms of a positive integer p that is its *period* and a non-negative integer h, where $h < p$, that is the stream's *phase*. The period denotes the number of ticks between successive firings for a state variable, and the phase denotes the offset into each period for when it fires. For a clock tick C, when $(C - h) \bmod p \equiv 0$, the variable fires; otherwise, it is idle.

Example 4 (Timed Semantics). Consider the stream specifications for m_2 and m_3 from Example 1. Suppose m_2 has period 3 and phase 0, and m_3 has period 3 and phase 1. Then the stream's timed semantics are as follows, where $\perp$ denotes "undefined" or "do not care":

$$
\begin{aligned}
\text{global clock} &= 0\ 1\ 2\ 3\ 4\ 5\ 6\ 7\ 8\ 9\ 10 \ldots \\
m_2 &= 1\ 1\ 1\ 2\ 2\ 2\ 1\ 1\ 1\ 2\ 2\ \ldots \\
m_3 &= \perp\ 0\ 0\ 0\ 1\ 1\ 1\ 2\ 2\ 2\ 1\ \ldots
\end{aligned}
$$

While the schedule of a monitor variable denotes when the variable fires, the schedule of a program variable denotes when the monitor samples it. Consequently, a sampling expression (i.e., *cType v n*) denotes that v is sampled at phase n in each period. For period p, we require $0 < n < p$. The constraint $0 < n$ ensures that the compiler has a tick to update state when variables are not being sampled (see Section 6). Recall the initial specification in Section 4.1: there we formalized "the engine is *immediately* shut off" by sampling the program variable *shutoff* in the tick just after sampling *temp*.

Given our model, we can state the correctness condition for a stream in a monitor specification to be implemented by a scheduled state variable:

Definition 2 (Stream Implementation). *We say that the state variable v with period p and phase h implements the stream σ if for all clock times C, $v(C) = \sigma(idx(C))$, where $idx(C) = \left\lfloor \frac{C-h}{p} \right\rfloor$ if $h \leq C$, and $idx(C) = \left\lceil \frac{C-h}{p} \right\rceil$ otherwise.*

6   Monitor Synthesis

In this section, we describe the synthesis of a Copilot specification to a state machine, which Atom [Haw08] compiles to C code. The state machine is represented by a set of state variables associated with each stream in the specification, an initial state, a state-update function for each variable, and a schedule for applying the state-update function. The synthesis algorithm is very simple and produces code with a low and uniform WCET. However, the simple algorithm requires us to make two additional well-formedness restrictions, generalizing Definition 1 slightly; we describe these additions in Section 6.1.

Besides synthesizing the specification, the compiler schedules the monitors within the overall periodic schedule of the observed program. The synthesis algorithm generates a schedule that (1) respects causality constraints—i.e., the data required to compute a value is available and that (2) interferes with the program's real-time constraints as little as possible. In our implementation, these two criteria are handled at different levels of the compiler. The purpose of (1) is to ensure that the Stream Implementation definition (Definition 2) holds. (2) is an optimization issue; the Atom scheduler handles (2) by optimizing the schedule (see Section 6.2).

Remark 1 (Array and List Notation). We store state values in arrays, and define some functions that operate over arrays and lists. We denote the value at index j in an array or list a by $a[j]$. The function $len(a)$ takes an array or finite list and returns the length of a. The array $<>$ is the empty array. The function l app a takes a finite list l and array a and returns an array a' formed by appending the values in l onto the front of a.

In the following, assume a monitor specification consists of a finite sequence of monitor variable definitions of the form

$$m_0 = exp_0, \ m_1 = exp_1, \ldots, \ m_n = exp_n$$

State. For each monitor variable m_i, its state contains the following:

- *History variables*: stream values are stored in a *history array*, a_i. The length of the history array is statically-computed from the monitor specification.
- *Update and output indexes*: two elements of the history array are respectively designated as an *update index* ($upIdx$), the index of the next-state value, and an *output index* ($outIdx$), the index of the current output value.

Additionally, for each unique sampling expression $cType$ v n, in a specification, we introduce a *temporary sampling variable* v_n that contains the value sampled from v at phase n in the current period. The variable v_n holds the sampled value until it is used in the next-state function.

State Update. The next-state value for stream m_i is computed by $nextSt(exp_i, 0)$, where

$$nextSt(e, \ k) = \text{case } e \text{ of}$$

$l ++ e'$	$\rightarrow$	$nextSt(e', \ k)$
$drop \ k' \ e'$	$\rightarrow$	$nextSt(e', \ k + k')$
$f(e_0, \ e_1, \ \ldots, \ e_n)$	$\rightarrow$	$f(nextSt(e_0, k), \ \ldots, \ nextSt(e_n, \ k))$
$var \ m_j$	$\rightarrow$	if $k < len(a_j) - 1$
		then $a_j[(k + outIdx_j) \bmod len(a_j)]$
		else $nextSt(exp_j, \ k - (len(a_j) - 1))$
$cType \ v \ n$	$\rightarrow$	v_n
$const \ c$	$\rightarrow$	c

Initial State. The initial state is computed as follows. For each monitor variable m_i, the initial state of history array $a_i = init(exp_i) \ app \ nextSt(exp_i, 0)$, where

$$init(e) = \text{case } e \text{ of}$$

$l ++ e'$	$\rightarrow$	$l \ app \ init(e')$
otherwise	$\rightarrow$	$<>$

$init(exp_i)$ may produce an empty array, but this array is always augmented by one last index with an initial arbitrary value. Initially, the next-state index points to that last index, while the output index is 0

For each temporary sampling variable v_n, its initial value is $\perp$, pronounced 'undefined', representing the undefined value of a program variable that has not been sampled ($\perp$ is polymorphic and a member of all types).

Example 5. The following are initial values of the history arrays:

specification	history array
$m_0 = [0, \ 1, \ 2] ++ extW64 \ x \ 3 + const \ 3$	$a_i = <0, \ 1, \ 2, \ \perp>$
$m_1 = var \ m_0 + var \ m_0$	$<0>$
$m_2 = drop \ 2 \ (var \ m_1)$	$<4>$

Scheduling. Each monitor variable in a specification has the same period, and each program variable is sampled once each period. Just like in Lustre, new logical clocks can be defined in terms of the underlying period [HCRP91]. This allows control over when variables are sampled. For example, in the following monitor, the program variable x sampled is only used every other period:

$$m_0 = [\mathbf{T}, \ \mathbf{F}] ++ var \ m_0$$
$$m_1 = \text{if } var \ m_0 \text{ then } (extW8 \ x \ 3) \text{ else } var \ m_1$$

The period for a monitor specification is either provided as an input to the compiler, or the compiler can compute the minimum necessary period. The period must satisfy the following constraint: let n be the largest phase n that appears in a sampling expression (of the form $cType \ v \ n$). Then the period p must satisfy the constraints: $1 < p$ and $n < p$. The first constraint ensures there are enough ticks per period to perform the actions described below, and the second constraint ensures all the program variables can be sampled within the period. Thus, we have the following order of actions each period:

- Phase 0: apply the state-update function for each monitor variable.
- Phase 1: increment the update and output indexes by 1 mod $len(a_i)$. The output is current for the current period from phase 1 until phase 0 of the next period.

Our algorithm ensures that the output for each stream is updated synchronously, in the same tick.

6.1   Well-Formedness Generalizations

The synthesis algorithm presented is simple and produces efficient code, but it requires two small generalizations to the well-formedness restrictions given in Definition 1. The algorithm guarantees that the Stream Implementation property (Definition 2) is satisfied for any Copilot specification satisfying these the constraints.

- We extend the restriction of no *loop* with a non-negative weight to no *closed walk* with a non-negative weight. Without the extension, the following specification is valid, but it requires pre-computing the next 3 elements of the stream generated by m_0:

$$m_0 = [0] \mathbin{++} var\ m_0 + 1$$
$$m_1 = drop\ 3\ (var\ m_0)$$

  A specification with a closed walk with a non-negative weight that does not contain a loop with a non-negative weight is semantically equivalent to some specification in which all closed walks have negative weights. For example, the following specification is equivalent to the preceding one but does not violate the new restriction:

$$m_0 = [0,\ 1,\ 2,\ 3] \mathbin{++} drop\ 3\ ((var\ m_0) + 1)$$
$$m_1 = drop\ 3\ (var\ m_0)$$

- Let $v_0, v_1, \ldots, v_n$ be a walk of a specification's dependency graph such that v_n is a program variable, and let w be the weight of the walk. Then we require that $w \le -init(exp_{v_0})$, where exp_{v_0} is the defining expression for monitor variable v_0. The intuition behind this requirement is that our synthesis algorithm does not keep track of previously-sampled values of external variables to be used in stream equations. For example, the following specification violates this condition:

$$m_0 = extW8\ x\ 2$$
$$m_1 = [0,\ 1,\ 2] \mathbin{++} drop\ 1\ (var\ m_0)$$

Our experience is that monitors violating these extended well-formedness constraints are relatively contrived.

6.2   Implementation

Copilot is implemented as an *embedded domain-specific language* (eDSL). In the eDSL approach, a DSL is a set of operators defined in a host language. A DSL specification defines data in the host language which can be manipulated; in our case, we rewrite the specification to C code. Because the DSL is embedded, there is no need to build custom compiler infrastructure—the host language's parser, lexer, type system, etc. can all be reused. In particular, the type system of Copilot is embedded in the type system of Haskell, which provides a Hindley-Milner polymorphic type system, extended with type classes [Jon02]. By using a well-tested implementation, we have strong guarantees of correctness, and we can keep the size of the compiler low (3000 lines of code at the time of writing). Finally, in a higher-order host language, one can write combinators over the DSL, acting as a macro system for the language. The architecture of our implementation of Copilot is shown in Figure 2. Copilot uses Atom, an open source eDSL (see Section 2) as an intermediate language that does the C-code generation and scheduler synthesis. Atom performs the schedule generation and optimization (optimization is not described in this paper), too. Informally, the Atom scheduler distributes events across the ticks of a period (without violating causality constraints) to minimize the WCET per tick.

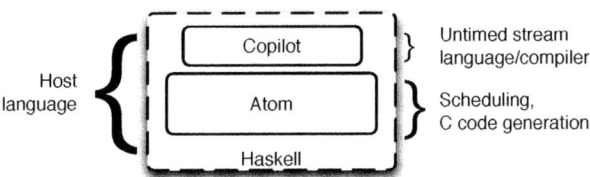

Fig. 2. The eDSL architecture for Copilot

The Copilot compiler has been tested against a simple interpreter on thousands of random streams, which discovered subtle issues, like the additional restrictions on the dependency graph presented in Section 6.1.

We have executed Copilot-generated specifications on the Arduino Duemilanove (ATmega328 microprocessor) as well as on ARM Cortex M3. The monitors generate C99 code, so any processor for which a C compiler exists is a potential target. However, the program's hard real-time guarantees depend on various hardware environmental assumptions; e.g., a cache can break hard real-time guarantees.

We have constructed several small examples to corroborate our design and approach. These examples are drawn from the domain of distributed and fault-tolerant systems and include simple distributed computations, a simple Byzantine agreement protocol, and a simple bus arbiter.

We are currently completing a more substantial case-study involving a fault-tolerant pitot tube sensor (using air pressure for measuring airspeed) on distributed ARM Cortex M3 microprocessors with injected faults.

Copilot will be released open-source (BSD3); please email the authors for an advance copy.

7   Conclusion

Summary. In the Introduction, we presented four constraints for a hard real-time monitoring framework: functionality, schedulability, certifiability, and SWaP overhead. We have presented a framework that together satisfies these constraints. In particular, our approach is based on sampling program variables and computing properties over the sampled values. Copilot-generated monitors can be integrated with the observed program without modifying its functionality or real-time guarantees. Finally, no real-time operating system is necessary for scheduling. Our language is a highly-constrained language that makes compilation simple and the ability to statically-compute memory and time usage straightforward. Nevertheless, it is powerful enough to encode typical monitoring formulas, such as past-time LTL and bounded LTL formulas.

Future Work. Beyond additional case-studies, one area of future work is to ensure that Copilot monitors are correct. One approach is to borrow from the coinductive verification techniques developed for hardware specifications, since our language is a stream language [Min98]. We have performed initial experiments using Frama-C [Fra] to verify the memory-safety of our generated C code.

We are current developing infrastructure to generate distributed monitors. This allows a global property to be specified for a distributed system, and to distribute the monitors to the system's nodes.

Finally, another topic of interest is to apply statistical techniques to distinguish systematic software faults from transient hardware faults [SLSR07].

Acknowledgements

This work is supported by NASA Contract NNL08AD13T. We thank Ben Di Vito for his direction and input.

References

[ACD⁺10] Axelsson, E., Claessen, K., Dvai, G., Horvth, Z., Keijzer, K., Lyckegrd, B., Persson, A., Sheeran, M., Svenningsson, J., Vajda, A.: Feldspar: a domain specific language for digital signal processing algorithms. In: 8th ACM/IEEE Int. Conf. on Formal Methods and Models for Codesign (2010)

[CDR04]   Chen, F., D'Amorim, M., Roşu, G.: A formal monitoring-base framewrok for software development analysis. In: Davies, J., Schulte, W., Barnett, M. (eds.) ICFEM 2004. LNCS, vol. 3308, pp. 357–373. Springer, Heidelberg (2004)

[DDE08]   Dwyer, M.B., Diep, M., Elbaum, S.: Reducing the cost of path property monitoring through sampling. In: Proceedings of the 23rd International Conference on Automated Software Engineering, pp. 228–237 (2008)

[DSS⁺05]   D'Angelo, B., Sankaranarayanan, S., Snchez, C., Robinson, W., Manna, Z., Finkbeiner, B., Spima, H., Mehrotra, S.: LOLA: Runtime monitoring of synchronous systems. In: 12th International Symposium on Temporal Representation and Reasoning, pp. 166–174. IEEE, Los Alamitos (2005)

[FL09]   Fishmeister, S., Lam, P.: On time-aware insrumentation of programs. In: RTAS 2009: 15h IEEE Real-Time and Embedded Technology and Application Symposium (2009)

[Fra]   Frama-C., http://frama-c.com/index.html (accessed August, 2010)

[GR04]   Goossens, J., Richard, P.: Overview of real-time scheduling problems (invited paper). In: Euro Workshop on Project Management and Scheduling (2004)

[Hav08]   Havelund, K.: Runtime verification of C programs. In: Suzuki, K., Higashino, T., Ulrich, A., Hasegawa, T. (eds.) TestCom/FATES 2008. LNCS, vol. 5047, pp. 7–22. Springer, Heidelberg (2008)

[Haw08]   Hawkins, T.: Controlling hybrid vehicles with Haskell. Presentation. Commercial Users of Functional Programming, CUFP (2008), http://cufp.galois.com/2008/schedule.html

[HCRP91]   Halbwachs, N., Caspi, P., Raymond, P., Pilaud, D.: The synchronous dataflow programming language Lustre. Proceedings of the IEEE 79(9) (September 1991)

[Inc92]   RTCA Inc. Software considerations in airborne systems and equipment certification, RCTA/DO-178B (1992)

[Jon02]   Jones, S.P. (ed.): Haskell 1998 Language and Libraries: The Revised Report (2002), http://haskell.org/

[KLKS04]   Kim, M., Lee, I., Kannan, S., Sokolsky, O.: Java-MaC: a run-time assurance tool for Java. Formal Methods in System Design 24(1), 129–155 (2004)

[Lam78]   Lamport, L.: Time, clocks, and the ordering of events in a distributed system. Communications of the ACM 21(7), 558–565 (1978)

[Min98]   Miner, P.: Hardware verification using coinductive assertions. PhD thesis, Indiana University, Bloomington, Adviser-Johnson, Steven D (1998)

[MP92]   Manna, Z., Pnueli, A.: The Temporal Logic of Reactive and Concurrent Systems. Springer, Heidelberg (1992)

[PMCR08]   Pellizzoni, R., Meredith, P., Caccamo, M., Rosu, G.: Hardware runtime monitoring for dependable cots-based real-time embedded systems. In: RTSS 2008: Proceedings of the 29th IEEE Real-Time System Symposium, pp. 481–491 (2008)

[PSM06]   Pike, L., Shields, M., Matthews, J.: A verifying core for a cryptographic language compiler. In: Proceedings of the 6th Intl. Workshop on the ACL2 Theorem Prover and its Applications, pp. 1–10. ACM, New York (2006)

[SLSR07]   Sammapun, U., Lee, I., Sokolsky, O., Regehr, J.: Statistical runtime checking of probabilistic properties. In: Sokolsky, O., Taşıran, S. (eds.) RV 2007. LNCS, vol. 4839, pp. 164–175. Springer, Heidelberg (2007)

[ZDG09]   Zhu, H., Dwyer, M., Goddard, S.: Predictable runtime monitoring. In: ECRTS 2009: 21st Euromicro Conference on Real-Time Systems, pp. 173–183 (2009)

StealthWorks: Emulating Memory Errors

Musfiq Rahman, Bruce R. Childers, and Sangyeun Cho

Computer Science Department, University of Pittsburgh, Pittsburgh PA 15260, USA

Abstract. A study of Google's data center revealed that the incidence of main memory errors is surprisingly high. These errors can lead to application and system corruption, impacting reliability. The high error rate is an indication that new resiliency techniques will be vital in future memories. To develop such approaches, a framework is needed to conduct flexible and repeatable experiments. This paper describes such a framework, StealthWorks, to facilitate research on software resilience by behaviorally emulating memory errors in a live system. We illustrate it to study program tolerance to random errors and in the development of a new software technique to continuously test memory for errors.

1   Introduction

Today's computing paradigms and applications owe much of their success to the availability of inexpensive high-capacity main memory. The capacity of computer memories has increased dramatically: A current laptop might have four gigabytes of memory and a server might have tens or hundreds of gigabytes. With the horsepower unleashed by chip multiprocessors, the pressure on memory capacity will only increase as future applications operate on even larger data sets and new execution environments (e.g., virtualization) gain popularity.

The ability to inexpensively construct a many-gigabyte main memory is thanks to increased DRAM chip density (i.e., more memory bits fit in a fixed chip area). Although DRAM improvements are a key enabler to numerous computing advancements, there is a sinister side to the story. As DRAM density improves, the smaller bit cells are more susceptible to manufacturing variations and sensitivities that can cause the cells to malfunction under certain environmental conditions. These malfunctions cause application corruptions, increased service disruption, and decreased system reliability. While it is commonly believed that the probability of "soft errors", which result from background radiation flipping a bit (a single-event upset, or SEU), is increased in large main memories, "hard errors" are *also likely*. Transient and hard errors happen due to intermittent and permanent failures in the memory circuits, rather than external events.

Indeed, a recent study about memory reliability for Google's data centers showed that there are 25,000 to 70,000 errors per billion device hours per year and more than 8% of DRAM chips are affected each year [7]. Of these errors, transient and hard errors were common. This result defies conventional wisdom that application memory corruptions are only plagued by SEUs. An important conclusion from this study is error correction techniques are necessary to achieve

G. Roşu et al. (Eds.): RV 2010, LNCS 6418, pp. 360–367, 2010.

the best reliability. However, these techniques do not come without cost. A typical hardware approach to protect against SEUs is a "SECDED" code, which requires eight extra memory bits per 64-bit word to repair one bit error. Even with this 12.5% information redundancy, the memory is still susceptible to multi-bit errors, which necessitates more sophisticated schemes, like chipkill [1]. Unfortunately, even a simple SECDED scheme is too expensive (in power and dollars) for most machines. Thus, the use of a scheme, like chipkill, is even more unlikely in the competitive marketplace of commodity computing. Given this situation, run-time verification and testing techniques that improve resilience without increasing system cost will serve a vital role [3–5].

To develop new software techniques for both soft and hard errors, a flexible and efficient framework is needed to model, insert and monitor memory errors in an experimentally repeatable and controlled manner. We developed such a framework, called StealthWorks, that can inject and emulate soft and hard errors and observe their impact on applications and the system. StealthWorks is hosted in an actual computer system, and thus, is a fast vehicle for emulation and study of errors. In this paper, we demonstrate StealthWorks with two case studies, one for soft errors and the other for hard errors. The first study illustrates StealthWorks in evaluating application vulnerability to single-event upsets by randomly injecting single bit flips. The second study demonstrates StealthWorks for the development of a novel software-based approach to improve resilience of legacy and commodity systems that cannot use or afford hardware error correction methods for multi-bit hard errors.

2   StealthWorks

Figure 1 shows the components in StealthWorks, which are grouped into the System-under-Test and the User Interface. The System-under-Test emulates memory errors in an actual machine's memory. The User Interface is a remote client for interacting with the System-under-Test.

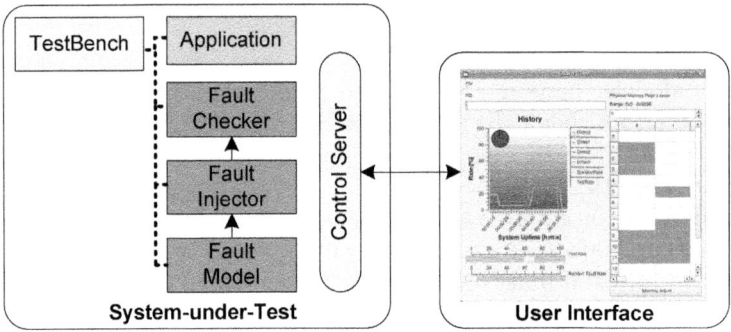

Fig. 1. StealthWorks framework

We focus on the System-under-Test, which has several modules. The Test Bench runs experiments through user scripts. The Fault Modeler determines the errors to inject and the Fault Injector emulates them. The Fault Checker intercepts program memory operations to check addresses for the presence of an error. Finally, the Control Server mediates communication between the System-under-Test and the User Interface. The Fault Modeler, the Fault Injector, and the Fault Checker form StealthWorks' core. Figure 2 shows how these core modules are organized and interact with one another. Next, we explain each module in the System-under-test.

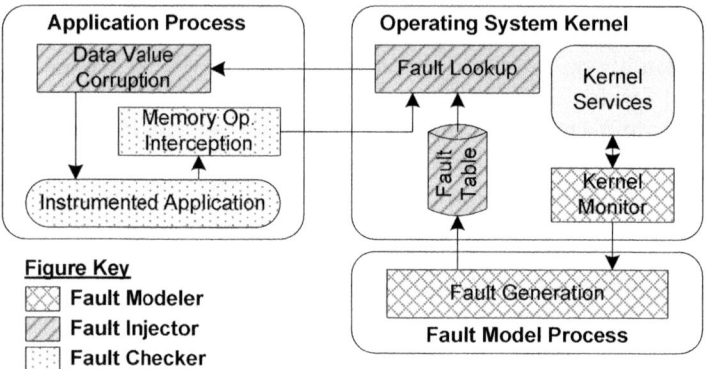

Fig. 2. Components comprising Fault Modeler, Fault Injector and Fault Checker

2.1   Test Bench

This component runs experiments through user-configurable scripts. An experiment includes the workload (how to run it), parameters for modeling memory errors, duration, and the statistics to collect. The scripts interact with the other StealthWorks modules.

2.2   Fault Modeler

The Fault Modeler hosts a user-specified *fault model*. This fault model determines what errors should be present in the memory. As shown in Figure 2, the Fault Modeler has two parts: Fault Generation and a Kernel Monitor. The user implements the fault model in Fault Generation with services provided by StealthWorks, including insert/delete an error, the Kernel Monitor, timers, event triggers, simulated system temperature, usage meters, age meters, and utility data types and functions. As shown in the figure, the fault model interacts with the Fault Injector through a database of errors, called the Fault Table. The fault model can insert and remove errors from the database.

The fault model indicates memory error addresses, error types, distribution, run-time causes, and how to corrupt data values for error types. A memory address with an error is indicated by a physical address since errors occur in hardware resources (i.e., physical pages). In addition to where to place errors, the fault model can optionally indicate how to corrupt data values. To corrupt a data value, the fault model marks a memory error address with a "corruption annotation". The annotation is user-defined. It can be used to specify the way to corrupt a value, such as a random bit flip, a stuck-at-0 error, etc. Fault Generation does not corrupt the actual data values because it cannot access these values directly. Instead, this is done by the Fault Injector (discussed next).

The Kernel Monitor collects information about system operation for the fault model. For instance, the Kernel Monitor can periodically sample memory utilization of different physical memory regions. Because the Kernel Monitor needs access to privileged information (e.g., page tables and allocation lists), it runs in the kernel and system calls are done (via wrapper functions) to interact with it.

We have implemented several example fault models. One model statically determines a fixed set of permanent errors, but it does not corrupt data values. It is useful to study how often a program touches an error location. An extended version can seed errors collected from a live system to create stress tests [5]. Another extension can corrupt data values for studying the inherent resilience of programs to hard faults [4]. A final example model considers the operating conditions identified in the Google study [7] as influential, including temperature, memory utilization, and device age, to determine when to insert errors.

2.3 Fault Injector

The Fault Injector emulates the errors generated by the Fault Modeler. It has three parts illustrated in Figure 2: the Fault Table, Fault Lookup, and Data Value Corruption. The Fault Table is a kernel hashtable of errors, which is indexed by physical memory word address. If an address is in the hashtable, it should be emulated by the Fault Injector as having an error. A hashtable entry records both the error type and the corruption annotation.

Fault Lookup is used by the Fault Checker to check whether a memory address has an error. It is invoked with a system call that passes the address. If an error is found, the system call returns a corruption annotation. If there is no error, a sentinel value is returned to indicate an error-free address. Because the Fault Checker intercepts memory operations, it operates on *virtual addresses*. Thus, Fault Lookup maps a virtual address to a physical one using the program's page table. The physical address is used to access the Fault Table.

Finally, Data Value Corruption changes data values, as indicated by the corruption annotation returned from Fault Lookup. For example, an annotation might indicate a stuck-at-0 fault for a particular bit. Data Value Corruption would set the stuck-at bit to 0 in the data value. Because it needs access to program data (instruction operands), it runs in the program's address space (user space). It is simplest and most efficient to perform the corruption in user space; it also avoids the difficulty kernel modification.

2.4   Fault Checker

The Fault Checker instruments program memory operations (instruction fetches and memory reads/writes) with dynamic binary translation (DBT) to gather an address trace. DBT can efficiently gather these address traces by optimizing instrumentation code in the context in which it is injected [2, 6, 8].

Each operation is intercepted to send the effective virtual memory address and access type (data/instruction, read/write, byte size) to the Fault Injector. Memory operations are rewritten to call an analysis payload shown in Figure 2 as "Memory Operation Interception". The analysis payload does a system call to inform the Fault Injector via Fault Lookup about the access. When Fault Lookup returns a corruption annotation, the Fault Checker invokes Data Value Corruption to determine the actual corrupted data value.

The current implementation of the Fault Checker can use either Pin [6] or Strata [8] DBT systems as the binary instrumenter. Pin offers easy-to-use interfaces to quickly craft the analysis payloads to corrupt data values. Strata provides lower-level facilities to inset and optimize the instrumentation code, which can lead to low instrumentation overhead [2, 8].

2.5   Control Server

This module mediates communication between the System-under-Test and the User Interface. It is a server that accepts connections from remote user interface clients. The Client Server understands commands and queries to control the System-under-Test and report information about an experiment. For example, it has a command to change the emulated temperature and a query to report application error rate.

3   Using StealthWorks

StealthWorks was developed in an ongoing project that aims to improve system reliability with software resiliency strategies. The framework has been used to run hundreds of experiments; we have found it to be robust and quite useful.

To illustrate StealthWorks' usage, we describe two studies. In the first study, we examine single-event upsets, which remain an important source of errors for deep submicron technology. In this study, we used StealthWorks to inject random SEUs into program data. We implemented a simple static fault model that determines ten random memory addresses to receive an SEU. The addresses are annotated with a "one-time bit flip" data value corruption. When a program is run, the Fault Checker determines whether a memory read operand touches an error address. If so, the Data Value Corruption flips a random bit in the word at the error address. Once an error is hit, it is removed. This experiment injects at most ten single-bit errors.

With this setup, we selected two example programs from SPEC2006 to determine whether they would run to completion with a correct result. We picked *tonto* and *mcf* because they are expected to touch a large number of memory pages and will likely hit the inserted errors. We ran each program ten times with the same errors. Out of the ten runs, *tonto* crashed eight times and *mcf* crashed five times. From a closer inspection, it appears that *tonto*'s control flow is more data dependent and susceptible to errors than *mcf*.

In the second study, we used StealthWorks to evaluate a new online technique to continuously test memory. This second study illustrates StealthWorks for another memory error source – multi-bit permanent errors, which cannot be corrected by traditional memory error correction. We developed a software-only memory testing and scrubbing technique for computers that cannot support or afford hardware error correction techniques. Our approach constantly tests an application's virtual memory pages; it guarantees that every memory page has been tested within a specified time limit. Pages with permanent errors are retired from page allocation. To keep run-time performance overhead low, the test strategy uses a spare core in a chip multiprocessor to concurrently test memory with program execution. In developing this approach, we relied extensively on StealthWorks for development and experimental evaluation.

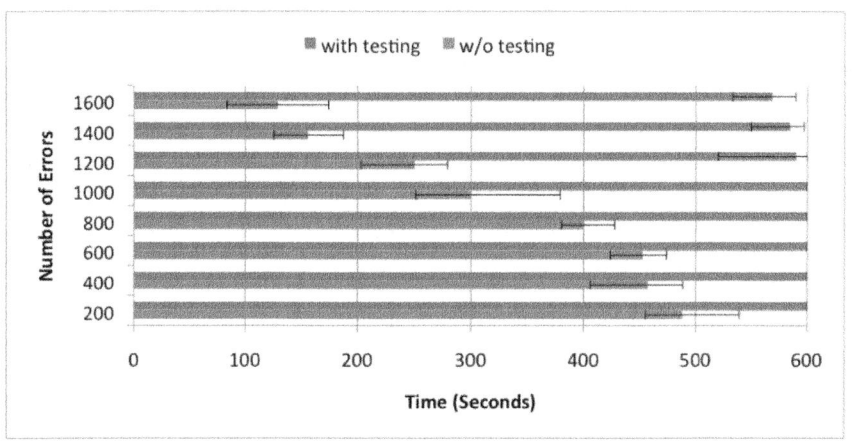

Fig. 3. Time to first fault from StealthWorks

Figure 3 shows one experiment that used StealthWorks to determine whether our online testing technique reduced application vulnerability. To measure vulnerability, we used StealthWorks to find the "time to first fault" (TTFF) of *mcf* when executed under a varying number of emulated errors in a 1-gigabyte memory. The figure compares our technique (bars labeled "w/testing") against a baseline without testing (bars labeled "w/o testing"). The X-axis is the amount of time until the first fault, and the Y-axis is the number of errors injected by StealthWorks. To determine a set of bars, we used the Monte Carlo method to do multiple trials since virtual-to-physical page mappings can change. Each trial was limited to the first ten minutes of *mcf*'s execution. The baseline (without testing) is also instrumented with StealthWorks to ensure that the execution times with and without testing are the same. This permits a fair comparison between TTFF for runs without and with testing. The figure shows the minimum and maximum of each trial as error bars.

As Figure 3 shows, without testing, *mcf* quickly encounters a memory location with an error. As expected, the time to the first fault decreased (more vulnerable) as the number of errors injected is increased. In comparison, our online testing approach let *mcf* tolerate a higher number of errors before the first fault was encountered.

The increased resilience comes at a small run-time cost; our continuous online testing strategy incurs a modest average 3% degradation in performance. This overhead comes from the additional memory pressure (on both the operating system kernel's memory allocator and the hardware memory subsystem) caused by the testing process. This experiment shows the benefit of StealthWorks – the framework permits development and study of software resiliency techniques with different scenarios.

4   Conclusion

Memory errors are surprisingly common and can lead to application failure. To mitigate errors, new resiliency techniques are needed. In this paper, we described an extensible framework, StealthWorks, that can be used to develop and evaluate methods to tolerate and correct memory errors. StealthWorks emulates memory errors in a live machine. We have found it to be a robust and useful framework for research on software resilience.

Acknowledgements

Christian DeLozier, Yang Hu and Yong Li implemented StealthWorks' control server and user interface client. This work is supported in part by the National Science Foundation awards CCF-0811295, CCF-0811352, and CNS-0702236.

References

1. Dell, T.J.: A white paper on the benefits of chipkill - correct ECC for PC server main memory. In: IBM Microelectronics Division (1997)
2. Kumar, N., Childers, B.R., Soffa, M.L.: Low overhead program monitoring and profiling. In: ACM SIGPLAN/SIGSOFT Workshop on Program Analysis for Software Tools and Engineering (PASTE 2005), pp. 28–34 (2005)
3. Li, M.-L., Ramachandran, P., Sahoo, S.K., Adve, S.V., Adve, V.S., Zhou, Y.: SWAT: An error resilient system. In: 4th Workshop on Silicon Errors in Logic - System Effects (2008)
4. Li, M.-L., Ramachandran, P., Sahoo, S.K., Adve, S.V., Adve, V.S., Zhou, Y.: Understanding the propagation of hard errors to software and its implications on resilient system design. In: Architecture Support for Programming Languages and Operating Systems (ASPLOS 2008), pp. 265–276 (2008)

5. Li, X., Huang, M.C., Shen, K.: A realistic evaluation of memory hardware errors and software system susceptibility. In: USENIX Conference (2010)
6. Luk, C.-K., Cohn, R., Muth, R., Patil, H., Klauser, A., Lowney, G., Wallace, S., Reddi, V.J., Hazelwood, K.: Pin: Building customized program analysis tools with dynamic instrumentation. In: ACM SIGPLAN Conference on Programming Language Design and Implementation (PDLI 2005), pp. 190–200 (2005)
7. Schroeder, B., Pinheiro, E., Weber, W.-D.: DRAM errors in the wild: a large-scale field study. In: Internaetional Conference on Measurement and Modeling of Computer Systems (SIGMETRICS 2009), pp. 193–204 (2009)
8. Scott, K., Kumar, N., Velusamy, S., Childers, B.R., Davidson, J.W., Soffa, M.L.: Retargetable and reconfigurable software dynamic translation. In: International Conference on Code Generation and Optimization (CGO 2003), pp. 36–47 (2003)

Efficient Data Race Detection
for Async-Finish Parallelism

Raghavan Raman[1], Jisheng Zhao[1], Vivek Sarkar[1], Martin Vechev[2], and Eran Yahav[2]

[1] Rice University
[2] IBM T. J. Watson Research Center
{raghav,jisheng.zhao,vsarkar}@rice.edu,
{mtvechev,eyahav}@us.ibm.com

Abstract. A major productivity hurdle for parallel programming is the presence of *data races*. Data races can lead to all kinds of harmful program behaviors, including determinism violations and corrupted memory. However, runtime overheads of current dynamic data race detectors are still prohibitively large (often incurring slowdowns of 10× or larger) for use in mainstream software development.

In this paper, we present an efficient dynamic race detector algorithm targeting the async-finish task-parallel parallel programming model. The async and finish constructs are at the core of languages such as X10 and Habanero Java (HJ). These constructs generalize the spawn-sync constructs used in Cilk, while still ensuring that all computation graphs are deadlock-free.

We have implemented our algorithm in a tool called TASKCHECKER and evaluated it on a suite of 12 benchmarks. To reduce overhead of the dynamic analysis, we have also implemented various static optimizations in the tool. Our experimental results indicate that our approach performs well in practice, incurring an average slowdown of 3.05× compared to a serial execution in the optimized case.

1 Introduction

Designing and implementing correct and efficient parallel programs is a notoriously difficult task, and yet, with the proliferation of multi-core processors, parallel programming will need to play a central role in mainstream software development. One of the main difficulties in parallel programming is that a programmer is often required to explicitly reason about the inter-leavings of operations in their program. The vast number of inter-leavings makes this task difficult even for small programs, and intractable for sizable applications. Unstructured and low-level frameworks such as Java threads allow the programmer to express rich and complicated patterns of parallelism, but also make it easy to get things wrong.

Structured Parallelism. Structured parallelism makes it easier to determine the context in which an operation is executed and to identify other operations that can execute in parallel with it. This simplifies manual and automatic reasoning about the program, enabling the programmer to produce a program that is more robust and often more efficient.

Realizing these benefits, significant efforts have been made towards structuring parallel computations, starting with constructs such as *cobegin-coend* [11] and *monitors*. Recently, additional support for fork-join task parallelism has been added in the form

G. Roşu et al. (Eds.): RV 2010, LNCS 6418, pp. 368–383, 2010.

of libraries [15,18] to existing programming environments and languages such as Java and .NET.

Parallel languages such as Cilk [5], X10 [8], and Habanero Java (HJ) [3] provide simple, yet powerful high level concurrency constructs that restrict traditional fork-join parallelism yet are sufficiently expressive for a wide range of problems. The key restriction in these languages is centered around the flexibility of choosing which tasks a given task can join to. The async-finish computations that we consider generalize the more restricted spawn-sync computations of Cilk, and similarly, have the desired property that the computation graphs generated in the language are deadlock-free [17] (unlike unrestricted fork-join computations).

Data Race and Determinism Detection. A central property affecting the correctness of parallel algorithms is data-race freedom. Data-race freedom is a desirable property as in some cases it can imply determinism [16,7]. For instance, in the absence of data races, all parallel programs with *async* and *finish*, but without *isolated* constructs, are guaranteed to be *deterministic*. Therefore, if we can prove data-race freedom of programs which do not contain *isolated* constructs, then we can conclude that the program is deterministic.

We present an efficient dynamic analysis algorithm that checks the presence of data races in async-finish style parallel computations. These constructs form the core of the larger X10, HJ and Cilk parallel languages. Using async, finish and isolated, one can express a wide range of useful and interesting parallel computations (both regular and irregular) such as factorizations and graph computations.

Our analysis is a generalization of Feng and Leiserson's SP-bags algorithm [12] which was designed for checking determinism of spawn-sync Cilk programs. The reason why the original algorithm cannot be applied directly to async-finish style of programming is that this model allows for a superset of the executions allowed by the traditional spawn-sync Cilk programs. Both, the SP-bags algorithm, as well as our extension to it, are sound for a given input: if a data race exists for that input, a violation will be reported.

Main Contributions. To the best of our knowledge, this is the first detailed study of the problem of data race detection for async-finish task-parallel programs as embodied in the X10 and HJ languages. The main contributions of this paper are:

- A dynamic analysis algorithm for efficient data race detection for structured async-finish parallel programs. Our algorithm generalizes the classic SP-bags algorithm designed for the more restricted spawn-sync Cilk model.
- An implementation of our dynamic analysis in a tool named TASKCHECKER.
- Compiler optimizations to reduce the overhead incurred by the dynamic analysis algorithm. These optimizations reduces the overhead by $1.59\times$ on average for the benchmarks used in our evaluation.
- An evaluation of TASKCHECKER on a suite of 12 benchmarks written in the HJ programming language[1]. We show that for these benchmarks, TASKCHECKER is able to perform data race detection with an average (geometric mean) slowdown of $4.86\times$ in the absence of compiler optimizations, and $3.05\times$ with compiler optimizations, compared to a sequential execution.

---

[1] These benchmarks also conform with version 1.5 of the X10 language.

2 Background

In this paper we present our approach to data race detection for an abstract language AFPL, *Async Finish Parallel Language*. We first present our language AFPL and informally describe its semantics. To motivate the generalization of the traditional SP-bags algorithm to our setting, we illustrate where our language allows for broader sets of computation dags than those expressible with the spawn-sync constructs in the Cilk programming language.

2.1 Syntax

Fig. 1 shows the part of the language syntax for AFPL that is relevant to parallelism. The language allows nesting of **finish** and **async** statements. That is, any statement can appear inside these two constructs. However, the language restricts the kind of statements that can appear inside **isolated** sections: no synchronization constructs such as async and finish are allowed inside isolated sections. However, isolated blocks may contain loops, conditionals, and other forms of sequential control flow.

$$Program: \quad P ::= \textbf{main} \; \{ \; \textbf{finish} \; \{ \; s \; \} \; \}$$
$$Statement: \; s ::= \textbf{finish} \; \{ \; s \; \}$$
$$| \quad \textbf{async} \; \{ \; s \; \}$$
$$| \quad \textbf{isolated} \; \{ \; r \; \}$$
$$| \quad ST(s)$$
$$| \quad s \; ; \; s$$
$$Restricted \quad r ::= RT(r)$$
$$Statement \qquad | \quad r \; ; \; r$$

Fig. 1. The syntax of synchronization statements for AFPL

To reflect that, we use the shortcut parametric macros ST and RT (to stand for standard statements and restricted statements respectively). $ST(s)$ will generate the set of usual statements and for any statement, it will replace its sub-statement, if necessary, with s. For instance, one of the several statements in the set for $ST(s)$ will be the conditional **if**(b) s **else** s, while for $ST(r)$, it will be **if**(b) r **else** r. The set of statements generated by RT includes all statements of ST except procedure calls. This restriction is placed to avoid synchronization constructs in methods called from within isolated sections.

While languages such as *X10* and *HJ* also allow for more expressive synchronization mechanisms such as futures, conditional isolated sections, clocks or phasers, the core of these languages is based around the constructs shown in Fig. 1. We note that a similar language, called Featherweight X10 (FX10) has been recently considered in [17]. FX10 considers a more restricted calculus (e.g. it has one large one-dimensional array for the global store) and does not support isolated sections. Our data race detection algorithm is largely independent of the sequential constructs in the language. For example, the sequential portion of the language can be based on the sequential portions of C, C++, Fortran or Java.

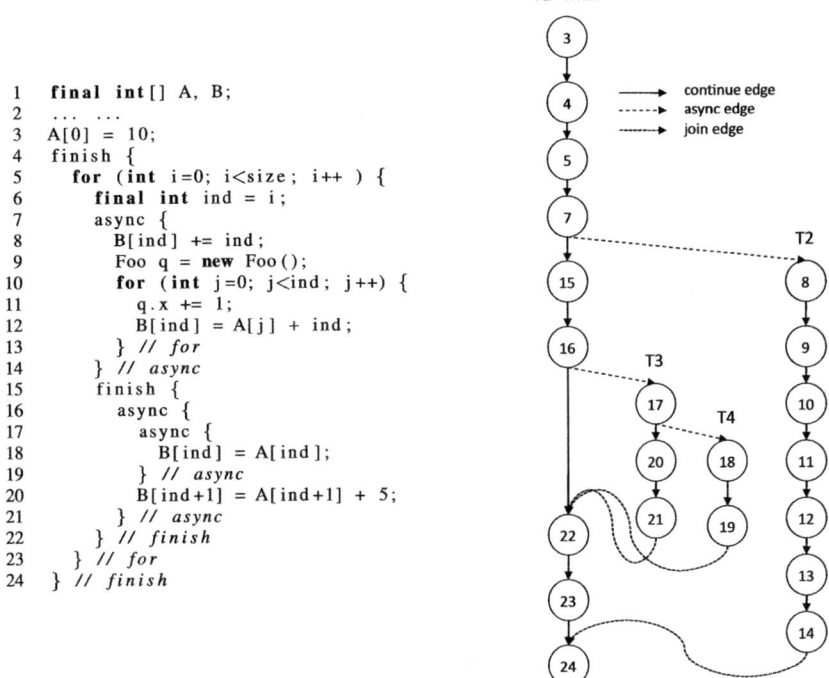

```
1    final int[] A, B;
2    ... ...
3    A[0] = 10;
4    finish {
5      for (int i=0; i<size; i++ ) {
6        final int ind = i;
7        async {
8          B[ind] += ind;
9          Foo q = new Foo();
10         for (int j=0; j<ind; j++) {
11           q.x += 1;
12           B[ind] = A[j] + ind;
13         } // for
14       } // async
15       finish {
16         async {
17           async {
18             B[ind] = A[ind];
19           } // async
20           B[ind+1] = A[ind+1] + 5;
21         } // async
22       } // finish
23     } // for
24   } // finish
```

Fig. 2. An example AFPL program and its computation graph

2.2   Informal Language Semantics

Next, we briefly discuss the relevant semantics of the concurrency constructs. For formal semantics of the async and finish constructs, see FX10 [17]. Initially, the program begins execution with the main task. When an **async** { s } statement is executed by task A, a new child task, B, is created. The new task B can now proceed with executing statement s in parallel with its parent task A. For example, consider the AFPL code shown in Fig. 2. Suppose the main task starts executing this piece of code. The async statement in line 7 creates a new child task, which will now execute the block of code in lines 7-14 in parallel with the main task. When a **finish** { s } statement is executed by task A, it means that task A must block and wait at the end of this statement until all descendant tasks created by A in s (including their recursively created children tasks), have terminated. That is, **finish** can be used to create a join point for all descendant tasks dynamically created inside its scope. In the example in Fig. 2, the finish in line 15 would wait for the tasks created by asyncs in lines 16 and 17 to complete. The statement **isolated** { s } means that the statement s is executed atomically with respect to other isolated statements[2].

---

[2] As advocated in [14], we use the *isolated* keyword instead of *atomic* to make explicit the fact that the construct supports weak isolation rather than strong atomicity.

2.3 Cilk vs. AFPL

Our data race detection algorithm, ESP-bags, presented in later sections, is an adaptation of the SP-bags algorithm [12] developed for the Cilk programming language. Unfortunately, the SP-bags algorithm cannot be applied directly to our language and needs to be extended. The reason is that our language supports a more relaxed concurrency model than the spawn-sync Cilk computations. The key semantic relaxation lays in the way a task is allowed to join with other tasks. In Cilk, at any given (join) point of the task execution, the task should join with *all* of its descendant tasks (including all recursive descendant tasks) created in between the start of the task and the join point. The join is accomplished by executing the statement **sync**. The sync statement in Cilk can be directly translated to a standard **finish** block, where the start of the finish block is the start of the procedure and the end of the finish block is the label of the sync statement. For instance, we can translate the following Cilk program:

$$\textbf{spawn } f1(); \textbf{sync}; \textbf{spawn } f2(); \textbf{sync}; s1;$$

into the following AFPL program:

$$\textbf{finish } \{ \textbf{ finish } \{ \textbf{ async } f1(); \}; \textbf{ async } f2(); \}; s1;$$

That is, each spawn statement is replaced by an async statement and each sync statement is replaced with a finish block, where the scope of the finish ranges from the start of the task to the label of the corresponding sync.

In contrast, with the use of nested finish operations in AFPL, it is possible for a task to join with *some* rather than all of its descendant tasks. The way these descendant tasks are specified at the language level is with the **finish** construct: upon encountering the end of a finish block, the task waits until all of the descendant tasks created inside the finish scope have completed.

The computation graph in Fig. 2 illustrates the differences between Cilk and AFPL. Each vertical sequence of circles denotes a task. Here we have four sequences for four tasks. Each circle in the graph represents a program label and an edge represents the execution of a statement at that label. Note that at label 22, the main task waits only for T3 and T4 and not for T2, which is not possible using the spawn-sync semantics used in Cilk.

Further, another restriction in Cilk is that every task must execute a sync statement upon its return. That is, a task cannot terminate unless all of its descendants have terminated. In contrast, in AFPL, a task can outlive its parents, i.e., a task can complete even while its children are still alive. For instance, in the example of Fig. 2, in Cilk, T3 would need to wait until T4 has terminated. That is, the edge from node 19 to 22 would change to an edge from 19 to 21. As we can see, this need not be the case in AFPL: task T3 can terminate before task T4 has finished.

More generally, the class of computations generated by the spawn-sync constructs is said to be *fully-strict* [6], while the computations generated by our language are called *terminally-strict* [2]. The set of terminally-strict computations subsumes the set of fully-strict computations. All of these relaxations mean that it is not possible to directly convert a AFPL program into the spawn-sync semantics of Cilk, which in turn implies that we cannot use its SP-bags algorithm immediately and we need to somehow generalize that algorithm to our setting. We show how that is accomplished in the next section.

3   ESP-Bags Algorithm

In this section, we briefly summarize the existing SP-bags algorithm used for spawn-sync computations. Then, we present our extension of that algorithm for detecting data races in AFPL programs. The original SP-bags algorithm was designed for Cilk's spawn-sync computations. As mentioned earlier, we can always translate spawn-sync computations into async-finish computations. Therefore, we present the operations of the original SP-bags algorithm in terms of async and finish, rather than spawn and sync constructs, so that the extensions are easily understood.

3.1   SP-Bags

We assume that each dynamic task (async) instance is given a unique task id. The basic idea behind the SP-bags algorithm is to attach two "bags", S and P, to each dynamic task instance. Each bag contains a set of task id's. When a statement E that belongs to a task A is being executed, the S-bag of task A will hold all of the descendant tasks of A that always precede E in any execution of the program. The S-bag of A will also include A itself since any statement G in A that executes before E in the sequential depth first execution will always precede E in any execution of the program. The P-bag of A holds all descendant tasks of A that may execute in parallel with E.

At any point during the depth-first execution of the program, a task id will always belong to at most one bag. Therefore, all these bags can be efficiently represented using a single disjoint-set data structure. The intuition behind the algorithm can be stated as follows: when a program is executed in depth-first manner, a write W_1 to a shared memory location L by a task τ_1 races with an earlier read/write to L by any task τ_2 which is in a P-bag when W_1 occurs and it does not race with read/write by any task that is in an S-bag when W_1 occurs. A read races with an earlier write in the same way.

Although the program being tested for data races is a parallel program, the SP-bags algorithm is a serial algorithm that performs a sequential depth-first execution of the program on a single processor. Each memory location is instrumented to contain two additional fields: a *reader* task id and a *writer* task id. The following table shows the update rules for the SP-bags algorithm:

Async A	$: S_A \leftarrow \{A\}, P_A \leftarrow \emptyset$
Task A returns to Task B	$: P_B \leftarrow P_B \cup S_A \cup P_A, S_A \leftarrow \emptyset, P_A \leftarrow \emptyset$
EndFinish F in a Task B	$: S_B \leftarrow S_B \cup P_B, P_B \leftarrow \emptyset$

When a task A is created, its S bag is initialized to contain its own task id, and its P bag is initialized to the empty set. When a task A returns to a task B in the depth-first execution, then both of its bags, S and P, are moved to the P bag of its parent, B, and its bags are reset. When a join point is encountered in a task, the P bag of that task is moved to its S bag.

In addition to the above steps, during the depth-first execution of a program, the SP-bags algorithm requires that action is taken on every read and write of a shared variable. Figure 3 shows the required instrumentation for *read* and *write* operations. For each operation on a shared memory location L, we only need to check those fields of L that could conflict with the current operation.

```
1   Read location L by Task t:
2       If L.writer is in a P-bag then Data Race;
3       If L.reader is in a S-bag then L.reader = t;

1   Write location L by Task t:
2       If L.writer is in a P-bag or L.reader is in a P-bag
3           then Data Race;
4       L.writer = t;
```

Fig. 3. Instrumentation on shared memory access. Applies both to SP-bags and ESP-bags.

3.2   ESP-Bags

Next, we present our extensions to the SP-bags algorithm. Recall that the key difference between AFPL and spawn-sync lays in the flexibility of selecting which of its descendent tasks a parent task can join to. The following table shows the update rules for the ESP-bags algorithm. The extensions to SP-bags are highlighted in **bold**.

Async A - fork a new task A : $S_A \leftarrow \{A\}, P_A \leftarrow \emptyset$	
*Task A returns to **Parent** B* : $P_B \leftarrow P_B \cup S_A \cup P_A, S_A \leftarrow \emptyset, P_A \leftarrow \emptyset$	
StartFinish F : $P_F \leftarrow \emptyset$	
EndFinish F in a Task B : $S_B \leftarrow S_B \cup P_F, P_F \leftarrow \emptyset$	

The key extension lays in attaching P bags, not only to tasks, but also to identifiers of finish blocks. At the start of a finish block F, the bag P_F is reset. Then, when a finish block ends in a task, the contents of its P bag are moved to the S bag of that task. Further, when during the depth-first execution a task returns to its parent, say B, B may be both a task *or* a finish scope. The actual operations on the S and P bags in that case are identical to SP-bags.

The need for this extension comes from the fact that at the end of a finish block, only the tasks created inside the finish block are guaranteed to complete and therefore will precede the tasks that follow the finish block. Therefore, only the tasks created inside the finish block need to be added to the S-bag of the parent task when the finish completes and those tasks created before the finish block began need to stay in the P-bag of the parent task.

This extension generalizes the SP-bags presented earlier. This means that the ESP-bags algorithm can be applied directly to spawn-sync programs as well by first translating then to async-finish as shown earlier, and the applying the algorithm. Of course, if we know that the finish blocks have a particular structure, and we know that translated spawn-sync programs do, then we can safely optimize away the P bag for the finish id's and directly update the bag of the parent task (as done in the original SP-bags algorithm).

3.3 Discussion

In summary, the ESP-bags algorithm works by updating the *reader* and *writer* fields of a shared memory location whenever that memory location is read or written by a task. On each such read/write operation, the algorithm also checks to see if the previously recorded task in these fields (if any) can conflict with the current task, using the S and the P bags of the current task. We now show an example of how the algorithm works for the AFPL code in Fig. 2. Suppose that the main task, T_1, starts executing that code. We refer to the finish in line 4 by F_1 and the first instance of the finish in line 15 by F_2. Also, we refer to the first instance of the tasks generated by the asyncs in lines 7, 16, and 17 by T_2, T_3, and T_4 respectively.

Table 1. ESP-bags Example

PC	T_1 S	F_1 P	T_2 S	F_2 P	T_3 P	T_3 S	T_4 S	B[0] Writer
1	$\{T_1\}$	-	-	-	-	-	-	-
4	$\{T_1\}$	∅	-	-	-	-	-	-
7	$\{T_1\}$	∅	$\{T_2\}$	-	-	-	-	-
8	$\{T_1\}$	∅	$\{T_2\}$	-	-	-	-	T_2
14	$\{T_1\}$	$\{T_2\}$	∅	-	-	-	-	T_2
15	$\{T_1\}$	$\{T_2\}$	∅	∅	-	-	-	T_2
16	$\{T_1\}$	$\{T_2\}$	∅	∅	∅	$\{T_3\}$	-	T_2
17	$\{T_1\}$	$\{T_2\}$	∅	∅	∅	$\{T_3\}$	$\{T_4\}$	T_2
*18	$\{T_1\}$	$\{T_2\}$	∅	∅	∅	$\{T_3\}$	$\{T_4\}$	T_4
19	$\{T_1\}$	$\{T_2\}$	∅	∅	$\{T_4\}$	$\{T_3\}$	∅	T_4
21	$\{T_1\}$	$\{T_2\}$	∅	$\{T_4,T_3\}$	∅	∅	∅	T_4
22	$\{T_1,T_4,T_3\}$	$\{T_2\}$	∅	∅	∅	∅	∅	T_4

Table 1 shows how the S and P bags of the tasks (T_1, T_2, T_3, and T_4) and the P bags of the finishes (F_1 and F_2) are modified by the algorithm as the code in Fig. 2 is executed. Each row shows the status of these S and P bags after the execution of a particular statement in the code. The PC refers to the statement number (from Fig. 2) that is executed. This table only shows the status corresponding to the first iteration of the for loop in line 5. The table also tracks the contents of the writer field of the memory location *B[0]*. The P bags of the tasks T_1, T_2, and T_4 are omitted here since they remain empty through the first iteration of the for loop.

In the first three steps in the table, the S and P bags of T_1, F_1, and T_2 are initialized appropriately. When the statement in line 8 is executed, the writer field of *B[0]* is set to the current task, T_2. Then, on completion of T_2 in line 14, the contents of its S and P bags are moved to the P bag of F_1. When the write to *B[0]* in line 18 (in Task T_4) is executed, the algorithm finds the task in its writer field, T_2, in a P bag (P bag of F_1). Hence this is reported as a data race. Further, when T_4 completes in line 19, the contents of its S and P bags are moved to the P bag of its parent T_3. Similarly, when T_3 completes in line 21, the contents of its S and P bags are moved to the P bag of its parent F_2. When the finish F_2 completes in line 22, the contents of its P bag are moved to the S bag of its parent T_1.

4   Handling Isolated Blocks

In this section, we briefly describe an extension to the ESP-bags algorithm to accommodate handling of isolated sections. Isolated sections are useful since they allow the programmer to write data-race-free parallel programs in which multiple tasks interact and update shared memory locations.

```
1    Isolated Read of location L by Task t:
2        If L.writer is in a P-bag then Data Race;
3        If L.isolatedReader is in a S-bag then L.isolatedReader = t;

1    Isolated Write of location L by Task t:
2        If L.writer is in a P-bag or L.reader is in a P-bag
3            then Data Race;
4        If L.isolatedWriter is in a S-bag then L.isolatedWriter = t;

1    Read location L by Task t:
2        If L.writer is in a P-bag or L.isolatedWriter is in a P-bag
3            then Data Race;
4        If L.reader is in a S-bag then L.reader = t;

1    Write location L by Task t:
2        If L.writer is in a P-bag or L.reader is in a P-bag
3            or L.isolatedWriter is in a P-bag or L.isolatedReader is in a P-bag
4            then Data Race;
5        L.writer = t;
```

Fig. 4. ESP-bags algorithm for AFPL, with support for *isolated* blocks

The extension to handle isolated sections includes checking that isolated and non-isolated accesses that may execute in parallel do not interfere. For this, we extend ESP-bags as follows: two additional fields are added to every memory location, *isolatedReader*, and *isolatedWriter*. These fields are used to hold the task that performs an *isolated* read or write on the location. We need to handle reads and writes from *isolated* blocks differently as compared to *non-isolated* operations. Fig. 4 shows the steps needed to be performed during each of the operations: *read, write, isolated-read*, and *isolated-write*.

5   Compiler Optimizations

The ESP-bags algorithm is implemented as a *Java* library. Recall that the ESP-bags algorithm requires that action is taken on every read and write to a shared memory location. To test a given program for data-race freedom using the ESP-bags algorithm, we need a compiler transformation pass that instruments read and write operations on shared memory locations in the program with appropriate calls to the library. In this section, we describe the static analyses that we used to reduce the instrumentation and hence improve the runtime performance of the instrumented program.

Main Task Check Elimination in Sequential Code Regions. A parallel program will always start and end with sequential code regions and will contain alternating parallel and sequential code regions in the middle. There is no need to instrument the operations in such sequential code regions. In an AFPL program, the sequential code regions are executed by the *main task*. Thus, in an AFPL program, there is no need to instrument the read and write operations in the sequential code regions of the main task.

Read-only Check Elimination in Parallel Code Regions. The input program may have shared memory locations that are written by the sequential regions of the program and only read within parallel regions of the program. Such read operations within parallel regions of the program need not be instrumented because parallel tasks reading from the same memory location will never lead to a conflict. To perform this optimization, the compiler implements an inter-procedural side-effect analysis [4] to detect potential write operations to shared memory locations within the parallel regions of the given program. If there is no possible write to a shared memory location M in the parallel regions of the program, that clearly shows that all accesses to M in the parallel regions must be read-only and hence the instrumentations corresponding to these reads can be eliminated.

Escape Analysis. The input program may include many parallel tasks. A race occurs in the program only when two or more tasks access a shared memory location and at least one of them is a write. Suppose an object is created inside a task and it never escapes that task, then no other task can access this object and hence it cannot lead to a data race. To ensure the task-local attribute, the compiler performs an inter-procedural escape analysis [10] that identifies if an object is shared among tasks. This also requires an alias analysis to ensure that no alias of the object escapes the task. Thus, if an object O is proven to not escape a task, then the instrumentations corresponding to all accesses to O can be eliminated.

Loop Invariant Check Optimization. If there are multiple accesses of the same type (read or write) to M by a task, then it is sufficient to instrument one such access because other instrumentations will only add to the overhead by unnecessarily repeating the steps. Suppose the input program accesses a shared memory location M unconditionally inside a loop, the instrumentation corresponding to this access to M can be moved outside the loop to prevent multiple calls to the instrumented function for M. In summary, given a memory access M that is performed unconditionally on every iteration of a sequential loop, the instrumentation for M can be hoisted out of the loop by using classical loop-invariant code motion.

Read/Write Check Elimination. In this optimization, we claim that if there are two accesses M_1 and M_2 to the same memory location in a task, then we can use the following rules to eliminate one of them.

1. If M_1 dominates M_2 and M_2 is a read operation, then the instrumentation for M_2 can be eliminated (since M_1 is either a read or write operation).
2. If M_2 post-dominates M_1 and M_1 is a read operation, then the check for M_1 can be eliminated (since M_2 is either a read or write operation). This rule tends to be

applicable in fewer situations than the previous rule in practice, because computation of post-dominance includes the possibility of exceptional control flow.

6   Evaluation

We report the performance results of our experiments on a 16-way (quad-socket, quad-core per socket) Intel Xeon 2.4GHz system with 30 GB memory, running Red Hat Linux (RHEL 5). The JVM used is the Sun Hotspot JDK 1.6. We applied the ESP-bags algorithm to a set of 8 Java Grande Forum (JGF) benchmarks shown in Table 2. Though we performed our experiments on different sizes of the JGF benchmarks, we only report the results of the maximum size in each case. We were unable to get the results of size B for MolDyn since the both the versions (original and instrumented) runs out of memory. We also evaluated our algorithm on 3 Shootout benchmarks and 1 EC2 challenge benchmark. All the benchmarks used were written in HJ using only the AFPL constructs and are available from [1].

Table 2. List of Benchmarks Evaluated

Source	Benchmark	Description
JGF (Section 2)	Series	Fourier coefficient analysis
	LUFact	LU Factorisation
	SOR	Successive over-relaxation
	Crypt	IDEA encryption
	Sparse	Sparse Matrix multiplication
JGF (Section 3)	MolDyn	Molecular Dynamics simulation
	MonteCarlo	Monte Carlo simulation
	RayTracer	3D Ray Tracer
Shootout	Fannkuch	Indexed-access to tiny integer-sequence
	Fasta	Generate and write random DNA sequences
	Mandelbrot	Generate Mandelbrot set portable bitmap file
EC2	Matmul	sMatrix Multiplication (two 1000*1000 double matrix)

Results of ESP-bags algorithm. Table 3 shows the results of applying the ESP-bags algorithm on our benchmarks. This table gives the original time taken for each benchmark, i.e., the time taken to execute the benchmark without any instrumentation. It also shows the slowdown of the benchmark when instrumented for the ESP-bags algorithm with and without the optimizations described in Section 5. The outcome of the ESP-bags algorithm is also included in the table, which clearly shows there are no data races in any of the benchmarks. The same was observed for all the input sizes. Hence all the benchmarks are free of data races for the inputs considered. Note that though RayTracer has some *isolated* conflicts, it is free of data races since there were no conflicts between isolated and non-isolated accesses.

Table 3. Slowdown of ESP-bags Algorithm

Benchmark	Number of asyncs	Time (s)	ESP-bags Slowdown Factor		Result
			w/o opts	w/ opts	
Crypt - C	1.3e7	15.24	7.63	7.29	No Data Races
LUFact - C	1.6e6	15.19	12.45	10.08	No Data Races
MolDyn - A	5.1e5	45.88	10.57	3.93	No Data Races
MonteCarlo - B	3.0e5	19.55	1.99	1.57	No Data Races
RayTracer - B	5.0e2	38.85	11.89	9.48	No Data Races (Isolated conflict)
Series - C	1.0e6	1395.81	1.01	1.00	No Data Races
SOR - C	2.0e5	3.03	14.99	9.05	No Data Races
Sparse - C	6.4e1	13.59	12.79	2.73	No Data Races
Fannkuch	1.0e6	7.71	1.49	1.38	No Data Races
Fasta	4.0e0	1.39	3.88	3.73	No Data Races
Mandelbrot	1.6e1	11.89	1.02	1.02	No Data Races
Matmul	1.0e3	19.59	6.43	1.16	No Data Races
Geo Mean			4.86	3.05	

ESP-bags slowdown. On an average, the slowdown of the benchmarks with the ESP-bags algorithm is $4.86\times$ without optimization. When all the static optimizations are applied, the average slowdown drops to $3.05\times$. The slowdown of all the benchmarks except LUFact is less than $10\times$. The slowdown for benchmarks like MolDyn, Monte-Carlo and Sparse are less than $5\times$. There is no slowdown in the case of Series because most of the code uses stack variables. In *HJ* none of the stack variables can be shared across tasks and hence we do not instrument any access to these variables. On the other hand, the slowdown for SOR and RayTracer benchmarks are around $9\times$.

Performance of Optimizations. We now discuss the effects of the compiler optimizations on the benchmarks. The static optimizations that were performed include check elimination in sequential code regions in the main task, read-only check elimination in parallel code regions, escape analysis, loop invariant check motion, and read/write check elimination. As is evident from the table, some of the benchmarks like SOR, Sparse, MolDyn, and Matmul benefit a lot from the optimizations, with a maximum reduction in slowdown of about 78% for Sparse. On the other hand, for other benchmarks the reduction is relatively less. The optimizations does not reduce the slowdown much for Crypt and LUFact because in these benchmarks very few instrumentations are eliminated as a result of the optimizations. In the case of MonteCarlo and RayTracer, though a good number of instrumentations are eliminated, a significant fraction of them still remain and hence there is not much performance improvement in these benchmarks due to optimizations. On an average, there is a 37% reduction in the slowdown of the benchmarks due these optimizations.

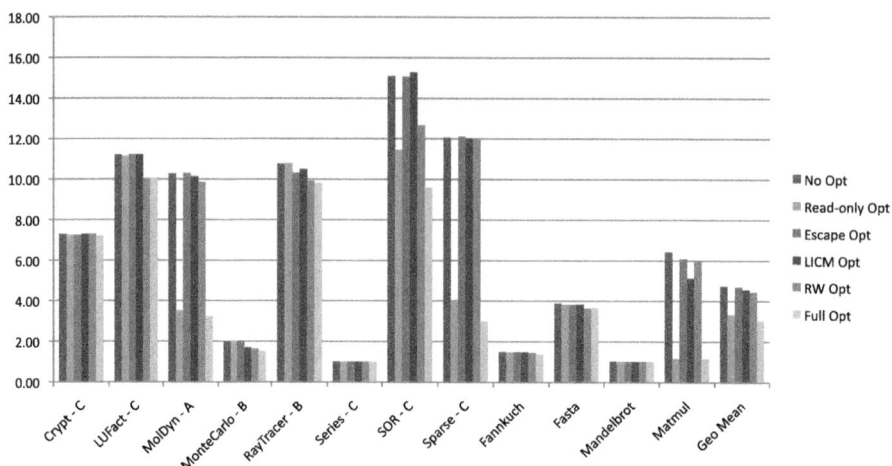

Fig. 5. Breakdown of static optimizations

Breakdown of the Optimizations. We now describe the effects of each of the static optimizations separately on the performance of the benchmarks. Figure 5 shows the breakdown of the effects of each of the static optimizations. The graph also shows the slowdown without any optimization and with the whole set of optimizations enabled. The Main Task Check Elimination optimization described in Section 5 is applied to all the versions included here, including the unoptimized version. This is because we consider that optimization as a basic step without which there could be excessive instrumentations.

The read-only check elimination performs much better than the other optimizations for most of the benchmarks, like MolDyn, SOR, and SparseMatmult. This is because in these benchmarks the parallel regions include reads to many arrays which are written only in the sequential regions of the code. Hence, this optimization eliminates the instrumentation for all these reads. It contributes the most to the overall performance improvement in the full optimized version. The read-write optimization works well in the case of SOR, but does not have much effect on other benchmarks. The Loop invariant code motion helps improve the performance of Montecarlo the most and the Escape analysis does not seem to help any of these benchmarks to a great extent.

Note that the performance of these four static optimizations do not directly add up to the performance of the fully optimized code. This is because some of these optimizations creates more chances for other optimizations. Hence their combined effect is much more than their sum. For example, the loop invariant code motion creates more chances for the Read-only and Read-Write optimization. So, when these two optimizations are performed after loop invariant code motion their effect would be more than that is shown here. Finally, we only evaluated the performance of these optimizations on the set of benchmarks shown here. For a different set of benchmarks, their effects could be different. But we believe that these static optimizations, when applied in combination, are in general good enough to improve the performance of most of the benchmarks.

7   Related Work

The original Cilk paper [12] introduces SP-bags for spawn-sync computations. We extend that algorithm to the more general setting of async-finish computations. An extension to SP-bags was proposed by Cheng et al. [9] to handle locks in Cilk programs. Their approach includes a data race detection algorithm for programs that satisfy a particular locking discipline. However, the slowdown factors reported in [9] were in the $33\times$ - $78\times$ range for programs that follow their locking discipline, and upto $3700\times$ for programs that don't. In this work, we detect data races in programs with async, finish, and isolated constructs. We outline and implement a range of static optimizations to reduce the slowdown factor to just $3.05\times$ on average.

A recent result on detecting data races by Flanagan et al. [13] (FastTrack) reduces the overhead of using vector clocks during data race detection. Their technique focuses on the more general setting of fork-join programs. The major problem with using vector clocks for race detection is that the space required for vector clocks is linear in the number of threads in the program and hence any vector clock operation also takes time linear in the number of threads. In a program containing millions of tasks that can run in parallel it is not feasible to use vector clocks to detect data races (if we directly extend vector clocks to tasks). Though FastTrack reduces this space (and hence the time for any vector clock operation) to a constant by using epochs instead of vector clocks, it needs vector clocks whenever a memory location has shared read accesses. Even one such instance would make it infeasible for programs with millions of parallel tasks. On the other hand, our approach requires only a constant space for every memory location and a time proportional to the inverse Ackerman function. Also, FastTrack just checks for data races in a particular execution of a program, whereas our approach can guarantee the non-existence of data races for all possible schedules of a given input. The price we have to pay for this soundness guarantee is that we have to execute the given program sequentially. But given that this needs to be done only during the development stage we feel our approach is of value.

Sadowski et al. [20] propose a technique for checking determinism by using interference checks based on happens before relations. This involves detecting conflicting races in threads that can run in parallel. Though they can guarantee the non-existence of races in all possible schedules of a given input, the fact that they use vector clocks makes these infeasible in a program with millions of tasks that can run in parallel.

The static optimizations that we use to eliminate the redundant instrumentations and hence reduce the overhead is similar to the compile-time analyses proposed by Mellor-Crummey [19]. His technique is applicable for loop carried data dependences across parallel loops and also for data dependences across parallel blocks of code. In our approach, we concentrate on the instrumentations within a particular task and try to eliminate redundant instrumentations for memory locations which are guaranteed to have already been instrumented in that task.

8   Conclusion

In this paper, we proposed a sound and efficient dynamic data-race detection algorithm called ESP-bags. ESP-bags targets the async-finish parallel programming model, which generalizes the spawn-sync model used in Cilk.

We have implemented ESP-bags in a tool called TASKCHECKER and augmented it with a set of static compiler optimizations that reduce the incurred overhead by $1.59\times$ on average. Evaluation of TASKCHECKER on a suite of 12 benchmarks shows that the dynamic analysis introduces an average slowdown of $4.86\times$ without compiler optimizations, and $3.05\times$ with compiler optimizations, making the tool suitable for practical use.

In future work, we plan to investigate the applicability of ESP-bags to the fork-join concurrency model.

Acknowledgements

We would like to thank Jacob Burnim and Koushik Sen from UC Berkeley, Jaeheon Yi and Cormac Flanagan from UC Santa Cruz, and John Mellor-Crummey from Rice University for their feedback on an earlier version of this paper.

References

1. Habanero Java, http://habanero.rice.edu/hj
2. Agarwal, S., Barik, R., Bonachea, D., Sarkar, V., Shyamasundar, R.K., Yelick, K.: Deadlock-free scheduling of X10 computations with bounded resources. In: SPAA 2007: Proceedings of the 19th symposium on Parallel algorithms and architectures, pp. 229–240. ACM, New York (2007)
3. Barik, R., Budimlic, Z., Cave, V., Chatterjee, S., Guo, Y., Peixotto, D., Raman, R., Shirako, J., Tasirlar, S., Yan, Y., Zhao, Y., Sarkar, V.: The habanero multicore software research project. In: OOPSLA 2009: Proceeding of the 24th ACM SIGPLAN conference companion on Object oriented programming systems languages and applications, pp. 735–736. ACM, New York (2009)
4. Barik, R., Sarkar, V.: Interprocedural Load Elimination for Dynamic Optimization of Parallel Programs. In: PACT 2009, Proceedings of the 18th International Conference on Parallel Architectures and Compilation Techniques, Washington, DC, USA, pp. 41–52. IEEE Computer Society, Los Alamitos (September 2009),
   http://dx.doi.org/10.1109/PACT.2009.32
5. Blumofe, R.D., Joerg, C.F., Kuszmaul, B.C., Leiserson, C.E., Randall, K.H., Zhou, Y.: Cilk: an efficient multithreaded runtime system. In: Proceedings of the Fifth ACM SIGPLAN Symposium on Principles and Practice of Parallel Programming, PPoPP, pp. 207–216 (October 1995)
6. Blumofe, R.D., Leiserson, C.E.: Scheduling multithreaded computations by work stealing. J. ACM 46(5), 720–748 (1999)
7. Bocchino, R., Adve, V., Adve, S., Snir, M.: Parallel programming must be deterministic by default. In: First USENIX Workship on Hot Topics in Parallelism, HOTPAR 2009 (2009)
8. Charles, P., Grothoff, C., Saraswat, V.A., Donawa, C., Kielstra, A., Ebcioglu, K., von Praun, C., Sarkar, V.: X10: an object-oriented approach to non-uniform cluster computing. In: Proceedings of the Twentieth Annual ACM SIGPLAN Conference on Obj ect-Oriented Programming, Systems, Languages, and Applications, OOPSLA, pp. 519–538 (October 2005)
9. Cheng, G.-I., Feng, M., Leiserson, C.E., Randall, K.H., Stark, A.F.: Detecting data races in cilk programs that use locks. In: Proceedings of the Tenth Annual ACM Symposium on Parallel Algorithms and Architectures (SPAA 1998), Puerto Vallarta, Mexico, June 28–July 2, pp. 298–309 (1998)

10. Choi, J.-D., Gupta, M., Serrano, M.J., Sreedhar, V.C., Midkiff, S.P.: Stack allocation and synchronization optimizations for Java using escape analysis. ACM Trans. Program. Lang. Syst. 25(6), 876–910 (2003), http://doi.acm.org/10.1145/945885.945892

11. Dijkstra, E.W.: Cooperating sequential processes, 65–138

12. Feng, M., Leiserson, C.E.: Efficient detection of determinacy races in cilk programs. In: SPAA 1997: Proceedings of the ninth annual ACM symposium on Parallel algorithms and architectures, pp. 1–11. ACM, New York (1997)

13. Flanagan, C., Freund, S.N.: Fasttrack: efficient and precise dynamic race detection. In: PLDI 2009: Proceedings of the 2009 ACM SIGPLAN conference on Programming language design and implementation, pp. 121–133. ACM, New York (2009)

14. Larus, J.R., Rajwar, R.: Transactional Memory. Morgan and Claypool (2006)

15. Lea, D.: A java fork/join framework. In: JAVA 2000: Proceedings of the ACM, conference on Java Grande, pp. 36–43. ACM, New York (2000)

16. Lee, E.A.: The problem with threads. Computer 39(5), 33–42 (2006)

17. Lee, J.K., Palsberg, J.: Featherweight x10: a core calculus for async-finish parallelism. In: PPoPP 2010: Proceedings of the 15th ACM SIGPLAN symposium on Principles and practice of parallel computing, pp. 25–36. ACM, New York (2010)

18. Leijen, D., Schulte, W., Burckhardt, S.: The design of a task parallel library. In: OOPSLA 2009: Proceeding of the 24th ACM SIGPLAN conference on Object oriented programming systems languages and applications, pp. 227–242. ACM, New York (2009)

19. Mellor-Crummey, J.: Compile-time support for efficient data race detection in shared-memory parallel programs. In: PADD 1993: Proceedings of the 1993 ACM/ONR workshop on Parallel and distributed debugging, pp. 129–139. ACM, New York (1993)

20. Sadowski, C., Freund, S.N., Flanagan, C.: SingleTrack: A dynamic determinism checker for multithreaded programs. In: Castagna, G. (ed.) ESOP 2009. LNCS, vol. 5502, pp. 394–409. Springer, Heidelberg (2009)

Run-Time Verification of Optimistic Concurrency

Ali Sezgin[1], Serdar Tasiran[1], Kivanc Muslu[1], and Shaz Qadeer[2]

[1] Koc University, Istanbul, Turkey
{asezgin,kmuslu,stasiran}@ku.edu.tr
[2] Microsoft Research, Redmond, WA, USA
qadeer@microsoft.com

Abstract. Assertion based specifications are not suitable for optimistic concurrency where concurrent operations are performed assuming no conflict among threads and correctness is cast in terms of the absence or presence of conflicts that happen in the future. What is needed is a formalism that allows expressing constraints about the future. In previous work, we introduced tressa claims and incorporated prophecy variables as one such formalism. We investigated static verification of tressa claims and how tressa claims improve reduction proofs.

In this paper, we consider tressa claims in the run-time verification of optimistic concurrency implementations. We formalize, via a simple grammar, the annotation of a program with tressa claims. Our method relieves the user from dealing with explicit manipulation of prophecy variables. We demonstrate the use of tressa claims in expressing complex properties with simple syntax.

We develop a run-time verification framework which enables the user to evaluate the correctness of tressa claims. To this end, we first describe the algorithms for monitor synthesis which can be used to evaluate the satisfaction of a tressa claim over a given execution. We then describe our tool implementing these algorithms. We report our initial test results.

1 Introduction

The main challenge in reasoning about concurrent programs is taking into account the interactions among threads on shared memory. An effective way to cope with the complexity of concurrent shared-memory programming is to specify and verify partial safety properties which are typically expressed as assertions over program variables.

For implementations based on optimistic concurrency, our experience suggests that expressing properties about concurrency control mechanisms in the form of assertions is unnatural and counter-intuitive. In optimistic concurrency, a thread accesses a shared resource as if there are no competing threads for the same resource and eventually validates whether this assumption was correct. If it was, then it *commits*; if not, it *rolls-back* any visible global change and, optionally, re-starts. Correctness in these implementations, such as those of non-blocking data structures or Software Transactional Memories (STM's) [1], cannot

G. Roşu et al. (Eds.): RV 2010, LNCS 6418, pp. 384–398, 2010.
© Springer-Verlag Berlin Heidelberg 2010

be easily expressed as variations of assertions. Instead, one needs to express the desired properties in terms of future behavior, for instance, what needs to hold at the present program state if the method call or transaction completes without conflict.

In our previous work [2], we have introduced tressa claims and incorporated prophecy variables in order to relate the program state at which a tressa claim is executed to the rest of the execution. Our objective was to simplify the use of QED [3] in reduction proofs of optimistic concurrent programs. Intuitively, tressa $\varphi(p)$ executed at state s expresses the belief that $\varphi(p)$ holds at s as long as the rest of the execution agrees with the *current* value of the prophecy variable p. For instance, imagine that the (boolean) return value res of a method m is mapped to the prophecy variable, $pRes$: An execution of m returns true iff $pRes$ is equal to true during the execution of m. Then, the expression tressa $pRes \Rightarrow \phi$ executed at state s claims that ϕ at s is required to hold only in those executions in which m returns true.

In this paper, we investigate the tressa construct with an eye towards specification and run-time verification. Tressa claims are suitable for specifying properties for optimistic concurrency because they provide a means to relate the outcome of a sequence of events yet to occur with the program state at which the tressa claim is executed. Reading in contrapositive form, the tressa claim of the previous paragraph expresses the requirement that if ϕ is false, then m should return false. This pattern appears often in optimistic concurrency if, for instance, ϕ expresses non-interference.

Instead of cluttering our specification methodology by prophecy variables, we define a grammar for expressing tressa claims. It is possible to address the value last/first written to or read from a variable by a particular subset of all active threads, or the value of a variable immediately after a desired method terminates. For instance, the above tressa claim would be replaced with tressaExit(res) $\Rightarrow$ $x = y$, where Exit(res) is the value of res immediately after m terminates. Thanks to this approach, the user is not required to look for and then annotate the proper places in the code where prophecy variables have to be managed, a process which is both error-prone and tedious.

The truth value of a tressa claim is a function of the program state where the tressa claim occurs and the execution suffix following this occurrence. Given the rather simple semantics, they are amenable to low complexity run-time verification which could help uncover subtle bugs of concurrency. Accordingly, we develop a run-time verification tool for tressa claim based specifications. We first describe monitor synthesis algorithms. We show that the complexity of monitor synthesis is linear in the sum of the size of the tressa claims checked during the execution.

We then present our framework which implements these algorithms. Our implementation is built on top of the CHESS tool [4]. CHESS allows complete coverage of interleaving executions up to a desired bound on the number of context switches. Since the number of context switches as well as the number of different variables and threads that manifest interesting bugs are typically small [5], the use of CHESS makes our tool stronger than random testing, that is, synthesizing tressa monitors over random interleavings. We demonstrate our tool over a sample of interesting implementations.

Related Work. The specification formalisms to generate monitors for run-time verification usually employ a variant of linear temporal logic, LTL [6,7,8]. As non-regular properties cannot be expressed in LTL, more expressive formalizations have recently been developed [9,10,11]. Our formalization is not more expressive than the latter formalizations; the strength in our approach comes from two aspects. First, tressa claims have a relatively simple syntax with intuitive constructs. This we believe will lead to a short learning phase. Second, the constructs we use transfer the burden of identifying, in the code, places corresponding to an event of interest from the user to the run-time verification tool. This removes the possibility of incomplete or erroneous annotation (with auxiliary variables) by the user. As far as the complexity of monitor synthesis and run-time verification is concerned, we propose an on-the-fly algorithm of linear time complexity in the number of tressa claims and of logarithmic space complexity in the length of the execution, on par with other recent work [9,10].

2   Motivation

In this section, we will give an example where assertion based reasoning fails to capture the natural correctness requirement.

Specifications with tressa claims. Consider the code given in Fig. 1 which is a simplified version of an atomic snapshot algorithm (e.g., [12]). The snapshot algorithm aims at obtaining a consistent view of a set (here, a pair) of addresses shared among concurrent threads each of which might either be trying to take

```
public Pair Snapshot(int a, int b)
{
 int va, vb, da, db;
 boolean s = true;

 atomic{ va = m[a].v; da = m[a].d; }         // Rda
 atomic{ vb = m[b].v; db = m[b].d; }         // Rdb

 // if method is to succeed, da and db form a consistent snapshot.

 atomic{ if (va<m[a].v) { s = false; } }     // Vala
 atomic{ if (vb<m[b].v) { s = false; } }     // Valb

 if (s) { return new Pair(da,db); }          // Comm
 else { return null; }                       // Abrt
}

public void Write(int a, int d)
{
 atomic{ m[a].d = d; m[a].v ++; }
}
```

Fig. 1. A collection that implements an atomic read of two distinct variables, Snapshot, and random access updates, Write

a snapshot or updating a shared address. For convenience, we assume that code blocks tagged with `atomic` are executed atomically (without interleaving).

The method `Snapshot` takes in two addresses, and tries to return a consistent pair of values stored in these two addresses. In any lock-based implementation, shared variables are accessed only after obtaining their exclusive ownership, e.g., via locks. This implementation, however, uses optimistic concurrency because as `m[b]` is being read (line `Rdb`), the lock for `m[a]` is not owned and any thread is free to update `m[a]`'s value. This is an *absence of conflict* assumption which needs to be eventually validated (the second round of reads of the same addresses at lines `Vala` and `Valb`). Each location is assumed to contain a version number which is incremented whenever a value is written by a call to `Write`. It is this version number which `Snapshot` uses in validation: a different (greater value) version number than the local copy indicates that its copy of the address is stale.

A correct snapshot algorithm should either terminate unsuccessfully and return a default value such as `null`, or, it should appear to take an instantaneous snapshot (of `m[a].d` and `m[b].d`) and return the values read. The implementation in Fig. 1 is correct in this sense. Intuitively, if the version number `m[a].v` has not been incremented by another concurrent write between lines `Rda` and `Vala`, then it is ensured that `m[a].d` is unchanged in this time interval, and `m[a].d` is equal to `da`. A similar argument holds for lines `Rdb`, `Valb`, `m[b].d` and `db`. It is most natural to put a claim about this desired property at the point in the program where it needs to hold, i.e., between `Rdb` and `Vala`.

Observe that if `Snapshot` is to terminate successfully, it must be the case that `m[a].d= da` and `m[b].d=db` between the lines `Rdb` and `Vala`. However, this guarantee is not about the past or the execution prefix, but rather of possible future behavior or the execution suffix. As such, any assertion, which can only relate execution prefixes to program states, placed between the first pair of reads and the rest of the method will fail to capture this property. For instance, we cannot assert `s==>(da==m[a].d)` between `Vala` and `Valb` because immediately after `m[a]` is found to be untouched (local and global version numbers are found to be equal at `Vala`), a context switch might occur and another thread might update `m[a]` which will violate the assertion. Assertions before `Vala` or after `Valb` will fail in a similar manner to express the desired property.

Generalizing the above arguments for arbitrary optimistic concurrency implementations, we can state that typically the programmer will need to specify a condition to be satisfied at the present state where the condition itself depends on the rest of the execution. For this class of specifications, we propose the use of tressa claims. Simply put, a tressa claim holds true only if the remaining part of the execution conforms to the claim. Capturing the remaining part of the execution is accomplished via special constructs (prophecy variables) denoting values of variables attained after a certain event occurs. This enables us to relate the present state to the eventual outcome and express the desired correctness property naturally.

```
...
atomic{ vb = m[b].v; db = m[b].d; }

tressa Exit(s) ==> (da==m[a].d && db==m[b].d);

atomic{ if (va<m[a].v) { s = false; } }
...
```

Fig. 2. A possible specification for Snapshot expressed in terms of future behavior

Now, consider the modification given in Fig. 2 containing a tressa claim. The claim states that if the method commits (in the future) (Exit(s), which denotes the value of s when Snapshot terminates, is true), the current values of the pair of da and db will constitute a consistent snapshot of addresses a and b. The claim is located where we expect the condition to hold and (the implicit prophecy variable) Exit(s) allows the claim to be checked for only successfully terminating Snapshot executions.

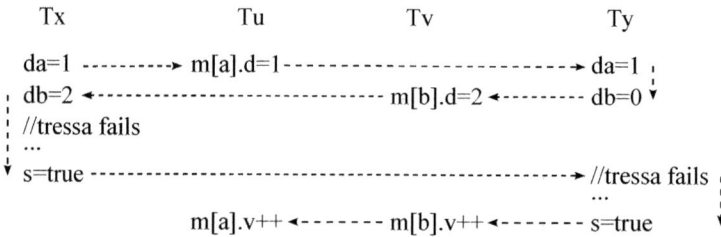

Fig. 3. An interleaving that exhibits an inconsistent snapshot

Bug Manifestation. In order to illustrate how tressa claims can help distinguish faulty behavior from correct ones, consider another implementation which uses the same Snapshot method, but has a broken non-atomic Write whose body is given as:

$$m[a].d = d; \; atomic\{ m[a].v ++; \}$$

That is, in the Write method, there can be arbitrarily many actions between the update of the data value, m[a].d, and the incrementing of the version number, m[a].v. This is a faulty implementation and the tressa claim we introduced in Fig. 2 will be violated in some executions and thus catch the bug. Incidentally, the underlying correctness criterion for our sample implementation is *linearizability* [13], but a discussion on linearizability goes beyond the scope of this paper. This buggy version allows executions which cannot be linearized, an example of which is given below.

Consider the execution given in Fig. 3. Dashed arrows represent time flow, each column represents the execution of a thread whose id is given at the top of each column and each row corresponds to a time instant when one of these threads makes a transition. In this sample execution, threads Tx and Ty execute Snapshot(a,b), taking snapshots of addresses a and b. Threads Tu and Tv execute Write(a) and Write(b) updating the contents of a and b, respectively. Assume that the initial value of each address is 0.

Thread Tx reads 0 for m[a].d, 2 for m[b].d. Thread Ty reads 1 for m[a].d, 0 for m[b].d. Since the version numbers are updated non-atomically, in this particular execution, both snapshot methods will conclude success and return their snapshot. However, both of the returned snapshots is inconsistent in any possible linearization of this sequence. This is an erroneous execution and the tressa should fail; it indeed does. When the tressa claim is evaluated in thread Tx, Exit(s) is true, because Tx does not observe any of the updates done by Tu and Tv and ends Snapshot deciding non-interference (s is set to true when Tx terminates), but da (0) is not equal to the current value of m[a].d (1). Similarly, the tressa of thread Ty also fails as its copy of Exit(s) is also true but the values of db (0) and m[b].d (2) are not equal.

Once the violation is generated, the user will be presented with the counter example which clearly identifies the failing tressa claims. Since the tressa claim depends on the outcome of the Snapshot method, and the values held in da and db after executing Rdb, its failure means that even though there was an interference from concurrent threads, the validation part of Snapshot failed to detect this. This would point to two possible sources of failure: (i) the validation part is erroneous, or (ii) the interference is not properly reported. In our case, it is the latter and the tressa violation helps the user identify the nature of the bug.

The tressa claim we gave above was an approximate specification of linearizability (or atomicity). This is for illustration purposes only. We will present other examples of tressa claims which express properties tailored to the implementation under consideration and not just general correctness criteria like linearizability.

3   Formalization

Programs. A *concurrent program text* is a collection of *procedures*, where each procedure is written according to a given grammar representing the underlying programming language. Each procedure has well-defined *entry* and *exit* points. Each well-formed sentence in the programming language assumed to be executing atomically is called a *statement*. A *program* is a mapping from a set of live threads Tid to the procedures of the program text. Intuitively, a program identifies which thread is running which procedure. We imagine a potentially infinite set of *program states*. Each program state holds all the necessary control information and the valuation of each program variable. We ignore the details of how this information is encoded in a program state. We distinguish a subset of program states, called the *initial states*, which are intuitively those states from which a program can start its execution.

Each program generates a set of *runs*, alternating sequences of program states and *dynamic statements*. For $t \in Tid$ and s a statement, the pair (t, s) is called a dynamic statement. Each run, $q_0 \xrightarrow{d_1} q_1 \ldots \xrightarrow{d_n} q_n$, where q_i's represent states, d_i's represent dynamic statements, satisfies the usual initial and transition conditions: The state q_0 is an initial state and for each triple $q_{i-1} \xrightarrow{d_i} q_i$, it is possible to make a transition from program state q_{i-1} to q_i by executing the dynamic statement d_i. The semantics of each transition is governed by the programming language.

Tressa Claims. A tressa claim is a special statement of the form tressa ϕ, where tressa is assumed to be part of the programming language lexeme and ϕ is a tressa predicate, an element of the set $Pred$ whose syntax is given below.

$$Pred : ::= rel_k(Expr^k) \mid Pred \wedge Pred \mid \neg Pred$$
$$Expr : ::= Term \mid f_k(Expr^k)$$
$$Term : ::= \mathsf{First}(var, AType, tSet) \mid \mathsf{Last}(var, AType, tSet, cond) \mid \mathsf{Exit}(var) \mid var$$
$$AType : ::= \mathsf{Rd} \mid \mathsf{Wr} \mid \mathsf{RW}$$

Each predicate is either the result of the application of some k-ary relation to k expressions ($Expr$) or a boolean combination of predicates. Each expression is either some term ($Term$) or some k-ary function f_k over expressions. $AType$ is the access type indicator: Rd is used for only read accesses, Wr for write accesses, and RW for read or write accesses.

Example. Our example is drawn from software transactional memory implementations. Consider the code given in Fig. 4, snippets from a program intended as a test harness for the Bartok STM implementation [14]. It starts by initializing the transaction (DTM.Start). The value stored in the shared object o1 is then transactionally read (DTM.OpenForRead) and this read value incremented by 1 is then transactionally written (DTM.OpenForUpdate) into o2. We require that if the transaction succeeds after doing these two operations, the values in o1 and o2 turn out to be exactly as updated by this transaction, i.e., (o1.d)+1=o2.d. This is expressed by the first tressa claim. We also require that an object that is only read (not updated) in a transaction should have its value constant throughout the execution span of a transaction that commits. In our code, o1 is one such object and the second tressa claim expresses this property.

As another interesting property, we want to express correct roll-back in the case of aborting a transaction. In our STM, each update is logged in a thread local list. As a variable is updated, an entry is inserted into this list, specifying the overwritten value. Then, to roll back the changes made to the shared address space, the list is traversed in reverse order, canceling the effect of each update until all the variable values are restored. In order to express correct undoing, we record the value of o2.d prior to the update done by this transaction in the local variable pre_start. We then require that the very last value written by an aborting transaction be equal to the initial value kept in pre_start. Notice that, due to the possibly more than one entry in the log list for o2.d, it would be harder to express this property using either assertions or temporal logical formulations.

```
public void Foo(Xact Tx) {
...
DTM.Start(Tx);                    //Transaction Tx starts
...
DTM.OpenForRead(Tx, o1);
tmp = o1.d;
tmp = tmp + 1;
...
DTM.OpenForUpdate(Tx, o2);
pre_start = o2.d;
o2.d = tmp;

tressa (Exit(success) ==> (o2.d == o1.d + 1);
...
// At every later read of o1.d
tressa (Exit(success) ==> (tmp == o1.d + 1));
...
success = DTM.Commit(Tx); // Transaction Tx attempts to commit.
                          // success==true if it commits.
if (!success) {
  done = false;
  tressa (Last(o2,Wr,{this},done)==pre_start);
  DTM.UndoUpdates(Tx);
  done = true;
}
}
```

Fig. 4. Specifying properties in a code built on the Bartok STM

Semantics. We will describe the valuation of each term using diagrams. For the following, we say that a dynamic statement (t, st) *matches* (v, a, T) if $t \in T$, st accesses v and the access type agrees with the access-type a.

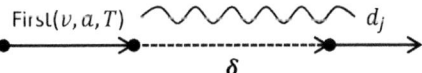

First(v, a, T) denotes the value of the variable v after the first occurrence of a matching dynamic statement in the execution suffix. If the action sequence represented by δ above does not contain any dynamic statement that matches (v, a, T), the value of the term is the value written (or the value read) by d_j, as the wavy line suggests. If no such d_j exists, First$(v, a, T) = \bot$.

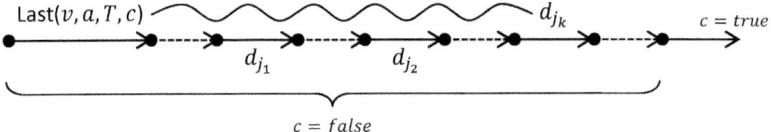

Last(v, a, T, c) denotes the value of the variable v after the last occurrence of a matching dynamic statement prior to c becoming true. In the diagram above, we assume that all d_{j_l} match (v, a, T) but only the very last one, d_{j_k}, determines the value of Last(v, a, T, c). If c stays false until termination or no matching statement occurs prior to c becoming true, Last(v, a, T, c) $= \bot$.

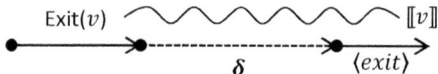

Exit(v) denotes the value of the variable v immediately after the procedure p in which the term occurs terminates. In the diagram above, letting t denote the thread which executed the instruction containing Exit(v), we assume that the number of calls to p and that of returns from p executed by t are equal (recursion is allowed). If the execution blocks before p terminates, Exit(v) $= \bot$.

A tressa claim is *ready* in a run if none of its terms evaluates to $\bot$. A program run *violates* tressa ϕ if tressa ϕ occurs during the run, the tressa claim is ready and ϕ evaluates to false. A program p *satisfies* a tressa claim tc if no instance of p has a run violating tc.

Let us further illustrate our formalization with the following example. Assume that ϕ is given as First(v, Rd, Tid) $=$ Last($x, \mathsf{Wr}, \{t\}, done$) and let ($t$, tressa ϕ) be the dynamic statement executed at q_i.

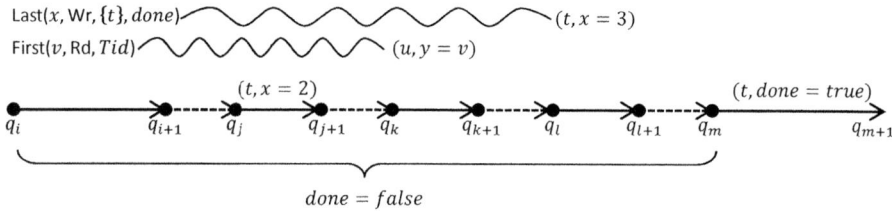

In the above diagram, we assume that the dashed lines represent sequences of statements that match neither (v, Rd, Tid) nor ($x, \mathsf{Wr}, \{t\}$). At q_j, an update to x is done by t, but since this is not the last matching statement prior to *done* becoming true, its value is ignored. Then, at q_k, the dynamic statement that matches (v, Rd, Tid) occurs. The value of v returned by this read determines the value of First(v, Rd, Tid) which we assume to be 5. At q_l, another update to x is done by t. According to the diagram, this is the last update to x by t prior to *done* becoming true at q_{m+1}. Thus, Last($x, \mathsf{Wr}, \{t\}, done$) $= 3$ in this run. Since all the terms of ϕ are determined by the execution segment ending at q_{m+1}, ϕ can be evaluated, which is found to be false. Thus, tressa ϕ fails. It is important to note that we need the execution segment $q_i \ldots q_{m+1}$ to evaluate the tressa claim but the claim itself fails at q_{i+1}.

4   Run-Time Verification

In this section, we first describe the algorithms we use to check tressa claims over a given run. Then, we give an overview of the implementation of these algorithms.

4.1   Monitoring Algorithm

In this section, we explain how a tressa claim occurring in a given run can be evaluated. We present an algorithm that manipulates the tressa claims it observes throughout the course of an execution. We first explain what is being done at each transition, then delve into specific operations.

Algorithm 1. Monitoring Transitions

1: **procedure** STEP($dstmt$)
2:     **for all** $te \in TressaTable$ **do**
3:         $te.termSet \leftarrow$ EvalTerms($te.termSet$,$dstmt$)
4:     **end for**
5:     **for all** $pred \in$ ParseStmt($dstmt$) **do**
6:         InitTressa($pred$)
7:     **end for**
8:     **for all** $te \in TressaTable$ **do**
9:         **if** $te.termSet = \emptyset$ **then**
10:             Check(te)
11:             Remove te from $TressaTable$
12:         **end if**
13:     **end for**
14: **end procedure**

Algorithm 1 shows the three phases that the monitor performs by each transition. It gets the label of the transition, the dynamic statement $dstmt$, as an input parameter. All the tressa claims which have been seen so far in the execution and whose value is not yet determined are kept in the $TressaTable$. In the first phase (lines 2-4), $TressaTable$ is traversed and each term whose value is yet to be determined is analyzed and any of its terms that becomes determined is evaluated (line 3). In the second phase (lines 5-7), all the tressa claims that occur in $dstmt$ are handled. In the third and final phase (lines 8-13), the tressa claims whose value can be calculated after this transition are found (line 9), their value is calculated (line 10) and is removed from $TressaTable$ (line 11). We should point out that the implementation of this algorithm is slightly different where each variable points to the set of terms that are affected by the accesses to that variable. Then, instead of checking all live tressa claims, only those terms which depend on the accessed variables are checked. We used this alternative algorithm for ease of presentation.

Algorithm 2 shows how a new tressa claim is handled. Each entry in the $TressaTable$ holds the predicate of the tressa claim and a set containing all the distinct terms of the predicate. These are assigned to a new entry, $tressaEntry$, at lines 2 and 3, respectively. Then, all the Val-terms are evaluated (lines 6-7) and each of these terms are removed from the set of undetermined terms (line 8). For all other term types, the value of the term is set to $\perp$ (line 9-10). For the Exitterms, we record the most recent value of the variable mentioned in the term (line 12-13). The resulting entry is inserted into the $TressaTable$ (line 14). Observe that if a tressa claim has only Val-terms, its value is ready to be evaluated immediately after it occurs in the execution.

Algorithm 2. Initializing for a New Tressa

1: **procedure** INITTRESSA(*pred*)
2:     *tressaEntry.pred* ← *pred*
3:     *tressaEntry.termSet* ← Parse(*pred*)
4:     *termSet* ← *tressaEntry.termSet*
5:     **for all** *term* ∈ *termSet* **do**
6:         **if** IsVTerm(*term*) **then**
7:             *term.val* ← EvalVTerm(*term*)
8:             *tressaEntry.termSet* ← *tressaEntry.termSet* \ {*term*}
9:         **else**
10:            *term.val* ← ⊥
11:        **end if**
12:        **if** IsETerm(*term*) **then**
13:            *term.preval* ← Eval(*term*)
14:        **end if**
15:    **end for**
16:    Insert *tressaEntry* into *TressaTable*
17: **end procedure**

Algorithm 3 shows how a set of terms is evaluated. It receives as input a term set, *termSet*, and a dynamic statement, *dstmt*. Each term in *termSet* initially has its value set to ⊥, denoting undetermined value. We evaluate each term depending on its type and *dstmt*. For instance, if the term is a First-term and if *dstmt* is a dynamic statement which matches the term (line 4), the value of the term is evaluated and assigned to the term (line 5).[1] Similar checks and assignments are made for each type except for the Val type as their values were already evaluated when the tressa was initialized as in Algorithm 2. If the term's value is determined, then it is removed from the set of undetermined terms (lines 13-14). The algorithm returns the new set of undetermined terms (line 17).

Algorithm 2 has time complexity linear in the length of the tressa claim where the length of a tressa claim is given as the number of distinct terms the claim contains. Algorithm 3 has time complexity linear in the number of terms the parameter *termSet* contains because each call takes constant time. Algorithm 1 then has time complexity $O(size_{tt})$ where $size_{tt}$ is the sum of the lengths of all tressa claims observed throughout the execution. In terms of space complexity, the only non-constant complexity comes from EvalETerm which counts the number of pending calls in case of recursion. This introduces a logarithmic space complexity in the length of the execution.

4.2   Implementation

We start by giving an architectural overview of the implementation. We then highlight several implementation related issues.

---

[1] The call to EvalETerm is simplified. Due to recursion, we actually keep track of the recursion depth by counting the number of pending calls.

Algorithm 3. Term Evaluation

1: **procedure** EVALTERMS(*termSet*,*dstmt*)
2:     *cSet* ← *termSet*
3:     **for all** *term* ∈ *cSet* **do**
4:         **if** IsFTerm(*term*) ∧ IsCompat(*term*,*dstmt*) **then**
5:             *term.val* ← EvalFTerm(*term*,*dstmt*)
6:         **end if**
7:         **if** IsLTerm(*term*) ∧ IsCompat(*term*,*dstmt*) **then**
8:             *term.val* ← EvalLTerm(*term*,*dstmt*)
9:         **end if**
10:        **if** IsETerm(*term*) ∧ IsCompat(*term*,*dstmt*) **then**
11:            *term.val* ← EvalETerm(*term*,*dstmt*)
12:        **end if**
13:        **if** *term.val* ≠ ⊥ **then**
14:           *termSet* ← *termSet* \ *term*
15:        **end if**
16:     **end for**
17:     **return** *termSet*
18: **end procedure**

Architecture. Figure 5 gives an operational description of our testing framework. In the first phase, the user annotates the test harness s/he wishes to verify with tressa claims according to a partial specification of correctness. The test harness is the input program wrapped with a specific test scenario. We currently accept programs written in C#, but in principle, any program written for the .NET framework can be easily handled.

In the second phase, we perform controlled executions of the given program. The annotated program is first processed by the Tressa library. The tressa library contains the code implementing the monitoring algorithm explained in Sec. 4.1. The output of this process, the original test harness along with its monitors, is fed into CHESS. The CHESS tool is responsible for two main tasks. First, it explores all possible interleavings of the Test Input (see below). Second, as each

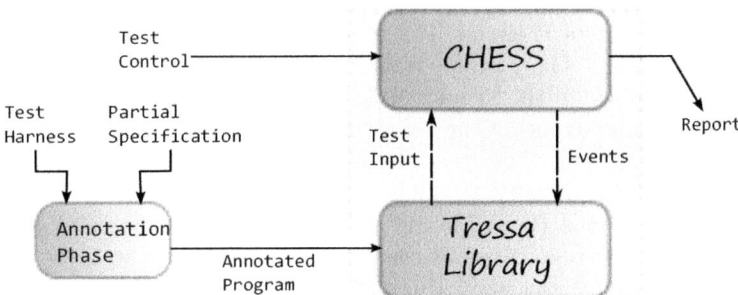

Fig. 5. The architectural diagram of the testing framework

interleaving is being executed, all memory accesses and method calls and exits are reported as events back to the Tressa library.

Tressa claims are evaluated as soon as they can be evaluated per the algorithm given in Sec. 4.1. If the tressa claim is satisfied, no further action is taken. Otherwise, the execution halts with a report specifying the failing tressa. CHESS can then be used to reproduce the failing execution for the analysis of the bug.

The CHESS Tool [4]. The use of CHESS is rather simple. The programmer specifies a particular test scenario on which s/he would like to check the outcome of her/his program. CHESS then runs the scenario so that all possible interleavings, up to a bound on the number of context switches specified by the programmer, are explored. It is well known that a concurrent program typically manifests its bug with only a few context switches over a few variables [4,5]. Thus, a small scenario with a context switch bound of two is likely to unravel subtle concurrency bugs. Case in point, the counter-example we gave in Sec. 2 for the buggy implementation (see Fig. 3), there is a single context switch per thread, there are four threads and two distinct addresses. Complete coverage of a set of interleavings reduces one degree of uncertainty about the outcome of a test-case. The user is still responsible for coming up with a scenario and a correct bound that would uncover the bug, but the additional uncertainty about whether the correct schedule would be chanced is removed.

Conceptually, CHESS achieves complete coverage by placing semaphores prior to all accesses to volatile variables or calls to synchronization methods from the C# System.Threading namespace such as the Thread.Start() method used for creating a thread or the Thread.Join() method used for waiting for a child thread to terminate. The places where semaphores are placed are the candidate context switching points. As CHESS explores a particular interleaving, each time a candidate context switching point is reached, exactly one semaphore is put in a non-blocking state which forces the scheduler to choose the desired thread. CHESS records down the set of interleavings it has already explored and as long as there remain unexplored interleavings, it resets the test harness, runs the program according to a new interleaving. A detailed explanation of the exact mechanism is beyond the scope of this paper.

The Tressa Library. The crux of the implementation lies in the Tressa library which implements the monitoring algorithm of Sec. 4.1. Tressa claims are generated by constructing a Tressa object whose constructor takes in its predicate in the form of a string. This string is then parsed into its constituent terms. Each term has a reference to the Tressa object it is part of. Additionally, for each of its terms, a handle denoting the term (its type and contents) and the variable referred to in the term is inserted into a global table.

An additional feature of CHESS has been crucial in the operation of the monitor implemented in the Tressa Library. As CHESS explores a particular execution, it keeps track of the relevant synchronization operations via an event generation mechanism. Each memory access, method call, method return and the like generate events which are then caught by CHESS in order to have complete control over the execution of the `Test Input`. We are making use of these events to instrument each memory access as well as the method calls/returns so that the monitoring algorithm is called at every relevant transition. For instance, every time a variable is read, it generates an event which supplies the address accessed, the value read. Thus, accesses to variables are instrumented. As a variable is accessed, it is checked whether there are terms dependent on it by inspecting the global table for an entry for that variable. If the variable's entry is non-empty, for each term in its entry, a check is performed to see whether the term becomes determined. This step can be seen as a call to the STEP with the instrumented instruction as its input parameter, *dstmt*.

Following the algorithms given in Sec. 4.1, when a term becomes determined, it is removed from the variable's entry. For each term about to be removed, we also check whether the owning tressa claim has still undetermined terms. If all the terms of a tressa claim become determined, the truth value of the predicate is calculated. If the predicate evaluates to false, the violation along with the tressa claim causing it is reported. Thanks to the bug reproduction capability of the CHESS tool, the user can then trace the buggy execution to see what the cause for the violation is. Currently, the Tressa library is implemented in C#. We are using the `CLR` wrapper of CHESS, and the overall system is run under the `.NET` framework.

5   Experiments

In this section, we report our experience with an initial proof-of-concept implementation where instrumentation of memory accesses is done manually. We are currently working on automating the instrumentation and will provide a public release of the implementation.

We have tried our framework on three programs: the atomic snapshot implementation (see Sec. 2), a concurrent stack implementation [15] and a model of the Bartok STM [14]. We ran the examples on a Mac laptop with 1GB of RAM running at 2.8GHz.

In the atomic snapshot implementation, we have tried both the correct and the buggy versions on the test scenario given in Fig. 3. As expected, thanks to full coverage provided by CHESS, the bug was caught by our implementation after exploring 191 different schedules. The correct implementation generated no violations in 979 total schedules which is the total number of schedules with at most two context switches per thread.

For the concurrent stack, we ran a test scenario of three threads, two of them pushing five elements, the third popping five elements. In the `push` method we placed the tressa claim $\mathsf{tressa}\,\mathsf{First}(\mathsf{top}, \mathsf{Wr}, \{t\}) = \mathsf{Val}(n)$ which expressed the property that the first write by the thread t currently executing the method into the stack (`top`) is equal to the element with which `push` is called (n). Contrary to our expectations, the tressa failed after 113 schedules. The reason was due to an elimination round which bypasses pushing if there is a concurrently pending pop operation. This example highlights that even deceptively simple looking tressa claims can be valuable tools in comprehending or debugging concurrent implementations. Later correcting this incorrect tressa claim removed the failure.

In the Bartok model, we uncovered a subtle bug by running a scenario with two threads, each running a transaction of at most two instructions. The bug was caught after 104 schedules, which takes about ten seconds, by the tressa claim tressa o.owner $\neq t \wedge$ o.IsOwned $\Rightarrow \neg\mathsf{Exit}(s)$. This claim, placed after a read of o, states that if o is currently owned by some other transaction, then this transaction should not commit. Corrected version was verified after completing all 112 possible schedules in approximately ten seconds.

References

1. Larus, J.R., Rajwar, R.: Transactional Memory. Morgan & Claypool (2006)
2. Sezgin, A., Tasiran, S., Qadeer, S.: Tressa: Claiming the future. In: VSTTE (2010)
3. Elmas, T., Qadeer, S., Tasiran, S.: A calculus of atomic actions. In: POPL 2009, pp. 2–15. ACM, New York (2009)
4. Musuvathi, M., Qadeer, S., Ball, T., Basler, G., Nainar, P.A., Neamtiu, I.: Finding and reproducing heisenbugs in concurrent programs. In: Draves, R., van Renesse, R. (eds.) OSDI, pp. 267–280 (2008)
5. Lu, S., Park, S., Seo, E., Zhou, Y.: Learning from mistakes: a comprehensive study on real world concurrency bug characteristics. In: ASPLOS, pp. 329–339 (2008)
6. Pnueli, A.: The temporal logic of programs. In: FOCS 1977: Foundations of Computer Science, pp. 46–57 (1977)
7. Havelund, K., Goldberg, A.: Verify your runs. In: VSTTE, pp. 374–383 (2005)
8. Leucker, M., Schallhart, C.: A brief account of runtime verification. J. Log. Algebr. Program. 78, 293–303 (2009)
9. Barringer, H., Goldberg, A., Havelund, K., Sen, K.: Rule-based runtime verification. In: Steffen, B., Levi, G. (eds.) VMCAI 2004. LNCS, vol. 2937, pp. 277–306. Springer, Heidelberg (2004)
10. Colombo, C., Pace, G.J., Schneider, G.: Dynamic event-based runtime monitoring of real-time and contextual properties. In: Cofer, D., Fantechi, A. (eds.) FMICS 2008. LNCS, vol. 5596, pp. 135–149. Springer, Heidelberg (2009)
11. Rosu, G., Chen, F., Ball, T.: Synthesizing monitors for safety properties: This time with calls and returns. In: Leucker, M. (ed.) RV 2008. LNCS, vol. 5289, pp. 51–68. Springer, Heidelberg (2008)
12. Afek, Y., Attiya, H., Dolev, D., Gafni, E., Merritt, M., Shavit, N.: Atomic snapshots of shared memory. J. ACM 40(4), 873–890 (1993)
13. Herlihy, M.P., Wing, J.M.: Linearizability: a correctness condition for concurrent objects. ACM Trans. Program. Lang. Syst. 12(3), 463–492 (1990)
14. Harris, T.L., Plesko, M., Shinnar, A., Tarditi, D.: Optimizing memory transactions. In: PLDI, pp. 14–25 (2006)
15. Hendler, D., Shavit, N., Yerushalmi, L.: A scalable lock-free stack algorithm. J. Parallel Distrib. Comput. 70, 1–12 (2010)

Who Guards the Guardians? — Toward V&V of Health Management Software

(Short Paper)

Johann Schumann[1], Ashok N. Srivastava[2], and Ole J. Mengshoel[3]

[1] SGT, Inc./ NASA Ames, Moffett Field, CA 94035
Johann.M.Schumann@nasa.gov
[2] NASA Ames, Moffett Field, CA 94035-0001
Ashok.N.Srivastava@nasa.gov
[3] Carnegie Mellon University, Moffett Field, CA 94035
Ole.J.Mengshoel@nasa.gov

1 Introduction

Highly complex and safety-critical systems are not only present in traditional areas such as the aerospace and nuclear power industries, but are also becoming ubiquitous in other areas including the automobile, health care, and the manufacturing industries. Integrated System Health Management (ISHM) systems are being created to detect, diagnose, predict, and potentially mitigate adverse events during the operation of such systems. ISHM systems obtain data from multiple sensors and perform reasoning about the state of health of the system based on data and physical models. Usually, major electromechanical or hydraulic subsystems in aircraft are monitored by an ISHM system.

More sophisticated ISHM systems detect and diagnose the root-cause of an anomaly and can also predict the remaining useful component life based on the sensor data. This prognostic capability is not only being used to increase safety, but also to substantially cut maintenance and environmental costs: in contrast to schedule based maintenance, where parts are replaced after a fixed time regardless of usage and deterioration, condition-based maintenance uses sensor data and estimates to only replace a component when it is necessary.

A modern ISHM system is a complex piece of software in itself. In the following, we therefore refer to it as Health Management Software (HMSW). Internally, the HMSW operates on a model of the component to be monitored [1,2,3]. Based upon sensor signals and other dynamic information, the HMSW detects if the component is working nominally, or if a failure has occurred. The failure will be identified and, if applicable, recovery actions started. It is obvious that such a system must work correctly and reliably. False alarms are not only a nuisance, but can lead to substantially higher maintenance costs or even safety-hazards if the operators get into the habit of ignoring the warning system. On the other hand, missed alarms can produce serious problems. So the question arises "Quis custodiet ipsos custodes?" ("Who guards the guardians?", Juvenal.)

G. Roşu et al. (Eds.): RV 2010, LNCS 6418, pp. 399–404, 2010.

Obviously, the HMSW must undergo rigorous verification and validation (V&V) to at least the same level of assurance as for the system monitored. However, there has been only limited research on that topic. Although there are many techniques for verifiable and verified monitors as well as reliable mitigation mechanisms, V&V challenges can be identified in the HMSW component, which performs reasoning in order to identify the fault and detect the most likely root causes. In this short paper, we will present major ISHM components, identify V&V challenges, and outline potential V&V approaches for HMSW.

2   ISHM Architecture

An ISHM system performs FDDR (Fault Detection, Diagnosis, and Recovery) by monitoring the *host system*. Based upon readings from *sensors*, the *ISHM engine* uses the *ISHM model* (which can be an explicit model or implicitly coded as a set of rules, for example) to determine if the system is working nominally, or if a failure has occurred (*diagnostics*) or will occur in the near future (*prognostics*).

Because most system faults manifest themselves in multiple ways, and a symptom can be caused by multiple faults, it is critical to determine the root-cause(s) of symptoms. Thus, the ISHM engine must be able to distinguish between potentially hundreds of potentially interacting root-causes. For example, low oil pressure and vibration could point to many different problems if looked at separately. Only when considered in combination, a worn-out engine bearing can be diagnosed. If present, a prognostic capability for an ISHM engine can be used to also estimate the remaining useful (safe) life of the system.

Depending on the application, an ISHM system must perform rapidly in order to provide suitable feedback to the operator and to be able to successfully mitigate the adverse event. Finally, most ISHM systems contains components that help to *mitigate* or recover from the error. In this paper, we focus on the HMSW core components: the ISHM engine and the ISHM model.

A wide range of FDIR modelling approaches are available; each of them may have several associated reasoning algorithms. These modelling approaches and algorithms are again supported by diagnostic software such as Livingstone [1], Hyde [2], or ProDiagnose [3,4]. Other software tools include TEAMS [5] and the Generic Modeling Environment (GME) [6].

3   V&V Challenges for ISHM

Although it is possible that the overall gain in safety and reliability of a system due to ISHM may be significant, it comes at a price. Poorly designed or malfunctioning HMSW can produce false alarms ("false positives") or can miss important failures ("false negatives"). A false alarm occurs if the HMSW system reports a failure, whereas the monitored system is working flawlessly. A continuously lit "Check Engine" light in the car can be such a nuisance signal. Although false alarms are not primarily a safety concern (in contrast to false negatives), they can severely impede the system operation by performing unnecessary fixes and reconfigurations. Moreover, they can lead to a situation where operators ignore the output of the system, thereby leading to other significant problems. Thus, the HMSW must be designed and validated carefully to avoid false negatives and false positive, and its implementation has to undergo rigorous V&V as errors will not only deliver unreliable results but can cause severe problems in the host system.

In addition, ISHM approaches can contain algorithmic elements, for which current V&V standards do not provide any guidance. For example, they may use nontraditional reasoning algorithms, some of which are "difficult" to perform V&V on, as they rely on randomization, iterative search, or large, complicated, or dynamic data structures.

We also note that the ISHM system is designed to detect adverse conditions in which the host system is in an off-nominal condition. Thus, the implications for V&V of the ISHM system and its underlying software must be able to accommodate off-nominal behavior in some of the inputs. This poses a significant challenge from a V&V perspective for traditional software, because the conditions of the off-nominal behavior are, by definition, unknown. Presumably, if a known off-nominal condition existed in the system, it would be removed during the design process. V&V research must address this issue to develop reliable and dependable HMSW.

4   Toward V&V of Health Management Software

In order to address the V&V issues discussed in Section 3, specific tools and techniques must be developed. In this paper, we want to focus on two critical ISHM components identified in Section 2: the analysis of the ISHM model, and the V&V of the ISHM engine, seen as a piece of code ("Code-level V&V"). We think that this separate analysis can be justified because in most approaches, the ISHM model is translated or compiled into a highly compact and efficient data structure, which is then accessed by the ISHM engine. For example, Bayesian networks (one class of ISHM models) can be translated into arithmetic circuits [8]. Other approaches transform rules and models into tables, which enable fast look-up and avoid the call to resource-consuming (iterative) reasoning algorithms.

Although health management can be seen as one approach for run-time verification and validation (failures are detected and mitigated with the system in operation), V&V of the HMSW will take place during its development and will not be performed while the HMSW is running.

4.1   Model-Level V&V

An ISHM model captures essential information about nominal and off-nominal operation of the host system on various levels of abstraction and is used by the ISHM engine to perform reasoning. Thus, V&V has to make sure that the model is *adequate* for the given domain and ISHM requirements and that it is as *complete* and *consistent* as possible. State-of-the-art V&V approaches include exhaustive model enumeration using a model checker, for example, Livingston Pathfinder [9].

Larger and hybrid models can be tested using parametric testing. This statistical approach combines n-factor combinatorial exploration with advanced data analysis [12] to exercise the ISHM model with wide ranges of sensor inputs and internal parameters. This approach scales to large systems, like fault detection models for the Ares I rocket [13].

For the goal of a complete model coverage during model validation, we have defined ISHM-specific coverage metrics (e.g., cover all failure modes, cover all reasoning paths) and used model checking with symbolic execution (e.g., Symbolic Pathfinder (SPF) [11]) as well as specific algorithms for the automatic generation of small test suites for full model coverage, which we are studying with ADAPT ISHM models [3]. Finally, sensitivity analysis for Bayesian Networks [8] is useful to assess the quality of the model parameters. The results of all these analysis techniques provide arguments about the quality of the model and its expected behavior.

4.2   Code-Level V&V

Since the health management functions are performed by software, this software—even if the model has been verified—has to undergo rigorous V&V ("code-level V&V"). Here, the HMSW is treated like a regular piece of software, which has to be tested and validated. In most cases, this will include testing according to established code coverage criteria, e.g., the MCDC (Modified Condition Decision Coverage) as required by the DO-178B standard [14], worst case execution time analysis, stack and memory analysis, etc.

Often, model translation and compilation (e.g., into arithmetic circuits [8]) eliminates or reduces the problems associated with non-traditional reasoning algorithms (see Section 3), and the resulting algorithms can be shown to have limited resource bounds and do not require dynamic memory allocation. The minimalistic ISHM engines that are the target of model translation and compilation might even be amenable to formal verification. Because of the high complexity of the model translation process, it is hard to provide any guarantees about the compiler implementation. In that case, techniques known from the area of compilers, like proof carrying code [15] might be applicable.

In all cases, the HMSW takes inputs from many different sources (hardware, sensors, software sensors, operating system, etc.) and thus has to interact with the host system as well as other software systems on multiple levels. The resulting HMSW architecture can therefore become rather complicated, requiring careful V&V. Research has been performed to develop architectures that provide specific capabilities for ISHM integration [16].

Code-level V&V for HMSW can utilize many V&V techniques that have been developed for traditional software. Their extension to handling code that is specific for HMSW is possible, but requires care. For example, ISHM specific notions and their meaning for HMSW V&V must be clearly defined. Otherwise, terminological misunderstandings (e.g., on terms like "non-deterministic", "search", or "recursive") can lead to unnecessary delays in V&V and certification.

5   Conclusions

ISHM systems have a growing potential in safety-critical areas. The health management software helps to ensure that the (hardware or software) system under scrutiny performs reliably and safely by monitoring the host system's behaviour during runtime.

Rigorous V&V of the HMSW is a prerequisite for widespread and safe applicability of such systems. Although approaches for V&V of monitors and fault recovery exist, we have identified V&V gaps in diagnosis and root cause analysis. We believe that by separating out model V&V from code-level V&V, different approaches can be combined to demonstrate that Health Management Software can correctly and reliably guard the monitored host system.

In this paper, we have presented V&V challenges and discussed how exhaustive techniques (based upon model checking and symbolic execution), parametric testing, and traditional code V&V techniques (like execution time analysis, code coverage, or stack analysis) could help to address the challenges.

References

1. Williams, B.C., Nayak, U.: A model-based approach to reactive self-configuring systems. In: Proceedings of AAAI 1996, pp. 971–978 (1996)
2. Narasimhan, S., Brownston, L.: Hyde: a general framework for stochastic and hybrid model-based diagnosis. In: Proc. DX 2007, pp. 162–169 (2007)
3. Mengshoel, O.J., Darwiche, A., Cascio, K., Chavira, M., Poll, S., Uckun, S.: Diagnosing faults in electrical power systems of spacecraft and aircraft. In: Proc. 10th Innovative Applications of Artificial Intelligence Conf. (IAAI 2008), pp. 1699–1705 (2008)
4. Ricks, B.W., Mengshoel, O.J.: Methods for probabilistic fault diagnosis: An electrical power system case study. In: Proc. PHM 2009 (2009)
5. Qualtech Systems Inc.: The Testability, Engineering and Maintenance System, TEAMS (1993), http://www.teamqsi.com
6. Manders, E.J., Biswas, G., Mahadevan, N., Karsai, G.: Component-oriented modeling of hybrid dynamic systems using the generic modeling environment. In: Proc. MDB/MOMPES, pp. 159–168. IEEE, Los Alamitos (2006)
7. Poll, S., Patterson-Hine, A., Camisa, J., Garcia, D., Hall, D., Lee, C., Mengshoel, O.J., Neukom, C., Nishikawa, D., Ossenfort, J., Sweet, A., Yentus, S., Roychoudhury, I., Daigle, M., Biswas, G., Koutsoukos, X.: Advanced diagnostics and prognostics testbed. In: Proc. DX 2007, pp. 178–185 (2007)
8. Darwiche, A.: Modeling and Reasoning with Bayesian Networks. Cambridge University Press, Cambridge (2009)
9. Lindsey, A.E., Pecheur, C.: Simulation-based verification of autonomous controllers via Livingstone Pathfinder. In: Jensen, K., Podelski, A. (eds.) TACAS 2004. LNCS, vol. 2988, pp. 357–371. Springer, Heidelberg (2004)
10. Pipatsrisawat, K., Darwiche, A., Mengshoel, O., Schumann, J.: Software Health Management: A Short Review of Challenges and Existing Techniques. In: Proc. SMC-IT (2009)
11. Pasareanu, C.S., Visser, W.: Symbolic execution and model checking for testing. In: Yorav, K. (ed.) HVC 2007. LNCS, vol. 4899, pp. 17–18. Springer, Heidelberg (2008)

12. Schumann, J., Gundy-Burlet, K., Pasareanu, C., Menzies, T., Barrett, T.: Software V&V support by parametric analysis of large software simulation systems. In: Proc. IEEE Aerospace. IEEE Press, Los Alamitos (2009)
13. Schumann, J., Bajwa, A., Berg, P.: Parametric testing of launch vehicle FDDR models. In: AIAA Space (2010)
14. DO-178B: Software considerations in airborne systems and equipment certification (1992), http://www.rtca.org
15. Necula, G.C.: Proof-carrying code. In: Proc. 24th ACM Symp. Principles of Programming Languages, pp. 106–119. ACM Press, New York (1997)
16. Dubey, A., Karsai, G., Kereskenyi, R., Mahadevan, M.: A Real-Time Component Framework: Experience with CCM and ARINC-653. In: IEEE International Symposium on Object-Oriented Real-Time Distributed Computing (2010)

Aspect-Oriented Instrumentation with GCC

Justin Seyster[1], Ketan Dixit[1], Xiaowan Huang[1], Radu Grosu[1],
Klaus Havelund[2], Scott A. Smolka[1], Scott D. Stoller[1], and Erez Zadok[1]

[1] Department of Computer Science, Stony Brook University, USA
[2] Jet Propulsion Laboratory, California Institute of Technology, USA

Abstract. We present the INTERASPECT instrumentation framework
for GCC, a widely used compiler infrastructure. The addition of plug-
in support in the latest release of GCC makes it an attractive platform for runtime instrumentation, as GCC plug-ins can directly add
instrumentation by transforming the compiler's intermediate representation. Such transformations, however, require expert knowledge of GCC
internals. INTERASPECT addresses this situation by allowing instrumentation plug-ins to be developed using the familiar vocabulary of Aspect-
Oriented Programming pointcuts, join points, and advice functions.
INTERASPECT also supports powerful customized instrumentation, where
specific information about each join point in a pointcut, as well as results
of static analysis, can be used to customize the inserted instrumentation.
We introduce the INTERASPECT API and present several examples that
illustrate how it can be applied to useful runtime verification problems.

1 Introduction

GCC is a widely used compiler infrastructure that supports a variety of input
languages, e.g., C, C++, Fortran, Java, and Ada, and over 30 different target machine architectures. GCC translates each of its front-end languages into
a language-independent intermediate representation, called `GIMPLE`, which then
gets translated to machine code for one of GCC's many target architectures.
GCC is a very large software system with over 100 developers contributing over
the years and a steering committee consisting of 13 experts who strive to maintain its architectural integrity.

In earlier work [5], we extended GCC to support *plug-ins*, allowing users to
add their own custom passes to GCC in a modular way without patching and
recompiling the GCC source code. Released in April 2010, GCC 4.5 [14] includes
plug-in support that is largely based on our design.

GCC's support for plug-ins presents an exciting opportunity for the development of practical, widely-applicable program transformation tools, including
program instrumentation tools for runtime verification. Because plug-ins operate
at the level of `GIMPLE`, a plug-in is applicable to all of GCC's front-end languages.
Transformation systems that manipulate machine code may also work for multiple programming languages, but low-level machine code is harder to analyze
and lacks the detailed type information that is available in `GIMPLE`.

G. Roşu et al. (Eds.): RV 2010, LNCS 6418, pp. 405–420, 2010.
© Springer-Verlag Berlin Heidelberg 2010

Implementing instrumentation tools as GCC plug-ins provides significant benefits but also presents a significant challenge: despite the fact that it is an intermediate representation, GIMPLE is in fact a low-level language, requiring the writing of low-level GIMPLE Abstract Syntax Tree (AST) traversal functions in order to transform one GIMPLE expression into another. Therefore, as GCC is currently configured, the writing of plug-ins is not for everyone but rather only for those intimately familiar with GIMPLE's peculiarities.

To address this challenge, we developed the INTERASPECT program instrumentation framework, which allows instrumentation plug-ins to be developed using the familiar vocabulary of Aspect-Oriented Programming (AOP). INTERASPECT is itself implemented using the GCC plug-in API for manipulating GIMPLE, but it hides the complexity of this API from its users, presenting instead an aspect-oriented API in which instrumentation is accomplished by defining *pointcuts*. A pointcut denotes a set of program points, called *join points*, where calls to *advice functions* can be inserted by a process called *weaving*.

INTERASPECT's API allows users to customize the weaving process by defining *callback functions* that get invoked for each join point. Callback functions have access to specific information about each join point; the callbacks can use this to customize the inserted instrumentation, and to leverage static-analysis results for their customization.

In summary, INTERASPECT offers the following novel combination of features:

- INTERASPECT builds on top of GCC, a compiler infrastructure having a large and dedicated following.
- INTERASPECT exposes an API, which encourages and simplifies open-source collaboration.
- INTERASPECT has access to GCC internals, which allows one to exploit static analysis and meta-programming during the weaving process.

To illustrate the practical utility of the INTERASPECT framework, we have developed a number of program-instrumentation plug-ins that use INTERASPECT for custom instrumentation. These include a *heap visualization* plug-in for anticipated use by the JPL Mars Science Laboratory software development team; an *integer range analysis* plug-in that finds bugs by tracking the range of values for each integer variable; and a *code coverage* plug-in that, given a pointcut and test suite, measures the percentage of join points in the pointcut that are executed by the test suite.

The rest of the paper is structured as follows. Section 2 provides an overview of GCC and the INTERASPECT framework architecture. Section 3 introduces the INTERASPECT API. Section 4 presents the three applications: heap visualization, integer range analysis, and code coverage. Section 5 summarizes related work, and Section 6 concludes the paper.

2 Overview of GCC and the INTERASPECT Architecture

As Fig. 1 illustrates, GCC translates all of its front-end languages into the GIMPLE intermediate representation for analysis and optimization. Each transformation

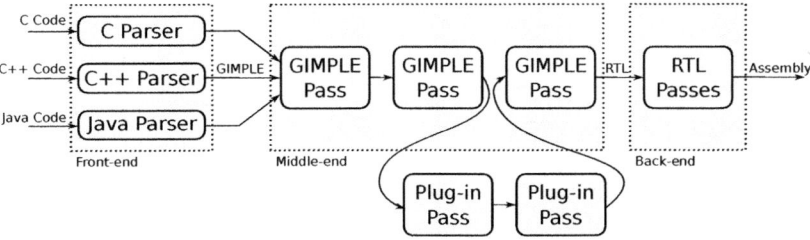

Fig. 1. A simplified view of the GCC compilation process

on GIMPLE code is split into its own *pass*. These passes, some of which may be *plug-ins*, make up GCC's *middle-end*. Moreover, a plug-in pass may be INTERASPECT-based, enabling the plug-in to add instrumentation directly into the GIMPLE code. The final middle-end passes lower the optimized and instrumented GIMPLE to the Register Transfer Language (RTL), which the *back-end* translates to assembly.

GIMPLE is a C-like three-address (3A) code. Complex expressions (possibly with side effects) are broken into simple 3A statements by introducing new, temporary variables. Similarly, complex control statements are broken into simple 3A (conditional) gotos by introducing new labels. Type information is preserved for every operand in each GIMPLE statement.

Fig. 2 shows a C program and its corresponding GIMPLE code, which preserves source-level information such as data types and procedure calls. Although not shown in the example, GIMPLE types also include pointers and structures.

```
int main() {                        1.   int main {
    int a, b, c;                    2.       int a, b, c;
    a = 5;                          3.       int T1, T2, T3, T4;
    b = a + 10;                     4.       a = 5;
    c = b + foo(a, b);      =>      5.       b = a + 10;
    if (a > b + c)                  6.       T1 = foo(a, b);
        c = b++ / a + (b * a);      7.       c = b + T1;
    bar(a, b, c); }                 8.       T2 = b + c;
                                    9.       if (a <= T2) goto fi;
                                    10.          T3 = b / a;
                                    11.          T4 = b * a;
                                    12.          c = T3 + T4;
                                    13.          b = b + 1;
                                    14.  fi: bar (a, b, c); }
```

Fig. 2. Sample C program and corresponding GIMPLE representation

A disadvantage of working purely at the GIMPLE level is that some language-specific constructs are not visible in GIMPLE code. For example, targeting a specific kind of loop as a pointcut is not currently possible because all loops look the same in GIMPLE. INTERASPECT can be extended with language-specific pointcuts, whose implementation would examine the AST.

INTERASPECT **architecture.** INTERASPECT works by inserting a pass that first traverses the GIMPLE code to identify program points that are join points in a

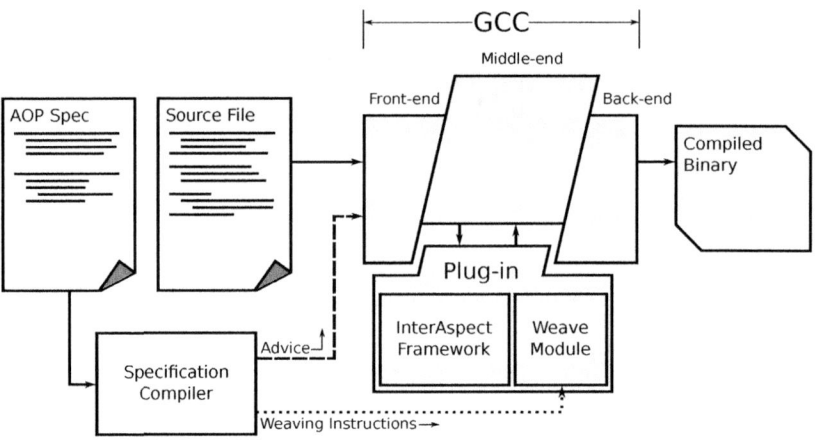

Fig. 3. Architecture of the INTERASPECT instrumentation framework for GCC

specified pointcut. For each such join point, it then calls a user-provided weaving callback function, which can insert calls to advice functions. Advice functions can be written in any language that will link with the target program, and they can access or modify the target program's state, including its global variables. Advice that needs to maintain additional state can declare static variables and global variables.

Unlike traditional AOP systems which implement a special AOP language to define pointcuts, INTERASPECT provides a C API for this purpose. We believe that this approach is well suited to open collaboration. Extending INTERASPECT with new features, such as new kinds of pointcuts, does not require agreement on new language syntax or modification to parser code. Most of the time, collaborators will only need to add new API functions.

As Fig. 3 illustrates, INTERASPECT can further serve as the instrumentation back-end for a traditional AOP specification language. The specification compiler's job is to split an AOP specification into pointcut definitions, associated weaving instructions, and advice code. The first two are sent to an INTERASPECT-based *weave module* for evaluation during the instrumentation plug-in pass, whereas the advice code is sent to GCC for compilation.

3   The INTERASPECT API

This section describes the functions in the INTERASPECT API, most of which fall naturally into one of two categories: (1) functions for creating and filtering pointcuts, and (2) functions for examining and instrumenting join points. Note that users of our framework can write plug-ins solely with calls to these API functions; it is not necessary to include any GCC header files or manipulate any GCC data structures directly.

Creating and filtering pointcuts. The first step for adding instrumentation in INTERASPECT is to create a pointcut using a *match* function. Our current implementation supports the four match functions given in Table 1, allowing one to create four kinds of pointcuts.

Table 1. *Match functions* for creating pointcuts

```
struct aop_pointcut *aop_match_function_entry();
    Creates pointcut denoting every function entry point.
struct aop_pointcut *aop_match_function_exit();
    Creates pointcut denoting every function return point.
struct aop_pointcut *aop_match_function_call();
    Creates pointcut denoting every function call.
struct aop_pointcut *aop_match_assignment_by_type(struct aop_type *type);
    Creates pointcut denoting every assignment to a variable or memory location that matches a type.
```

Using a function entry or exit pointcut makes it possible to add instrumentation that runs with every execution of a function. These pointcuts provide a natural way to put instrumentation at the beginning and end of a function the way one would with before-execution and an after-returning advices in a traditional AOP language. A call pointcut can instead target calls to a function. Call pointcuts can instrument calls to library functions without recompiling them. For example, in Section 4.1, a call pointcut is used to intercept all calls to `malloc`.

The assignment pointcut is useful for monitoring changes to program values. For example, we use it in Section 4.1 to track pointer values so that we can construct the heap graph. We plan to add several new pointcut types, including pointcuts for conditionals and loops. These new pointcuts will make it possible to trace the complete path of execution as a program runs, which is potentially useful for coverage analysis, profiling, and symbolic execution.

After creating a match function, a plug-in can refine it using *filter* functions. Filter functions add additional constraints to a pointcut, removing join points that do not satisfy those constraints. For example, it is possible to filter a call pointcut to include only calls that return a specific type or only calls to a certain function. Table 2 summarizes filter functions for call pointcuts.

Table 2. *Filter functions* for refining function-call pointcuts

```
void aop_filter_call_pc_by_name(struct aop_pointcut *pc, const char *name);
    Filter function calls with a given name.
void aop_filter_call_pc_by_param_type(struct aop_pointcut *pc, int n, struct aop_type *type);
    Filter function calls that have an $n^{th}$ parameter that matches a type.
void aop_filter_call_pc_by_return_type(struct aop_pointcut *pc, struct aop_type *type);
    Filter function calls with a matching return type.
```

Instrumenting join points. INTERASPECT plug-ins iterate over the join points of a pointcut by providing an iterator callback to the *join* function, shown in Table 3. INTERASPECT then calls the iterator callback for each join point so that it can instrument the join point with a call to an *advice* function.

Table 3. *Join function* for iterating over a pointcut

```
void aop_join_on(struct aop_pointcut *pc, join_callback callback, void *callback_param);
    Supply callback function with any data structure as callback_param.
```

Callback functions use *capture* functions to examine values associated with a join point. Capture functions expose two kinds of values: static values that are known at compile time and runtime values that will not be known until program execution time. Static values, such as the name of the variable assigned by an assignment statement, are directly readable in the callback itself. The callback cannot access runtime values, such as the values assigned by an assignment statement, but it can pass them as parameters to advice functions, so that they are available to instrumentation code at runtime. These runtime values are represented in the callback function as special aop_dynval objects. Capture functions are specific to the kinds of join points they operate on. Tables 4 and 5 summarize the capture functions for function-call join points and assignment join points, respectively.

Table 4. *Capture functions* for function-call join points

```
const char *aop_capture_function_name(aop_joinpoint *jp);
    Captures the name of the function called in the given join point.
struct aop_dynval *aop_capture_param(aop_joinpoint *jp, int n);
    Captures the value of the n^th parameter passed in the given function join point.
struct aop_dynval *aop_capture_return_value(aop_joinpoint *jp);
    Captures the value returned by the function in a given call join point.
```

AOP systems like AspectJ [17] provide Boolean operators, such as *and* and *or*, to refine pointcuts. The INTERASPECT API could be extended with corresponding operations. Even without them, a similar result can be achieved in INTERASPECT by including the appropriate logic in the callback. For example, a plug-in can instrument calls to malloc *and* calls to free by joining on a pointcut with all function calls and using the aop_capture_function_name facility to add advice calls only to malloc and free. Simple cases like this can furthermore be handled by using regular expressions to match function names, which will be added to the framework.

After capturing, a callback can add an advice function call before or after the join point using the *insert* function of Table 6. The aop_insert_advice function takes any number of parameters to be passed to the advice function at runtime, including values captured from the join point and values computed during instrumentation by the plug-in itself.

Table 5. *Capture functions* for assignment join points

```
const char *aop_capture_lhs_name(aop_joinpoint *jp);
```
    Captures the name of a variable assigned to in a given assignment join point, or returns NULL if the join point does not assign to a named variable.
```
enum aop_scope aop_capture_lhs_var_scope(aop_joinpoint *jp);
```
    Captures the scope of a variable assigned to in a given assignment join point. Variables can have global, file-local, and function-local scope. If the join point does not assign to a variable, this function returns AOP_MEMORY_SCOPE.
```
struct aop_dynval *aop_capture_lhs_addr(aop_joinpoint *jp);
```
    Captures the memory address assigned to in a given assignment join point.
```
struct aop_dynval *aop_capture_assigned_value(aop_joinpoint *jp);
```
    Captures the assigned value in a given assignment join point.

Using a callback to iterate over individual join points makes it possible to customize instrumentation at each instrumentation site. A plug-in can capture values about the join point to decide which advice function to call, which parameters to pass to it, or even whether to add advice at all. In Section 4.2, this feature is exploited to uniquely index named variables during compilation. Custom instrumentation code in Section 4.3 separately records each instrumented join point in order to track coverage information.

Table 6. *Insert function* for instrumenting a join point with a call to an advice function

```
void aop_insert_advice(struct aop_joinpoint *jp, const char *advice_func_name,
                       enum aop_insert_location location, ...);
```
    Insert an advice call, before or after a join point (depending on the value of location), passing any number of parameters. A plug-in obtains a join point by iterating over a pointcut with aop_join_on.

Function duplication. INTERASPECT provides a *function duplication* facility that makes it possible to toggle instrumentation at the function level. Although inserting advice at the GIMPLE level creates very efficient instrumentation, users may still wish to switch between instrumented and uninstrumented code for high-performance applications. Duplication creates two or more copies of a function body (which can later be instrumented differently) and redefines the function to call a special advice function that runs at function entry and decides which copy of the function body to execute.

When joining on a pointcut for a function with a duplicated body, the caller specifies which copy the join should apply to. By only adding instrumentation to one copy of the function body, the plug-in can create a function whose instrumentation can be turned on and off at runtime. Alternatively, a plug-in can create a function that can toggle between different kinds of instrumentation. Section 4.2 presents an example of using duplication to reduce overhead by sampling.

4   Applications

To demonstrate INTERASPECT's flexibility, we present several example applications of the API. The plug-ins we designed for these examples provide instrumentation that is tailored to specific problems (memory visualization, integer range analysis, code coverage). Though custom-made, the plug-ins themselves are simple to write, requiring only a small amount of code.

4.1   Heap Visualization

The heap visualizer uses the INTERASPECT API to expose memory events that can be used to generate a graphical representation of the heap in real time during program execution. Allocated objects are represented by rectangular nodes, pointer variables and fields by oval nodes, and edges show where pointer variables and fields point.

In order to draw the graph, the heap visualizer needs to intercept object allocations and deallocations and pointer assignments that change edges in the graph. Fig. 4 shows a prototype of the visualizer using Graphviz [2], an open-source graph layout tool, to draw its output. The graph shows three nodes in a linked list during a bubble-sort operation. Each node is labeled with its size, its address in memory, and the addresses of its fields. Variables that point to NULL or to an invalid memory location are drawn with a dashed border. Edges are labeled with the line number of the assignment that created the edge, as well as the number of assignments to the source variable that have occurred so far.

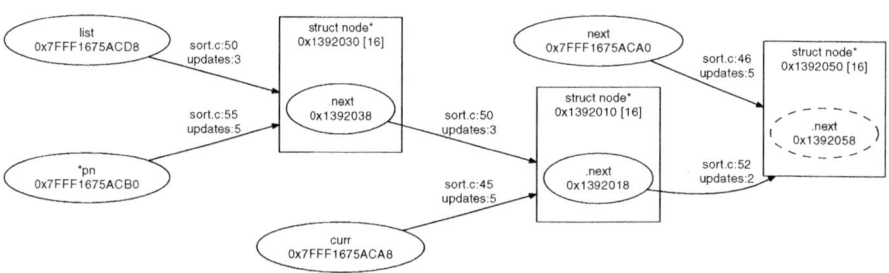

Fig. 4. A visualization of the heap during a bubble sort operation on a linked list

The INTERASPECT code for the heap visualizer instruments each allocation (call to malloc) with a call to the heap_allocation advice function, and it instruments each pointer assignment with a call to the pointer_assign advice function. These advice functions update the graph. Instrumentation of other allocation and deallocation functions, such as calloc and free, is handled similarly.

The INTERASPECT code in Fig. 5 instruments calls to malloc. The function instrument_malloc_calls constructs a pointcut for all calls to malloc and then calls aop_join_on to iterate over all the calls in the pointcut. Only a short main

```
static void instrument_malloc_calls()
{
  /* Construct a pointcut that matches calls to: void *malloc(unsigned int). */
  struct aop_pointcut *pc = aop_match_function_call();
  aop_filter_call_pc_by_name(pc, "malloc");
  aop_filter_call_pc_by_param_type(pc, 0, aop_t_all_unsigned());
  aop_filter_call_pc_by_return_type(pc, aop_t_all_pointer());

  /* Visit every statement in the pointcut. */
  aop_join_on(pc, malloc_callback, NULL);
}

/* The malloc_callback() function executes once for each call to malloc() in the target
   program.  It instruments each call it sees with a call to heap_allocation(). */
static void malloc_callback(struct aop_joinpoint *jp, void *arg)
{
  struct aop_dynval *object_size;
  struct aop_dynval *object_addr;

  /* Capture the size of the allocated object and the address it is allocated to. */
  object_size = aop_capture_param(jp, 0);
  object_addr = aop_capture_return_value(jp);

  /* Add a call to the advice function, passing the size and address as parameters.
     (AOP_TERM_ARG is necessary to terminate the list of arguments
     because of the way C varargs functions work.) */
  aop_insert_advice(jp, "heap_allocation", AOP_INSERT_AFTER,
                    AOP_DYNVAL(object_size), AOP_DYNVAL(object_addr),
                    AOP_TERM_ARG);
}
```

Fig. 5. Instrumenting all memory allocation events

function (not shown) is needed to set GCC to invoke `instrument_malloc_calls` during compilation.

The `aop_match_function_call` function constructs an initial pointcut that includes every function call. Additional `filter` functions narrow down the pointcut to include only calls to `malloc`. First, `aop_filter_call_pc_by_name` filters out calls to functions that are not named `malloc`. Then, `aop_filter_pc_by_param_type` and `aop_filter_pc_by_return_type` filter out calls to functions that do not match the standard `malloc` prototype, which takes an unsigned integer as the first parameter and returns a pointer value. This filtering step is necessary because a program could define its own function with the name `malloc` but a different prototype.

For each join point in the pointcut (in this case, a statement that calls `malloc`), `aop_join_on` calls `malloc_callback`. The two `capture` calls in the callback function return `aop_dynval` objects for the call's first parameter and return value: the size of the allocated region and its address, respectively. Recall from Section 3 that an `aop_dynval` serves as a placeholder during compilation for a value that will not be known until runtime. Finally, `aop_insert_advice` adds the call to the advice function, passing the two captured values. Note that INTERASPECT chooses types for these values based on how they were filtered. The filters used here restrict `object_size` to be an unsigned integer and `object_addr` to be some kind of pointer, so INTERASPECT assumes that the advice function `heap_allocation` has the prototype:

```
void heap_allocation(unsigned long long, void *);
```

To support this, INTERASPECT code must generally filter runtime values by type in order to capture and use them.

The INTERASPECT code in Fig. 6 tracks pointer assignments, such as

```
list_node->next = new_node;
```

The aop_match_assignment_by_type function creates a pointcut that matches assignments, which is additionally filtered by the type of assignment. For this application, we are only interested in assignments to pointer variables.

```
static void instrument_pointer_assignments()
{
  /* Construct a pointcut that matches all assignments to a pointer. */
  struct aop_pointcut *pc = aop_match_assignment_by_type(aop_t_all_pointer());

  /* Visit every statement in the pointcut. */
  aop_join_on(pc, assignment_callback, NULL);
}

/* The assignment_callback function executes once for each pointer assignment.
   It instruments each assignment it sees with a call to pointer_assign(). */
static void assignment_callback(struct aop_joinpoint *jp, void *arg)
{
  struct aop_dynval *address;
  struct aop_dynval *pointer;

 /* Capture the address the pointer is assigned to, as well as the pointer address itself. */
  address = aop_capture_lhs_addr(jp);
  pointer = aop_capture_assigned_value(jp);

  aop_insert_advice(jp, "pointer_assign", AOP_INSERT_AFTER,
                    AOP_DYNVAL(address), AOP_DYNVAL(pointer),
                    AOP_TERM_ARG);
}
```

Fig. 6. Instrumenting all pointer assignments

For each assignment join point, assignment_callback captures address, the address assigned to, and pointer, the pointer value that was assigned. In the above examples, these would be the values of &list_node->next and new_node, respectively. The visualizer uses address to determine the source of a new graph edge and pointer to determine its destination.

The function that captures address, aop_capture_lhs_addr, does not require explicit filtering to restrict the type of the captured value because an address always has a pointer type.

The value captured by aop_capture_assigned_value and stored in pointer has a void pointer type because we filtered the pointcut to include only pointer assignments. As a result, INTERASPECT assumes that the pointer_assign advice function has the prototype:

```
void pointer_assign(void *, void *);
```

4.2   Integer Range Analysis

Integer range analysis is a runtime tool for finding anomalies in program behavior by tracking the range of values for each integer variable [12]. A range analyzer can learn normal ranges from training runs over known good inputs. Values that fall outside of normal ranges in future runs are reported as anomalies, which can indicate errors. For example, an out-of-range value for a variable used as an array index may cause an array bounds violation.

Our integer range analyzer uses sampling to reduce runtime overhead. Missed updates because of sampling can result in underestimating a variable's range, but this trade-off is reasonable in many cases. Sampling can be done randomly or by using a technique like Software Monitoring with Controlled Overhead [15].

INTERASPECT provides function-body duplication as a means to add instrumentation that can be toggled on and off. Duplicating a function splits its body into two copies. A *distributor block* at the beginning of the function decides which copy to run. An INTERASPECT plug-in can add advice to just one of the copies, so that the distributor chooses between enabling or disabling instrumentation.

Fig. 7 shows how we use INTERASPECT to instrument integer variable updates. The call to aop_duplicate makes a copy of each function body. The first argument specifies that there should be two copies of the function body, and the

```
static void instrument_integer_assignments()
{
  struct aop_pointcut *pc;

  /* Duplicate the function body so there are two copies. */
  aop_duplicate(2, "distributor_func", AOP_TERM_ARG);

  /* Construct a pointcut that matches all assignments to an integer. */
  pc = aop_match_assignment_by_type(aop_t_all_signed_integer());

  /* Visit every statement in the pointcut. */
  aop_join_on_copy(pc, 1, assignment_callback, NULL);
}

/* The assignment_callback function executes once for each integer assignment.
   It instruments each assignment it sees with a call to int_assign(). */
static void assignment_callback(struct aop_joinpoint *jp, void *arg)
{
  const char *variable_name;
  int variable_index;
  struct aop_dynval *value;
  enum aop_scope scope;

  variable_name = aop_capture_lhs_name(jp);

  if (variable_name != NULL) {
    /* Choose an index number for this variable. */
    scope = aop_capture_lhs_var_scope(jp);
    variable_index = get_index_from_name(variable_name, scope);

    aop_insert_advice(jp, "int_assign", AOP_INSERT_AFTER,
                      AOP_INT_CST(variable_index), AOP_DYNVAL(value),
                      AOP_TERM_ARG);
  }
}
```

Fig. 7. Instrumenting integer variable updates

second specifies the name of a function that the distributor will call to decide which copy to execute. When the duplicated function runs, the distributor calls `distributor_func`, which must be a function that returns an integer. The duplicated function bodies are indexed from zero, and the `distributor_func` return value determines which one the distributor transfers control to.

Using `aop_join_on_copy` instead of the usual `aop_join_on` iterates only over join points in the specified copy of duplicate code. As a result, only one copy is instrumented; the other copy remains unmodified.

The callback function itself is similar to the callbacks we used in Section 4.1. The main difference is the call to `get_index_from_name` that converts the variable name to an integer index. The `get_index_from_name` function (not shown for brevity) also takes the variable's scope so that it can assign different indices to local variables in different functions. It would be possible to directly pass the name itself (as a string) to the advice function, but the advice function would then incur the cost of looking up the variable by its name at runtime. This optimization illustrates the benefits of INTERASPECT's callback-based approach to custom instrumentation.

The `aop_capture_lhs_name` function returns a string instead of an `aop_dynval` object because variable names are known at compile time. It is necessary to check for a `NULL` return value because not all assignments are to named variables.

To better understand InterAspect's performance impact, we benchmarked this plug-in on the compute-intensive `bzip2` compression utility using empty advice. The instrumented `bzip2` contains advice calls at every integer variable assignment, but the advice functions themselves do nothing, allowing us to measure the overhead from calling advice functions independently from actual monitoring overhead. With a distributor that maximizes overhead by always choosing the instrumented function body, we measured 24% runtime overhead. Function duplication by itself contributes very little to this overhead; when the distributor always chooses the uninstrumented path, the overhead from instrumentation was statistically insignificant.

4.3   Code Coverage

A straightforward way to measure code coverage is to choose a pointcut and measure the percentage of its join points that are executed during testing. INTERASPECT's ability to iterate over each join point makes it simple to label join points and then track them at runtime.

The example in Fig. 8 adds instrumentation to track coverage of function entry and exit points. To reduce runtime overhead, the `choose_unique_index` function assigns an integer index to each tracked join point, similar to the indexing of integer variables in Section 4.2. Each index is saved along with its corresponding source filename and line number by the `save_index_to_disk` function. The runtime advice needs to output only the set of covered index numbers; an offline tool uses that output to compute the percentage of join points covered or to list the filenames and line numbers of covered join points. For brevity we omit the actual implementations of `choose_unique_index` and `save_index_to_disk`.

```
static void instrument_function_entry_exit()
{
  struct aop_pointcut *entry_pc;
  struct aop_pointcut *exit_pc;

  /* Construct two pointcuts: one for function entry and one for function exit. */
  entry_pc = aop_match_function_entry();
  exit_pc = aop_match_function_exit();

  aop_join_on(entry_pc, entry_exit_callback, NULL);
  aop_join_on(exit_pc, entry_exit_callback, NULL);
}

/* The entry_exit_callback function assigns an index to every join
   point it sees and saves that index to disk. */
static void entry_exit_callback(struct aop_joinpoint *jp, void *arg)
{
  int index, line_number;
  const char *filename;

  index = choose_unique_index();
  filename = aop_capture_filename(jp);
  line_number = aop_capture_lineno(jp);

  save_index_to_disk(index, filename, line_number);

  aop_insert_advice(jp, "mark_as_covered", AOP_INSERT_BEFORE,
                    AOP_INT_CST(index), AOP_TERM_ARG);
}
```

Fig. 8. Instrumenting function entry and exit for code coverage

5 Related Work

Aspect-oriented programming was first introduced for Java with AspectJ [10,17]. There, weaving takes place at the bytecode level. The AspectBench Compiler (abc) [3] is a more recent extensible research version of AspectJ that makes it possible to add new language constructs (see for example [4]). Similarly to INTERASPECT, it manipulates a 3A intermediate representation (Jimple) specialized to Java.

Other frameworks for Java, including Javaassist [7] and PROSE [19], offer an API for instrumenting and modifying code, and hence do not require the use of a special language. Javaassist is a class library for editing bytecode. A source-level API can be used to edit class files without knowledge of the bytecode format. PROSE has similar goals.

AOP for other languages such as C and C++ has had a slower uptake. AspectC [8] was one of the first AOP systems for C, based on the language constructs of AspectJ. ACC [18] is a more recent AOP system for C, also based on the language constructs of AspectJ. It transforms source code and offers its own internal compiler framework for parsing C. It is a closed system in the sense that one cannot augment it with new pointcuts or access the internal structure of a C program in order to perform static analysis.

The XWeaver system [21], with its language AspectX, represents a program in XML (srcML, to be specific), making it language-independent. It supports

Java and C++ . A user, however, has to be XML-aware. Aspicere [20] is an aspect language for C based on LLVM bytecode. Its pointcut language is inspired by logic programming. Adding new pointcuts amounts to defining new logic predicates. Arachne [9,11] is a dynamic aspect language for C that uses assembler manipulation techniques to instrument a running system without pausing it.

AspectC++ [22] is targeted towards C++. It can handle C to some extent, but this does not seem to be a high priority for its developers. For example, it only handles ANSI C and not other dialects. AspectC++ operates at the source-code level and generates C++ code, which can be problematic in contexts where only C code is permitted, such as in certain embedded applications. OpenC++ [6] is a front-end library for C++ that developers can use to implement various kinds of translations in order to define new syntax and object behavior. CIL [13] (C Intermediate Language) is an OCaml [16] API for writing source-code transformations of its own 3A code representation of C programs. CIL requires a user to be familiar with the less-often-used yet powerful OCaml language.

Additionally, various low-level but mature tools exist for code analysis and instrumentation. These include the BCEL [1] bytecode-instrumentation tool for Java, and Valgrind [23], which works directly with executables and consequently targets multiple programming languages.

6   Conclusions

We have presented INTERASPECT, a framework for developing powerful instrumentation plug-ins for the GCC suite of production compilers. INTERASPECT-based plug-ins instrument programs compiled with GCC by modifying GCC's intermediate language, GIMPLE. The INTERASPECT API simplifies this process by offering an AOP-based interface. Plug-in developers can easily specify pointcuts to target specific program join points and then add customized instrumentation at those join points. We presented several example plug-ins that demonstrate the framework's ability to customize runtime instrumentation for specific applications.

As future work, we plan to add pointcuts for all control flow constructs, thereby allowing instrumentation to trace a program run's exact path of execution. We also plan to investigate API support for pointcuts that depend on dynamic information, such as AspectJ's cflow, by introducing filters that are evaluated at run-time. Dynamic pointcuts can already be implemented in INTERASPECT with advice functions that maintain and use appropriate state, but API support would eliminate the need to write those advice functions.

Acknowledgements. We thank the anonymous reviewers for their valuable comments. Part of the research described herein was carried out at the Jet Propulsion Laboratory, California Institute of Technology, under a contract with the National Aeronautics and Space Administration. Research supported in part by AFOSR Grant FA9550-09-1-0481, NSF Grants CCF-0926190, CCF-0613913, and CNS-0831298, and ONR Grants N00014-07-1-0928 and N00014-09-1-0651.

References

1. BCEL, `http://jakarta.apache.org/bcel`
2. AT&T Research Labs. Graphviz (2009), `http://www.graphviz.org`
3. Avgustinov, P., Christensen, A.S., Hendren, L., Kuzins, S., Lhoták, J., Lhoták, O., de Moor, O., Sereni, D., Sittampalam, G., Tibble, J.: abc: An extensible AspectJ compiler. In: Proceedings of the Fourth International Conference on Aspect-Oriented Software Development. ACM Press, New York (2005)
4. Bodden, E., Havelund, K.: Racer: Effective race detection using AspectJ. In: International Symposium on Software Testing and Analysis, Seattle, WA, pp. 155–165. ACM, New York (2008)
5. Callanan, S., Dean, D.J., Zadok, E.: Extending GCC with modular GIMPLE optimizations. In: Proceedings of the 2007 GCC Developers' Summit, Ottawa, Canada (July 2007)
6. Chiba, S.: A metaobject protocol for C++. In: Proceedings of the ACM Conference on Object-Oriented Programming Systems, Languages, and Applications, pp. 285–299 (October 1995)
7. Chiba, S.: Load-time structural reflection in Java. In: Bertino, E. (ed.) ECOOP 2000. LNCS, vol. 1850, p. 313. Springer, Heidelberg (2000)
8. Coady, Y., Kiczales, G., Feeley, M., Smolyn, G.: Using AspectC to improve the modularity of path-specific customization in operating system code. In: Proceedings of the 9th ACM SIGSOFT Symposium on the Foundations of Software Engineering, pp. 88–98 (2001)
9. Douence, R., Fritz, T., Loriant, N., Menaud, J.-M., Ségura-Devillechaise, M., Südholt, M.: An expressive aspect language for system applications with Arachne. In: Proceedings of the 4th international conference on Aspect-oriented software development. ACM Press, New York (2005)
10. AspectJ, `http://www.eclipse.org/aspectj`
11. Arachne, `http://www.emn.fr/x-info/arachne`
12. Fei, L., Midkiff, S.P.: Artemis: Practical runtime monitoring of applications for errors. Tech. Rep. TR-ECE-05-02, Electrical and Computer Engineering, Purdue University (2005), `http://docs.lib.purdue.edu/ecetr/4/`
13. Necula, G.C., McPeak, S., Rahul, S.P., Weimer, W.: CIL: Intermediate language and tools for analysis and transformation of C programs. In: Horspool, R.N. (ed.) CC 2002. LNCS, vol. 2304, pp. 213–228. Springer, Heidelberg (2002)
14. GCC 4.5 release series changes, new features, and fixes, `http://gcc.gnu.org/gcc-4.5/changes.html`
15. Huang, X., Seyster, J., Callanan, S., Dixit, K., Grosu, R., Smolka, S.A., Stoller, S.D., Zadok, E.: Software monitoring with controllable overhead. International Journal on Software Tools for Technology Transfer (STTT) (2010) (accepted for publication)
16. Objective Caml, `http://caml.inria.fr/index.en.html`
17. Kiczales, G., Hilsdale, E., Hugunin, J., Kersten, M., Palm, J., Griswold, W.G.: An Overview of AspectJ. In: Knudsen, J.L. (ed.) ECOOP 2001. LNCS, vol. 2072, pp. 327–355. Springer, Heidelberg (2001)
18. ACC, `http://research.msrg.utoronto.ca/ACC`

19. Nicoara, A., Alonso, G., Roscoe, T.: Controlled, systematic, and efficient code replacement for running Java programs. In: Proceedings of the ACM EuroSys Conference, Glasgow, Scotland, UK (April 2008)
20. Aspicere, `http://sailhome.cs.queensu.ca/~bram/aspicere`
21. Rohlik, O., Pasetti, A., Cechticky, V., Birrer, I.: Implementing adaptability in embedded software through aspect oriented programming. In: IEEE Mechatronics & Robotics, pp. 85–90 (2004)
22. Spinczyk, O., Lohmann, D.: The design and implementation of AspectC++. Know.-Based Syst. 20(7), 636–651 (2007)
23. Valgrind, `http://valgrind.org`

Runtime Verification for Software Transactional Memories

Vasu Singh

Institute of Science and Technology, Austria

Abstract. Software transactional memories (STMs) promise simple and efficient concurrent programming. Several correctness properties have been proposed for STMs. Based on a bounded conflict graph algorithm for verifying correctness of STMs, we develop TRACER, a tool for runtime verification of STM implementations. The novelty of TRACER lies in the way it combines coarse and precise runtime analyses to guarantee sound and complete verification in an efficient manner. We implement TRACER in the TL2 STM implementation. We evaluate the performance of TRACER on STAMP benchmarks. While a precise runtime verification technique based on conflict graphs results in an average slowdown of 60x, the two-level approach of TRACER performs complete verification with an average slowdown of around 25x across different benchmarks.

1 Introduction

Software transactional memory (STM) [18,23] holds promise as a programming paradigm for managing concurrency. STM gives the programmer an intuitive interface, and at the same time allows maximal concurrency on part of the underlying system. STM takes over the responsibility of correct synchronization of concurrent programs, making programming easier for the programmer. With this shift of responsibility, the verification of STM implementations becomes more important.

Over time, several correctness properties have been proposed for STMs. To start with, some basic correctness notions like serializability and strict serializability [20] were borrowed from the database community. As research grew in STM implementations, it was noticed [6,17] that these correctness notions are often insufficient for STMs. This led to the formalization of a new correctness property called opacity [15].

Despite the different correctness properties, a central theme in correctness of STMs is to require a sequential execution of a subset of transactions. While database notions required a sequential execution only for the committing subset of transactions, new correctness properties like opacity also restrict the behavior of aborting transactions. Opacity requires that there exists a sequential execution consisting of all transactions (committed, aborted, and active). These different correctness properties can be captured using conflict graphs [20]. Conflict graphs are a common technique to study correctness properties in databases. A conflict graph represents an execution, where the transactions of the execution are the

G. Roşu et al. (Eds.): RV 2010, LNCS 6418, pp. 421–435, 2010.

vertices in the graph, and the conflicts between transactions are directed edges. Conflict graphs reduce the problem of checking correctness of an execution to checking that a graph is acyclic.

Static verification of STMs has been addressed using model checking [12,13,14] and theorem proving [4,5]. However, static verification is often limited in application to STM algorithms due to the inherent complexity of STM implementations. Moreover, static verification often does not fill the gap between the STM algorithm and the optimizations introduced in the STM implementations by the programmer or the underlying compiler and hardware. Although Guerraoui et al. [14] verify STM algorithms under relaxed memory models, these approaches cannot be extended to real world STM implementations. The complexity of the STM implementations thus calls for efficient runtime verification techniques which can be coupled with the STM implementations to check correctness of executions on-the-fly.

This paper first describes a compositional framework to construct conflict graphs for different correctness properties of STMs. We formalize correctness properties as a set of conflicts on a subset of vertices in the conflict graph. As the size of a conflict graph increases with the number of transactions in the execution, it is essential to remove completed transactions to keep the conflict graph bounded. This pruning of the conflict graph has to be carefully done in order to maintain all conflicts introduced by the completed transactions being pruned. Several methods have been proposed for pruning conflict graphs [3,8,12,13,16]. We describe a bounded conflict graph based algorithm for verifying STM implementations. This algorithm is adapted from our earlier work on static verification of STMs [12,13].

The main contribution of this paper is the use of the bounded conflict graph algorithm to develop TRACER, a novel, sound and complete, runtime verification tool for STM implementations. Soundness and completeness imply that TRACER declares a history to be correct if and only if the history is indeed correct with respect to the given correctness property. TRACER instruments every transactional memory access, and every transaction commit and abort with the required instructions to modify the conflict graph. We observe that the approach of changing the conflict graph precisely at every step has a huge impact on performance of TRACER. This is due to the expensive operations required to maintain the precise set of edges in the conflict graph. Thus, we build two modes in TRACER: a coarse mode and a precise mode. The coarse verification mode uses Bloom filters [1] for fast and inaccurate (overapproximate) storage of access sets, and runs our conflict graph algorithm using these inaccurate access sets. The overapproximation of access sets often results in spurious cycles in the conflict graph. When such a cycle is detected, the precise verification mode is triggered. The precise verification runs a precise conflict graph algorithm to verify the correctness of the execution. While the coarse mode accounts for the soundness and efficiency of TRACER, the precise mode guarantees the completeness of TRACER.

We implement TRACER as a part of TL2 [6], a state-of-the-art STM implementation. We evaluate the performance of TRACER on STAMP benchmarks [2]. These benchmarks include different domains of parallel computing, and provide a versatile data access pattern for STMs. To emphasize the importance of the coarse verification technique in improving the efficiency, we first measure the time taken by directly adopting a precise verification technique. We observe that the precise construction of the conflict graph slows down the execution by up to 150x in the worst case, and around 60x on average with 8 threads on an 8-core machine. Then, we turn on the coarse verification, and show that the intermediate sound but incomplete verification step can drastically improve the speed of execution, by reducing the slow down to 60x in the worst case, and around 25x on average with 8 threads on an 8-core machine.

This paper proceeds as follows. Section 2 describes a framework for correctness properties in STMs. Section 3 describes the bounded conflict graph based algorithm. Section 4 presents our runtime verification tool TRACER. Section 5 evaluates the performance of TRACER. Section 6 presents related work and Section 7 concludes the paper.

2 Framework

We first present a general framework to describe a shared memory system consisting of a set $T = \{t_1 \ldots t_k\}$ of *threads* that communicate by executing commands on a set $X = \{x_1 \ldots x_n\}$ of *shared variables*.

2.1 Histories

Operations. The threads execute sequences of operations, whose subsequences (transactions) should execute as if atomically. To distinguish the start and end point of a sequence of operations that should be atomic, we define special operations: *start* to start a new sequence, operation *commit* to finish a sequence successfully (commit), and *abort* to finish a sequence with a failure (abort). We define a set *Oper* of *operations* as $(\{start, commit, abort\} \cup (\{rd, wr\} \times X)) \times T$. A *history* $h \in Oper^*$ is a sequence of operations. Let H be the set of all histories. Given a history h, we refer to its ith operation as operation i.

Transactions. A *transaction* of a thread t is a subsequence $oper_1 \ldots oper_n$ of a history h such that (i) $oper_1$ is a *start* operation, (ii) either operation $oper_n$ is the last operation of t in h, or we have $oper_n \in \{commit, abort\}$, and (iii) all operations $oper_2, \ldots, oper_{n-1}$ are read or write operations.[1]

We say that a history h is *sequential* if, for every transaction x in h, every operation between the first operation of x and the last operation of x in h is a part of x. A transaction T is *committed* (resp. *aborted*) in a history h if the last operation of T is a *commit* operation (resp. an *abort* operation).

2.2 Conflicts

A conflict enforces an order between a pair of operations in a history. Many of the correctness properties in STMs require a justifying serial history such that the

---

[1] We do not consider nested transactions in this work.

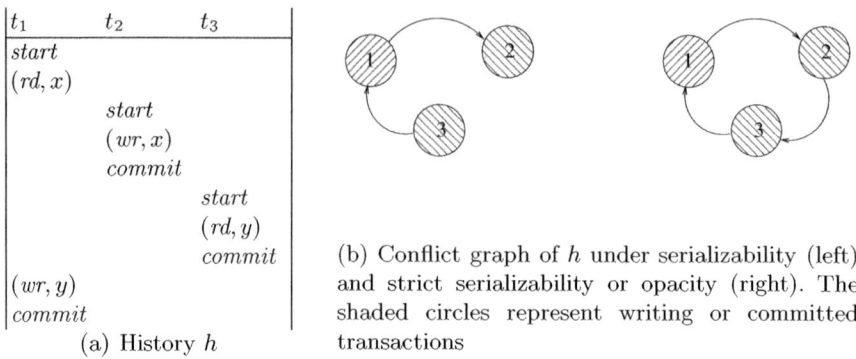

(a) History h

(b) Conflict graph of h under serializability (left) and strict serializability or opacity (right). The shaded circles represent writing or committed transactions

Fig. 1. Conflict graphs for checking correctness of a history

order of conflicting operations is the same as the one in the original history. We define a *conflict* c as a function $c : H \times Oper \times Oper \rightarrow \mathbb{B}$. We define two conflicts that allow us to specify serializability, strict serializability, and opacity. Note that one can define new conflict functions and adapt our verification algorithm for those conflicts.

- *access* conflict $c_{ac}(h, i, j) =$ true if $i < j$ and operations i and j are accesses of a variable x and one of them is a write.
- *real time* conflict $c_{rt}(h, i, j) =$ true if $i < j$ and operation i is a commit of a transaction and operation j is the start of a transaction.

2.3   Conflict Graphs

Given a set C of conflicts and a history h, a *conflict graph* of the history h with respect to C is a directed graph $G = (V, E)$ such that the vertices V are the set of transactions in h, and E is a set of directed edges such that there is an edge $e \in E$ from a vertex v_1 to a vertex v_2 if and only if there is an operation i in transaction v_1 and an operation j in transaction v_2 and a conflict $c \in C$ such that $c(h, i, j) =$ true.

2.4   Correctness Properties

We define a *correctness property* as $\pi = \langle C, f \rangle$, where C is a set of conflicts and $f : V \rightarrow \mathbb{B}$ is a function on the vertices. Given a correctness property $\pi = \langle C, f \rangle$, we say that a history h is correct with respect to the π if there does not exist a cycle $v_0, \ldots v_n$ in the conflict graph of h, where for all i such that $0 \leq i \leq n$, we have $f(v_i) =$ true. We now characterize some correctness properties.

Serializability is captured using the access conflict, and the vertices that correspond to transactions that are sure to commit. Formally, the correctness property *serializability* is defined as $\langle C_{ser}, f_c \rangle$, where we have $C_{ser} = \{c_{ac}\}$ and $f_c(v) =$ true if the transaction corresponding to vertex v has committed or written to a variable. *Strict serializability* is defined as $\langle C_{sser}, f_c \rangle$, where we have $C_{sser} = \{c_{ac}, c_{rt}\}$. In other words, strict serializability adds the real-time ordering requirement for committed transactions to serializability. *Opacity* is defined as $\langle C_{sser}, f \rangle$, where $f(v) =$ true for all vertices. Intuitively, opacity enforces strict serializability for all transactions: committed, aborted, or active.

Figure 1 shows an example of a history and its conflict graph under different correctness properties. While the history is serializable, it is neither strictly serializable nor opaque. This is because the transaction of thread 2 has a real time conflict with the transaction of thread 3, which creates a cycle in the conflict graph for strict serializability and opacity. Consider the case when the transaction of thread 3 does not commit: then, there is a cycle in the conflict graph for opacity, but not in the conflict graph for strict serializability.

3 The Conflict Graph Algorithm

It is straightforward to produce conflict graphs where the number of vertices is the number of transactions. However, as an STM execution consists of millions of transactions, it becomes impractical to check for cycles in the conflict graph. We thus present an algorithm that constructs conflict graphs bounded in the number of threads instead of the number of transactions. This algorithm is adapted from our earlier work [12] on static verification of STM algorithms. The idea of the algorithm is to remove committed transactions from the conflict graph after capturing their access sets in the form of prohibited access sets of active transactions. For example, let a transaction read a variable x and write a variable y. Let another transaction read variable y before the write by the first transaction. Now, if the first transaction commits, it is sufficient to remember for the second (active) transaction that it is prohibited to read/write to y or write to x. Algorithm 1 presents an incremental algorithm that creates and uses the bounded conflict graphs to verify a history with respect to a correctness property $\langle C, f \rangle$. We consider the access and real-time conflicts, and thus the algorithm can be used for checking serializability, strict serializability, and opacity. The algorithm can be adapted for other conflicts.

Description. We now define some functions that we use in Algorithm 1. The function $status : V \to \{$active, aborted, committed, pending$\}$ describes the status of the transaction corresponding to a vertex. The function $writing : V \to \mathbb{B}$ describes whether a transaction corresponding to a vertex writes to a variable or not. The functions $rs : V \to 2^{Obj}$ and $ws : V \to 2^{Obj}$ describe the read and write sets of the active transaction corresponding to a vertex, respectively. Similarly, the functions prs and pws describe the prohibited read and write sets of the active transaction corresponding to a vertex. Together, we call the read and write sets as the *access sets* of the transactions, and the prohibited read and write sets as the *prohibited sets*. We adapt the colored DFS algorithm for detecting cycles in the conflict graph as shown in Algorithm 2. Our algorithm ensures that if a cycle is found in the conflict graph, then all transactions in the cycle satisfy the function f in the correctness property $\langle C, f \rangle$.

Complexity. To get a practical runtime verification tool, it is important to design the data structures for verification in a way that the cost of instrumentation for each operation in Algorithm 1 is minimal. Software transactions consist of a long sequence of reads and writes followed by a commit operation. Moreover, in a transaction, it is often the case that the number of reads is more than the number of writes. Thus, it is important to keep the overhead associated with the instrumentation of a read low. The access sets and the prohibited sets for verification as described above have to be stored differently from the access sets of the STM implementation. The access sets of STM implementations are often stored as linked lists, as the only required operation is insertion. But, for verification access sets, we often need to search in the sets. For example, the instrumentation for the read operation requires an insertion into the read set of the transaction, and a search in the write set of all other transactions. Assuming access sets are implemented as binary search trees, the instrumentation has a cost $O(k \cdot \log n)$ in the worst case. Similarly, a write operation requires an insertion into the write set of the transaction, and a search in the read and write sets of

---

Algorithm 1. Incremental algorithm for verifying a history with respect to the correctness property $\langle C, f \rangle$

On an operation *start* by transaction t:
    add a new vertex t to the conflict graph
    set $status(t)$ as active
    if $c_{rt} \in C$ **then**
        for all vertices $u \neq t$
            if $status(u) = $ pending **then**
                add edge from u to t
    return 1

On an operation (rd, x) by transaction t:
    if $x \in $ prs(t) **then**
        add edge from t to t
    if $c_{ac} \in C$ **then**
        for all vertices $u \neq t$
            if u writes to x **then**
                add edge from u to t
    return $acyclic(G, f)$

On an operation (wr, x) by transaction t:
    set $writing(t)$ as true
    if $x \in $ pws(t) **then**
        add edge from t to t
    if $c_{ac} \in C$ **then**
        for all vertices $u \neq t$
            if u reads or writes x **then**
                add edge from u to t
    return $acyclic(G, f)$

Algorithm 1. continued

On an operation *commit* by transaction t:
  set $status(t)$ as committed
  for all vertices $u \neq t$
    if there is an edge from t to u **then**
      for all vertices $u' \neq t$ **then**
        if there is an edge from u' to t **then**
          add edge from u' to u
      set $status(u)$ as pending
      if $c_{ac} \in C$ **then**
        $\mathsf{pws}(u) = \mathsf{pws}(u) \cup \mathsf{pws}(t) \cup \mathsf{ws}(t) \cup \mathsf{rs}(t)$
        $\mathsf{prs}(u) = \mathsf{prs}(u) \cup \mathsf{prs}(t) \cup \mathsf{ws}(t)$
  if $acyclic(G, f) = 0$ **then** *return* 0
  set $writing(t)$ as false
  set $\mathsf{rs}(t), \mathsf{ws}(t), \mathsf{prs}(t)$, and $\mathsf{pws}(t)$ to $\emptyset$
  remove all edges (v_1, v_2) where $v_1 = t$ or $v_2 = t$
  return 1

On an operation *abort* by transaction t:
  set $status(t)$ as aborted
  set $writing(t)$ as false
  set $\mathsf{rs}(t), \mathsf{ws}(t), \mathsf{prs}(t)$, and $\mathsf{pws}(t)$ to $\emptyset$
  remove all edges (v_1, v_2) where $v_1 = t$ or $v_2 = t$
  return 1

---

all other transactions. A commit operation is expensive as it requires to copy the read and write sets into the prohibited access sets. Thus, the commit requires an instrumentation of cost $O(k \cdot n \cdot \log n)$. An abort operation removes the incoming and outgoing edges from a vertex, and thus requires $O(k)$ instrumentation.

4   The **TRACER** Tool

We develop TRACER, an online runtime verification tool for checking the correctness of execution of STM implementations. We instrument every load and store instruction on transactional variables, and every commit and abort instruction according to Algorithm 1. The execution of TRACER is completely synchronized with the history produced by the STM implementation. This implies that if an STM implementation is run with TRACER, it is guaranteed not to produce an incorrect history. Moreover, the completeness of TRACER guarantees that if an STM implementation produces a correct history, then TRACER does not raise any errors. To achieve soundness and completeness efficiently, TRACER runs two levels of verification. The first level gives an incomplete answer, but in a sound and fast manner. The second level guarantees complete verification. The working of the two modes is described in more detail below, and illustrated in Figure 2.

Algorithm 2. Algorithm for detecting cycles in the conflict graph G with respect to a correctness property $\langle C, f \rangle$

```
acyclic(G, f) :
    for all vertices v
        if f(v) = true then
            v.mark = white
        else
            v.mark = black
    for all vertices v
        if v.mark = white then
            if visitTwice(G, v) then
                return false
    return true

visitTwice(G, v) :
    set v.mark = grey
    for all edges (v, v') ∈ G
        if v'.mark = grey then
            return true
        if v'.mark = white then
            if visitTwice(G, v') then
                return true
    v.mark = black
    return false
```

4.1 Coarse Verification

Our coarse verification technique uses Bloom filters [1] to store the access and prohibited sets of all threads. Bloom filters give a fast, though overapproximate, means of storing these sets. The time required for insertion and search in a Bloom filter is constant. However, the precision of storage decreases as the number of accesses of a transaction increases. Bloom filters give an $O(k)$ instrumentation for read, write, commit, and abort operations. We implement Bloom filters of size B. For our implementation, we vary B from 32 bits to 256 bits. For a memory address x, the function bloom(x) gives a B-bit binary number. Now, we list the instructions for search, insertion, and multiple insertion using Bloom filters.

```
search(x, b)        :    (b & bloom(x)) = bloom(x)
add(x, b)           :    b := b | bloom(x)
add(b',b)           :    b := b | b'
```

Note the constant time instruction for adding a set of addresses from one access set to another using Bloom filters. This is often required in the commit operation of Algorithm 1. Note that for a transaction with read set represented as b, the operation search(x,b) may return true even if the transaction never read x. Due to the overapproximation, the coarse verification technique may find cycles in the conflict graph even if the history satisfies the required correctness property. To tackle this situation, the coarse verification maintains a record of

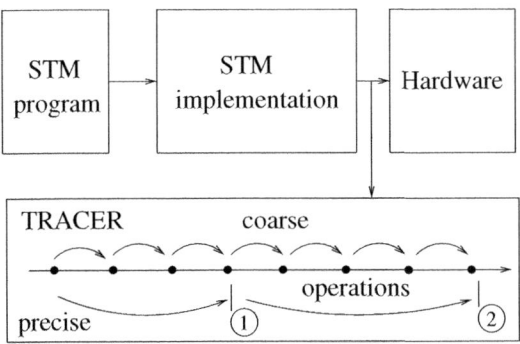

Fig. 2. The working of TRACER

the history. When a cycle is observed by the coarse verification technique, the precise verification technique is triggered to find out whether the cycle observed is spurious or indeed genuine. If the precise verification finds the cycle to be genuine, the history is reported back as erroneous. Otherwise, the predecessor relation of the coarse verification is reset to be the predecessor relation of the precise verification, and the coarse verification is continued.

4.2   Precise Verification

The precise verification technique is responsible for the completeness of our results. This requires the precise verification technique to remember the exact access sets for every transaction. We implement the access sets as hash tables. When the precise verification technique is triggered, it starts from the state of the precise conflict graph when the precise verification technique was last triggered. It executes Algorithm 1 for all operations invoked since then. This ensures no repetition of work. Note that in many cases, TRACER ends up performing a precise verification regularly due to false alarms generated by the coarse verification. However, as the precise verification in this case is performed by one particular thread, it is very efficient in terms of cache performance, and easily covers the extra overhead of the coarse verification. In other words, updating the precise conflict graph and looking for cycles in the precise conflict graph at every step is very expensive. The coarse verification does away with most of the overhead, and still guarantees sound verification. Whenever correctness is under doubt, the precise verification step catches up with the coarse verification to check whether the counterexample generated is genuine or spurious. These points are marked as ① and ② in Figure 2.

5   Evaluation of **TRACER**

We implement TRACER as part of the TL2-x86 implementation. We use the STAMP benchmarks to evaluate our tool by verifying serializability of the obtained histories. We briefly describe the STAMP benchmarks and the TL2 algorithm here.

5.1   STAMP Benchmarks

STAMP consists of eight different benchmarks from a variety of application domains that may benefit from STMs: computational biology, security, engineering, and machine learning. Different benchmarks are characterized by their transaction length and the size of access sets. *Bayes* implements an algorithm for Bayesian network learning. This benchmark consists of long transactions with relatively large read and write sets. *Genome* is an application for gene sequencing, which matches numerous DNA segments to construct the original source. The transactions, read and write sets are all moderate sized. *Intruder* is a security application for detecting intrusion in networks. It has relatively short transactions and small read and write sets. *Kmeans* implements the kmeans-algorithm to cluster a set of objects into a set of partitions. The transactions in Kmeans are small with small read and write sets. *Labyrinth* implements a routing algorithm in a three dimensional grid between a start and an end point. It has large read and write sets, and long transactions. *SSCA2* is a scientific application for efficient graph construction, using adjacency arrays and auxiliary arrays. The transactions in SSCA2 are small, with small read and write sets, and little contention. *Vacation* is an application from online transaction processing domain that emulates a travel reservation system. The transactions are of medium length, with moderate read and write sets. *Yada* is based on Ruppert's algorithm for Delaunay mesh refinement, and consists of long transactions.

5.2   Integrating **TRACER** with TL2

Transactional Locking II (TL2) is an efficient lock-based STM algorithm. TL2 uses a global clock and version numbers for checking the correctness of the execution. Now, we describe in brief how TL2 works and the instrumentation that we introduce.

On the start of a transaction t, the transaction t reads the value of the global clock and stores it locally as gc. We instrument the read of the global clock with the TRACER *start transaction*. On a transactional read of variable x, the transaction checks the version number of x and whether x is locked. If the version number is not more than gc and x is not locked, the transaction reads the variable. We instrument the read of x with the TRACER *read variable x*. It is again checked that the version number is not more than gc and that x is not locked: otherwise the transaction is aborted. On a transactional write of x, the variable is locally updated. Note that the conflict graph is not updated on a local write. On a commit, the transaction in TL2 acquires the locks for all variables it writes to. Then, the transaction checks that the version number for all read variables has not changed since the transaction performed the read. If this does not hold, the transaction aborts. Otherwise, the transaction writes globally to the written variables, and then commits. We instrument the global write of variable

Table 1. Average execution time (in seconds) and slowdown with only precise verification. The slowdown is with respect to the execution of the uninstrumented TL2 STM implementation.

Benchmark	1 thread	2 threads	4 threads	8 threads
Bayes	3.45 (1.02x)	3.70 (1.04x)	3.72 (1.05x)	3.74 (1.07x)
Genome	4.58 (2.95x)	17.41 (20.70x)	26.07 (48.51x)	45.93 (88.71x)
Intruder	1.629 (7.22x)	5.90 (23.04x)	14.13 (46.47x)	51.93 (159x)
Kmeans	1.887 (7.12x)	4.53 (17.69x)	10.93 (47.39x)	28.34 (89.05x)
Labyrinth	0.288 (1.154x)	0.171 (1.14x)	0.110 (1.07x)	0.125 (1.37x)
SSCA2	30.56 (1.333x)	33.79 (2.28x)	47.34 (4.07x)	69.03 (7.61x)
Vacation	1.92 (4.36x)	4.463 (20.23x)	5.616 (43.19x)	14.71 (94.3x)
Yada	2.39 (2.61x)	7.928 (9.65x)	14.083 (24.86x)	36.742 (58.69x)

x with the TRACER *write variable x*, and the final cleanup phase of the commit with the TRACER *commit transaction*. Moreover, we instrument the cleanup of the abort with the TRACER *abort transaction*.

5.3   Results

We run our experiments on a quad dual core Intel Xeon 1.86 GHz server. First of all, we execute the uninstrumented TL2 STM implementation with the STAMP benchmarks. Then, we run TRACER to verify serializability in three different modes: only the precise verification, only the coarse verification, and then both verification techniques together. We average every execution for 10 runs.

Only precise verification. Table 1 shows the execution time and the slowdown without the coarse verification step. We observe very large slowdown as we increase the number of threads.

Only coarse verification. Table 2 gives the results of running only the coarse verification. We observe that the slowdown is very less as compared to the precise verification. However, the number of false alarms drastically increases as the number of threads increases in many of the benchmarks. As the size of the conflict graph increases, the chances of a spurious cycle due to overapproximation increases.

Both coarse and precise verification. Table 3 gives the results of running TRACER with both coarse and precise verification strategies. In this case, we get a larger slowdown than that achieved by running only the coarse verification strategy. However, we do not get any false alarms. Moreover, the slowdown observed is significantly less than running only the precise verification step (Table 1). For example, with 8 threads, the slowdown is at most 58x in the *Vacation* benchmark. With only the precise verification step, the slowdown is as high as 159x in the *Intruder* benchmark. Moreover, with 1 thread, as there are no cycles, the precise

Table 2. Average execution time (in seconds), slowdown, and number of false alarms per execution in TRACER without precise verification. The slowdown is with respect to the execution of the uninstrumented TL2 STM implementation.

Benchmark	1 thread	2 threads	4 threads	8 threads
Bayes	3.431 (1.01x)	3.62 (1.01x)	3.68 (1.04x)	3.70 (1.06x)
	0	9	11	12
Genome	3.821 (2.46x)	5.274 (6.27x)	6.67 (12.41x)	17.97 (34.71x)
	0	3549	4812	7207
Intruder	0.79 (3.5x)	1.70 (6.64x)	5.72 (18.81x)	16.39 (50.19x)
	0	9341	10256	10482
Kmeans	0.848 (3.2x)	1.751 (6.21x)	4.341 (18.82x)	11.11 (34.91x)
	0	12623	28843	30347
Labyrinth	0.282 (1.13x)	0.169 (1.13x)	0.109 (1.07x)	0.102 (1.12x)
	0	1	3	5
SSCA2	27.732 (1.21x)	19.98 (1.35x)	16.06 (1.38x)	22.67 (2.50x)
	0	1327	3681	12148
Vacation	1.06 (2.41x)	1.54 (6.98x)	2.46 (18.92x)	8.378 (53.7x)
	0	1742	2319	4026
Yada	1.311 (1.43x)	2.447 (2.98x)	5.354 (9.45x)	10.881 (17.38x)
	0	4281	9122	14253

Table 3. Average execution time (in seconds) and slowdown in TRACER with both coarse and precise verification turned on. The slowdown is with respect to the execution on the uninstrumented TL2 STM implementation.

Benchmark	1 thread	2 threads	4 threads	8 threads
Bayes	3.433 (1.01x)	3.63 (1.01 x)	3.69 (1.04 x)	3.70 (1.06 x)
Genome	3.868 (2.49x)	8.2 (9.75x)	15.1 (28.1x)	26.56 (51.3x)
Intruder	0.81 (3.6x)	2.59 (10.23x)	6.12 (20.05x)	15.67 (47.9x)
Kmeans	0.846 (3.2x)	4.031 (14.3x)	7.75 (33.6x)	13.78 (43.3x)
Labyrinth	0.283 (1.13x)	0.171 (1.14x)	0.112 (1.09x)	0.103 (1.12x)
SSCA2	27.732 (1.21x)	20.12 (1.36x)	16.975 (1.45x)	23.92 (2.64x)
Vacation	1.06 (2.41x)	1.79 (8.12x)	2.75 (21.17x)	9.12 (58.5x)
Yada	1.312 (1.43x)	3.89 (4.73x)	7.871 (13.9x)	15.21 (24.3x)

verification step is never triggered and the slowdown due to instrumentation is exactly same as the one obtained in the coarse verification step.

Analysis and Discussion. We observe that combining the coarse and the precise analyses yields results closer to the only-coarse analysis as compared to the only-precise analysis. The large part of the overhead is due to the acquisition and release of the global lock for every instrumentation. To justify this, we measured the time of instrumentation after turning off both the coarse and precise verification (and just storing the sequence of operations). The time is nearly the same as that for the coarse verification. Basically, STM implementations are designed to be highly efficient, and their performance increases almost linearly with the number of processors available. However, any online runtime verification would need to sequence the order of operations, which requires certain synchronization for every transaction access. As the number of threads increases, the penalty of synchronization increases. Moreover, the size of the conflict graph increases with the number of threads. This makes the performance of TRACER deteriorate as compared to the uninstrumented STM implementation when the number of threads increases.

6   Related Work

Several dynamic tools [7,10,21] for verifying race freedom in concurrent programs have been built. These tools cannot be directly used to verify STM implementations as STMs often contain data races for reasons of performance. Tools [8,9,11] for detecting atomicity violations in multithreaded programs have been developed. These tools can indeed be adapted to prove atomicity of transactions in STM implementations. However, the performance of these tools is not known under STM benchmarks, which generally consist of large access sets and millions of transactions per execution.

Manovit et al. [19] used testing to find errors in STM implementations. Their approach is more suited for offline verification of STM implementations. Runtime verification for serializability of transactional memories based on conflict graphs has been done by Chen et al. [3]. This work uses hardware support to reduce the overhead of instrumentation. On the other hand, we provide an online runtime verification tool that relies on multiple levels of verification to provide efficiency.

There is considerable amount of work on static verification of STM algorithms. Tasiran [24] verified the correctness of the Bartok STM. The author manually proves the correctness of the Bartok STM algorithm, and uses assertions in the Bartok STM implementation to ensure that the implementation refines the algorithm. Cohen et al. [5] model checked STM applied to programs with a small number of threads and variables, against the strong correctness property of Scott [22]. Guerraoui et al. [12,13] used model checking to verify the correctness of STM algorithms. They also check the correctness of STM algorithms under relaxed memory models [14]. However, due to state space explosion with model checking, their verification techniques cannot be easily extended to STM implementations.

7   Conclusion

We presented a framework to verify STM implementations with respect to different correctness properties like serializability, strict serializability, and opacity.

Our framework can be extended to other correctness properties that can be expressed in terms of cycles in a conflict graph. We developed and implemented TRACER, an efficient tool for sound and complete verification of STM implementations. TRACER combines a fast, coarse analysis with a precise analysis to verify executions of STM implementations at run-time. On average, TRACER has an overhead of around 25x for the STAMP benchmarks.

We believe that there is a lot of room for improvement in the performance that we obtain. As TRACER freezes the execution of all threads on every transactional memory access, TRACER has higher overhead when the number of threads is large. We target performance obtained by dynamic tools for data race detection and atomicity violations [11,10], which achieve complete verification with slowdown of 10x. In future work, we shall explore techniques for more efficient instrumentation. For example, we plan to use more sophisticated locking techniques for updating the transactional access sets. Also, we plan to study inexpensive algorithms for sound but incomplete updates to the conflict graphs and cycle detection.

References

1. Bloom, B.H.: Space/time trade-offs in hash coding with allowable errors. Communications of the ACM 13(7), 422–426 (1970)
2. Minh, C.C., Chung, J., Kozyrakis, C., Olukotun, K.: STAMP: Stanford transactional applications for multi-processing. In: Proceedings of The IEEE International Symposium on Workload Characterization (September 2008)
3. Chen, K., Malik, S., Patra, P.: Runtime validation of transactional memory systems. In: International Symposium on Quality Electronic Design, pp. 750–756 (2008)
4. Cohen, A., O'Leary, J., Pnueli, A., Tuttle, M.R., Zuck, L.: Verifying correctness of transactional memories. In: International Conference on Fomal Methods in Computer Aided Design, pp. 37–44. IEEE Computer Society, Los Alamitos (2007)
5. Cohen, A., Pnueli, A., Zuck, L.D.: Mechanical verification of transactional memories with non-transactional memory accesses. In: Gupta, A., Malik, S. (eds.) CAV 2008. LNCS, vol. 5123, pp. 121–134. Springer, Heidelberg (2008)
6. Dice, D., Shalev, O., Shavit, N.N.: Transactional locking II. In: Dolev, S. (ed.) DISC 2006. LNCS, vol. 4167, pp. 194–208. Springer, Heidelberg (2006)
7. Elmas, T., Qadeer, S., Tasiran, S.: Goldilocks: A race and transaction-aware java runtime. In: ACM SIGPLAN Conference on Programming Language Design and Implementation, pp. 245–255 (2007)
8. Farzan, A., Madhusudan, P.: Monitoring atomicity in concurrent programs. In: Gupta, A., Malik, S. (eds.) CAV 2008. LNCS, vol. 5123, pp. 52–65. Springer, Heidelberg (2008)
9. Flanagan, C., Freund, S.N.: Atomizer: A dynamic atomicity checker for multithreaded programs. In: ACM SIGPLAN Symposium on Principles of Programming Languages, pp. 256–267 (2004)
10. Flanagan, C., Freund, S.N.: FastTrack: Efficient and precise dynamic race detection. In: ACM SIGPLAN Conference on Programming Language Design and Implementation, pp. 121–133 (2009)

11. Flanagan, C., Freund, S.N., Yi, J.: Velodrome: A sound and complete dynamic atomicity checker for multithreaded programs. In: ACM SIGPLAN Conference on Programming Language Design and Implementation, pp. 293–303 (2008)

12. Guerraoui, R., Henzinger, T.A., Jobstmann, B., Singh, V.: Model checking transactional memories. In: ACM SIGPLAN Conference on Programming Language Design and Implementation, pp. 372–382. ACM, New York (2008)

13. Guerraoui, R., Henzinger, T.A., Singh, V.: Nondeterminism and completeness in model checking transactional memories. In: Palamidessi, C. (ed.) CONCUR 2000. LNCS, vol. 1877, pp. 21–35. Springer, Heidelberg (2000)

14. Guerraoui, R., Henzinger, T.A., Singh, V.: Software transactional memory on relaxed memory models. In: Bouajjani, A., Maler, O. (eds.) CAV 2009. LNCS, vol. 5643, pp. 321–336. Springer, Heidelberg (2009)

15. Guerraoui, R., Kapałka, M.: On the correctness of transactional memory. In: ACM SIGPLAN Symposium on Principles and Practice of Parallel Programming, pp. 175–184. ACM, New York (2008)

16. Hadzilacos, T., Yannakakis, M.: Deleting completed transactions. In: ACM SIGACT-SIGMOD Symposium on Principles of Database Systems, pp. 43–46 (1986)

17. Herlihy, M., Luchangco, V., Moir, M., Scherer, W.N.: Software transactional memory for dynamic-sized data structures. In: ACM SIGACT-SIGOPS Symposium on Principles of Distributed Computing, pp. 92–101. ACM, New York (2003)

18. Herlihy, M., Moss, J.E.B.: Transactional memory: Architectural support for lock-free data structures. In: International Symposium on Computer Architecture, pp. 289–300. ACM, New York (1993)

19. Manovit, C., Hangal, S., Chafi, H., McDonald, A., Kozyrakis, C., Olukotun, K.: Testing implementations of transactional memory. In: International Conference on Parallel Architectures and Compilation Techniques, pp. 134–143 (2006)

20. Papadimitriou, C.H.: The serializability of concurrent database updates. Journal of the ACM 26(4) (1979)

21. Savage, S., Burrows, M., Nelson, G., Sobalvarro, P., Anderson, T.E.: Eraser: A dynamic data race detector for multithreaded programs. ACM Trans. Comput. Syst. 15(4), 391–411 (1997)

22. Scott, M.L.: Sequential specification of transactional memory semantics. In: ACM SIGPLAN Workshop on Transactional Computing (2006)

23. Shavit, N., Touitou, D.: Software transactional memory. In: ACM SIGACT-SIGOPS Symposium on Principles of Distributed Computing, pp. 204–213. ACM, New York (1995)

24. Tasiran, S.: A compositional method for verifying software transactional memory implementations. Technical Report MSR-TR-2008-56, Microsoft Research (2008)

Optimized Temporal Monitors for SystemC*

Deian Tabakov and Moshe Y. Vardi

Rice University,
6100 Main Str. MS-132,
Houston, TX 77005, USA
{dtabakov,vardi}@rice.edu

Abstract. SystemC is a modeling language built as an extension of
C++. Its growing popularity and the increasing complexity of designs
have motivated research efforts aimed at the verification of SystemC
models using assertion-based verification (ABV), where the designer asserts properties that capture the design intent in a formal language such
as PSL or SVA. The model then can be verified against the properties
using runtime or formal verification techniques. In this paper we focus
on automated generation of runtime monitors from temporal properties.
Our focus is on minimizing runtime overhead, rather than monitor size or
monitor-generation time. We identify four issues in monitor generation:
state minimization, alphabet representation, alphabet minimization, and
monitor encoding. We conduct extensive experimentation on a synthetic
workload and identify a configuration that offers the best performance
in terms of runtime overhead.

1   Introduction

SystemC (IEEE Standard 1666-2005) is a system modeling language built as an
extension of C++, providing libraries for modeling and simulation of systems
on chip. It leverages the object-oriented encapsulation and inheritance mechanisms of C++ to allow for modular designs and IP transfer/reuse [1]. Various
libraries provide further functionality, for example, SystemC's Transaction-Level
Modeling (TLM) library defines structures and protocols that streamline the
development of high-level models. Thanks to its open-source license, actively
involved community, and wide industrial adoption, SystemC has become a *de
facto* standard modeling language, within a decade after its first release.

The growing popularity of SystemC and the increasing complexity of designs
have motivated research efforts aimed at the verification of SystemC models
using *assertion-based verification* (ABV) – an essential method for validation of
hardware-software models [2]. With ABV, the designer asserts properties that
capture design intent in a formal language, e.g., PSL[1] [3] or SVA[2] [4]. The

---

* For   a   longer   version   of   this   paper,   as   well   as   source   code,   see
http://www.cs.rice.edu/~vardi/papers. Work supported in part by NSF
grants CCF-0613889, and CCF-0728882, BSF grant 9800096, and a gift from Intel.
[1] *Property Specification Language*, IEEE Standard 1850-2007.
[2] *SystemVerilog Assertions*, IEEE Standard 1800-2005.

G. Roşu et al. (Eds.): RV 2010, LNCS 6418, pp. 436–451, 2010.

model then is verified against the properties using runtime verification or formal verification techniques.

Most ABV efforts for SystemC focus on *runtime verification* (also called *dynamic verification, testing,* and *simulation*). This approach involves executing the model under verification (MUV) in some environment, while running monitors in parallel with the model. The monitors observe the inputs to the MUV and ensure that the behavior or the output is consistent with the asserted properties [1]. The complementary approach of *formal verification* attempts to produce a mathematical proof that the MUV satisfies the asserted properties. Our focus in this paper is on runtime verification.

A successful ABV solution requires two components: a formal declarative language for expressing properties, and a mechanism for checking that the MUV satisfies the properties. There have been several attempts to develop a formal declarative language for expressing temporal SystemC properties by adapting existing languages (see [5] for a detailed discussion). Tabakov et al. [5] argued that standard temporal property languages such as PSL and SVA are adequate to express temporal properties of SystemC models, after extending them with a rich layer of Boolean assertions that capture the event-based semantics of SystemC, which, together with existing clock-sampling mechanisms in PSL and SVA, enables specification of properties at different levels of abstraction. Tabakov and Vardi then showed [6] how a nominal change of the SystemC kernel enables monitoring temporal assertions expressed in the framework of [5] with overhead of about 0.05% – 1% per monitor (note that [6] used hand-generated monitors, while this work focuses on automatically generated monitors).

The second component needed for assertion-based verification, a mechanism for checking that the MUV satisfies the asserted properties, requires a method for generating runtime monitors from formal properties. For simple properties it may be feasible to write the monitors manually (c.f., [7]); however, in most industrial workflows, writing and maintaining monitors manually would be an extremely high-cost, labor-intensive, and error-prone process [8]. This has inspired both academia and industry to search for methods for automated generation of monitors from temporal properties.

Formal, automata-theoretic foundations for monitor generation for temporal properties have been laid out in [9], which showed how a deterministic finite word automaton (DFW) can be generated from a temporal property such that the automaton accepts the finite traces that violate the property. Many works have elaborated on that approach, cf. [10, 11, 12, 13, 14, 15]); see the discussion below of related work. Many of these works, e.g. [10], handle only safety properties, which are properties whose failure is always witnessed by a finite trace. Here, as in [12], we follow the framework of [9] in its full generality and we consider all properties whose failure may be witnessed by a finite trace. For example, the failure of the property "eventually q" can never be witnessed by a finite trace, but the failure of the property "always p and eventually q" may be witnessed by a finite trace.

Apriori it is not clear how monitor size is related to performance, and most works on this subject have focused on underlying algorithmics or heuristics to generate smaller monitors or on fast monitor generation. This paper is an attempt to shift the focus toward optimizing runtime overhead that monitor execution adds to simulation time. We believe that this reflects more accurately the priorities of the industrial applications of monitors [10]. A large model may be accompanied by thousands of monitors, most of which are compiled once and executed many times, so lower runtime overhead is a crucial optimization criterion, much more than monitor size or monitor-generation time. In this paper we identify several algorithmic choices that need to be made when generating temporal monitors for monitoring frameworks implemented in software. We conduct extensive experimentation to identify the choices that lead to superior performance on a synthetic SystemC loads.

We identify four issues in monitor generation: *state minimization*, should nondeterministic automata be determinized online or offline; *alphabet representation*, should alphabet letters be represented explicitly or symbolically; *alphabet minimization*, should inconsistent alphabet letters be eliminated; and *monitor encoding*, how should the transition function of the monitor be expressed. These options give us a *configuration space* of 27 different ways of generating a monitor from nondeterministic automata.

Lacking an extensive benchmark suite of SystemC models and temporal properties, we evaluate performance on a synthetic workload. We use a model representing an adder [6]. Its advantages are that it is scalable and creates events at many different level of abstractions. For temporal properties we use linear temporal formulas. We use a mixture of pattern and random formulas, giving us a collection of over 1,300 temporal properties. Our experiments identify a specific configuration that offers the best performance in terms of runtime overhead.

2 Related Work

Most related papers that deal with monitoring focus on simplifying the monitor or reducing the number of states. Using smaller monitors is important for in-circuit monitoring, say, for post-silicon verification [16], but for pre-silicon verification, using lower-overhead monitors is more important. Very few prior works focus on minimizing runtime overhead.

Several papers focus on building monitors for *informative prefixes*, which are prefixes that violate input assertions in an "informative way." Kupferman and Vardi [9] define informative prefixes and show how to use alternating automata to construct nondeterministic finite word automata (NFW) of size $2^{O(\psi)}$ that accept informative prefixes of ψ. Kupferman and Lampert [17] use a related idea to construct NFW automata of size $2^{O(\psi)}$ that accept at least one prefix of every trace that violates a safety property ψ. Two constructions that build monitors for informative prefixes are by Geilen [14] and by Finkbeiner and Sipma [13]. Neither provide experimental results. Armoni et al. [10] describe an implementation based on [9] in the context of hardware verification. Their experimental results focus on both monitor size and runtime overhead. They showed that the overhead is significantly lower than that of commercial simulators. Stolz and Bodden [18] use monitors constructed from alternating automata to check specifications of Java programs, but do not give experimental results.

Morin-Allory and Borione [19] show how to construct hardware modules implementing monitors for properties expressed using the *simple subset* of PSL. Pierre and Ferro [20] describe an implementation based on this construction, and present some experimental results that show runtime overhead, but do not present any attempts to minimize it. Boulé and Zilic [16] show a rewriting-based technique for constructing monitors for the simple subset of PSL. They provide substantial experimental results, but focus on the monitor size and not on runtime overhead.

D'Amorim and Roşu [12] show how to construct monitors for *minimal bad prefixes* of temporal properties without any restrictions whether the property is a safety property or not. They construct a nondeterministic finite automaton of size $2^{O(\psi)}$ that extracts the safety content from ψ, and simulate a deterministic monitor on the fly. They present two optimizations: one reduces the size of the automaton, while the other searches for a good ordering of the outgoing transitions so that the overall expected cost of running the monitor would be smallest. They measure experimentally the size of the monitors for a few properties, but do not measure their runtime performance. A similar construction, but without any of the optimizations, is also described by Bauer et al. [11].

3   Theoretical Background

Let AP be a finite set of atomic propositions and let $\Sigma = 2^{AP}$ be a finite alphabet. Given a temporal specification ψ, we denote the set of models of the specification with $\mathcal{L}(\psi) = \{w \in \Sigma^\omega \mid w \models \psi\}$. Let $u \in \Sigma^*$ denote a finite word. We say that u is a *bad prefix* for $\mathcal{L}(\psi)$ iff $\forall \sigma \in \Sigma^\omega : u\sigma \notin \mathcal{L}(\psi)$ [9]. Intuitively, a bad prefix cannot be extended to an infinite word in $\mathcal{L}(\psi)$. A *minimal bad prefix* does not have a bad prefix as a strict prefix.

A *nondeterministic Büchi automaton* (NBW) is a tuple $\mathcal{A} = \langle \Sigma, Q, \delta, Q^0, F \rangle$, where Σ is a finite alphabet, $Q \neq \emptyset$ is a finite set of states, $\delta : Q \times \Sigma \to 2^Q$ is a transition function, $Q^0 \subseteq Q$ is a set of initial states, and $F \subseteq Q$ is a set of accepting states. If $q' \in \delta(q, \sigma)$ then we say that we have a transition from q to q' labeled by σ. We extend the transition function $\delta : Q \times \Sigma \to 2^Q$ in the usual way to $\delta : 2^Q \times \Sigma^* \to 2^Q$. A *run* of $\mathcal{A}$ on a word $w = a_0 a_1 \ldots \in \Sigma^\omega$ is a sequence of states $q_0 q_1 \ldots$, such that $q_0 \in Q^0$ and $q_{i+1} \in \delta(q_i, a_i)$ for some $a_i \in \Sigma$. For a run r, let $Inf(r)$ denote the states visited infinitely often. A run r of $\mathcal{A}$ is called *accepting* iff $Inf(r) \cap F \neq \emptyset$. The word w is accepted by $\mathcal{A}$ if there is an accepting run of $\mathcal{A}$ on w. For a given Linear-Time Logic (LTL) or PSL/SVA formula ψ, we can construct an NBW that accepts precisely $\mathcal{L}(\psi)$ [21]. We used SPOT [22], an LTL-to-Büchi-automata tool, which is among the best available in terms of performance [23]. Using our framework for PSL or SVA would require an analogous translator.

A *nondeterministic automaton on finite words* (NFW) is a tuple $\mathcal{A} = \langle \Sigma, Q, \delta, Q^0, F \rangle$. An NFW can be determinized by applying the *subset construction*, yielding a *deterministic automaton on finite words* (DFW) $\mathcal{A}' = \langle \Sigma, 2^Q, \delta', \{Q^0\}, F' \rangle$, where $\delta'(S, a) = \bigcup_{s \in S} \delta(s, a)$ and $F' = \{S : S \cap F \neq \emptyset\}$. For a given NFW $\mathcal{A}$, there is a canonical minimal DFW that accepts $\mathcal{L}(\mathcal{A})$ [24]. In the remainder of this paper, given an LTL formula ψ, we use $\mathcal{A}_{NBW}(\psi)$ to mean an NBW that accepts $\mathcal{L}(\psi)$, and $\mathcal{A}_{NFW}(\psi)$ (respectively, $\mathcal{A}_{DFW}(\psi)$) to mean a an NFW (respectively, DFW) that rejects (respectively, accepts) the minimal bad prefixes of $\mathcal{L}(\psi)$.

Building a monitor for a property ψ requires building $\mathcal{A}_{DFW}(\psi)$. Our work is based on the construction by d'Amorim and Roşu [12], which produces $\mathcal{A}_{NFW}(\psi)$. Their construction assumes an efficient algorithm for constructing $\mathcal{A}_{NBW}(\psi)$ (e.g., [22], when the specification is expressed in LTL, or [25], when the specification is in PSL). We sketch their construction and then we show how we construct $\mathcal{A}_{DFW}(\psi)$.

Given an NBW $\mathcal{A} = \langle \Sigma, Q, \delta, Q^0, F \rangle$ and a state $q \in Q$, define $\mathcal{A}^q = \langle \Sigma, Q, \delta, q, F \rangle$. Intuitively, $\mathcal{A}^q$ is the NBW automaton defined over the structure of $\mathcal{A}$ but replacing the set initial states with $\{q\}$. Let $empty(\mathcal{A}) \subseteq Q$ consist of all states $q \in Q$ such that $\mathcal{L}(\mathcal{A}^q) = \emptyset\}$, i.e., all states that cannot start an accepting run. The states in $empty(\mathcal{A})$ are "unnecessary" in $\mathcal{A}$ because they cannot appear on an accepting run. We can compute $empty(\mathcal{A})$ efficiently using nested depth-first search [26]. Deleting the states in $empty(\mathcal{A})$ is functionality available in SPOT.

To generate a monitor for ψ, d'Amorim and Roşu build $\mathcal{A}_{NBW}(\psi)$ and remove $empty(\mathcal{A}_{NBW}(\psi))$. They then treat the resulting automaton as an NFW, with all states taken to be accepting states. That is, the resulting NFW is $\mathcal{A} = \langle \Sigma, Q', \delta', Q^0 \cap Q', F \cap Q' \rangle$, where $Q' = Q - empty(\mathcal{A})$, and δ' is δ restricted to $Q' \times \Sigma$. When started with $\mathcal{A}_{NBW}(\psi)$, we call the resulting automaton $\mathcal{A}_{NFW}^{dR}(\psi)$.

Theorem 1. [12] $\mathcal{A}_{NFW}^{dR}(\psi)$ *rejects precisely the minimal bad prefixes of* ψ.

From now on we refer to $\mathcal{A}_{NFW}^{dR}(\psi)$ simply as $\mathcal{A}_{NFW}(\psi)$. $\mathcal{A}_{NFW}(\psi)$ is not useful as a monitor because of its nondeterminism. d'Amorim and Roşu describe how to use $\mathcal{A}_{NFW}(\psi)$ to simulate a deterministic monitor. Their description is in terms of nondeterministic multi-transitions and binary transition trees [12]. Instead of introducing these formalisms, here we use instead the approach in [10,27], which presents the same concept in automata-theoretic terms. The idea in both papers is to represent $\mathcal{A}_{DFW}(\psi)$ symbolically, and perform the subset construction on the fly, as we read the inputs from the trace. Given $\mathcal{A}_{NFW}(\psi) = \langle \Sigma, Q, \delta, Q^0, Q \rangle$ and a finite trace $a_0, \ldots, a_{n-1}$, we construct a run $P_0, \ldots, P_n$ of $\mathcal{A}_{DFW}(\psi)$ as follows: $P_0 = \{Q^0\}$ and $P_{i+1} = \bigcup_{s \in P_i} \delta(s, a_i)$. The run is accepting iff $P_i = \emptyset$ for some $i \geq 0$, which means that we have read a bad prefix. Notice that each P_i is of size linear in the size of $\mathcal{A}_{NFW}(\psi)$, thus we have avoided the exponential blowup of the determinization construction, with the price of having to compute transitions on the fly [10,27].

Another way of constructing a monitor from $\mathcal{A}_{NFW}(\psi)$ is to determinize it explicitly using the subset construction. In the worst case the resulting $\mathcal{A}_{DFW}(\psi)$ is of size exponential of the size of $\mathcal{A}_{NFW}(\psi)$, which is why explicit determinization has rarely been used. We note, however, that we can minimize $\mathcal{A}_{DFW}(\psi)$, getting a minimal DFW. (If the minimal DFW has a single state, then either the property is not satisfiable, or it can never have a bad prefix.) It is not clear, *a priori*, what impact this determinization and minimization will have on runtime overhead.

4   Monitor Generation

We now describe various issues that arise when constructing $\mathcal{A}_{DFW}(\psi)$.

STATE MINIMIZATION. As noted above, we can describe $\mathcal{A}_{DFW}(\psi)$ symbolically. We discuss in detail below how to express $\mathcal{A}_{DFW}(\psi)$ as a collection of C++ expressions. The alternative is to feed $\mathcal{A}_{NFW}(\psi)$ into a tool that constructs a minimal equivalent $\mathcal{A}_{DFW}(\psi)$. Here we use the `BRICS Automaton` tool [28]. Clearly, determinization and minimization, as well as subsequent C++ compilation, may incur a nontrivial computational cost. Still such a cost might be justifiable if the result is reduced *runtime* overhead, as assertions have to be compiled only once, but then run many times. A key question we want to answer is whether it is worthwhile to determinize $\mathcal{A}_{NFW}(\psi)$ explicitly, rather than on the fly.

ALPHABET REPRESENTATION. In our formalism, the alphabet Σ of $\mathcal{A}_{NFW}(\psi)$ is $\Sigma = 2^{AP}$, where AP is the set of atomic propositions appearing in ψ. In practice, tools that generate $\mathcal{A}_{NBW}(\psi)$ (SPOT in our case) often use $\mathcal{B}(AP)$, the set of Boolean formulas over AP, as the automaton alphabet: a transition from state q to state q' labeled by the formula θ is a shortcut to denote all transitions from q to q' labeled by $\sigma \in 2^{AP}$, when σ satisfies θ. When representing $\mathcal{A}_{DFW}(\psi)$ symbolically, we can use formulas as letters. Automata-theoretic algorithms for determinization and minimization of NFWs, however, require comparing elements of Σ, which makes it impractical to use Boolean formulas for letters. We need a different way, therefore, to describe our alphabet. `BRICS Automaton` represents the alphabet of the automaton as Unicode characters, which have 1-to-1 correspondence to the set of 16-bit integers. Below we show two ways to describe the alphabet of $\mathcal{A}_{NFW}(\psi)$ in terms of 16-bit integers.

The explicit approach is to represent Boolean formulas in terms of their satisfying truth *assignments*. Let $AP = \{p_1, p_2, \ldots, p_n\}$ and let $\mathcal{F}(p_1, p_2, \ldots, p_n)$ be a Boolean function. An *assignment* to AP is an n-bit vector $\mathbf{a} = [a_1, a_2, \ldots, a_n]$. An assignment $\mathbf{a}$ *satisfies* $\mathcal{F}$ iff $\mathcal{F}(a_1, a_2, \ldots, a_n)$ evaluates to 1. Let A^n be the set of all n-bit vectors and let $I : A^n \rightarrow \mathbb{Z}_+$ return the integer whose binary representation is $\mathbf{a}$, i.e., $I(a) = a_1 2^{n-1} + a_2 2^{n-2} + \ldots + a_n 2^0$. We define $sat(\mathcal{F}) = \{I(a) : a \text{ satisfies } \mathcal{F}\}$. Thus, the explicit representation of the automaton $\mathcal{A}_{NFW}(\psi) = \langle \mathcal{B}(AP), Q, \delta, Q^0, F \rangle$ is $\mathcal{A}_{NFW}^{ass}(\psi) = \langle \{0, \ldots, 2^n - 1\}, Q, \delta_{ass}, Q^0, F \rangle$, where $q' \in \delta_{ass}(q, z)$ IFF $q' \in \delta(q, \sigma)$ and $z \in sat(\sigma)$.

The symbolic approach to alphabet representation leverages the fact that Ordered Binary Decision Diagrams (*BDDs*) [29] provide canonical representation of Boolean functions. A BDD is a rooted, directed acyclic graph with one or two terminal nodes labeled **0** or **1**, and a set of variable nodes of out-degree two. The variables respect a given linear order on all paths from the root to a leaf. Each path represents an assignment to each of the variables on the path. For a fixed variable order, two BDDs are the same iff the Boolean formulas they represent are the same. The symbolic approach enumerates all Boolean formulas that appear as transition labels in $\mathcal{A}_{NFW}(\psi)$ using their BDD representation (in our case, such representation is computed by SPOT), and assigns each unique formula a unique integer. We thus obtain $\mathcal{A}_{NFW}^{bdd}(\psi)$ by replacing transitions labeled by Boolean formulas with transitions labeled by the corresponding integers. While the size of $\mathcal{B}(AP)$ is doubly exponential in $|AP|$, the automaton $\mathcal{A}_{NBW}(\psi)$ is exponential in $|\psi|$, so the number of Boolean formulas used in the automaton is at most exponential in $|\psi|$.

Here we provide both $\mathcal{A}_{NFW}^{ass}(\psi)$ and $\mathcal{A}_{NFW}^{bdd}(\psi)$ as inputs to BRICS Automaton, producing, respectively, minimized $\mathcal{A}_{DFW}^{ass}(\psi)$ and $\mathcal{A}_{DFW}^{bdd}(\psi)$. We note that neither of these two approaches is *a priori* a better choice. LTL–to–automata tools use Boolean formulas rather than assignments to reduce the number of transitions in the generated *nondeterministic* automata, but when using $\mathcal{A}_{DFW}^{bdd}(\psi)$ as a monitor, the trace we monitor is a sequence of truth assignments, and $\mathcal{A}_{DFW}^{bdd}(\psi)$ is not deterministic with respect to truth assignments.

ALPHABET MINIMIZATION. While propositional temporal specification languages are based on Boolean atomic propositions, they are often used to specify properties involving non-Boolean variables. For example, we may have the atomic propositions a==0, a==1, and a>1 in a specification involving the values of a variable int a. This means that not all assignments in 2^{AP} are consistent. For example, the assignment (a==0) && (a==1) is not consistent. By eliminate inconsistent assignments we may be able to reduce the number of letters in the alphabet exponentially. Identifying inconsistent assignments requires calling an SMT (Satisfiability-Modulo-Theory) solver [30]. Here we would need an SMT solver that can handle arbitrary C++ expressions of type bool. Not having access to such an SMT solver, we used the compiler as an improvised SMT solver.

A set of techniques called *constant folding* allow compilers to reduce constant expressions to a single value at compile time (see, e.g., [31]). When an expression contains variables instead of constants, the compiler uses *constant propagation* to substitute values of variables in subsequent subexpressions involving the variables. In some cases the compiler is able to deduce that an expression contains two mutually exclusive subexpressions, and issues a warning during compilation. We construct a function that uses conjunctions of atomic propositions as conditionals for dummy if/then expressions, and compile the function (we use gcc 4.0.3). To gauge the effectiveness of this optimization we apply it using two sets of conjunctions. *Full alphabet minimization* uses all possible conjunctions involving propositions or their negations, while *partial alphabet minimization* uses only conjunctions that contain each atomic proposition, positively or negatively.

We compile the function and then parse the compiler warnings that identify inconsistent conjunctions. Prior to compiling the Büchi automaton we augment the original temporal formula to exclude those conjunctions from consideration. For example, if (a==0) && (a==1) is identified as an inconsistent conjunction, we augment the property ψ to $\psi \wedge \mathbf{G}(!((a == 0) \wedge (a == 1)))$.

MONITOR ENCODING. We describe five ways of encoding automata as C++ monitors. Not all can be used with all automata directly, so we identify the transformations that need to be applied to an automaton before each encoding can be used.

The strategy in all encodings is to construct the run $P_0, P_1, \ldots$ of the monitor using two bit-vectors of size $|Q|$: current[] and next[]. Initially next[] is zeroed, and current[j] = 1 iff $q_j \in Q^0$. Then, after sampling the state of the program, we set next[k] = 1 iff current[j] = 1 and if there is a transition from q_j to q_k that is enabled by the current program state. When we are done updating next[] we assign it to current[], zero next[], and then repeat the process at the next sample point. Intuitively, current[] keeps track of the set of automaton states that are reachable after seeing the execution trace so far, and next[] maintains the set of automaton states that are reachable after completing the current step of the automaton. The details of the way we update current[] and next[] are reflected in the different encodings.

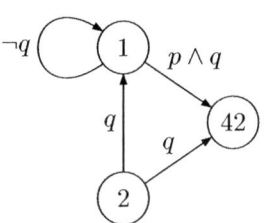

Fig. 1. A (nondeterministic) automaton with Boolean formula transitions

The two encodings front_nondet and back_nondet expect that the automaton transitions are Boolean formulas, and do not assume determinism. Thus, front_nondet and back_nondet can be used with $\mathcal{A}_{NFW}(\psi)$ directly. They can also be used with $\mathcal{A}_{DFW}^{ass}(\psi)$ and $\mathcal{A}_{DFW}^{bdd}(\psi)$, once we convert back the transition labels from integers to Boolean formulas as follows. In $\mathcal{A}_{DFW}^{ass}(\psi)$, we calculate the assignment corresponding to each integer, and use that assignment to generate a conjunction of atoms

```
if (current[1]) {
    if (p && q) {next[42] = 1;}
    if (!q) {next[1] = 1;}
}
if (current[2]) {
    if (q) {next[42] = 1;}
    if (q) {next[1] = 1}
}
```
        (a) front_nondet encoding

```
next[1] =(current[1] && !q) ||
         (current[2] && q);

next[42]=(current[1] && (p && q)) ||
         (current[2] && q);
```
        (b) back_nondet encoding

Fig. 2. Illustrating front_nondet and back_nondet encoding

or their negations. In $\mathcal{A}^{bdd}_{DFW}(\psi)$ we relabel each transition with the Boolean function whose BDD is represented by the integer label.

The front_nondet encoding uses an explicit if to check if each state s of current[] is enabled. For each outgoing transition t from s it then uses a nested if with a conditional that is a verbatim copy of the transition label of t to determine if the destination state of t is reachable from s. The back_nondet encoding uses a disjunction that represents all of the ways in which a state in next[] can be reached from the currently reachable states. Encoding the automaton in Fig. 1 is illustrated in Fig. 2.

The three encodings front_det_switch, front_det_ifelse, and back_det assume that the automaton is deterministic and that the transitions are integers corresponding to assignments. Thus, these three encodings can be used only with $\mathcal{A}^{ass}_{DFW}(\psi)$. At the beginning of each step of the automaton we use the state of the MUV (i.e., the values of all public and private variables) [5] to derive an assignment $\mathbf{a}$ to the atomic propositions in $AP(\psi)$. We then calculate an integer representing the relevant model state $mod\_st = I(\mathbf{a})$, where $\mathbf{a}$ is the current assignment, and use mod_st to drive the automaton transitions. The back_det encoding is similar to back_nondet in that it encodes the automaton transitions as a disjunction of the conditions that allow a state in next[] to be enabled. The difference is that here the transitions are driven by mod_st instead of Boolean functions. See Fig. 4 for an illustration of this encoding. The front_det_switch and front_det_ifelse encodings differ in the C++ constructs that we use to take advantage of the determinism in the automaton; see Fig. 5 for an illustration of the encodings of the automaton in Fig. 3.

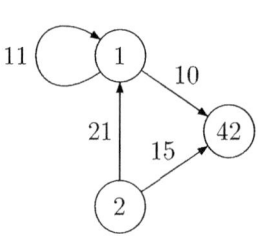

Fig. 3. A deterministic automaton with integer transitions

```
// Calculate the value of mod_st
int mod_st = 0;
mod_st += q ? 16 : 0;
mod_st += p ?  8 : 0; //...
next[1]  = (current[1] && (mod_st == 11) ||
           (current[2] && (mod_st == 21);
next[42] = (current[1] && (mod_st == 10)) ||
           (current[2] && (mod_st == 15));
```

Fig. 4. Illustrating back_det

CONFIGURATION SPACE. The different options give us 27 possible combinations for generating a monitor, summarized in Table 1.

```
// Calculate the value of mod_st          // Calculate the value of mod_st
int mod_st = 0;                           int mod_st = 0;
mod_st += q ? 16 : 0;                     mod_st += q ? 16 : 0;
mod_st += p ?  8 : 0; //...               mod_st += p ?  8 : 0; //...
if (current[1]) {                         if (current[1])
  if (mod_st==10) {next[42] = 1;}           switch(mod_st) {
  else if (mod_st==11) {next[1] = 1;}         case 10: next[42] = 1; break;
  else {error();}                             case 11: next[1] = 1; break;
}                                             default: error();
if (current[2]) {                           }
  if (mod_st==15) {next[42] = 1;}         if (current[2])
  else if (mod_st==21) {next[1] = 1;}       switch(mod_st) {
  else {error();}                             case 15: next[42] = 1; break;
}                                             case 21: next[1] = 1; break;
                                              default: error();
                                            }
```

(a) front_det_ifelse encoding   (b) front_det_switch encoding

Fig. 5. Illustrating front_det_ifelse and front_det_switch

Table 1. The configuration space for generating monitors

State Minimization	Alphabet Representation	Alphabet Minimization	Monitor Encoding
no	N/A		front_nondet
	BDDs	none	back_nondet
			front_nondet
		partial	back_nondet
yes	assignments		front_det_ifelse
		full	front_det_switch
			back_det

5   Experimental Issues

SYSTEMC MODEL: Our experimental evaluation is based on the Adder[3] model presented in [6]. The Adder implements a squaring function by using repeated incrementing by 1. We used the Adder to calculate 100^2 with 1,000 instances of a monitor for the same property. Since we are mostly concerned with monitor overhead, we focus on the time difference between executing the model with and without monitoring. We established a baseline for the model's runtime by compiling the Adder model with a virgin installation of SystemC (i.e., without the monitoring framework of [6]) and averaging the runtime over 10 executions. To calculate the monitor overhead we averaged the runtime of each simulation over 10 executions and subtracted the baseline time. Notice that the overhead

---

[3] Source code available at http://www.cs.rice.edu/∼vardi/memocode10.tar.bz2

as calculated includes the cost of the monitoring framework and the slow-down due to all 1,000 monitors.

PROPERTIES: We used specifications constructed using both pattern formulas and randomly generated formulas. We used LTL formulas, as we have access to explicit-state LTL-to-automata translators (SPOT, in our case), but the framework is applicable to any specification language that produces NBWs.

We adopted the pattern formulas used in [32] and presented below:

$$lu(n) := (\ldots(p_1\mathbf{U}p_2))\ldots\mathbf{U}p_n)\mathbf{U}p_{n+1} \qquad qq(n) := \bigwedge_{i=1}^{n}(\mathbf{F}p_i \vee \mathbf{G}p_{i+1})$$

$$ru(n) := p_1\mathbf{U}(p_2\mathbf{U}(\ldots(p_n\mathbf{U}p_{n+1})\ldots))$$

$$c1(n) := \bigvee_{i=1}^{n}\mathbf{GF}p_i \qquad rr(n) := \bigwedge_{i=1}^{n}(\mathbf{GF}p_i \vee \mathbf{FG}p_{i+1})$$

$$c2(n) := \bigwedge_{i=1}^{n}\mathbf{GF}p_i \qquad ss(n) := \bigvee_{i=1}^{n}\mathbf{G}p_i$$

In addition to these formulas we also used bounded $\mathbf{F}$ and bounded $\mathbf{G}$ formulas, and a new type of nested $\mathbf{U}$ formulas, presented below:

$$f1(n) := \mathbf{G}(p \rightarrow (q \vee \mathbf{X}q \vee \ldots \vee \mathbf{XX}\ldots\mathbf{X}q))$$

$$f2(n) := \mathbf{G}(p \rightarrow (q \vee \mathbf{X}(q \vee \mathbf{X}(q \vee \ldots \vee \mathbf{X}q)\ldots)))$$

$$g1(n) := \mathbf{G}(p \rightarrow (q \wedge \mathbf{X}q \wedge \ldots \wedge \mathbf{XX}\ldots\mathbf{X}q))$$

$$g2(n) := \mathbf{G}(p \rightarrow (q \wedge \mathbf{X}(q \wedge \mathbf{X}(q \wedge \ldots \wedge \mathbf{X}q)\ldots)))$$

$$uu(n) := \mathbf{G}(p_1 \rightarrow (p_1\mathbf{U}(p_2 \wedge p_2\mathbf{U}(p_3 \ldots (p_n \wedge p_n\mathbf{U}p_{n+1})))\ldots)$$

In our experiments we replaced the generic propositions p_i in each pattern formula with atomic formulas (a==100^2-100(n-i-1)), where a is a variable representing the running total in the Adder. Since most pattern formulas assert some form of eventuality, using such atomic propositions ensures that failure of the property cannot be detected until the last few cycles of the simulation. This forces the monitor to stay active during the entire duration of the simulation, which makes it easier to measure monitoring overhead. For each pattern we scaled up the formulas until all 27 configurations either timed out or crashed. Most configurations can be scaled up to $n = 5$, except for the bounded properties, which can be scaled to $n = 17$. We identified 127 pattern formulas for which at least one configuration could complete the monitoring task.

The random formulas that we used were generated following the framework of [33]. For each formula length there are two parameters that control the number of propositions used and the probability of selecting an $\mathbf{U}$ or a $\mathbf{V}$ operator (formula length is calculated by adding the number of atomic propositions, the number of logical connectives, and the number of temporal operators). We varied the number of atomic propositions between 1 and 5, the probability of selecting an $\mathbf{U}$ or a $\mathbf{V}$ was one of $\{0.1, 0.3, 0.7, 0.95\}$, and we varied the formula length from 5 to 30 in increments of 5. We used the same style of atomic propositions as in the pattern formulas. For each combination of parameters we generated 10 formulas at random, giving us a total of 1200 random formulas.

6 Results

We ran all experiments on Ada, Rice's Cray XD1 compute cluster.[4] Each of Ada's nodes has two dual core 2.2 GHz AMD Opteron 275 CPUs and 8GB of RAM. We ran with exclusive access to a node so all 8GB of RAM were available for use. We allowed 8 hours (maximal job time on Ada) of computation time per configuration per formula for generating Büchi automata, automata-theoretic transformations, generating C++ code, compilation, linking with the Adder model using the monitoring framework presented in [6], and executing the monitored model 10 times.

We first evaluate the individual effect of each optimization. For each formula we partition the configuration space into two groups: those configurations that use the optimization and those that do not. We form the Cartesian product of the overhead times from both groups and present them on a scatter plot.

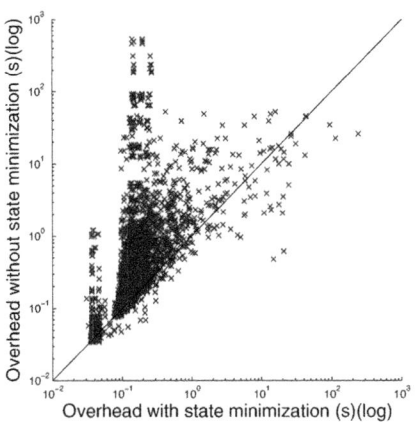

Fig. 6. Monitor overhead with and without state minimization. State minimization lower the overhead by orders of magnitude.

STATE MINIMIZATION. In Fig. 6 we show the effect of state minimization on the runtime overhead. A few outliers notwithstanding, using state minimization dramatically lowers the runtime overhead of the monitor. This result can be explained partly by the size of the automaton with and without optimization. For some formulas we see four orders of magnitude smaller automata. State minimization sometimes produces bigger automata, which is not surprising as nondeterministic automata can be exponentially more succinct than the equivalent minimal deterministic ones [24]. Our data show that when the minimized automaton ($\mathcal{A}^{bdd}_{DFW}(\psi)$ or $\mathcal{A}^{ass}_{DFW}(\psi)$) has more states than the unminimized automaton ($\mathcal{A}_{NFW}(\psi)$), generating a monitor

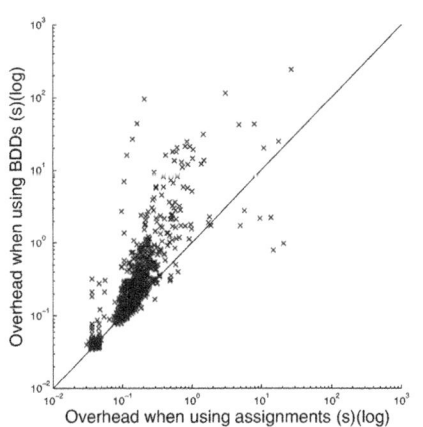

Fig. 7. Using assignments for alphabet representation leads to better performance than using BDDs

---

[4] rcsg.rice.edu/ada

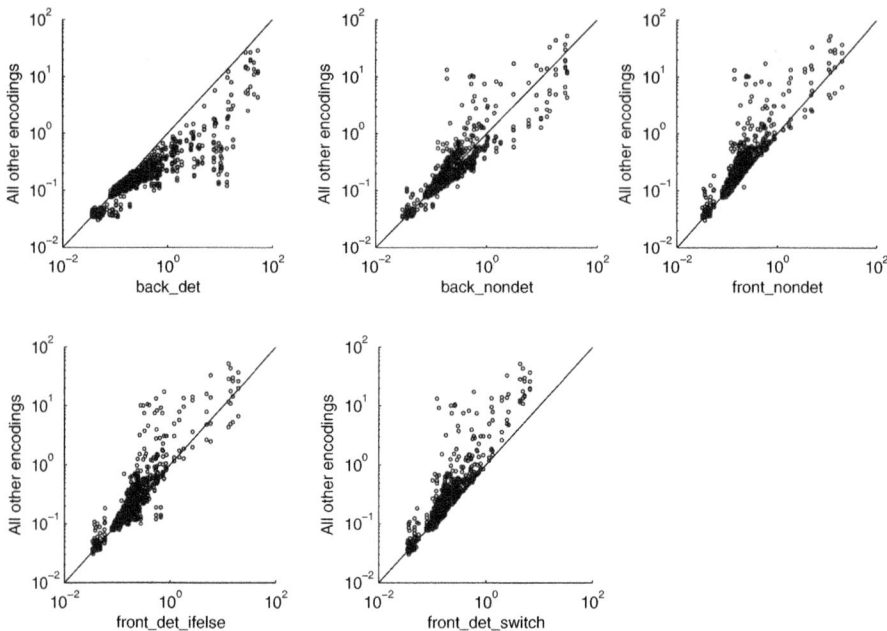

Fig. 8. Comparison of the monitor overhead when using different encodings. Each subplot shows the performance when using one of the encodings (x-axis) vs. all other encodings (y-axis).

using $\mathcal{A}_{NFW}(\psi)$ leads to smaller runtime overhead. This observation can be used as a heuristic.

ALPHABET REPRESENTATION. Fig. 7 shows that using assignments leads to better performance than BDD-based alphabet representation. Our data shows that in the vast majority of cases, using assignments leads to smaller automata, which again suggests a connection between monitor size and monitor efficiency.

ALPHABET MINIMIZATION. Our data shows that partial– and full– alphabet minimization typically slow down the monitor. We think that the reasons behind it are two-fold. On one hand, the performance of gcc as a decision engine to discover mutually exclusive conjunctions is not very good (in our experiments it was able to discover only 10%–15% of the possible mutually exclusive conjunctions). On the other hand, augmenting the formula increases the formula size, but SPOT cannot take advantage of the extra information in the formula and typically generates bigger Büchi automata. If we manually augment the formula with *all* mutually exclusive conjunctions we do see smaller Büchi automata, so we believe this optimization warrants further investigation.

MONITOR ENCODING. Finally, we compared the effect of the different monitor encodings (Fig. 8). Our conclusion is that no encoding dominates the others, but two (front_nondet and front_det_switch) show the best performance relative to all others (front_det_switch has a slight edge over front_nondet), and back_det has the worst performance.

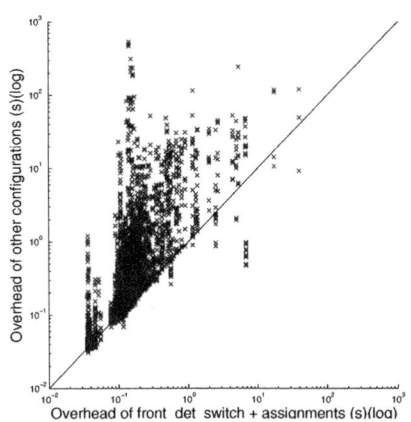

BEST CONFIGURATION: The final check of our conclusion is presented in Fig. 9, where we plot the performance of the winning configuration against all other configurations. There are a few outliers, but overall the configuration gives better performance than all others.

Based on the comparison of individual optimizations we conclude that front_det_switch encoding with assignment–based state minimization and no alphabet minimization is the best overallconfiguration.

Fig. 9. Best overall performance

7 Discussion

Together with the specification formalism proposed in [5], and the monitoring framework described in [6], this work provides a general ABV solution for temporal monitoring of SystemC models. We have identified a configuration that generates low-overhead monitors and we believe that it would serve as a good default setting. We note, however, that practical use of our tool may involve monitoring tasks that are different than the synthetic load that we used for our tests. Recent developments in the area of self-tuning systems show that even highly optimized tools can be improved by orders of magnitude using search techniques over the configuration space (c.f., [34]). Thus we have left the user full control over tool configuration.

Acknowledgment. We thank Kristin Y. Rozier for her code for generating the random formulas used in our experiments.

References

1. Grotker, T., Liao, S., Martin, G., Swan, S.: System Design with SystemC. Kluwer Academic Publishers, Norwell (2002)
2. Gupta, A.: Assertion-based verification turns the corner. IEEE Design and Test of Computers 19, 131–132 (2002)
3. Eisner, C., Fisman, D.: A Practical Introduction to PSL. Springer, New York (2006)

 4. Vijayaraghavan, S., Ramanathan, M.: A Practical Guide for SystemVerilog Assertions. Springer, New York (2005)
 5. Tabakov, D., Vardi, M., Kamhi, G., Singerman, E.: A temporal language for SystemC. In: FMCAD 2008: Proc. Int. Conf. on Formal Methods in Computer-Aided Design, pp. 1–9. IEEE Press, Los Alamitos (2008)
 6. Tabakov, D., Vardi, M.: Monitoring temporal SystemC properties. In: Proc. 8th Int'l Conf. on Formal Methods and Models for Codesign, pp. 123–132. IEEE, Los Alamitos (2010)
 7. Geist, D., Biran, G., Arons, T., Slavkin, M., Nustov, Y., Farkas, M., Holtz, K., Long, A., King, D., Barret, S.: A methodology for the verification of a "system on chip". In: Proc. 36th Design Automation Conference, DAC 1999, pp. 574–579. ACM, New York (1999)
 8. Abarbanel, Y., Beer, I., Gluhovsky, L., Keidar, S., Wolfsthal, Y.: Focs: Automatic generation of simulation checkers from formal specifications. In: Emerson, E.A., Sistla, A.P. (eds.) CAV 2000. LNCS, vol. 1855, pp. 538–542. Springer, Heidelberg (2000)
 9. Kupferman, O., Vardi, M.: Model checking of safety properties. Formal methods in System Design 19(3), 291–314 (2001)
10. Armoni, R., Korchemny, D., Tiemeyer, A., Vardi, M., Zbar, Y.: Deterministic dynamic monitors for linear-time assertions. In: Havelund, K., Núñez, M., Roşu, G., Wolff, B. (eds.) FATES 2006 and RV 2006. LNCS, vol. 4262, Springer, Heidelberg (2006)
11. Bauer, A., Leucker, M., Schallhart, C.: Monitoring of real-time properties. In: Arun-Kumar, S., Garg, N. (eds.) FSTTCS 2006. LNCS, vol. 4337, pp. 260–272. Springer, Heidelberg (2006)
12. D'Amorim, M., Roşu, G.: Efficient monitoring of ω-languages. In: Etessami, K., Rajamani, S.K. (eds.) CAV 2005. LNCS, vol. 3576, pp. 364–378. Springer, Heidelberg (2005)
13. Finkbeiner, B., Sipma, H.: Checking finite traces using alternating automata. Form. Methods Syst. Des. 24(2), 101–127 (2004)
14. Geilen, M.: On the construction of monitors for temporal logic properties. Electr. Notes Theor. Comput. Sci. 55(2) (2001)
15. Giannakopoulou, D., Havelund, K.: Automata-based verification of temporal properties on running programs. In: Int. conf. on Automated Software Engineering, Washington, DC, USA, p. 412. IEEE, Los Alamitos (2001)
16. Boulé, M., Zilic, Z.: Generating Hardware Assertion Checkers. Springer Publishing Company, Incorporated, Heidelberg (2008)
17. Kupferman, O., Lampert, R.: On the construction of fine automata for safety properties. In: Graf, S., Zhang, W. (eds.) ATVA 2006. LNCS, vol. 4218, pp. 110–124. Springer, Heidelberg (2006)
18. Stolz, V., Bodden, E.: Temporal assertions using AspectJ. Electron. Notes Theor. Comput. Sci. 144(4), 109–124 (2006)
19. Morin-Allory, K., Borrione, D.: Proven correct monitors from PSL specifications. In: DATE 2006: Proc. Conf. on Design, automation and test in Europe, European Design and Automation Association, pp. 1246–1251 (2006)
20. Pierre, L., Ferro, L.: A tractable and fast method for monitoring SystemC TLM specifications. IEEE Transactions on Computers 57, 1346–1356 (2008)
21. Vardi, M., Wolper, P.: Reasoning about infinite computations. Information and Computation 115(1), 1–37 (1994)

22. Duret-Lutz, A., Poitrenaud, D.: SPOT: An extensible model checking library using transition-based generalized Büchi automata. In: Modeling, Analysis, and Simulation of Computer Systems, pp. 76–83 (2004)
23. Rozier, K.Y., Vardi, M.Y.: LTL satisfiability checking. In: Bošnački, D., Edelkamp, S. (eds.) SPIN 2007. LNCS, vol. 4595, pp. 149–167. Springer, Heidelberg (2007)
24. Hopcroft, J., Ullman, J.: Introduction to Automata Theory, Languages, and Computation. Addison-Wesley, Reading (1979)
25. Bustan, D., Fisman, D., Havlicek, J.: Automata construction for PSL. Technical report, The Weizmann Institute of Science (2005)
26. Courcoubetis, C., Vardi, M., Wolper, P., Yannakakis, M.: Memory efficient algorithms for the verification of temporal properties. Formal Methods in System Design 1, 275–288 (1992)
27. Tabakov, D., Vardi, M.Y.: Experimental evaluation of classical automata constructions. In: Sutcliffe, G., Voronkov, A. (eds.) LPAR 2005. LNCS (LNAI), vol. 3835, pp. 396–411. Springer, Heidelberg (2005)
28. Møller, A.: dk.brics.automaton (2004), http://www.brics.dk/automaton/
29. Bryant, R.: Graph-based algorithms for Boolean-function manipulation. IEEE Trans. on Computers C-35(8) (1986)
30. de Moura, L.M., Bjørner, N.: Z3: An efficient SMT solver. In: Ramakrishnan, C.R., Rehof, J. (eds.) TACAS 2008. LNCS, vol. 4963, pp. 337–340. Springer, Heidelberg (2008)
31. Cooper, K.D., Torczon, L.: Engineering a Compiler. Morgan Kaufmann, San Francisco (2004)
32. Geldenhuys, J., Hansen, H.: Larger automata and less work for LTL model checking. In: Valmari, A. (ed.) SPIN 2006. LNCS, vol. 3925, pp. 53–70. Springer, Heidelberg (2006)
33. Daniele, M., Giunchiglia, F., Vardi, M.Y.: Improved automata generation for linear temporal logic. In: Halbwachs, N., Peled, D.A. (eds.) CAV 1999. LNCS, vol. 1633, pp. 249–260. Springer, Heidelberg (1999)
34. Hoos, H.H.: Computer-aided design of high-performance algorithms. Technical report, University of British Columbia (2008)

Runtime Verification of Stochastic, Faulty Systems

Cristina M. Wilcox and Brian C. Williams

Massachusetts Institute of Technology, Cambridge, MA, 02141, USA
cwilcox@alum.mit.edu, williams@csail.mit.edu
http://groups.csail.mit.edu/mers/

Abstract. We desire a capability for the lifelong verification of complex embedded systems that degrade over time, such as a semi-autonomous car. The field of runtime verification has developed many tools for monitoring the safety of software systems in real time. However, these tools do not allow for uncertainty in the system's state or failure, both of which are essential for monitoring hardware as it degrades. This work augments runtime verification with techniques from model-based estimation in order to provide a capability for monitoring the safety criteria of mixed hardware/software systems that is robust to uncertainty and hardware failure.

We begin by framing the problem as runtime verification of stochastic, faulty, hidden-state systems. We solve this problem by performing belief state estimation over the combined state of the Büchi automata representing the safety requirements and the probabilistic hierarchical constraint automata representing the embedded system. This method provides a clean framing of safety monitoring of mixed stochastic systems as an instance of Bayesian filtering.[1]

Keywords: stochastic systems, hidden state, belief state update.

1 Introduction

1.1 Runtime Verification for Faulty Embedded Systems

The field of runtime verification seeks to check software correctness at runtime. Runtime verification complements testing methods by providing a framework for automated testing that can be extended into a capability for monitoring a system post-deployment. With a runtime verification capability in place, an operational system can detect deviations from formally specified behavior and potentially take corrective action, providing a capability for fault-tolerance which is desirable for safety critical systems.

Runtime verification has also been used in complex *mixed systems*, that is, systems that involve a mix of hardware and software [10, 2]. However, runtime

---

[1] This research was supported in part by the Ford-MIT Alliance agreement of 2007, and by a grant from the Office of Naval Research through Johns Hopkins University, contract number 960101.

G. Roşu et al. (Eds.): RV 2010, LNCS 6418, pp. 452–459, 2010.

verification for such systems assumes observability of properties to be monitored. We argue that for complex hardware systems, such as a space probe or a car, the system's state is generally unobservable, due to the high cost of sensing all variables reliably. Hence, in order to perform safety monitoring of these mixed systems, this thesis extends proven runtime verification techniques so that they handle systems with hidden states.

To deal with hidden states, we draw upon inference techniques from the field of Model-based diagnosis (MBD) [14], which are based on a model of the system components and constraints. MBD applies conflict-directed search techniques in order to quickly enumerate system configurations, such as failure modes, that are consistent with the model and observations. These techniques are suitable for mixed systems and scale well to systems with large numbers of components [8,14].

A second issue, not directly addressed by runtime verification, is that complex systems with long life cycles experience performance degradation due to seemingly random hardware failure. Many systems function well when manufactured, but may become unsafe over time, especially when they are in use for longer than their intended life span. For example, car owners occasionally fail to have their vehicles inspected promptly, which can result in a component, such as the braking system, receiving more use than it was designed for. We want to be able to detect any breaches of safety due to wear and tear in such a situation.

Thus, this work advocates the use of a plant model that incorporates stochastic behavior [14], allowing wear and tear to be modeled as stochastic hardware failure. With such a model, specification violations resulting from performance degradation can be detected online and recovery action can be taken, such as the removal of unsafe functions.

1.2 Architecture of the Proposed Solution

We propose a capability for the monitoring of formal specifications for mixed systems that are written in Linear Temporal Logic (LTL) [11]. Linear Temporal Logic is a well studied logic that is similar to plain English and expressive enough to capture many important high-level safety requirements. Additionally, we allow requirements to be written over hidden system states.

Our safety monitoring capability will also have a model of the stochastic, faulty plant captured as a Probabilistic Hierarchical Constraint Automaton (PHCA) [14]. This automaton representation allows for the abstract specification of embedded software, as well as the specification of discrete hardware modes, including known failure modes. Additionally, stochastic transitions may be specified in order to model random hardware failure. Such a model of the system allows the safety monitoring capability to identify hidden system state, including in the case of sensor failure, unmodeled failures, intermittent failures, or multiple faults.

Given sensory information, the safety monitoring capability will then compute online the likelihood that the LTL safety requirements are being met. We accomplish this by framing the problem as an instance of belief state update over the combined state of the Büchi Automaton and Probabilistic Hierarchical Constraint Automaton, as described in Section 4.2.

Together, LTL and PHCA offer an orderly specification method for performing safety monitoring of mixed stochastic systems. Viewing safety monitoring as belief state update on a hybrid of BA and PHCA state provides a clean framing of the problem as an instance of Bayesian filtering.

1.3   Related Work

Some examples of the successful application of runtime verification techniques in software systems are JPaX, by Havelund and Roşu [6], DBRover, by Drusinsky [3], and MaC [7], by Kim *et al.* In this paper we build on such work by extending these techniques to deal with mixed stochastic systems.

Peters and Parnas [10], and Black [2] have developed monitors for runtime verification of systems that include hardware, but these works do not consider hidden state, which is the primary focus of this paper. Sistla and Srinivas [13], and Sammapun *et al.* [12] present sound monitoring algorithms for software systems exhibiting probabilistic behavior, but neither work is concerned with properties written over hidden system states, and thus their methods do not suffice for the purpose of safety monitoring of mixed systems.

Runtime verification has been moving towards the monitoring of general properties for mixed stochastic systems, but no work we are aware of has attempted to monitor properties written over unobservable system states. Additionally, no work has employed a system model appropriate for faulty hardware systems. The approach presented in this paper provides these novel capabilities.

2   Temporal Logic and Büchi Automata

2.1   Linear Temporal Logic

In this paper we consider safety requirements written in next-free Linear Temporal Logic (LTL) [11,5]. An LTL statement α may be comprised of propositions connected with the usual boolean operators ($\neg$, $\wedge$, $\vee$, $\rightarrow$), as well as the temporal operators always ($\square$), eventually ($\lozenge$), until ($\mathcal{U}$), and release ($\mathcal{R}$). These operators are formally defined as is usual in the literature.

2.2   LTL to NBA Conversion

In order to automate the monitoring of a Linear Temporal Logic statement Λ, it may be converted into a nondeterministic Büchi Automaton (NBA) and executed on the finite program trace W. To perform this conversion, we use the method specific to Büchi Automata on finite inputs described by Giannakopoulou and Havelund in [5], which is based on earlier work [4] on converting LTL to a form of Büchi Automaton for the purposes of model checking. This method results in NBA with finite-trace semantics.

2.3   Nondeterministic Büchi Automata

Nondeterministic Büchi Automata (NBA) extend nondeterministic finite automata (NFA) to operate on infinite-length words, allowing us to use a nondeterministic Büchi Automaton to represent the language of a Linear Temporal Logic statement [1].

A nondeterministic Büchi Automaton is a tuple $\langle Q, Q_0, F, \Sigma, T \rangle$, such that Q is a finite set of states, $Q_0 \subseteq Q$ is a set of start states, $F \subseteq Q$ is a set of accepting states, Σ is the input alphabet, and the transition function is $T : Q \times \Sigma \to 2^Q$.

We refer to Q hereafter as the *safety state* of the physical system. The alphabet Σ of a NBA consists of all possible physical configurations of the system. These NBA are modified from canonical NBA to accept finite traces.

2.4   Deterministic Büchi Automata

Runtime verification for stochastic systems as described in this paper requires a model of the safety requirements with a complete transition function, which a NBA does not guarantee. We obtain this function by converting the NBA of the safety requirements into a deterministic Büchi Automaton (DBA). A DBA is defined similarly to an NBA except that it may only have one start state $q_0 \in Q$, and the transition relation $T : Q \times \Sigma \to Q$ must be complete.

NBA on finite traces can be converted to an equivalent deterministic Büchi automaton without loss of expressiveness through subset or powerset construction. A method for doing so is described by Giannakopoulou in [5].

After conversion, a DBA contains a special state $q_\varnothing$ that denotes a violation of the safety requirements, and is the only non-SAFE state of the DBA.

3   The Probabilistic Hierarchical Constraint Automata Model

When safety properties are written over hidden system states, runtime verification of these properties requires a model of system behavior. We use the *Probabilistic Hierarchical Constraint Automaton* (PHCA) [14] formalism because it allows us to concisely and accurately model mixed hardware/software systems that degrade or fail, such as planetary rovers or cars. PHCA allow for probabilistic behavior, which is a reasonable model of random hardware failure.

PHCA are derived from HMMs. Like an HMM, a PHCA may have hidden states and transition probabilistically. Unlike an HMM, PHCA introduce the notion of constraints on states as well as a hierarchy of component automata. Systems are modeled as a set of individual PHCA components that communicate through shared variables. Discrete modes of operation representing nominal and faulty behavior are specified for each component. Components may transition between modes probabilistically or based on system commands. Additionally, modes and transitions may be constrained by the modes of other components.

For an example and more detail, the reader is referred to [9]. Note that another model providing the transition and observation probabilities required in Section 4.2 may be substituted, such as a less sophisticated HMM.

4   Runtime Verification for Stochastic Systems

Traditional runtime verification does safety monitoring of software systems in which state can be directly observed. In this section we extend the problem to that of safety monitoring of mixed hardware / software systems that can fail, and solve this problem by incorporating stochastic behavior and hidden state.

If it is assumed that the state of a mixed system is observable, then runtime verification may be used to monitor the safety of such a system. However, due to incomplete or faulty sensing, it is not realistic to assume that the state of an embedded system is generally observable. Therefore, in the case in which the system state x is hidden and Λ involves these hidden states, we estimate the safety of the system as a belief distribution, as described in Section 4.1. Section 4.2 derives an expression for this belief distribution in terms of system probabilities.

4.1   Extension to Hidden-State

Our system is drawn as a time-evolving graphical model in Figure 1.

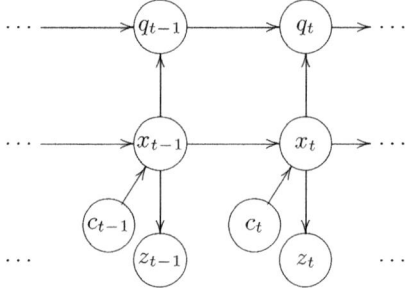

Fig. 1. A graphical model of an embedded system. The commands into the system are represented by c, observations z, physical system (hardware *and* software) state is x, and safety state is q. Subscripts denote time. Arrows denote conditional dependencies.

In this graphical model, q is the safety state of the system, defined as the state of the Deterministic Büchi Automaton (DBA) that describes a safety constraint on the system. Under the assumption that x is observable, the state q_t of the DBA at time t may be calculated from available information. However, when we remove the assumption that x is observable, q_t may no longer be directly calculated; the problem of safety monitoring can no longer be solved by runtime verification methods alone.

Instead, we want a capability that will evaluate the safety of the system given the available information: a safety specification Λ, a plant model Φ, the control sequence $c_{1:t}$, and observation sequence $z_{1:t}$.[2] This capability estimates

---

[2] Here subscripts denote time, hence $z_{1:t}$ is the vector of z's from time 1 to t.

the *probability* that the system remains consistent with Λ, that is, the probability that the system is SAFE. Let Q denote the set of states of the DBA for Λ, and let Q_{SAFE} denote the set $Q/q_\varnothing$. That is, Q_{SAFE} is the set Q with the trap state $q_\varnothing$ removed. The probability $\mathbf{P}(\text{SAFE})$ is then equivalent to the probability of being in a SAFE state of the DBA at time t:[3]

$$\mathbf{P}(\text{SAFE}) = \mathbf{P}(q_t \in Q_{\text{SAFE}})$$

This probability can be derived from the probability distribution over states q of the DBA at time t, given the commands and observations, by summing over the SAFE states Q_{SAFE}:

$$\mathbf{P}(\text{SAFE}) = \sum_{q^j \in Q_{\text{SAFE}}} \mathbf{P}(q_t^j | z_{1:t}, c_{1:t}) \tag{1}$$

Thus the problem of stochastic safety monitoring of embedded systems reduces to the problem of finding the probability distribution over DBA states q, conditioned on the history of observations and commands. This probability distribution over q is often called a *belief state*, hence we abbreviate it as $\mathbf{B}(q_t)$.

4.2   Calculating Safety Belief

Let y_t represent the complete system state $< q_t, x_t >$ and let $\mathbf{B}(y_t)$ denote the belief over y at time t, that is $\mathbf{B}(y_t) = \mathbf{P}(q_t, x_t | z_{1:t}, c_{1:t})$. The graphical model in Figure 1, viewed in terms of y, is equivalent to a canonical hidden Markov model:

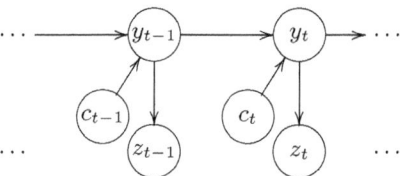

Fig. 2. Graphical model from Figure 1 with clustered state $y = q \otimes x$

The belief $\mathbf{B}(q_t)$ is obtained by marginalizing x_t out of $\mathbf{B}(y_t) = \mathbf{P}(q_t, x_t | z_{1:t}, c_{1:t})$:

$$\mathbf{B}(q_t) = \mathbf{P}(q_t | z_{1:t}, c_{1:t}) = \sum_{x_t} \mathbf{P}(q_t, x_t | z_{1:t}, c_{1:t}) \tag{2}$$

and $\mathbf{B}(y_t) = \mathbf{P}(y_t | z_{1:t}, c_{1:t})$ is obtained through standard HMM filtering:

$$\mathbf{B}(y_t) = \eta \mathbf{P}(z_t | y_t) \sum_{y_{t-1}} \mathbf{P}(y_t | y_{t-1}, c_t) \mathbf{B}(y_{t-1}) \tag{3}$$

---

[3] Summing over all states of the automaton except the trap state is necessary for the correct monitoring of liveness conditions.

Equation (3) computes the belief state over the combined system state y, which can also be thought of as the combined DBA / PHCA state. To obtain a relation in terms of functions specified by these models, we manipulate (3) further by expanding y in the observation probability $\mathbf{P}(z_t|y_t)$ and the transition probability $\mathbf{P}(y_t|y_{t-1}, c_t)$, giving us (4). Applying the Chain Rule and simplifying based on conditional independence arguments yields (5):

$$\mathbf{B}(y_t) = \eta \mathbf{P}(z_t|q_t, x_t) \sum_{y_{t-1}} \mathbf{P}(q_t, x_t|q_{t-1}, x_{t-1}, c_t) \, \mathbf{B}(y_{t-1}) \qquad (4)$$

$$= \eta \, \mathbf{P}(z_t|x_t) \sum_{y_{t-1}} \mathbf{P}(q_t|x_t, q_{t-1}) \mathbf{P}(x_t|x_{t-1}, c_t) \, \mathbf{B}(y_{t-1}) \qquad (5)$$

Substituting Equation (5) into (2) produces the following, where η is a normalization constant:

$$\mathbf{B}(q_t) = \eta \sum_{x_t} \mathbf{P}(z_t|x_t) \sum_{y_{t-1}} \mathbf{P}(q_t|x_t, q_{t-1}) \mathbf{P}(x_t|x_{t-1}, c_t) \, \mathbf{B}(y_{t-1}) \qquad (6)$$

Equation (6), which computes the belief state over the BA, is similar to the standard Forward algorithm for HMM belief state update (3). First, the next state is stochastically predicted based on each previous belief $\mathbf{B}(y_t)$ and on the transition probabilities of the models, then this prediction is corrected based on the observations received. An additional sum marginalizes out x_t, and the result is normalized by η. The observation probability $\mathbf{P}(z_t|x_t)$ and the transition probability $\mathbf{P}(x_t|x_{t-1}, c_t)$ are both functions of the model of the physical system. In an HMM, these are specified as a part of the model of the system. For PHCA, these system-wide probabilities must be calculated from the specified component transition and observation probabilities [14, 8]. The transition probability $\mathbf{P}(q_t|x_t, q_{t-1})$ in Equation (6) can be obtained from the transition function T_{D} of the specified deterministic Büchi Automaton as follows:

$$\mathbf{P}(q_t|x_t, q_{t-1}) = \begin{cases} 1 & \text{if } T_{\mathrm{D}}(q_{t-1}, x_t) = q_t \\ 0 & \text{otherwise} \end{cases} \qquad (7)$$

The cost of computing (6) is entirely dependent on the sizes of Q and X. In order to find the probability of each q_t, we must loop twice over these sets. If n is the size of the combined set, $n = |Q \times X|$, then we have a time complexity of $O(n^2)$, and a space complexity of $O(n)$.

Finally, given the belief state determined by Equation (6), the probability that the system is currently SAFE is given by:

$$\mathbf{P}(\text{SAFE}) = \sum_{q_t \in Q_{\text{SAFE}}} \eta \sum_{x_t} \mathbf{P}(z_t|x_t) \sum_{y_{t-1}} \mathbf{P}(q_t|x_t, q_{t-1}) \mathbf{P}(x_t|x_{t-1}, c_t) \, \mathbf{B}(y_{t-1}) \qquad (8)$$

5   Summary

In this paper we extended traditional runtime verification to deal with faulty mixed hardware/software systems by assuming a stochastic plant with hidden state, and then performing belief state update on the combined state of the deterministic Büchi Automata representing the safety requirements and the Probabilistic Hierarchical Constraint Automata representing the plant behavior. This method is innovative in its allowance for hidden state and probabilistic failure.

Preliminary validation has shown that our method is capable of quickly and accurately detecting safety violations on small models. Further work will seek to characterize the utility of these methods on larger models.

References

1. Baier, C., Katoen, J.P.: Principles of Model Checking. The MIT Press, Cambridge (2008)
2. Black, J.: System Safety as an Emergent Property. Ph.D. thesis, Carnegie Mellon University, Pittsburgh, PA (April 2009)
3. Drusinsky, D.: The Temporal Rover and the ATG Rover. In: Havelund, K., Penix, J., Visser, W. (eds.) SPIN 2000. LNCS, vol. 1885, pp. 323–330. Springer, Heidelberg (2000)
4. Gerth, R., Peled, D., Vardi, M.Y., Wolper, P.: Simple on-the-fly automatic verification of linear temporal logic. In: IFIP Conf. Proc., vol. 38, pp. 3–18 (1995)
5. Giannakopoulou, D., Havelund, K.: Automata-based verification of temporal properties on running programs. In: 16th IEEE International Conference on Automated Software Engineering, San Diego, CA (2001)
6. Havelund, K., Roşu, G.: Java pathexplorer - a runtime verification tool. In: The 6th International Symposium on AI, Robotics and Automation in Space (May 2001)
7. Kim, M., Kannan, S., Lee, I., Sokolsky, O., Viswanathan, M.: Java-MaC: a runtime assurance approach for Java programs. Formal Methods in System Design 24(2), 129–155 (2004)
8. Martin, O.B., Chung, S.H., Williams, B.C.: A tractable approach to probabilistically accurate mode estimation. In: Proc of iSAIRAS 2005, Munich, Germany (September 2005)
9. Mikaelian, T., Williams, B.C., Sachenbacher, M.: Model-based monitoring and diagnosis of systems with software-extended behavior. In: AAAI 2005, Pittsburgh, PA, pp. 327–333 (July 2005)
10. Peters, D.K., Parnas, D.L.: Requirements-based monitors for real-time systems. IEEE Transactions on Software Engineering 28(2) (February 2002)
11. Pnueli, A.: The temporal logic of programs. In: 18th Annual Symposium on Foundations of Computer Science (FOCS 1997), pp. 46–57 (1977)
12. Sammapun, U., Sokolsky, O., Lee, I., Regehr, J.: Statistical runtime checking of probabilistic properties. In: Sokolsky, O., Taşıran, S. (eds.) RV 2007. LNCS, vol. 4839, pp. 164–175. Springer, Heidelberg (2007)
13. Sistla, A.P., Srinivas, A.R.: Monitoring temporal properties of stochastic systems. In: Logozzo, F., Peled, D.A., Zuck, L.D. (eds.) VMCAI 2008. LNCS, vol. 4905, pp. 294–308. Springer, Heidelberg (2008)
14. Williams, B., Chung, S., Gupta, V.: Mode estimation of model-based programs: Monitoring systems with complex behavior. In: Proc. of the International Joint Conference on Artificial Intelligence, Seattle, WA, pp. 579–585 (2001)

Low-Overhead Bug Fingerprinting for Fast Debugging

Cristian Zamfir and George Candea

School of Computer and Communication Sciences
École Polytechnique Fédérale de Lausanne (EPFL), Switzerland

Abstract. There is a gap between the information available at the time of a software failure and the information actually shipped to developers in the corresponding bug report. As a result, identifying the cause of the bug based on this bug report is often difficult. To close this gap, we propose *bug fingerprints*—an augmentation of classic automated bug reports with runtime information about how the reported bug occurred in production.

Classic automated bug reporting systems contain at most a coredump that describes the final manifestation of a bug. In contrast, bug fingerprints contain additional small amounts of highly relevant runtime information that helps understand how the bug occurred. We show how these "fingerprints" can be used to speed up both manual and automated debugging. As a proof of concept, we present DCop, a system for collecting such runtime information about deadlocks and including it in the corresponding bug reports. The runtime overhead introduced by DCop is negligible (less than 0.17% for the Apache Web server), so it is suitable for use in production.

1   Introduction

Software debugging is time-consuming and labor-intensive, with most of the work going into understanding how the reported bug occurred in the field. For example, 70% of the concurrency bugs reported to Microsoft take days to months to fix [4]. This labor-intensive aspect makes software debugging expensive. Our work is aimed at reducing the often needless labor involved in debugging.

A classic bug report contains at best a coredump that describes the final state of the failed application. State-of-the-art automated bug reporting systems, such as Windows Error Reporting (WER) [3], produce a trimmed version of the coredump, which reduces the overhead and privacy problems of a full coredump. Most other software relies on users to provide a coredump and a description of how to manually reproduce the bug.

The absence of precise information about how the bug occurred in the field leads to incorrect diagnosis. Non-deterministic bugs are particularly hard to reproduce and diagnose, forcing developers to guess the cause of the failure based on the bug report. Since bug reports offer no runtime information about how the bug occurred, guessing often leads to incorrect fixes; e.g., one study reports that 30% of concurrency bugs are initially fixed incorrectly [8]. Ideally, developers should not have to rely so much on guessing.

There do exist tools that help reduce guessing by employing full system record-replay [2]. However, they can incur runtime recording overheads that make them impractical for in-production use. Other approaches use post-factum analysis to eliminate

G. Roşu et al. (Eds.): RV 2010, LNCS 6418, pp. 460–468, 2010.

completely the need for runtime recording (execution synthesis [15]), or to require less recording (ODR [1], SherLog [14]). However, post-factum analysis may not be effective for all bugs and can involve substantial compute time at the developer's site.

The inherent trade-off between runtime recording overhead and the fidelity/ease of subsequently reproducing bugs forms a spectrum of solutions, with full system replay [2] at one end, and execution synthesis [15] at the other. This spectrum is still poorly understood, and an important question remains: which is the least amount of information that is practical to record at runtime, yet still makes it easy to diagnose bugs of a certain type.

Our observation is that, given a class of bugs, it is possible to record a small amount of bug-specific runtime information with negligible overhead, and this information can substantially improve debugging. Based on this observation, we propose *bug fingerprints*, small additions to classic bug reports that contain highly relevant "breadcrumbs" of the execution in which the bug occurred. These breadcrumbs ease the reconstruction of the sequence of events that led to the failure.

We show that this idea works for deadlocks, an important class of concurrency bugs. We built DCop, a prototype deadlock fingerprinting system for C/C++ software—it keeps track at runtime of each thread's lock set and the callstacks of the corresponding lock acquisitions; when a deadlock hangs the application, this information is added to the bug report. DCop's runtime overhead is negligible (e.g., less than 0.17% for the Apache Web server), yet these breadcrumbs enable faster, even automated, debugging.

In the rest of this paper we describe the design of DCop (§2), evaluate it (§3), discuss the generalization of bug fingerprints to other bug types (§4), illustrate the use of fingerprints for automated debugging (§5), review related work (§6), and conclude (§7).

2   Deadlock Fingerprints

Despite being frequent (e.g., 30% of the bugs reported in [8] are deadlocks), deadlock bug reports are scarce, because deadlocks do not produce a coredump—instead, they render the application unresponsive. Normal users restart the application without submitting a bug report, while expert users may attach a debugger to the program and capture each thread's callstack. Systems such as WER can be used to create a coredump, but it is still hard to debug deadlocks based on this information that describes only the end state.

Deadlocks become straightforward to debug if we have information on how the program acquired *every* mutex involved in the deadlock. In particular, the callstacks of the calls that acquired mutexes *held* at the time of deadlock, together with the callstacks of the *blocked* mutex acquisitions, provide rich information about how the deadlock came about. Alas, the former type of callstack information is no longer available at the time of the deadlock, and so it does not appear in the coredump.

Fortunately, it is feasible to have this information in every bug report: First, the amount of information is small—typically one callstack per thread. Second, it can be maintained with low runtime overhead, because most programs use synchronization infrequently. As it turns out, even for lock-intensive programs DCop incurs negligible overhead.

DCop's deadlock fingerprints contain precisely this information. Regular deadlock bug reports contain callstacks, thread identifiers, and addresses of the mutexes that are requested—but not held—by the deadlocked threads. We call these the *inner* mutexes, corresponding to the innermost acquisition attempt in a nested locking sequence. Additionally, deadlock fingerprints contain callstack, thread id, and address information for the mutexes that are already held by the threads that deadlock. We call these the *outer* mutexes, because they correspond to the outer layers of the nested locking sequence. Outer mutex information must be collected at runtime, because the functions where the outer mutexes were acquired are likely to have already returned prior to the deadlock.

We illustrate deadlock fingerprints with the code in Fig. 1a, a simplified version of the global mutex implementation in SQLite [11], a widely used embedded database engine. The bug occurs when two threads execute *sqlite3EnterMutex()* concurrently. Fig. 1b shows the classic bug report, and Fig. 1c shows the deadlock fingerprint.

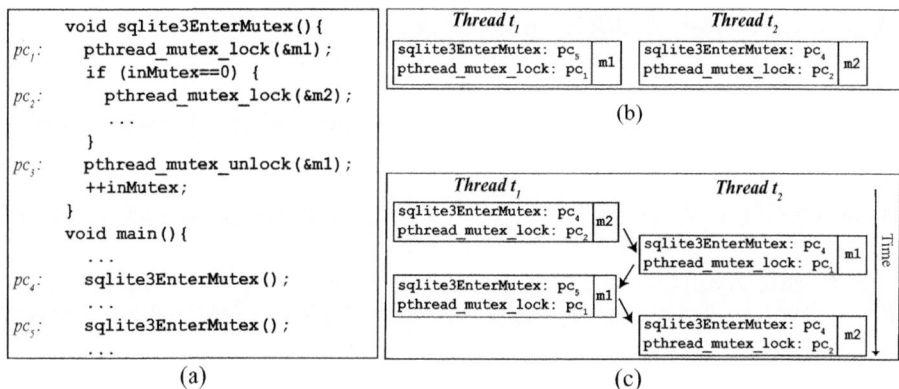

Fig. 1. (a) SQLite deadlock bug #1672. (b) Regular bug report. (c) DCop-style deadlock fingerprint.

A regular bug report shows the final state of the deadlocked program: t_1 attempted to lock mutex m_1 at pc_1 and t_2 attempted to lock mutex m_2 at pc_2—we invite the reader to diagnose how the deadlock occurred based on this information. The bug report does not explain how t_1 acquired m_2 and how t_2 acquired m_1, and this is not obvious, since there are several execution paths that can acquire mutexes m_1 and m_2.

The deadlock fingerprint (Fig. 1c) clarifies the sequence of events: t_1 acquired m_2 at pc_2 in a first call to *sqlite3EnterMutex*, and t_2 acquired m_1 at pc_1. This allows a developer to realize that, just after t_1 unlocked m_1 at pc_3 and before t_1 incremented the *inMutex* variable, t_2 must have locked m_1 at pc_1 and read variable *inMutex*, which still had the value 0. Thus, t_2 blocked waiting for m_2 at pc_2. Next, t_1 resumed, incremented *inMutex*, called *sqlite3EnterMutex* the second time, and tried to acquire m_1 at pc_1. Since m_1 was held by t_2 and m_2 was held by t_1, the threads deadlocked. This is an example of how DCop can help debug the deadlock and reveal the data race on *inMutex*.

To acquire this added information, DCop uses a lightweight instrumentation layer that intercepts the program's synchronization operations. It records the acquisition callstack for currently held mutexes in a per-thread event list. A deadlock detector is run whenever the application is deemed unresponsive, and it determines whether the cause is a deadlock.

The runtime monitor is designed to incur minimal overhead. First key decision was to avoid contention at all costs, so each thread records the callstack information for its lock/unlock events in a thread-local private list. The private lists are merged solely when a deadlock is found (and thus the application threads are stuck anyway). This avoids introducing any additional runtime synchronization.

A second design choice was to trim the private lists and keep them to the minimum required size: every time a mutex is unlocked, DCop finds the corresponding lock event in the list and discards it—mutexes that are no longer held cannot be involved in deadlocks. Thus, DCop only keeps track of mutexes that have not yet been released, and so the size of a per-thread event list is bounded by the maximum nesting level of locking in the program. In our experience, no event lists ever exceeded 4 elements.

As a result of this design, DCop's runtime overhead is dominated by obtaining the backtrace on each mutex acquisition. To reduce this overhead to a minimum, DCop resolves backtrace symbols offline, since this is expensive and need not be done at runtime.

The deadlock detection component of DCop is activated when the user stops an application due to it being unresponsive. The detector processes each thread's list and creates a resource allocation graph (RAG) based on the events in the lists. The RAG contains a vertex for each active thread and mutex, and edges correspond to mutex acquisitions (or acquisition requests that have not succeeded yet). Edges are labeled with the thread id of the acquiring thread and the callstack corresponding to the lock operation. Once the RAG is constructed, the detector checks for cycles in the graph—a RAG cycle corresponds to a deadlock. If a deadlock is found, the detector assembles the corresponding fingerprint based on the callstacks and thread identifiers found on the cycle's edges.

DCop's deadlock detector has zero false positives. Furthermore, since the size of the threads' event lists is small, assembling a deadlock fingerprint is fast.

We implemented DCop inside FreeBSD's `libthr` POSIX threads library; our changes added 382 LOC. One advantage of recording fingerprints from within the existing threading library is the opportunity to leverage existing data structures. For example, we added pointers to DCop's data structures inside the library's own thread metadata structure. An important optimization in DCop is the use of preallocated buffers for storing the backtrace of mutex acquisitions—this removes memory allocations from the critical path.

3   Performance Evaluation

Having discussed DCop's design, we now turn our attention to the key question of whether it is suitable for use in production? We evaluate DCop's performance on a workstation with two Intel 4×1.6GHz-core CPUs with 4GB of RAM running FreeBSD 7.0.

First, we employ DCop on interactive applications we use ourselves, such as the emacs text editor. There is no perceptible slowdown, leading to the empirical conclusion that user-perceived overhead is negligible. However, since recording mutex operations adds several instructions at each synchronization operation, (e.g., obtaining the backtrace for a lock operation), some lock intensive programs may exhibit more overhead.

Next, we use DCop for the Apache Web server with 50 worker threads. We vary the number of concurrent clients and, for each concurrency level, we execute 5×10^5 GET requests for a 44-byte file. In Fig. 2 we compare the aggregate request throughput to a baseline without DCop. The overhead introduced by DCop is negligible throughout, with the worst-case being a less than 0.17%

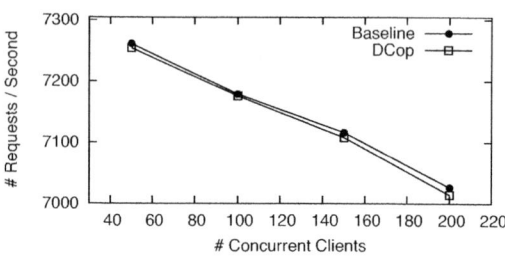

Fig. 2. Comparative request throughput for the Apache 2.2.14 server at various levels of client concurrency

drop in throughput for 200 concurrent clients. Both baseline and DCop throughput decrease slightly with concurrency level, most likely because there are more clients than worker threads. The maximum synchronization throughput (lock operations/second) reaches 7249 locks/second.

To analyze DCop's overhead in depth, we wrote a synchronization-intensive benchmark that creates 2 to 1024 threads that synchronize on 8 shared mutexes. Each thread holds a mutex for δ_{in} time, releases it, waits for δ_{out} time, then tries to acquire another mutex. δ_{in} and δ_{out} are implemented as busy loops, thus simulating computation done inside and outside a critical section. The threads randomly call multiple functions within the microbenchmark, in order to build up highly varied callstacks ("fingerprints").

We measure how synchronization throughput varies with the number of threads. In Fig. 3 we show DCop's overhead for δ_{in}=1 microsecond and δ_{out}=1 millisecond, simulating a program that grabs a mutex, updates in-memory shared data structures, releases the mutex, and then performs computation outside the critical section. The worst case overhead is less than 0.33% overhead. The decreasing overhead shows that indeed DCop introduces no lock contention. Instead,

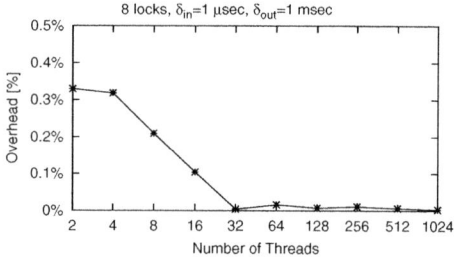

Fig. 3. Overhead of collecting deadlock fingerprints as a function of the number of threads

the application's own contention amortizes DCop's overhead.

We repeat the experiment for various combinations of $1 \leq \delta_{in} \leq 10^4$ and $1 \leq \delta_{out} \leq 10^4$ microseconds, simulating applications with a broad range of locking patterns. The measured overhead ranges from 0.06% in the best case to 0.77% in the worst case. The maximum measured synchronization throughput reaches 831,864 locks/second.

These results confirm that DCop introduces negligible runtime overhead, thus making it well suited for running in production, even for server applications. We hope this advantageous cost/benefit trade-off will encourage wider adoption of deadlock fingerprinting.

4   Generalizing Bug Fingerprinting

Having seen how bug fingerprinting works for deadlocks, we now turn our attention to generalizing bug fingerprinting to other kinds of bugs. In §5 we discuss how bug fingerprints can be employed in automated debugging.

In essence, a bug fingerprint serves to *disambiguate executions*: when faced with a bug report, a developer must find (guess) which of the many (often infinite) possible executions of the software could have led to the observed failure. The bug report provides clues for trimming down the set of possible executions, and the bug fingerprint should narrow it down to only a handful of possibilities. Fingerprint information must be small, to avoid undue recording overheads. Choosing what runtime information to include in a given fingerprint is therefore specific to each class of bugs. We illustrate this process with two examples: data races and unchecked function returns.

A bug fingerprint for a data race-induced failure contains information on the races that manifested during execution prior to the failure in the bug report. This way, it is possible to determine which potential data races influenced the execution and which did not. However, monitoring memory accesses efficiently is not easy.

An efficient data race fingerprinting system employs static analysis to determine offline, prior to execution, which memory accesses are potential data races. It then monitors at runtime only these accesses. There are two options to perform such monitoring with low overhead: debug registers and transactional memory (TM). x86 debug registers [6] can be configured to deliver an interrupt to a monitor thread whenever two memory accesses to the same address are not ordered by a happens-before relation and at least one of the access is a write (i.e., a data race occurred). The corresponding program counters and memory address are then saved for later inclusion in the bug report, should a failure occur. One drawback is that today's CPUs can monitor only a small set of addresses at a time, so debug registers can be used to watch only a subset of the statically-discovered potential races. An alternative approach is to use the conflict detection mechanism of TM to detect data races, and record the fingerprint. If TM features are available in hardware, this can be done quite efficiently.

Another interesting class of bugs appears in code that "forgets" to check all possible return values of a library function. For example, not checking whether a socket `read()` call returned -1 can lead to data loss (if caller continues as if all data was read) or even memory corruption (if return value is used as an index). For such unchecked-return bugs, the fingerprint contains (a) the program locations where a library function call's return value was not checked against all possible return values, and (b) the actual return value. Such fingerprinting can be done with low overhead by statically analyzing the program binary to determine the places in the program where library calls are not properly checked (e.g., using the LFI callsite analyzer [9]), and monitoring at runtime only those locations.

For most bug types, a general solution is to incrementally record the execution index [12] and include it in the bug fingerprint. The execution index is a precise way to identify a point in an execution and can be used to correlate points across multiple executions. Such a bug fingerprint can be used to reason with high accuracy about the path that the program took in production, but has typically high recording overhead (up to 42% [12]). It is possible to reduce the overhead by recording only a partial execution index (e.g., by sampling) that, although less precise, can still offer clues for debugging.

It is practical to fingerprint any class of bugs, as long as the runtime information required to disambiguate possible executions that manifest the bug can be recorded efficiently. Fingerprinting mechanisms can leverage each other, so that collecting fingerprints for n classes of bugs at the same time is cheaper than n times the average individual cost.

5   Debugging Using Deadlock Fingerprints

Augmenting bug reports with bug fingerprints can substantially speed up debugging. For example, a developer debugging a deadlock can get from the deadlock fingerprint all mutexes involved in the deadlock and the callstacks corresponding to their acquisition calls. This allows the developer to insert breakpoints at all outer mutex locations and understand how the deadlock can occur.

Bug fingerprints are also an excellent aid for automated debuggers, like ESD [15]. ESD is based on execution synthesis, an automated technique that starts from a bug report and finds an execution path and a thread schedule that reproduce the bug deterministically, with no human intervention. The technique employs a static analysis phase, that proceeds backward from the coredump and identifies critical transitions that take the program to the state contained in the coredump. Then a forward symbolic execution phase searches for the necessary inputs and thread schedule to reproduce the bug.

Bug signatures can improve the efficiency of execution synthesis, since they help disambiguate between possible executions. The more execution paths appear to be likely to reach the end state contained in the coredump, the longer ESD has to search. Bug signatures, however, contain clues that can substantially prune this search space.

For example, a major challenge in execution synthesis for deadlocks is identifying the thread schedule that leads to deadlock. DCop's deadlock fingerprints narrow down the set of possible schedules, thus reducing search time. In preliminary measurements, we find that for a program with three threads and an average lock nesting level of three, the thread schedule synthesis phase of ESD can be reduced by an order of magnitude. Similarly, in the case of data races, we expect orders of magnitude improvement in search performance, if data race fingerprints are available.

The combination of low-overhead bug fingerprinting with ESD-style automated debugging promises to improve the productivity of software developers. Thus, we consider a combined deployment to be an appealing solution for the software industry.

6   Related Work

Runtime support for debugging ranges from classic bug reporting systems, that provide a partial or complete coredump, to heavyweight whole-system record-replay systems.

Special hardware can be used to make the latter approach faster. In between these extremes, there exist multiple approaches that record less information and use post-factum analysis to reconstruct the missing pieces offline. We briefly survey this spectrum of solutions.

The state of the art in automated bug reporting systems, such as Windows Error Reporting [3], collect bug reports from a large number of users. These bug reports reveal some information about the bug (e.g., the end state of the application), but not how the application got there. Bug fingerprints enrich bug reports with bug-specific runtime information that can help these systems classify failures more accurately. As shown earlier, bug fingerprints preserve the low runtime overhead of classic bug reporting systems.

FDR [13] uses modified hardware to perform efficient execution recording. It piggybacks on the cache coherence hardware to record thread ordering information. While this approach can help debugging, it requires hardware features that are not available today and that are uncertain to exist in the future. In contrast, a system like DCop can be used today, without requiring any hardware or software changes.

Other approaches record system execution at the virtual machine level and use this information to deterministically replay executions. They are highly precise, but can incur significant overhead (e.g., up to 260% for Revirt [2]); recording multiprocessor executions has typically several orders of magnitude higher overhead. Bug fingerprints operate at a higher level: they leverage knowledge about the bug class to identify minute pieces of runtime information that help reproduce the bugs with minimal recording. Although they require more human effort and they lack the precision of VM-based record-replay, bug fingerprints are an effective debugging aid with virtually no runtime overhead.

R2 [5] performs record-replay at the library level, and can interpose at high-level APIs to reduce the recording overhead. R2 offers the flexibility of choosing what exactly to record, so it is in essence a mechanism for performing selective recording. We believe R2 could be used to obtain fingerprints for certain classes of bugs, although R2 has limited support for nondeterministic executions. That being said, DCop incurs two orders of magnitude less overhead than R2 on Apache, for identical workloads.

ODR [1] and PRES [10] are recent systems for replaying concurrency bugs; they trade runtime overhead for post-factum analysis time, and thus explore new points in the spectrum of solutions. The benefit of deterministic replay comes at a cost of more than 50% runtime overhead, which makes them less compelling for production use. In DCop we forgo the goal of deterministic replay in exchange for negligible runtime overhead.

Dimmunix [7] also collects deadlock fingerprints, but for a different reason: immunity against deadlocks. Once a deadlock occurs, Dimmunix records a signature of the deadlock that is then used to identify and avoid that same deadlock pattern in subsequent executions. Since DCop is focused on collecting fingerprints, not on avoidance, it can perform the collection with two orders of magnitude less runtime overhead and produce fingerprints that are richer than Dimmunix's signatures.

7 Conclusions

This paper described *bug fingerprints*, an augmentation of classic bug reports with run-time information about how the reported bug occurred. Fingerprints contain clues that substantially help in both manual and automated debugging. A proof-of-concept system fingerprints deadlocks with negligible overhead (less than 0.17% for Apache). We discussed how to extend this approach to other types of bugs, and argued that coupling bug fingerprints with automated debugging techniques can make debugging more efficient.

References

1. Altekar, G., Stoica, I.: ODR: Output-deterministic replay for multicore programs. In: Symp. on Operating Systems Principles (2009)
2. Dunlap, G.W., King, S.T., Cinar, S., Basrai, M., Chen, P.M.: ReVirt: Enabling intrusion analysis through virtual-machine logging and replay. In: Symp. on Operating Systems Design and Implementation (2002)
3. Glerum, K., Kinshumann, K., Greenberg, S., Aul, G., Orgovan, V., Nichols, G., Grant, D., Loihle, G., Hunt, G.: Debugging in the (very) large: ten years of implementation and experience. In: Symp. on Operating Systems Principles (2009)
4. Godefroid, P., Nagappan, N.: Concurrency at Microsoft – An exploratory survey. In: CAV Workshop on Exploiting Concurrency Efficiently and Correctly (2008)
5. Guo, Z., Wang, X., Tang, J., Liu, X., Xu, Z., Wu, M., Kaashoek, M.F., Zhang, Z.: R2: An application-level kernel for record and replay. In: Symp. on Operating Systems Design and Implementation (2008)
6. Intel. Intel Architecture Software Developer's Manual, Vol. 2: Instruction Set Reference (1999)
7. Jula, H., Tralamazza, D., Zamfir, C., Candea, G.: Deadlock immunity: Enabling systems to defend against deadlocks. In: Symp. on Operating Systems Design and Implementation (2008)
8. Lu, S., Park, S., Seo, E., Zhou, Y.: Learning from mistakes – a comprehensive study on real world concurrency bug characteristics. In: Intl. Conf. on Architectural Support for Programming Languages and Operating Systems (2008)
9. Marinescu, P.D., Banabic, R., Candea, G.: An extensible technique for high-precision testing of recovery code. In: USENIX Annual Technical Conf. (2010)
10. Park, S., Xiong, W., Yin, Z., Kaushik, R., Lee, K.H., Lu, S., Zhou, Y.: Do you have to reproduce the bug at the first replay attempt? – PRES: Probabilistic replay with execution sketching on multiprocessors. In: Symp. on Operating Systems Principles (2009)
11. SQLite (2010), http://www.sqlite.org/
12. Xin, B., Sumner, W.N., Zhang, X.: Efficient program execution indexing. In: Conf. on Programming Language Design and Implementation (2008)
13. Xu, M., Bodik, R., Hill, M.D.: A "flight data recorder" for enabling full-system multiprocessor deterministic replay. In: Intl. Symp. on Computer Architecture (2003)
14. Yuan, D., Mai, H., Xiong, W., Tan, L., Zhou, Y., Pasupathy, S.: SherLog: error diagnosis by connecting clues from run-time logs. In: Intl. Conf. on Architectural Support for Programming Languages and Operating Systems (2010)
15. Zamfir, C., Candea, G.: Execution synthesis: A technique for automated debugging. In: ACM SIGOPS/EuroSys. European Conf. on Computer Systems (2010)

ESAT: A Tool for Animating Logic-Based Specifications of Evolvable Component Systems

Djihed Afifi, David E. Rydeheard, and Howard Barringer

The University of Manchester, School of Computer Science,
Kilburn Building, Oxford Road, Manchester, M13 9PL, United Kingdom
{djihed,david,howard}@cs.man.ac.uk

1 Introduction

An increasingly important area of runtime monitoring is the incorporation of techniques for diagnosis and repair, for example, in autonomic control applications [9], in robotics, and in e-business process change [12]. In particular, a runtime monitor becomes a 'supervisor' - a process which not only monitors but may evolve the running system dynamically. In [4], a framework for the logical modelling of hierarchically structured supervised component systems was set out. The modelling captures the following key behavioural concepts: at runtime, a supervisory component can (i) monitor its supervisee to ensure conformance against desired behaviour, (ii) analyse reasons for non-conformance, should that arise, (iii) evolve its supervisee in a pre-programmed way following diagnosis, or via external stimulus received from higher-level supervisory components. Structurally, components may contain sub-components, actions over the state of the component, and programs over the actions. In this logical framework, components are specified by first-order logic theories. Actions are either basic revisions to the state of the component or combinations of actions. Crucially, a supervisory component is treated as a logical theory meta to its supervisee, thus providing access to all facets of the supervisee's structure. A supervisory component program is executed meta to its supervisee's program. Synchronisation between the two may occur through a variety of schemes, from lock-step synchronisation to asynchronous execution with defined synchronisation points. A supervisory program action may evolve its supervisee by making changes to its state, to its actions, to its sub-components, or to its program. This occurs in the logical framework via a theory change induced from the meta-level.

The logical framework introduces a new design methodology whereby evolutionary concerns are built into system designs at various levels. The hierarchical aspect of this framework allows for localised monitoring and evolution, improving the manageability of evolution in large systems. As the logic for specifying supervised component systems is revision-based, programs over the actions can be directly executed. This execution is performed using ESAT, the Evolvable Systems Animator Tool. ESAT is written in Java and makes use of automatic theorem provers to simulate systems. ESAT animates abstract logical specifications of evolvable systems. The tool was developed in order to support case

G. Roşu et al. (Eds.): RV 2010, LNCS 6418, pp. 469–474, 2010.

studies which explored and tested this particular design methodology and to prototype systems. Furthermore, the animation of logical models enables the reasoning and verification of various properties of models of evolvable systems. ESAT differs from other formal specification tools such as Perfect Developer [6] and Maude [11] in its support for meta-level descriptions and runtime evolutionary change.

2   ESAT: Evolvable Systems Animator Tool

2.1   Input Component Specifications

An overview of the tool is given in Fig. 1. The input to the tool is a textual representation of component schema definitions. Figure 2 outlines an example specification of an autonomic rover system. It consists of three specifications of theories: *Rover* is an abstract description of an autonomous rover system, *Planner* is a specification of a supervisor as a planning agent, and *Supervised_Rover* combines instances of the previous specifications. The logic of the specification is a many-sorted (typed) first-order logic with enumerated types, sub-typing, product types and lists. A schema may declare types, functions, predicates, sub-components, constraints, an initial state, actions and a program. In addition to the system-wide types such as *Int* and *String*, a schema may introduce its own types as well as functions. A schema may introduce predicates as either: (i) *observation* predicates: the state of a component is defined as a subset of the positive ground atoms of these predicates (ii) *abstraction* predicates: other predicates that may appear in the schema's constraints or actions. For a supervisor component, special predicates are used for its meta relation with its supervisee. As an example, the supervisor formula "$holds(\phi, c)$" is used to denote that an object formula ϕ holds at the supervisee level at an object configuration named by the supervisor as c. A schema may define sub-components that will be instantiated from other schemas. Components can be either standalone or supervisor-supervisee pairings. The constraints of a schema are a set of parametrised schematic first-order logic formulae. Actions can be one of four kinds (i) basic actions specified in a STRIPS-style via pre-conditions, and additions and deletions of state atomic formulae, i.e. via state revisions. Pre-conditions may contain free variables that are bound at execution time, (ii) paired actions: the pairing of a supervisor action with a supervisee action, (iii) joint actions: the lock step parallel execution of several actions from several components, (vi) choice actions: the non-deterministic choice between several actions. ESAT incorporates a guarded choice language (with non-deterministic choice) with iteration for specifying a program for each component.

2.2   Animation

For animating a specification, ESAT provides both a command line interface (CLI) and a graphical user interface (GUI). The CLI simulates an input specification from start to finish (or to a pre-determined action count execution limit) without user intervention and is suitable for running large simulations. The GUI

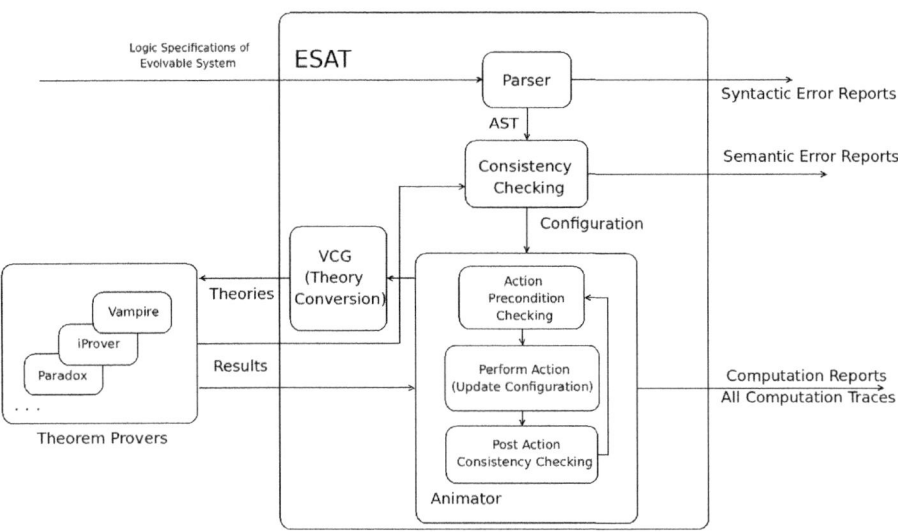

Fig. 1. ESAT Overview

Rover

OBSERVATION PREDICATES
    $at : Point$
    $next : Point$
    $blocked : Points$

ABSTRACTION PREDICATES
    $obstruction : Point \times Point$
    $between : Point \times Point \times Point$

CONSTRAINTS
    $geometry \stackrel{dfn}{=} \ldots$

ACTIONS
    $view(h : Point, P : Points)$
    pre $\{at(h), blocked(Q)\}$
    add $\{blocked(P \cup Q)\}$
    del $\{blocked(Q)\}$

    $setHeading(t : Point) \cdots$
    $drive \cdots$

PROGRAM
    NULL.

INITIALLY
    $\{\}$

Supervised_Rover

COMPONENTS
    $ER : (P : Planner()$ META TO $R : Rover())$

PROGRAM
    $\cdots$

META *Planner*

TYPES
    $ConfigName$

CONSTANTS
    $c_R : ConfigName$

FUNCTIONS
    $s : ConfigName \rightarrow ConfigName$
    $replan : Point \times Point \times Points \rightarrow$ PROGRAM

OBSERVATION PREDICATES
    $holds :$ FORMULAE $\times ConfigName$
    $evolve : \ldots$
    $current : ConfigName$
    $goal : Point$

CONSTRAINTS
    $EWC \stackrel{dfn}{=} \ldots$

ACTIONS
    $query(P :$ FORMULAE$) \ldots$
    $observe(P :$ FORMULAE$, c : ConfigName) \ldots$
    $rePlan(p_s, p_d : Point) \ldots$

PROGRAM
    $[\ goal(p) \wedge current(c) \wedge holds(at(s), c) \wedge$
            $start \neq p \rightarrow rePlan(s, d)$
    $\|\ goal(p) \wedge current(c) \wedge holds(at(p), c)$
            $\rightarrow query(at(p))$
    $]^*$

INITIALLY
    $\{current(c_R)\}$

Fig. 2. Rover Example Specification

allows for running, pausing and stepping through a simulation, and provides detailed feedback about the actions being executed and the state of the system at any point during animation.

The input specification is animated by executing its programs and producing a tree of all traces. This animation requires the use of automated theorem provers (see [1]) in order to: (i) Verify the consistency of the theory and of the state of each component at system start-up, after executing actions and after performing evolutions. This checking may throw logical error reports when the theory of a component does not have a model i.e. it is unsatisfiable, (ii) Establish the validity of each action's pre-conditions from the component's theory and state, (iii) Check that the meta-level relations hold, i.e. that the supervisee's reflection in the supervisor in each supervisor-supervisee pair is correct.

ESAT can use any automated theorem prover for first-order logic which supports the TPTP [16] format and which has the capability to determine the satisfiability of a set of formulae and the deducibility of a formula from a formula set.

Although the component specifications use typed formulae, these are encoded as untyped first-order formulae by ESAT as TPTP input to the theorem provers. The translation from typed to untyped logic adds axioms and predicates to encode typing information (see [8]). When a decision is required from a theorem prover, multiple provers may be fired in parallel: theorem provers differ in their proof capability and speed of decision making. The tool supports using different theorem provers for satisfiability and deducibility. We found that using multiple theorem provers increases the overall simulation speed by an average of 30% in our case studies as it is often the case that one theorem prover will be particularly fast at the given problem. We have experimented with 14 theorem provers and model finders, with the main emphasis on Paradox [5], iProver [10], Vampire [14] and E [15].

The animation of a system potentially generates a large number of proof obligations. As the overhead of discharging proof obligations can be as much as 90% of the running time, the simulation of a simple system may spend a substantial amount of time communicating theories and results with theorem provers. A simple caching mechanism is used by ESAT to eliminate, in the examples we have run, over 60% of these obligations. For each component, the caching mechanism associates a mini-cache that stores the list of previously proven formulae as well as the the set of previously unproven sets of formulae. In the case of a cache hit, the lookup is much faster than firing external theorem provers. The caching also improves the performance of theorem provers by supplying the previously proven formulae as axioms. On the Rover system, the caching mechanism reduces the simulation time from 6 minutes to 90 seconds.

A problem with running large system simulations is the complexity of the execution trace and the difficulty of inspecting a tree of traces in a linear fashion. The tool facilitates system modelling and execution by providing a GUI with the following views:

- A text editor with syntax highlighting for creating system specification files. Import statements can be used to include schema definitions from multiple files.
- A trace viewer that graphically displays a system's execution trace. The user can step through the execution of a specification's programs. The proof obligations that were generated for each action are displayed for inspection. Statistics about the number of proof obligations, the provers that successfully returned a result and the proof obligations that were eliminated using the caching mechanism are summarised in this view.
- A configuration viewer that graphically displays the system's component tree and the properties of each component such as its state and program. This view is helpful for examining evolutions that change the hierarchical structure of a system.
- A theory editor for testing logical theories. In this view, the user can directly write theories in the input format of the theorem provers and test satisfiability or deducibility. Proof obligations that were generated during the simulation of a specification can be verified here to examine the model generated in satisfiability mode or the proof generated in deducibility mode. This is useful for refining the theories of the component schema specifications.

3   Concluding Remarks

ESAT has been used on a variety of case studies which include (i) an evolvable version of the traditional 'blocks world' in which a supervisor monitors a table and blocks being moved around the table, and can invoke changes to the system e.g. changing the table size or number of tables, (ii) a simple model of a banking system comprising a network of ATMs in which not only are there standard local evolutions such as stocking notes and upgrading card readers, but also diagnostic system-wide recognition of potential fraud and evolution of security mechanisms, and (iii) an abstraction of a hierarchic reactively planned autonomous rover where a putative rover's exploration plan can be updated by supervisors as more information about the environment and the rover's internal state is received and analysed. The development of the tool and animation of these case studies enabled us to thoroughly test both the mathematical setting and the syntactic descriptions of this logical framework for evolvable systems. In the future, we see ESAT as both a tool for prototyping evolvable systems and also as part of a runtime monitoring system of implemented (e.g. in Java) evolvable systems.

ESAT is still under development. Currently, only TPTP theorem provers that accept classical first-order logic are used to determine the computation steps. System specifications that use arithmetic or other theories such as lists or arrays need to axiomatise the theories as first-order logic formulae suitable for these provers, e.g. Presburger Arithmetic. In the future, TPTP theorem provers that support arithmetic such as SPASS+T [13] and MetiTarski [2] will be explored. Also, a new verification condition generator needs to be implemented to use SMT solvers that support the INTS, REALS and ARRAYS theories, such as Z3 [7] and CVC [3]. Furthermore, ESAT can be extended to enable the runtime monitoring and evolution of components written as real Java programs.

References

1. Afifi, D., Rydeheard, D., Barringer, H.: Automated reasoning in the simulation of evolvable systems. In: Workshop on Practical Aspects of Automated Reasoning (PAAR 2010), Edinburgh, UK (2010)
2. Akbarpour, B., Paulson, L.C.: Towards automatic proofs of inequalities involving elementary functions. PDPAR 2006: Pragmatical Aspects of Decision Procedures in Automated Reasoning, p. 27 (2006)
3. Barrett, C., Tinelli, C.: CVC3. In: Damm, W., Hermanns, H. (eds.) CAV 2007. LNCS, vol. 4590, pp. 298–302. Springer, Heidelberg (2007)
4. Barringer, H., Gabbay, D., Rydeheard, D.: Modelling evolvable component systems: Part I: A logical framework. Logic Jnl IGPL 17(6), 631–696 (2009)
5. Claessen, K., Sörensson, N.: New techniques that improve MACE-style model finding. In: Proc. of Workshop on Model Computation, MODEL (2003)
6. Crocker, D.: Perfect developer: A tool for object-oriented formal specification and refinement. tools exhibition notes at formal methods europe. In: Tools Exhibition Notes at Formal Methods Europe, p. 2003 (2003)
7. De Moura, L., Bjørner, N.: Z3: An efficient SMT solver. In: Ramakrishnan, C.R., Rehof, J. (eds.) TACAS 2008. LNCS, vol. 4963, pp. 337–340. Springer, Heidelberg (2008)
8. Enderton, H.B., NetLibrary, I.: A mathematical introduction to logic. Academic Press, New York (1972)
9. Kephart, J.O., Chess, D.M.: The vision of autonomic computing. Computer 36(1), 41–50 (2003)
10. Korovin, K.: iProver - an instantiation-based theorem prover for first-order logic (system description). In: Armando, A., Baumgartner, P., Dowek, G. (eds.) IJCAR 2008. LNCS (LNAI), vol. 5195, pp. 292–298. Springer, Heidelberg (2008)
11. Lincoln, P., Clavel, M., Eker, S., Meseguer, J.: Principles of maude. In: Meseguer, J. (ed.) Electronic Notes in Theoretical Computer Science, vol. 4, Elsevier Science Publishers, Amsterdam (2000)
12. Oquendo, F., Warboys, B., Morrison, R., Dindeleux, R., Gallo, F., Garavel, H., Occhipinti, C.: ArchWare: Architecting Evolvable Software. In: Oquendo, F., Warboys, B.C., Morrison, R. (eds.) EWSA 2004. LNCS, vol. 3047, pp. 257–271. Springer, Heidelberg (2004)
13. Prevosto, V., Waldmann, U.: Spass+ t. ESCoR: Empirically Successful Computerized Reasoning 192, 88 (2006)
14. Riazanov, A., Voronkov, A.: The design and implementation of VAMPIRE. AI Communications 15(2-3), 91–110 (2002)
15. Schulz, S.: E-a brainiac theorem prover. AI Communications 15(2), 111–126 (2002)
16. Sutcliffe, G., Suttner, C.B.: The TPTP Problem Library: CNF Release v1.2.1. Journal of Automated Reasoning 21(2), 177–203 (1998)

A Tool Which Mines Partial Execution Traces to Improve Static Analysis

Gianluca Amato, Maurizio Parton, and Francesca Scozzari

Università "G. d'Annunzio" di Chieti e Pescara – Dipartimento di Scienze, Italy

Abstract. We present a tool which performs abstract interpretation based static analysis of numerical variables. The novelty is that the analysis is parametric, and parameters are chosen by applying a variant of principal component analysis to partial execution traces of programs.

Abstract interpretation based static analysis [5] may be used to prove run-time properties of program variables such as "all the array indexes are contained within the correct bounds". It discovers assertions which hold when execution reaches specific program points. The expressive power of assertions depends on the particular choice of the *abstract domain*. The simplest abstract domain for numerical properties is the *interval domain* [4], which allows assertions of the form $m \leq x \leq M$ where x is a program variable and m, M are constants.

A lot of research is devoted to explore the trade-off between precision, expressive power and computational cost of abstract domains. In this context, we have recently proposed a family of parametric *parallelotope domains* [1]. They are similar to the interval domain, except that intervals are expressed in a non-standard basis in the vector space of variable's values. The non-standard basis is the parameter of the domain: given a change of basis matrix A, our domain includes all the assertions of the form $\boldsymbol{m} \leq A\boldsymbol{x} \leq \boldsymbol{M}$, where $\boldsymbol{x}$ is the vector of program variables and A is fixed for the entire analysis. When the basis is cleverly chosen, parallelotopes approximate the invariants with a greater precision than intervals, as illustrated in Figures 1, 2 and 3 on a partial execution trace.

In order to find the "optimal" basis, we propose a new technique based on a pre-analysis of the partial execution traces of the program. First, we collect the values of numerical variables in all the program points for different inputs. Then, we apply to the sample data a statistical technique called *orthogonal simple component analysis* (OSCA) [2], which is a variant of *principal component analysis* (PCA). It finds a new orthonormal coordinate system maximizing the variance of the collected values. More explicitly, PCA finds new axes such that the variance of the projection of the data points on the first axis is the maximum among all possible directions, the variance of the projection of the data points on the second axis is the maximum among all possible directions which are orthogonal to the first axis, and so on. If we apply PCA to the values collected from partial executions traces of the program in Figure 1, we get the new basis (x', y') in Figure 3. OSCA returns an approximation of PCA such that the principal components are proportional to vectors of small integers, a property which helps the

G. Roşu et al. (Eds.): RV 2010, LNCS 6418, pp. 475–479, 2010.

```
xyline = function(x)
{
    assume(x>=0)
    y=-x
    while(x>y) {
①       x= x-1
        y= y+1
    }
}
```

Fig. 1. The example program xyline

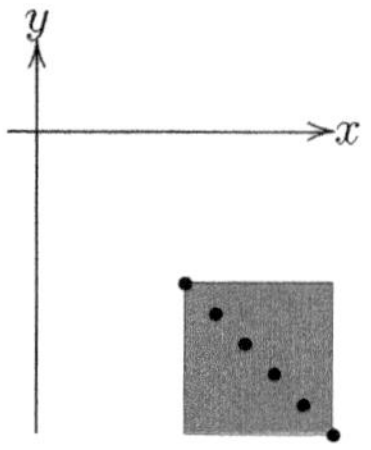

Fig. 2. Interval abstraction of a partial execution trace, observed at program point ①

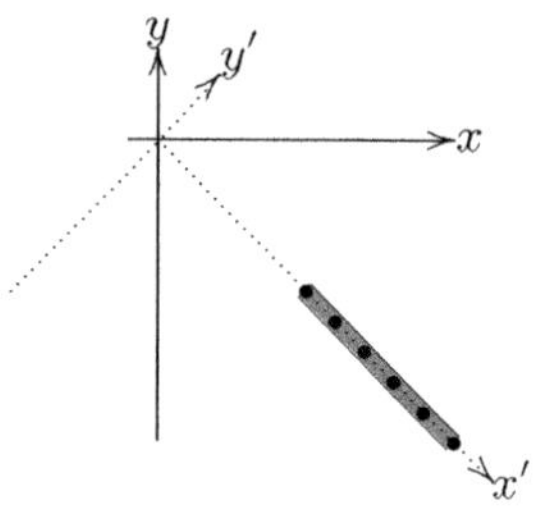

Fig. 3. Parallelotope abstraction with axes rotated by 45 degrees

correct implementation of parallelotope operators. For the program in Figure 1, OSCA finds the change of basis matrix $\begin{bmatrix} 1 & 1 \\ -1 & 1 \end{bmatrix}$ whose columns correspond to the axes (x', y') in Figure 3. Whereas the standard analysis on the interval domain is not able to discover any invariant for the while-statement, the parallelotope domain is able to find out that $x + y = 0$ and the combined analysis finds out that $x \geq -1, y \leq 1, x + y = 0$, at the program point ①.

1   Using the Tool

We have implemented in the R programming language a tool which performs the following steps:

1. Given a program written in an imperative fragment of the R language, the tool instruments the program in order to collect variables's values in all the program points.
2. On the collected values, the tool computes the PCA (using the standard R library), which is afterward refined to get the OSCA. The result is a matrix which describes the (hopefully) optimal basis.
3. The tool performs a static analysis of the program using intervals, parallelotopes and their combination. As a result, it returns a set of assertions for each program point.

The easiest way to use the tool is to start the R interactive environment, load the tool and the program to analyze, and use the function compare.analyses. When the function to analyze has no arguments, it is enough to use:

```
compare.analyses( <function name> )
```

If the function requires some arguments, we need to provide user-supplied values. These are not needed for the static analysis, but as input for the instrumented program. User-supplied values are passed in the second argument of compare.analyses as a list of value assignments, where each value assignment is a map from variable names to values. For instance, if we want to analyze the example program xyline, using the input values $10, 20, 50$ for x, we write

```
compare.analyses(xyline,list(list(x=10),list(x=20),list(x=50)))
```

Note that in R the type list is used both for lists and maps.

The result of compare.analyses is a list with five components. The first two components are the matrices generated by PCA and OSCA. In our case:

```
         x           y                          x  y
PC1   0.7072070   0.7070065          PC1   -1  1
PC2  -0.7070065   0.7072070          PC2    1  1
```

The other three components are the results of the static analyses with the domains of boxes, parallelotopes and their combination. The tool returns a set of assertions for each program point, which are generally displayed as an annotated program.

```
"[ y=0 ]"                  "[ ]"                      "[ y=0 : ]"
assume(x > 0)              assume(x > 0)              assume(x > 0)
"[ 0<=x , y=0 ]"           "[ ]"                      "[ 0<=x , y=0 : -x+y<=0 , 0<=x+y ]"
y = -x                     y = -x                     y = -x
"[ 0<=x , y<=0 ]"          "[ x+y=0 ]"                "[ 0<=x , y<=0 : -x+y<=0 , x+y=0 ]"
while ({                   while ({                   while ({
    "[ ]"                      "[ x+y=0 ]"                "[ -1<=x , y<=1 : -x+y<=2 , x+y=0 ]"
    x > y                      x > y                      x > y
}) {                       }) {                       }) {
    "[ ]"                      "[ -x+y<=0 , x+y=0 ]"      "[ 0<=x , y<=0 : -x+y<=0 , x+y=0 ]"
    x = x - 1                  x = x - 1                  x = x - 1
    "[ ]"                      "[ -x+y<=1 , x+y=-1 ]"     "[ -1<=x , y<=0 : -x+y<=1 , x+y=-1 ]"
    y = y + 1                  y = y + 1                  y = y + 1
    "[ ]"                      "[ -x+y<=2 , x+y=0 ]"      "[ -1<=x , y<=1 : -x+y<=2 , x+y=0 ]"
}                          }                          }
"[ ]"                      "[ 0<=-x+y , x+y=0 ]"      "[ -1<=x<=0 , 0<=y<=1 : 0<=-x+y<=2 , x+y=0 ]"
```

The analysis with the box domain does not depend on the result of the PCA. In this case, the analyses is not able to determine any constraints, if not the trivial ones before the beginning of the while. For the parallelotope domain, the axes are rotated according to the change of basis matrix in the second component, and therefore the domain is able to express intervals of the form $m \leq -x + y \leq M$ and $m \leq x + y \leq M$. The tool shows that, at the end of the program, the constraints $0 \leq -x + y$ and $x + y = 0$ hold, but it cannot prove any upper bound for $-x + y$. Finally, the domain which combines boxes and parallelotopes enhances the precision of both analyses.

The function compare.analyses takes many optional parameters which may heavily modify the result of the analyses. For example, the parameter vars allows to specify the list of variables to be considered during the analysis. The standard behaviour includes all the variables in the program since, for most domains, considering more variables (and thus more relationships) improves the result of the static analysis. Our tool shows that, in some cases, reducing the space of variables may considerably improve the precision of the parallelotopes and combined domains.

For example, consider the standard bubblesort program on the right. If we perform an analysis with the standard parameters, the combined domain proves that "[0<=b , 0<=j , 0<=t : 0<=b]". The result of the OSCA is the matrix

```
function(k) {
  b = 100
  while (b>=1) {
    j=1
    t=0
    while (j<=(b-1)) {
      if (k[j]>k[j+1]) {
        tmp = k[j+1]
        k[j+1] = k[j]
        k[j]=tmp
        t=j
      }
      j=j+1
    }
    if (t==0) return(k)
    b=t
  }
  return(k)
}
```

	b	j	t	tmp
PC1	0	−1	−1	1
PC2	0	1	0	1
PC3	0	−1	2	1
PC4	1	0	0	0

It is worth noting that the variable *tmp* is included in the first three simple components, although it contains values from the array k, hence it is not correlated to the variables b, j and t which are used to index the array.

If we perform the analysis with the option vars=c("b","j","t") which excludes the variable *tmp*, we get the change of basis matrix:

	b	j	t
PC1	0	1	1
PC2	0	−1	1
PC3	1	0	0

and the combined domain is able to find more precise constraints:

"[1<=b<=100 , 0<=j<=100 , 0<=t<=99 : 0<=j+t<=199 , −100<=−j+t<=0 , 1<=b<=100]"

If the result of the statistical analysis of traces is not satisfactory, the tool has an option to provide a user-supplied change of basis matrix.

2   Implementation

The tool has been almost entirely implemented in R. This has at least three advantages. First of all, the analyzed language is R itself, and not an ad-hoc, artificial language. The second advantage is that we exploit metaprogramming on R, viewing a program both as a list and a function. Finally, R is very well-suited for statistical applications and manipulation of vectors, which are native types. On the contrary, the main disadvantage is that the performance of the analyzer in R is not comparable to other analyzers', since R uses a call-by-value semantics and is not well-suited for manipulating complex data structures. Anyway, we believe that it is a good choice for rapid prototyping.

The program to be analyzed is instrumented by inserting, at each program point, a call to a function which collects the values of variables. The same function can also interrupt the program after a certain number of steps. The option whileonly considers only a single program point for each while cycle, just before checking the while guard. From several experiments, it does not seem to make a lot of difference.

The instrumented program is executed and the collected values are stored in a matrix, which is fed to the native function *prcomp* which computes PCA. The resulting matrix is then refined by the OSCA, that we have implemented by scratch, since, at the best of our knowledge, there exists no available implementation. The resulting change of basis matrix is the input for the static analysis. Since static analysis must return only correct results, we need to ensure that numerical approximations do not introduce any error. In the case of the box domain, it is enough to appropriately round the result of operations in such a way that boxes are always overapproximated. To this aim, we have written a small foreign procedure (in C language) to change the floating point rounding mode of the CPU. For the parallelotope and combined domains, we have used exact rational arithmetic through the GMP library. We also wrote a wrapper library, to support infinite values.

3 Conclusion

This is the first tool which uses partial trace information for feeding a subsequent static analysis. The tool is still a prototype, which should be improved in many ways. We may use techniques of code coverage to improve the quality of partial execution traces. We may partition the set of program variables into groups and perform PCA separately on each group. We may also partition the program code itself, and perform a different PCA on each partition. As a future work, the tool could also be extended with different statistical methods, in order to discover better bases, and with a user-friendly front-end, especially for parameter tuning. Moreover, porting the code of the parallelotope domain to a faster programming language, possibly within some well-known library such as APRON [6] or PPL [3], would make it available to a wider community, while improving performance. Finally, the tool is available at the web page http://www.sci.unich.it/~amato/random.

References

1. Amato, G., Parton, M., Scozzari, F.: Deriving numerical abstract domains via principal component analysis. To appear in Proc. Static Analysis Symposium (2010)
2. Anaya-Izquierdo, K., Critchley, F., Vines, K.: Orthogonal simple component analysis: a new, exploratory approach. To appear in the Annals of Applied Statistics (2010)
3. Bagnara, R., Hill, P.M., Zaffanella, E.: The Parma Polyhedra Library: Toward a complete set of numerical abstractions for the analysis and verification of hardware and software systems. Science of Computer Programming 72(1-2), 3–21 (2008)
4. Cousot, P., Cousot, R.: Static determination of dynamic properties of programs. In: Proc. Int'l Symposium on Programming, pp. 106–130 (1976)
5. Cousot, P., Cousot, R.: Abstract interpretation and applications to logic programs. The Journal of Logic Programming 13(2-3), 103–179 (1992)
6. Jeannet, B., Miné, A.: APRON: A library of numerical abstract domains for static analysis. In: Bouajjani, A., Maler, O. (eds.) CAV 2009. LNCS, vol. 5643, pp. 661–667. Springer, Heidelberg (2009)

LarvaStat: Monitoring of Statistical Properties

Christian Colombo, Andrew Gauci, and Gordon J. Pace

Department of Computer Science, University of Malta, Malta

Abstract. Execution paths expose non-functional information such as system reliability and performance, which can be collected using runtime verification techniques. Statistics gathering and evaluation can be very useful for processing such information for areas ranging from performance profiling to user modelling and intrusion detection. In this paper, we give an overview of LarvaStat — a runtime verification tool extending LARVA [2] with the ability to straightforwardly specify real-time related statistical properties. Being automaton-based, LarvaStat also makes explicit the overhead induced by monitoring.

1 Introduction

Runtime verification tools mainly focus on the analysis of system traces for the verification of functional aspects of the system. However, system executions are also rich in information related to non-functional system properties, such as system security, dependability and performance. LarvaStat extends the runtime verification tool LARVA [2] with the capability of collecting statistical information, and verifying non-functional requirements based on such statistics. Taking security as an example application area, LarvaStat allows for the characterisation of suspicious user behaviour through statistical evaluation, which can subsequently be used to blacklist users deemed suspicious. This mechanism has been applied to develop an intrusion detection system based on techniques presented in [4] and an integrated system profiler used for measuring system performance.

LarvaStat's statistical constructs are based on the notion of *incrementally computable statistics* [5], characterising a class of statistics which can be efficiently evaluated in both time and space. An incrementally computable statistic involves (i) storing the current statistic's valuation, and (ii) executing an update function when a new value is to be added to the input data set. Many statistics such as the count, average, maximum, minimum and variance all admit incrementally computable behaviour, although others, such as the median, do not.

All statistics LarvaStat collects are themselves exposed to the monitoring tool as *statistical events* — exposing the latest statistic valuation upon each update. This allows for (i) writing specifications based on these events (such as blocking users upon the statistic valuation exceeding a certain threshold); and (ii) the specification of *multilayered statistics* — statistics over statistics, such as the mean of the maximum download file size.

Moreover, it is often the case that statistics are required to be collected only for certain subtraces. For example, a statistic intent on counting the number of bytes sent during some communication is only interested from the moment of opening to that of

G. Roşu et al. (Eds.): RV 2010, LNCS 6418, pp. 480–484, 2010.

closing of a communication channel. LarvaStat allows for the specification of *intervals of interest* for statistics.

2   LarvaStat

LarvaStat is an event-driven runtime verification framework, and is concerned with interpreting observed event information. Parametrised events can be either observable system actions (such as a method call), timer events, automata-generated events or a combination thereof.

Definition 1. *Given a set* basicevent *of basic events (parametrised over a set of values V) and set* timer *of timer variables, we define a composite parametrised event* event *as either (i) a basic event, (ii) a timeout on a timer (over* $\mathbb{R}$*), (iii) a choice between events through the general choice operator* $\sum$*, or (iv) the complement of an event* $(\bar{e})$*.*

$$\text{event} ::= \text{basicevent} \mid \text{timer} @ \delta \mid \sum 2^{\text{event}} \mid \overline{\text{event}}$$

The first statistical construct is the *statistic aggregator*, and is defined as (i) an initial statistic valuation (eg. initialising the count), and (ii) an update rule (eg. incrementing the count upon the occurrence of an event).

Definition 2. *A statistical aggregator ranging over* Γ *is defined through (i) the initial memory value* $\gamma_0 \in \Gamma$*; and (ii) the update rule entailing a parametrised event (triggering the update), a condition (acting as an event filter), an update function on the memory, and an event on which to signal the updated value. We assume that values over* Γ *can be mapped to V to pass the value over the output event.*

$$\text{event} \times V \rightarrow (\text{cond} \times (\Gamma \rightarrow \Gamma)) \times \text{event}$$

Note that cond *stands for a condition on the system state and timer configuration.*

Given a sequence of timestamps, basic events and system states $(t_i, e_i(v_i), \theta_i)$ (with i ranging from 1 to n) and statistical aggregator with initial memory γ_0 and update action (in, s, out), statistical events would be triggered at each point in the trace where a basic event $e_i(v_i)$ triggers in and such that the condition is triggered — c holds, where $(c, u) = s(v_i)$. At each such position, γ (starting with value γ_0) is updated to $u(\gamma)$, with the result being output as an event: $out(u(\gamma))$. Formal definitions of trace semantics of event triggering are given in [2].

Example 1. A statistical aggregator counting the number of bytes sent requires memory storage containing the current amount, and is initialised to 0. The statistic is updated on each basic even *send(v)* (*v* represents the number of bytes sent), with the update action defined as: $(send, \lambda v.(\lambda x.true, \lambda n.n + v), result)$.

See Fig. 1(a) for an example *point statistic* written in LarvaStat, specifying a statistic aggregator for counting the number of successful user logins.

LarvaStat also supports statistics evaluated over intervals of interest, defined as a statistic aggregator and an interval characterisation. This interval dictates which system trace subsequence is relevant to the specified statistic aggregator. Intervals are characterised by identifying the opening and closing events (eg. an interval specifying the opening and closing of a connection channel). Through the use of timers, one can use this approach to define intervals by giving the opening event and the duration of time during which to calculate the statistic (eg. a statistic counting the number of user downloads in the first thirty minutes of logging in).

Definition 3. *Statistics aggregation over an interval of interest is defined as (i) a statistic aggregator; (ii) the event and condition marking the interval opening* event $\times V \rightarrow$ cond; *and (iii) the event and condition marking the interval closing* $V \rightarrow$ (event $\times V \rightarrow$ cond).

Note that the closing event is also parametrised by the parameter given to the opening event. Every time an opening event (satisfying the condition) is triggered, a new statistic aggregator is created and initialised, which continues calculating the value until the closing event appears.

Example 2. A statistical aggregator over interval of interest evaluating the number of bytes sent on a per connection basis is defined through (i) the statistic aggregator defined in example 1, (ii) interval opening *(openConnection,λport.true)*, and (iii) interval closing $\lambda port_0.(closeConnection, \lambda port_1.port_0 = port_1)$. Note that it is assumed that both *openConnection* and *closeConnection* are parametrised by the port number.

See Fig. 1(b) for an example *interval statistic* written in LarvaStat, specifying the statistic aggregator over interval of interest defined above (ignoring port number to simplify presentation).

3   Case Study

LarvaStat has been used for implementing a probabilistic intrusion detection and integrated system profiler sitting above an ftpd server implemented in Java[1]. The system profiler is responsible for quantifying system performance, whereas the intrusion detection system observes user behaviour, with the aim of capturing suspicious behaviour through the use of misuse detection and anomaly detection techniques [4]. Moreover, given that the monitoring of users is expensive, an additional mechanism has been implemented for the probabilistic choice of users to monitor. This choice is dependent on two parameters: *user risk factor* and *system load*. Both parameters are extrapolated from statistical information collected by LarvaStat.

System profiling is carried out by quantifying the current system load (assuming that the server's performance is tightly bound to bandwidth usage and the current count of logged in users), and analysing system load history for predictive purposes. For example, counting the number of currently logged in users is specified through three statistics, as seen in Fig. 1(a). *UsersLoggedIn* counts the number of user logins, *UsersLoggedOut* counts the number of log out events, while *CurrentUserCount* is a layered statistic which listens to the previous two statistics.

The intrusion detection uses various techniques, (i) a Markov chain analysing the user's command sequence, with each ftpd command being related to a risk factor, and

---

[1] http://www.anomic.de/AnomicFTPServer

marking the user as suspicious if the command sequence exceeds a threshold; and (ii) the use of statistical moments for the characterisation of abnormal user behaviour, monitoring each user's download and upload behaviour patterns, and assuming a statistically predictable pattern.

```
POINTSTAT UsersLoggedIn : Integer {          INTERVALSTAT byteCount : Integer {
  INIT {UsersLoggedIn.setValue(new Integer(0));}   INIT{byteCount
  EVENTS {successfulLogin()}                          .setValue(new Integer(0));}
  UPDATE {UsersLoggedIn.setValue(            EVENTS{sendInfo}
       UsersLoggedIn.getValue() + 1);}       CONDITION{ }
}                                            INTERVAL {
POINTSTAT UsersLoggedOut : Integer {...}       OPEN  [ downloadStarting ]
POINTSTAT CurrentUserCount : Integer {         CLOSE [ downloadComplete ]
  INIT{CurrentUserCount.setValue(            }
                   new Integer(0));}         UPDATE{ byteCount.setValue(
  EVENTS{ UsersLoggedIn_Event |                      byteCount.getValue()
       UsersLoggedOut_Event }                               + bufferSize); }}
  UPDATE{ CurrentUserCount.setValue(
      UsersLoggedIn.getValue() -
      UsersLoggedOut.getValue()); }}
```

Fig. 1. LarvaStat statistic construct examples (a) and (b)

Fig. 2 shows automata (which are processed by LARVA) which are automatically generated by LarvaStat to calculate the statistics *UsersLoggedIn* and *byteCount* from the description in Fig. 1. Transitions are tagged by the event which fires them, the event which they fire, and the action to update the statistic. The initial state is tagged with the action to initialise the statistic. LarvaStat does not extend LARVA's expressivity, but rather is a syntactic sugar for the intuitive high-level specification of statistical properties.

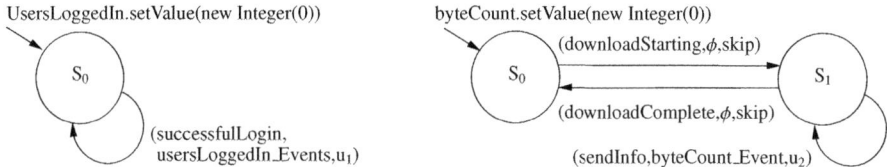

Fig. 2. DATEs executing statistical constructs (a) and (b)

The case study contains the specification of twenty statistics, some of which are evaluated on the system, whereas others are evaluated on a per user basis. All statistics are incrementally computable and intuitively defined, while also being implemented without altering a line of the underlying ftpd system code.

System overhead was measured by simulating multiple users logging in concurrently and exhibiting varied download and upload behaviour patterns. This setting was run multiple times with and without the additional intrusion detection system, whereby the system on average exhibited approximately a 9% processing overhead while being monitored.

4   Related Work and Conclusions

Three existing related approaches have been identified. The approach in [5] specifies a framework focusing on the asynchronous collection of statistics over runtime executions. This is achieved by presenting a Linear Temporal Logic extension focused on evaluating numerical queries on the trace, and admits a tractable evaluation strategy given complete trace knowledge. Lola [3] is another tool, and presents a functional stream computation language allowing for the expression of system properties, numerical queries as well as guaranteeing bounded memory requirements. EAGLE [1] is a third approach, whose use of meta operators allows for the encoding of multiple formalisms such as interval temporal logics, finite state automata, as well as logics for the expression of numerical queries. Our approach supports real-time related statistics collection, and enables interval masking over traces. The automaton-based approach, also makes explicit the overhead induced by monitoring over and above that due to statistics state storage and update.

LarvaStat shows the potential of applying runtime verification techniques for the collection of non-functional metrics about the system being monitored, which can then be used to verify properties over these metrics. By extending an existing runtime verification tool, the resulting framework is able to both collect statistics over system executions, as well as monitoring system properties quantified through statistical queries. The ftpd case study, shows the applicability of the approach, by adding probabilistic intrusion detection and a system profiler to an existing tool.

References

1. Barringer, H., Goldberg, A., Havelund, K., Sen, K.: Rule-based runtime verification. In: Steffen, B., Levi, G. (eds.) VMCAI 2004. LNCS, vol. 2937, pp. 44–57. Springer, Heidelberg (2004)
2. Colombo, C., Pace, G., Schneider, G.: Dynamic event-based runtime monitoring of real-time and contextual properties. In: Cofer, D., Fantechi, A. (eds.) FMICS 2008. LNCS, vol. 5596, pp. 135–149. Springer, Heidelberg (2009)
3. D'Angelo, B., Sankaranarayanan, S., Sánchez, C., Robinson, W., Finkbeiner, B., Sipma, H.B., Mehrotra, S., Manna, Z.: Lola: Runtime monitoring of synchronous systems. In: 12th International Symposium on Temporal Representation and Reasoning (TIME), pp. 166–174 (2005)
4. Denning, D.E.: An intrusion-detection model. IEEE Transactions on Software Engineering 13, 222–232 (1987)
5. Finkbeiner, B., Sankaranarayanan, S., Sipma, H.B.: Collecting statistics over runtime executions. Electr. Notes Theor. Comput. Sci. 70(4), 36–55 (2002)

WS-PSC Monitor: A Tool Chain for Monitoring Temporal and Timing Properties in Composite Service Based on Property Sequence Chart[*]

Pengcheng Zhang[1], Zhiyong Su[2], Yuelong Zhu[1], Wenrui Li[1], and Bixin Li[3]

[1] College of Computer and Information Engineering, Hohai University, Nanjing, China
[2] Wuxi Huishi Technology Co., Ltd, Wuxi, China
[3] School of Computer Science and Engineering, Southeast University, Nanjing, China
{pchzhang,ylzhu,liwenrui}@hhu.edu.cn,
zhiyongsu@gmail.com, bx.li@seu.edu.cn

Abstract. Web service composition is a new paradigm to develop distributed and reactive software-intensive systems. Due to the autonomous attribute of each basic service, validation of composite services must be extended from design time to run-time. In this paper, we describe a novel tool chain called WS-PSC Monitor to monitor temporal and timing properties in composite service based on graphical specification property sequence chart and timed property sequence chart. The tool chain provides a completely graphical front-end which can make software designers do not have to deal with any particular textual and logical formalism.

Keywords: Composite service, run-time monitor, property sequence chart, timed property sequence chart.

1 Introduction

In recent years, the idea of software as a service has added a new paradigm to the service oriented architecture(SOA). In SOA, basic services are seen as autonomous agents acting according to certain contracts. For example, through work flow languages BPEL [6], service requestors may compose existing basic services to provide more powerfully composite services. For such systems, verification is particularly challenging as the overall behavior of such systems depends heavily on the involved agents, which renders the analysis of such systems prior to execution next to impossible [5]. Consequently, runtime analysis techniques, such as runtime monitoring [2], are being pursued as a lightweight verification technique complementing traditional verification techniques, such as model checking and testing, and establishes another trade-off point between these forces.

The property specifications for monitored properties focus mostly on logic-based or scenario-based specification formalisms. Logic-based formalisms are often more expressive than scenario-based formalisms. However, scenario-based

---

[*] This work is supported partial by the Fundamental Research Funds for the Central Universities under Grant No.2009B04314 and 948 project of Ministry of Water Resources under Grant No.201016.

G. Roşu et al. (Eds.): RV 2010, LNCS 6418, pp. 485–489, 2010.

approaches provide a graphical modeling formalism that is widely accepted in industrial practice. Consequently, this paper focuses on monitoring temporal and timing properties of a composite service based on existing graphical specification formalisms Property Sequence Chart(PSC) [1] and Timed Property Sequence Chart (TPSC) [8], since PSC and TPSC specifications are *as simple as possible, without losing expressive power*. A corresponding tool chain called WS-PSC Monitor is developed.

2   The Approach

2.1   Theoretical Foundations

Monitors are typically generated automatically from some high-level specifications. As defined in [5], the generated monitor is a device that reads a finite trace and yields a certain result (for example, true, false or inconclusive). To ensure the correctness of the monitor itself and to reduce costs, different monitoring approaches have been developed over the last years to automatically generate monitors for high-level property specification formalisms.

According to the formal semantics of PSC [1], we have defined four different functions of the message in PSC specifications [9], i.e. *Constraint, NextCorrect, NextFail*, and *NextIgnore*. The messages constrained by the messages are contained in *Constraint* function; the next expected messages are contained in *NextCorrect* according to the PSC specifications; the next unexpected messages are contained in *NextFail*; the next ignored messages are contained in *NextIgnore*. The four functions of each occurred message in PSC can be counted iteratively, and results are placed into a Property Database. The Property Database is used as monitor for further analyzing temporal properties.

According to the formal semantics of TPSC [8], we can also define the formal translational semantics that maps TPSC specifications into a corresponding timed Büchi automata(TBAs) [10]. The rules are divided into basic and compositional rules. Basic rules discuss how to translate single TPSC into a TBA while compositional rules show how to compose these basic automata with structured operators, such as *par, loop* and *alt*. The generated TBAs are also used as monitor for analyzing timing properties.

2.2   Framework Overview

The flow of the WS-PSC Monitor framework is shown in Figure 1 and divided into the following steps:

1) AOP(Aspect-Oriented Programming) based approach [4] is used to extend the BPEL engine. According to PSC and TPSC specifications, the monitoring aspects are automatically generated to intercept the messages among the interactions of each basic service. The **interceptor** intercepts the run-time messages in BPEL-based composite service, then sends these messages to the **Observer**;

2)According to property types, the **observer** can classify the intercepted messages. If property type is temporal property, the observer can only record all the interaction messages; if property type is timing property, the observer needs also to record the time frames for each interaction message.

3)The informal requirements are represented by PSC and TPSC specifications, where PSC specifications are used to represent temporal properties and TPSC specifications are used to represent timing properties.

4)We can use the two translators of the system and translate PSCs and TPSCs into **property database** and **timed Büchi automata**, respectively.

5)**Analyzers** receive the intercepted messages and the properties represented by PSC and TPSC, then Analyzers check whether the runtime information satisfies the desired properties. If property type is temporal property, **Analyzer1** is used. If property type is timing property, **Analyzer2** is used.

6)The analysis results are shown for designers. Then designers can further analyze and correct the possible errors in the systems.

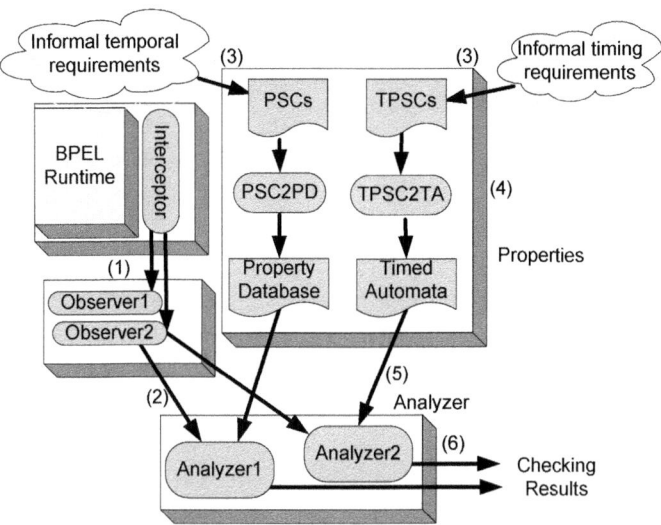

Fig. 1. The framework of tool chain WS-PSC Monitor

2.3   The Implementation

The tool is developed on the Eclipse Rich Client Platform (RCP). It has 122 java classes and about 20 thousand lines of codes. Figure 2 shows the main user interface with *Prop3* of a TA (TeleAssistant) BPEL composite service, which is a software and telecommunication-based service which is designed to help patients needing daily assistance in remote areas. The tool has the following additional components and interfaces: *Navigator, TPSC Editor, Automata view, Property view, BPEL files view, Message view* and *Console*. The navigator is used to manage and show the opened projects and files. The PSC and TPSC Editor allows users to manually specify temporal properties in PSC and timing properties in

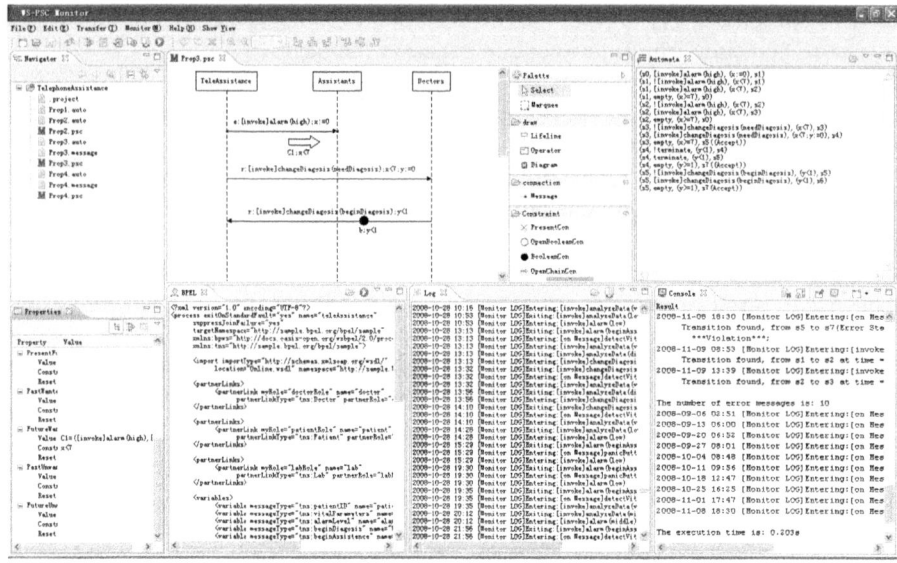

Fig. 2. The main interface of the tool WS-PSC monitor

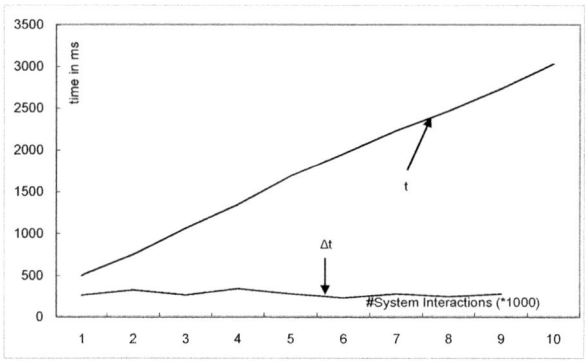

Fig. 3. The performance measurement of the tool WS-PSC monitor

TPSC, respectively. There is a *Palette window*, which is used to help users to drag and drop the PSC or TPSC elements. The lifeline or message elements of each property can be shown in the property view, where the first message *e:[inv]alarm(high)* of *Prop3* and its constraint is shown under clock constraints in the screen shot. The Automata view is used to show the generated TBA for the property in the PSC or TPSC Editor. We use the textual representation of TBA. The BPEL files view shows the monitored BPEL specification and the message view shows the monitored messages including its time information. Finally, the Console is used to show that whether the collected messages satisfying the desired timing property and the time the algorithm takes.

The performance measurement of the monitoring approach is presented in Figure 3, where t shows the time for checking the trace for TBA and $\triangle t$ shows the time consumed for monitoring 1000 system interactions. From the curves, we can see that the time for the process will grow when the number of system interactions increases and it will just take about 3000 ms even when the number of system interactions is 10^5. The curve for $\triangle t$ shows that the time consumed per 1000 system interaction is between 250ms and 300ms.

3   Conclusion

This demonstration of WS-PSC tool chain aims to show the process of monitoring temporal and timing properties in composite services by the use of PSC and TPSC specifications. Compare to other approaches, our approach provides a complete graphical front-end for software designers that do not have to deal with any particular textual and logical formalisms. In the future, we will extend this work to automatically generate monitors for probabilistic properties from Probabilistic TPSC (PTPSC) specifications [7,3].

References

1. Autili, M., Inverardi, P., Pelliccione, P.: Graphical scenarios for specifying temporal properties: an automated approach. Automated Software Engineering 14(3), 293–340 (2007)
2. Delgado, N., Gates, A.Q., Roach, S.: A taxonomy and catalog of runtime software-fault monitoring tools. IEEE Trans. Software Eng. 30(12), 859–872 (2004)
3. Grunske, L., Zhang, P.: Monitoring probabilistic properties. In: ESEC/FSE, pp. 183–192 (2009)
4. Kiczales, G., Lamping, J., Mendhekar, A., Maeda, C., Lopes, C.V., Loingtier, J.-M., Irwin, J.: Aspect-oriented programming. In: Aksit, M., Matsuoka, S. (eds.) ECOOP 1997. LNCS, vol. 1241, pp. 220–242. Springer, Heidelberg (1997)
5. Leucker, M., Schallhart, C.: A brief account of runtime verification. J. Log. Algebr. Program. 78(5), 293–303 (2009)
6. WS-BPEL. Web services business process execution language version 2.0, committee specification. OASIS (2007)
7. Zhang, P., Grunske, L., Tang, A., Li, B.: A formal syntax for probabilistic timed property sequence charts. In: Proc. of ASE, 500–504 (2009)
8. Zhang, P., Li, B., Grunske, L.: Timed property sequence chart. Journal of System and Software 83(3), 371–390 (2010)
9. Zhang, P., Li, B., Muccini, H., Sun, M.: An approach to monitor scenario-based temporal properties in web service compositions. In: Ishikawa, Y., He, J., Xu, G., Shi, Y., Huang, G., Pang, C., Zhang, Q., Wang, G. (eds.) APWeb 2008 Workshops. LNCS, vol. 4977, pp. 144–154. Springer, Heidelberg (2008)
10. Zhang, P., Li, B., Sun, M.: Extending PSC for monitoring the timed properties in composite services. In: Proc. of APSEC, pp. 335–342 (2008)

Author Index